Library of
Davidson College

The Social Scene

WINTHROP PUBLISHERS, INC.

Cambridge, Massachusetts

The Social Scene

A Contemporary View of the Social Sciences

Robert S. Browne
Howard E. Freeman
Charles V. Hamilton
Jerome Kagan
A. Kimball Romney

Special Acknowledgments

The editors and publisher of this volume wish to acknowledge especially the important contributions made by a number of colleagues who gave most generously of their time and knowledge. This volume has undergone a number of changes in various stages of the manuscript. Among those whose advice and assistance were most helpful in designing and perfecting the manuscript are: Arthur B. Hayes III, Montgomery College; Wallace W. Culver, Montgomery College; John Davis, South Texas Junior College; Edward H. Ferguson, San Jacinto College; William Frever, Oakland Community College; Robert Moseley, Rockland Community College; Elbridge Smith, State University of New York at Cobleskill; Reginald Touchton, Florida Junior College; and Richard G. Fritz, Northern Virginia Community College.

An excellent and very valuable teacher's manual has been prepared by Jeffrey C. Bertsch of Florida Junior College.

While the editorial contributions of the publisher and the criticisms of our colleagues have helped to perfect this volume, it would not have come about at all without the invaluable assistance of the Two Year Division of Prentice-Hall. Among the Prentice-Hall representatives and managers who helped us to shape this work, we wish to acknowledge the assistance of Robert Haltiwanger, General Manager; Angus McDonald, Regional Manager; Gary Gutchell, Regional Manager; and particularly, George Ragland, Regional Manager. Harold Balmer, Weldon Rackley, Doug Garber, Richard Reiner, Chuck Murphy and Ron Harris provided meaningful advice and direction.

The imagination, versatility and unfailing assistance of Muriel Harman, at Winthrop Publishers, have also been of indispensable help.

Cover by Joe Guertin

Copyright © 1972 by Winthrop Publishers, Inc.
17 Dunster Street, Cambridge, Massachusetts 02138

All rights reserved. No part of this book may be reproduced in any form or by any means without permission in writing from the publisher. Printed in the United States of America 0–87626–837–8, Current printing (last number):10 9 8 7 6 5 4 3 2 1.

Library of Congress Catalog Card Number: 70–170115.

Contents

ix   *Preface*

1   *Introduction: The Domain of the Social Sciences*

20   **Introduction to Psychology**

     Concepts:

     Schema
30   *Recognition Memory for Words, Sentences, and Pictures*, Roger N. Shepard

     Concept
38   *The Cross-Cultural Generality of Visual-Verbal Synesthetic Tendencies*, Charles E. Osgood

     Motive
46   *Effects of Social Class and Race on Responsiveness to Approval and Disapproval*, David L. Rosenhan

     Attention
56   *The Determinants of Attention in the Infant*, Jerome Kagan

     Cognitive Transformations
71   *Presleep Experiences and Dreams*, Herman A. Witkin and Helen B. Lewis

     Avoidance Behavior
77   *Vicarious Extinction of Avoidance Behavior*, Albert Bandura, Joan E. Grusec, and Frances L. Menlove

     Emotion
87   *Cognitive Effects of False Heart-Rate Feedback*, Stuart Valins

     Psychopathology
99   *The Case of Dawn*, G. W. Goethals and D. S. Klos

114 **Introduction to Sociology**

Concepts:

Group
122 *The Cash Posters: A Study of a Group of Working Girls*, George C. Homans

Norm
135 *Sex As Work: A Study of Avocational Counseling*, Lionel S. Lewis and Dennis Brissett

Role
146 *The Hasher: A Study of Role Conflict*, Louis A. Zurcher, Jr., David W. Sonenschein and Eric L. Metzner

Social Stratification
159 *Social Class and Campus Dating*, Ira L. Reiss

Bureaucracy
174 *The Navy Disbursing Officer As A Bureaucrat*, Ralph H. Turner

Social Institution
182 *To Comfort and to Challenge*, Charles Glock, Benjamin Ringer, and Carl R. Babbie

Deviance
192 *Stripteasers: The Anatomy and Career Contingencies of A Deviant Occupation*, James K. Skipper, Jr., and Charles H. McCaghy

Social Disorganization
208 *Wincanton: The Politics of Corruption*, John A. Gardiner with the assistance of David J. Olson

226 **Introduction to Anthropology**

Concepts:

Race
235 *The Study of Race*, S. L. Washburn

Chronology
247 *Tree Rings—The Archaeologist's Time-Piece*, Emil W. Haury

Socio-Linguistics
257 *The Logic of Nonstandard English*, William Labov

Life Cycle
278 *A Yoruba Market-Woman's Life*, Janheinz Jahn

Socialization

290 *Maternal Care and Infant Behavior in Japan and America*, William Caudill and Helen Weinstein

Practices

301 *The Sexual Life of Savages: in North-Western Melanesia*, Bronislaw Malinowski

Culture Relativity

310 *Shakespeare in the Bush*, Laura Bohannan

Culture Change

319 *Fathoms and Feet, Acres and Tons: An Appraisal*, Keith Gordon Irwin

336 **Introduction to Economics**

Concepts:

Scarcity

350 *Scarcity, Competitive Behavior, and Economics*, Alchian and Allen

Exchange

359 *The Economic Organization of a P.O.W. Camp*, R. A. Radford

Poverty

370 *The Merchant and the Low-Income Consumer: The Poor Pay More*, David Caplovitz

Capitalism

383 *Litton Industries: Big Brother as a Holding Company*, David Horowitz and Reese Erlich

Property

397 *Pollution, Property and Prices*, J. H. Dale

Socialism

410 *Ujamaa—The Basis of African Socialism*, Julius Nyerere

The Corporate State

417 *The Greening of America*, Charles Reich

430 **Introduction to Political Science**

Concepts:

Sovereign Power

443 *Stability and Change in Africa*, Julius Nyerere

Legitimacy
455   *"Hell No, We Won't Go!"*, John Cooney and Dana Spitzer

Representation
467   *We Will Exercise Our Rights*, Steve Wasserman

Interest Groups
473   *The Food and Drug Administration and the Pill*, Alice J. Wolfson and Phillip E. Wolfson

Justice
480   *If You Were On Welfare*, Richard M. Elman

Liberty
485   *Americans Betrayed*, Morton Grodzins

Ideology
495   *The Black Revolution: A Primer for White Liberals*, Charles V. Hamilton

Revolution
500   *A Double Deception: The Problem of Aggression*, Howard Zinn

511   *Glossary*

Preface

The Social Scene is designed to introduce the student to the social sciences. Although there are a number of different pedagogical approaches to introducing the social sciences, we believe we have chosen a relatively unique one. This book is meant to be read, understood, and enjoyed by persons without previous training in the social sciences.

We have chosen a relatively simple approach. Our emphasis is on acquainting the student with the key concepts that are used by persons in the fields of psychology, sociology, anthropology, economics and political science.

The book is organized by sections—one for each of the various disciplines. The main introduction to the book provides a broad overview of the social sciences. A major purpose of the introductions to each of the sections is to present and define the disciplines and to integrate the various readings contained in the sections. The section introductions also indicate overlaps in concepts and ideas and identify some of the areas in which the research or ideas of persons in one social science correspond with those in another. A determined effort has been made to identify the interrelationships that exist between the various social science disciplines and to show the student the value of looking at human behavior and social processes from different perspectives. The readings are actual research documents reporting the work of social scientists in the various disciplines. They have been chosen to illustrate key concepts.

In developing the book, each of the editors selected a small list of key concepts with which persons educated in social sciences should be familiar. Since it is difficult to get two social scientists to agree on what a minimum set of concepts for students should be, the editors have selected those concepts on which there was reasonable agreement. In selecting these, we constantly asked ourselves not only what was currently popular and fashionable in the social sciences, but also what lasting ideas, notions and views were embodied in these concepts. An effort was made to select readings which conveyed more than a formal definition of the concepts, but rather, showed the student how they are used in looking at a particular slice of human behavior and social life.

The student who completes this book should have more than an expanded vocabulary. In every field of knowledge there are important ideas and thoughts, and without a set of terms it is difficult to communicate ideas. Some of the concepts in social science are familiar because they have been adopted from everyday language. Others are familiar because their popularity has made them common language. For, in the language of the social sciences, like in any other language, once you have a minimum set of "concepts" or terms, it is easy to build on them.

While the readings have been selected to illustrate specific concepts, they contain many important substantive ideas. They provide the student with a broad exposure to the ideas, thoughts, methods and research of social scientists in the various disciplines.

It should be noted that we have also tried as much as possible to select readings that would capture the interest of students. Some of them touch upon major social issues that are relevant to college students. Others border on the esoteric and hopefully will fan the curiosity of the student. As we have noted, however, in both our writing and our selections we have aimed at material which persons without previous training in the social sciences would find interesting and understand. At times some editing has been required of the research material. Most of the articles, however, appear in their original form, or we have indicated by ellipses where we have omitted material.

Not all of the instructors using this volume will agree with the order in which the social sciences have been presented. The decision to start with psychology and move from there into sociology, anthropology, economics and political science is an arbitrary one. We have carefully organized the book so that instructors could acquaint the student with the social sciences in a different order than that presented, or indeed reshuffle the presentation of papers within sections.

The book is a collaborative effort of a publisher and the editors of this volume. Mr. James Murray III, President of Winthrop Publishers, Inc., has had long experience in the development of educational materials in the social sciences and is responsible for many of the social science publications of Winthrop's parent company, Prentice-Hall, Inc. He and the editors individually and collectively reviewed the several prominent approaches to introducing the social sciences in colleges and universities throughout the country. Many well-written volumes exist. Some provide broad overviews of the various social sciences, but can be criticized for their lack of depth and a failure to acquaint the student firsthand with research literature in the field. Others are quite penetrating but suffer from their narrowness of scope. We have tried to provide a volume that by itself may be used by the instructor for a course in the social sciences. At the same time, we believe it can serve as a companion volume to a general introduction of the social sciences, which, because it is broad and sweeping, fails to delve deeply into the literature and knowledge base of the fields.

As we have mentioned, this book is meant to be used and enjoyed by persons with no previous training in the social sciences. We do feel, however, that all students share a common interest in the social world about them and in the behavior of man. We hope that the contents of this volume will intensify their interest and further develop their intellectual outlook and their concern with the social affairs of the community and the society.

Finally, a note should be added about the editors of this volume. Although we differ in discipline of primary interest, academic affiliation and past experience, all of us share a set of common characteristics. We regard ourselves as working social scientists; persons who have a mutual interest in the general nature of the social sciences and a respect for the specific expertise of individuals in each of these sciences. All of us have taught in a variety of educational institutions and have done extensive research in our respective fields. All of us have a commitment to the use of science for the betterment of our fellow man, and for the improvement of our social conditions. We have attempted in this volume both to try to impart some of our concern with the use of science for social action and our scholarly interest in human behavior and social life.

We encourage the student to pursue further work in the social sciences; but we hope that this volume will provide him with a broad survey of our various disciplines.

Robert S. Browne
Howard E. Freeman
Charles V. Hamilton
Jerome Kagan
A. Kimball Romney

Photograph Credits

P. 15 by Frank Siteman, STOCK, Boston; p. 18 by Ellis Herwig, STOCK, Boston; p. 31 by Ted Rozumalski, BLACK STAR; p. 37 by Arthur Furst; p. 51 by Ernest Baxter, BLACK STAR; p. 54 by Arthur Furst; p. 69 by A. Hakim Raquib; p. 109 by A. Hakim Raquib; p. 112 by Dennis Brack, BLACK STAR; p. 123 by Dennis Brack, BLACK STAR; p. 140 by Patricia Gross, STOCK, Boston; p. 147 by Hugh Rodgers, MONKMEYER; p. 158 by St. Louis Post Dispatch, BLACK STAR; p. 161 by St. Louis Post Dispatch, BLACK STAR; p. 193 by A. Hakim Raquib; p. 196 by Arthur Furst; p. 220 by Norman Hurst, STOCK, Boston, © 1968 by Norman Hurst; p. 221 by Norman Hurst, STOCK, Boston, © 1971 by Norman Hurst; p. 224 by Kirk Steven, BLACK STAR; p. 241 by John Moss, BLACK STAR; p. 244 by EDITORIAL PHOTOCOLOR ARCHIVES, INC.; p. 253 by Joe Clarke, BLACK STAR; p. 263 by Marion Bernstein, EDITORIAL PHOTO-COLOR ARCHIVES, INC.; p. 272 by A. Hakim Raquib; p. 281 by Holzgraf, MONKMEYER; p. 286 by A. Abbas, BLACK STAR; p. 292 by Roland Lange, BLACK STAR; p. 307 by Norman Myers, BLACK STAR; p. 331 by St. Louis Post Dispatch, BLACK STAR; p. 334 by Fred Anderson, BLACK STAR; p. 375 by Norman Hurst, STOCK, Boston, © 1971 by Norman Hurst; p. 377 by A. Hakim Raquib; p. 405 by John Collier, BLACK STAR; p. 428 by A. Hakim Raquib; p. 462 by Andrew Sacks, EDITORIAL PHOTOCOLOR ARCHIVES, INC.; p. 471 by Tower News Service, EDITORIAL PHOTOCOLOR ARCHIVES, INC.; p. 498 by A. Hakim Raquib; p. 509 by Claus C. Meyer, BLACK STAR.

Acknowledgments

"Recognition Memory for Words, Sentences and Pictures" by Roger N. Shepard. From *Journal of Verbal Learning and Verbal Behavior*, Volume XI, 1967, 156–163. Reprinted by permission. "The Cross-Cultural Generality of Visual-Verbal Synesthetic Tendencies" by Charles E. Osgood. Reprinted from *Behavioral Science*, Volume 5, No. 2, 1960, by permission of James G. Miller, M.D., Ph.D., Editor. "Effects of Social Class and Race on Responsiveness to Approval and Disapproval" by David L. Rosenhan. From *Journal of Personality and Social Psychology*, IV, 1966, pp. 253–259. Reprinted by permission. "The Determinants of Attention in the Infant" by Jerome Kagan. From *American Scientist*, Volume 58, 1970. Reprinted by permission. "Presleep Experiences and Dreams" by Herman A. Witkin and Helen B. Lewis. From *Experimental Studies in Dreaming*, edited by Herman A. Witkin and Helen B. Lewis. Copyright © 1967 by Random House, Inc. Reprinted by permission of the publisher. "Vicarious Extinction of Avoidance Behavior" by Albert Bandura, Joan E. Grusec and Frances L. Menlove. From *Journal of Personality and Social Psychology*, V, 1967, pp. 16–23. Reprinted by permission. "Cognitive Effects of False Heart-Rate Feedback" by Stuart Valins. From *Journal of Personality and Social Psychology*, IV, 1966, pp. 400–408. Reprinted by permission. "The Case of Dawn" by G. W. Goethals and D. S. Klos. Abridged from pages 329–360 of George W. Goethals and Dennis S. Klos, *Experiencing Youth: First-Person Accounts*. Copyright © 1970 by Little, Brown and Company. Reprinted by permission. "The Cash Posters: A Study of a Group of Working Girls" by George C. Homans. From *American Sociological Review*, XIX, December 1954, pp. 724–733. Reprinted by permission. "Sex as Work: A Study of Avocational Counseling" by Lionel S. Lewis and Dennis Brissett. From *Social Problems*, Vol. 15, #1, Summer 1967, pp. 8–18. Reprinted by permission of The Society for the Study of Social Problems. "The Hasher: A Study of Role Conflict" by Louis A. Zurcher, David W. Sonenschein, and Eric L. Metzner. From *Social Forces*, XLIV, June 1966, pp. 505–514. Reprinted by permission. "Social Class and Campus Dating" by Ira L. Reiss. From *Social Problems*, Vol. 13, #2, Fall 1965, pp. 193–205. Reprinted by permission of The Society for the Study of Social Problems. "The Navy Disbursing Officer as a Bureaucrat" by Ralph H. Turner. From *American Sociological Review*, XLL, June 1947, pp. 342–348. Reprinted by permission of The American Sociological Association. "To Comfort and To Challenge" by Charles Y. Glock, Benjamin B. Ringer, and Earl R. Babbie. From *To Comfort and To Challenge*, chapter 9, pp. 202–216. University of California Press, 1967. Originally published by the University of California Press; reprinted by permission of The Regents of the University of California. "Stripteasers: The Anatomy and Career Contingencies of A Deviant Occupation" by

James K. Skipper, Jr. and Charles H. McCaghy. From *Social Problems*, Winter, 1970, Vol. 17, #3, pp. 391–405. Reprinted by permission of The Society for the Study of Social Problems. "Wincanton: The Politics of Corruption" by John A. Gardiner, with the assistance of David J. Olson. From the President's Commission on Law Enforcement and Administration of Justice: Task Force Reports: Organized Crime, Appendix B, pp. 61–70, 78–79. "The Study of Race" by Sherwood L. Washburn. Reproduced by permission of the American Anthropological Association from *American Anthropologist*, Vol. 65, No. 3, 1963. "Tree Rings—The Archaeologist's Time-Piece" by Dr. Emil W. Haury. Reproduced by permission of the Society for American Archaeology from *American Antiquity*, Vol 1, No. 2, 1935. "The Logic of Non-Standard English" by William Labov. From the Georgetown Monograph Series on Languages and Linguistics, Number 22, 1969. Reprinted by permission. "A Yoruba Market-Woman's Life" by Janheinz Jahn. Reprinted by permission of Grove Press, Inc. Translated by Oliver Coburn. Copyright © 1962 by Faber and Faber Ltd. Reprinted by permission of Faber and Faber Ltd. from *Through African Doors* by Janheinz Jahn. "Maternal Care and Infant Behavior in Japan and America" by William Caudill and Helen Weinstein. From *Psychiatry* (1969) 32: 12–43. "The Sexual Life of Savages: in North-Western Melanesia" by Bronislaw Malinowski. From *The Sexual Life of Savages* by Bronislaw Malinowski. Reprinted by permission. "Shakespeare in the Bush" by Laura Bohannan. From *Natural History*, LXXV (1966) pp. 28–33. Copyright © 1966 by *Natural History* magazine. "Fathoms and Feet, Acres and Tons: An Appraisal" by Keith Gordon Irwin. From *Scientific Monthly*, Vol. 72, pp. 9–17, January 1951. Reprinted by permission. "Scarcity, Competitive Behavior, and Economics" by Armen A. Alchian and William R. Allen. From *Exchange and Production Theory in Use* by Armen A. Alchian and William R. Allen. Copyright © 1964, 1967, 1969 by Wadsworth Publishing Company, Inc., Belmont, California. Reprinted by permission of the publisher. "The Economic Organization of a POW Camp" by R. A. Radford. From *Economica*, XII, November 1945, pp. 290–317. Reprinted by permission. "The Merchant and the Low-Income Consumer: The Poor Pay More" by David Caplovitz. Reprinted with permission of The Macmillan Company from *The Poor Pay More* by David Caplovitz. Copyright ©1963 by The Free Press of Glencoe, a Division of The Macmillan Company. "Litton Industries: Big Brother as a Holding Company" by David Horowitz and Reese Erlich. From *Ramparts*, October, 1968. Copyright © by Ramparts Magazine, Inc., 1968. Reprinted by permission of the Editors. "Pollution, Property, and Prices" by J. H. Dale. Reprinted from *Pollution, Property and Prices* by J. H. Dale by permission of University of Toronto Press. Copyright © 1968 University of Toronto Press. "The Greening of America" by Charles Reich. From *The Greening of America* by Charles Reich. Copyright © 1970 by Charles A. Reich. Reprinted by permission of Random House, Inc. Originally appeared in the *New Yorker*. "Hell No, We Won't Go" by John Cooney and Dana Spitzer, from *TRANS-action*, September 1969. Copyright © September, 1969 by TRANS-action, Inc., New Brunswick, New Jersey. Reprinted by permission. "We Will Exercise Our Rights" by Stephen Wasserman. From *The High School Revolutionaries*, edited by Marc Libarle and Tom Seligson. Copyright © 1970 by Marc Libarle and Tom Seligson. Reprinted by permission of Random House, Inc. "The Food and Drug Administration and the Pill" by Alice J. and Phillip E. Wolfson. From *Social Policy*, Vol. I, No. 3, (September/October 1970). Reprinted by permission of the publisher, International Arts and Sciences Press, Inc., White Plains, New York. "If You Were on Welfare" by Richard M. Elman. From *Saturday Review*, Vol. LIII, No. 21, May 23, 1970, pp. 27, 28, 29, 61.

Reprinted by permission of International Famous Agency. Copyright © 1970 by Saturday Review, Inc. "Americans Betrayed" by Morton Grodzins. From *Americans Betrayed* by Morton Grodzins. Copyright © 1949 by The University of Chicago Press. Reprinted by permission of the publisher. "Black Revolution: A Primer for White Liberals" by Charles V. Hamilton. From *Progressive*, January 1969. Reprinted by permission. "The Double Deception: The Problem of Aggression" by Howard Zinn. From *Vietnam: The Logic of Withdrawal* by Howard Zinn, chapter 7. Copyright © 1967 by Howard Zinn. Reprinted by permission of Beacon Press.

The Social Scene

Introduction: The Domain of the Social Sciences

Science is a vast enterprise involving innumerable persons in literally every country of the world. Science advances understanding and enables people to explain their behavior and the environment in which they live. Through the application of scientific findings, people have developed an extensive number of products and procedures that extend life, improve our physical and psychological well-being and give us more control over our destinies. Unfortunately, the same approach has led to the development of lethal weapons and other destructive devices. The constructive or destructive use of science has come to depend, however, upon ethical and moral questions.

Precisely because science is so vast, no scientist or group of scientists can be technically competent in all areas. For this reason science is generally separated into three families or domains—the physical and biological sciences and the social sciences–which may or may not overlap. Within each of these three families there is further specialization.

The Social Scene provides an introduction to the **social sciences** which can be defined briefly as the study of the behavior of people in human society. As we shall see, the social sciences are sometimes also called the behavioral sciences. We will begin by defining more completely the term **social sciences** and then by considering the major disciplines—psychology, sociology, anthropology, economics, and political science—that are encompassed by this term.

What Are the Social Sciences?

A recent report of a distinguished commission to the National Science Foundation offered the following definition of the **social sciences:**

The **social sciences** are intellectual disciplines that study man as a social being by means of the scientific method. It is their focus on man as a member of **society** and on the **groups** and **societies** he forms, that distinguishes the **social sciences** from the physical and biological sciences (National Science Foundation, 1969, p. 7).

A review of the outlook and needs of the **social sciences** describes them as *dealing with the behavior of people, their relations with other human beings and the environment they share* (National Academy of Sciences—Social Science Research Council, 1969, p. 19).

The five **social sciences** generally regarded as essential social science disciplines—psychology, sociology, anthropology, economics, and political science—are in many ways difficult to define and to distinguish from one another. They share a concern with **social processes** and the products and consequences of **social relationships** The bonds between the various disciplines are real. They provide the different perspectives necessary to obtain a rounded picture of human behavior and of human **societies** An individual's actions take place within an environment and this environment is composed of people, the traditions they have inspired, and the objects they have produced.

It bears emphasis that there are large overlaps between the social science disciplines, as well as overlaps with several of the biological and physical sciences. Indeed, a number of special disciplines, areas that fall between the more traditionally established ones, have grown up and achieved an autonomy of their own. Perhaps the best-known such discipline is **social psychology**, which is concerned with the individual in relation to his group behavior and group processes. Social psychology has dual parentage in psychology and sociology and both disciplines continue to contribute to its development (Sherif and Sherif, 1969, pp. 18–19).

We will continue to emphasize the interrelationships between the various **social sciences**; it is necessary, however, both for analytical purposes and to achieve an effective allocation of work, to split the **social sciences** into disciplines, and to consider each one separately.

Psychology

Psychology can be thought of as a science of individual behavior and mental processes; it studies the individual as he acts in his natural environment or in the laboratory. It includes observable phenomena, such as gestures and speech, physiological changes like heart rate and sweating, and thought processes that must be inferred from answers to problems and dreams. Psychologists study the nature and organization of **mental processes** in people; they also determine his **motivations**. Psychologists deal with the **mental abilities** and **aptitudes** of individuals; their capacities for learning, thinking and emotional expression. The most common application of psychology concerns learning and education problems, problems of personnel selection in industry, and concerns of clinical assessment and care of mental illness.

Psychology is interrelated with sociology; it deals with individual behavior as it takes place in a complex social environment. The investigations of psychologists working in laboratories on experiments with birds, lower mammals and primates provide us with a knowledge of the brain and its mechanisms, the forces that motivate individuals, the problems of mental disorders and the ways that we learn. These studies can then be applied to human infants, growing children, and adults of all ages. Psychology is in part also a life science closely related to biology. The behavior of people naturally depends on neurological and physiological processes.

Sociology

Sociology is the discipline that investigates the collective behavior of individuals. We have seen that psychologists study the individual in his environment. Sociologists also study the behavior and motivation of individuals as they relate to each other and undertake activities in **groups** and organizations. Sometimes sociology is referred to as the science of **society**. It studies the structure, functions and various features of **societies** and **communities** such as families, religious **groups**, professions, occupations, race relations, and so on. In addition, sociology is applied to a large extent to the many social problems in the **community** such as crime, violence, and **poverty**. In this sense sociology is interrelated with anthropology, economics and political science, because **poverty** is a cultural, political and economic as well as a sociological problem.

Anthropology

Anthropology sometimes is difficult to distinguish from sociology; both disciplines study the **societies** *in which people live and the social forms and structures within which individual and group behavior takes place.* Anthropology is a generic name for a number of even further specialized fields including **social anthropology, archaeology, physical anthropology** and **linguistics**. Traditionally, anthropologists have studied pre-literate and developing **cultures**. More recently anthropologists are studying **cultures** of industrialized **societies**, such as the United States. While many anthropologists continue to study pre-literate **societies**, Indian tribes, South Sea Islanders, and so on, more and more anthropologists are focusing their work on urban **groups** and seeking to understand **kinship** patterns, friendship relationships, the **values** and **beliefs** that characterize the contemporary urban center. Anthropologists have produced fruitful work on important contemporary problems such as **poverty**, ghetto life, minority **groups** and mental health.

Anthropologists who specialize in **physical anthropology** are concerned with the **evolution** of the human body, the antiquity of people and the development of human and social qualities. **Archaeology** is closely linked to **physical anthropology**. Archaeologists are concerned with early people and their **culture**. Through the physical residue of earlier times, they are putting together art objects, buildings, and burial mounds in an effort to reconstruct earlier civilizations which have no recorded histories. **Social** and **cultural anthropology** is concerned with the organization, arrangement, **beliefs** and **values** of **groups** of people. In **linguistics**, anthropologists study the universals of human language and thought and their links to the behavior and social life of people.

Economics

Economics is sometimes defined as the study of the allocation of available productive resources among competing uses. The work of economists is focused on employment, **inflation** and **deflation**, economic growth, fiscal and monetary policies, international payments, taxation, monopolies, manpower, labor markets, union movements, agricultural and industrial production and the inequities resulting from the distribution of income.

The theories and work of economists strongly influence the domestic and international policies of our government and the workings of both large and small businesses in the United States. Although many economists are engaged in generalized economic studies of a national or international scope, a number of them focus on highly specific topics, such as the problems involved in producing goods or of marketing and selling products. **Economic indicators** such as prices, wages and unemployment figures are well-known to us, and the public is probably more familiar with the areas of examination of economists than with any of the other **social sciences**. We worry constantly, for example, about **inflation** or recession. Economists provide indicators on these economic problems for persons and local or national governments.

Political Science

Political science investigates the ways in which people govern themselves. It is concerned with the goals of the political system, the structural relationships in that system, the patterns of **individual** and **group behavior** which help explain how the system functions, and the development of laws and social policies. Political scientists study a variety of phenomena involved in the process of government including political parties, **interest groups**, communication and public opinions, **bureaucracy**, and public administration.

In the United States, political scientists have provided us with considerable information about voting habits, such as the reasons underlying which persons vote and why they vote for certain individuals. They have also analyzed problems associated with the way local and national governments are developed and organized, as well as problems of international tensions such as those between competing **ideologies**. Some political scientists study the local **communities** in which they live; others are concerned with the development and processes of government in new nations or in remote

communities. Some political scientists focus on broad ideological issues such as the emergent organizations of governments under **communism, socialism** and various other ideologies. Others are more microscopic in that they investigate and concern themselves with the way particular departments operate at a city or state government level. The political scientist, then, investigates political processes that set up and enforce various rules of collective behavior to realize group interests and to protect individual rights. He is concerned with patterns of interpersonal and **group behavior** which contribute to the ways in which various political systems function, and with the goals and structural relationships of political systems.

The Concept of the Behavioral Sciences

We have mentioned that the **social sciences** are sometimes described as the **behavioral sciences**. Many persons use the terms interchangeably. For a significant number, however, the concepts have somewhat different meanings, although the definitions of both are fuzzy. The term **behavioral sciences** was invented both to eliminate from consideration those aspects of the **social sciences** that are not directly concerned with behavior (such as **archaeology**) and to allow such fields as psychiatry and physiology to be included as **behavioral sciences**. The term is a more recent one than the term **social sciences**.

How Social Scientists Work

Basically all scientists follow the same rules in their work (Freeman and Jones, 1970, pp. 3–4). They subscribe to a methodology or philosophy, if you will, which is commonly known as the scientific method.

Social scientists are trained to share a common outlook and to be aware of a wide set of techniques, although between disciplines there are differences in the emphasis given to the range of these techniques.

There are a number of rules in common, as Berelson and Steiner (1964) note. Their discussion is as brief and clear-cut as any:

The procedures are public: The results and the methods are both communicable and communicated. The scientific report contains a detailed description of just what was done and how. The description is adequate if, and only if, another competent practitioner of the science can follow each step of the investigation. In addition:

The definitions are precise: Here again, the procedure must be crystal-clear. As an example, the statement "aggressive subjects were found to have greater dependence on their fathers than non-aggressive subjects" is inadequate as a scientific report. How was aggressive defined and measured? By what test or procedures and by what specific scores? Where was the cut-off point between aggressive and non-aggressive subjects? How was dependence on the father revealed?

The data-collecting is objective: Once the investigation is underway, the investigator is bound to follow the data, whatever way they may fall—for or against his hypothesis (however cherished), and for or against his personal preferences. Biased procedures in collecting data have no place in science, nor has biased perception of the results. As a result:

The findings are replicable: Because of the openness of the inquiry, another scholar can test the findings by seeking to reproduce them. This is why "artistic sensitivity" or "clinical insight" is itself not sufficient, though it may of course suggest hypotheses. And, although all persons in the social sciences strive for replicability, the ability to repeat is more difficult in studying certain problems.

The purposes are explanation, understanding, and prediction: The scientist wants to know why and how, and to be able to prove it. If he can, then he can predict the conditions under which the specified behavior will occur. And if he can do that, then the question of control enters in as well. We have achieved a great deal of control over nature in the physical and biological sciences, and some in economic affairs; but the matter inevitably becomes more sensitive with the prospect that the behavioral sciences will enable us to control ourselves, or each other.

Thus, there are a variety of procedures and techniques used by social scientists. In broad terms, one can think about three different approaches which are commonly employed in the **social sciences**; the experiment, the survey, and the case study.

An *experiment* is any investigation that includes two elements: manipulation or control of some variable and systematic observation or measurement of the results. Experiments are common to all fields of science and those undertaken in the **social sciences** differ only by subject matter from ones in other fields. However, particularly in psychology, and to some extent in sociology, much of the investigation which is undertaken is by experiment. The basic design is the same. Some experiments in **social science** are carried out in laboratories; these are mainly studies undertaken with animals and are conducted under conditions that are as sterile and as well-controlled as research of a biological or physical nature. Other experiments are carried out in **communities** which are being investigated. Many of these experiments are complicated because of the realities of the everyday environment. One of the limitations of such experiments is the difficulty of manipulating and controlling the complex world in which we live. Another limitation is the concern for the well-being and privacy of subjects which might be otherwise affected by experiments.

The *survey*, known to many of us because of public opinion polling, is a common means of assessing political views, consumer preferences and the like. A wide variety of surveys are undertaken each year by social scientists, mainly by economists and political scientists. The surveys differ greatly in the topics considered and in their extent. (They also differ in whether they are carried out with selected subgroups from the population, or whether they are broad national studies of representative samples.) Generally, however, surveys are more concerned with factual and behavioral data rather than with delving deeply into the psychological recesses of individuals regarding their **beliefs**, **values** and **motives**.

Finally, there are *case studies*, either of single individuals or organizations, or of comparisons of several different people or **groups**. Much of the work of anthropologists consists of case studies. The survey measures many persons on a few characteristics, usually on one point in time. The case study typically examines quite intensively many characteristics of one or a few units, such as a **community**. Usually, case studies extend over relatively long periods of time. They may be of a particular person, perhaps during adolescence, or of a particular **community** during a period of rapid change in its ethnic or racial composition, or of a particular social class of persons in a city, or of any other special or definable **group**.

In addition an important source of information to social scientists is regularly collected information, public reports or other types of public records. For example, much economic analysis is based upon the information uniformly and regularly collected by federal, state and local governments. Sociologists often make use of statistics collected by police departments, the FBI and other law enforcement agencies in trying to understand **deviant behavior** and the crime problem. Many of these records are quite suitable for research; others are limited in accuracy and specificity.

It should be noted that there are widely divergent methods and techniques used in collecting data. *One of the dimensions running throughout the* **social sciences** *is the extent to which a particular study is quantitative—reported in numerical terms—or qualitative—reported in verbal statements*. Descriptions in terms of statistics, such as averages, and those reported in terms of "more" or "less" are equally valuable. However, the use of quantitative methods depends to a large extent on the particular field of inquiry. Likewise sometimes events, behavior or incidents are directly observed. At other times they are reported by the subjects themselves, and still at other times by individuals who are only marginally involved in some particular process or event. Some social scientists depend heavily on what is called **participant observation**, where the scientists literally become or have been and continue to be a part of the **groups** that they study. Others are much more detached and sit in their offices, directing large staffs of highly–trained interviewers who seek out appropriately designated informants. Both in terms of scope and intensity the key attribute of all scientific investigation seems to be systemization and replicability.

Any discussion of scientific method, however brief, must explicitly acknowledge the limitations that exist within all of the **social sciences** in conforming to generally-accepted ideas of scientific rigor. In certain of the disciplines, and when studying a number of critical research problems, opportunities for replication and precision are very limited. For example, anthropologists who use a **semi-participant observation approach** in studying a particular society at a particular time simply cannot repeat their investigations exactly. Limitations of time and money require that some studies be undertaken with less than perfectly developed instruments, or with measures whose reliability and validity are questionable. Nevertheless, regardless of the limitations of particular studies or work in the particular disciplines, social scientists hold in common with all scientists the attitude that it is important to strive to meet the general criteria for scientific work.

Finally, it should be pointed out that while social scientists try to operate with a set of procedures that emphasize objectivity, the choice of the problems they study and sometimes the way they go about studying these problems are related to who they are and what their values are. Social science is not "value free" in the sense of deciding what to study and when to undertake an investigation. However, scientific rigor is important in determining how one conducts a study. Indeed, there are continual accusations from both the radical right and left that the problem-selection process is dominated by persons whose values do not represent theirs. They feel that the "wrong" problems are often worked on and that they are being disenfranchised from using social science to advance their interests. Whether or not their accusations are justified is not a matter for this volume. However, perhaps the fact that these accusations exist clarifies the difference between objectivity in how social science operates and subjectivity in what social science emphasizes.

The Basic and Applied Social Sciences

As is probably apparent from the discussion so far, the social sciences, like all science, contribute *both* to the knowledge base and to the solution and resolution of practical problems and issues. Often, a distinction is made between basic and applied science. The difference lies not so much in the actual steps or procedures that the scientists employ, but rather in the problems they select for their study and their concern for immediate practical applications. There is certainly a great difference between a social scientist who analyzes poverty in the biblical era and one who is concerned with poverty now. Different also are the investigator who studies public administration in the colonial period and the political scientist who studies problems of governmental administration in Washington today.

Recently, the social sciences and related disciplines have been more concerned with the immediacy of their work. There is a tendency on the part of social scientists and government, industry and community leaders to apply the knowledge, theories, techniques and procedures of the social sciences to the contemporary community and its many problems. (Freeman and Sherwood, 1970). The applied emphasis of the social sciences differs considerably. For instance, economics has long-term and historical links to government, industry and people of action, while sociology and anthropology have been traditionally more distant from the policy-maker and practitioner. Psychologists serve as therapists, vocational counselors and assessors of aptitudes and mental ability.

The social sciences like all science have a dual function. They serve to help people cope with their environment and at the same time to explore and to understand the world about them. In other words, simultaneously there is an interest in application and an interest in understanding. The balance between basic work and applied activities is often the subject of controversy among persons identified with the various social science disciplines. But while many social scientists hold that the primary goal of the social sciences is the discovery and verification of generalizations on social behavior, whether or not they are immediately useful in programs to improve social life and social conditions, given our troubled times, the applied perspective seems to be gaining adherents.

As we have noted, the social sciences were reviewed by the National Academy of Sciences and the Social Science Research Council (1969) which determined how useful they were in dealing with the many interpersonal and social problems that we face today. For the purpose of their report they chose an example from each of the social sciences to show how that particular social science has been useful:

Psychology—It is largely the work of psychologists that led to the development of computer instruction and reading improvement programs. This approach has raised the reading levels of hundreds of thousands of children throughout the country and revolutionized a part of our general educational system.

Sociology—Sociologists' studies of segregation in schools provided information that led to both federal and local efforts to modify the racial composition of public schools.

Anthropology—Comparative studies of child rearing by anthropologists in which differences were found from one culture to the next have proved valuable to therapists and counselors in providing guidance to parents on the development of their children.

Economics—the development of economic indicators which provide figures at regular intervals on such matters as the cost of living, unemployment, and production of manufactured goods, are invaluable in planning the industrial and technical development of the country.

Political Science—Information and analysis by political scientists on nation building and the ramifications of social change in educational programs, occupational distributions and the like around the world have been used by our government, international organizations and private groups in establishing policies toward the developing nations.

The social sciences are far from having all the answers to the problems facing contemporary society. They are limited in method, theory and the manpower necessary to meet the many demands made upon them for new knowledge and improved application of existing knowledge. Social scientists in many ways have not been able to meet the expectations of persons in the community who are convinced that the very existence of people and progress toward better social conditions can come from the so-called "scientific method." But the potential is there and the work and accomplishments we can now see are convincing evidence of the promise of the **social sciences**.

Finally, it should be noted that there are a wide variety of practicing professionals—social workers, educators, persons in the medical specialties such as psychiatry, public health and rehabilitation, lawyers engaged in a variety of criminal and civil practices, city planners, recreation workers and the like whose knowledge base is drawn primarily from the **social sciences**. These practicing professionals and technicians, as well as, of course, responsible and intelligent laymen, gain much from an understanding of the **social sciences**. Many of their clinical and practice techniques, their procedures and perspectives are predicated on principles derived from the theories and research of the **social sciences**. In fact, in recent years, there has been a growing awareness and understanding of the **social sciences** on the part of socially concerned individuals, as well as professionals and technicians, in the fields of health, education and welfare, and medicine.

We have mentioned both the complex interrelationships between the **social sciences** and their potential contributions to problem-solving. Many of the problems that the world faces today require the combined efforts of persons in all of the **social science** disciplines, since these problems are beyond the interest and abilities of persons in any single discipline. Sometimes, one **social science** has more to offer than another; generally all of the **social sciences** can be brought into play in analyzing complex social problems. This is certainly true of such complex crises as international conflict in Viet Nam or the Middle East, or of our ecological environment, where noise pollution is of great concern to psychologists, air and water pollution of concern to economists and especially political scientists, who are concerned with the many political aspects of pollution. The **social sciences** cannot individually or collectively pretend to have pat solutions to any of these very complicated issues. Rather, their contribution to any solution is to provide a detailed analysis of the problem. They can also present options which can be elected to reduce the problem, and the benefits and consequences of implementing alternate programs. For example, **the social sciences** have made important contributions to understanding the causes and effects of **poverty**.

An Analysis of Poverty from the Multidisciplinary Approach of the Social Sciences

Poverty is both difficult to define and to measure; it has different meanings to various **groups** in the **community**. Its meaning depends upon the economic, social and psychological environment and the cultural **values** held by community members, particularly those with power and influence. Also, its definition has changed with time. A century ago, one would have been regarded as impoverished if he lacked the most basic necessities of food, clothing and shelter. As industrialization, urbanization and the **gross national product (GNP)** increased while human suffering and inequalities spread, social leaders began to question the assumption that **poverty** was the normal condition of the masses. Their definition of want, however, meant lacking sufficient resources to ward off starvation, to provide the most basic medical care, to supply a minimum of clothing and shelter, and to be able to survive a reasonable number of years as an adult (Freeman & Jones, 1970, 80–81). Today's poor, in contrast to the skilled and semi-skilled laborers who immigrated to this country, are external aliens in the affluent country of their birth.

To quote Michael Harrington (Ferman & Kornbluh, 1968:vii):

> They are the rejects of the past. They are the people who have been driven off farmlands, workers displaced by technological advancement, old folks who face **poverty** in their declining years, women left alone to raise the children, unemployed teenagers and youths who have dropped out of school but cannot find jobs. This is a new kind of **poverty** in a new kind of **society.** This is the first **poverty** of automation, the first **poverty** of the minority poor, and a **poverty** that under present conditions could become hereditary, transmitted from **generation** to **generation,** unless the typical cycles of **poverty** are broken.

Today the definition of **poverty** includes many more people than those who are literally "starving to death." We regard all persons as entitled to more than the minimum amounts of food and the bare necessities.

As we have seen, any attempt to define **poverty** must bring into play all of the **social sciences**. Economists emphasize monetary terms, or dollars, in defining **poverty,** but recognize that **poverty** cannot be defined solely in terms of dollars. Definitions of the poor must take into account the living conditions of the entire **community**, of the fortunate as well as of the impoverished, whether the poor are living in the city or in the country. Specifically we shall see in the economics section, where the **concept** of **poverty** is introduced, that the poor people of lower class Harlem are obliged to pay more for lower quality goods than those people who live in the upper class neighborhoods of New York City.

It is also necessary to assess the **values** of **community** members and their leadership regarding what constitutes a right and proper existence. Thus, in the very task of describing the conditions of **poverty**, economists work with sociologists and anthropologists to develop a perspective which is concerned with the quality of life as well as one's income and expenditures. The various methods of sociology and anthropology are used to obtain information about the living conditions of the economically deprived, as well as the **values** of policy-makers and the views of the general public concerning what constitutes acceptable living standards. For instance, federally-sponsored surveys are continually being undertaken to assess the types of goods that Americans want and need. Other surveys are undertaken to determine the levels and characteristics of the unemployed.

Psychologists use the term "relative deprivation" to identify the gap or distance between an individual's own situation and the life circumstances of groups with which he identifies—groups which psychologists and sociologists aptly refer to as a person's "reference group." Also, the importance of the community leader, the policy and decision-maker, in defining poverty has been stressed. What he believes and does greatly influence the ordinary citizens' views on poverty. The political scientist has a critical role in the identification of community leaders, the sources of their power and what determines and influences their behavior.

Each of the various social sciences is brought to bear not only in *defining* the problem of poverty and *identifying* the poor, but also in the search for the *causes* of poverty. For example, psychologists have provided a great deal of documentation that the social and economic backgrounds of children are associated with markedly different experiences for social stimulation and therefore the acquisition of knowledge. Differences in the type of interaction that children enjoy or suffer during their early lives have continued impact on their motivation and ability to perform intellectual tasks and thus to adapt to a society in which certain talents are increasingly rewarded. For example, psychologists have discovered that even the phenomena of learning the dominant language of a society is influenced by familial environment. This occurs, it seems, because children learn how to speak from listening to their parents and friends. In middle-class homes, children hear the language of the majority and are continually encouraged to develop facility in language. In certain poor, minority-group homes, the child hears a different language and is less frequently rewarded for being "a good talker." Moreover, poor children are usually chastised and punished more often than middle-class children and therefore build up an expectation of criticism from adults. This especially influences how they react to praise and punishment from others. In the section on psychology the reading by David Rosenhan specifically documents the influence that poverty and social class have on the motivation and responsiveness of children.

Anthropologists work closely with psychologists to identify the number of possible cultural differences between the environment of the poor and the more fortunate in the United States. They refer to the "culture of poverty." Anthropologists such as Oscar Lewis point out that the way of life of the poor, their values and behavior patterns represent aspects of a different social system. (Lewis, 1966) These anthropologists maintain that the poor are characterized by different cultural goals and values which deviate from those held by the majority. While not all social scientists totally accept the "culture of poverty" viewpoint, it is generally held that:

The behavior of lower-class persons is usually outside the mainstream of cultural control. They exist in a milieu impoverished to the point where social learning is retarded because impulse and immediate feelings rather than normative planning tend to control their behavior, their interest in educational or occupational achievements is very limited. Concerned primarily with subsistence rather than status achievements, they have few aspirations. In contrast to those in the working class, lower-class persons seek jobs that pay good money now. They do not seriously consider the potential for steady employment and advancement. (Komarovsky, 1969, pp. 199–200).

The work of sociologists on the causes of **poverty** has revealed that for many community members there is only a limited potential within our **social structure** for occupational and social mobility—the possibility of persons improving their economic and social lot. For example, economic mobility, for the most part, depends on education. For the lower classes, quality education is limited because neither their home lives nor the resources of the available schools are adequate. These factors only tend to reinforce the **poverty** of the poor.

The sociologists' work is closely related to economic analyses of the labor force and economic conditions of life in the United States. Economists have provided invaluable statistical evidence on the present and future economic growth of the country. They are continually projecting the supply and demand for various types of labor. This data is essential for understanding the problem of **poverty**. Since the importance of the different causes of **poverty** changes from time to time, without up-to-date data and trend information provided by economists, it would be extremely difficult to determine the shifting importance of these changes for the poor.

Then too, political scientists and sociologists have pointed sharply to the alienation of the poor. Political scientists have documented the lack of opportunity for persons with limited income to participate fully in the political and social affairs of the country. Studies show the consequences and ramifications of their rejection. Alienation of the poor reduces motivation to involve themselves in various types of educational and social activities essential for economic advancement. Political scientists continually analyze the data on voting and participation in community activities to monitor the progress being made by the disenfranchised, and the extent to which alienation and **poverty** are interrelated.

The work of social scientists does not stop at trying to understand the *causes* of **poverty**. Rather, they have been very active in the development of a wide range of programs to control and ameliorate the suffering of the poor. They have participated in the design of a variety of programs to rehabilitate the lot of specific individuals among the poor. An example is the development of vocational training centers for persons who have never had the opportunity to learn a skill or who need special training because of physical and mental disabilities. Sociologists have also promoted what are referred to as structural opportunity programs. These programs seek to modify the opportunities for social participation and to reduce irrational barriers to employment and education. Changes in admission policies at universities, the development of community colleges, the establishment of skill-training centers, legal assistance for the poor and so on have all been stimulated by the work of social scientists.

A major ongoing effort is the involvement of the poor in the political process. While some question the tactics of certain programs, including some social scientists, there is considerable agreement that it is important for community members of low income not only to share in decisions relating to the amelioration and control of their own social problems, but also to perceive of themselves as having a voice and a **role** in the general life of the **community**. For example, in the health area, new programs that involve setting up community health centers have boards composed of local residents who influence policies. Or, by removing such barriers as literacy tests, it is possible to encourage larger numbers of poor people to vote in local and state elections. Also, modifications in the economic support of the poor, and a shift from a poorly-organized, ineffective welfare system to proposals for some form of guaranteed annual income or negative income tax has been stimulated and developed by economists and other social scientists.

Many social scientists have been extremely vocal in pointing out, to policy-makers and the public in general, the relationship between international problems and conflicts and the problem of **poverty** in the nation. They have demanded a reordering of our national priorities in favor of the poor. Analyses have been conducted of the consequences of our foreign policy in Viet Nam and Indo-China to determine how much these international and defense commitments drain off what could be applied to domestic programs. Like the matter of participation of the poor in community programs and efforts designed to improve their lot, the views of social scientists on the relationship between the domestic and international arenas have not gone unchallenged. However, social scientists have performed an invaluable service to the **community** by constantly pointing up the importance of this relationship.

Social scientists have also provided a constant reminder of the relationship between **poverty** and discrimination. They have pointed out the need to remove the racial and ethnic barriers that prevent the full participation of Blacks, Mexican-Americans, American Indians, Puerto Ricans and women in the economic and social life of the country. They have pointed to the strong connection between discriminatory behavior and economic deprivation in American **society**. Some community members and politicians are not in agreement with the views of social scientists concerning the need for strong action to maximize equality and remove discrimination. Nevertheless, the evidence provided by social scientists, and their influence and presence on the public and political scenes, have been important stimuli to social change.

The many ways in which social scientists have involved themselves in the problem of **poverty** illustrates the increasing **role** outside the classroom of persons from the several disciplines. More and more, teaching and scholarship are going hand in hand with social action and social change.

Psychology, Sociology, Anthropology, Economics and Political Science all provide a different perspective on problems of contemporary society. They contribute to our understanding of these problems by increasing our knowledge base, and by providing empirical evidence of the problems of people and approaches to their solution. The vast contemporary problems of ecology, pollution, over-population, race-relations and international conflict are all problems with which social scientists are intimately involved. Social scientists are increasingly meeting the demand for relevance.

References

Berelson, Bernard and Gary A. Steiner
    1964   *Human Behavior: An Inventory of Scientific Findings.* New York: Harcourt, Brace & World.

Biesanz, John and Mavis Biesanz
    1969   *Modern Society: An Introduction to Social Science.* Englewood Cliffs, New Jersey: Prentice-Hall.

Ferman, Louis A. and Joyce Kornbluh (eds.)
    1968   *Poverty in America,* Rev. ed. Ann Arbor: University of Michigan Press.

Freeman, Howard E. and Wyatt C. Jones
    1970   *Social Problems: Causes and Controls.* Chicago: Rand McNally.

Freeman, Howard and Clarence C. Sherwood
    1970   *Social Research and Social Policy.* Englewood Cliffs, New Jersey: Prentice-Hall.

Komarovsky, Mirra
    1969   "Blue Collar Marriage." From Roach, Gross, Gursslin. *Social Stratification in the United States.* Englewood Cliffs, New Jersey: Prentice-Hall.

Lewis, Oscar
    1966   *La Vida: A Puerto Rican Family in the Culture of Poverty.* San Juan & New York: Random House.

National Academy of Sciences—Social Science Research Council
    1969   *The Behavioral and Social Sciences: Outlook and Needs.* Washington, D.C.: National Academy of Science.

National Science Foundation—National Academy of Sciences
    1969   *Knowledge Into Action: Improving the Nation's Use of the Social Sciences.* Washington, D.C.: U.S. Government Printing Office.

Sherif, Muzafer and Carolyn W. Sherif
    1969   *Social Psychology.* New York: Harper & Row.

Psychology

Psychology

Introduction to Psychology

Concepts:

Schema
Recognition Memory for Words, Sentences, and Pictures, Roger N. Shepard

Concept
The Cross-Cultural Generality of Visual-Verbal Synesthetic Tendencies Charles E. Osgood

Motive
Effects of Social Class and Race on Responsiveness to Approval and Disapproval, David L. Rosenhan

Attention
The Determinants of Attention in the Infant, Jerome Kagan

Cognitive Transformations
Presleep Experiences and Dreams, Herman A. Witkin and Helen B. Lewis

Avoidance Behavior
Vicarious Extinction of Avoidance Behavior, Albert Bandura, Joan E. Grusec, and Frances L. Menlove

Emotion
Cognitive Effects of False Heart-Rate Feedback, Stuart Valins

Psychopathology
The Case of Dawn, G. W. Goethals and D. S. Klos

Introduction to Psychology

The psychology of people is complicated. For this reason, it helps to have a simplified blueprint of the basic elements that psychologists regard as important to an understanding of mental processes and behavior—what they regard as "the psychological system." A useful analogy is the building of a house. This process requires first of all a set of *basic units,* like wood, nails, brick, plaster, pipe and wire. Using these materials (the basic units), the builder undertakes a series of *procedures,* such as sawing, wiring, soldering and putting up studs. The result of applying these procedures to the basic units is a set of new *forms* like walls, rooms and, of course, the final house. The house, however, does not resemble the original materials, and is a *new structure.*

Let us see how this analogy pertains to human psychology. A person consists of a series of *basic units,* much like the nails, wood and wire in the house. These basic units are referred to by psychologists as *structures.* In the same way that builders undertake a series of procedures, in creating a house, these psychological structures are manipulated by psychological *processes,* which use outside information to produce a new set of psychological *products.* The ideas to be illustrated in the first set of articles describe some of the *structures, processes* and *products* that psychologists regard as significant and meaningful.

Structures

The *basic units* or *structures* used in psychology are broken down further into *associations* between events that occur close to each other in time or space; **schemata** for people or objects experienced and the *structures* used for *problem-solving,* which include **concepts**, rules and finally **motives**. In our Introduction we shall deal with and define further only three of these *structures*, namely, **schemata, concepts** and **motives**.

SCHEMA

A **schema** *can be defined as an abstract representation of experience* and is probably the first psychological structure to develop. For instance, an infant begins to establish **schemata** for events during the first few weeks of his life. The best way to appreciate a **schema** is to pick up a magazine and to look at a picture for a few moments and then to put it down. You now have some idea what was in that picture; what it was about, and how it was arranged. That idea, while not an exact photographic copy, is a **schema**. The important thing to remember about a **schema** is that it preserves the relationship among the individual elements in the picture. You know that some things are on top of others, although you certainly do not know the exact distance between the elements. A person can develop **schemata** for any experience, picture, speech, music, smell and touch. There are melodies you are able to recognize as familiar, and your capacity to recognize that you have heard them in the past is explained by the fact that you possess a **schema** for that musical experience.

The first reading by Roger Shepard illustrates man's enormous capacity to create and store a great many **schematas** in a short period of time. In Shepard's experiment, adults looked at over 600 different pictures, words, or sentences, devoting less than 10 seconds to each. After looking at 600 pictures, the adults would not have been able to spontaneously remember many of the pictures, but when they were shown a pair of pictures, one of which was in the pile they looked at and the other a new picture, and were asked to point to the one they had seen earlier, most adults were able to recognize over 95% of the pictures. Some recognized them all. This awesome performance can only be explained by assuming that the mind created some representation of each picture. The **schemata** permitted correct recognition. The results of Shepard's experiment indicate that our mind is full of hundreds of thousands of representations of past experience which we cannot always recreate while sitting alone in our room. However, if a particular situation that is in some way related to a past event occurs, we often are able to remember that a certain experience happened to us some time in our past.

We shall see, in the anthropology section, that **schemata** are important for **linguistics**, since **language** depends upon abstract representations or symbols of shared experiences. As the article by Roger Shepard indicates, the psychological aspects of recognition memory are critical to **linguistics** and to communication.

CONCEPT

A second important *structure* is the **concept**. The main difference between a **schema** and a **concept** can be appreciated by imagining the differences between a 3-year-old and a chemist, both looking at a picture of the chemical formula for the cellular substance DNA. The chemist is likely to say to himself, "DNA molecule." The child, who does not have this **concept**, can only represent its pictorial qualities as a **schema**. If we turn the molecule around the child might not realize that he had seen the picture before; the chemist would say that it is still the DNA molecule, regardless of its orientation in space. What is different about these two representations? The major difference is that the chemist has a mental structure consisting of a set of essential elements, which, in the case of DNA, include the 4 paired bases, the sugar and phosphate molecules and the connecting structures that hold the bases together in a twisted ladder.

A **concept** *is an arbitrary way of representing a common set of events or attributes that "stick" together across a variety of experiences.* A **concept** is never a particular event but always an abstraction of many events. It stands for the few shared qualities that are common to many situations. Consider the drawing of a cross. The 8-month-old represents this particular event as a **schema** while an adult represents it as the sign of the **concept** of Christian religion and thinks of it in its relationship to the church. Religion is a **concept** because there is no single object called religion, but rather many events that are characterized by a reference to God, church and commitment to moral principles. Religion, as a **concept**, summarizes those dimensions. The **concept** dog, refers to the set of dimensions hair, tail, four legs, an elongated face, friendly to people, and a barking sound. Without **concepts** people cannot order their world or share their ideas. Indeed, the **concept** of **"concept"** is vital to intellectual pursuits, as is evidenced by the organization of this volume.

In the next section on sociology we will see that sociologists use the term **norm** to refer to standards upon which community members agree. **Norms** have no applicability, however, unless a significant number of the members of a **community** evaluate them in the same way. In this sense, **norms** are for the sociologist a kind of **concept**.

There are three important qualities of **concepts**. The first concerns the degree to which **concept** refers to abstract entities, like justice, or to concrete, real objects, like dogs and cats. The second concerns the complexity or simplicity of the **concept**, for example, whether it has many or few dimensions. **Society** is a complex **concept**, for it has many dimensions. Nail is a simple **concept** for it has few dimensions. The third important quality of a **concept** pertains to the dimensions that are most central to its meaning. A barking sound is more central to the **concept** of dog than is an elongated face (consider a bull dog, for example). Some very important central dimensions of **concepts** include the ideas of good vs. bad, strong vs. weak, active vs. passive. The goodness or badness of a **concept** is critical because this evaluation is tied to the experiences of pleasure and pain. Early in a child's life he learns to call objects and events that cause him distress, bad; those that bring him pleasure, good. Food, warmth, mother, ice cream are good; sickness, bruises, spankings are bad. Moral standards are also **concepts** that are closely associated with the dimension good vs. bad. For example, the **concepts** steal and lie are moral standards, for most children believe that these are bad actions. Professor Charles Osgood of the University of Illinois has studied the conceptual dimensions used by people all over the world and has found that they tend to conceptualize events and objects on similar dimensions; the three most important being, *good* vs. *bad*, *strong* vs. *weak* and *active* vs. *passive*. Osgood says that people from four different language **cultures** conceptualize simple drawings in the same way. For example, most people regard the **concept** "bad" as *thick* and *crooked*, while the concept "good" is seen as *rounded* and *large*. Osgood's work suggests that all human beings must encounter a similar set of experiences which lead them to regard these **concepts** in a similar way.

MOTIVE

Motive is a third important *structure* after **schema** and **concept**. **Motive** refers to the idea of some goal that has not yet been attained; it refers to the mental representation of that desired event. A **motive** is neither the action that attains the goal nor the feeling of excitement, tension or pain that may accompany it. The actions and thoughts of human beings are often aimed at goals, where a goal is an experience the person desires. Many children have dreamed of flying to Disneyland or of yelling at their mother, but this wish was never acted upon. If we define **motive** as the idea that stands for the wanted experience, gratification of the **motive** is a little bit like finding a name on the tip of one's tongue; or like experiencing the match between idea and desired event. **Motive** is important in explaining why a lot of our actions are influenced by anticipations of the future. We cannot account for all of a person's behavior or predict his future actions unless we invent a word to explain intention. We need to explain why someone suddenly stops what he is doing and initiates new action without any provocation from the external environment. Or, why a person rises from a quiet library chair, leaves the room and returns ten minutes later. The word **motive** is as good as any in explaining why a person displays behavior that is inappropriate to the situation.

One of the important determinants of **motive** is the reaction of other people to one's actions. The article by David Rosenhan, in addition to pointing out that social class is often more of a determinant than **race** on motivational responsiveness, also indicates that children are especially motivated to learn by how adults will react to them, and adult approval or disapproval is often a major determinant of a child's motivation.

In fact, the next section on sociology indicates that sociologists are also concerned with **motive**. A reading in this section, called *Wincanton: The Politics of Corruption*, describes a situation in which the public is exploited for **motives** of economic gain by corrupt politicians, and indicates that economic gain is a major motivation in American **society**.

Motive was originally introduced into psychology to bear the burden of the notion of "cause" which was popular in natural sciences. Sigmund Freud made this an essential theme in his psychoanalytic theory, and he called the basic human causes "id impulses," suggesting that they could be conscious or unconscious **motives**. We now believe that some actions are not derived from **motives**; that some are unlearned reflexes like sneezing and coughing. Others are expected or habitual reactions to certain feeling states or situations. An American child sits in a chair to eat; a Japanese child kneels on a pillow; a New York commuter at an airport stands at a lunch counter. These specific actions are not motivated but are rather appropriate to the context. There are, however, many behaviors that are attempts to gratify **motives**. Four major subdivisions of **motives** are *sensory, control of uncertainty, hostility* and *mastery*.

Processes

Now that we have considered three important psychological *structures*—**schema**, **concept** and **motive**, we turn to two important *processes* which act on these structures and permit them to eventually become new *products*. The first process is the state called **attention**; the second process concerns the complex mental **transformations** that act on **motives**, **schemata**, and **concepts** to produce new ideas. Let us consider **attention** first.

ATTENTION

Attention is simultaneously the most critical, yet the most fragile psychological state. It is highly-selective, for we cannot attend to all aspects of our environment with equal facility. The mind can only work on one event at a time. There are many experiments that show that if two different messages are heard simultaneously through both ears, it is impossible to understand both messages. You can try this experiment in an environment where there are two conversations going on, a conversation you are having with someone and a background conversation several feet away. Notice how hard it is to understand both conversations at once. You can try to understand pieces of each one by shifting your **attention** back and forth very rapidly; but it is not possible to attend to both of them with equal intensity. **Attention** *involves focusing on one segment of experience and ignoring others.* **Attention** is a little like the beam of a flashlight in a dark room. If the attentional beam is broad, you can notice changes in those aspects of the room on which the beam falls. If the beam is narrow and focused on a small sector of the room, you are oblivious to changes in the dark parts of the room. You are less sensitive to changes in sights and sounds that are outside the narrow area of your concentration. You tend to learn most about a particular event when you are attending closely to it. Hence, if you knew when a person was attending to a lecture, and to what he was attending, you would know the knowledge he was acquiring. In fact, if brain waves become better predictors of particular states of **attention**, humans may some day become more adept at predicting and, perhaps, even controlling, states of **attention**.

The article on **attention** deals with those factors that determine sustained **attention** in the young child during the first 3 years of life. The young infant is born with innate tendencies to focus **attention** on events that change, like moving lights or stimuli that have much black-white contour contrast. However, by two months of age, experience has taken over and the child tends to invest long periods of **attention** on events that are discrepant from his **schema**. *The general principle states that the person will be maximally attentive to those events that are neither completely familiar nor completely novel but, like the baby-bear's porridge, "just right."* Toward the end of the first year, a new factor emerges: the richness of **concepts** and rules that the child actuates to help him understand discrepant events. We must differentiate between *immediate* and *delayed* understanding of an event. Delayed understanding occurs when it is impossible to comprehend an unusual event on first encounter and one has to activate a set of **concepts** and rules to aid in the explanation. For example, suppose one is on an airplane and hears an unusual sound from the engine. If you know very little about engines, there is nothing you can do or think about to explain the disturbing sound. However, if you have a lot of knowledge about how jet motors operate, these ideas will be activated and various explanations will be tried out, while you are attending to the unusual sound. The immediate understanding of an event is called **recognition**; delayed understanding following activation of **concepts** and rules is called **interpretation**. By the time the child is a year old he is already influenced by these three major determinants of **attention**, and will be influenced by them for the rest of his life.

COGNITIVE TRANSFORMATIONS

The mind is *not* an inert blackboard receiving information but a tree that manufactures new substances like chlorophyll. Chlorophyll is one essential product in every tree. But the presence of chlorophyll cannot be explained by noting that basic units such as water, light and chemicals pour into the plant from the outside. The water, sun and chemicals are necessary for the manufacture of chlorophyll, but complicated structures within the leaf transform these 3 elements into the new structure we call chlorophyll. Similarly, the mind takes in information from the outside and continually produces new mental *products*. It is impossible to understand the content of the mind only by knowing what was put in from the outside. Human creativity is an obvious example of this idea, for a creative product is, by definition, a product which few people had thought of before. Therefore, it could not have been experienced. A new invention, a new discovery, or a creative poem are products that could only have been generated by complex mental **transformations**.

The human dream is a good example of the importance of **cognitive transformations**. We have images and thoughts in dreams that have never been experienced before. That is one reason why we call dreams bizarre, nightmarish, or crazy. Mental processes act on our **schemata**, our **concepts**, and the day's events to produce the content of our dreams. Psychologists believe they may learn something about these transformational processes by studying human dreams. One method of performing these studies is to give people a controlled experience just before they go to sleep and to determine if the content of subsequent dreams is related to the content of the controlled experience. If it is, we may be able to decipher how the mind transforms the original information. The selection by Herman Witkin and Helen Lewis describes what adults dream after they have watched two highly dramatic films, one concerning a live birth, and the other a circumcision rite performed in an aboriginal tribe. Since a person shows certain rapid eye movements (called REM's) when he is dreaming, and his brain waves assume a particular form, the experimenter was able to tell when the subject was dreaming by recording the eye movements and brain waves of the sleeping adults. The subject was then awakened and asked to describe the dream he was having at that moment. By relating the content of that dream to the film he saw earlier, the scientists were able to obtain clues as to how the mind transforms information into dreams.

Products

The last class of important psychological ideas refers to *products* that result from the complex interrelationships of *structures* and *processes*. These products include the *complicated behaviors* people display, as well as **emotional states**, **beliefs** about the self, **fears** and **symptoms**.

AVOIDANCE BEHAVIOR AND ITS CURE

Some children, as well as adults, possess strong **fears** of objects or places. These fears may be acquired as a result of having experienced **fear** during an event, or of being told by other people that certain objects might hurt them. These **fears** and anxieties in children may be based on **beliefs**, which are transmitted to the child by such diverse sources as mothers or the mass media. This **avoidance behavior**, based on the unquestioning acceptance of social **beliefs** can often be reduced by increasing contact and communication with other members of **society**. Many mothers, for example, tell their children to be afraid of lightning, and the children shortly acquire a **fear** of thunderstorms. These two processes produce many children who are afraid of animals and objects, even man's best friend, The Dog. Since **fear** sustains avoidance of the dog, any procedures that reduce the **fear** should affect the child's tendency to approach the feared animal or object. There are many ways to reduce a child's **fear**. One can merely expose him to others who are engaged in the feared activity. Many young women, for example, entering college have not had prior sexual experience because of anxiety or guilt. They often experience a sharp reduction in **fear** when they learn that their roommates, or other students whom they respect, are engaging in sexual relationships with minimal distress. Within several months, their own behavior may change dramatically. This reduction of anxiety follows recognition that members of the peer **group** are displaying the feared behavior. This can be a major basis for behavioral change. Many of the changes in attitudes in our own society snowball because people meet and talk with those who hold different attitudes. The changing attitudes toward women's place in society, marijuana, or the Viet Nam war during the 1960's and 1970's are classic examples of this process. The article by Professors Bandura, Grusec and Menlove shows how fear of dogs can be alleviated in young children merely by having the frightened child watch other children approach and play with the animal.

EMOTION

The concept of emotion has been a perennially puzzling problem to people. Every human being has felt a sudden increase in his heart-beat, tightness of stomach, sweating of palms, or throbbing of head when he is insulted, sexually aroused, or confronted by a dangerous animal. *This interrelationship between distinctive external events and strong, salient, internal feelings is called emotion.* For instance, the external and internal effects of poverty or the fact that poor people are even more deprived and pay more for what they get, as mentioned in the economics section, can have long-term emotional consequences on individuals. Rituals, such as death rites, important to anthropologists in their study of communities are also institutionalized occasions for strong emotions. The controversy over emotion concerns whether there are separate internal, physiological states that might be specific to each emotion. For instance, is there a distinctive change in physiological arousal specific to anger, joy, depression or excitement? Some psychologists claim that this is true and believe that if we understood how the central nervous system worked, we could find places in the brain that discharged when the person experienced a particular emotion. Experiments by physiological psychologists have shown that there are specific areas in the brain that, when stimulated, will make an animal behave as if he were in a state of rage, contentment, or sexual excitement. An opposing view argues that since there are so many subtle differences in human emotions it would be impossible for a distinctive physiological state to accompany each of our emotions. Consider the differing connotations of the emotion "sadness." We have emotional words like, grief-stricken, mournful, sad, depressed, quiet, apathetic, lonely and alienated. It is unlikely that there are different physiological states to match each of these affect words.

This controversy between specific and nonspecific physiological states has led to the assumption that there are a small number of distinctive physiological feeling states that alert the person, force him to pay attention to how he feels, and provoke him to understand these feelings. A person wants to interpret why his heart is beating faster or why he feels uncomfortably warm. He has a problem and he assesses the physical context; the people with whom he is interacting; the events that have just occurred; his own thoughts; and arrives at an answer, usually unconsciously. The "answer" is an emotional state. The person may feel a pain in his leg, an emptiness in his stomach and a slight throbbing in his head. If he is sitting alone in a hotel room, 1000 miles from home, he may decide he is lonely. If he is driving home from work at 7:00 p.m., he may decide he is fatigued. The reading by Valins implying that the specific situation influences the emotional state a person subsequently assumes is carried one step further by showing that it is not even necessary to have a distinct physiological state. One can experience an emotional state of excitement *without any change* in physiology. Valins had college men look at attractive pin-up photos while they listened to a heartbeat which they *believed* was their own. It was, however, a tape-recorded heartbeat. Professor Valins made this "taped" heartbeat increase with certain pictures and remain the same for others. When the men were asked which of the photographed women they considered most attractive, they selected the ones that were accompanied by the increased heartbeat. It seems that many people have learned to associate certain physiological changes with "interest and excitement" and mere knowledge that there *might* be a physiological change is enough to trigger the affect state. This argument has strong implications for the **emotion** of **fear**. Suppose one overheard a person in a plane say "My palms are sweating but I am not afraid." Is this passenger afraid or not? It is likely that the person has learned that when palms sweat, one is afraid, although this association need not be true, for the palms might be sweating because the person had made a motoric adjustment to prepare himself for the plane's take-off. Hence, **emotions**, which most people regard as a fundamental biological process, are governed by complex interactions of **schemata** and **concepts**, and properly needs to be seen as a social process as well.

PSYCHOPATHOLOGY

A mental **symptom** is a complicated product that involves feelings of distress and anxiety, as well as the notion that one is not adjusted to **society**. From the standpoint of the afflicted individual, the **symptoms** he usually feels are pain, discomfort, or mental stress; from the standpoint of the **community**, the same **symptoms** often are viewed as a reflection of the individual's nonconformity. Sociologists refer to such symptomatic forms of behavior as **deviant behavior**, or as we shall see in the next section, individuals may be classified or considered together as a **deviant group** because they manifest similar non-normative behavior. **Deviant behavior** is always the result of the violation of some **norm**; the **norm** being what the **community** views as "right" and "proper." In this discussion, we are focusing on **symptoms** of an emotional nature, although other types of non-normative behavior such as being in an unusual occupation may be viewed as **deviant**.

Psychology is an immature science and does not understand all the causes of extreme **fear** and anxiety. These phenomena are difficult to study for we do not have sensitive methods with which to investigate them. At the moment, one way to investigate anxiety is to talk to people who are experiencing or have experienced this state. As indicated in the earlier section on **motives**, one important cause of extreme distress is uncertainty about one's worth or **value**. Extreme uncertainty about the self generates anxiety and the person strives to resolve the uncertainty and reduce the **fear**. The last selection by Goethals and Klos is an excerpt from an autobiography of a young college woman. She was experiencing the most serious form of anxiety: namely, uncertainty about her ability to run her life. This state led her to assume that she was not in control of her life, and that some foreign agent outside her, or more seriously, *inside her*, was running her everyday affairs. She concluded she had no control over this alien "other" who was directing daily experience. Although this was a frightening feeling, it reduced uncertainty about the future for she was not responsible, if *someone else* was in control. Therefore, the terrifying responsibility of directing one's life and of making decisions was removed. Although the woman experienced extreme anxiety, if one encountered her on the street, she would have appeared normal. She was even able to obtain acceptable grades and pass her courses at college.

Before beginning the readings, the student should keep in mind three important ideas that have been introduced in this section. The human being is a psychologically *active* organism, *selecting* from his environment things to which he can attend, *transforming* them to fit his **schemata**, **concepts** and **motives**, and *producing* new systems of behavior or changing old ones. The person is continually trying to keep the "system" in balance; trying to protect himself from exposure to **schemata**, **concepts**, and **motives** which he does not understand or which conflict with those he possesses; and simultaneously seeking new experiences which are related to what he knows and with which he feels he can deal.

SCHEMA

Recognition Memory for Words, Sentences, and Pictures

ROGER N. SHEPARD

The results of a variety of laboratory experiments have indicated that there are rather severe limitations on the amount of information that a human [Subject] can retain from a single exposure to a set of stimuli. In his well known paper on the subject, Miller (1956) cites Hayes' finding that typical *Ss* can accurately recall lists of no more than about five monosyllabic words . . . This seems puzzling since, intuitively, what we can retain from a single picture, if not "worth a thousand words," surely exceeds what could be encoded in just five monosyllables.

The present experiments were based on the conviction that objective measures that are more in line with our intuitive feelings of memory capability could be obtained by applying **recognition techniques** to complex, meaningful stimuli (like pictures). Three experiments are reported in which the stimuli were, respectively, words (of two levels of familiarity), short sentences, and about 750 colored pictures carefully selected for their variety and memorability.

Method

Basically the same procedure was followed in all three experiments. Except for Exp. I (in which, unfortunately, the number of stimuli was somewhat smaller), each *S* first looked through an *inspection series* of 612 visual stimuli, one stimulus at a time at his own rate, and then looked through a *test series* of 68 pairs each of which contained one new stimulus (not previously presented) and one old stimulus (already included in the preceding inspection

series). The *S's* task was always to indicate, for each test pair, which of the two stimuli he recognized as old. This "forced-choice" technique avoids difficulties of possible response biases (or non-optimal criteria) that beset the simpler technique in which test stimuli are presented singly and in which each is separately judged to be either "new" or "old" (cf. Shepard and Chang, 1963). The stimuli to be presented in the inspection and test series, both, and the stimuli to be presented in just the test series were always drawn at random from the same initial population; and the old stimulus was always randomly assigned to one of the two positions within each test pair.

EXPERIMENT I: WORDS

Subjects. The Ss were 17 students at Harvard University.

Stimuli. The basic population of stimuli consisted of 600 English common nouns and adjectives each of which was between five and seven letters in length. Of these, 300 were selected to be *frequent* in written English on the basis that, in the count of Thorndike and Lorge (1944), each occurred at least 100 times per million sampled words (examples: "child," "office," "supply"). The other 300 were chosen to be *rare* on the basis that, in the same count, each occurred less than once per million (examples: "ferule," "julep," "wattled"). For the inspection series, each word was typed in the center of a separate 3 × 5-in. blank white card while, for the test series, the two words in each pair were typed one above the other on each card.

Procedure. An inspection series of 540 single words was constructed by drawing and intermingling, at random 270 "frequent" and 270 "rare" words from the total population of 600. The remaining 60 words, together with a random subset of 60 of the words previously selected for the inspection series, were then used to construct 60 test pairs in such a way that each possible (ordered) combination consisting of a frequent or rare old type of item together with a frequent or rare new type of item occurred just 15 times. The resulting deck of 600 cards was given to each *S* with the instruction to proceed through the cards in order and, for each of the test pairs (on the last 60 cards), to write a "T" or a "B" on a response sheet to indicate that the "top" or "bottom" member of the pair was judged to be the old word.

EXPERIMENT II: SENTENCES

Subjects. A new group of 17 Harvard students served as *Ss* in the main part of this second experiment.

Stimuli. The initial population of stimuli consisted of 1360 short English sentences originally developed at the Harvard Psycho-Acoustic Laboratory for purposes of articulation testing (Egan, 1944). (Examples: "A dead dog is no use for hunting ducks." "The colt reared and threw the sick rider.") The sentences were typed on separate 3 × 5-in. cards as before.

Procedure. Each of the 17 *Ss* was given a deck containing 612 of the sentences followed by 68 test pairs. The manner of construction of the deck and the instructions given to the *Ss* were essentially the same as in Exp. I. As a supplement to this main experiment, two additional *Ss* (friends of *E*) agreed to undertake the same task with an inspection series of double length, containing 1224 sentences.

EXPERIMENT III: PICTURES

Subjects. The *Ss* were 34 technical and clerical employees of the Bell Telephone Laboratories.

Stimuli. The basic population of stimuli consisted of 748 colored pictures each of which was glued on a separate 5 × 8-in. white card. The principal criteria for selection of stimuli for this population, while entirely subjective, were intended to insure that the pictures would be both (a) individually of high salience and memorability and (b) collectively of low similarity and confusability. The pictures (including colored prints, photographs, and other illustrations) were culled from a variety of sources—particularly advertisements in magazines. Usually, in an effort to maximize salience, a single object was cut out of the original picture and pasted on the card. The cards were not presented directly to the Ss in this experiment, but were first photographed on successive frames of 16-mm color film and then projected onto a screen in front of S. The S pressed a key to advance the film to each new frame at a self-paced rate.

Procedure. As in the preceding experiment, an inspection series of 612 individual stimuli was immediately followed by a test series of 68 pairs. This time, however, the two pictures in each test pair were projected side-by-side (rather than one above the other) and Ss were asked to indicate whether the old picture was the one on the left or right.

For 16 of the Ss in this last experiment, an additional variation was introduced in order to explore the effect of a delay between the inspection and test series. Following the first series of 68 test pairs (which was administered immediately after the inspection series), a *second* such series (constructed of *different* test pairs) was also administered after a delay of either 2 hours, 3 days, 1 week, or about 4 months. Four different Ss were assigned, at random, to each of these four conditions of delay. The delayed test series was constructed from the 68 remaining new pictures paired with 68 old pictures not included in the first test series. Each of the 16 Ss in the delayed test condition was also asked to indicate, for each choice (of a left or right picture as "old"), how confident he was that his choice was correct. A three-point scale was provided for this purpose: "possibly" correct, "probably" correct, and "certainly" correct.

Results

Table 1 presents . . . [the] percent correct recognitions in each of the three experiments. For all three types of stimuli, [Subjects] were remarkably accurate in recognizing, in each test pair, the stimulus that had appeared in the preceding inspection series. Their performance was particularly impressive in the case of the pictorial stimuli used in Exp. III. . . .

The fact that, on the average, Ss were more successful in recognizing the old word when it was rare (92.5% correct) than when it was common (84.4% correct) may reflect a greater immunity of the rare words to **proactive interference** from words seen by Ss prior to their experimental session. Another possible explanation is suggested by the observation that, whereas the words occurring frequently in written English did indeed seem thoroughly familiar, the rare words seemed to vary widely in subjective familiarity. Thus, if each S found only, say, about a quarter (rather than a half) of the words in the inspection series to be truly strange and unfamiliar, these particular words might have been better remembered either because they were strange or because they stood out simply by being in the minority (cf., von Restorff, 1933; Smith, 1949; Nachmias, 1958).

In previous experiments in which three-digit numbers were used as stimuli, the ability to recognize an old stimulus was

TABLE 1

Percent Correct Recognitions of the Old Stimulus in Test Pairs following Inspection Sequences of Words, Sentences, or Pictures

Experiment	No. Ss	Length of inspection series	Percent correct on test pairs Mean %
I. Words	17	540	88.4
(old) (new)			
freq. freq.			82.1
freq. rare			86.7
rare freq.			93.0
rare rare			92.0
II Sentences	17	612	89.0
(double deck)	2	1224	88.2
III. Pictures	34	612	96.7
(after delay of)			
2 hr	4		99.7
3 days	4		92.0
7 days	4		87.0
120 days	4		57.7

found to decrease systematically with the number of other stimuli intervening between the original presentation of that stimulus and the subsequent test (Shepard and Teghtsoonian, 1961; Shepard and Chang, 1963). Although the words used here were retained much longer than the three-digit numbers used before, on the average the words may be subject to this same sort of decline. In particular, *Ss* recognized 90.8% of the old words from the last half of the inspection series, but only 86.1% of the old words from the first half. . . .

EXPERIMENT II: SENTENCES

Although the mean percent correct choices (of the old member of test pairs) was about the same for sentences as it was for words, the prior inspection series was about 13% longer in the case of the sentences. Thus memory capacity may actually be somewhat greater in the case of the sentences. Interestingly, the two supplementary *Ss* who tried the double inspection series (of 1224 sentences) performed about as well as the 17 *Ss* who were given the standard inspection series (of 612 sentences). However, this is a very small sample for the double series and, furthermore, these two *Ss* were chosen specifically for their motivation to undertake such a protracted and demanding task.

EXPERIMENT III: PICTURES

The *Ss* discriminated between new and old stimuli best when those stimuli were meaningful, colored pictures. Although a different population of *Ss* was used, the difference between the **mean performance** for the pictures and that for the sentences (after equally long inspection series) is probably reliable ($t = 4.7$, $p < .01$, after arcsine transformation). Actually, as is to be expected when average performance is so close to 100%, the distribution of performances in Exp. III was highly skewed. For this experiment at least, then, the **median** (98.5% correct) is probably preferable to the mean as an indicator of typical performance.

As anticipated from previous results (e.g., Strong, 1913), there was a very marked effect of delay on performance in the second test series. There was also a corresponding decline in the confidence that Ss expressed in their choices. The average percents of choices (both correct and incorrect) that were rated "certain" were 66, 45, 33, and 12% after delays of 2 hours, and 3, 7, and 120 days, respectively. Despite this marked decline, even after a delay of 1 week, memory for these pictorial stimuli was nearly equivalent to that found for the verbal materials (sentences or words) when the test followed immediately. (It is presumed, here, that performance on the delayed test was not appreciably affected by the earlier experience with the nondelayed test, since entirely different pictures were used for the two tests.)

A record was kept of the time taken by each of the 34 Ss to look through the entire inspection series of 612 stimuli (in Exp. III only). These times ranged from a maximum of 129 min down to a minimum of 15 min (taken by the one S who made more than 7 errors in the immediately following series of 68 test pairs). The distribution of Ss with respect to average time spent looking at each picture had a mean of 5.9 sec and SD of 2.4 sec.

Discussion

Evidently, after 20 or more years of absorbing visual information, Ss are still able to take in as many as 612 further pictures without any particular effort and, then, discriminate these from pictures not previously seen with (median) accuracy of over 98%.[1]

RELATION TO EARLIER EVIDENCE ON
MEMORY CAPACITY

There have, of course, been suggestions—particularly from memory reports obtained from Ss under **hypnotic regression** (Gerard, 1953, p. 118; Reiff and Scheerer, 1959, pp. 194–204), or electrical stimulation of the brain (Penfield, 1958), as well as from so-called **"eidetic"** Ss (Haber and Haber, 1964), that, really, everything that is ever taken in at all may in some sense be retained forever after without any loss or distortion in its original richness and detail. Moreover, recent biochemical speculations have suggested possible mechanisms for storing information of this order of magnitude (e.g., see Gaito, 1963; Szilard, 1964, p. 1099). Of course, in order to reconcile such a theory of perfect retention with the empirical *fact* of imperfect recognition or recall (and with the deterioration of performance generally found with delayed tests), errors must be attributed to failures merely of retrieval and not to failures of retention itself. However, in the absence of more conclusive evidence, the

---

[1] In an article that appeared after the present paper had already been submitted for publication, Nickerson (1965) has just reported a similar experiment on recognition memory in which, in general agreement with the present finding, there was an overall 95% correct discrimination between new and old pictures. However, Nickerson used (a) a smaller number of pictures which, moreover, were restricted entirely to black-and-white photographs, (b) a "yes-no" rather than a forced-choice procedure, and (c) the type of method (introduced by Shepard and Teghtsoonian, 1961) in which the test trials are interspersed within the inspection series itself (rather than assembled in a block at the end).

hypothesis of universally perfect retention can safely be regarded as little more than an interesting conjecture.

The present experiments were directed toward the more immediately accessible question as to how much information normal human *Ss* can assimilate *and* retrieve under normal conditions (i.e., without recourse to hypnosis, brain stimulation, drugs, etc.). Probably as a result of careful selection of highly memorable stimulus materials (and, possibly, the adoption of a self-paced rate), performance measured here was substantially superior to performances previously measured in similar experiments (like the early experiment by Strong, 1912, in which, after an inspection series of only 150 pictures, *Ss* classified test stimuli as new or old with only about 69% over-all success). . . .

QUANTITATIVE ESTIMATION OF
INFORMATION RETAINED

In the nondelayed test in Exp. III the median performance (98.5%) was close to 100% correct and, in fact, nine out of the 34 *Ss* did achieve exactly 100%. Hence it seems reasonable to suppose that, from a single exposure to the inspection series, *Ss* can at least retain something of the order of magnitude of 612 bits (i.e., the information needed to specify whether each one of the 612 stimuli was old or new). . . .

These new results do not, of course, take us very far towards the goal of understanding the *mechanisms* of storage and retrieval of information. They do, however, suggest that some progress in this direction may eventually be achieved through systematic attempts to determine just what are the critical properties of sets of stimuli (like the pictures used here) that enable *Ss* to attain these higher levels of performance.

References

Cofer, C. N., and Musgrave, B. S. (Eds.), *Verbal behavior and learning: Problems and processes.* New York: McGraw-Hill, 1963.

Egan, J. P. Articulation testing methods II Harvard Univer.: Psycho-Acoustic Laboratory, OSRD Report No. 3802, November 1944.

Egan, J. P. Recognition memory and the operating characteristic. Indiana Univer.: Hearing and Communication Laboratory, Technical Note AFCRC–TN–58–51, 1958.

Gaito, J. DNA and RNA as memory molecules. *Psychol. Rev.,* 1963, 70, 471–480.

Gerard, R. W. What is memory? *Scientific American,* 1953, 189, No. 3, 118–126.

Haber, R. N., and Haber, R. B. Eidetic imagery: I. Frequency. *Percept. motor skills,* 1964, 19, 131–138.

Luce, R. D. A threshold theory for simple detection experiments. *Psychol. Rev.,* 1963, 70, 61–79.

Miller, G. A. The magical number seven, plus or minus two: Some limits on our capacity for processing information. *Psychol. Rev.,* 1956, 63, 81–97.

Nachmias, J. The effect of stimulus-heterogeneity on free recall. *Amer. J. Psychol.,* 1958, 71, 578–582.

Nachmias, J., and Sternberg, S. An analysis of the recognition process. Paper read at the fourth annual meeting of the Psychonomic Society, August, 1963.

Nickerson, R. S. Short-term memory for complex meaningful visual configurations: A demonstration of capacity. *Canad. J. Psychol.,* 1965, 19, 155–160.

Penfield, W. Some mechanisms of consciousness discovered during electrical stimulation of the brain. *Proc. Natl. Acad. Sci.,* 1958, 44, 51–66.

Reiff, R., and Scheerer, M. *Memory and hypnotic age regression.* New York: International Univer. Press, 1959.

Shannon, C. E. A mathematical theory of communication. *Bell Syst. Tech. J.,* 1948, 27, 379–423.

Shepard, R. N., and Chang, J.-J. Forced-choice tests of recognition memory under steady-state conditions. *J. verb. Learn. verb. Behav.*, 1963, 2, 93–101.

Shepard, R. N., and Teghtsoonian, M. Retention of information under conditions approaching a steady state. *J. exp. Psychol.*, 1961, 62, 302–309.

Smith, M. H. Influence of isolation on immediate memory. *Amer. J. Psychol.*, 1949, 62, 405–411.

Sperling, G. The information available in brief visual presentations. *Psychol. Monogr.*, 1960, 74, No. 11 (Whole No. 498).

Strong, E. K. The effect of length of series upon recognition memory. *Psychol. Rev.*, 1912, 19, 447–462.

Strong, E. K. The effect of time-interval upon recognition memory. *Psychol. Rev.*, 1913, 20, 339–372.

Szilard, L. On memory and recall. *Proc. Natl. Acad. Sci.*, 1964, 51, 1092–1099.

Teghtsoonian, R. One-trial learning directly observed. *Canad. J. Psychol.*, 1964, 18, 304–310.

Thorndike, E. L., and Lorge, I. *The teacher's word book of 30,000 words.* New York: Teachers College, Columbia Univer., 1944.

von Restorff, H. Über die Wirkung von Berichsbildung im Spurenfeld. *Psychol. Forsch.*, 1933, 18, 299–342.

Yntema, D. B., and Trask, F. P. Recall as a search process. *J. verb. Learn. verb. Behav.*, 1963, 2, 65–74.

CONCEPT

The Cross-Cultural Generality of Visual-Verbal Synesthetic Tendencies

CHARLES E. OSGOOD

Introduction

. . . This project . . . was concerned with the ways in which language or culture, or both, may produce differences in **cognitive processes**; *or*, conversely, the degree to which certain cognitive processes may be independent of differences in language or culture, and hence general across language/culture groups. . . . [T]ranslation-equivalent forms of the semantic differential (Osgood, Suci, & Tannenbaum, 1957) were given to subjects in several Southwest Indian communities, as well as to Mexican-Spanish and Anglo subjects. . . .

The usual form of the semantic differential requires the subject to judge verbal concepts (e.g., HORSE, CORN, MAN) against verbally defined scales (e.g., *strong-weak, active-passive, good-bad*). Problems of translation equivalence therefore enter at two places. In the present experiment the concepts to be judged are verbal, but the 'scales' are visual—binary pictorial alternatives with which the subject must selectively associate the verbal concept being judged. Thus, instead of the bipolar words *thin-thick*, the subject sees a *thin* line paired with a *thick* line, and he simply points to whichever drawing seems to 'go best' with the concept being judged; instead of the bipolar adjectives *angular-rounded*, he sees a jagged, *angular* line-drawing paired with a *rounded* line-drawing. The difference between the drawings in each pair is restricted to a single dimension, e.g., angularity, size, nearness, etc. . . .

[One purpose of the work was to ask] Do the Navajo, like ourselves, see HAPPY as more *up* and SAD as more *down*? Do the Japanese, like ourselves, conceive of EXCITEMENT as *colorful* and CALM as *colorless*? And if certain differences in visual **metaphor** do appear, can these be related to what we know about the differences in culture? A third purpose was to see if those terms in Navajo, Mexican-Spanish, and Japanese selected as translation-equivalent to verbal opposites in English actually function as opposites in the meaningful judgments of non-Anglo subjects. Treating our paired visual alternatives as a sort of **projective** device, can the choices for GOOD be shown to be the mirror-image of those for BAD, for example? A final, and somewhat supplementary, purpose was to study similarities and differences in the **connotations** of both color terms and actual color samples. Can it be shown, for example, that Navajos and Anglos may differ widely in their connotative meanings of the words "blue" and its correlate in Navajo, yet agree closely on their meanings for a specific BLUE color chip? This analysis was restricted to the Navajo/Anglo comparison.

Method

SUBJECTS

The **synesthesia** experiment was run on four groups of subjects, each representing a different language/culture base. [Navajo, Mexican-Spanish, American (Anglo) and Japanese . . .] It should be noted, first, that all but the Anglo subjects were bilingual to some degree with respect to English, and, second, that there are marked differences in education (and perhaps intelligence) between the Anglo and Japanese groups on the one hand and the Navajo and Mexican-Spanish on the other. The phenomena of visual synesthesia with which we are dealing here may be largely independent of these variables, but nevertheless they should be kept in mind in interpreting the results.

MATERIALS

The verbal concepts used in this study are listed in Table 1. . . . Although the concepts are given here only in English, in administering the experiment the translation-equivalent terms in the subject's native language were given by the experimenter or interpreter. The equivalents for Japanese were determined by the back-translation technique (using different bilinguals in the two stages). . . .

TABLE 1

Verbal Concepts Used in Synesthesia Experiment

1. HEAVY	*10. QUIET	*20. NOISY
2. GOOD	11. BLUE	*21. GREY
3. FAST	12. BAD	22. SLOW
4. HAPPY	13. LIGHT	23. WHITE
*5. UP	*14. DOWN	24. CALM
*6. ENERGETIC	15. BLACK	25. MAN
*7. LOOSE	16. WOMAN	26. YELLOW
8. STRONG	*17. LAZY	27. WEAK
9. EXCITEMENT	*18. TIGHT	28. SAD
	19. GREEN	

Pictorial Alternatives Used in Synesthesia Experiment
(see Figure 1)

1. up-down	6. dark-light	*11. diffuse-concentrated
2. vertical-horizontal	7. crooked-straight	
3. homogeneous-heterogeneous	8. hazy-clear	12. large-small
4. colorless-colorful	*9. blunt-sharp	*13. near-far
5. thick-thin	10. rounded-angular	

*These concepts and visual alternatives were omitted in the materials given to Mexican-Spanish subjects.

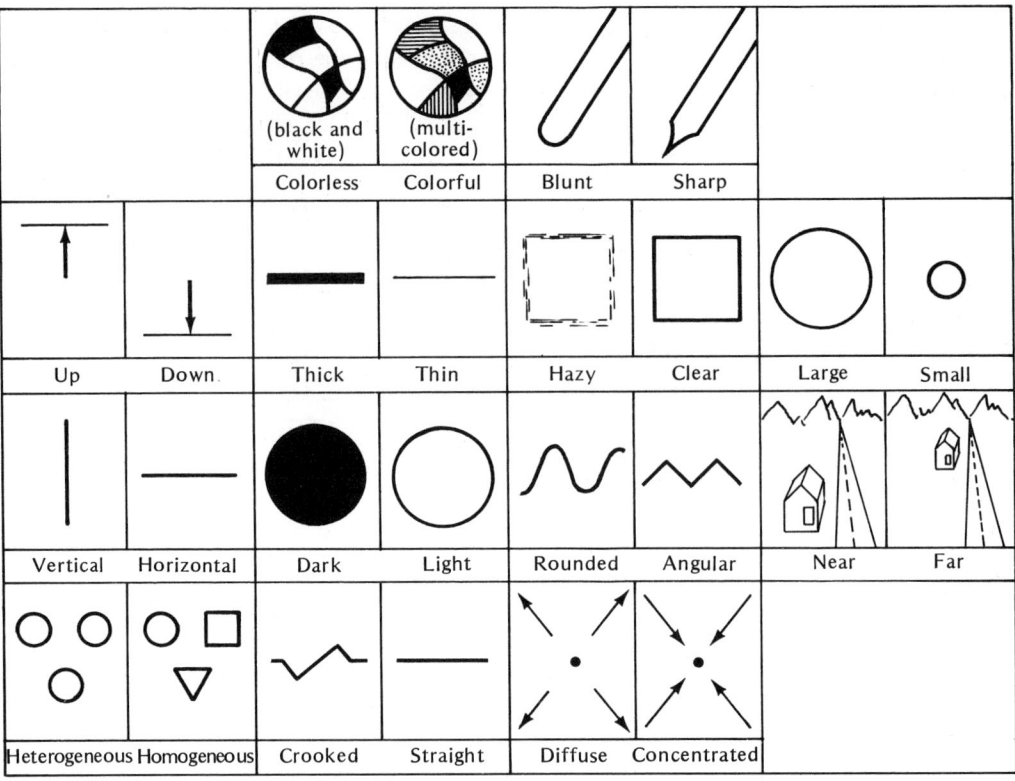

Figure 1

The visual alternatives, or 'scales,' used in this study are displayed in Figure 1 and listed *verbally* in Table 1. The labelling of these visual alternatives is somewhat arbitrary and is done only to facilitate talking about them. The subjects were given no verbal characterizations, although they may well have done some spontaneous labelling. Each pair of visual alternatives was drawn on a single card, so that the order of presentation could be varied if desired; the left-right orientation on each card was as shown in Figure 1.

Procedure

The general procedure was to name one of the concepts to be judged [in Table 1] and then run through the series of cards, having the subject point to or otherwise indicate which of the two visual alternatives [pictures] on each card seemed most appropriate to that concept. Then the next concept would be named and run through in the same fashion. Thus, in effect, the subject judged whether HEAVY (in his own language) seemed more *up* or *down, vertical or horizontal, homogeneous or heterogeneous,* and so forth through the 13 alternatives; then he did the same thing for the concept GOOD, and so on through the test. . . .

Results

. . . Anglos agree among themselves that HEAVY is *down, colorless, thick, dark, concentrated,* and *near;* Navajos see HEAVY as *thick, dark, crooked, blunt, large* and *near*; Mexican-Spanish see it as *down, horizontal, heterogeneous, thick, dark, crooked, hazy*, and *large*; Japanese agree among themselves that HEAVY is *down,* *colorless, thick, dark, crooked, hazy, concentrated, large, near,* and *blunt*. The synesthetic associations for other concepts ... can be explored by the reader ...

... [W]e may now consider specific

TABLE 2

Significant (Approx. .01 Level) Synesthetic Agreements and Disagreements Among Anglo, Navajo and Japanese Groups

ANGLOS, NAVAJOS AND JAPANESE AGREE THAT:		ANGLOS, NAVAJOS AND JAPANESE DISAGREE ON WHETHER:	
HEAVY	is down, thick, dark and near.	HEAVY	is crooked (A) or straight (N, J).
GOOD	is homogeneous and bright.		
FAST	is thin, bright, and diffuse.		
HAPPY	is colorful and bright.	HAPPY	is rounded (A) or angular (N, J).
UP	is up and diffuse.	UP	is large (N) or small (J).
ENER-GETIC	is colorful.	ENER-GETIC	is heterogeneous (A) or homogeneous (N); is thin and light (N) or thick and dark (J).
LOOSE	is hazy, rounded and blunt.		
STRONG			
EXCITE-MENT	is colorful.		
QUIET	is horizontal.		
BLUE		BLUE	is thick, dark and straight (A) or thin (J), or light and crooked (N).
BAD	is heterogeneous, colorless, thick, dark and crooked.	BAD	is angular (A) or rounded (N); is blunt (N) or sharp (J).
LIGHT (weight)	is thin and bright.	LIGHT	is clear (N) or hazy (J).
DOWN	is down and crooked.	DOWN	is thick (A, J) or thin (N); is hazy (N) or clear (J).
BLACK	is colorless, dark, thick, and concentrated.		
WOMAN	is colorful, thin and bright.		
LAZY	is blunt.	LAZY	is straight (A) or crooked (N).
TIGHT	is clear and angular.	TIGHT	is dark and small (A, J) or bright and large (N).
GREEN	is colorful.	GREEN	is thin and diffuse (A, J) or thick and concentrated (N).
NOISY	is crooked.		
GREY		GREY	is thin (N) or thick (J).
SLOW	is down, horizontal and blunt.	SLOW	is thick (A, J) and dark (A) or thin and bright (N).
WHITE	is thin and bright.		
CALM	is bright.	CALM	is large (A) or small (N).
MAN	is thick.		
YELLOW	is colorless, bright and hazy.		
WEAK	is thin and bright.	WEAK	is colorless (N) or colorful (J).
SAD	is colorless.	SAD	is blunt (A, N) or sharp (J).

agreements and—particularly—disagreements. Table 2 summarizes this information. It is restricted to comparisons among Anglos, Navajos, and Japanese; not only does the small N for Mexican-Spanish limit the possible significance of comparisons, but the other three groups represent extreme variations in both language families and culture. While inspecting Table 2 it should be kept in mind that *thick, near, homogeneous,* etc., refer to the visual alternatives shown in Figure 1. . . .

. . . FAST is *thin, bright,* and *diffuse;* LOOSE is *hazy, rounded* and *blunt;* ENERGETIC and EXCITEMENT are *colorful;* BAD is *heterogeneous, colorless, thick, dark,* and *crooked;* NOISY is *crooked;* SLOW is *down, horizontal,* and *blunt;* and so forth.[1] The visual alternatives selected here are not denoted by the verbal concepts and their translation equivalents; rather, they are connoted on a synesthetic (or metaphoric) basis.

The significant disagreements are open to a number of different interpretations: (1) Differences in the metaphorical extensions of the visual dimensions themselves. This may be the case as between Anglos and Japanese, on the one hand, and Navajo on the other, for the scales *thick-thin, dark-light* and *straight-crooked.* (2) Differences in the denotative meanings of verbal concepts, and hence unsuccessful translation. This is certainly the case for Anglo *vs.* Navajo meanings of BLUE (cf., results for color study below). (3) Differences in the connotative implications of translation-equivalent verbal concepts. This may be the case for Anglo *vs.* Navajo meanings of ENERGETIC, LAZY, FAST, SLOW, and TIGHT. It is obviously impossible to choose among these alternative interpretations on the basis of these data alone. In passing it may be noted that there were almost four times as many significant disagreements between Navajo and the other two groups as between Anglo and Japanese. . . .

. . . [One] question was: *can cross-language and cross-culture generality of* **visual-verbal synesthesia** *be demonstrated?* There is ample evidence for visual-verbal synesthesia within our own culture. As early as 1921, Lundholm (1921) reported data on the "feeling tones" of lines: that SAD was represented by large, downward-directed curves; that MERRY was represented by small, upward-directed lines; that GENTLE was represented by large, horizontally-directed curves, and so on. Poffenberger and Barrows (1924) confirmed and extended the relationships reported by Lundholm. Karowski, Odbert and Osgood (1942) were able to demonstrate similar relationships between word meanings and the synesthetic drawings of photistic visualizers. More recently, Scheerer and Lyons (1957), Hochberg and Brooks (1956), and McMurray (1958) have reported Western intracultural consistencies in relating line drawings and/or verbally defined visual dimensions to connotative meanings or feeling-tones. As far as I am aware, the present study is the first attempt to demonstrate that the visual-verbal synesthetic relationships characteristic of our own language/culture community are shared by peoples who speak different languages and enjoy different cultures—the Navajo, the Japanese, and the Mexican-Spanish living in the American Southwest. The over-all similarities in synesthetic tendencies across these groups are impressive—when the synesthetic relationships that are significant (.01 level) intraculturally are tested for cross-cultural

---

[1] The one case of cross-cultural agreement that goes against the writer's intuitive grain is that of CALM being seen as *bright,* but in this he must be idiosyncratic.

agreement, approximately 90% of the relationships prove to be in the same direction. We can conclude with confidence, then, that the determinants of these synesthetic relations are shared by humans everywhere—to the extent that our sample of "everywhere" is representative.

A [second] question in which we were interested was: *are terms which are translation-equivalent to functional opposites in our language also functionally opposed in other language/culture groups?* The answer to this question is important for several reasons: For one thing, the semantic differential as a measuring instrument is based on the assumption that 'true' opposites do 'slice up' the semantic space into meaningfully opposed regions; for another thing, the notion of logical opposition has always had a fundamental and primitive status in Western philosophical thought—is this merely a figment of our Western language structure, or is it really fundamental to human thinking wherever it may occur? Again, to the extent that our sample of human languages and cultures is representative, the answer is clear and compelling: peoples who use different languages and have grown up in different cultural settings also utilize meaningful opposition as a pillar of their logical constructions. This conclusion was obtained under conditions in which the verbal opposites were separated in time of judgment and were determined by association with purely visual alternatives. This over-all conclusion is not countered by the occasional negative instances which were found: Landar's (1957) analysis of four Navajo folk tales implies that for the Navajo the logical opposition is between *moving-stationary,* the Anglo *fast-slow* as translated being degrees of moving; the failure of *energetic-lazy* to function as an opposition for the Japanese is also tagged as a translation problem.[2] For 11 of the 12 Anglo oppositions described functional opposition is demonstrated for the other language/culture groups as well. . . .

Despite impressive over-all similarities across the language/culture groups studied in visual synesthetic tendencies, there are some clear-cut differences on particular relations . . .

. . . [T]here are probably some "real" cultural differences in visual synesthesia that cannot be explained away as artifactual on any of the above grounds. For one thing, it seems possible that the Navajo do not utilize an activity factor in connotative meaning to the same extent that Anglos do . . . Anglos clearly display a third activity factor which is only suggested in the Navajo data. For another thing, we noted that both in terms of significant differences in correlations among the visual alternatives and in the over-all correlations of the visual-alternative matrices, the Southwest-living Navajo and Mexican-Spanish agreed with each other as against the Anglos and Japanese. The shift of the Mexican-Spanish, from "allegiance" with the Anglos on concept meanings to "allegiance" with the Navajo on visual scale meanings, was particularly striking. Does this mean that growing up in the visual environment provided by the Southwest helps to organize the dimensions of the visual frame of reference in a somewhat different way than elsewhere?

This research obviously has bearing on the Sapir-Whorf "Weltanschauung" hypothesis–but in support of the converse. Most of the discussion and research relat-

---

[2] Both Professor Seizo Ohe (at the Center for Advanced Study in the Behavioral Sciences, Stanford, 1958) and a Japanese friend agreed that the terms we used for "energetic" and "lazy" were not really opposites in their language.

ing to this hypothesis has been designed to demonstrate that differences in language do produce differences in "world view," and certainly there is both observational (Carroll, 1956) and experimental (Brown & Lenneberg, 1954; Lenneberg & Roberts, 1956) evidence for this view. The present study and others along the same line (Kumata, 1957; Kumata & Schramm, 1956; Suci, 1957; Triandis & Osgood, 1958) strongly support the position that, for certain aspects of cognitive behavior at least, "world view" may remain relatively stable despite differences in both language and culture. The apparent conflict between these two sets of findings disappears if one makes a distinction between two general classes of cognition—which, for lack of better terms, I shall call *denotative* and *connotative*. The phenomena which seem to display generality across human groups regardless of language or culture are essentially connotative—the affective "feeling tones" of meaning which contribute to synesthesia, metaphor and the like. The phenomena which display dependence upon the structure and lexical categorizing of language seem to be essentially denotative—the multitudinous and arbitrary sets of correlations between perceptual events and linguistic events (i.e., the "rules of usage" of any language code). The distinction I am making has the status of an hypothesis, not a conclusion, but the meager evidence available seems to be consistent with it.

Finally, we may inquire into the reasons behind similarities in connotative systems despite language/culture differences. First, by virtue of being members of the human species, people are equipped biologically to react to situations in certain similar ways—with autonomic, emotional reactions to rewarding and punishing situations (evaluation), with strong or weak muscular tension to things offering great or little resistances (potency), and so on—and hence they can form connotative significances for perceived objects and their linguistic signs varying along the same basic dimensions. Such connotative reactions enter into a wide variety of meaningful situations, are therefore broadly generalized, and provide a basis for synesthetic and metaphorical transpositions. Beyond this shared connotative framework, there are many specific relations between human organisms and their generally similar environments whose stability can be the basis for synesthetic and metaphorical translations. These may be either innate to the species or developed by learning under similar conditions. An example of the former (innate) basis may be the common association of the red end of the spectrum with warmth and activity and the blue end with coldness and passivity. An example of the latter (acquired) basis may be the common association of visually large with auditorily loud—it is simply a characteristic of the physical world that as any noise-producing object approaches or is approached, increases in visual angle are correlated with increases in loudness. These "homotropisms" and experiential **contingencies** may be expressed in language but are independent of the structure of any particular language.

References

Brown, R. W. & Lenneberg, E. H. A study in language and cognition. *J. abnorm. soc. Psychol.*, 1954, 49, 454–462.

Carroll, J. B. (Ed.). *Language, thought and reality: Selected writings of Benjamin Lee Whorf.* New York: Wiley, 1956.

Casagrande, J. B. The Southwest Project in Comparative Psycholinguistics: A progress report. Social Science Research Council, 1956, Item 10, 41–45.

Hochberg, J. & Brooks, V. An item analysis of physiognomic connotation. Unpublished study, privately distributed, 1956.

Karowski, T. F., Odbert, H. S., & Osgood, C. E. Studies in synesthetic thinking: II. The role of form in visual responses to music. *J. gen. Psychol.*, 1942, 26, 199–222.

Kimura, T. Apparent warmth and heaviness of colours. *Japanese J. Psychol.*, 1950, 20, 33–36.

Kumata, H. A factor analytic investigation of the generality of semantic structure across two selected cultures. Unpublished doctoral dissertation, University of Illinois, 1957.

Kumata, H. & Schramm, W. A pilot study of cross-cultural methodology. *Publ. Opin. Quart.*, 1956, 20, 229–237.

Landar, H. J. Four Navajo summer tales. Report of the Southwest Project in Comparative Psycholinguistics, 1957.

Lenneberg, E. H. & Roberts, J. M. The language of experience. *Suppl. int. J. Amer. Linguistics*, 1956, 22, 33.

Lundholm, H. The affective tone of lines: Experimental researches. *Psychol. Rev.*, 1921, 28, 43–60.

McMurray, G. A. A study of "fittingness" of signs to words by means of the semantic differential. *J. exp. Psychol.*, 1958, 56, 310–312.

Odbert, H. S., Karowski, T. F., & Eckerson, A. B. Studies in synesthetic thinking: I. Musical and verbal association of color and mood. *J. gen. Psychol.*, 1942, 26, 153–173.

Osgood, C. E., Suci, G. J. & Tannenbaum, P. H. *The measurement of meaning.* Urbana: The Univ. of Illinois Press, 1957.

Poffenberger, A. T. & Barrows, B. E. The feeling value of lines. *J. appl. Psychol.*, 1924, 8, 187–205.

Ross, R. T. Studies in the psychology of the theatre. *Psychol. Record*, 1938, 2, 127–190.

Scheerer, M. & Lyons, J. Line drawings and matching responses to words. *J. Pers.*, 1957, 25, 251–273.

Suci, G. J. An investigation of the similarity between the semantic spaces of five different cultures. Report for the Southwest Project in Comparative Psycholinguistics, 1957.

Triandis, H. C. & Osgood, C. E. A comparative factorial analysis of semantic structures in monolingual Greek and American college students. *J. abnorm. soc. Psychol.*, 1958, 57, 187–196.

Wexner, L. B. The degree to which colors (hues) are associated with mood-tones. *J. appl. Psychol.*, 1954, 38, 432–435.

Effects of Social Class and Race on Responsiveness to Approval and Disapproval

DAVID L. ROSENHAN

Recent concern with the academic failure of the culturally deprived or the culturally different has yielded a number of hypotheses regarding the potential sources of this failure (cf. Passow, 1963; Riessman, 1962). Since the term culturally deprived implies primarily lower-class children, and particularly those who are nonwhite, these hypotheses have sought to explain the failures of these children in terms of characteristics that are presumed to be possessed primarily by the lower class. Thus, their relatively impoverished status is seen as relevant to their academic failure. So, too, their transient status in the community, their unstable parental **identifications**, their negative self-images, the degree to which they are encouraged to achieve—all these and others are seen as potential sources for the academic performance discrepancies between young children from the lower and middle classes (cf. Passow, 1963, for a discussion of these issues).

Empirical research in this area has been meager and, to a large extent, inconclusive. Douvan (1956) has reported that lower-class children are less responsive to the idea of being correct than middle-class children. Zigler and Kanzer (1962) demonstrated further that middle-class children were more responsive to abstract reinforcers, that is, reinforcers directed at performance, while lower-class children responded more to concrete reinforcers, or those reinforcers that generally connoted praise. However, a replication of this study by Rosenhan and Greenwald (1965) did not bear out the findings. No differences were found between middle- and lower-class children in their tendency to respond to performance (i.e., abstract) or person (i.e., concrete) reinforcers.

The present study takes a social class interaction position (cf. Clark, 1963; Rosenhan, 1965) and examines the notion that the lower-class child may be more alienated than the middle-class child in a middle-class school system. Taking alienation to mean a lack of relationship with one's environment (English & English, 1958) and particularly an inability to comprehend environmental expectancies, the argument runs as follows: For the middle-class child, the middle-class school may be seen as an extension of his middle-class home. Often, long before he has entered first grade, he anticipates going to school and has learned something about school from his parents. Commonly enough, he has been introduced to some of the materials that he will subsequently encounter in school. Moreover, he is reasonably familiar with middle-class institutions and is comfortable with middle-class people. Thus, for this child, the school is a comfortable situation with which he often has prior familiarity. For the lower-class child, however, the situation may be quite different. In his environment, attending school may not be an especially high-status activity. He has probably received little if any of the **vicarious and anticipatory reinforcement** that the middle-class child receives prior to going to school. Indeed, what with the larger family that he tends to come from and the greater need for both of his parents to be employed, the school may have subtly acquired negative reinforcing properties in the sense that it may be viewed as a repository in order to permit the parents greater freedom. From whatever source, then, it is conceivable that the lower-class child experiences greater alienation in middle-class institutions and with middle-class people than does the middle-class child.

In the present study we examine one hypothesis derivable from the above proposition: If lower-class children are more alienated in a middle-class institution, they should be more responsive to praise than middle-class children would be. By the same token, the performance of lower-class children should be more disrupted by disapproval than that of their middle-class peers. In general, the relationship of a lower-class child to middle-class institutions can be viewed in much the same way that a Westerner might experience, say, an Oriental wedding. Feeling quite unfamiliar with the rites and rituals, he would be more delighted than an Oriental would be by a remark that approved of his behavior. On the other hand, having done something that evoked disapproval, he would be more disturbed by the criticism than would one who was relatively more at home at such ceremonies.

In order to test the hypothesis, a middle-class male experimenter verbally reinforced the performance of first-grade lower- and middle-class subjects in a binary-choice game. Half of the subjects were given positive reinforcement when they made the correct response. No reinforcement was offered for incorrect responses. The remaining subjects were given negative reinforcement for incorrect responses, with no reinforcement given for correct responses.

It has been suggested (Riessman, 1962) that the Negro lower-class child suffers an especial handicap in that his color leads him to acquire a negative-identity image more rapidly and more deeply than the white child. We examine this hypothesis in this experiment by considering separately the effects of disapproval and approval on

TABLE 1

Composition of the Sample and Performance of the Subjects (N=12 in Each Group)

| | CA[a] | | Socioeconomic class | | Responses to left lever (percentage of 160 trials) | |
Subject group	M	Range	M	Range	M	Range
Middle-class white						
Approval	6:1	5:10–6:6	1.4	1–3	60	04
Disapproval	6:2	5:11–6:4	1.4	1–3	62	03
Lower-class white						
Approval	6:2	5:10–6:7	5.8	5–7	64	06
Disapproval	6:3	5:9–6:8	6.0	5–7	55	04
Lower-class Negro						
Approval	6:3	5:11–6:10	6.4	6–7	63	09
Disapproval	6:1	5:9–6:11	6.0	5–7	55	04

[a] At time of testing.

white and Negro lower-class children. (Negro middle-class children were not available for this study.) If both the alienation and the negative-identity hypotheses are correct, then Negro children should be more positively affected by approval than white children and more negatively affected by disapproval.

Method

SUBJECTS

Subjects were 72 first-grade boys who were drawn from two public schools of mixed socioeconomic class.[1] Socioeconomic class was determined on the basis of parental occupation (Warner, Meeker, & Eells, 1949, p. 140). Subjects were randomly assigned to the approval and disapproval conditions. Twenty-four subjects were middle- and 48 were lower-class children. Of the lower-class children, half were Negro and half were white. A comparable Negro middle-class sample could not be obtained. Table 1 describes the composition of the groups.

A middle-class white male experimenter conducted the study. He was told that the experiment dealt with the effects of approval and disapproval on probability learning, but was not aware of the social class hypotheses. Nor did he realize that the subjects had been presorted on the basis of social class and race.

APPARATUS

A black metal box, measuring 7 × 12 × 7 inches, served as the binary-choice apparatus. Mounted on the lower right and left corners of the panel was a toggle-type automatic-return switch which the subject manipulated. The subject's responses activated either of two lights on the experimenter's clipboard indicating which lever the subject had depressed. The experimenter then responded accordingly. The apparatus is described fully in Rosenhan (in press).

---

[1] The assistance of the Trenton School System, and particularly of Olive Brown, director of instruction, Lester Blinn, and Merle Lloyd, principals, is gratefully acknowledged.

PROCEDURE

The experimenter met the subject outside of his classroom and chatted with him on the way to the experimental room. Once inside, the subject was seated before a low table on which was the binary-choice game. The experimenter instructed the child in the use of the switches and, for the approval condition, told him that "each time you press the right button, I will say 'right.'" For the disapproval condition, the instructions were reversed, namely, "each time you press the wrong button, I will say 'wrong.'" The instructions were repeated several times.

Prior to the training trials, the subject was administered four practice trials, for which the first and last trials were correct (i.e., they were reinforced for the approval condition; for the disapproval condition the second and third practice trials were negatively reinforced).

When it was clear that the subject understood the instructions, he was administered 160 training trials. A **reinforcement ratio** of 70 : 30 to the left and right levers, respectively, was employed. That is, for the approval condition the left lever was positively reinforced 70% of the time, and the right lever 30% of the time. For the disapproval condition the reinforcement ratio was reversed—70% of the right and 30% of the left lever presses were negatively reinforced. Reinforcements were randomized in blocks of 20 trials. Thus, the response behavior demanded—pressing the left lever—was the same for both the approval and disapproval conditions and constituted the dependent variable for this study.

Results

Three **analyses of variance** were applied to the mean performance data shown in

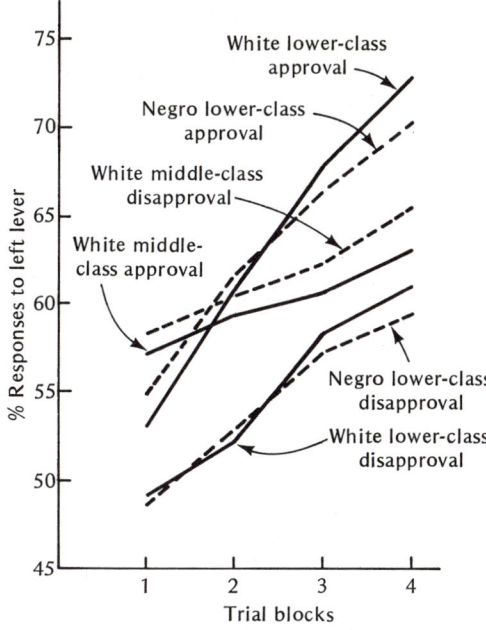

Fig. 1. Mean performance of subjects by experimental group and blocks of 40 trials

Table 1. The first analysis considered the effects of approval and disapproval on lower-class children. It examined whether Negro and white boys responded differentially to these reinforcers. As will be seen in Table 2, no race differences emerged either as main effects or in interaction with other variables. The effects of reinforcers were such that lower-class children were much more responsive to approval than to disapproval.

The trials' main effect in this as in the subsequent analysis indicates that the tendency to respond to the left lever increased over the four blocks of trials. The subject's performance began at or near the 50% level and increased as he gained more experience with the reinforcement contingencies. The interaction between trials and the reinforcer valence demonstrated that the subject's tendency to respond to the left lever rose under approval conditions but remained relatively stable (and low) under conditions of disapproval. Figure 1 presents the data across trials for these lower-class subjects and for the middle-class subjects.

The second analysis of variance (Table 2) examined the responsiveness of lower- and middle-class white children to approval and disapproval. Again, the main effects of the reinforcement dimension were significant. However, they interacted with social class such that compared to middle-class boys, the performance of lower-class boys was facilitated by approval and retarded by disapproval.

Looking now to the between-blocks-of-trials analysis, we find that the main effects of trials are marked: The subjects' performances improve over trials. The Trials × Social Class interaction is seen in Figure 1, where the early performance of lower-class subjects in the approval condition is below that of middle-class subjects in either condition. Terminal performance of lower-class subjects under approval is, however, higher than that of any other group.

Approximately similar results obtained from the third analysis which considered the effects of approval and disapproval on lower-class Negroes and middle-class whites (Table 2). While the overall effect of approval was greater than that of disapproval, lower-class Negroes performed better with approval and worse with disapproval than did middle-class whites. And while the performance of all groups improved over the four blocks of trials, the amount of improvement for Negroes in

TABLE 2

Summary of the Analyses of Variance for the Color and Class Comparisons

		I Lower class: White versus Negro subjects		II White subjects: Lower versus middle class		III Lower-class Negro versus middle-class white	
Source	df	MS	F	MS	F	MS	F
Between subjects	1	1.5052	.06	16.9216	1.27	28.5208	1.30
Groups (A)	1	577.5469	22.05*	97.7552	7.32*	102.0833	4.65**
Reinforcers (B)	1	.0469	.00	194.0052	14.53*	200.0833	9.12*
A × B	1						
Error (b)	44	26.1928		13.3509		21.9461	
Within subjects							
Trials (C)	3	313.4219	125.39	179.8108	158.26*	133.1875	71.94*
A × C	3	3.8108	1.52	38.6302	34.00*	19.4097	10.48*
B × C	3	13.3524	5.34*	4.5469	4.00*	1.3889	.75
A × B × C	3	1.0191	.41	6.4358	5.66*	2.3889	1.29
Error (w)	132	2.4995		1.1362		1.8513	

*$p < .05$.
**$p < .01$.

the approval condition (whose initial performance was below that of the middle-class boys in either condition) was substantially greater than it was for middle-class whites.

Discussion

It is clear from these data that identical reinforcers—approval or disapproval—have differential effects according to the social class of the subject. Taking performance to mean the number of times the subjects pressed the left lever, the performance of lower-class subjects was substantially improved under conditions of approval relative to middle-class subjects. Under conditions of disapproval, however, lower-class boys performed more poorly than their middle-class peers.

The data are consistent with the view that lower-class children, at least on entry into middle-class institutions and with middle-class people, are unfamiliar with their surroundings and therefore experience a greater sense of alienation than do middle-class boys. This presumed sense of alienation leaves them especially sensitive to external social reinforcers that convey approval or disapproval of their behavior. Unable, as it were, to assure themselves that they are legitimate members of the environment in which they find themselves, they rely more heavily than middle-class children on external indexes of the quality of their performance.

At the same time we have an instance where alienation is not necessarily deleterious to performance. If learning is viewed as the tendency to respond to the more reinforced lever, then for lower-class children, approval facilitated learning. And while the **paradigm** is limited to a brief experimental event and to a small sample of performance, the data are sufficiently encouraging to speculate that the longer term effects of middle-class approval might produce a generally elevated performance in lower-class children. Long-term disapproval, on the other hand, might have relatively enduring opposite effects, reducing the performance of lower-class children far below what it might be under other conditions.

It is also possible and consistent with the above interpretation that lower- and middle-class children differ in their approaches to a positively reinforced **binary-choice** game. While children of both classes may recognize that the left lever is correct more often than the right one, middle-class children employ a problem-solving approach, attempting to get each item correct. Lower-class children, on the other hand, may tend to employ the more conservative strategy of maximizing their correct responses. Such differences in strategy are consistent with the relative **incentive** value of praise for lower- and middle-class children, since, in general, the greater the value of the reward the more the subject will tend to maximize (cf. Tune, 1964; Weir, 1964).

Under conditions of negative reinforcement, a problem-solving approach might similarly hold for middle-class children, the problem in this instance being the avoidance of wrong responses. Maximizing, on the other hand, makes little psychological sense where negative reinforcement is concerned, since locating rewards may be more important for the subject than avoiding punishment.

A problem-solving versus maximizing interpretation of these data, however, is limited by the fact that the children apparently did not achieve asymptotic performance (see Figure 1). Clearly, additional trials would have been necessary in order to reach asymptote, yet it is doubtful that such young children could have handled more trials. Moreover, an internal analysis of responses, such as the number of consecutive times the subject depressed the left lever (cf. Rosenhan, 1966) was not possible in this study because the responses to the levers were summarized on counters, rather than individually recorded. Nevertheless, a strategy interpretation remains a distinct possibility for these data.

ALTERNATIVE INTERPRETATIONS OF THESE FINDINGS

Differential child-rearing practices in lower- and middle-class homes: The effect of reinforcer adaptation and variability. Sears, Maccoby, and Levin (1957) have shown that social classes differ in their methods of child rearing. Specifically, lower-class parents are more prone to employ physical punishment with their children while middle-class parents use verbal persuasions and penalties. It is conceivable that by the time the middle-class child is 6 years old, he has become relatively adapted to **(satiated on?)** verbal reinforcers such that neither approval nor disapproval affect him deeply or differentially. For lower-class children, however, who are relatively less adapted to verbal methods of behavior control, approval and disapproval have more potent effects.

There is in fact some experimental evidence that can be interpreted to support the notion that middle-class children are to some extent satiated on verbal reinforcers. Gewirtz and Baer (1958) compared the responses to approval of children who had been experimentally satiated with or deprived of approval for a brief period of time. They found that compared to a matched untreated control group, deprived children were more responsive to approval. Subsequent evidence (Rosenhan, in press) demonstrated that deprived subjects were more responsive to both approval and disapproval than were satiated subjects. The combined data would be consistent with the view that young middle-class children are relatively **adapted** to verbal reinforcement regardless of **valence**, that their responsiveness to such reinforcers increases only after periods of deprivation. While comparable data are not available for lower-class children, they might conceivably be more "deprived of sociality" than their middle-class peers and hence more responsive to it (cf. Zigler, 1961; Zigler & Williams, 1963).

If there is some difficulty with this interpretation, it rests with the strong effects of disapproval on lower-class children. For while lower-class parents tend to utilize physical means of punishment, they do not use such means exclusively. Presumably it is combined with verbal disapproval such that lower-class children ought to have become adapted to both kinds of disapproval, or perhaps to disapproval in general. Their performance in the disapproval condition, relative to middle-class children, indicates clearly that this is not the case, weakening thereby a child-rearing interpretation of these data or requiring a more complex model.

Anxiety. The data are clearly interpretable within an anxiety framework; namely, lower-class children are more anxious in a middle-class setting than are middle-class children. Thus, for lower-class children, approval reduces anxiety while disapproval heightens it. Since middle-class children, on the other hand, are presumed to be quite secure in this setting, neither approval nor disapproval affects them strongly.

Such an interpretation is not inconsistent with an alienation view of lower-class children's behavior in that these children may be anxious because they are alienated. Offered by itself, of course, an anxiety interpretation gives no clue as to why lower-class children should be more anxious. And since no independent measures of anxiety were obtained it was felt that the alienation interpretation offered was the more appropriate one at this time.

Intelligence. Probability learning has been conceptualized as a problem-solving task in which the subject devises strategies to maximize his gain (i.e., to get the most correct answers). As such, one might expect intelligence to play something of a role. Numerous studies have shown that relative to the lower class, middle-class children possess superior IQs (cf. Deutsch & Brown, 1964), and one would therefore have expected such children to have performed better under all conditions. Since this did not in fact occur, an interpretation that rests on social class differences in intelligence is not appropriate to these data.

CLASS VERSUS COLOR

While there is considerable evidence that young children are perceptive of and sensitive to racial differences, these differences do not appear to affect their responsiveness to verbal reinforcement. Ordinarily, one might have expected Negro lower-class children to experience most alienation with a middle-class white experimenter, by virtue of the combined effects of both class and color differences. Thus, their responsiveness to both approval and disapproval should have been heightened relative to lower-class white children. Since this did not occur it can be argued that, at least for very young boys, social class differences rather than color differences are the critical variables that determine responsiveness in reinforcement situations. It should be noted that a similar failure to obtain differences between Negro and white lower-class children, this time in a simple conditioning task, occurred previously (Rosenhan & Greenwald, 1965).

Clearly, the failure to obtain race differences in performance in two studies may simply reflect the restricted range of the experimental paradigms employed. Perhaps different experimental tasks or conditions might have elicited the presumed racial differences. At the same time, we note that this experiment *was* sufficiently sensitive to distinctions of social class which were presumably based on the same dynamics of alienation that should have affected Negro behavior more deeply than in fact they did. Thus, the argument that the experiment considers a restricted range of behavior is only partially compelling.

It is also possible that the tendency to be sensitive to racial differences reflects primarily the tendency to distinguish people and behaviors that are within one's social class from those that are outside of it. In other words, racial differences may be one aspect of social class differences, particularly insofar as relatively few Negroes are in the middle class. In any event, it seems clear that as far as the performance of young children is concerned (as distinguished from perceptions and attitudes), class is far more significant than color.

References

Clark, K. B. Educational stimulation of racially disadvantaged children. In A. H. Passow (Ed.), *Education in depressed areas*. New York: Teachers College, Columbia University, Bureau of Publications, 1963. Pp. 142–162.

Deutsch, M., & Brown, B. Social influences in Negro-white intelligence differences. *Journal of Social Issues,* 1964, 20, 24–35.

Douvan, E. Social status and success striving. *Journal of Abnormal and Social Psychology,* 1956, 52, 219–233.

English, H. B., & English, A. C. *A comprehensive dictionary of psychological and psychoanalytical terms.* New York: Longmans, Green, 1958.

Gewirtz, J. L., & Baer, D. M. The effect of brief social deprivation on behaviors for a social reinforcer. *Journal of Abnormal and Social Psychology,* 1958, 56, 49–56.

Passow, A. H. *Education in depressed areas.* New York: Teachers College, Columbia University, Bureau of Publications, 1963.

Riessman, F. *The culturally deprived child.* New York: Harper, 1962.

Rosenhan, D. *Cultural deprivation and learning: An examination of method and theory.* (Res. Memo. 65–4) Princeton, N. J.: Educational Testing Service, 1965.

Rosenhan, D. Double alternation in children's binary-choice responses: A dilemma for theories of learning and arousal. *Psychonomic Science,* 1966, 4, 431–432.

Rosenhan, D. Aloneness and togetherness as drive conditions in children. *Journal of Experimental Research in Personality,* in press.

Rosenhan, D., & Greenwald, J. A. The effects of age, sex, and socioeconomic class on responsiveness to two classes of verbal reinforcement. *Journal of Personality,* 1965, 33, 108–121.

Sears, R. R., Maccoby, E. E., & Levin, H. *Patterns of child rearing.* Evanston, Ill.: Row, Peterson, 1957.

Tune, G. S. Response preferences: A review of some recent literature. *Psychological Bulletin,* 1964, 61, 286–302.

Warner, W. L., Meeker, M., & Eells, K. *Social class in America.* Chicago: Science Research Associates, 1949.

Weir, M. W. Developmental changes in problem-solving strategies. *Psychological Review,* 1964, 71, 473–490.

Zigler, E. Social deprivation and rigidity in the performance of feebleminded children. *Journal of Abnormal and Social Psychology,* 1961, 62, 413–421.

Zigler, E., & Kanzer, P. The effectiveness of two classes of verbal reinforcers on the performance of middle- and lower-class children. *Journal of Personality,* 1962, 30, 157–163.

Zigler, E., & Williams, J. Institutionalization and the effectiveness of social reinforcement: A three-year follow-up study. *Journal of Abnormal and Social Psychology,* 1963, 66, 197–205.

ATTENTION

The Determinants of Attention in the Infant

JEROME KAGAN

The evolution of a science is recorded in what are usually gradual but are sometimes abrupt changes in the central question asked, the concepts preferred, and the subject judged convenient for study. Nineteenth-century physiologists asked how sensory events were transferred from **receptor surface** to brain, conceived of a process requiring energy transmission, and studied animal forms with accessible **afferent nerves.** Physiologists now believe they know how a flash of light travels from the retina inward but remain puzzled over what happens when afferent nerves release their information at the end of the journey. This question has generated the concepts of inhibition and arousal and has attracted investigators to organisms whose brains are accessible to surgery and electrical recording.

Psychology too has experienced a dramatic shift in preferred question, process, and organism. Until recently behavioral scientists wanted to understand how an animal learned a new habit, be it running a maze or pressing a bar with its paw. The solution seemed to require theoretical and empirical inquiry into the phenomena surrounding motivation, reinforcement, and the hypothetical connections between external stimulus and response. This conception of the problem led naturally to the selection of small mammals which allowed close control of experimental conditions. Psychologists have recently redirected their interest from the puzzle of response acquisition to the mystery of mental processes. This shift is due to several factors. Neurophysiologists have found that the brain's electrical activity covaries more closely with states of attention than with patterns of behavior. The **psycholinguists** have reminded psychology of the profound chasm between knowing and acting: the young child understands sentences long before he utters them, and all of us possess the competence to generate many more rules than we will ever use. Piaget's lifetime effort to outline a developmental history of the stages of human reasoning has catalyzed inquiry into the structure of thought in the child.

These lines of investigation have been supplemented by events in other sectors. Existentialism, drug experience, and popularizations of psychopathology have aroused interest in the quality of inner feelings at the expense of concern with the pragmatic outcome of action. Public recognition that the majority of school failures are poor children has led public and private institutions to increase their support of scientific exploration of children's thought. And the concept of **critical period**, an idea born in experimental embryology and nurtured in comparative psychology, has prompted scientists to examine more carefully the early months of human development. These diverse forces have found a common aim in study of the mental processes of the young child.

A six-month-old infant displays a remarkable ability to focus his attention on interesting events, and he will maintain prolonged orientations to the face of a stranger, the movement of a leaf, or a lively conversation. He seems to be quietly absorbing information and storing it for future use. Since acquiring knowledge about the environment depends so intimately upon how the infant distributes his attention, and for how long, it is important to ask what governs these processes. This question has stimulated fruitful research from which an outline of preliminary principles is emerging.

Early determinants of fixation time: contrast and movement

The most obvious index of attentiveness to visual events is the length of orientation to an object–called **fixation time.** Like any response it has multiple determinants; the relative power of each seems to change as the infant grows. **Ontogenetically**, the earliest determinant of length of orientation to a visual event derives from the basic nature of the central nervous system. The infant is predisposed to attend to events that possess a high rate of change in their physical characteristics. Stimuli that move or possess **light-dark contrast** are most likely to attract and hold a newborn's attention. A two-day-old infant is more attentive to a moving or intermittent light than to a continuous light source; to a design with a high degree of black-white contrast than to one of homogeneous hue (Haith 1966; Salapatek and Kessen 1966; Fantz 1966; Fantz and Nevis 1967). These facts come from experiments in which stimuli varying, for example, in degree of black-white contrast (e.g., a black triangle on a white background versus a totally gray stimulus) are presented to infants singly or in pairs while observers or cameras record the length of orientation to each of the stimuli. In general, the newborn's visual search behavior seems to be guided by the following rules: (1) If he is alert and the light is not too bright, his eyes open. (2) Seeing no light, he searches. (3) Seeing light but no edges, he keeps searching. (4) Finding contour edges, his eyes focus on and cross them (Haith 1968).

The attraction to loci of maximal contrast and movement is in accord with knowledge about **ganglion potentials** in the

Fig. 1. One of a set of random designs shown to four-month infants

boards of constant area but varying numbers of squares. The total number of inches at which black borders white increases as the number of squares increases. Karmel (1966) has suggested, on the basis of studies with young infants, that the longest fixations are devoted to figures with a moderate amount of edge.

Although indices of attention to auditory events are more ambiguous than those to visual ones, intermittent tones, which have a high rate of change, elicit more sustained interest, as evidenced by motor quieting, than continuous tones (Eisenberg 1964; Brackbill 1966). Nature has apparently awarded the newborn an initial bias in his processing of experience. He does not have to learn what he should examine, as the nineteenth-century empiricists argued. The preferential orientation to change is clearly adaptive, for the source of change is likely to contain the most information about the presence of his mother or danger.

The role of discrepancy from schema

The initial disposition to attend to events with a high rate of change soon competes with a new determinant based on experi-

retinas of vertebrates. Some ganglion cells respond to a light going on; others to its going off; still others to both. Since an object moving across a visual field stimulates a set of cells for a short period, it creates onset and offset patterns similar to those of an intermittent light. Figures that contain dark lines on light backgrounds serve better as onset stimuli than do solid patterns because the change in stimulation created by the border of dark on light elicits more frequent firing of nerve cells, and this phenomenon may facilitate sustained attention (Kuffler 1952, 1953).

The preference for attending to objects with high contrast is dependent, however, on the size of the figure; there seems to be an optimal area that maintains fixation at a maximum. Four-month-old infants shown designs of varying areas (Fig. 1) were most attentive to the moderately large designs (Fig. 2) (McCall and Kagan 1967). Similarly there is a non-linear relation between the total amount of black-white edge in a figure and attention. Consider a series of black-and-white checker-

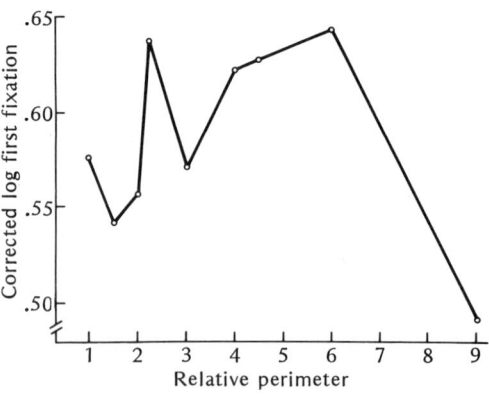

Fig. 2. Relation between fixation time and approximate area of random design in four-month infants

ence. The child's encounters with events result, inevitably, in some mental representation of the experience, called a schema. A schema is defined as an abstraction of a sensory event that preserves the spatial or temporal pattern of the distinctive elements of the event. A schema is to be regarded as a functional property of mind that permits an organism to recognize and retrieve information. The schema does not necessarily involve a motor response. It is neither a detailed copy of the event nor synonymous with the language label for the event. An example from a recent experiment may be useful here.

A four-year-old looked through a set of 50 magazine pictures illustrating objects, people, or scenes, many of which he had never seen before and could not name when asked. He spent only a few seconds on each picture and flipped through the 50 in less than three minutes. He was then shown 50 pairs of pictures; one of each pair was the picture he saw earlier, the other was new. He was asked to point to the picture he saw before. Although he could recall spontaneously only three or four, the average four-year-old recognized over 45 of the 50 pictures. Some children recognized them all. Since some of the pictures showed objects the child had never seen (say, a lathe or a slide rule), it is unlikely that his performance can be totally explained by assuming that each picture elicited a language label or a fragmentary motor response. What hypothetical entity shall we invoke to explain the child's ability to recognize over 90 percent of the scenes? If we use the concept schema to refer to the processes that permitted recognition, we can say that each picture contained a unique configuration of salient elements, and the schema preserved that configuration, without necessarily preserving an exact spatial analogue of the event. Some psychologists might use the older term **memory engram** to convey the meaning we attribute to schema. The schema for a visual event is not a photographic copy, for minor changes in the scenes viewed initially do not produce changes in the child's performance. Nor is the schema synonymous with a visual image, for the child is also able to recognize a series of different melodies or sound patterns after brief exposure to each. Early twentieth-century biologists used the concept of the gene to explain demonstrated properties of cells and nuclear material, though no one knew the gene's structure. We use the concept of schema to account for properties of mind, even though we cannot specify its structure.

The notion of schema helps to explain the older infant's distribution of attention. Toward the end of the second month, fixation time is influenced by the degree to which the child's memory for a particular class of events resembles the specific external event encountered originally. Thus the length of orientation to a picture of a strange face is dependent on the child's schema for the faces he has seen in the past. Events which are moderately **discrepant** from his schema elicit longer fixations than very familiar events or ones that are completely novel and bear no relation to the schema. The relation of fixation time to magnitude of discrepancy between schema and event is assumed to be **curvilinear**; this assumption is called the discrepancy hypothesis.

The neurophysiologist describes this attentional phenomenon in slightly different language.

The prepotent role of novelty in evoking the **orienting reflex** suggests that this response is not initiated directly by a stimulus, in the customary sense of the term, but rather by a change in its intensity, pattern or other parameters. A comparison of present with previous stimulation seems of prime significance, with an orienting reflex being evoked by each point of disagreement. The concept of a cortical neuronal model . . . accounts for this induction of the orienting reflex by stimuli whose characteristic feature is their novelty. This model preserves information about earlier stimuli, with which aspects of novel stimulation may be compared. The orienting reflex is evoked whenever the parameters of the novel stimulus do not coincide with those of the model [Magoun 1969, p. 180].

Although an orienting reflex can often be produced by any change in quality or intensity of stimulation, duration of sustained attention seems to be influenced by

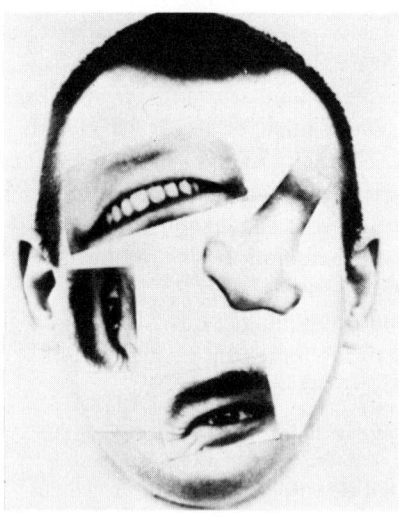

Fig. 3. Achromatic faces shown to infants

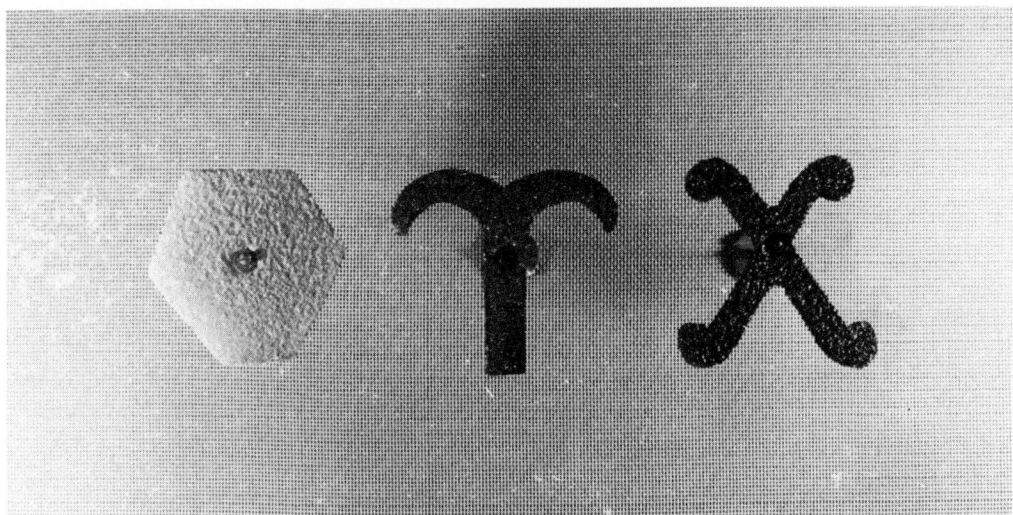

Fig. 4. One of the two standard mobiles shown to infants in the laboratory

the degree of discrepancy between event and related schema. Consider some empirical support for the discrepancy hypothesis. One- or two-week-old infants look equally long at a black-and-white outline of a regular face (upper right Fig. 3) and a meaningless design, for contrast is still the major determinant of attention at this early age. Even the eight-week-old attends equally long to a three-dimensional model of a head and an abstract three-dimensional form (Carpenter 1969). But four-month-old infants show markedly longer fixations to the two regular faces in Figure 3 than to the design in Figure 1 (McCall and Kagan 1967). The four-month-old has acquired a schema for a human face, and the achromatic illustrations are moderately discrepant from that schema. However, if the face is highly discrepant from the schema, as occurs when the components are rearranged (the lower faces in Fig. 3), fixation time is reduced (Wilcox 1969; Haaf and Bell 1967). The moderately discrepant face elicits more sustained attention than the extremely discrepant form at 16 weeks, but not during the first eight weeks of life (Fantz and Nevis 1967; Wilcox 1969; Lewis 1969). The differences in length of fixation to a normal face and to an equally complex but distorted face is greatest between three and six months of age, when infants normally display long fixations to faces. After six months fixation times to photographs of faces drop by over 50 percent and are equally long for both regular and irregular faces (Lewis 1969).

This developmental pattern confirms the discrepancy hypothesis. Prior to two months, before the infant has a schema for a human face, photographs of either regular or irregular faces are treated as nonsense designs and elicit equal periods of attention. Between two and four months the schema for a human face is established, and a photograph of a strange face is optimally discrepant from that schema. During the latter half of the first year, the schema for a face becomes so firmly established that photographs of regular or irregular faces, though discriminable, elicit short and equal fixations.

A second source of support for the discrepancy hypothesis comes from experiments in which an originally **meaningless stimulus** is presented repeatedly (usually 5 to 10 times), and afterward a variation of the original stimulus is shown to the infant. Fixation time typically decreases with repetitions of the first stimulus; but when the variation is presented, fixation times increase markedly (McCall and Melson 1969). In one experiment four-month-old infants were shown a stimulus containing three objects (a doll, a bow, and a flower) for five 30-second presentations. On the sixth trial the infants saw a stimulus in which one, two, or all three objects were replaced with new ones. Most infants showed significantly longer fixations to the changed stimulus than to the last presentation of the original (McCall and Kagan 1970).

The most persuasive support for the curvilinear hypothesis comes from an experiment in which a new schema was established experimentally (Super, Kagan, Morrison, Haith, and Weiffenbach, unpublished). Each of 84 firstborn Caucasian infants, four months old, was shown the same three-dimensional stimulus composed of three geometric forms of different shape and hue for 12 half-minute periods (Fig. 4). Each infant was then randomly assigned to one of seven groups. Six of these groups were exposed at home to a stimulus that was of varying discrepancy from the standard viewed in the laboratory. The mother showed the stimulus, in the form of a mobile, to the child 30 minutes a day for 21 days. The seven experimental groups were as follows (Fig. 5):

Group 1: Control standard. These infants were exposed to the same stimulus they saw in the laboratory at four months.
Group 2: Subtraction. These infants were shown a four-element stimulus constructed by adding a fourth element to the three-element standard seen in the laboratory. ("Subtraction" referred to the later laboratory session [see below], which used only three elements.)
Group 3: Serial rearrangement. Infants exposed to a stimulus in which the three elements of the original standard were rearranged in the horizontal plane.
Group 4: Asymmetric rearrangement. Infants shown the three-element stimulus rearranged in an asymmetric form.
Group 5: Ninety-degree rotation. Infants shown a stimulus in which the three horizontal elements in the standard were rearranged in a vertical plane.
Group 6: Extreme discrepancy. Infants shown a mobile consisting of many more elements of different shapes and colors than those of the standard.
Group 7: No-mobile control. Infants exposed to no stimulus during the 21-day experimental period.

	Standard	
Group	XOT	OTX
Standard control	XOT	OTX
Subtraction	☐XOT	☐OTX
Serial rearrangement	OTX	XOT
Asymmetric rearrangement	O X T	T O X
90° rotation	X O T	O T X
Extreme discrepancy	[mobile figures]	[mobile figures]
No-home-mobile control	None	None

Fig. 5. Schematic illustration of the mobiles infants saw at home for 21 days

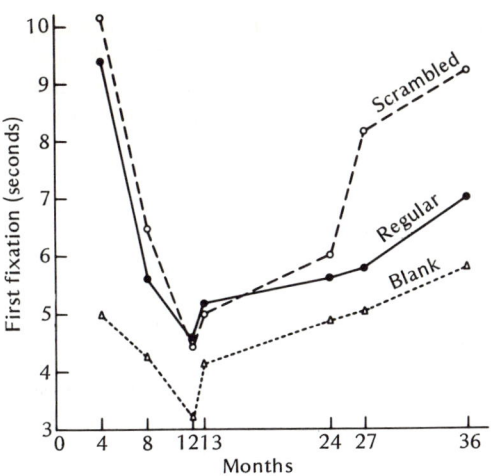

Fig. 6. Relation between fixation time to faces and age of child

Three weeks later each subject was brought back to the laboratory and shown the same stimulus viewed initially at four months. The major dependent variable was the change in fixation time between the first and second test sessions. Figure 6 illustrates these change scores for total fixation time across the first six trials of each session.

The infants who saw no stimulus at home are the referent group to which all the other groups are to be compared. These infants showed no change in fixation time across the three weeks, indicating that the laboratory stimulus was as attractive on the second visit as on the first. The infants who developed a schema for the asymmetric and vertical rotation mobiles (moderate discrepancy) showed the smallest drop in interest across the three weeks. By contrast, the infants who experienced a minimal (groups 2 and 3) or major discrepancy (group 6) showed the greatest drop in interest. (Analysis of variance for total fixation time across the first six trials yielded an F ratio of 5.29 and a probability value of less than .05.) There was a curvilinear relation between attention and stimulus-schema discrepancy. Although the existing data are still not conclusive, they clearly support the discrepancy hypothesis.

The onset of a special reaction to discrepancy between two and three months is paralleled by other physiological and behavioral changes in the infant. Temporal characteristics of the **cortical evoked potential** to a visual stimulus approach adult form, growth of **occipital neurons** levels off, and the alpha rhythm of the **electroencephalogram** becomes recognizable (Ellingson 1967). The Moro reflex—the spreading and coming together of the arms when the head is suddenly dropped a few inches—begins to disappear, crying decreases, babbling increases, decreased attention to repeated presentations of a visual event becomes a reliable phenomenon (Dreyfus-Brisac 1958; Ellingson 1967), and three-dimensional representations of objects elicit longer fixations than two-dimensional ones (Fantz 1966). Perhaps the infant's capacity to react to discrepancy at this age reflects the fact that the brain has matured enough to permit the establishment of long-term memories and their activation by external events.

The effect of the infant's hypotheses

As the child approaches the end of the first year he acquires a new kind of cognitive structure which we call hypotheses. A hypothesis is an interpretation of some experience accomplished by mentally transforming an unusual event to the form the child is familiar with. The "form he is familiar with" is the schema. The cognitive structure used in the transformation is the hypothesis. Suppose a five-year-old notes a small bandage on his mother's face; he will attempt to find the reason for the bandage and may activate the hypothesis, "She cut her face." A five-month-old will recognize his mother in spite of the bandage but will not try to explain its presence.

To recognize that a particular sequence of sounds is human speech, rather than a telephone, requires a schema for the quality of a human voice. Interpretation of the meaning of the speech, on the other hand, requires the activation of hypotheses, in this case linguistic rules. The critical difference between a schema and a hypothesis resembles the difference between recognition and interpretation. **Recognition** is the assimilation of an event as belonging to one class rather than another. The performance of the four-year-old in the experiment with 50 pictures illustrates the recognition process. The child requires only a schema for the original event in order to answer correctly. **Interpretation** involves the additional process of activating hypotheses that change the perception of an event so that it can be understood. It is assumed that the activation of hypotheses to explain discrepant events is accompanied by sustained attention. The more extensive the repertoire of hypotheses—the more knowledge the child has—the longer he can work at interpretation and the more prolonged his attention. The child's distribution of attention at an art museum provides a final analogy. He may be expected to study somewhat unusual pictures longer than extremely realistic ones or surrealistic ones because he is likely to have a richer set of hypotheses for the moderately discrepant scenes. The richer the repertoire of hypotheses, holding discrepancy of event constant, the longer the child will persist at interpretation. There is as yet no body of empirical proof for these ideas, but data that we shall consider agree with these views.

In sum, three factors influence length of fixation time in the infant. High rate of change in physical aspects of the stimulus is primary during the opening weeks, discrepancy becomes a major factor at two months, and activation of hypotheses becomes influential at around 12 months. These three factors supplement each other; and a high-contrast, discrepant event that activates many hypotheses should elicit longer fixation times from an 18-month-old than a stimulus with only one or two of these attributes.

Two parallel investigations attest to the potential usefulness of the complementary principles of discrepancy and activation of hypotheses. In the first, one-, two-, and three-year-old children of middle class families in Cambridge, Massachusetts, and of peasant Indian families from a village in the Yucatan peninsula were shown color prints of male faces—Caucasian for the American children and Indian for the Mexican children (Finley 1967). Fixation time to the faces increased with age. The largest increase between two and three years of age occurred to the discrepant, scrambled face rather than to the nondiscrepant, regular face; the former required the activation of more hypotheses in order to be assimilated.

In the second study 180 white, firstborn boys and girls from the Cambridge area viewed the clay faces in Figure 7 repeatedly at 4, 8, 13, and 27 months of age. There was a U-shaped relation between age and fixation time. Fixation decreased from 4 to 13 months but increased between 13 and 27 months. The longer fixations at 4 months reflect the fact that

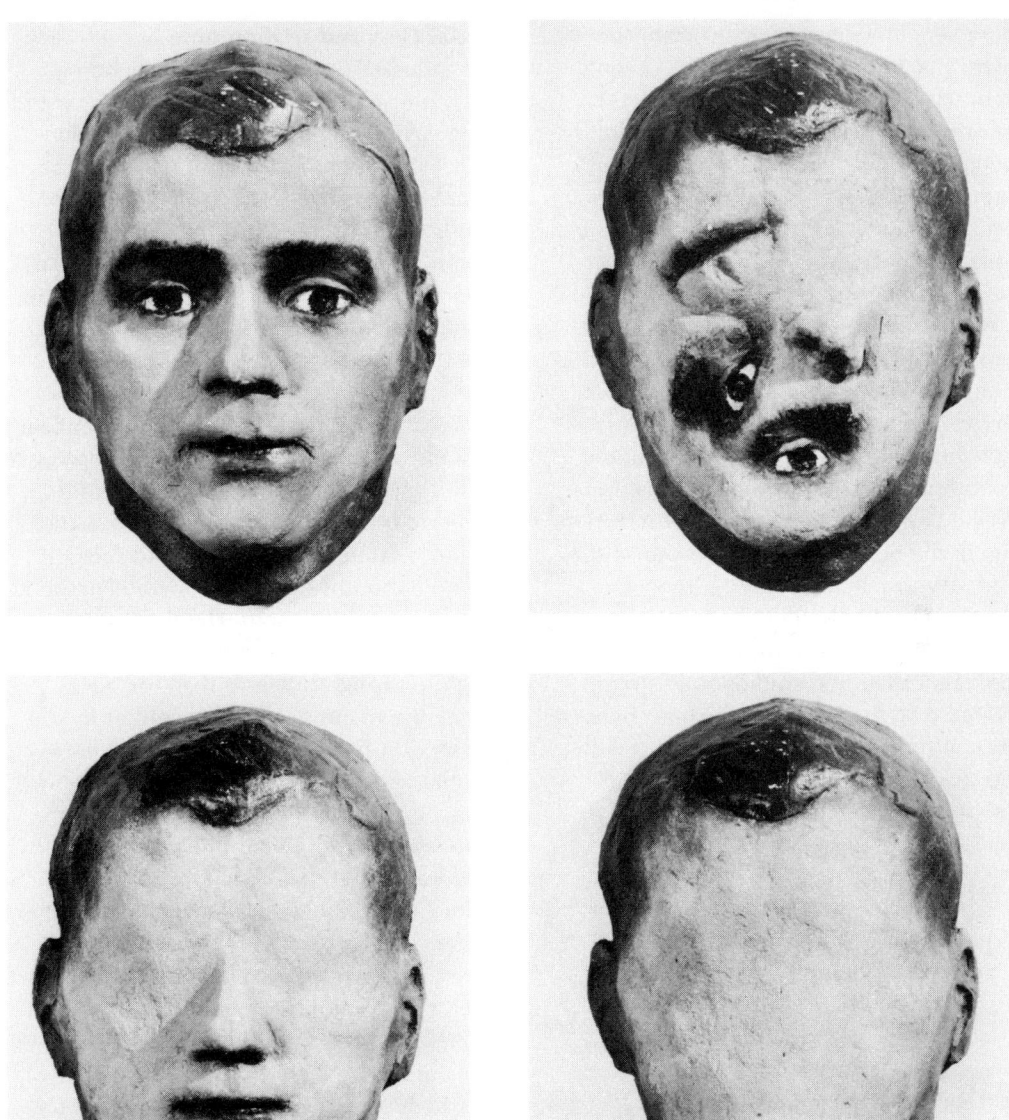

Fig. 7. Clay masks shown to children at 4, 8, 13, and 27 months

these stimuli were discrepant from the infant's acquired schema for his parents' faces. Fixations decreased at 8 and 13 months because these masks were less discrepant but did not yet activate a long train of hypotheses in the service of **assimilation**. Between one and two years fixations rose because the child was activating hypotheses to resolve the discrepancy.

As with the first study, the largest increase in fixation time, between 13 and 27 months, occurred to the scrambled face. The children's spontaneous comments indicated that they were trying to understand how a face could be so transformed. "What happened to his nose? Who hit him in the nose?" asked a two-year-old. And, "Who that, Mommy? A monster, Mommy?" said another.

The function resulting from combining the data of the two studies is illustrated in Figure 8. The U-shaped relation between fixation time and age is concordant with the theoretical argument given earlier.

Social class and fixation time

The number of hypotheses surrounding a class of events should covary, in part, with language competence. Hence any experiences that promote acquisition of language should be associated with longer fixation times toward the end of the first year.

The positive correlation between parental educational level and the child's linguistic competence is well known and well documented (see, for example, Cazden 1966). Thus a positive relation between parental education and fixation time should appear toward the end of the first year and grow with time. The data on 180 firstborns indicated that parental education was not highly related to fixation time to faces at 4 and 8 months but was moderately related (correlation coefficient [r] = about 0.4) at 13 and 27 months, and this relation was slightly stronger for girls than for boys. Since the majority of infants either increased in fixation time or showed no essential change between 13 and 27 months, we computed the change in first fixation between 13 and 27 months for each child and correlated that change with parental educational level as well as independent indexes of verbal ability at 27 months. There was a positive relation between increase in fixation time and parents' educational level for the girls (r = .31) but not for boys (r = −.04); 27-month-old girls with the highest vocabulary scores showed the largest increases in fixation time.

It is not clear why the relation between parental education and sustained attention should be stronger for girls than for boys. Other investigators have also reported closer **covariation** in girls than boys between social class and various indexes of cognitive development including IQ scores and school grades. Moss and Robson (1968) studied the relation between amount of face-to-face interaction mother

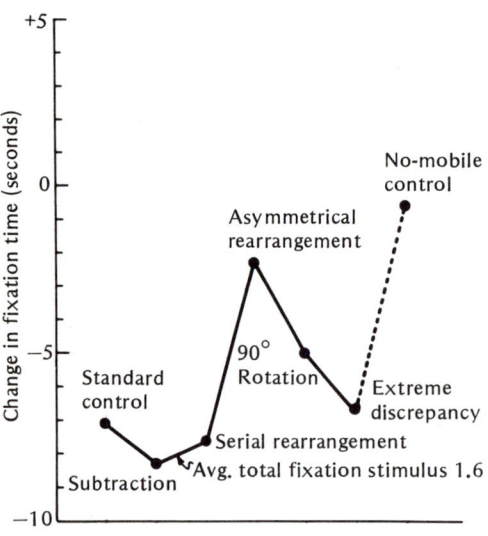

Fig. 8. Change in fixation time for each of the experimental groups

and infant had in the home and the three-month-old infant's fixation time to photographs of faces in the laboratory. The association was positive for girls ($r = .61$, $p < .01$) and close to zero for boys. Hess, Shipman, Brophy, and Bear (1968, 1969) and Werner (1969) have reported more substantial correlations for girls than boys between maternal education or verbal ability, on the one hand, and the child's IQ or level of reading achievement on the other. There seems to be a general tendency for indexes of maternal intellectual ability and, by inference, maternal concern with the child's mental development, to be better predictors of cognitive development in daughters than sons.

One interpretation of this puzzling phenomenon rests on the fact that girls are biologically less variable than boys (Acheson 1966). This implies that fewer infant girls would display extreme degrees of irritability, activity, or attentiveness. Let us assume the following principle: the more often the mother attempts to interest her child in an event the stronger the child's tendency to develop a general sensitivity to change and a capacity for sustained attention to discrepancy. This principle is likely to be less valid for infants who temperamentally have a tendency toward apathy or hyper-vigilance. There are many functional relations in nature that lose their validity when one of the variables assumes an extreme value, and this may be another instance of that phenomenon.

An alternative explanation of the stronger covariation for girls than boys between maternal intelligence and the child's mental development assumes greater differences between well and poorly educated mothers in their treatment of daughters than of sons, especially in maternal actions that promote attention and language acquisition. A mother seems more likely to project her motives, expectations, and self-image on her daughter than on her son, and is more likely to assume that her daughter will come to resemble her. Many poorly educated mothers feel less competent than the college graduate and have greater doubts about their daughters' potential for intellectual accomplishment. Such a mother may set or supply lower standards and less enthusiastic as well as less consistent encouragement to her infant girl to learn new skills. The well educated mother sets higher aspirations and acts as though she held the power to catalyze her child's development.

The situation with sons is somewhat different. Most mothers, regardless of class background, believe their sons will have to learn how to support a family and achieve some degree of independence. Hence mothers of all classes may be more alike in energizing the cognitive development of sons. The restricted range of acceleration of sons, compared with daughters, would result in closer covariation for girls between social class and indexes of cognitive development.

This argument finds support in observations of the mother-child interaction in the home. Well educated mothers are more likely to talk to their four-month-old daughters than mothers with less than a high school education. But this class difference in maternal "talkativeness" does not occur for sons. Observations of an independent sample of 60 mother-daughter pairs at 10 months of age (Tulkin, unpublished) also indicates that middle, in contrast to lower, class mothers spend significantly more time in face-to-face contact with their daughters, vocalize more often to them, and more frequently reward their attempts to crawl and stand. A final source of data is the home observations on some of the 180 children at 27 months. The observer noted each instance in which the mother reproved the child for disobeying a rule. Mothers of all social classes were more likely to reprove sons than daughters. However, reproval for incompetence at a task was most frequently meted out by the well educated mothers of daughters; there was no comparable class difference for mothers of sons.

Thus, independent and complementary evidence supports the idea that differential pressures toward intellectual competence are more likely to covary with social class for mother-daughter than for mother-son pairs. It has usually been assumed that the girl is more concerned with acceptance by parents and teachers than the boy, and that this particular motive for intellectual accomplishment covaries with social class; but intellectual achievement among boys is spurred by more varied motives, including hostility, power, and identification with competent male figures—motives less closely linked to social class. However valid these propositions, they are not operative during the first year of life.

Implications

The influence of contrast, discrepancy, and activation of hypotheses on distribution of attention is probably not limited to the first two years of life. Schools implicitly acknowledge the validity of these principles for older children by using books with contrasting colors and unusual formats and by emphasizing procedures whose aim is to ensure that the child has a relevant hypothesis available when he encounters a new problem. A child who possesses no hypothesis for solution of a problem is likely to withdraw from the task. Many children regard mathematics as more painful than English or social studies because they have fewer strategies to use with a difficult problem in arithmetic than for one in history or composition. The school might well give children more help in learning to generate hypotheses with which to solve problems, and put less pressure on them to accumulate facts.

The principles discussed in this paper are also related to the issue of incentives for acquiring new knowledge. The behaviorist, trying to preserve the theoretical necessity of the concept of reinforcement, has been vexed by the fact that the child acquires new knowledge in the absence of any demonstrable external reward. However, the process of assimilating a discrepant event to a schema has many of the characteristics of a pleasant experience and therefore is in accord with the common understanding of a reward. The central problem in educating children is to attract and maintain focused attention. The central theoretical problem in understanding mental growth is to discern the factors that are continually producing change in schema and hypothesis. Solution of these two problems is not to be found through analyses of the environment alone. We must decipher the relation between the perceiver and the space in which he moves, for that theme, like Ariadne's thread, gives direction to cognitive growth.

References

Acheson, R. N. 1966. Maturation of the skeleton. In F. Falkner, ed. *Human development.* Philadelphia: W. B. Saunders, pp. 465–502.

Brackbill, Y., G. Adams, D. H. Crowell, and M. C. Gray. 1966. Arousal level in newborns and preschool children under continuous auditory stimulation. *J. Exp. Child Psychol.* 3:176–88.

Carpenter, G. C. Feb. 1969. Differential visual behavior to human and humanoid faces in

early infancy. Presented at Merrill-Palmer Infancy Conference, Detroit, Mich.

Cazden, C. B. 1966. Subcultural differences in child language. *Merrill-Palmer Quart.* 12: 185–219.

Dreyfus-Brisac, C., D. Samson, C. Blanc, and N. Monod. 1958. L'électroencéphlograme de l'enfant normal de moins de trois ans. *Etudes néo-natales* 7:143–75.

Eisenberg, R. B., E. J. Griffin, D. B. Coursin, and M. A. Hunter. 1964. Auditory behavior in the neonate. *J. Speech and Hearing Res.* 7: 245–69.

Ellingson, R. J. 1967. Study of brain electrical activity in infants. In L. P. Lipsitt and C. C. Spiker, eds. *Advances in child development and behavior.* New York: Academic Press, pp. 53–98.

Fantz, R. L. 1966. Pattern discrimination and selective attention as determinants of perceptual development from birth. In A. H. Kidd and J. J. Rivoire, eds. *Perceptual development in children.* New York: International Universities Press.

Fantz, R. L., and S. Nevis. 1967. Pattern preferences in perceptual cognitive development in early infancy. *Merrill-Palmer Quart.* 13:77–108.

Finley, G. E. 1967. Visual attention, play, and satiation in young children: a cross cultural study. Unpublished doctoral dissertation, Harvard Univ.

Haaf, R. A., and R. Q. Bell. 1967. A facial dimension in visual discrimination by human infants. *Child Devel.* 38:893–99.

Haith, M. M. 1966. Response of the human newborn to visual movement. *J. Exp. Child Psychol.* 3:235–43.

Haith, M. M. March 1968. Visual scanning in infants. Paper presented at regional meeting of Society for Research in Child Development. Clark Univ., Worcester, Mass.

Hess, R. D., V. C. Shipman, J. E. Brophy, and R. M. Bear. 1968 and (follow-up phase) 1969. The cognitive environments of urban preschool children. Report to the Graduate School of Education, Univ. of Chicago.

Karmel, B. Z. 1966. The effect of complexity,

amount of contour, element size and element arrangement on visual preference behavior in the hooded rat, domestic chick, and human infant. Unpublished doctoral dissertation, George Washington Univ., Washington, D.C.

Kuffler, S. W. 1952. Neurons in the retina: Organization, inhibition, and excitation problems. *Cold Spring Harbor Symposium in Quantitative Biology* 17:281–92.

Kuffler, S. W. 1953. Discharge patterns and functional organization of mammalian retina. *J. Physiol.* 16:37–68.

Lewis, M. 1969. Infants' responses to facial stimuli during the first year of life. *Devel. Psychol.* no. 2, pp. 75–86.

McCall, R. B., and J. Kagan. 1967. Attention in the infant: effects of complexity, contour, perimeter, and familiarity. *Child Devel.* 38: 939–52.

McCall, R. B. and J. Kagan. 1970. Individual differences in the infant's distribution of attention to stimulus discrepancy. *Developmental Psychology* 2:90–98.

McCall, R. B., and W. H. Melson. March 1969. Attention in infants as a function of the magnitude of discrepancy and habituation rate. Paper presented at meeting of the Society for Research in Child Development. Santa Monica, Calif.

Magoun, H. W. 1969. Advances in brain research with implications for learning. In K. H. Pribram, ed., *On the biology of learning*. New York: Harcourt, Brace & World, pp. 171–90.

Moss, H. A. 1967. Sex, age and state as determinants of mother-infant interaction. *Merrill-Palmer Quart.* 13:19–36.

Moss, H. A., and K. S. Robson. 1968. Maternal influences on early social-visual behavior. *Child Devel.* 39:401–8.

Salapatek, P., and W. Kessen. 1966. Visual scanning of triangles by the human newborn. *J. Exp. Child Psychol.* 3:113–22.

Super, C., J. Kagan, F. Morrison, and M. Haith. An experimental test of the discrepancy hypothesis. J. Genet. Psychol. (in press)

Tulkin, S. Social class differences in mother-child interaction. Unpublished.

Werner, E. E. 1969. Sex differences in correlations between children's IQs and measure of parental ability and environment ratings. *Devel. Psychol.* 1:280–85.

Wilcox, B. M. 1969. Visual preferences of human infants for representations of the human face. *J. Exp. Child Psychol.* 7:10–20.

COGNITIVE TRANSFORMATIONS

Presleep Experiences and Dreams

HERMAN A. WITKIN
AND HELEN B. LEWIS

From observations made on himself and his patients, Freud (1953) demonstrated that the contents of a dream are often continuations of emotionally charged experiences of the day. The still-active daytime feelings and thoughts, to which Freud gave the name "day's residue," are worked over, so that they usually appear in the dream in altered form—that is, transformed—rather than directly. A key question in the study of dreams is how the thoughts and feelings stirred in the waking state are transformed into the language of the dream. One way of investigating this problem is to arrange for a known presleep experience, experimentally induced, which may be identified in the content of ensuing dreams. The presleep event may then serve as one reference point or "tracer element" for studying the forms and processes of transformation. We assume that the experimentally induced presleep experience contributes to the "day's residue" and that having this reference reduces the number of steps of inference involved in unraveling the ensuing dreams. . . .

Procedure

Our experimental procedure has the following main components: (1) the presleep psychological event; (2) a study, on some occasions, by means of a special technique, of the hypnagogic reverie state intervenning between the presleep event and the time of falling asleep; (3) reports from the subject of his experience in all subsequent dream periods, identified by the concomitant occurrence of rapid eye movements (REM) and Stage 1 EEG; (4) recordings of **autonomic activity** during the presleep psychological event and during subsequent sleep; (5) an extended inquiry at the end of the sleep session into each dream and the entire laboratory experience; (6) an intensive clinical study of each subject.

The Presleep Psychological Event

The Emotionally Charged Films. In casting about for a method of presleep stimulation, we considered it necessary to have a medium which could be used to provide both exciting and neutral experiences and which could be readily duplicated from subject to subject. Films seemed to meet these requirements particularly well.

We have used two emotionally charged films in our studies. One is a medical teaching film showing the birth of a baby; the other is an anthropological documentary of a subincision initiation rite practiced by a primitive Australian group. Both films are capable of arousing a range of strong reactions. The material in both is sexually exciting. Both show mutilation of or injury to the body, particularly the sexual organs, thereby arousing feelings about physical aggression. They also provide opportunities for "looking" at usually forbidden sights. Previous studies of the subincision film by Lazarus, et al. (1962), have found strong physiological reactions to it. The films are described in greater detail later . . .

The Dream Monitoring Procedure

. . . [T]he simultaneous occurrence of rapid, conjugate eye movement (REM periods) and Stage 1-EEG sleep may be taken to signify the presence of dreaming. In our study the subject went to bed immediately after the presleep event. He was awakened by a loud buzzer during each subsequent REM-Stage 1-EEG period and asked to report what had been going through his mind. After he gave his spontaneous report, he was questioned briefly in order to establish such characteristics of the dream experience as representation of the self, quality of feelings, extent of activity, and nature of surroundings. The entire report was tape-recorded. By this procedure it was possible to obtain much, although not all, of the subject's dream product following a presleep event. On-the-spot failure to recall dreams could also be determined. . . .

Dream Content in Relation to Presleep Experience

The dream content we have recovered appears often to have a clear relation to the presleep stimulus employed. In many instances, as we have noted, identification of an element in the dream as related to the presleep stimulus relies on the interpretation of a symbolic or metaphoric dream translation. Identification of the dream elements as related to the presleep stimulus also depends frequently on the subject's associations. The essence of the present procedure is that the introduction of known "tracer" stimuli permits more objective judgment of the appropriateness of such interpretation.

To illustrate the relation of the dream yield to the presleep stimulus, we shall now review the dreams reported at subsequent REM awakenings, after we have given a description of the content of the presleep event.

Birth Film. The birth film is in color and has a sound track. The first part describes the Malmstrom Vacuum Extractor and discusses its advantages as a method of delivery. The second part shows the exposed vagina and thighs of the woman, painted with iodine, in other words, brown. The arm of the obstetrician is seen inserting the vacuum extractor into the vagina; the gloved hands and arms of the obstetrician, covered with blood, are then shown pulling periodically on a chain protruding from the vagina. The cutting motion of an episiotomy is also shown. The baby is then delivered with a gush of blood. The film ends by illustrating that only a harmless swelling of the skin of the baby's head results from the vacuum extraction method.

So that the reader may form an impression of the dream yield of an entire sleep session, we present, first, three full texts of all the dreams reported by Mr. A after the birth film.

While watching the film just before going to sleep, Mr. A was observed to be breathing harder, to make swallowing movements, and not to take his gaze off the film for an instant. At the end he was very eager to discuss the film, which the experimenter tried to avoid. He said that he had seen books on deliveries (his wife had been a nurse), but this film was a "shocker" with "blood and all." He asked why this method was used in preference to Caesarean delivery and spontaneously mentioned that he "had to remember" the name of "Malmstrom."

Before seeing the film, Mr. A commented on the EEG recording paper, which is full of lines and markings, asking, "Is that the way I look?" He remarked further, with some sarcasm, that he ought to put some of his EEG recordings in a frame and hang them up.

First Awakening[1]   12:45 p.m.   REM, abrupt

S: Yes. Yes, I can hear you. Go ahead.
E: Was anything going through your mind?
S: No, I really just, uh, I was dreaming about (p) let me see, a group of college boys walking down the lane, in the lane, in the uh, in the park, singing, and they were outside there in the distance, and there was a group of girls and all, dressed in white sitting on the park benches, uh . . carrying flowers, I think. Um, it was dark and they were covering, uh, they were wearing white gloves, I remember long, you know, long white gloves (P) and there was, uh, let's see (P) I'm trying to think of the details . . they were trying to hide something, or something . . lots of flowers in the park. Yellow ones, I think. Regular flowers.
E: Did you recognize anybody in the dream?
S: Uh. No. There's nobody I could recognize.
E: Were you in the dream?
S: No, I wasn't. I couldn't particularly single out anybody that I could recognize in the dream. (p) I had to make a special effort to retain the . . you know, it disappears after a very few seconds, if I don't make a constant effort to retain it.
E: Where there any feelings connected with it?
S: No. I, uh, I guess you might say I was a passive observer of the scene. I had no feelings either way of what was going on. It had been going on maybe a few minutes, I guess, then I woke up. At the beginning, some time earlier it had something to do about insects, uh bees. I was catching bees. Somebody was catching bees and letting them go on flowers, you know,

---

[1] In these transcripts two dots are used to indicate some hesitation on the subject's part, (p) to indicate a slight pause, and (P) to indicate a long pause. Three dots indicate minor deletions of repetitions from the text. The time noted at the beginning of each report is the time of awakening. At the far right is indicated the stage of sleep from which the subject was awakened and the method of awakening.

pollinating the flowers. I think . . uh . . just came to a park there, uh, trying to control them so I could pollinate yellow flowers, and uh (p) and uh, uh, I don't know. Could you ask me another question?

E: Did you say you were catching the bees?

S: At first, the beginning there they were uh, they were in a laboratory or something being used to . . for experimental purposes. They were being used to pollinate flowers, well that was way back, hard to remember the beginning of the dream. As you go along you get more involved, um, one things leads to another. Yes, that's about it, you know. These bees were pollinating these flowers, and uh (p) they were bright yellow, shining almost in the dark, and uh, these girls didn't want to see, uh, these boys to see them. They didn't want to see them, so they were trying to hi . . to cover up their elbows and holding their arms so that they wouldn't be seen, the gloves wouldn't be seen. The whiteness of the gloves wouldn't be seen in the dark. (p) Way off in the distance you could hear them singing as they were walking along the walks. (p) That's about it.

E: You said it was dark?

S: Yes, very dark.

E: Do you remember what you were dreaming just when you woke up?

S: Yes. At that point they were walking in the distance singing with uh the girls sitting on the benches in the foreground listening, and clutching their elbows (p) trying to keep, I think, the bright flowers from being seen, you know. Sort of, I think there was possibly a glow, a yellowish glow on the flowers where the bees had been around previously. (p) I guess that's it.

Second Awakening   2:50 p.m.   REM, abrupt

S: Yes, I can hear you. Go ahead.

E: Okay. Would you tell me anything that was going through your mind?

S: Yes, (*inaudible*) looking out the window. And I could see the part of the airplane near the wing (*inaudible*) the fuselage. I found myself in an airplane flying along, and uh some people . . ooh, just before that I was sitting in the (p) now let me think. (p) I don't know, at the moment you woke me up I was flying around in the airplane looking out, sort of, like (*inaudible*) looking out well, not through a window, exactly, looking out through a (p) a like a hole. Well, anyhow, I could see the part of the airplane where the wing is attached, the body of the plane. And just above me and . . to my left was a hole, and through the hole was protruding a coil of wire, and there was a man holding a . . the end of the wire . . big wire, and he had his finger through the end of it. One loop at the end of it, pulling it, it was attached to the . . the other part of the wire was attached to a door, and when he pulled the wire, the door would go up and down and the wire . . his hand would pull the wire and would cause him, the door would go up, he'd let it go back in, the door would go down, and uh, it was sort of a troop carrier plane, people, parachutists, jumping out of the airplane. Actually, I don't think I saw anybody jump, but I got the impression that it was that kind of airplane. Anyway I was explaining it to the uh other fellow, I was explaining that the plane was actually (*inaudible*). He was telling me that, uh, about somebody who was making these wires. He went into the business of making these wires. (p) Let me see, now I remember very little of what he said. (p) Uh, we were flying alone at the time. Just before that I was talking to somebody. (P) It was a baseball player, I suppose I was, too. He was telling me about all of his children . . how many he had. I was telling him how many children I had. It seems we had large families, the two of us. And um, he was telling me how everyone called him "lover" or something like that, and uh, (p) let me see, uh, he was also (p) a pretty good baseball player, and he was on the same team I was, and he was in the running for some honor, he was going for the best player on the team or something like that. He was ahead of me, and I was sort of behind him (p) on, you know, on the team as well as in the department of having children. He was ahead of me. And we were talking a little, sitting facing each other, on these boxes or stools. I think that was it; we were sitting on stools. (p) And then it, uh, switched from that to the dream I was telling you about when I woke up. Let's see, it went

from there to the airplane. (P) Is there anything else I could tell you?
E: Who was the other person?
S: Not anyone that I could recognize or name. (P) But uh, (p) it's the name of some well known baseball player. I forget his name right now, but I think he was on the Dodgers, Los Angeles Dodgers. (P) During the last season, I was rooting for him, you know, to win the pennant. (P) I don't know. That's about it. Anything else I can tell you?
E: Were there any feelings connected with the dream?
S: Feelings? No. I was just talking, that's all. No., there weren't any special feelings. I was just talking. (P) Can I tell you anything else?
E: Do you have anything else to tell?
S: Let me think now. (P) No, I guess that about covers it.
E: Okay, good night. . . .

Subincision Film. The second charged film we used is a silent film, in black and white, made by Géza Róheim of a subincision rite practiced by an **aboriginal** Australian group, the Arunta (Spencer and Gillen, 1927). It shows a number of older men preparing for the initiation of four young men. All the men are naked. Each initiate lies down across the backs of the other initiates, who are perched on all fours close to each other. An incision is made with a sharp stone along the ventral surface of the penis and the scrotum. The bleeding penis is then seen being held over a fire. The faces of the initiates clearly reflect their anguish. A hairdressing ritual is also shown. The film ends with a rhythmic ritual dance.

Classic symbolic transformations, as well as condensed and distorted representations, appear in the dream after the subincision film, as they did after the birth film. Like the birth film, the subincision film also evokes a variety of themes. If one compares the dreams of the same subject after the birth and subincision films, one can also glimpse a personal style of **imagery**, an observation we are pursuing in our further systematic studies.

Here is the text of a dream which Mr. A had after seeing the subincision film.

Second Awakening   4:40 p.m.   REM, abrupt
S: Yes. I was just dreaming about . . let's see now . . I was dreaming about two characters, one facing . . two cowboy types . . you know, like you see on television, facing each other, and one is holding a gun on the other one, and the other one was telling . . telling him that that's no special gun he's got . . it's um . . old Western action type gun, and he remembered he knew a friend of his who had one who was in some kind of contest or other and he wasn't too successful with it . . I forgot the exact words. That's about it. All dressed up in their usual outfits . . cowboys . . clothes . . and the surrounding scene was, I think . . I don't know. I can't remember exactly the surrounding scene. Maybe there were some people around, but I'm not sure. This fellow who was holding the gun, he wasn't talking at all. He was just pointing it at him, and (p) I could see from this other fellow's viewpoint you know . . this gun looming up in front of me . . kinda like I was looking right into it. (p) Uh, that's it I guess. (P) Go ahead. Can you hear me? Well, that's it.
E: Anything at all more you could tell me about these two people?
S: They were tall, I think one fellow was dressed in dark clothes and the other fellow was dressed in lighter clothes. You know the general outfit. They wear tall hats turned up at the brim (p) all the rest. One was a heavy fellow . . the one who was dark dressed was a heavy man, and the other one was more slender, I think. He talked with a deep voice . . the one who was dressed in the dark outfit (p) there was a sort of a cowboy twang in his voice.
E: Were they doing anything?
S: They were standing there facing each other. One was holding a gun on the other one . . pointing the gun at him. The other one was doing the talking . . the one who was having the gun pointed at him . . and he'd look at the

gun, and nothing else . . he couldn't see anything else around him . . everything was blurred around him except for the barrel of the gun pointing. You know, I could see it from his uh . . viewpoint, it's like I was looking into it. All I could see was the gun . . the barrel of the gun, you know, pointing directly at me . . and I could see the sight, big sight . . pointing directly at me . . and with the gunsight on top of two winglike projections. I was looking directly into the gun, and all I could see was the barrel and above it was the gunsight, and the two winged-like projections on either side of it, like some gunsights have. (P) With the center post in the middle, if you know what a gunsight looks like.

In this text we have what appears to be a classic symbolic representation of the penis as a gun. Once again, as in his dream of the girls hiding something following the birth film, A is in the position of the victim. He is looking right into the barrel of the gun which is being "held on him," "the one who is doing the talking." One can sense a double reference both to the film and to being the experimental subject who does the talking. Again, as in his dreams following the birth film, the imagery of the dream has something of an opposite quality to the film. Instead of naked men, A sees cowboys who are all dressed up in special outfits, and the whole quality of the action is as if on television, that is, not to be taken too seriously.

Mr. B had a dream after the subincision film that he was "holding something in my hand like a piece of chalk or a cigarette, between my thumb and forefinger." An image or experience of holding the penis seems to have entered the dream, transformed into "holding a cigarette" or a "piece of chalk." The dream also specified that the events taking place were "in the lower right-hand corner" of "whatever scene or impression I had." In the inquiry at the end of the session the "lower right-hand corner" was identified as the part of the wall of the bedroom on which the film had been projected.

Mr. B also had two dreams about cats and began the end-of-session inquiry with the remark, "I guess I had cats on my mind." In one dream a cat was "playing around" a sewing machine, and B was "concerned that the needle wouldn't pierce him." The second dream was clearly about Mr. B's cat, which is described in the inquiry as a "male, but he's been altered." In the associative inquiry, B negated any connection between the altered cat and the theme of the subincision film, immediately after he himself had made the connection.

After the subincision film C dreamed that he was being "dismantled" and that some girls in a library were "grabbing books off the shelves," as if, C said in the inquiry, "it had been their last chance."

. . . Thus it seems possible to obtain in the laboratory dreams and enough of their relevant clinical context to permit their study in the manner followed in clinical work. More important, our procedure makes it possible to put to experimental test a number of concepts about dream phenomena, some of them implicit in the clinical method of dream interpretation. Some of the hypotheses which may be checked by this procedure are being examined in a more systematic repetition of the preliminary study described. These hypotheses deal with dream transformation, sequence effects in dreams of the same night, dream recall and defenses, and personal styles of dreaming.

AVOIDANCE BEHAVIOR

Vicarious Extinction of Avoidance Behavior

ALBERT BANDURA, JOAN E. GRUSEC, AND FRANCES L. MENLOVE

Recent investigations have shown that **behavioral inhibitions** (Bandura, 1965a; Bandura, Ross, & Ross, 1963; Walters & Parke, 1964) and **conditioned emotional responses** (Bandura & Rosenthal, 1966; Berger, 1962) can be acquired by observers as a function of witnessing **aversive stimuli** administered to performing subjects. The present experiment was primarily designed to determine whether preexisting avoidance behavior can similarly be extinguished on a vicarious basis. The latter phenomenon requires exposing observers to modeled stimulus events in which a performing subject repeatedly exhibits approach responses toward the feared object without incurring any aversive consequences.

Some suggestive evidence that **avoidance responses** can be extinguished vicariously is furnished by Masserman (1943) and Jones (1924) in exploratory studies of the relative efficacy of various psychotherapeutic procedures. Masserman produced strong feeding inhibitions in cats, following which the inhibited animals observed a cage mate, that had never been negatively conditioned, exhibit prompt approach and feeding responses. The observing subjects initially cowered at the presentation of the **conditioned stimulus**, but with continued exposure to their fearless companion they advanced, at first hesitantly and then more boldly, to the goal box and consumed the food. Some of the animals, however, showed little reduction in avoidance behavior despite prolonged food deprivation and numerous **modeling trials**. Moreover, avoidance responses reappeared in a few of the animals after the normal cat was removed, suggesting that in the latter cases the modeling stimuli served merely as temporary external inhibitors of avoidance responses. Jones (1924) similarly obtained variable results in extinguishing children's phobic responses by having them observe their peers behave in a nonanxious manner in the presence of the avoided objects.

If a person is to be influenced by modeling stimuli and the accompanying consequences, then the necessary observing responses must be elicited and maintained. In the foregoing case studies, the models responded to the most feared stimulus situation at the outset, a modeling procedure that is likely to generate high levels of emotional arousal in observers. Under these conditions any avoidance responses designed to reduce vicariously instigated aversive stimulation, such as subjects withdrawing or looking away, would impede vicarious extinction. Therefore, the manner in which modeling stimuli are presented may be an important determinant of the course of vicarious extinction.

Results from psychotherapeutic studies (Bandura[1]) and experiments with infrahuman subjects (Kimble & Kendall, 1953), reveal that avoidance responses can be rapidly extinguished if subjects are exposed to a graduated series of aversive stimuli that progressively approximate the original intensity of the conditioned fear stimulus. For the above reasons it would seem advisable to conduct **vicarious extinction** by exposing observers to a graduated sequence of modeling activities beginning with presentations that can be easily tolerated; as observers' emotional reactions to displays of attenuated approach responses are extinguished, the fear-provoking properties of the modeled displays might be gradually increased, concluding with interactions capable of arousing relatively strong emotional responses.

If emotion-eliciting stimuli occur in association with positively reinforcing events, the former cues are likely to lose their conditioned aversive properties more rapidly (Farber, 1948) than through mere repeated nonreinforced presentation. It might therefore be supposed that vicarious extinction would likewise be hastened and more adequately controlled by presenting the modeling stimuli within a favorable context designed to evoke simultaneously competing positive responses.

The principles discussed above were applied in the present experiment, which explored the vicarious extinction of children's fearful and avoidant responses toward dogs. One group of children participated in a series of modeling sessions in which they observed a fearless peer model exhibit progressively longer, closer, and more active interactions with a dog. For these subjects, the modeled approach behavior was presented within a highly positive context. A second group of children was presented the same modeling stimuli, but in a neutral context.

Exposure to the behavior of the model contains two important stimulus events, that is, the occurrence of approach responses without any adverse consequences to the performer, and repeated observation of the feared animal. Therefore, in order to control for the effects of exposure to the dog per se, children assigned to a third group observed the dog in the positive context but with the model absent. A fourth group of children participated in the positive activities, but they were never exposed to either the dog or the model.

---

[1] A. Bandura, "Principles of Behavioral Modification," unpublished manuscript, Stanford University, 1966.

In order to assess both the generality and the stability of vicarious extinction effects, the children were readministered tests for avoidance behavior toward different dogs following completion of the treatment series, and approximately 1 month later. It was predicted that children who had observed the peer model interact nonanxiously with the dog would display significantly less avoidance behavior than subjects who had no exposure to the modeling stimuli. The largest decrements were expected to occur among children in the modeling-positive context condition. It was also expected that repeated behavioral assessments and the general disinhibitory effects of participation in a series of highly positive activities might in themselves produce some decrease in avoidance behavior.

Method

SUBJECTS

The subjects were 24 boys and 24 girls selected from three nursery schools. The children ranged in age from 3 to 5 years.

PRETREATMENT ASSESSMENT OF AVOIDANCE BEHAVIOR

As a preliminary step in the selection procedure, parents were asked to rate the magnitude of their children's fearful and avoidant behavior toward dogs. Children who received high fear ratings were administered a standardized performance test on the basis of which the final selection was made.

The strength of avoidance responses was measured by means of a graded sequence of 14 performance tasks in which the children were required to engage in increasingly intimate interactions with a dog. A female experimenter brought the children individually to the test room, which contained a brown cocker spaniel confined in a modified playpen. In the initial tasks the children were asked, in the following order, to walk up to the playpen and look down at the dog, to touch her fur, and to pet her. Following the assessment of avoidance responses to the dog in the protective enclosure, the children were instructed to open a hinged door on the side of the playpen, to walk the dog on a leash to a throw rug, to remove the leash, and to turn the dog over and scratch her stomach. Although a number of the subjects were unable to perform all of the latter tasks, they were nevertheless administered the remaining test items to avoid any assumption of a perfectly ordered scale for all cases. In subsequent items the children were asked to remain alone in the room with the animal and to feed her dog biscuits. The final and most difficult set of tasks required the children to climb into the playpen with the dog, to pet her, to scratch her stomach, and to remain alone in the room with the dog under the exceedingly confining and fear-provoking conditions.

The strength of the children's avoidant tendencies was reflected not only in the items completed, but also in the degree of vacillation, reluctance, and fearfulness that preceded and accompanied each approach response. Consequently, children were credited 2 points if they executed a given task either spontaneously or willingly, and 1 point when they carried out the task minimally after considerable hesitancy and reluctance. Thus, for example, children who promptly stroked the dog's fur repeatedly when requested to do so received 2 points, whereas subjects who held back but then touched the dog's fur briefly obtained 1 point. In the item requiring the children to remain alone in the room with the dog, they received 2 points if they approached the animal and played with her, and 1 point if they were willing to remain in the room but avoided any contact with the dog. Similarly, in the feeding situation children were credited 2 points if they fed the dog by hand, but a single point if they tossed the biscuits on the floor and thereby avoided close contact with the animal. The maximum approach score that a subject could attain was 28 points.

On the basis of the pretreatment assessment, the children in each nursery school were grouped into three levels of avoidance behavior, with the corresponding scores ranging from 0 to 7, 8 to 17, and 18 to 20 points. There were approximately the same number of children, equally divided between boys and girls, at each of the three avoidance levels. The subjects from each of these groups were then assigned randomly to one of four conditions.

TREATMENT CONDITIONS

Children who participated in the *modeling-positive context* condition observed a fearless peer model display approach responses toward a cocker spaniel within the context of a highly enjoyable party atmosphere.

There were eight 10-minute treatment sessions conducted on 4 consecutive days. Each session, which was attended by a group of four children, commenced with a jovial party. The children were furnished brightly colored hats, cookie treats, and given small prizes. In addition, the experimenter read stories, blew large plastic balloons for the children to play with, and engaged in other party activities designed to produce strong positive affective responses.

After the party was well under way, a second experimenter entered the room carrying the dog, followed by a 4-year-old male model who was unknown to most of the children. The dog was placed in a playpen located across the room from a large table at which the children were seated. The model, who had been chosen because of his complete lack of fear of dogs, then performed prearranged sequences of interactions with the dog for approximately 3 minutes during each session. One boy served as the model for children drawn from two of the nursery schools, and a second boy functioned in the same role at the third school.

The fear-provoking properties of the modeled displays were gradually increased from session to session by varying simultaneously the physical restraints on the dog, the directness and intimacy of the modeled approach responses, and the duration of interaction between the model and his canine companion. Initially, the experimenter carried the dog into the room and confined her to the playpen, and the model's behavior was limited to friendly verbal responses ("Hi, Chloe") and occasional petting. During the following three sessions the dog remained confined to the playpen, but the model exhibited progressively longer and more active interactions in the form of petting the dog with his hands and feet, and feeding her wieners and milk from a baby bottle. Beginning with the fifth session, the dog was walked into the room on a leash, and the modeled tasks were mainly performed outside the playpen. For example, in addition to repeating the feeding routines, the model walked the dog around the room, petted her, and scratched her stomach while the leash was removed. In the last two sessions the model climbed into the playpen with the dog where he petted her, hugged her, and fed her wieners and milk from the baby bottle.

It would have been of interest to compare the relative efficacy of the graduated modeling technique with bold displays of approach behavior from the outset. However, pretest findings showed that when modeled displays are too fear provoking, children actively avoid looking at the performances and are reluctant to participate in subsequent sessions. The latter approach would therefore require additional procedures designed to maintain strong attending behavior to highly aversive modeling stimuli.

Children assigned to the *modeling-neutral context* condition observed the same sequence of approach responses performed by the same peer model except that the parties were omitted. In each of the eight sessions the subjects were merely seated at the table and observed the modeled performances.

In order to control for the influence of repeated exposure to the positive atmosphere and to the dog per se, children in the *exposure-positive context* group attended the series of parties in the presence of the dog with the model absent. As in the two modeling conditions, the dog was introduced into the room in the same manner for the identical length of time; similarly, the dog was confined in the playpen during the first four sessions and placed on a leash outside the enclosure in the remaining sessions.

Children in the *positive-context* group participated in the parties, but they were never exposed to either the dog or the model. The main purpose of this condition was to determine whether the mere presence of a dog had an adverse or a beneficial effect on the children. Like the third condition, it also provided a control for the possible therapeutic effects of positive experiences and increased familiarity with amiable experimenters, which may be particularly influential in reducing inhibitions in very young children. In addition, repeated behavioral assessments in which subjects perform a graded series of approach responses toward a feared object without any aversive consequences would be expected to produce some direct extinction of avoidance behavior. The inclusion of the latter two control groups thus makes it possible to evaluate the changes effected by exposure to modeling stimuli over and above those resulting from general disinhibition, direct extinction, and repeated observation of the feared object.

POSTTREATMENT ASSESSMENT OF AVOIDANCE BEHAVIOR

On the day following completion of the treatment series, the children were readministered the performance test consisting of the graded sequence of interaction tasks with the dog. In order to determine the generality of vicarious extinction effects, half the children in each of the four groups were tested initially with the experimental animal and then with an unfamiliar dog; the remaining children were presented with the two dogs in the reverse order.[2] The testing sessions were separated by an interval of 1½ hours so as to minimize any transfer of emotional reactions generated by one animal to the other.

The unfamiliar animal was a white mongrel, predominantly terrier, and of approximately the same size and activity level as the cocker spaniel. Two groups of 15 children, drawn from the same nursery-school population, were tested with either the mongrel or the spaniel in order to determine the aversiveness of the two animals. The mean approach scores with

---

[2]The authors are especially indebted to Chloe and Jenny for their invaluable and steadfast assistance with a task that, at times, must have been most perplexing to them.

the spaniel ($M = 16.47$) and the mongrel ($M = 15.80$) were virtually identical ($t = .21$).

FOLLOW-UP ASSESSMENT

A follow-up evaluation was conducted approximately 1 month after the posttreatment assessment in order to determine the stability of modeling-induced changes in approach behavior. The children's responses were tested with the same performance tasks toward both animals, presented in the identical order.

After the experiment was completed, the children were told that, while most dogs are friendly, before petting an unfamiliar dog they should ask the owner. This precautionary instruction was designed to reduce indiscriminate approach behavior by children who were in the modeling conditions toward strange dogs which they would undoubtedly encounter.

MEASUREMENT PROCEDURE

The same female experimenter administered the pretreatment, posttreatment, and follow-up behavioral tests. To prevent any possible bias, the experimenter was given minimal information about the details of the study and had no knowledge of the conditions to which the children were assigned. The treatment and assessment procedures were further separated by the use of different rooms for each activity.

In order to provide an estimate of interscorer reliability, the performances of 25% of the children, randomly selected from pretreatment, posttreatment, and follow-up phases of the experiment, were scored simultaneously but independently by another rater who observed the test sessions through a one-way mirror from an adjoining observation room. The two raters were in perfect agreement on 97% of the specific approach responses that were scored.

A dog's activity level may partly determine the degree of fear and avoidance exhibited by the children; conversely, timorous or unrestrained approach responses might differentially affect the animals' reactivity. Therefore, during the administration of each test item, the animals' behavior was rated as either passive, moderately active, or vigorous. The raters were in perfect agreement in categorizing the dogs' activity levels on 81% of the performance tests.

Changes in children's approach-response scores across the different phases of the experiment, and the number of subjects in each treatment condition who were able to carry out the terminal performance task served as the dependent measures.

Results

The percentages of test items in which the animals behaved in a passive, moderately active, or vigorous manner were 55, 43, and 2, respectively, for the model-positive context group; 53, 44, and 2 for children in the model-neutral context condition; 52, 45, and 3 for the exposure-positive context group; and 57, 41, and 2 for the positive-context subjects. Thus, the test animals did not differ in their behavior during the administration of performance tasks to children in the various treatment conditions.

APPROACH RESPONSES

Table 1 presents the mean increases in approach behavior achieved by children in each of the treatment conditions in different phases of the experiment with each of the test animals.

The children's approach responses toward the two dogs did not differ either in the posttreatment assessment ($t = 1.35$) or in the follow-up phase ($t = .91$) of the study. Nor were there any significant effects ($t=1.68$) due to the order in which the test animals were presented following completion of the treatment series. A t-test analysis also disclosed no significant change ($t=1.50$) in mean approach scores between measurements conducted in the posttreatment and the follow-up phases of the experiment. Moreover, analysis of variance of the posttreatment scores revealed no significant Treatment × Dogs ($F=2.15$) or Treatment × Order ($F=.30$) interaction effects. The data were therefore combined across phases and test animals in evaluating the major hypotheses.

An analysis of covariance, in which adjustments were made for differences in initial level of avoidance, was computed for mean approach responses performed by children in the various groups. The results reveal that the treatment conditions had a highly significant effect on the children's behavior ($F=5.09$, $p<.01$). Tests of the differences between the various pairs of treatments indicate that subjects in the modeling-positive context condition displayed significantly more approach behavior than subjects in either the exposure ($F=9.32$, $p<.01$) or the positive-context ($F=8.96$, $p<.01$) groups. Similarly, children who had observed the model within the neutral setting exceeded both the exposure ($F=6.57$, $p<.05$) and positive-context groups ($F=4.91$, $p<.05$) in approach behavior. However, the data yielded no significant differences between either the two modeling conditions ($F=.04$) or the two control groups ($F=.76$).

WITHIN-GROUP ANALYSIS OF APPROACH RESPONSES

The approach scores obtained by the different groups of children in preexperimental and subsequent tests are summarized graphically in Figure 1. Within-group analyses of changes between initial performance and mean level of approach behavior following treatment disclose significant increases in approach behavior for children in the modeling-positive context group ($t=7.71$, $p<.001$) and for those who observed the modeling performance within the neutral setting ($t=5.80$, $p<.001$). Although the positive context group showed an increment in approach behavior ($t=5.78$, $p<.001$), children who were

TABLE 1

Mean Increases in Approach Responses as a Function of Treatment Conditions, Assessment Phases, and Test Animals

Phases	Treatment conditions			
	Modeling—positive context	Modeling—neutral context	Exposure—positive context	Positive context
Posttreatment				
Spaniel	10.83	9.83	2.67	6.08
Mongrel	5.83	10.25	3.17	4.17
Follow-Up				
Spaniel	10.83	9.33	4.67	5.83
Mongrel	12.59	9.67	4.75	6.67
Combined data	10.02	9.77	3.81	5.69

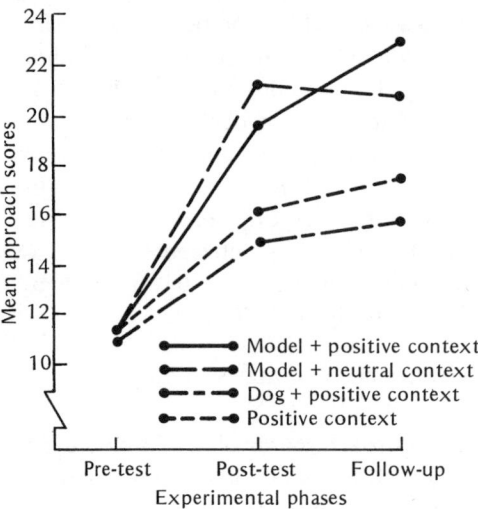

Fig. 1. Mean approach scores achieved by children in each of the treatment conditions on the three different periods of assessment

merely exposed to the dog in the positive context achieved a small, but nonsignificant ($t=1.98$), reduction in avoidance responses.

TERMINAL PERFORMANCES

Another measure of the efficacy of modeling procedures is provided by comparisons of the number of children in each condition who performed the terminal approach behavior at least once during the posttreatment assessment. Since the frequencies within the two modeling conditions did not differ, and the two control groups were essentially the same, the data for each of the two sets of subgroups were combined. The findings show that 67% of the children in the modeling treatment were able to remain alone in the room confined with the dog in the playpen, whereas the corresponding figure for the control subjects is 33%. The χ^2 value for these data is 4.08, which is significant beyond the .025 level.

Within the control groups, the terminal performances were attained primarily by subjects who initially showed the weakest level of avoidance behavior. The differences between the two groups are, therefore, even more pronounced if the analysis is conducted on the subjects whose pretreatment performances reflected extreme or moderately high levels of avoidance behavior. Of the most avoidant subjects in each of the two pooled groups, 55% of the children in the modeling conditions were able to perform the terminal approach behavior following the experimental sessions, while only 13% of the control subjects successfully completed the final task. The one-tailed probability for the obtained $\chi^2 = 4.74$ is slightly below the .01 level of significance.

The relative superiority of the modeling groups is also evident in the follow-up phase of the experiment. Based on the stringent criterion in which the most fearful task is successfully performed with *both* animals, a significantly larger number of children in the modeling conditions (42%) than in the control groups (12%) exhibited generalized extinction ($\chi^2 = 4.22$, $p < .025$). Moreover, not a single control subject from the two highest levels of avoidance behavior was able to remain alone in the room confined in the playpen with each of the dogs, whereas 33% of the most avoidant children in the modeling conditions successfully passed both terminal approach tasks ($\chi^2 = 4.02$, $p < .025$).

Discussion

The findings of the present experiment provide considerable evidence that avoidance responses can be successfully extinguished on a vicarious basis. This is shown in the fact that children who experienced a gradual exposure to progressively more fearful modeled responses displayed extensive and stable reduction in avoidance behavior. Moreover, most of these subjects were able to engage in extremely intimate and potentially fearful interactions with test animals following the treatment series. The considerable degree of **generalization of extinction** effects obtained to the unfamiliar dog is most likely due to similar stimulus properties of the test animals. Under conditions where observers' avoidance responses are extinguished to a single animal, one would expect a progressive decrement in approach behavior toward animals of increasing size and fearfulness.

The prediction that vicarious extinction would be augmented by presenting the modeling stimuli within a highly positive context was not confirmed, although subjects in the latter condition differed more significantly from the controls than children who observed approach behavior under neutral conditions. It is entirely possible that a different temporal ordering of emotion-provoking modeling stimuli and events designed to induce anxiety-inhibiting responses would facilitate the vicarious extinction process. On the basis of evidence from conditioning studies (Melvin & Brown, 1964) the optimal treatment procedure might require repeated observational trials, in each of which aversive modeling stimuli are immediately followed by positively reinforcing experiences for the observers. These temporal prerequisites depend upon the abrupt presentation and termination of the two sets of stimulus events that cannot be readily achieved with live demonstrations. It would be possible, however, to study the effects of systematic variations in the temporal spacing of critical variables if modeling stimuli were presented pictorially. Apart from issues of economy and control, if pictorial stimulus material proved equally as efficacious as live modeling, then skillfully designed therapeutic films could be developed and employed in preventive programs for eliminating common fears and anxieties before they become well established and widely generalized.

Although children in both the exposure and the positive-context groups showed some increment in approach behavior, only the changes in the latter group were of statistically significant magnitude. Apparently the mere presence of a dog had some mild negative consequences that counteracted the facilitative effects resulting from highly rewarding interactions with amiable experimenters, increased familiarity with the person conducting the numerous tests of avoidance behavior, and any inevitable direct extinction produced by the repeated performance of some approach responses toward the test animals without any adverse consequences. As might be expected, the general **disinhibitory** effects arising from these multiple sources occurred only in the early phase of the experiment, and no significant increases in approach behavior appeared between the posttreatment and follow-up assessments.

The data obtained in this experiment demonstrate that the fearless behavior of a model can substantially reduce avoidance responses in observers, but the findings do not establish the nature of the mechanism by which vicarious extinction occurs. There are several possible explanations of vicariously produced effects (Bandura, 1965b; Kanfer, 1965). One interpretation is in terms of the informative value of modeling stimuli. That is, the repeated evocation of approach responses without any adverse consequences to another person undoubtedly conveys information to the observer about the probable outcomes of close interactions with dogs. In the present study, however, an attempt was made to minimize the contribution of purely cognitive factors by informing children in all groups beforehand that the test animals were harmless.

The nonoccurrence of anticipated aversive consequences to a model accompanied by positive affective reactions on his part can also extinguish in observers previously established emotional responses that are vicariously aroused by the modeled displays (Bandura & Rosenthal, 1966). It is therefore possible that reduction in avoidance behavior is partly mediated by the elimination of conditioned emotionality.

Further research is needed to separate the relative contribution of cognitive, emotional, and other factors governing vicarious processes. It would also be of interest to study the effects upon vicarious extinction exercised by such variables as number of modeling trials, distribution of extinction sessions, mode of model presentation, and variations in the characteristics of the models and the feared stimuli. For example, with extensive sampling in the modeled displays of both girls and boys exhibiting approach responses to dogs ranging from diminutive breeds to larger specimens, it may be possible to achieve widely generalized extinction effects. Once approach behaviors have been restored through modeling, their maintenance and further generalization can be effectively controlled by response-contingent reinforcement administered directly to the subject. The combined use of modeling and reinforcement procedures may thus serve as a highly efficacious mode of therapy for eliminating severe behavioral inhibitions.

References

Bandura, A. Influence of models' reinforcement contingencies on the acquisition of imitative responses. *Journal of Personality and Social Psychology*, 1965, 1, 589–595.(a)

Bandura, A. Vicarious processes: A case of no-trial learning. In L. Berkowitz (Ed.), *Advances in experimental social psychology*. Vol. 2. New York: Academic Press, 1965. Pp. 1—55. (b)

Bandura, A., & Rosenthal, T. L. Vicarious classical conditioning as a function of arousal level. *Journal of Personality and Social Psychology*, 1966, 3, 54–62.

Bandura, A., Ross, D., & Ross, S. A. Vicarious reinforcement and imitative learning. *Journal of Abnormal and Social Psychology*, 1963, 67, 601–607.

Berger, S. M. Conditioning through vicarious instigation. *Psychological Review*, 1962, 69, 450–466.

Farber, I. E. Response fixation under anxiety and non-anxiety conditions. *Journal of Experimental Psychology*, 1948, 38, 111–131.

Jones, M. C. The elimination of children's fears. *Journal of Experimental Psychology*, 1924, 7, 383–390.

Kanfer, F. H. Vicarious human reinforcement: A glimpse into the black box. In L. Krasner & L. P. Ullman (Eds.), *Research in behavior modification*. New York: Holt, Rinehart & Winston, 1965. Pp. 244–267.

Kimble, G. A., & Kendall, J. W., Jr. A comparison of two methods of producing experimental extinction. *Journal of Experimental Psychology*, 1953, 45, 87–90.

Masserman, J. H. *Behavior and neurosis*. Chicago: University of Chicago Press, 1943.

Melvin, K. B., & Brown, J. S. Neutralization of an aversive light stimulus as a function of number of paired presentations with food. *Journal of Comparative and Physiological Psychology*, 1964, 58, 350–353.

Walters, R. H., & Parke, R. D. Influence of response consequences to a social model on resistance to deviation. *Journal of Experimental Child Psychology*, 1964, 1, 269–280.

EMOTION

Cognitive Effects of False Heart-Rate Feedback

STUART VALINS

Although there is considerable evidence that emotional states are accompanied by physiological changes (Duffy, 1962; Woodworth & Schlosberg, 1962), until recently there was little indication that these internal events facilitate the development of emotional behavior. Several experiments have now shown that emotional behavior is affected by the experimental manipulation of **sympathetic activity**. Emotional behavior is more readily learned when the **sympathetic nervous system** is intact than when it is surgically **enervated** (Wynne & Solomon, 1955), and more readily manifested during **epinephrine-induced** states of sympathetic activation than during states of relative inactivation (Latané & Schachter, 1962; Schachter & Singer, 1962; Schachter & Wheeler, 1962; Singer, 1963).

In an attempt to account for the influence of autonomic arousal on emotional behavior, Schachter (1964) has emphasized the importance of the cognitive effects of internal events. Within his cognitive-physiological theory of emotion, physiological changes are considered to function as stimuli or cues and are represented cognitively as feelings or sensations. These feelings, in turn, arouse further cognitive activity in the form of attempts to identify the situation that precipitated them. Emotional behavior results when the feeling state is attributed to an emotional stimulus or situation. The optimum conditions for the development of an emotion are thus present when an individual can say, "That stimulus [emotional] has affected me internally." In accord with these notions, it has been found that when subjects are **pharmacologically aroused** and exposed to stimuli designed to induce emotion, more emotional behavior is manifested when the arousal state is attributed to the emotional situation than when it is attributed to the injection (Schachter & Singer, 1962). Furthermore, the results of a recent experiment suggest that the effects of internal cues on emotional behavior may be mediated by an alteration in the perceived intensity of the emotional stimulus. Nisbett and Schachter (1966) found that when a series of electric shocks were administered to subjects who were in a mild state of fear, the shocks were judged to be more painful by those subjects who correctly attributed their internal symptoms to the shocks than by subjects who incorrectly attributed their symptoms to a pill.

Once it is granted that internal events can function as cues or stimuli then these events can now be considered as a source of cognitive information. They can, for example, result in cognitions such as, "My heart is pounding," or "My face is flushed." As potential cognitive information, however, these events are subject to the same mechanisms that process any stimulus before it is represented cognitively. Such mechanisms can result in their being denied, distorted, or simply not perceived. It is thus plausible that the cognitive representation of an internal event can be nonveridical; a particular reaction can fail to register or can be misperceived, and a non-existent reaction can be represented cognitively. Mandler (1962) also has questioned the **veridicality** of internal sensations and suggests that:

. . . someone may learn to make statements about his internal private events under the control of environmental stimuli or irrelevant internal stimuli. Thus, I could say, "I am blushing," in an embarrassing situation without showing any signs of peripheral vasodilation. Or I may have learned to talk about tenseness in my stomach in a stress situation without stomach events exerting any influence on such a remark [p. 317].

If cognitive representations of internal events are important for emotional behavior, then these nonveridical representations of physiological changes should have the same effects as veridical ones. They will be evaluated by reference to a precipitating situation and result in emotional behavior if the situation is an emotional one. Using Mandler's example, his "symbolic" blusher should be equally embarrassed with or without the presence of peripheral vasodilation. He should be less embarrassed, however, if he now has a mirror at his disposal and observes that he is not blushing. Embarrassment should be greatest only when he *thinks* that he has blushed in response to the situation.

The present experiment represents an attempt to determine the effects of nonveridical cognitive cues concerning internal reactions on the labeling of emotional stimuli. This will be accomplished by manipulating the extent to which a subject believes his heart has reacted to slides of seminude females and by observing the effects on his "liking" for the slides. The research of Schachter and his associates suggests that if a subject were covertly injected with epinephrine and shown a slide of a nude female, he would interpret his internal sensations as due to the nude stimulus and he would label the girl as more attractive than if he had been injected with placebo and he had experienced no internal sensations. If, however, it is the cognitive effect of internal events that influences emotional behavior, then this same influence should be observed when subjects think that they have reacted to a given stimulus, regardless of whether they have indeed reacted. As such, it is hypothesized that the cognition, "That girl has affected my heart rate," will induce subjects to consider the girl more attractive or appealing than the cognition, "That girl has not affected my heart rate."

These effects are predicted regardless of whether the heart-rate feedback matches the subjects' stereotyped expectations. Most of us would expect that, if anything, our heart rates would increase in response to photographs of nude females. How would we interpret our heart-rate changes, however, if the rate remained normal to some photographs but decreased substantially to others? If all of the photographs were of attractive females, we could not interpret a decrease as indicating that a girl is a "dog." If we felt it necessary to evaluate these reactions at all, it is likely that we would interpret any change in our heart rates as indicating greater attraction or appeal. Only if all of the photographs were relatively unattractive would we expect that a decrease in heart rate be interpreted as less attraction. Thus, under the appropriate cognitive conditions (highly attractive females), feedback indicating that heart rate has decreased should affect the labeling of emotional stimuli in a manner similar to that of feedback indicating that heart rate has increased.

Procedure

Male introductory psychology students, whose course requirements included 6 hours of participation in experiments, volunteered for a psychophysiological experiment. When the subject arrived at the laboratory, the experiment was described as a study of physiological reactions to sexually oriented stimuli. These reactions were allegedly being recorded while the subjects viewed 10 slides of seminude females. Two groups of subjects were led to believe that they were hearing an amplified version of their hearts beating while watching the slides and heard their "heart rates" change markedly to half of them. Two other groups of subjects heard the identical sounds, but did not associate them with their own heart beats. Several measures of the attractiveness of each slide were subsequently obtained from all subjects and used to evaluate the effects of the heart-rate feedback.

BOGUS HEART-RATE CONDITIONS

Subjects in these conditions were told that the experiment was concerned with heart-rate reactions to sexually oriented stimuli. It was explained that:

Most of our research is conducted over at the Bell Medical Research Building. We have all sorts of electronic wizardry and sound proof chambers over there. Right now there are several experiments being conducted and our facilities at Bell are too overcrowded. Because of this situation, we are doing this experiment here, and are forced to use a fairly crude but adequate measure of heart rate. In our other lab we record heart rate using electrodes which are taped to the chest. They pick up the electrical impulses from the heart which are then recorded on a polygraph. Here we are recording heart rate the way they used to do it 30 years ago. I will be taping this fairly sensitive microphone to your chest. It picks up each major heart sound which is amplified here, and initiates a signal on this signal tracer. This other microphone then picks up the signal and it is recorded on this tape recorder (the signal tracer, amplifier, and tape recorder were on a table next to the subject). By appropriately using a stop watch and this footage indicator, I can later determine exactly where each stimulus occurred and evaluate your heart rate reaction to it.

Unfortunately, this recording method makes it necessary to have audible sounds. They would be a serious problem if we were employing a task which required concentration. Since our procedure does not require concentration, it won't be too much of a problem and it is not likely to affect the results. All that you will be required to do is sit here and look at the slides. Just try to ignore the heart sounds. I will be showing the slides from the next room through this one-way screen. I'll tape this microphone to your chest and after recording your resting heart rate for a while, I will present 10 slides to you at regular intervals. Then I will record your resting heart rate again for several minutes and I will repeat the same slides again in the same order.

After taping the microphone to the subject's chest, the experimenter started the tape recorder and left the room. The sounds which these subjects were hearing were in reality prerecorded. A concealed wire from the tape recorder fed these sounds into the signal tracer speaker. Twenty subjects heard a tape recording which indicated that their heart rates had increased substantially to five slides, but had not changed to five others (heart-rate increase group); 20 other subjects heard a tape recording which indicated that their heart rates had decreased substantially to five of the slides, but had not changed to the other five (heart-rate decrease group).[1]

EXTRANEOUS SOUND CONDITIONS

Subjects in these conditions thought that the experiment was investigating vasomotor reactions to sexually oriented stimuli. They were told that:

Most of our research is conducted over at the Bell Medical Research Building. We have all sorts of electronic wizardry and sound proof chambers over there. I am doing this experiment now because of the conflicting results which we have obtained in two other identical experiments which we have done over at Bell. One experiment was done in a completely sound proof chamber. Another one was done in an office in which extraneous sounds could be heard, bells ringing in the hallway, people walking up and down, etc. Well, the results in these two experiments were not the same. We feel that it is possible that the results may have been different due to the extraneous sounds which were heard in the experiment where the subject was in an office. To determine whether extraneous sounds can affect finger temperature reactions to sexual stimuli, throughout this experiment you will hear sounds from this tape recorder, sounds that are completely meaningless but are just our way of controlling and producing extraneous sound. Later I will compare your finger temperature reactions to sexual stimuli with those of subjects who do not hear any sounds. I can then assess the physiological effects of the extraneous sounds and determine whether they were the reason why we obtained directionally different results in the two other experiments.

---

[1] It should be mentioned that Gerard and Rabbie (1961) and Bramel (1963) have used a similar technique in order to make subjects think that they were more or less frightened or homosexual. They accomplished this by allowing subjects to see dial readings which purportedly indicated internal reactions to experimental stimuli, but which were actually under the control of the experimenter. These investigators, however, were not primarily concerned with the evaluation and labeling of internal states. Their manipulations included detailed explanations of the "meaning" of the dial readings, so that subjects had no choice but to later indicate that they were or were not frightened or homosexual. In contrast, subjects in the present experiment were (a) specifically instructed to ignore the bogus heart sounds, (b) told nothing about the meaning of heart-rate changes, and (c) told that the experimenter could not hear the heart sounds and thus would not know for some time how the subject had reacted. It is the purpose of the present experiment to determine whether subjects will *spontaneously* label their feelings toward a stimulus by reference to their knowledge of how their hearts have reacted.

These sounds have absolutely no meaning for you. Just try to ignore them. I will be showing the slides from the next room through this one-way screen. I'll tape this thermistor to your finger and after recording your resting finger temperature for a while, I will present 10 slides to you at regular intervals. Then I will record your resting finger temperature again for several minutes and I will repeat the same slides again in the same order.

A dummy thermistor was then taped to the subject's finger, the tape recorder started, and the experimenter left the room. Ten of these subjects (sound increase group) heard the same tape recording as the heart-rate increase group, and 10 (sound decrease group) heard the same recording as the heart-rate decrease group. The sounds emanated from the signal tracer as in the experimental conditions, but the subjects were now told that it was just an elaborate speaker.

TAPE RECORDINGS

The tape recordings were made by recording square wave pulses produced by a Hewlett-Packard low-frequency signal generator, a signal tracer used as a capacitance network, and an external speaker. Pulses of a given frequency per minute could be varied over a wide range.

Heart beat and sound increase recording. This recording began with the pulse rate varying every 5 seconds between 66 and 72 beats per minute (BPM). At the start of the third minute the rate increased in 5-second segments from 72 to 84 and then to 90 BPM. It then decreased to 84, 78, and to 72 BPM, and subsequently continued to vary between 66 and 72 BPM. The identical rate increase was recorded at minutes 5, 8, 10, 11, 15, 17, 20, 22, and 23. The rate continued to vary between 66 and 72 BPM at minutes 4, 6, 7, 9, 12, 13, 14, 16, 18, 19, 21, and 24.

Heart beat and sound decrease recording. This recording was the same as the previous one except for the minutes at which the rate increased. At the start of the third minute for this recording, the rate decreased from 66 to 54 and then to 48 BPM. It then increased to 54, 60, and to 66 BPM, and subsequently continued to vary between 66 and 72 BPM. This same decrease in rate was recorded whenever an increase had been recorded on the other tape.

COORDINATION OF SLIDES WITH TAPE RECORDINGS

Ten color slides were made from photographs of seminude females which had been published by *Playboy* magazine. The slides were projected at 1-minute intervals, each for 15 seconds. The first slide was presented approximately 1 minute, 58 seconds after the tape-recorded sounds had begun so that a marked change in the rate of the sounds was evident 2 seconds afterward. Since the remaining nine slides were presented at 1-minute intervals, this same slide-sound change contingency was apparent for slides 3, 6, 8, and 9. Slides 2, 4, 5, 7, and 10 were presented at the minutes when no change in the rate of the sounds occurred. After the tenth slide (Minute 12 on the tape recording), there was a 3-minute break during which the rate of the sounds varied between 66 and 72 BPM. The slides were then repeated in the same manner starting at Minute 15. The slide order was also systematically rotated within conditions so that each slide was followed by a sound change as often as it was not.

To further clarify the procedure, consider the experimental situation as viewed by a subject who thought he was hearing his heart beating. For 2 minutes, he hears it beating at what appears to be a normal and reasonable rate. The first slide is then presented, and shortly afterward he notices a marked change in his heart rate. After 15 seconds of observing the slide, his heart rate gradually returns to what has been established as normal. The second slide is presented, but there is not any noticeable effect on his heart rate. It continues to vary between 66 and 72 BPM. After seeing all 10 slides, it is apparent that 5 of them have affected his heart rate, but the other 5 have not. This conclusion is reinforced when, after a 3-minute period of normal heart rate, the slides are shown again, and the same ones affect his heart rate, while the others have no effect.

ATTRACTIVENESS MEASURES

The effects of heart-rate feedback were assessed by determining the extent to which it influenced the subject's opinions of how attractive the girls were. Three measures of these opinions were obtained: (a) attractiveness ratings which were made immediately after the bogus feedback, (b) choice of photographs as remuneration, (c) attractiveness rankings made several weeks after the experiment.

Slide ratings. After the second presentation of the slides, the experimenter disengaged the apparatus and briefly discussed the slides with the subject. The subject was then told that 12 slides were originally being used but that 2 were eliminated in order to shorten the procedure. It was explained that the experimenter was now considering reducing the number of slides to 7 or 8. He was asking a number of subjects to rate the slides so that only the 7 or 8 most attractive or appealing ones would be included. The slides were quickly shown again to the subject and, using a 100-point scale ranging from "Not at all" to "Extremely," he rated them as to: "How attractive or appealing each girl is to you."

Photograph choices. The subject then completed a short questionnaire which was followed by an intensive interview to determine whether he had accepted the experimental deceptions. The physiology of sexual arousal was also discussed, but no mention was ever made of the true purpose of the experiment or of the experimental deceptions. The experimenter apologized for being unable to pay the subject and offered to give him some photographs of the girls which had been donated by the publisher. The 10 photographs from which the slides had been made were casually spread on a table, and the subject was told to take 5. The experimenter left the room and thanked the subject before he made his choices. As the subject was leaving, he was intercepted and the photographs taken back. It was explained that the photographs had been offered to the subject only to determine if there were differences in attractiveness estimates relating to slide versus photograph modes of presentation.

Delayed photograph rankings. Three weeks after participating in the experiment, the subject received a letter from a fictitious "social scientist." The letter requested the subject's cooperation for an attitude survey and asked him to permit an interviewer to question him. Approximately 1 week later an interviewer arrived at the subject's dormitory room and described the survey as a study of undergraduate attitudes toward the psychological and physical characteristics of members of the opposite sex. The subject first ranked three sets of photographs, each consisting of a model in 12 different dresses, according to how attractive the girl was in each photograph. He then ranked 12 photographs of seminude females on the same dimension. Ten of these photographs were those which he had seen in the experiment proper. After ranking these photographs, the interviewer questioned the subject as to whether he had previously seen them and determined whether he had associated the interview with the original experiment. It should be emphasized that throughout these interviews, the subjects were totally unaware that the feedback in the original experiment was nonveridical.

Results

ADEQUACY OF THE EXPERIMENTAL MANIPULATIONS

In order to be effective, the manipulation of differential heart-rate feedback must be accurately perceived by the subjects and adequately accepted as a reflection of their internal reactions. Although they were instructed to ignore the bogus heart sounds, the subjects' interest in their reactions and the amplification of the sounds resulted in all subjects being aware of the different slide-sound change contingencies. The bogus heart beats were also accepted as veridical. None of the 40 experimental subjects had substantial suspicions that the sounds might not be their heart beats. Several had what they described as momentary doubts when first hearing the sounds, but these were quickly forgotten or dispelled. The slightly varying sound rate during the first 2 minutes seemed quite reasonable and served, as intended, to convince the subjects of the veridicality of the bogus beats. The bogus heart-rate reactions to the different slides were also accepted as veridical. Although the heart-rate decrease subjects were overwhelmingly surprised by this feedback, they simply considered as wrong their previous expectations of how they react to these stimuli. Suspicions concerning the veridicality of the feedback were also not increased when the subjects were confronted with a marked discordance between their presumed heart-rate reactions and their initial "liking" for a slide. This discordance was apparently reconciled by many subjects in precisely the manner which was predicted. They changed their estimates of how attractive the girls were.

HEART-RATE FEEDBACK AND ATTRACTIVENESS MEASURES

It was hypothesized that the **cue** function of internal events affects the labeling of emotional stimuli. A nonveridical cognitive cue which indicates that one has reacted markedly to a slide of a seminude female should, in this situation, be interpreted as indicating that the stimulus object is attractive or appealing.

Slide ratings. The prerecorded sounds were played throughout the first two presentations of the slides. During the third presentation, the tape recorder was turned off, and the subjects rated the attractiveness or appeal of each girl. If heart-rate feedback has had the predicted effect, the experimental subjects, in comparison to the control subjects, should rate the slides followed by a change in the sound rate (reinforced) as more attractive than the slides not followed by a change (nonreinforced). Table 1 presents the mean ratings of the reinforced and nonreinforced slides for each of the experimental groups and for the combined control groups. When the sounds were not considered heart beats, they had virtually no effect on the subjects' ratings. Since the control groups rated the reinforced and nonreinforced slides similarly, it is evident that the sounds alone did not have any differential excitatory effects.

It can be seen, however, that when subjects thought the sounds were their heart beats, there was a substantial effect of differential feedback on their ratings. Subjects in the heart-rate decrease condition

TABLE 1

Mean Slide Attractiveness Ratings

Slides	Conditions		
	Heart-rate increase ($N=20$)	Heart-rate decrease ($N=20$)	Sound increase + sound decrease ($N=10+10$)
Reinforced	72.42	69.26	60.86
Nonreinforced	54.11	62.57	63.76
Difference	18.31	6.69	−2.90

Note.—All p values reported are 2-tailed. p value of difference score comparisons (t tests): heart-rate increase versus sound increase and decrease, $p < .001$; heart-rate decrease versus sound increase and decrease, $p < .05$; heart-rate increase versus heart-rate decrease, $p < .05$.

rated the reinforced slides 6.69 points higher than the nonreinforced ones; subjects in the heart-rate increase condition rated the reinforced slides 18.31 points higher than the nonreinforced ones. Each of these differences is significantly greater than that of the combined control groups. The heart-rate increase feedback also had a greater effect than the decrease feedback. Subjects in the former condition apparently lowered their ratings of the nonreinforced slides as well as raising their ratings of the reinforced ones. The effects of the manipulations are more clearly portrayed in Table 2 which presents the number of subjects in each condition who rated the reinforced slides higher than the nonreinforced ones. This analysis shows that the bogus feedback affected the ratings of the majority of the subjects in the experimental conditions, whereas extraneous sounds had little effect in the control conditions.

Photograph choices. Differential heart-rate feedback has obviously affected the subjects' ratings of the slides. It may be asked, however, to what extent these ratings are truly indicative of the way subjects feel about these stimuli. Will they now, for example, choose more photographs of the reinforced nudes than the nonreinforced ones as remuneration for participating in the experiment? It will be recalled that each subject selected five photographs. Table 3 tabulates the number of subjects in each condition who chose three or more of the previously reinforced nudes and the number choosing two or less. It can be seen that a significant number of experimental subjects chose more of the photographs that had been reinforced than photographs that had not been reinforced. The data for the heart-rate decrease condition alone are not quite significant, whereas that of the control groups appear

TABLE 2

Number of Subjects Rating Reinforced Slides Higher and Number Rating Them Lower than Nonreinforced Slides

Reinforced slides rated	Conditions			
	Heart-rate increase ($N=20$)	Heart-rate decrease ($N=19$)[a]	Heart-rate increase + decrease ($N=20+19$)[a]	Sound increase + sound decrease ($N=10+10$)
Higher	17	15	32	9
Lower	3	4	7	11
p value (sign test)	.002	.02	.001	ns

[a] One subject rated the reinforced and nonreinforced stimuli identically.

TABLE 3

Number of Subjects Choosing Three or More Reinforced Photographs and Number Choosing Two or Less

	Conditions			
No. of reinforced photographs chosen	Heart-rate increase ($N=20$)	Heart-rate decrease ($N=20$)	Heart-rate increase + decrease ($N=20+20$)	Sound increase + sound decrease ($N=10+10$)
3 or more	15	14	29	6
2 or less	5	6	11	14
p value (sign test)	.04	ns	.007	ns

just as strong, but in the opposite direction. An analysis of the mean number of reinforced nudes chosen by each group, however, shows that the heart-rate decrease subjects chose significantly more than that expected on a chance basis, but the control groups did not choose significantly less. The control groups chose an average of 2.25 reinforced photographs ($t=1.55$, ns), whereas the heart-rate decrease subjects chose 3.10 reinforced photographs ($t=2.41$, $p<.05$), and the heart-rate increase subjects chose 3.20 reinforced photographs ($t=2.45$, $p<.05$). With the exception that, on this measure the experimental groups did not differ from one another, the analysis of photograph choices clearly supports that of the ratings. A marked change in heart rate which is considered as effected by a nude female is interpreted as attraction and results in greater liking for the stimulus.

Delayed photograph rankings. It may also be asked whether the observed effects of the heart-rate feedback are temporary or whether they are sufficiently substantial to result in relatively long-lasting cognitive change. In order to answer this question, interviews were conducted with the subjects 4–5 weeks after the experiment proper. During the course of these interviews, the subjects were asked to rank, from most to least attractive, 12 photographs of seminude females. Since 10 of these photographs were used in the experiment proper, an analysis of these rankings permits an evaluation of the relative permanency of the feedback effects. It should be mentioned that the interviewer made every effort to avoid allowing the subjects to associate the interview procedure with the original experiment. Since the source of the photographs was identified as *Playboy* magazine, the subjects did not think it unusual that two experiments would be using similar stimuli. The subjects were, in fact, quite surprised when subsequently informed of the true purpose of the interview. In addition, most of the subjects appeared to rank the photographs on the basis of how they felt at the moment. They were not aware of, or at least did not verbalize, any tendency to rank them according to their previous attractiveness estimates.

It can be seen in Table 4 that the analysis of the delayed photograph rankings is generally consistent with the previous analyses. In comparison to the control subjects, more of the experimental subjects ranked the reinforced photographs as more attractive than the nonreinforced ones ($\chi^2=4.57$, $p<.05$). Thus, differential heart-rate feedback has had effects which

TABLE 4

Number of Subjects Ranking Reinforced Photographs Higher and Number Ranking Them Lower than Nonreinforced Photographs

	Conditions			
Reinforced photographs ranked	Heart-rate increase ($N=20$)	Heart-rate decrease ($N=20$)	Heart-rate increase + decrease ($N=20+20$)	Sound increase + sound decrease ($N=10+9$)[a]
Higher	14	14	28	7
Lower	6	6	12	12
p value (sign test)	ns	ns	.02	ns

[a] One subject could not be contacted for the interview.

are relatively long lasting (mean delay = 31.25 days). Presumed internal reactions have served as cues and have resulted in distinctly different evaluations of emotional stimuli.

Discussion

The major hypothesis of this study has received considerable experimental support. When a subject thought that his heart had reacted markedly to certain slides of seminude females, he rated these slides as more attractive and chose them more often than slides that he thought had not affected his heart rate. These results are exactly what one would have expected had heart-rate changes and veridical feelings of palpitation been pharmacologically induced to some slides but not to others. The mechanism operating to produce these effects is presumably the same regardless of the veridicality of the feedback. Internal events are a source of cognitive information and, as Schachter has proposed, individuals will want to evaluate and understand this kind of information. When an emotional explanation is prepotent, they will label their reactions accordingly. This process is apparently what has been observed in the present experiment. The subjects did attempt to evaluate their reactions, and, having done so, the conditions were such that it was most appropriate for them to explain their reactions by referring to the slides and to interpret them as indicating varying degrees of attraction.

A given heart-rate reaction, however, was not always evaluated as attraction. Post-experimental interviews revealed that, at times, a particular reaction was attributed to surprise, since the subject was daydreaming, and the presentation of the slide shook him out of his reverie, or to a sudden fit of coughing or sneezing, or to a slight resemblance to a former girl friend. It was often evident that these alternative explanations were sought when subjects could not convince themselves that they liked a particular slide. In such cases, it was apparently necessary for them to explain their reactions by referring to other causes. The subjects' attempts to label their reactions suggest that the attractiveness estimates reflected more than shallow verbal definitions of internal reactions. A number of subjects seemed to actively persuade themselves that a reinforced nude was attractive. They reported looking at the slide more closely, and it was evident that they attempted to justify the feedback by magnifying the girl's positive characteristics. Although these subjects realized that they were looking for an explanation for the feedback, they did not feel that they were distorting the slide. Closer inspection simply showed them what their "subconscious" knew all the time. The girl's breasts or buttocks were indeed nicer than they originally thought. Although there is no systematic evidence available, it would be difficult to explain how the feedback could still have effects after several weeks were it not for a process similar to this active self-persuasion.

It is of some interest to consider whether the heart-rate feedback had a direct physiological excitatory effect. If the bogus heart-rate changes resulted in actual physiological change, the differential attractiveness ratings might be attributed to veridical internal cues rather than nonveridical ones. Although physiological variables were not measured, there is little reason to suspect that the bogus feedback had any direct effects other than cognitive ones. If these auditory stimuli had excitatory effects that were not due to their "meaning," then the extraneous-sound subjects should have manifested differential attractiveness ratings depending upon the slide-sound change contingencies. However, the differences observed for these subjects, between their ratings of the reinforced and nonreinforced stimuli, were slight and in a direction opposite to that which would be expected. Furthermore, when subjects rated their awareness of palpitations or actual *feeling* of heart beating during the experiment (4-point scale, ranging from "Not at all" to "An intense amount"), the experimental subjects reported experiencing *fewer* palpitations than did the control subjects. This effect was **significant** for the heart-rate increase versus extraneous-sound comparison (.6 versus 1.10, $p<.05$) and has subsequently been replicated ($p<.06$). Analysis of the data of this replication, which include galvanic skin response and heart-rate measurements, also reveals that subjects exposed to the heart-rate increase and sound increase manipulations react alike physiologically. It is thus likely that the observed effects of bogus heart-rate feedback are primarily a result of cognitive factors and not physiological ones. In fact, the bogus feedback appears to mask veridical feedback by diverting the subject's attention from his actual internal reactions.

The cognitive manipulations and processes which have been emphasized in the present experiment bear some similarity to current techniques and theory concerned with the extinction of maladaptive emotional behavior. Using systematic **desensitization therapy** (Wolpe, 1958) **phobic** patients have been treated by teaching them to perform responses to phobic objects that are incompatible with the fear responses usually generated. In an experimental study, Lang and Lazovik (1963) trained snake-phobic subjects in deep muscle relaxation. The subjects were subsequently hypnotized during each of 11 therapeutic sessions and instructed to relax while imagining a number of situations in which a snake was involved. Subjects participating in this treatment were later observed to be less frightened by snakes, and approximately half of them could even be induced to touch or pick up a live snake. The extinction of these well-established behaviors is presumably due to the resulting incompatibility between the induced muscular relaxation and the physiological changes ordinarily accompanying states of fear. Consider the treatment, however, from a subject's point of view.

Whereas in the past he has been physiologically upset when thinking about snakes, he can now think about them without experiencing as many marked internal sensations. His musculature is now completely relaxed and results in his being able to say, "Thinking about snakes no longer affects me internally." Similar cognitions concerning internal events have effectively influenced the labeling of emotional stimuli in the present experiment. It would seem reasonable that such cognitions are also induced during desensitization therapy and might be the primary factor contributing to the successful treatment of phobic patients. If this is so, the rather tedious muscular relaxation procedure could be replaced with another manipulation of the cognitive representation of internal events. It may be possible to eliminate phobic behaviors solely by inducing nonveridical cognitions concerning internal reactions. Such cognitions could be manipulated so that they would be incompatible with the knowledge of how one usually reacts when frightened. Snake-phobic subjects, for example, who are led to believe that thinking about or seeing snakes does not affect them internally, might reevaluate their attitudes toward snakes and become less frightened by them.

References

Bramel, D. Selection of a target for defensive projection. *Journal of Abnormal and Social Psychology,* 1963, 66, 318–324.

Duffy, E. *Activation and behavior.* New York: Wiley, 1962.

Gerard, H., & Rabbie, J. Fear and social comparison. *Journal of Abnormal and Social Psychology,* 1961, 62, 586–592.

Lang, P. J., & Lazovik, A. D. Experimental desensitization of a phobia. *Journal of Abnormal and Social Psychology,* 1963, 66, 519–525.

Latané, B., & Schachter, S. Adrenalin and avoidance learning. *Journal of Comparative and Physiological Psychology,* 1962, 65, 369–372.

Mandler, G., Emotion In, *New directions in psychology.* New York: Holt, Rinehart & Winston, 1962. Pp. 267–343.

Nisbett, R., & Schachter, S. Cognitive manipulation of pain. *Journal of Experimental Social Psychology,* 1966, 2, 227–236.

Schachter, S. The interaction of cognitive and physiological determinants of emotional state. In L. Berkowitz (Ed.), *Advances in experimental social psychology.* Vol. 1. New York: Academic Press, 1964. Pp. 49–80.

Schachter, S., & Singer, J. E. Cognitive, social, and physiological determinants of emotional state. *Psychological Review,* 1962, 69, 379–399.

Schachter, S., & Wheeler, L. Epinephrine, chlorpromazine, and amusement. *Journal of Abnormal and Social Psychology,* 1962, 65, 121–128.

Singer, J. E. Sympathetic activation, drugs, and fright. *Journal of Comparative and Physiological Psychology,* 1963, 56, 612–615.

Wolpe, J. *Psychotherapy by reciprocal inhibition.* Palo Alto: Stanford University Press, 1958.

Woodworth, R. S., & Schlosberg, H. *Experimental psychology.* New York: Holt, Rinehart & Winston, 1962.

Wynne, L. C., & Solomon, R. L. Traumatic avoidance learning: Acquisition and extinction in dogs deprived of normal peripheral autonomic function. *Genetic Psychology Monographs,* 1955, 52, 241–284.

PSYCHOPATHOLOGY

The Case of Dawn

G. W. GOETHALS AND D. S. KLOS

. . . We moved to Atlanta when I was twelve. The huge modern schools rather awed me. My mother, in her most embellished manner, told us how exciting living near the city would be, but she was also afraid. She didn't even attempt driving downtown until six months after we had arrived, and then when she finally ventured out it was with such caution and infrequency that my aunt declared that she was tired of chauffering my mother all over looking at rug samples and house-hunting. I remember the night we arrived in Atlanta, a tired rather unsophisticated family drinking warm drinks in a sort of fuzzy wonder at the Woolworth's which was part of a tremendous shopping complex outside of Atlanta. It was about eleven p.m.; very late for all of us (my father still gets up at 6 a.m. every day), and there were so many fluorescent lights and so many sounds of traffic that I was dazzled. My mother and father argued about directions the whole way. We ended up at about midnight at the apartment buildings where we were to live for several months until a house was found. It looked like an old redevelopment project, nothing but dull brick rectangles three floors high hugged in by parking lot. But I loved it. I loved the City already. I loved the sense of countless people. Ever since, the sound of heavy traffic all night long through an open window evokes in me real feeling: and it is the feeling of being surrounded, and comforted. . . .

Junior high school was the most excruciating period I lived through until my sophomore and junior years at college. I was impossibly silent in classes, by far the shyest and most afraid student in the school. It was attributed by my mother to the change of atmosphere, but neither Don nor Jenny had any such obvious social reactions to the move. Although I was very conscientious about my work, it was in junior high school that I first had difficulties in any academic subject—I got C's in Science. After having won the scholarship at school it was hard to take, but the A's in English and my success in writing poetry was compensation. What could not be compensated for was the fact that I had no friends. The closest thing I ever had to a "chum" was the girl next door, an attractive and rather snobbish girl whose father worked for the State Department and had just moved from Switzerland. But I was not in any way intimate with her; we were in the same grade and went to school together, but shared neither friends, nor confidences. I do recall staring emptily and somehow hungrily at her bedroom window lit up at nights, hoping to catch a glimpse of her.

If I was afraid with people in a situation where I was expected to communicate with them, such as in classes, I was even more afraid of being alone. I was terrorized by noises and shadows when left alone in the house at night. And after bedtime I lay in bed for hours paralyzed by my imagination; I had many nightmares and often sleepwalked, as did Jenny; and we put bells on the doorhandle to our bedroom to alert each other if one of us should start wandering. The house was new, and there were centipedes on the ground floor for the first three years; this too was a source of terror for me, and even when in high school Don left for college and I got his room, I used to have nightmares from which I would awaken to see the wall next to my bed crawling with every kind of bug. I'm not sure how often there actually were bugs and how often I invented them, but certainly there was a real basis for some of my fears, since I was always having to drop books on centipedes. But I still think I see spiders or bugs on my sheets and the wall next to my bed sometimes in the middle of the night; often I am certain enough of it to rush from bed and not return for half-an-hour, until I can convince myself of the impossibility of it. . . .

My high school years were much better. I had my own bedroom, and I began to excel in my courses. I found that I could get into advanced placement courses in not only English but also math and French; and I began to acquire extracurricular credits in art at an institute in Atlanta and in human kindness by teaching retarded children to swim at the YMCA. Out of an atmosphere of emotional frustration, I was able to use my talent in writing and in the arts to convince myself of the existence of creative possibility, of hope. I began to believe I could do everything. In one respect this was hopelessly untrue: I never made friends. I had numbers of acquaintances at school, and I was the favorite of most of my teachers; but I never invited anyone home, nor was I invited to anyone else's house. It was not for nothing that when I was awarded the Most Studious award at a school dance in my senior year, I was not there to accept it; I heard later that after announcing my name a number of times they decided I was studying and were confirmed in their choice. The times of greatest joy were notably (a) when I received both first place and honorable mention in different categories of a national writing contest, and was given a beautifully headswelling introduction at a school assembly, where I was also awarded prizes in the state French and Spanish contests and various other awards, and (b) when I got acceptances from all the colleges of my choice on the same day in my senior year. It was a time when all things could be done, and I looked forward to college as the arena for the accomplishment of all things.

I began masturbating in my sophomore year in high school, sometimes with the aid of neighborhood pets; but I never went out on a date until my junior year, when I met a strange broody melancholic character who decided he was in love with me after an evening discussing Camus, and then with a bull-doggish looking boy from my high school who invited me to the senior prom. It was most uncomfortable, and I hated kissing him because he was uncommunicative and nervous and awkward, and because I felt nothing toward him; whereas the other suitor had rather mystified and intrigued me, and I was elated when he rather gently and meaningfully kissed me one day behind the front door. But after my senior year in high school my mother, as a combination reward and educational experiment, decided I should travel to Europe. I went to Belgium for a session at a sterile Protestant school and a visit with the wealthy family of a prefect of one of the provinces. My first real sexual experiments took place at the hands of the son in this family, a handsome huge boy with a talent for sexual diversity; and there at the age of 16 had intercourse for the first time. There was no pain, and the pleasure was immense; but I think throughout it, as has been true ever since, I was more concerned with being a successful partner and evoking the most pleasure in the man than with "forgetting" myself and slipping into orgasm unconsciously. When I arrived at college, I felt tremendously experienced and excited, and during my first year there I had only the mildest case of freshman doldrums. I kept in touch with my family but was relieved to experience the self-determination that my separation from them had brought. Now at a distance from the turmoil, I began to actively wish that my parents would get a divorce, that my mother would find someone in whom to confide (I was no longer so selfishly cruel as I had been in junior high school, condemning my mother silently for an affair that she had with a rather slick married man whom I detested) and realize her fantasies, and that my father would be spared the contention which sent him off to work at 6:30 a.m. and kept him away until 8 or 9 at night at his office. I myself felt that my fantasies were being realized; I basked in the sensations of scholarliness: the books and wood-panelled reading rooms, the tolerance of diversity, high teas and jolly-ups. My roommate was a rather stuffy masculinely energetic girl from Baltimore with whom I had long wishful discussions revealing her narrow-mindedness and inordinate stinginess with her possessions. (She used to tell me that if she were to lend out her hair-dryer or scales to hallmates, as she was occasionally asked to do, they would be returned broken or late or not at all; and she used to suspect that people had been in her drawers if anything looked out of place.) In spite of her surface liberalism her tremendous capacity for gossip ended up revealing her rather strong prejudices. She once told me that she had been asked out by a Jewish boy from Baltimore who seemed very nice but she had just never been out with a JEW before and she wasn't sure she could bring herself to do it. I recall being quite vehement in the defence of the unknown gentleman, which was to be quite amusing in light of the fact that he was Stephen Silbiger, whom I would one day marry. I did not meet him that year, though, and was anyway very involved with a senior whom I met at a jolly-up near the end of my freshman year. In my anxiousness to get tangible evidences of being liked, I came on very hard at mixers and even in classes; and this particular boy was quick to respond in kind. We seldom talked, and anyway he was sick of school and glad to be graduating. He was what I should have recognized as a jock. But he was out to make me and I was out to be made, and it happened that way. There was a rather painful episode about a girl in Beverly, Mass., whom he loved; he told me that on his last night in town, after calling me up at two in the morning (which infuriated my roommate) and telling me to come to the Gotham Hotel, where we went through the whole Mr. and Mrs. Smith cliché as I tried to be cheerful. But it was a cold night and I had been ordered out of bed a little too brusquely to be told that there was nothing between us but that he needed to f——— someone and he loved this chick in Beverly. I remember he had cut himself shaving over his remarkably bad complexion, and when I awoke the next morning I found blood all over my face. The next morning he didn't talk to me and we left, by plan, pretending not to know each other....

Late in the summer I met a girl by the name of Anna, who invited me to share an apartment with her that fall. I was delighted; not only was Anna troubled by emotional difficulties also but she seemed to want privacy, to dislike intimate friendships with girls, and to be a good writer with many of my ambitions in the literary field. We got a lovely apartment with a fireplace right in the Square (something I had always dreamed of since living at the Health Center) and furnished it rather elegantly and simply. We developed an easy symbiotic style of living together, going our own ways and politely asking each other to share food and give judgments on each other's poetry. I think her sense of delicacy was slightly offended by my having various male friends over for the night so often, but she was perhaps more hurt by the fact that she had no one than by my apparent promiscuity. She knew that essentially I was as lonely as she. During the summer I had gotten to know a group of seniors living together who were very kind to me and who invited me over to cook dinner for them during the latter part of the summer practically every night. Although I started off f———ing the one of them I had originally met (he was the first case of real impotence I had ever run into and in fact we never really actually f———ed at all, he was very tormented by his inability to actually carry out intercourse), he left for Denmark and became engaged there to a girl with whom he had no sexual relations. After he left I became intimate with one of his roommates, a gentle energetic life-loving boy who was very fair and kind to me and who seemed to enjoy f———ing as much as I did (and I did most certainly love it).

When Anna and I early in the fall decided to have a party to reacquaint ourselves with the outside world, he was one of the people I invited, although by that time the relationship was very painlessly and gently tapering off. One of Anna's invited guests was a tall rather handsome junior by the name of Stephen Silbiger, and I saw him for the first time that night through the door to Anna's bedroom where he was sitting with Anna and her most sympathetic friends listening to her troubles. I didn't have time in my hostessing fervor to stop and think about it, or even to really register who he was; I was too busy flitting around trying to satisfy everybody as both hostess and as a person and feeling a little annoyed when the drinking started and people began coming in hordes most of whom we didn't know. Anna (in an agony of nerves and nervousness) split without saying anything to me. I felt as though I had been left to handle a party which had gotten out of control. I had grass in my bedroom and didn't want the place to be busted. The noise was getting louder and people were bringing in yards of ale. In my general anxiety, I forgot completely about the dark appealing face I had glimpsed through the bedroom door, and it was not until the next day, when he knocked on the door after the debris of the party had been cleaned up, that I really met Stephen.

Stephen and Dick knocked on the door to our apartment when I was there with the brother of the boy I had been f—--ing over the summer. I was turning this boy on and generally leading up to having him stay the night. He was very gentle and sweet and I wanted (as his brother had once said he wished) for him to have "a good woman" the first time. When I answered the door I expected that they were there to see Anna, but they said that they had heard that I had some grass and they were having a hard time getting through the "dry" spell before harvest and would like to buy a little. I was really disappointed not to be able to ask them to stay and smoke with me, particularly since both of them looked very strange and interesting to me and I was dying to talk to someone who had run the gamut at school and would provide some feedback, rather than the awkward and reticent boy in the other room. I asked them into my bedroom and poured out some grass into an envelope to lay it on them, by which gesture they seemed rather surprised and very grateful. I told them I could get unlimited amounts through Will and could probably arrange a deal.

Later that week Stephen called to see if the deal could go through and he picked me up in his Volvo and we went over to cop. Will was out and we returned to Cambridge. In the car Stephen asked me if I would come over and have a smoke at his apartment, but I was reluctant since I had a paper due the next day. But as usual I was easily talked into going, and I discovered that he was into soul music (which I loved) and Dylan (which I hated). Smoking the first time with him was very stiff and unrelaxed for me; but he rolled over on the bed and we could really feel each other, and I felt immediately more at ease. I remember I got as excited as I ever had with all my clothes on, and Stephen said he came a couple of times before we even f—--ed. It was a very successful evening for me, but had no real emotional content. That I was looking for a deeper relationship must have been true, because I remember thinking as I told him of my studies toward conversion to Judaism that since he was Jewish he would understand what I saw in Buber and what I strove for in myself. As it turned out he was something of an alienated Jew, but he must have been interested anyway, because the next day he called to invite me to go to Marblehead with him. We loaded my alpaca rug and fur coat into the car and spent a wonderful day staring at the sea which I had always loved so much. All of this fit very easily into romantic molds for me, and I was truly happy for the first time in many months. Not only was it the source of relief from loneliness, but Stephen took over from the beginning and insisted on paying off my bills, which amounted to a good $500 and were causing me all kinds of agony and nightmares, since creditors kept phoning and threatening. At the time I was considering doing a few weekend lays for a pimp I had met during the summer, but couldn't quite carry it out, more out of fear than any revulsion: the idea itself rather appealed to me. At any rate Stephen's entrance into my life was heralded by a joy and an elimination of fears that quite surprised me. And yet I never quite gave myself to him any more than I had given myself to anyone else. It was to take many months before I knew him well enough to reveal things to him that no one else knew; it took Stephen a long time and a lot of painful discussion to make me trust him that much.

On October 21 we drove to Washington to attend the march. We were speeding on meth as we drove and the sunset and sunrise were only long instants apart. In those intervening instants we shared wonderful optimistic fantasies about Stephen resuming his writing in a dedicated way, about our going to Japan together the following summer, and about having three weddings. It was during that trip that Stephen asked me to marry him. I said I couldn't decide so quickly and he was glad to wait; then a half-hour later I just said "Yes." It was delightful to have made the decision so quickly and so happily. And by the time we arrived in Washington I was ready to learn how to be in love all over again. . . .

By Thanksgiving, we had exchanged all of the basic intimacies about our former "love" relationships (I could not fairly be said to have had any clear love relationships), about our families, and some of our own secrets. But I was still faking orgasms with Stephen, and it disturbed me, since it seemed to me that complete honesty was the only real way of giving oneself entirely to another person, and since secretiveness had always been my weapon against people. Somehow there was no time that seemed appropriate for such a revelation: certainly not just before or after intercourse, and yet at any other time I convinced myself that it wasn't that important a secret. We did discuss at great lengths, though, my growing apprehensions about marriage; I put up every kind of resistance to it, and whatever resistance I actually showed on the surface was prompted by a far larger pool of fear than I ever told Stephen. I could not remember having ever seen a successful marriage, that is, one in which a working, cooperative, loving relationship had persisted for very long. I had promised myself since I was in high school that I would marry someone who would find me socially convenient (I saw myself as a well-mannered and elegant runner-of-a-house and giver-of-parties) in return for his quite certain economic means. Moreover, in my conception of realistic marriage, each partner would have an understanding with the other by which each could f—— whomever he chose to, as long as his obligations to and respect for the other were not infringed upon. This was totally at odds with Stephen's conception of marriage, as he had imagined it with Lynn (who certainly seemed to me to be the Ideal Wife type) and as he had seen it happen with both of his brothers. He had only happy visions of companionship and sharing, and eventually of children; and slowly he allowed my imprisoned fantasies to emerge into possibility by his words. I was not convinced until after we were married that it could be the source of such happiness, and I'm sure I caused him much suffering and anxiety by being so resistant. As for my dissociation of sexuality and love, it still has not been overcome. It was one of the most painful things to me that Stephen had had a relationship in which sexuality had been nothing more or less than a beautiful extension of love and trust, while I saw sexuality as a route toward that love and trust. I felt as though I could never offer him what Lynn had, and indeed as the relationship progressed it became clear that anything I had with Stephen he had already felt with Lynn in its original and first-love form, while for me everything we did was new and nothing was to be taken for granted. . . .

We decided to get our own apartment. The difficulties with Anna and the cramped quarters in Stephen's apartment made it not only desirable but practical to look for our own place. We found a lovely apartment which we fell in love with, leased, and spent a week painting. It was as though the most tangible parts of our dreamings were being realized. I had been delighted to find that Stephen loved cars and driving, since I always had been given to great speeds and skillful steering; we were both excited about getting an Alfa after the Volvo was sold. We both loved soul music, and I had a good collection (which Stephen was to jokingly refer to as one of the reasons he married me); our tastes in most things generally coincided. The only source of real disturbance to me in Stephen's habits was his daily grass habit; he began to deal on a fairly large scale that winter in order to earn money, and for many months I was fearful of a bust, particularly since we lived so close to a head shop. But gradually I began to see that not only could he do anything he chose to while stoned (which I still cannot) but that it was a source of great pleasure and relaxation to him. On those terms, I learned to accept it. Now I am still a much less frequent user than he, but haven't had a thought in months about being busted, other than a sort of pioneerish conviction that it should be legalized and that the social effects of grass are not only not dangerous, but can even be very useful in a person's mode of dealing with the world. I am convinced that it will, by force of logic, eventually be legalized, and I now take the position that to be busted would help the cause, since it will be the number of supposedly "respectable" people who are discovered smoking that will tip the balance of opinion in favor of the drug, since reports by commissions obviously have had no effect. I do however still strongly object to dealing speed or acid, because I know that they can get out of hand. Stephen has no real convictions on this point, feeling that people for whom a drug is harmful are not likely to buy it— yet this is not true of speed freaks, who get their eight-hour highs at the expense of their lives eventually. But for the most part we don't deal speed, and never acid, so that that point of contention is avoided. . . .

When we returned to Cambridge I prepared to resume school. But that term was interrupted by a series of attacks which I now believe to have been psychotic episodes, in which I would feel totally commanded by my former guardian, the Other Woman in me. She would come over me like an electrical current and force me to act in very strange and unfortunate ways. This was a terrible period for Stephen, because I knew that it was a battle of strengths, his against hers, whoever she was; I somehow no longer could do any more. Exhausted, I was taken over. Usually when I felt that it was going to happen (and I could feel it in a very physical way, trembling and apprehension and excitement from the inside), I would tell Stephen and he would pin me on the bed and hold me down until the violence passed. The attacks were directed against him, and I was told by my alter ego that she, not Stephen, possessed me and that one of them had to be killed, or failing that, that I had to be. And so I told Stephen to please fight her when she took over, and he did. I will never admire anybody more than I do him for his courage and compassion and endurance during those days. When I was "taken over" and began to fight him, he would pin me down and hit me, often until my face bled; and then when it passed and I came out of it, crying and confused, he covered me with kisses. He would alternately swear and strike out at the "bitch" when she appeared (and Stephen told me that my face changed drastically when this transference took place although I had no sense of anything except intense apprehension) and then chant Hebrew prayers to me when I asked him after the fit until I fell asleep. I remember that on the third or fourth night of these "attacks" he was so exhausted from fighting me and from making the violent changes of emotion that were required, that he began to cry as he was holding me down, and I couldn't stand it: I just felt as though I were going under a drug or something and couldn't stay with him and comfort him and hold him and thank him. It was the most wonderful thing anyone has ever done for me. And after that week the Woman never reappeared in such strength, preferring to catch me when I was alone and never again challenging Stephen. . . .

. . . Although the attacks ended, I was still terrified of being left alone in the apartment and became very afraid at night when the telephone rang, thinking that it would be my mother. After every telephone call from her (which always ended up in a yelling session) I collapsed in tears and became quite unmanageable for an hour or more. Gradually though, under the influence of Stephen's amazing love, my distress at these phone calls decreased until by early spring I felt quite able and controlled again. During the month of March, as a token gesture to my mother (who sent me clippings and wrote little notations in the margins about how my children would be deformed if I continued to use contraceptive pills or to smoke pot) I went off pills, assuming that rhythm would be contraceptive enough if I were careful. Six days before my period was due (one day before what is normally considered the infertile period) I began to feel creepy again (if you will forgive the expression) and felt full-force the power of the old other voice urging me to get Stephen to f——— me; but the voice expressed itself mainly in the strongest sexual desire I ever felt, and I convinced Stephen that it would be all right, believing that myself.

In April I made an appointment with a physician; the pregnancy test was positive. I was both elated and afraid, and I remembered with a kind of bitter amusement that this would be the second time around for Stephen and that the pattern was repeating itself. What was such a source of joy and love for me would be a repeat experience for him. I felt rather acutely that Lynn's pregnancy had outdone mine and that Stephen's joy in hers must have been enhanced since it was the first time he had made a baby in anyone. Lynn had given him support instead of problems as I had. But when I told Stephen, it was with positive joy; and he responded with smiling.

As it turned out, that same afternoon I had an appointment with Dr. Roberts, and he immediately had me put in the infirmary, afraid of the disturbances that he felt the new condition would create in me after the initial numb disbelief. The next week was a very depressing one: I didn't want to kill that peculiar combination of Stephen and me that was growing in me, and yet from all sides I was told that to have the child would be disastrous. Stephen took me to a metropolitan hospital where I was given a battery of tests and several interviews by two psychiatrists. I was classified as an hysteric and was eligible for a therapeutic interruption under state law. The only remaining hitch was the anaesthetic consent which had to be signed by a parent. It was plain that I could not tell my mother; I was quite certain that she would fly up immediately and worsen everything. I knew that my father would be jolted, but the chances were better. I tried to reassure him over the phone after writing him a letter, and although he was hit hard in his Puritan core (as he had been by our living together before we were married, refusing even to come into the apartment), he came through with the signature and agreed not to tell my mother. I made a number of phone calls to my mother to prevent her calling home at night not to find me there; but as if by instinct she called anyway on the night before the abortion was to be performed; Stephen immediately called me and said she had demanded that I call her back "when I got in"; and so from my bed at the hospital having asked the nurses to keep out for a few minutes so there would be no telltale noises, I called her up and went through an agonizing half-hour being lectured about parking tickets and not writing letters.

The operation was incredibly smooth and painless and I was out the next day. I felt emptier but relieved.

There are two areas which in this stream of associations I have failed to touch. One is that of work. It has always been characteristic of me that I was healthiest when I was busiest, and during the first few months with Stephen, I was working full time in the emergency ward of a hospital, until I was too exhausted to go on. Stephen would drop me off and pick me up every night, and his dependability and calm was wonderful. But one of the unfortunate trends in my association with Stephen has been a gradual loss of drives and concentrated energies toward working; I get my schoolwork done in spurts, and haven't held a job since that spring. At the beginning of the relationship I was particularly worried about my inability to write poetry as I lived with him longer and longer; and it was only during the summer months when he was working that I got any real writing done. I am still battling with myself for the poetic inspiration that used to come so easily. On the other hand, this form of expression has been supplanted gradually by my interest in psychodynamics and their social implications. I have been doing my best work since I came to school in my social science courses. Although I have neglected my artwork, I feel capable of turning it out if I had the time, so that the loss of inspiration seems to be limited to my long-time poetic talent.

The other topic I should touch briefly on is drugs. As I have already described, I have come not to scorn Stephen's dependence on a smoke in the evenings and even sometimes before starting the day off, but to see it as a part of his psychodynamic relation to the world. And I myself have learned to overcome the tendency to become suspicious and fearful when smoking grass, having replaced it with a very healthy relaxation and general rosiness which usually puts me to sleep. . . .

The only really bad experiences with drugs that I had after meeting Stephen occurred when I was the most disturbed. At the height of the period of being afraid to be left alone, I was stoned one night when Stephen had to go out for something, and I remember huddling on the bed afraid of noises. Someone knocked on the door, and I answered it to find what appeared to me to be a terrible figment of my imagination—a young man with only one arm. He went into the usual magazine selling spiel, with the added dimension that he was a Vietnam veteran, but my mind was racing in all kinds of unholy paranoid directions; and even after I got him to leave (after convincing him, I'm sure, that I was thoroughly mad) I thought for two days that he was following me around and would catch up with me eventually. Fortunately in Stephen's company those feelings can be relatively short-lived. I used to find myself falling into that kind of misinterpretation of the attitudes of others toward me quite frequently when I was stoned, but that has completely disappeared now.

One other momentous event which I left out was the confession which I finally made to Stephen that I had never had an orgasm with any man, and not even with him. I was afraid to tell him because then I could be accused of having lied every time we had had intercourse by my exaggerated ecstasies, and also because I sensed that an integral part of his joy in intercourse came from the sensation of giving me such joy and release. His reaction was initially one of disbelief and a passing disappointment, followed immediately by eloquent reassurances that he loved me, that we would be married anyway OF COURSE, and that with a lot of love and persistence he would bring me around. Since then I have held rather desperately on to that dream—that this relationship will join my dissociated concepts of sexuality and love in eventual orgasm, and I have cried in frustration after intercourse many times, wanting so much to give him the gift of my unconscious and complete surrender, but unable to make it happen.

The marriage date was June 5. In late April invitations were to be sent out. I made a brief visit home (ostensibly to make arrangements with my mother for the wedding) sometime in March which had the usual dramatics and confrontations, in one of which I ended up on the bed in my room crying and trying to block out my mother's words with my hands over my ears. I moved so close to the wall to get away from her that the bed slipped out and I ended up on the floor, which was good occasion for my mother to call me childish and to capitalize beautifully on my humiliating position behind the bed. But the arrangements were somehow made, with every eye toward economy in order to give them little to complain about (my wedding gown was a simple evening dress which cost less than that of the attendants!). I had written a girl I had met the summer before and known for only two months to ask her to be my bridesmaid. Somehow no one I knew, not even Mimi who had shared my propensities for self-torture and self-examination when I was in my black period at college, was friend enough to be an obvious choice for bridesmaid, and I had felt that this girl and I had had an affinity which convinced me that she would accept. She did, but with the condition that she couldn't pay for the dress and her transportation (she had her problems too), and although I wrote offering to pay for one or the other, she never wrote back and, in the end, my only bridesmaid was Jenny.

Stephen has now decided to see a psychiatrist whom he had heard lecture and particularly admired. I, having quite effectively asserted my emancipation from my family with the help of Stephen's con-

tinuous and unselfish support, am now cementing my career ambitions in the direction of clinical psychology, although my love for creative writing and for art could very possibly pre-empt these newer ambitions. What happens to us in the future is largely dependent upon whether Stephen is able (by hook or by crook) to obtain a deferment when he graduates, since he is quite certain of his disinclinations to go on to graduate school. Once that point is decided, we will have to find a way in which to allow ourselves to grow away from the past which still influences each of us in its indirect ways, and to find our own modes for dealing with a social world. Such a development will have to take place somewhere away from the strain of social expectations and acceleration, in a place where we shall be able to postpone meeting those external demands until internal organization can be completed. On the whole I am immensely optimistic: I have already managed to separate myself emotionally as well as physically from my mother's turmoil in order to begin to straighten out my own in some effective way (I was hardly upset at all by a recent telephone conversation with my mother in which she revealed that SOMEHOW she had discovered that I had had the abortion and had, moreover, provided my sister with grass and explicit guides to its use when she asked it of me this year, even though she called me a "murderer" in effect and was very abusive); my misinterpretations of the attitudes of others toward me is diminishing noticeably, and moreover I am less concerned now than I used to be about what they think, which appears to me to be a healthy trend; I haven't seen Dr. Roberts in months, or had a recurrence of "psychotic" delusions (such as the bleeding broomhandles I had seen when I was at my worst); and Stephen is very much aware of his difficulties and their nature, which is the first step toward dealing with them when he gets a chance. Our avoidance of parties and visiting is largely functional in allowing us to get holds on ourselves before we try to deal with the complications of social interaction; I can see only love, promise and mutual trust in the future. Remembering the trend of things, from my petrified silence being driven home in the car by my mother when she was drunk, along the lines of my conviction that I was ugly (which lasted in its most unrealistic forms until only a few months ago), to the fear I felt when Stephen was considering seeing Lynn with me over our spring vacation just before we were married—all reflecting the undependability of other people with respect to myself, and my reaction of mistrust—remembering these things in the light of my present sense of fullness, of solidity, of essential trust, makes me feel very lucky. And if it didn't have such dangerous implications, I would say that my angel was right: I have been looked after. Things are on the way up.

Sociology

Sociology

Introduction to Sociology

Concepts:

Group
The Cash Posters: A Study of a Group of Working Girls, George C. Homans

Norm
Sex As Work: A Study of Avocational Counseling, Lionel S. Lewis and Dennis Brissett

Role
The Hasher: A Study of Role Conflict, Louis A. Zurcher, Jr., David W. Sonenschein and Eric L. Metzner

Social Stratification
Social Class and Campus Dating, Ira L. Reiss

Bureaucracy
The Navy Disbursing Officer As A Bureaucrat, Ralph H. Turner

Social Institution
To Comfort and to Challenge, Charles Glock, Benjamin Ringer, and Carl R. Babbie

Deviance
Stripteasers: The Anatomy and Career Contingencies of A Deviant Occupation, James K. Skipper, Jr., and Charles H. McCaghy

Social Disorganization
Wincanton: The Politics of Corruption, John A. Gardiner with the assistance of David J. Olson

Introduction to Sociology

Sociology involves the collective experiences of individuals. It attempts to describe and understand persons' **social relationships** with each other. Sociologists also study the **social structures** and **social processes** of **groups** and **communities**.

Each person enters a social situation with a psychological *structure* and a set of biophysiological characteristics. His behavior in each situation is determined, however, not only by what he brings to it but by how, as a psychological and physical being, he interacts and meshes with others who are involved in the same situation or event. These situations create the **social relationships** in which he is enmeshed. People leave such situations somewhat different from when they entered. As they move from social event to social event, from one point to the next, from one moment to another they are constantly changing their **social relations**. People are products of their social world and their relationships in this world. These differences are reflected in their psychological *structures* and influence the psychological *products*—the individual behavior of persons.

But in the same way as each event in the psychological world of people is related to their other experiences, situations are also linked together. Social events are neither idiosyncratic, that is, peculiar, nor independent. There is a fabric to social life that provides continuity to people's existence. This fabric is referred to as the **social structure**. The **social structure** can be thought of as a complicated three-dimensional grid in which the boxes are of different sizes and often intricate pathways are required in order to move back and forth through the grid.

An individual's biological and psychological characteristics greatly influence his behavior and his relations with fellow members of his **community**. However, these characteristics by themselves are not sufficient to understand the behavior of community members. The properties of social life are determined by the outlines of the **social structure**, and by the marks the **social structure** leaves on individuals as they experience life in different **groups**, **communities** and **societies**.

The regularities of social life are dependent upon **social relationships** between community members and the character of the **social structure** in which the relationships take place. Likewise, disruptions and social disorder often result from the failure of the consummation of **social relationships** in ways which are consistent with the motivations and expectations of the persons involved. Disruptions also occur from contradictions and confusion in the structural arrangements of a **group** or **community**.

Group

A key concept in understanding the social life of people is **group**. In any given day we come into contact with endless individuals in a variety of different circumstances. Many of these meetings are casual, and have minimal consequences for the individual or his future individual and social development. However, a **group** involves a number of persons, an aggregate or collective, who communicate with each other over a reasonable span of time and who are engaged in a similar task or who share similar goals. In the anthropology section we shall see that one's group affiliations may not necessarily be a selective process, but rather that one's **race** may act as a determinant of the **group** to which he belongs.

Sociologists have evolved a number of different classifications of **groups**. Perhaps the most common is the distinction between **primary** and **secondary groups**. This distinction is usually made between those **groups** in which there is face to face, physical contact among members and those in which group interaction consists of formalized communication and indirect contacts between members. For example, physicians who belong to a medical club in a single hospital which has weekly meetings and poker games would be regarded as a **primary group**. But the American Medical Association, a national professional body, would be regarded as a **secondary group**.

We will see also in the anthropology section that **societies** are a type of **group**. In primitive **societies** these **groups** are bonded together by **kinship** ties; in more complex **societies, group** ties are usually ordered around **families** or work.

Everyone belongs to a variety of **primary** and **secondary groups**. Some are composed of family members, friends, or persons that share our particular interests. George Homans, in *The Cash Posters*, provides a careful description of a work **group**. He describes a collectivity of girls who perform common tasks and who develop a series of social arrangements between themselves—not only to get the job done, but in order to gain personal satisfactions and rewards for each work day. Homans' study is instructive for a number of reasons. It demonstrates that all individuals are not viewed in the same way by each group member; as in all **groups**, a **social structure** exists. In this instance, the **social structure** is of a relatively primitive and simple type. Nevertheless, it is clear that both characteristics—related to the way the girls act on the job, and those that are part of the judgmental criteria of the larger social world—are involved in how the girls see themselves and each other. How persons they come into contact with in the work situation see them is also important.

Homans demonstrates also how individual characteristics of the girls—their psychological *structures*—are related not only to work effectiveness but to their social positions in the **group**. His study emphasizes that psychological *structures, processes* and *products* operate in the context of group life and **social structure**.

Norm

In his discussion of the cash posters, Homans describes how the group members manage to get along with each other and to undertake consistently, if not well, a relatively routine and repetitive job. They have to have certain agreements—explicit or implicit—about how to behave with each other, and with outsiders with whom they must necessarily become involved. *The term* **norms** *refers to this type of agreement about what constitutes right and proper conduct.* **Norms** exist in all areas of social life. The cash posters have **norms** about how many cards per hour they should be able to process; about how they should behave toward their supervisor and toward each other. **Norms** are consensual arrangements that exist about how we view different aspects of social life; about work activities; about family life and play, and even about sexual conduct, as the study by Lewis and Brissett shows.

The study by Lewis and Brissett is an analysis of marriage manuals, which finds that sex in marriage seems to be regarded as work. In other words, there seems to be a pervasive **norm** that sex which is fun is not right and proper. **Norms** generally function to maintain the stability of **groups** and to regularize the participation of its members.

The Lewis and Brissett article is instructive in its discussion of **norms**, for it demonstrates that **norms** are neither independent of each other or of the general **ethos** or **value patterns** of society. **Norms** must fit one another, and the **values** held by different community members. The analysis of fifteen marriage manuals provides convincing evidence that **norms** do not arise spontaneously in **groups**, and are not necessarily generated there. The various **groups** in which we exist are affiliated, sometimes closely and sometimes loosely, with each other. These **groups** also are regulated and influenced by outside inputs, including, of course, the mass media.

We will make the distinction in the anthropology section between **beliefs** and **practices**. This distinction is similar to the way **norms** are divided. For instance, there are ideological **norms**—things we believe but do not necessarily expect people to do most of the time. There are also behavioral **norms**—**norms** that define and regulate "right and proper" conduct.

Role

Norms determine how each of us behaves in a **group**. At a given point in time many demands are made upon one's psychological and physical person. Often there is conflict between the **norms** and an individual's actions in different interpersonal relationships. All of us are labelled in many different ways—father, husband, professor, author, church deacon, political activist may characterize a single individual that we know. Each of these labels is referred to as a **status**, a particular position that involves a series of rights and duties (i.e., normative **expectations**) for the individual occupying that position. *A person's behavior in a particular status is what is referred to as a role.* In most interpersonal situations and group situations, as indicated, we tend to be looked at in more than one of our **statuses**. Different people regard us in different ways. When our role behavior is sometimes not consistent with our **status** the situation is one of **role conflict**.

Zurcher, Sonenschein and Metzner describe the "hasher," the college male who does a variety of chores around the kitchens of sororities and fraternities to earn food and occasionally a few dollars a month. According to their paper, conflicts of both a personal and interpersonal nature arise because **norms** prescribe different behavior for college students and low-level blue-collar workers. These differences must be confronted by students working part-time around sorority houses and part-time sharing the **status** of "fellow students." The **role** of the hasher in the sorority house demands behavior inconsistent with the expectations of a college student. Individuals who occupy both these **roles** have to resolve the disparities as best they can, often by developing defense mechanisms of both an individual and a social nature.

Norm, **group**, **role**, and **social control** constitute key concept in understanding social life and **social behavior**. In the three papers that deal with these concepts, numerous references to problems of **social stratification** appear. In the last paper on the hasher, for example, the point that this occupational category is of low **social status** is explicitly made, for it has much to do with the conflicts that ensue for an individual who works around a sorority house in such a position. In all **groups**, and within the larger **society**, there tend to be vertical rankings of individuals.

Social Stratification

In most **societies**, particularly complex ones, no single ranking completely describes the vertical structural system. Sometimes we are judged solely on the basis of physical characteristics. Sometimes we are evaluated solely on the basis of economic criteria, but rarely is economic status the only ranking that makes a difference. Sometimes judgments are made on our family backgrounds, **race** and ethnicity.

Both sociologists and the general public talk about a **social stratification** system, and the term **social class** is part of our common language. The differences which define where one falls are often based on a multitude of dimensions, and are quite subtle and difficult to measure. Nevertheless, a few more or less objective characteristics of individuals, such as education and occupation, are of critical importance in determining how individuals are regarded by others, and how they regard themselves.

Reiss in his article on **social class** and campus dating discusses a common view that individuals tend to be ranked by potential dates and mates on college campuses in terms of their social characteristics and perhaps those of their parents. Reiss reviews previous studies, which suggest that there is indeed a scale of social desirability among potential dates. He reports that an earlier study suggested that the rating-dating system was based on popularity, that is on having a "good line," dress, social graces, and so on. His view, based upon his own research, is that not only in casual dating but also in serious dating there is an underlying campus **social stratification** system. It operates regarding both who one takes out and who one marries. It confirms that the social characteristics of one's parents, as well as one's own attributes, are determinants of **status** within the **social structure** of a college **community**.

The determination of one's place in the **social structure** is important in other arenas than the college **community**. The article on the hasher emphasizes that opportunities are regulated by one's position in the **social structure**. Persons concerned with social justice must be constantly concerned about the matter of the relevancy of social characteristics. For example, the concept of beauty which is used to determine Miss America's qualifications is quite distinct from those used to determine the beauty of Hottentot women. For the Hottentots, the size of a woman's behind determines her beauty.

As a general policy, however, sociologists advocate that the **social structure** be modified to allow for increased participation by those now denied opportunities on the basis of irrelevant social characteristics, such as skin color and family background, which are used as determinants of what we can do and who we will be.

Bureaucracy

As **groups** increase in size and complexity, the system of regulations—the **norms** that govern the conduct of individuals and determine the procedures and modes of conduct—are made much more specific and formal. **Bureaucracies** function to depersonalize social activities or relationships and to minimize the importance of the individual and his personality in determining the activities that occur within a particular **group**. Sometimes the term **bureaucracy** is used in a pejorative sense. One of the cherished **values** in many societies is a retention of the individual's **values** and the personality aspirations during social encounters. **Bureaucracies**, when they operate well, are efficient to the point where the consequences to the person are a price many are willing to pay. Other times the costs to the individual are too great. "Dropping out" on the part of young and old is a response to the loss of individual autonomy because of bureaucratic arrangements.

But no **bureaucracy** works perfectly. Some, of course, are more efficient and effective than others. In describing the Navy disbursing officer, Turner discusses **bureaucracies** and some of the characteristics of the social **role** of the disbursing officer that render bureaucratic arrangements imperfect. The article also is instructive for its discussion of the **social stratification** system in which the Navy disbursing officer operates. The Navy disbursing officer is also an illustration of another work **role**. Because he occupies other **statuses** and performs **roles** as friend and quasi-friend to many of those that are part of his **group**, some bureaucratic issues are confronted.

Social Institution

A **social institution** is the most general level of social organization. Institutions usually appear in a horizontal relationship to one another. They are the units that promote and develop broad mechanisms of **social control**; they are responsive to the modification of **norms**; they define relationships among and within social **groups**. They are, if we can recall the grid which forms the outlines of the **social structure**, the major pivotal points, the girders around which various clusters of **norms** and subgroups, circulate. Thus, we can talk about such institutions as the economic domain and the **family**.

In the anthropology section we shall consider the relationship between **social institutions** and **culture change**. It is interesting to note, however, the turmoil of contemporary **society** over the change of a **culture** and the reluctance of **social institutions** and of those in power to follow the changes in **society**. The reading in the economics section by Charles Reich, from *The Greening of America*, addresses itself to some of these antagonisms between **social institutions** and **culture change**.

In contemporary **society** the religious institution has been a source of conflict. In part the tenuous position of the religious institution is associated with the erosion of its influence and the dominance of other **social institutions**, such as the educational institution. However, the bureaucratic arrangements within the religious institution have not proved particularly flexible, but have been slow to adapt to the sweeping changes that have taken place in the **norms** of **society**.

According to Glock and Ringer, the church's commitment has been to two functions: to comfort and to challenge; to care, as they say, for the "halt, the lame and the blind, and those who are weary and heavily laden"; and at the same time to be influential in everyday life. Their study suggests, however, that the religious institution has overextended itself in its comforting function, and underperformed in its challenging one. They cite, for example, the limited participation of the religious institution with respect to civil rights.

The article is instructive in other ways. As good sociologists, Glock and Ringer recognize that one cannot change the functions of **social institutions** without changing the organizational arrangements—**bureaucracies**—within institutions. Thus they spend time discussing the need for a modification in the structure of the religious institution, and finally they relate the structural changes advocated to some ideas about program development. All institutions need to be constantly surveyed and scrutinized, and many of the efforts of the disenfranchised and the dissatisfied are directed to modification of institutional arrangements. The concept of **social institutions** is critical to an understanding of social life, and Glock and Ringer's paper alerts us to some of the considerations within one of them.

In the anthropology section, an article by a distinguished anthropologist is included to illustrate the concept of **race**. Washburn makes an impassioned plea for an understanding of social differences based on skin color. It can, of course, be maintained that the church, as a key **social institution**, has vigorously challenged unproductive views and **values** on such issues as skin color. It would seem that if the church were to become a mediating force in the development of a more responsive social morality in the country, pleas such as that of Dr. Washburn in his article on **race** would become unnecessary.

The articles up to this point have been directed at illuminating concepts that allow us to describe and analyze various levels of the social order. But, as all of us know, community life is hardly utopian. Not all individuals and **groups** conform to the **norms** and the regulations of the **social institutions**. The social order is hardly placid, and there exists within the **social structure** a variety of **groups** whose behaviors set them apart from most individuals and other **social groups**.

Deviance

Sometimes **deviants** and **deviant groups** raise or are believed to raise so many disturbances for the workings of the social system that strenuous efforts are undertaken to eradicate them or at least to control them and keep their members in line. In some cases, however, **deviant groups** are tolerated or accorded a special place within the **social structure**; often, it is argued, because the activities that they undertake are rewarding and valued positively by a significant proportion of those who have influence on the social control and regulatory processes. The article by Skipper and McCaghy describes one such **group**—stripteasers.

This article is particularly instructive in illustrating that not only are characteristics of individuals important and critical, but that it is necessary for persons who enter this deviant **role** to be exposed to a series of career contingencies which lead to their particular occupational choice. **Deviant behavior**, particularly those types that are caused primarily by social characteristics and events rather than by one's biological makeup, do not spring up instantaneously. Rather, persons performing deviant **roles**, whether they are stripteasers, heroin pushers, or corrupt businessmen, have experienced a series of career contingencies that are passed through before their deviant conduct becomes routinized and regularized.

Social Disorganization

The final paper in this section illustrates the concept of **social disorganization**. The concepts selected and illustrated earlier in this section apply equally well to situations in which there is a lack of conformity to the social **norms** of community life and to situations in which the **social order** is based upon a less than desirable set of actions by individuals within the **community**. **Social disorganization** refers to a situation in which behaviors and conditions that exist are rooted in the goals and aspirations of a few individuals who are concerned with their own remuneration, power, influence, and recognition, rather than being linked to the social functions required for the conduct of group and community life. Gardiner describes a real **community**, under a pseudonym, in which virtually all the social control mechanisms have been overtaken by criminal elements for motives of economic exploitation, and many of the **norms** superseded by conduct that leads to the aspirations of just a few. The article also shows how it is possible for leaders within all the **social institutions** of a **community** to become perverted. It should be obvious that there is a link between the concept of **deviance** and that of **social disorganization**. **Deviance** is attached to the **role** behavior of individuals, while disorganization is associated with characteristics of the **social structure**. **Deviance** and **social disorganization** are of course, proportionate to the order of social life.

In the economics section a relationship will be made between **poverty** and **social disorganization**. Poor people most often live in areas which are socially disorganized, and very often become the victims of merchants who do not subscribe to socially recognized **norms**. As the reading on *The Poor Pay More* indicates, Harlem is a type of disorganized **community** in which the economic exploitation of the poor is not regulated.

This section has linked the concepts and the general views offered in the psychology section with the sociology concepts and stressed the importance of the individual and his psychological *structure* for social behavior. As we move on to the anthropology section it should be possible to see the links between the concepts of sociologists and psychologists in the study of the **social structures** and **cultures** of **societies**.

The Cash Posters: A Study of a Group of Working Girls

GEORGE C. HOMANS

Since the Western Electric researches, few studies of single groups of workers have been reported, and even fewer that combined the measurement of individual effectiveness with the systematic observation of social behavior and the interviewing of all the group members. I shall describe briefly here a study that did combine these features.[1] It is a study of the ten girl "cash posters" in an accounting division of a certain company, and it formed part of a study of the division as a whole, which I carried on from December 1949 through April 1950. Since it deals with only one group and that group had only ten members, it can hardly hope to establish general hypotheses about small group behavior. Several such studies, made with comparable methods, might hope to do so, and they would provide the indispensable background to more **macroscopic studies** of worker behavior, made by questionnaires. But by itself the present one can only be called a case study of the relations between repetitive work, individual behavior, and **social organization** in a clerical group.

Method of Study. I have described elsewhere my procedure in introducing myself into the company and the division.[2] I chose to study this particular division largely because the nature of some of the

---

[1] The research reported here was made possible financially by the Laboratory of Social Relations, Harvard University.

[2] G. C. Homans, "Status among Clerical Workers," *Human Organization,* 12 (Spring, 1953), pp. 5–10.

jobs allowed the keeping of reliable output records, and because the layout of the "floor" allowed an unobstructed view of what went on. My first step was to occupy a small table at the back of the room. With this as a base of operations, I spent about a month introducing myself to each of the workers, learning the various clerical procedures, and getting a general impression of behavior in the division. Any constraint due to the presence of a stranger seemed to end after I attended the Christmas office party, and from then on I could get no evidence that the workers' behavior was different from what it had been before I came in.

The second stage of the study, which took 14 working days, was systematic observation of interaction in the room, specifically of who talked to whom, and how often. With 60 persons in the room, I soon found I could not keep a continuous interaction record, and so I adopted a sampling procedure. Every 15 minutes I scanned the room like a radar beam and made a note of which persons were talking together at that time. This method, plus the distances at which most of the observations were made, precluded systematic recording of originations, receipts, and durations of interaction. I could only see *which persons* were interacting. It also precluded recording the content of interaction, except when it took place, as it often did, right in front of me. In this case I did not record content systematically, but only if it seemed to throw light on social relations.

The third and longest phase of the study consisted of individual interviews with the supervisors and workers, conducted on company time in a private room away from the office floor. Before the interview, I asked each worker if she was willing to talk to me; they all agreed except one, whom I did not press further, and who was not one of the cash posters. The interviews, which lasted from one to two hours, were nondirective except in two respects. After explaining again the purpose of the study, I always began the main body of the interview with the question: "How do you like your job?" That is, the initial focus of the interview was on **attitudes** toward the job. I did not press for information on "personal problems," which rarely came up, or on life outside the job, which often did, but I did not discourage talking about these matters if they arose. Then at some point in the course of the interview, as the question came up naturally, I asked, "Who are your close friends in here?" I wanted to get further systematic information on social organization. I recorded each interview, as I remembered it, as soon as possible after it ended.

During the interviewing period, I kept in touch with the division every day, to make arrangements for the next interviews and to hear the latest gossip. When the interviews were over, I returned for two weeks to my table on the floor, to check my first impressions and to make further brief interaction records to determine whether my original results were badly out of line. They were not.

The management also gave me the basic personnel data on the workers and, if they were kept, their output and accuracy records. The whole study took four months and a half. Let me say here, as I have said before, that I enjoyed my association with a fine body of American men and women. In fact I had a wonderful time.

The Cash Posting Job. The division contained sixty persons, doing several different clerical jobs. I am concerned here with only ten of the workers and only one of the jobs—the ten girls that did the "cash posting."

The cash posting job was next to the

bottom of the grades that made up the usual channel of advancement in the division. At the time of the study, a poster made 42.23 dollars for a 40-hour, 5-day week. The posters were all high-school graduates, young in age, and relatively new to the company, as promotion to cash poster from lower grades came fairly rapidly. The reason for this was that the company required girls to leave the company when they married, and most marrying takes place at the ages represented by the cash posters. So vacancies on the job were frequent, but promotion to higher grades took place much more slowly. None of the girls looked forward to cash posting or to work in the company as a permanent job.

The day before a girl left the company to get married, the others, in the afternoon "relief" period, decorated her desk and covered it with candy and presents. Since none of the supervisors felt he should take it on, the girls assigned me the job of handing out the presents and, far more unnerving, of pinning a corsage on the girl who was leaving. In this way I came to be of some use in division society.

One supervisor, who also had special clerical work to do, was in charge of cash posters, and he reported to the division head.

All the reader needs to know about the company is that it had a large number of customers to whom it sent out monthly bills. It was the business of the division to account for the payment of these bills. Because there were so many of them, they were not all sent out on the first of the month but some on every working day. The bills were printed by machine from punch-cards, whereupon the cards were brought to the division and placed in files, ten in number, which ran in four rows up and down the floor. Although old-fashioned bookkeeping had long disappeared from the company, its language was still preserved, and so the files were called "ledgers," and the cards, since they represented unpaid bills, were called the "arrears."

As customers paid their bills, their cash and checks, together with the bill stubs, went to the cashier's office, not on the floor. There the receipts were added, and from there bundles of stubs, each wrapped in an adding-machine tape showing the total of each bundle, came to the desk occupied by the posters' supervisor, which was close in front of my own. He arranged them on the desk in order of size. A cash poster took the first bundle in order, went to the appropriate ledger and, flipping through the arrears cards, pulled out the cards whose printed numbers corresponded to those on the stubs in her "tape." This was called "pulling cash" or more formally "cash posting"—another survival of the language of ledger-books. The removal of a card from the arrears meant that a customer would not be billed again for that amount next month.

When she had pulled all the cards corresponding to stubs in her bundle ("tape"), the cash poster brought cards, stubs, and tape back to the supervisor's desk, took the first new tape, and repeated the process. The pulled cards and tape were sent down to the machine room, where the cards were mechanically counted and added. This addition revealed any failure of cards and tape to balance and thus any mistakes —wrong cards pulled—that the poster had made. Since each poster kept a record of which tapes she had worked on, it was easy to calculate how many cards she pulled and how many errors she made per hour of work. These output and accuracy records were written up daily and placed in a drawer of the supervisor's desk for the posters to see. The cash posters did look at them, and in summary form they were made available to me.

Ninety per cent of all bills were paid in the exact amount shown on the stub. In the case of over- or under-payments, the posters had to perform certain operations on the cards besides simply pulling them, but for the sake of brevity these will not be described. The number of such payments in a tape, the number of stubs in a tape, and the degree to which the cards corresponding to the stubs were concentrated in a single ledger affected the speed at which the tape could be completed. But the order in which the tapes were picked up equalized these variations, in the long run, among the cash posters.

Besides cash posting, the girls spent some time every afternoon working on "collection stubs." This was a job of determining, before the company put pressure on delinquent customers, whether long-overdue bills had been recently paid. No output records could be kept of this work. When they finished it, the girls returned to pulling what they illogically called "next day's cash."

Cash posting was the only "production" job in the division—the only one it had to stay caught up with every day. And no girl was accepted as a cash poster unless, by the end of her training period, she could pull, on the average, 300 cards an hour. This was called the "quota," and it served as a standard of minimum output. The records show that all the girls did, on the average, make the quota; most of them did not find this hard to do, and some of them made a great deal more. In theory, the supervisor "bawled out" a girl if she failed for two days in a row to make the quota. In fact, he rarely had to, and when he did the bawling out was gentle. But neither did he praise a girl when she made a high record, and there was no incentive payment. The public output records themselves seemed to suffice to keep output up. One of my field notes reads as follows: "Murphy, LoPresti,[3] and others gathered around their boss's desk looking at the output records with cries of 'I made it!'"

The fact is that cash posting looked to an outsider like a hard and dull job. A number of girls who were offered it had turned it down. The supervisors wisely felt that they would have a still harder time getting recruits and getting out production if they tried to bear down on a group of young girls like this one.

The girls liked their immediate boss. He never tried to use "human relations skills." He was frank and outspoken when they broke the rules, but they felt they knew where they stood with him and said—which is the highest of all praise from workers—"He's fair." Or even, "He's a man!" For his part he said, "I have a good bunch of girls working for me. I really don't think you could get a better one anywhere. Of course, some of them carry the others. They're not all equally fast. But they do a good job, even the slowest of them. Some of them are so good they really ought to have something better than they have now."

The cash posters were on their feet most of the day, moving, "tapes" in hand, from ledger to ledger. This gave them many chances for social contact, both with members of their own job group and with other workers, many of whom also worked at the ledgers. They made the most of their opportunities, especially as they were convinced they could do their work without concentrating on it—they could work and talk at the same time. In theory, talking was discouraged. In practice, the super-

---

[3] All names are fictitious but faithful to ethnic background.

visors made little effort to stop it, except when it got so loud they thought it disturbed some of the older workers. In part, they felt that they could not stop it; in part, that talking did not always get in the way of work. As one of them said, "If you get them on the carpet for talking or making mistakes, you usually find that the girl who talks most or has made the mistake is one of your best girls."

The cash posters spent most of their time on their feet, but they were also assigned small tables, four in one place and six in another, where they could work on collection stubs or where, if they had to pull many cards in a single ledger, they could bring the card tray to work on it seated. Assignment to neighboring tables was an important factor in the formation of friendships. In the last half-hour of the last working day of the year, all tables were reassigned in accordance with the supervisor's plan, secret until then. The girls took their new seats to the accompaniment of squealing and giggling. This move was supposed, among other things, to break up **cliques** that might get in the way of work.

The characteristics of the cash posting job should by now be clear. It was an exceedingly routine and repetitive clerical job, which could be done with little concentration by girls whose main interests were not in the job itself and who were not deeply concerned with promotion in the company. In view of the fact that it required no previous outside training, such as stenography, it paid well. It required no cooperation among the girls but allowed much social interaction. Little pressure was put on the girls to work fast, and morale was generally good.

Attitudes toward the Job. I opened the interviews with the question, "How do you like your job?" And nine out of the ten cash posters said they liked it, the next comment usually being, "It's a job," *i.e.* better than no job at all. Since the interviews were non-directive, I got no further systematic information on the reasons why they liked the job, but I suspect that the frequency with which they spontaneously mentioned some of its features is a pretty good index of their importance to the posters. Only one feature of the job was mentioned favorably by more than half (6) of the girls, and that was the general friendliness of the group and the "niceness" of the people in the division. The only other attitude expressed by more than half (6) may be summed up as: "I do my work and get my quota and that's all."

A characteristic comment was Elizabeth Rourke's: "Then there was an opening on cash posting. I learned the job in three weeks. Most of them take four. I got so I could do 297, so they qualified me and forgot about the last three. After all, a job's a job. It really isn't hard to get the quota. Of course, you have to keep working, but if you do, you don't have any trouble getting over 300. That's all I worry about. As long as I get over 300 I don't care. Sometimes they bawl you out, if you don't make 300 two days in a row. But half the time I think Al Johnson (former boss of the cash posters) is kidding. He says, 'Aren't you ever going to stop talking?' I have to talk, and I think that a lot of the time it helps you to talk. You speed up a little afterwards so's to be sure to make your quota. It makes you feel better. Half the time you can do your work with your eyes and talk at the same time. The other day I wasn't thinking of what I was doing—I guess I was thinking of something else—and I made 400. I don't usually do that, but Dotty Murphy does it all the time. It's just as easy for her to get 400 as it is for me to get 300. But if you do make 400 no one says anything. You don't get anything for it.

You don't get any more pay, so what good does it do you to get 400? Then they might expect you to get 400 all the time."

This last remark is characteristic of situations where restriction of output exists. And other remarks of the same kind were made, for instance: "If you pull a lot of cards, you spoil the job for the other girls. They're expected to pull that many too." In point of fact no one in the room remembered a time when the quota had been anything but 300: it had never been raised. It served as a floor under output, but a glance at the output records later in this paper will show that output varied greatly above the quota. No group norm put a ceiling on output. A couple of years before, when relations between the posters and a former division head were strained, there may have been some restriction. And when Lillian Granara became the first cash poster in recent history to pull over 400 cards an hour, she said she was criticised for doing so. But such behavior seems to have disappeared at the time of my study. When Murphy began to match Granara's performance, she escaped attack. Only the two posters, Asnault and Burke, who had been on the job in the old days expressed, in interviews, disapproval of the speed at which others were working; and on the floor no girl brought effective pressure on any other to keep her output down.

The attitudes characteristic of restriction of output were present in the group; the thing itself was not, certainly not as an organized group practice. But neither did the girls feel under any pressure to work particularly fast. Indeed the lack of pressure may have been the very thing that helped some of them to work, in fact, very fast indeed.

Social Organization. Besides forming a job-group, the cash posters formed a distinct social group, in the following sense.

The interaction count showed that only one cash poster (Burke) interacted more often with members of other job groups than with her own. The so-called ledger clerks formed the largest job-group in the division and the one next above the posters in the ladder of promotion, though their pay was the same. Only one of the ledger clerks interacted more often with the cash posters than with members of her own group. This was O'Brien, the youngest of the ledger clerks and the one who had been most recently a cash poster. This tendency of the cash posters to interact with one another took place in spite of the fact that nothing in the work itself or in the layout of the room prevented their interacting more often with members of other job-groups.

Within this over-all unity of the posters, sub-groups could be mapped out both by **sociometric choice** and by interaction. The sociogram resulting from answers to the interview question: "Who are your close friends in here?" is shown in Figure 1. It reveals two main trios: Donovan, LoPresti, and Murphy on one side and Asnault,

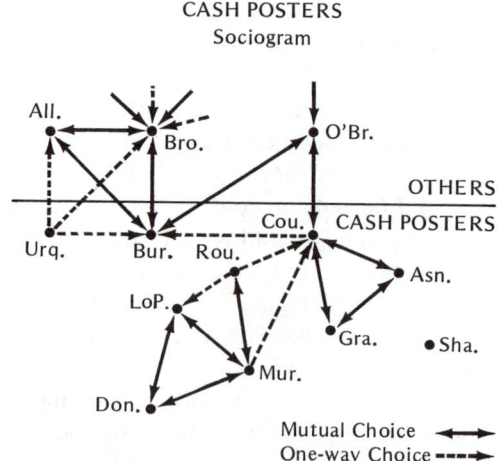

Figure 1.

Coughlin, and Granara on the other, with Rourke a link between the two. The first trio was linked by Coughlin to O'Brien, the newest of the ledger clerks. Burke, though generally popular and friendly, did not express close friendship with any cash poster but was attached to a ledger clerk clique centering around Brooks. Urquhart, the newest cash poster, chose three of this clique but was chosen by none. And Shaugnessy, a true isolate, neither chose nor was chosen.

That these choices represented real social groupings is best shown by data of another sort. Once in the morning and once in the afternoon, the girls left the floor for ten minutes to take their "relief" periods. At these times the same girls regularly gathered at the same places. O'Brien, Coughlin, Asnault, Granara, and Rourke regularly went "downstairs," and Shaugnessy attached herself to them. Murphy, LoPresti, and Donovan went to the "wash room." Burke went to the "vault" with the group that included Allen and Brooks, and more and more often, as time went on, Urquhart attached herself to this group. Not surprisingly, friendship choice and interaction off the floor were closely related.

The most important determinant of clique formation was the position of a poster's table during her first year on the job. Girls who sat near one another then had many chances to interact and tended to become friends, and the friendships once made were apt to persist even after seating arrangements were changed, as they were every New Year's Eve. This was true of both the main trios of the sociogram. As Granara said, "The girls I go around with in here are Ann (Coughlin) and Marie (Asnault). We sat together last year and we used to talk. We'd pass by and call each other 'stupid' and things like that. Other people would think it was an insult, but it's just a joke with us. Ann used to go and have lunch with Shirley (Allen) and Kay (Burke) and Susan (Brooks) and people like that, but now she goes around with us."

Although the girls were observably and by their own recognition divided into cliques, I could observe no hostility between them, and most of the posters spoke favorably of the general friendliness in the division. Murphy said there had been some hostility in the past: "In those days there was a lot of jealousy in here. We were divided into two sides—the girls with their chairs over by the window and the girls inside. You know the way we were set up last year. We would speak to each other, but one group would think the others were trying to get ahead of them." She mentioned the matter of overtime. In that year, Murphy, Donovan, LoPresti, and Urquhart sat together "inside," the others "by the window." While I was in the room, the posters got no overtime work.

Just as I could observe no hostility between the posters' cliques, so I could observe no systematic differences between them in off-the-job activities. But there were some differences between the two groups—they might almost be called moieties—that provided the larger social structure of the division. The older women were not much interested in organized social activities, and leadership in them fell to the younger ledger clerks, notably Brooks and O'Brien. When the office gave a party, these two were elected co-chairmen. Two bowling teams from the office occasionally played against one another, and Brooks and O'Brien were captains of the teams. A tall and beautiful girl and a good bowler, Brooks received more friendship choices than any other person in the division, and was fourth in total interactions. O'Brien interacted more than

TABLE 1

Cash Posters

	Age	Time on Job	Late-ness	Cards Per Hour	Errors Per Hour	Interaction Jan. 9–26				Soc. Choices		
						In	Out	Total	Range	In	Out	Total
Asnault	22	3–5	6	363	.57	38	8	46	13	2	0	2
Burke	26	2–5	3	306	.66	11	53	64	24	2	3	5
Coughlin	20	2–0	4	342	.40	38	20	58	17	4	1	5
Donovan	20	1–9	7	308	.79	20	10	32	14	2	0	2
Granara	21	1–3	6	438	.65	27	10	40	16	2	0	2
Lo Presti	25	–11	8	317	.03	40	8	56	14	3	0	3
Murphy	19	–7	0	439	.62	52	34	92	22	3	0	3
Rourke	17	–4	3	323	.82	33	27	60	16	1	0	1
Shaugnessy	23	–2	16	333	.44	13	2	16	9	0	0	0
Urquhart	18	–2	11	361	.49	21	9	32	13	0	0	0

anyone save Murphy, whom I shall speak of later. The sociogram shows that each headed a different circle of friends, though there were important links of friendship, notably that of Burke with O'Brien, between the two groups.

Compared to the O'Brien group, the Brooks group contained a higher proportion of girls that lived in the suburbs of the city—particularly the "better" suburbs—and they engaged in what were, in their view, somewhat more sophisticated activities, for instance, a skiing week-end. O'Brien, Coughlin, Asnault, and Granara were asked on this party but did not go. As one of the Brooks group (Allen) said: "I used to think that city girls were sophisticated, but when I came in here I found that the country girls knew twice as much as the city girls. By country girls I mean people like Susan Brooks, Kay Burke and myself. Kay likes classical music. The city girls haven't been anywhere, and all they are interested in is getting married when they are 18, sitting at home, and going out to the movies once a week. When I talk about music, they just say, 'Don't say those names to me.'" It is easy to exaggerate these differences and in any event they were not very important to the cash posters, as only two of their number were members of the Brooks group: Burke centrally and Urquhart peripherally.

All I need say in summary of this brief section on social organization is that certain familiar relationships between the distributions of interaction, interpersonal sentiment, and differences in off-the-job activity have turned up here as they turn up in many observational studies of working groups.[4] Friendship choice was associated with interaction off the job. Cliques, defined by frequent interaction and friendship choice between members, tended to display mutual hostility and different styles of off-the-job activity, though the tendencies were slight. Note also the influence of "external" factors, such as differences in

---

[4] See G. C. Homans, *The Human Group*, New York: Harcourt, Brace, and Co., 1950, especially Chs. 4 and 5.

social background and assignments to seats and job, in setting initial values of interaction and activity variables.

Individual Effectiveness. I turn now to the behavior of individual cash posters, especially in relation to effectiveness on the job. Table 1 summarizes the quantitative data I obtained in the study. The "time on job" column gives in years and months the length of time each girl had been cash posting at the time I began the study. The "lateness" column gives the total number of times each girl was late in the five months of the study. Absences are not included, because they seemed, far more than latenesses, to be determined by forces beyond the girls' control. The "cards per hour" column gives the five-months' average of output. The output of only one of the girls, Urquhart, showed the characteristics of a learning curve by being higher every successive month. "Errors per hour" is the same kind of figure as "cards per hour." The "interaction" columns show the number of times a girl was seen talking to another girl during the period in which I counted interactions by the method described above. The figures show the times she talked to another cash poster (in) and the times she talked to some other worker (out). These are raw scores. The "total" figures are corrected to make up for the absences of certain of the girls. "Range" is the number of *different* persons a girl talked to. "Sociometric choices" are those *received* by a girl, either from other cash posters (in) or from other workers in the division (out). The way choices were *given* is shown in the sociogram (Figure 1).

Ten cases is a small number on which to base statistical relationships. Yet there is at least one significant correlation among these figures: frequency of interaction is significantly related to sociometric choices received.[5] Popular girls talked, and were talked to, a great deal. This finding may seem to run counter to one of Bales and his associates. Tabulating the data from twelve meetings of five-man discussion groups, these investigators appear to have found an over-all relationship between interactions *initiated* and "liking" choices received. But the *top* men in interaction initiated were not highly chosen on a "liking" question. Indeed they were only third, on the average, in likes, and received *most* dislikes. Unlike my finding, high interactors were not popular. What can account for the difference in the findings?

The members of the Bales groups were working on problems, common to all the members, which they were to solve by discussion. In moving towards a solution, the most frequent interactors seem to have taken control of their groups. At least they were the most highly chosen on the question, "Who gave the most guidance?" And as Bales writes, "The more 'directive' and 'constricting' the quality of activity, the more likely it is to arouse negative reactions."[6] Or as I should put it, the authority, recognized or unrecognized, of one person over another will tend to cut down the other's liking for the person in authority.[7]

Unlike the Bales groups, the cash posters were working on individual jobs. Their interactions were largely "social:" not directed to common tasks. The person in authority over them was their boss; no one

---

[5] $P = .024$ by Fisher's Exact Test; population divided into those above the median and those below on each variable.

[6] R. F. Bales, "The Equilibrium Problem in Small Groups," in T. Parsons, R. F. Bales, and E. A. Shils, *Working Papers in the Theory of Action*, Glencoe, Ill.: The Free Press, 1953, pp. 146–147.

[7] G. C. Homans, *The Human Group*, pp. 244–248.

of them had much occasion to exercise control over the others. These differences in the conditions (external system) under which the groups were brought together go far to account for differences in the findings. Let us remember Claude Bernard's *dictum:* "The experimenter will be convinced that phenomena can never be contradictory if they are observed under the same conditions, and he will know that, if they show variations, this necessarily results from the intervention or interference of other conditions, which mask or modify these phenomena."[8]

To return to the data on the cash posters, one relationship that would be important if it did exist is in fact absent. Contrary to the theory that talking interfered with work, the figures show no correlation—for this kind of work and this kind of workers—between output and frequency of interaction. Indeed the lowest producer and the highest were the two most frequent talkers.

Inspection of the table shows that a girl whose score was extreme on one of the measures was also extreme on the others. The number of individuals is too small to establish as general hypotheses the relationships thus suggested. Instead I shall briefly describe a few of the posters as each exhibiting a distinct constellation of traits, in the hope that other researchers will discover similar constellations.

The Isolate. Mildred Shaugnessy was more often late than the others. She interacted far less than they. She named no one, and was named by no one, as a close friend. Her low interaction was not just the result of her having been in the division a short time. Urquhart had been a cash poster just as briefly, interacted quite a lot, named three girls as friends, and was gaining acceptance. Shaugnessy was the only girl the others expressed any hostility toward, usually giving the reason that she made personal remarks she thought were funny but they did not. She came from a "poor" section of the city, and appeared to this observer less well-dressed than the others. She was not married, but it was believed in the division that she was not living at home, that she had had some kind of quarrel with her family. In her interview, she expressed more attitudes that differed from the modal ones in her group than did any of the others. In particular, she expressed general approval of all the bosses, in spite of the fact that they often "called" her for being late—the other girls were much more selective in their approval—and she said that talking got in the way of posting. She had to concentrate; the other girls were more apt to feel that talking helped work. How far this was a rationalization of the circumstance that people did not in fact talk to her I cannot tell. As a job she would like to have, she mentioned a telephone switchboard of her own in a small hotel, that is, an isolated job. Other studies have found a relationship between absenteeism and failure to be accepted as a member of an organized group at work.[9] In this case I believe lateness to be more closely linked to acceptance. If one is not liked at work, one will be that much less eager to go to work—though Shaugnessy did not make this connection. She has since left the employ of the company to get another job.

The Low Producer. Catherine Burke was a tall, heavy girl, but I doubt that her phys-

---

[8]C. Bernard, *Introduction a l'Etude de la Médicine Expérimentale,* Paris: Flammarion, 1952, p. 113.

[9]See especially E. Mayo, *The Social Problems of an Industrial Civilization,* Boston: Harvard Graduate School of Business Administration, 1945, Ch. V.

ical slowness had much to do with the fact that her output was lower than that of any other cash poster. She had been a cash poster longer than any other girl but one; she expressed no liking for the job, but she had several times refused "promotion" to ledger clerk, saying "It's too much trouble." (The job did not carry any more pay.) Her choice and interaction pattern reflected the facts that she was popular and that many of her friendships were with girls who had moved out of cash posting. Only one poster talked more than she did, but unlike all the others, Burke talked far more with other members of the division than with posters. She tied with Coughlin on sociometric choices, but again, and unlike Coughlin, her choices came more from the others than from the posters. She talked to more *different* people not only than any other poster but than any other person in the whole division. She was also the only cash poster who had any higher education—two years at a Catholic junior college. She got a job in the company because her father had worked in it for many years. The family had done well, lived in a "good" suburb, and her brother had an excellent job in public relations. By reputation she had the most active social life outside the office; she belonged to more outside organizations and spoke of herself as "the traveller of the division:" "In the summer I'm always coming in on Friday with a bag and coming in with it again on Monday morning." Popular though she was, she believed in keeping her social life at the office and her social life outside separate. "I don't believe in having your friends come from the office. Most of my close friends are not in here. They are the girls I went to college with. When I talk to them I find out that I am getting a lot more pay than they are. I tell them that cash posting is something pretty wonderful. I don't let them in on the truth." Perhaps the best way to sum up this fine and able girl is to say that she was bored with the work of the division and wasted on it. Even more than the others, her deepest interests were outside cash posting and indeed the company—just as her interactions were.

She was also a survivor of days when relations with the bosses were much less good than they were in my time. As she said, "Some of the girls that have come in recently think that we (Asnault and herself) are silly. They try to get four or five hundred and walk their legs off. I tell them they don't know how we had to fight to get things the way they are now." She has since left the company to enter a Catholic religious order.

The Accurate Worker. Helen LoPresti's record was remarkable for her extraordinarily small number of mistakes. This cannot be related to her social position; her interaction and sociometric scores were in no way extreme. She herself explained her accuracy by an experience in her past. During the war she had worked for a firm, famous for its efficiency and high-pressure methods, that runs a chain of department stores. As she said, "I worked for a man who was a buyer in jewelry, and kept his figures for him. If I didn't have them right, he would be out hundreds of dollars. He couldn't do the work himself. He had to trust me. So when I work here, I try to be accurate . . . and of course that slows me down on production." Intelligent and conscientious, she won rapid promotion in the firm and became supervisor of a small number of other girls. She went on to say: "The girls were inexperienced, and it got so that I was doing all the work. I tried to do it all myself. I was too efficient for my own good. I would do the work after hours and take it home with me. Finally it got to be too much for me. I'm sensitive. I was worrying about everything and I couldn't stand it, so I quit." A girl who wants everything done just right may have trouble delegating work to others. Certainly she is under especially heavy strain in a firm like the one LoPresti worked for. Not only does the firm put her under pressure, but she puts it on herself. Cash posting allowed LoPresti to do everything right without being under pressure, and she liked it: "You have nothing to worry about. You do your work and that's that. I worry about a lot of things. Am I normal, you must be asking yourself? Well, *am* I normal?"—Interviewer: "Don't be silly." (Giggle from both.)—LoPresti: "I don't want to get into a spot like I was in at ———." (Note the interviewer's non-directive technique.) LoPresti has since been promoted in the company.

The High Producer. I could never develop any subtle social or psychological theory to account for the behavior of Dorothy Murphy. For me, she simply had a high activity rate: she had the highest output among the posters, and she also talked more than anyone else in the room. Her interview was the longest: I had to stop it so that she could take her "relief" period. She was never late. A stocky girl, she never, unlike her nearest rival, gave the slightest appearance of making an effort to work fast, and she herself felt that if she concentrated she did not do so well. It may be significant that she reported a very energetic mother, active in association work, and a father who probably, as production manager of a factory, had a better job than the fathers of the other cash posters. She was easily intelligent enough to go to college. Both her brothers had gone, and her family could have afforded it, but she did not want to. And yet she cannot have been without ambition. Although she liked her present job, she was the only poster who had formally applied for transfer to some other division. She has since transferred to a division where the chances for advancement were greater than they were in ours, and as a result this very effective girl has moved higher in the company than any of the former cash posters.

The Popular Girl. Ann Coughlin received most sociometric choices from other cash posters and tied with Burke in total choices received. In other respects her record was not remarkable. She talked often but not very often; her output was neither low nor high—and this fact itself may be significant. Unlike Murphy, she had wanted to go to college, but her family could not afford it. She can best be described as a sweetheart—strong in all the less sophisticated and more familial virtues. She stands in sharp contrast to the social isolate, and she was the only girl who said, "I *love* my job." She has since left the company to get married.

I have tried to describe a small group of working girls—a study clinical in intent but employing some systematic observations of work effectiveness and social organization. I have described the attitudes of the girls toward a job that was highly repetitive, done without restriction of output or pressure for production from supervision. The analysis of social organization brought out again some familiar generalizations. Finally, I have tried to describe certain constellations of traits in individual behavior, related to work effectiveness, to social position in the group and outside, and to the worker's past history, that may prove suggestive to other researchers. In conclusion, let me express the hope that the kind of research described here will not be wholly abandoned in favor of more macroscopic investigations.

Sex As Work: A Study of Avocational Counseling

LIONEL S. LEWIS
AND DENNIS BRISSETT

It is commonly accepted that America is a society of **leisure**. The society is said to have shifted from one of **production** to one of **consumption**.[1] The American of today spends little time working; he has a great deal of time to play.

With this surfeit of leisure, Americans have been called upon to engage in forms of consumption quite unknown to their inner-directed predecessors. There exist extensive opportunities for play, but little knowledge of how to conduct oneself in this play. As Riesman has remarked, "To bring the individual into unfrightening contact with the new range of opportunities in consumption often requires some guides and signposts."[2] Knowing how to play has become problematic; it is something the individual must learn. He must, in a word, be socialized into the art of play.

Faced with this necessary **socialization**, the consuming American seeks out persons to teach him how to play. Very often this involves engaging the services of avocational counselors. The term avocational counseling ". . . describe[s] the activities undertaken by a number of relatively rapidly growing professions in the United States, including travel agents, hotel men, resort directors, sports teachers and coaches, teachers of the arts, including

---

[1] Leo Lowenthal, "The Triumph of Mass Idols," in *Literature, Popular Culture, and Society*, Englewood Cliffs, New Jersey: Prentice-Hall, 1961, pp. 109–140.

[2] David Riesman (with Nathan Glazer and Reuel Denney), *The Lonely Crowd*, Garden City, New York: Doubleday Anchor Books, 1953, p. 341.

dancing teachers, and so on."[3] Each of the various counselors supplies the American public with advice on play and leisure. The advice of one such group of counselors is the subject matter of this paper.

Quite recently, Nelson Foote has observed that sex, since it is becoming increasingly dissociated from procreation, is becoming more and more a kind of play activity. He states that "the view that sex is fun can . . . hardly be called the invention of immoralists; it is every man's discovery."[4] The arena of consumption is extended to include the realm of man's sexual activity, and the avocational counselor finds himself a place advising people on the vicissitudes of sex as play.

Concomitant with this increasing amount of leisure time, and the attendant problem of learning how to play, it has been observed that the play of most Americans has become a laborious kind of play. "Fun, in its rather unique American form, is grim resolve. . . . We are as determined about the pursuit of fun as a desert-wandering traveler is about the search for water. . . ."[5] Consumption, to most Americans, has become a job. Like work, play has become a duty to be performed. This interpretation is supported by the emergence of what Wolfenstein has labeled a "fun morality." Here "play tends to be measured by standards of achievement previously applicable only to work . . . at play, no less than at work, one asks: 'Am I doing as well as I should?' "[6] Consumption very definitely has become production.

It is the purpose of this paper to examine the products of the avocational counselors of marital sex and to inquire as to their depiction of man's sexual behavior. If it is true that play is becoming work in the mass society, it might be necessary to amend Foote's notion of the character of sexual play. In focusing on how marital sex is handled by these avocational counselors, we will show how sex, an area of behavior usually not thought of as involving work, has been treated as such. We will emphasize how general work themes are presented as an essential part of sexual relations, and how the public is advised to prepare for sex just as they are advised to prepare for a job.

Marriage Manuals

The avocational counselors of sex with the widest audience are those who write what are frequently referred to as marriage manuals. These manuals are designed to explain all aspects of the sexual side of marriage. Their distribution is wide: many are in paperback and are readily available in drug stores; many can be found in multiple copies in public and university libraries; and some are distributed by facilities which offer services in sex, fertility, and contraception, such as Planned Parenthood clinics.

Fifteen manuals were selected from a listing of almost 50 for analysis in this study. They are listed under References. The first criterion for using a manual was wide circulation. This was determined by number of printings and number of copies sold. For example, one volume (15) in 1965 was in its forty-fifth printing and had sold more than one-half million copies in the United States; a second (13) was in its forty-eighth printing and had sold almost six hundred thousand; a third (3) was in its thirtieth

---

[3]Riesman, loc. cit.
[4]Nelson Foote, "Sex as Play," in Eric Larrabee and Rolf Meyersohn, editors, *Mass Leisure*, Glencoe, Illinois: Free Press, 1958, p. 335.
[5]Jules Henry, *Culture Against Man*, New York: Random House, 1963, p. 43.
[6]Martha Wolfenstein, "The Emergence of Fun Morality," in Eric Larrabee and Rolf Meyersohn, op. cit., p. 93.

136 Sociology

printing[7] and has "been read by" two million eight hundred thousand;[8] and a fourth (5) advertises on its cover "over a million and a half copies in print." Other criteria were that the book be still read and available. The fifteen volumes ranged from 14 page pamphlets to full-sized, indexed, hard-bound books.

Each manual was read by both authors, and principal themes were recorded. Notes were taken, compared, and classified. Only material about whose meaning both authors agreed was utilized in drawing conclusions about the themes in a book.

Working at Sex

Marital sex, as depicted by the marriage manuals, is an activity permeated with qualities of work. One need not even read these books, but need only look at the titles or the chapter headings to draw this conclusion. Thus, we have books titled *The Sex Technique in Marriage* (10), *Modern Sex Techniques* (14), *Ideal Marriage: Its Physiology and Technique* (15). There are also chapters titled "How to Manage the Sex Act (3)," "Principles and Techniques of Intercourse (7)," "The Fourth Key to Soundly Satisfying Sex: A Controlled Sexual Crescendo (5)."

From the outset, as we begin to read the books, we are warned not to treat sex frivolously, indeed not to play at sex:

An ardent spur-of-the-moment tumble sounds very romantic. . . . However, ineptly arranged intercourse leaves the clothes you had no chance to shed in a shambles, your plans for the evening shot, your birth control program incomplete, and your future sex play under considerable better-be-careful-or-we'll-wind-up-in-bed-again restraint (5, pp. 34–35).

In other words, marital sex should not be an impromptu performance.

Moreover, sex should not be approached with a casual mien. Rather, we are counseled, sexual relations, at least good sexual relations, are a goal to be laboriously achieved. It is agreed that "satisfactory intercourse is the basis for happy marriage." However, it is added, "It does not occur automatically but must be striven for (12, p. 39)." In the plain talk of the avocational counselor, "Sexual relations are something to be worked at and developed (7, p. 6)."

This work and its development are portrayed as a taxing kind of endeavor; as behavior involving, indeed requiring, a good deal of effort. That sex involves effort is a pervasive theme in the 15 manuals. From the start one is advised to direct his effort to satisfying his or her mate so that mutual climax is achieved, sexual activity is continual, and one's partner is not ignored after climax. Thus, we are told:

Remember, *couple* effort for *couple* satisfaction! That's the key to well-paced, harmonious sex play (5, p. 62).

Certain positions of intercourse are also seen as particularly taxing, in fact so taxing that certain categories of people are advised not to use them. One author, in discussing a particularly laborious position, remarks that "This is no position for a couple of grandparents, no matter how healthy and vigorous they are for their age, for it takes both effort and determination (4, p. 201)." Quite obviously, certain kinds of marital sex are reserved only for those persons who are "in condition."

The female is particularly cautioned to work at sex, for being naturally sexual seems a trait ascribed only to the male.

---

[7] We were unable to obtain this most recent printing, and our copy was the twenty-ninth printing.

[8] These figures were published in *Newsweek*, October 18, 1965, p. 100.

The affinity of sex to her other work activities is here made clear: "Sex is too important for any wife to give it less call upon her energy than cooking, laundry, and a dozen other activities (5, p. 36)." To the housewife's burden is added yet another chore.

Even the one manual that takes great pains to depict sex as sport, injects the work theme. It is pointed out that:

You certainly can [strive and strain at having a climax]—just as you can . . . help yourself to focus on a complex musical symphony. . . . Just as you strive to enjoy a party, when you begin by having a dull time at it. Sex is often something to be worked and strained at—as an artist works and strains at his painting or sculpture (6, p. 122).

Sex, then, is considered a kind of work; moreover, a very essential form of labor. Regular sexual activity is said, for instance, to contribute to "physical and mental health (7, p. 27)," and to lead to *spiritual unity* (14, frontpiece)." In the majestic functionalist tradition, "A happy, healthy sex life is vital to wholesome family life, which in turn is fundamental to the welfare of the community and of society (1, XIII)." Marital sex, most assuredly, is the cornerstone of humanity, but not any kind of marital sex—only that which leads to orgasm. "It is the orgasm that is so essential to the health and happiness of the couple . . . (10, p. 80)."

Indeed it is the orgasm which may be said to be the *product* of marital sexual relations. It is the *raison d'être* for sexual contact, and this orgasm is no mean achievement. In fact,

Orgasm occasionally may be the movement of ecstasy when two people together soar along a Milky Way among stars all their own. This moment is the high mountaintop of love of which the poets sing, on which the two together become a full orchestra playing a fortissimo of a glorious symphony (4, pp. 182–183).

In masculine, and somewhat more antiseptic terms, "ejaculation is the aim, the summit and the end of the sexual act (15, 133)." Woe be to the couple who fail to produce this state as there are dire consequences for the unsuccessful, particularly for the woman.

When the wife does not secure an orgasm, she is left at a high peak of sexual tension. If this failure to release tension becomes a regular thing, she may develop an aversion to starting any sex play that might lead to such frustrations. . . . Repeated disappointments may lead to headaches, nervousness, sleeplessness, and other unhappy symptoms of maladjustment (1, p. 65).

So important is it to reach orgasm, to have a product, that all the other sexual activities of marriage are seen as merely prosaic ingredients or decorative packaging of the product.

In fact, orgasm as a product is so essential that its occasion is not necessarily confined to the actual act of intercourse, at least for the women. Numerous counselors indicate that it may be necessary for the man to induce orgasm in the woman during afterplay. "A woman who has built up a head of passion which her husband was unable to requite deserves a further push to climax through intensive genital caress . . . (5, p. 111)." Particularly in the early years of marriage, before the husband has learned to pace his orgasm, he may have to rely on the knack of digital manipulation. In one author's imagery, "Sometimes it may be necessary for the husband to withdraw and continue the stimulation of his wife by a rhythmic fondling of clitoris and vulva until orgasm is attained (1, p. 66)."

The central importance of experiencing orgasm has led many of the authors to deemphasize the traditional organs of intercourse. The male penis (member) is particularly belittled. It is considered "only one of the instruments creating sensation in the female, and its greatest value lies as a mental stimulant and organ of reproduction, not as a necessary medium of her sexual pleasure." The same author adds, ". . . the disillusioning fact remains that the forefinger is a most useful asset in man's contact with the opposite sex . . . (14, p. 71)." Furthermore, this useful phallic symbol should be directed primarily to the woman's seat of sensation, the clitoris. Only a man who is ignorant of his job directs his digital attention to the vulva, the female organ that permits conventional union.

One must often deny himself immediate pleasure when manufacturing the orgasm. One author, in referring to an efficient technique to attain orgasm, states that: "Unfortunately, some men do not care for this position. This, however, should be of little importance to an adequate lover, since his emotions are the less important of the two (14, p. 122)." Likewise, the woman may have to force herself in order to reach orgasm, even though she may not desire the activity which precedes it. It is specified that "If you conscientiously work at being available, you may ultimately find the feminine role quite satisfying even in the absence of ardor or desire (5, p. 38)." The work ethic of the sexual side of marriage, then, is one resting quite elaborately on what has been referred to as the "cult of the orgasm."

Still, one cannot easily perform one's job; its intricacies must first be mastered. After all, ". . . there is considerably more in the sexual relationship than . . . at first thought (8, p. 136)." "Remember that complete development of couple skills and adaptations takes literally years (5, p. 206)." There is a great deal to be learned. One author talks of eight steps "in order to facilitate sexual arousal and lead, finally, to satisfactory orgasm" and of seven "techniques which she and her mate may employ to help her attain full climax (6, pp. 124–126)."

All of this requires a good deal of mastery that is necessary if the sex relationship is not to undergo "job turnover." Firstly, in the face of incompetence, the marriage partner may, at times, turn to auto-eroticism. One author stipulates that "There cannot be a shadow of a doubt that faulty technique, or total lack of it on the man's part, drives thousands of wives to masturbation as their sole means of gratification (3, p. 140)." Moreover, if sexual skills are not acquired, the husband or wife may seek out new partners for sexual activity. The woman is admonished that adequate sexual relations will keep a man from "The Other Woman . . . (4, pp. 264–265)." The male also must be proficient in sexual encounters for "it is the male's habit of treating . . . [sexual relationships] as such [mechanically] which causes much dissatisfaction and may ultimately drive the wife to someone who takes it more seriously (14, p. 77)."

Learning Sex: Passive and Active

Marital sex is said to necessitate a good deal of preparation if it is to be efficiently performed. In one author's words: "This [complete satisfaction] cannot be achieved without study, practice, frank and open discussion . . . (12, p. 45)." This overall preparation seems to involve both a passive and an active phase. The passive phase seems most related to an acquisition of information previous to engaging in sexual, at least marital sexual, relations. The active phase best refers to the training, one might say on-the-job training, that the married couple receive in the sexual conduct of wedlock.

The matter of passive preparation receives a great deal of attention from the avocational counselors. Thirteen of the fifteen books call attention to the necessity of reading, studying and discussing the various facets of sexual relationships. After listing a number of these activities, one author advises that "If the two of them have through reading acquired a decent vocabulary and a general understanding of the fundamental facts listed above, they will in all likelihood be able to find their way to happiness (1, p. 20)." Another counselor cites the extreme importance of reciprocal communication by noting that ". . . the vital problem . . . must be solved through intelligent, practical, codified, and instructive discussion . . . (14, p. 7)." The general purpose of all this learning is, of course, to dispel ignorance, as ignorance is said to lead to "mistakes at work," and such cannot be tolerated. The learning of the other partner's physiology is particularly emphasized, most counselors devoting at least one chapter and a profusion of illustrations to relieve the ignorance of the marriage partners. One author, however, quite obviously feels that words and pictures are insufficient. Presenting a sketch of the woman's genitals, he asserts that "It should be studied; on the bridal night . . . the husband should compare the diagram with his wife's genital region . . . (14, p. 18)."

Together with learning physiology, the various manuals also stress the critical im-

portance of learning the methodology of marital sex. Sexual compatibility seems not a matter of following one's natural proclivities, but rather "The technique of the sexual relation has to be learned in order to develop a satisfactory sex life (13, p. 172)." One must know one's job if one is to be successful at it. Not surprisingly, to like one's job also requires a learning experience, particularly for the woman. As one book scientifically asserts:

There is a striking consensus of opinion among serious specialists (both men and women) that the average woman of our time and clime must *learn* to develop specific sexual enjoyment, and only gradually attains to the orgasm in coitus. . . . they [women] have to *learn how* to feel both voluptuous pleasure and actual orgasm (15, p. 262).

In summary, then, passive learning involves the mastering of physiology and techniques. By the desexualized female of the marriage manuals, the fine art of emotional experience and expression is also acquired. And the naturally inept male must learn, for:

If the husband understands in even a general way the sexual nature and equipment of his wife, he need not give the slightest offense to her through ignorant blundering (1, p. 20).

This learning process, according to most of the manuals, eventually becomes subject to the actual experience of matrimonial sex. The marriage bed here becomes a "training" and "proving" ground. Again, wives seem particularly disadvantaged: "Their husbands have to be their guides (3, p. 108)." However, generally the training experience is a mutual activity. As one author suggests in his discussion of the various positions for coitus,

In brief, the position to be used is not dictated by a code of behavior but should be selected as the one most acceptable to you and your mate. To find this you will examine your own tastes and physical conformations. By deliberate application of the trial and error method you will discover for yourselves which is most desirable for you both (11, p. 11).

In training, rigorous testing and practice is a must. In the words of one manual "experimentation will be required to learn the various responses within one's own body as well as those to be expected from one's beloved . . . (9, p. 7)," and also, "After a variable time of practice, husband and wife may both reach climax, and may do so at the same time (11, p. 10)."

Both the husband and wife must engage in a kind of "muscular control" training if the sex act is to be efficiently performed. The woman's plight during intercourse is picturesquely portrayed with the following advice. "You can generally contract these muscles by trying to squeeze with the vagina itself . . . perhaps by pretending that you are trying to pick up marbles with it (5, p. 97)." Fortunately, the man is able to practice muscular control at times other than during intercourse. Indeed, the man, unlike the woman, is permitted to engage in activities not normally related to sexual behavior while he is training. It is advised that "You can snap the muscles [at the base of the penile shaft] a few times while you are driving your car or sitting in an office or any place you happen to think of it . . . (5, p. 96)." The practice field, at least for the male, is enlarged.

In general, then, a careful learning and a studied training program are necessary conditions for the proper performance of marital sex. As seems abundantly true of all sectors of work, " 'Nature' is not enough . . . . Man must pay for a higher and more complex nervous system by study, training, and conscious effort . . . (7, p. 34)."

The Job Schedule

As in most work activities, the activity of marital sex is a highly scheduled kind of performance. There is first of all a specification of phases or stages in the actual conduct of the sex act. Although there is disagreement here, some authors indicating four or five distinct phases (15, p. 1), the consensus of the counselors seems to be that "Sexual intercourse, when satisfactorily performed, consists of three stages, only one of which is the sex act proper (11, p. 7)."

The sexual act therefore is a scheduled act and the participants are instructed to follow this schedule. "All three stages have to be fitted into this time. None of them must be missed and none prolonged to the exclusion of others (8, p. 155)." Practice and study is said to insure the proper passage from one phase to another (12, p. 42). Moreover, to guarantee that none of the phases will be excluded, it is necessary to engage in relations only when the sexual partners have a sizable amount of time during which they will not be distracted: ". . . husbands and wives should rarely presume to begin love-play that may lead to coitus unless they can have an hour free from interruptions (1, p. 51)." Even then, however, the couple must be careful, for there is an optimal time to spend on each particular phase. For instance, "Foreplay should never last less than fifteen minutes even though a woman may be sufficiently aroused in five (14, p. 43)." Likewise, the epilogue to orgasm should be of sufficient duration to permit the proper recession of passion.

Given this schedule of activity, the marriage manuals take great pains to describe the various activities required at each particular phase. It is cautioned, for instance, that "all contact with the female genital region . . . should be kept at an absolute minimum (14, pp. 42–43)" during foreplay. The man is warned furthermore to "refrain from any excessive activity involving the penis (14, p. 77)" if he wishes to sustain foreplay. Regarding afterplay, the advice is the same; the partners must not permit themselves "any further genital stimulation (15, p. 25)."

The "job specification" is most explicit, however, when describing the actual act of intercourse. It is particularly during this stage that the sexual partners must strain to maintain control over their emotions. Innumerable lists of "necessary activities" are found in the various manuals. The adequate lovers should not permit themselves to deviate from these activities. Sometimes, in fact, the male is instructed to pause in midaction, in order to ascertain his relative progress:

After the penis has been inserted to its full length into the vagina, it is usually best for the husband to rest a bit before allowing himself to make the instinctive in-and-out movements which usually follow. He needs first to make sure that his wife is comfortable, that the penis is not pushing too hard against the rear wall of the vagina, and that she is as ready as he to proceed with these movements (1, p. 61).

Techniques

The "labor of love" espoused by the avocational counselors is one whose culmination is importantly based on the proper use of sexual technique. In fact, ". . . *miserable failure results from ignorance of technique* (3, p. 49)." Indeed "no sex relationship will have permanent value unless technique is mastered . . . (8, p. 177)." Thirteen of the fifteen books devote considerable space to familiarizing the reader with the techniques of sexual activity. These discussions for the most part involve enumerating the various positions of intercourse, but also include techniques to induce, to prolong, to elevate, and to minimize passion. Many times the depiction of particular coital positions takes on a bizarre, almost geometric, aura. In one such position, "The woman lies on her back, lifts her legs at right angles to her body from the hips, and rests them on the man's shoulders; thus she is, so to speak, doubly cleft by the man who lies upon her and inserts his phallus; she enfolds both his genital member and his neck and head. At the same time the woman's spine in the lumbar region is flexed at a sharp angle . . . (15, p. 218)." Often, however, the mastery of sexual technique seems to involve little more than being able to keep one's legs untangled, ". . . when the woman straightens her right leg the man, leaving his right leg between both of hers, puts his left one outside her right, and rolls over onto his left side facing her (1, 58)."

At times, in order to make love adequately, it is required of the participants that they supplement their technique with special equipment. Some of this equipment, such as lubricating jellies, pillows, and birth control paraphernalia, is simple and commonplace. Others are as simple but not as common, such as chairs, foot-high stools, and beds with footboards or footrails. Some, like aphrodisiacs, hot cushions, medicated (carbonic acid) baths, and sitz baths, border on the exotic. Still others actually seem to detract from the pleasure of intercourse. In this vein would be the rings of sponge rubber which are slipped over the penis to control depth of penetration and the various devices which make the male less sensitive, such as condoms and a local anesthetic applied to the glans.

This equipment that minimizes stimulation, while not particularly inviting, might be said to give greater pleasure than still other techniques that are suggested to add variety to the sex life. The latter, in fact, seem cruelly painful. For instance,

. . . both partners tend to use their teeth, and in so doing there is naught abnormal, morbid or perverse. Can the same be said of the real love-bite that breaks the skin and draws blood? Up to a certain degree—yes (15, p. 157).

Indeed, a certain amount of aggression should be commonplace.

. . . both of them can and do exult in a certain degree of male aggression and dominance. . . . Hence, the sharp gripping and pinching of the woman's arms and nates (15, p. 159).

At times, the authors seem to go so far as to indicate that the proper performance of the sex act almost requires the use of techniques that create discomfort. The element of irksomeness becomes an almost necessary ingredient of the conduct of marital sex.

Concluding Remarks

The kinds of impressions assembled here seem to support the notion that play, at least sexual play in marriage, has indeed been permeated with dimensions of a work ethic. The play of marital sex is presented by the counselors quite definitely as work.

This paradox, play as work, may be said to be an almost logical outcome of the peculiar condition of American society. First of all, it seems that in America, most individuals are faced with the problems of justifying and dignifying their play. In times past, leisure was something earned, a prize that was achieved through work. In the present era, it might be said that leisure is something ascribed or assumed. Indeed, as Riesman and Bloomberg have noted, "leisure, which was once a residual compensation for the tribulations of work, may become what workers recover from at work."[9]

The American must justify his play. It is our thesis that he has done this by transforming his play into work. This is not to say that he has disguised his play as work; it is instead to propose that his play has become work.[10] To consume is, in most cases, to produce. Through this transformation of play, the dignity of consumption is seemingly established; it is now work, and work is felt to carry with it a certain inherent dignity. The individual now is morally free to consume, and moreover free to seek out persons to teach him how to consume, for learning how to play is simply learning how to do one's job in society.

This transformation of play into work has been attended by another phenomenon that is also quite unique to contemporary American society. Given the fact that work has always been valued in American society, a cult of efficiency has developed. As a consequence, the productive forces in America have become very efficient, and an abundance of consumer goods has been created. So that such goods will be consumed, Americans have been socialized into being extremely consumption oriented. As Jules Henry[11] has noted, the **impulse controls** of most Americans have been destroyed. The achievement of a state of general satisfaction has become a societal goal. To experience pleasure is almost a societal dictum.

Thus there seem to be two antagonistic forces operating in American society. On the one hand, there is an emphasis on work and, on the other hand, there is an emphasis on attaining maximum pleasure. These two themes were recurrent in the fifteen manuals which we read, and as one writer put it:

> . . . it may well be that the whole level of sexual enjoyment for both partners can be stepped up and greatly enriched if the man is able to exercise a greater degree of deliberation and management (1, p. 33).

It was as if the avocational counselors were trying to solve a dilemma for their audience by reminding them to both "let themselves go" while cautioning them that they should "work at this." If sex be play, it most assuredly is a peculiar kind of play.

References

Oliver M. Butterfield, Ph.D., *Sexual Harmony in Marriage,* New York: Emerson Books, 1964 (sixth printing).

Mary Steichen Calderone, M.D., M.S.P.H., and Phyllis and Robert P. Goldman, *Release from Sexual Tensions,* New York: Random House, 1960.

Eustace Chesser, M.D., *Love Without Fear,* New York: The New American Library, 1947 (twenty-ninth printing).

Maxine Davis, *Sexual Responsibility in Marriage,* New York: Dial Press, 1963.

John E. Eichenlaub, M.D., *The Marriage Art,* New York: Dell Publishing Co., 1961 (fourteenth printing).

---

[9]David Riesman and Warner Bloomberg, Jr., "Work and Leisure: Tension or Polarity," in Sigmund Nosow and William H. Form, editors, *Man, Work, and Society,* New York: Basic Books, Inc., 1962, p. 39.

[10]Many investigators have observed the intertwining of work and play. We are here only interested in one aspect of admixture, the labor of play.

---

[11]Henry, *op. cit.,* pp. 20–21.

Albert Ellis, Ph.D., and Robert A. Harper, Ph.D., *The Marriage Bed,* New York: Tower Publications, 1961.

Bernard R. Greenblat, B.S., M.D., *A Doctor's Marital Guide for Patients,* Chicago: Budlong Press, 1964.

Edward F. Griffith, *A Sex Guide to Happy Marriage,* New York: Emerson Books, 1956.

Robert E. Hall, M.D., *Sex and Marriage,* New York: Planned Parenthood-World Population, 1965.

Isabel Emslie Hutton, M.D., *The Sex Technique in Marriage,* New York: Emerson Books, 1961 (revised, enlarged, and reset edition following thirty-fifth printing in 1959).

Lena Levine, M.D., *The Doctor Talks with the Bride and Groom,* New York: Planned Parenthood Federation, 1950 (reprinted, February 1964).

S. A. Lewin, M.D., and John Gilmore, Ph.D., *Sex Without Fear,* New York: Medical Research Press, 1957 (fifteenth printing).

Hannah M. Stone, M.D., and Abraham Stone, M.D., *A Marriage Manual,* New York: Simon and Schuster, 1953.

Robert Street, *Modern Sex Techniques,* New York: Lancer Books, 1959.

Th. H. Van de Velde, M.D., *Ideal Marriage: Its Physiology and Technique,* New York: Random House, 1961.

The Hasher: A Study of Role Conflict

LOUIS A. ZURCHER, JR.
DAVID W. SONENSCHEIN
AND ERIC L. METZNER

The effect of **role conflict** upon **personal** and **social adjustment** has been of considerable interest to social scientists. Typically, the individual's reaction to a role conflict situation has been described in terms of traditional defense mechanisms. Burchard, for example, writing of the contradictory behavioral expectations facing the military chaplain, describes four representative solutions to the officer-clergyman conflict: (1) Rationalization (Someone has to carry the gospel to these boys), (2) Compartmentalization (Render therefore unto Caesar the things which are Caesar's and unto God the things that are God's), (3) Repression (I don't see any conflict), (4) Withdrawal (I'd rather not talk about it).[1] Cousins, reporting the behavior of subjects in experimentally contrived role conflict, observed "rationalization, displacements, and wish fulfilling fantasy" as modal responses.[2]

Role conflict, however, is experienced within the broad scope of perceived social environment. **Defense mechanisms**, as solutions to the conflict situation, are not isolated from the social context in which that conflict takes place. In fact, it is likely that a role conflict which has been perpetuated by a continuing set of social conditions will be accompanied by a similarly continuing, socially determined, set of defense mechanisms. The individual who must enact the

---

[1] W. Burchard, "Role Conflicts of Military Chaplains," *American Sociological Review*, 19 (August 1954), pp. 528–535.

[2] A. N. Cousins, "Social Equilibrium and the Psychodynamic Mechanisms," *Social Forces*, 30 (December 1951), pp. 202–209.

conflicting roles will be provided, usually informally, with the socially acceptable means whereby he can alleviate, at least temporarily, that conflict.

In this paper, the authors will present an example of perpetuated role conflict in a university setting. It will be seen that the informal organization supporting one of the role enactments provides each participant with a socially legitimized set of defenses (part of the role expectations) by which he can abate the conflict.

A number of studies have discussed the **adjustment** the college student must make to the conflicts between the behavioral expectations of college life and the behavioral expectations he has internalized from his family association.[3] Among the parental expectations for the college student are "good grades, conscientious study, writing home regularly, spending money carefully, and preparing for a future occupation." Conflicting with these, are the peer-group expectations of "parties, campus politics, fraternity affairs, dating, athletics, and nights out with the boys."[4] Other sources of conflict, within the college life itself, are situations in which the individual must enact two college roles whose behavioral patterns are conflicting. The role of the fraternity man *vs.* the role of student, has been discussed in that context.[5] A second example, which this paper presents, involves the role conflict inherent in the dual enactment of the roles of "college man" and "hasher" in a sorority.

---

[3]See, for example, E. Hartshorne, *Undergraduate Society and the College Culture* (Cambridge: Harvard University Press, 1943).

[4]A. R. Lindesmith and A. L. Strauss, *Social Psychology* (New York: Dryden Press, 1949), p. 616.

[5]D. Krech, R. S. Crutchfield, and E. L. Ballachey, *Individual In Society* (New York: McGraw-Hill Book Co., 1962), pp. 405, 496.

The individual entering college for the first time has, through exposure to a popularized and dramatized stereotype, come to perceive the status of "college man" as incorporating the following characteristics and role expectations: (1) a young man who deserves a white-collar or "clean" occupation of more than average prestige, (2) a sophisticate, above average in intelligence, taste, and *savoir faire*—able to smoke a pipe with an air of casual indifference, (3) a "lover," a "man of the world" who dominates and manipulates the tender young coeds, (4) a "hail fellow well met" who can, at any time spontaneously join in an impromptu frolicsome venture. These expectations are repeatedly reinforced in the informal academic setting.

Hashers at the subject university are male college undergraduate students who are employed as attendants in the kitchens of sororities and fraternities (in this paper, we will focus our attention on the unique social situation of the sorority hasher). In return for their work, hashers are given meals and, in some cases of additional responsibility, a few dollars a month. The job consists of setting tables; washing and drying dishes, silver, and utensils; cleaning up the kitchen; mopping floors; disposing of garbage; general handy work; and, on occasion, carrying luggage for the girls. As it can be seen, the tasks are in general very similar to those of the "K. P." of military fame.

Even though it is part-time work, the job of hasher can be classified as what Becker calls a "service occupation."[6] According to Becker, the service occupations are "distinguished by the fact that the worker in them comes into more or less direct and personal contact with the ultimate consumer of the product of his work, the client for whom he performs the service. Consequently, the client is able to direct or attempt to direct the worker at his task and to apply sanctions of various kinds . . ."[7] Becker sees as characteristic of such jobs that the workers consider "the client unable to judge the proper worth of the service and resent bitterly any attempt on his part to exercise control over the work. A good deal of conflict and hostility arises as a result, and methods of defense against outside interference become a preoccupation of the members."[8]

The hasher occupies the lowest level in the functional work hierarchy of the kitchen. At the top of the hierarchy is the house mother, then the cooks (in order of longevity), the head hasher, and finally, the hashers themselves (in order of longevity). This chain-of-command is rigidly enforced—a policy not unusual in an organized kitchen work setting. Whyte, for example, describes the elaborate restaurant kitchen status system in which even the kinds of vegetables worked with and the levels of food preparation are related to position in the staff hierarchy.[9] Orwell writes of the rigid caste system existing in the hotel restaurant where he was employed, in which the staff "had their prestige graded as accurately as that of soldiers, and a cook or waiter was as much above a kitchen helper as a captain above a private."[10] The hasher in the sorority house, since he is the low man on the totem pole,

---

[6]Howard S. Becker, "The Professional Dance Musician and His Audience," *The American Journal of Sociology*, 57 (September 1951), pp. 136–144.

[7]*Ibid.*, p. 136.

[8]*Ibid.*, p. 136.

[9]W. F. Whyte, *Human Relations in the Restaurant Industry* (New York: McGraw-Hill Book Co., 1948).

[10]George Orwell, *Down and Out in Paris and London* (London: Secker and Warburg, 1933), p. 70.

is expected to accept without question the assignments handed out by the cooks and by the head hasher (though there is considerably more latitude for complaining or "bitching" about a task assigned by the latter). Furthermore, as part of his job, the hasher is expected to be neat, quietly efficient, and at all times polite to the girls. He is not to speak with them when serving (unless asked a question), and, by house rule, he is not to attempt to date them during his off-duty hours.

The position of hasher in a sorority thus brings with it the behavioral **expectations** of (1) menial or "dirty" work, (2) low prestige, (3) a marked lack of sophistication, and (4) manifest subservience to and strict social distance from a group of college coeds.

It appears, therefore, that the individual who must enact both the role of college man and hasher experiences conflict, and it will be seen that this conflict manifests itself in the way the hashers perceive themselves, the way they behave in the work situation, their attitudes toward and behavior with the girls for whom they work, and the attitudes of the girls toward and their behavior with the hashers. Furthermore, components within the informal organization of the work situation will be observed to provide the individual with group-structured defenses to the role conflict. These defenses become an integral part of the hasher role enactment and are learned along with the formal requirements of the job.

Procedure

The two junior authors (one a senior in cultural anthropology and the other a senior in psychology), both of whom had been hashers in a total of five different sororities for three years previous to the present study, observed as participators[11] in the hasher group of a large, campus housed, nationally affiliated sorority (85 girls, ten hashers). The systematic observations were conducted during the course of ten months, a little more than the full academic year. The participant observers, cognizant of the hypotheses and familiar with role theory, kept daily records of relevant attitudes, behaviors, statements, and patterns of interaction of (1) the hashers, (2) the sorority girls, and (1) and (2) *vis-à-vis* each other. The three authors met several times a week to discuss the data and to focus attention for the periods of observation to follow.[12]

The subject sorority was one of the largest on the university campus. At the time of the study, and for a number of years before, the subject sorority was not among those considered by the students to be popular or "in," but rather among those considered to be "unreal." Furthermore, and perhaps to be expected because

---

[11] The two junior authors occupied the role of "complete participator" in Gold's continuum of participant-observers. That is, they themselves were hashers, and members of the work group were not aware of the fact that they were being observed. See Raymond L. Gold, "Roles in Sociological Field Observations," *Social Forces*, 36 (March 1958), pp. 217–223.

[12] In addition to the work by Gold cited above, the authors are indebted to the following for various participant-observer techniques: Howard S. Becker, "Problems of Inferences and Proof in Participant-Observation," *American Sociological Review*, 23 (December 1958), pp. 652–660; Mortimer Sullivan, Stuart Queen, and Ralph Patrick, "Participant Observation as Employed in the Study of a Military Training Program," *American Sociological Review*, 23 (December 1958), pp. 660—667; Jackson Toby, "Variables in Role Conflict Analysis," *Social Forces*, 30 (March 1952), pp. 323–327; Roger Heyns and Ronald Lippitt, "Systematic Observational Techniques," in Gardner Lindzey (ed.), *Handbook of Social Psychology*, Vol. 1 (Cambridge, Mass.: Addison-Wesley, 1954), pp. 370–404.

of the girls' awareness of the relatively low status of their house in the Panhellenic system, the social distance maintained between the members and the hashers was rigid and extreme.

The work setting of hashers in this particular sorority house would be, the authors felt, one in which there was a high degree of role conflict, and one in which the defenses to such conflict would be clearly manifested.

Conclusions based upon the data from **participant observation** in the subject sorority provided the framework for a series of open-ended interview questions.[13] Though the main focus of this investigation was the case study analysis of a specific conflict engendering work situation(in one sorority), interviews were conducted with 48 hashers, 50 members, and 21 staff personnel of seven of the remaining 13 sororities on the university campus, thus attempting to establish the degree, if any, to which the conclusions could be generalized. Including the subject sorority house, the sample consisted of: two "large" houses (65 or more members, eight to ten hashers, and two full-time cooks); three "medium" houses (50–65 members, six to eight hashers, and two cooks on separate shifts); and three "small" houses (less than 50 members, five or fewer hashers, and one full-time cook). Independent of size, the eight sorority houses in the sample varied in prestige (indicated by the number of "rushees," number of student body

---

[13]The purpose of the open-ended interviews was to explore, in sororities other than the subject house, the following broad phenomena: What did the hashers think of their jobs? How did they get along with the girls? What did the girls think of the hashers? How did the house mothers and the cooks view the interaction between the hashers and the girls? What were the formal house rules and expectations relevant to the hasher work situation?

In each interview situation, at least the following questions were asked with the intent being to get the respondents talking, and to probe with further, more specific questions when the opportunity arose: (1) *Hashers:* What do you think of the job of hasher? Advantages? Disadvantages? When is the job most enjoyable? When is the job least enjoyable? Why did you choose hashing as a part-time job? Do you intend to continue hashing while you are a student? What do you think of the girls in this sorority? What do you think their attitude is toward the hashers? How do the hashers and girls get along, generally? Have you worked for any other houses? If so, how do the work situations compare? What is your idea of a "good house" for which to work? A "bad house?" Do you do any extra things for the girls in this house? Do you represent them in intramural sports? Do any of the hashers in the house date a member? Would you recommend the job of hasher to a good friend? (2) *Girls:* What do you think of the job of hasher for a college man? What do you think of the hashers in your own sorority? What is your idea of a "good hasher?" A "bad hasher?" How do you think the hashers and the members get along, generally? What are the names of the hashers who work in your sorority house? How do you think the hasher crew of your house compares with those of other houses? Do you think the members should date hashers? Have you ever dated a hasher? Do you ever find it difficult to get a hasher to do what you ask him to do? Do you have a "turn-about" day? Tell me about it. (3) *House Mothers* and *Cooks:* What do you think of the job of hasher for a college man? What is your idea of a good hasher employee? A bad hasher employee? Are there any particular work or disciplinary problems that you have with the hashers? How, in general, do the girls get along with the hashers? The hashers with the girls? What is your opinion of hashers and members dating? Is there a formal or informal house rule against such dating? What is the hasher turnover rate in this house? Have you worked for other houses? If so, how do the hashers here compare with those in the others? Are there any differences among the houses with which you have been associated in the way the hashers and the girls get along? In this sorority, do you have a "turn-about" day? Tell me about it.

and club offices held by members, number of queens, cheerleaders, pompon girls, etc., and by student opinion). Two were high prestige or "top" houses; four were of average prestige; and two were low prestige or "loser" houses. It was felt that this sample of sororities was fairly representative of the entire university population of houses, though at the onset, since the authors were aware of the limitations of participant observation and open-ended, informal interviews, no sweeping generalizations were intended.

Results and Discussion

It is immediately apparent to the observer that the hasher is not proud of his work and that he prefers not to be identified with the job. As MacIver has pointed out, men in our society tend to be judged according to the work which they pursue,[14] and the stereotype representing the occupational levels similar to that of the hasher is distasteful to the aspiring college man. Table 1 presents the mean prestige ranks assigned by 276 freshman and sophomore students in basic social science classes to ten part-time jobs typically held by male college students. As indicated in the table, the male students, on the average, rank the job of hasher last. The female students rank the jobs of off-campus restaurant helper and movie usher lower than the job of hasher. None of the student evaluators were fraternity or sorority members.

The college student has, in general, a middle-class view of work—that is, work should enhance one's prestige, provide for the realization of one's talents, and be satisfying and desirable in itself. This view is in contrast to that of the lower class

TABLE 1

Mean Prestige Ranks Assigned by Lower Division Students to Ten Typical Part-time Jobs Held by Male College Students

	Average Rank By Sex	
Part-time Job	Males (N=112)	Females (N=164)
Bellboy	6.8	6.8
Grocery Clerk	5.9	5.8
Life Guard	4.0	3.5
Hasher	7.4	7.0
Stock Clerk	4.9	5.0
Gas Station Attendant	6.1	6.0
Off-campus Restaurant Helper	7.1	7.1
Reader	2.8	2.6
Library Assistant	3.4	2.9
Movie Usher	6.6	7.5

which sees work as an unpleasant but necessary means of securing food and shelter, and as being neither interesting nor desirable in itself.[15] To the members of the lower class who must pursue such "drudgery," the college student imputes low intelligence, irresponsibility, and generalized inferiority.[16] The hasher then finds himself in the unique situation of having middle-class definitions and expectations of work, but performing tasks and conforming to expectations which clearly are representative of a lower-class job.

When in a position in which he must profess the nature of his employment, the hasher's admission is inevitably quickly followed by a qualifying statement: "It's a

---

[14] R. M. MacIver, *Society: A Textbook of Sociology* (New York: Rinehart & Co., 1937).

[15] Krech, Crutchfield, and Ballachey, *op. cit.*, p. 283.

[16] Helen M. Davidson, F. Reissman, and Edna Meyers, "Personality Characteristics Attributed to the Worker," *Journal of Social Psychology*, 57 (June 1962), pp. 155–160.

means to an end," "I'm just doing this until I find something more suitable," "It's the only job I could get with hours that won't interfere with my class schedule," and so on. The *temporary* nature of the job is stressed, and a point is made of demonstrating to the questioner that the hasher's primary role is that of student. (Table 1 indicates the high student ranking of the "scholarly" student related jobs of reader and library assistant.) The hasher's friends and acquaintances are often observed to ask him why he does such work, thus indicating a violation of their expectations of him as a college man. Sometimes a hasher will describe, with a leer, his job as an opportunity to "get near all those girls," and will gloss over the unpleasant realities of his task. In fact, some of the hashers interviewed stated that they initially took the job with the hope that they would "get the inside track" to a covey of coeds. This hope, of course, vanished in the face of the blunt reality of sorority girl-hasher social distance.

In the subject sorority house, there is a formal rule forbidding dating between the hashers and the sorority girls, and social intercourse within the house is maintained at as impersonal, employer- employee level as possible. Fraternization has been discouraged to the point where the girls and the hashers both feel uncomfortable if they have to interact on a level other than that called for by the job.

The no-dating rule in the subject sorority has been rigidly followed only for the last two years. The older hashers often speak of those "good old days a couple of years ago" when the girls were "somehow much nicer." Pertinent here is the hasher's definition of the sorority member who is a "good kid." In every case interviewed, the hasher's description of this ideal sorority girl centered on the attribute of "naturalness"—that is, a tendency to "be herself" and not to "look down" on the hasher, thus not stressing his subservient role. A good house to work for is one in which you are "treated like a human being." Good kids and good houses, then are those that treat the individual less like a hasher and more like a college man. W. F. Whyte observed that a conflict situation resulted among restaurant personnel when persons of high status had their activities initiated by persons perceived by them to be of lower status.[17] Many of the hashers are upper classmen, yet they must take orders from and wait on freshman girls. Any sorority member who minimizes this status threat is appreciated by the hasher as a "good kid."

Whyte also noted that in the restaurant under his observation it was not uncommon for female employees to initiate the action of male employees—e.g., waitresses giving orders to male cooks. Since in our society the male sex role generally includes the expectation that he be the originator of action between the sexes, that he dominate in heterosexual interpersonal relations, Whyte saw the role reversal in the restaurant as a key source of employee dissatisfaction. He cites a number of occasions where male employees contrived ways to avoid having to receive direct orders from female employees.[18] Similarly, in an analysis of some of the factors contributing to alienation from work, Blauner observed that "jobs differ in the degree to which they permit the particular 'manly virtues' that in our society are deemed ap-

---

[17] W. F. Whyte, "The Social Structure of the Restaurant," *American Journal of Sociology,* 54 (January 1949), pp. 302–310.

[18] *Ibid.,* pp. 305–307.

propriate to a 'real man.'"[19] One of the factors Blauner emphasizes is the degree to which the job allows sexual expression and status dominance with respect to women. It can be seen that the job of hasher includes both the sex role reversal that Whyte viewed as disruptive of the work situation and the lack of sexual expression and status dominance over women that Blauner saw as being a contributing factor to alienation from work. (Note, as indicated in Table 1, the high prestige position of the life guard, a very masculine job.)

The kitchen, called "The Inside" by the hasher, is his stronghold—within it he is in close association with other like-situated individuals. In the dining room, "The Outside," are "them," the girls. Interaction through the swinging doors might best be described as studied aloofness on the part of the girls and overt hostility on the part of the hashers. Orwell writes of the "double door between us (kitchen help and waiters) and the dining room" and contrasts the spontaneity of emotion, the relative relaxation, and the we-feeling of the kitchen with the controlled, tense, and guarded interaction with the customers. "It is an instructive sight," continues Orwell, "to see a waiter going into a hotel dining room. The set of his shoulders alters; all the dirt and hurry and irritation have dropped off in an instant. He glides over the carpet, with a solemn priest-like air."[20] Scott describes a similar phenomenon in the paddock, the private world of the professional jockeys and handlers. According to Scott, when in the paddock with his peers, the jockey or the handler "can no longer fake his behavior . . . The paddock represents that point where ordinary vigilance in role deception cannot be sustained."[21] Becker's description of the deliberately maintained self-isolation of the dance-band musician provides an interesting parallel to the hasher's kitchen stronghold. Becker observes that "the musician is, as a rule, spatially isolated from the audience, being placed on a platform barrier that prevents any direct interaction. This isolation is welcomed because the audience, being made up of squares, is felt to be potentially dangerous . . . Musicians, lacking the usually provided physical barriers, often improvise their own and effectively segregate themselves from their audience."[22]

The hasher, of course, is not able to isolate himself from the "clients" as readily as the dance-band musician or even the professional waiter. He must interact with the girls in the sorority house, on the campus, and often in the classroom. Neither is he so obligated, on the other hand, to restrain himself from insulting the "clients." Though hashers are formally expected to be polite to the girls "no matter what," and though they are still bound by the "gentleman" expectation for college men, they often are not subtle in their demonstrations of displeasure with the girls.

The girls very often refer to the individual as "hasher," rather than by given name, and are quite free with orders and criticism. Any praise usually takes on a con-

---

[19] Robert Blauner, *Work, Self, and Manhood: Some Reflections on Technology and Identity*, paper read at the annual meeting of the American Sociological Association, Montreal, Canada, September, 1964.

[20] Orwell, *op. cit.*, p. 86.

[21] Marvin B. Scott, "A Note on the Place of Truth," *Berkeley Journal of Sociology*, 8 (June 1963), p. 38.

[22] Becker, *op. cit.*, p. 142.

descending tone—"nice hasher," "nice boy," and so on. The girl's view of the hasher in the subject sorority house is revealed by the fact that one of the initiation requirements for a pledge is that she sing a love song to a hasher while he sits on her lap. This is taken to be one of the initiation rites that "humbles the pledges." (Ironically, the hashers themselves use this as a kind of initiation rite for entrance into their informal work group. That is, the newest hasher is the one who is made available to the pledge for the love song, and after he has been so used, he is told by his fellow hashers that he now knows "what working in the sorority is really like.")

The hashers seem to get much satisfaction from "getting the girls' goats." The kitchen often resounds with gleefully shared exclamations like "Boy, did I get *her* mad!" and "I sure told *her* off!" Spilling of food while serving, ignoring an order, sharp answers to criticism, and any other verbal aggression is rewarded with the plaudits of the other hashers—"That'll show them"; "That'll shape her up!" While in the kitchen the hashers will often deliberately make noises (loud talking, whistling, banging of pots and pans) with the intent of disturbing the girls. In the subject sorority, the hashers will save the food scraps from the preparation phase of the meal, and while the girls are eating will overload the garbage disposal unit and convulse with laughter as the mechanism emits loud and excruciating gurgles, whines, and crunches. "It's hard to tell," reported one chuckling hasher, "which garbage disposals sound the worst—the ones out in the dining room, or the one in the kitchen."

Orwell describes the kitchen personnel's disdain for the customer of the hotel restaurant—a disdain developed as a defense against the "superiority" of the customer.

One waiter told Orwell that, "as a matter of pride, he had sometimes wrung a dirty dishcloth into the customer's soup before taking it in, just to be revenged upon a member of the bourgeoisie."[23] Another waiter scolded Orwell, "Fool! Why do you wash that plate? Wipe it on your trousers. Who cares about the customers? They don't know what's going on. What is restaurant work? You are carving a chicken and it falls on the floor. You apologize, you bow, you go out; and in five minutes you come back by another door—with the same chicken. That is restaurant work!"[24] So also is it hasher revenge. Besides the deliberate casualness toward dropped food and the amused "what they don't know won't hurt them attitude," on numerous other occasions in the subject sorority minor assaults were made on foods to be served to the girls—e.g., a marble tossed into a gelatin and grape salad mold; a small amount of grass thrown in with cooking spinach ("for those cows"); each dinner roll "thrown around the bases" from one hasher to another before it was placed in the serving basket; a drop or two of blood from the cut finger of a hasher splashed into a pot of soup ("This ought to make those bloodsuckers happy!"); green food coloring added to the milk; salt shaker tops loosened so they would fall off in the girls plates; etc. The actions themselves are, of course, less significant than the glee with which they are shared by the hashers who are "getting to the girls."

An extremely interesting phenomenon revealed by the participant observation (and confirmed in other than the subject sorority by interviews) is the nature of the derisive terms the hashers have for the

---

[23] Orwell, *op. cit.*, p. 113.
[24] *Ibid.*, p. 114.

girls. Almost always, the names have animal referents, and the animal is most often the pig—"Here they come, let's slop the troughs"; "Souee" and "Oink-Oink" grumbled (on the kitchen side of the swinging door) as the hashers walk out of the kitchen to serve the food; "What do the pigs want now"; "Let's go clean out the feeding pens"; "Mush, you huskies!" The records contain a startling number of this kind of statement, as well as many other derogatory comments about the girl's manners, breeding, and femininity. It would appear that the hashers are projecting feelings of their own "low born" position upon the girls. It is almost as if they are saying, "See, we aren't so bad, look at those slobs out in the dining room!"

The physical appearance of the sorority girls is also called into question by the hashers. "They've all had their faces remolded, and they still can't get dates." "A guy would have to be pretty hard up to take out one of these dogs." "They must have an 'ugly requirement' in order to get into this sorority." The hasher lets his peers know that even if he *could* date one of the girls in the sorority, he wouldn't. Thus is some modicum of control gained by the hasher over the emasculating "no dating" situation.

Within the kitchen, escape mechanisms of various sorts are everywhere apparent. Horseplay is the order of the day, with episodic food throwing and water splashing bouts, word fads, running "in group" jokes, and general zaniness. Of particular interest are the sets of activities which the hashers in the subject sorority house referred to as "bits." A "bit" is a relatively organized session of play-acting, originally arising spontaneously, and having a central theme and roles for each of the hashers. During the "bit" everything in the work setting, people, actions, and utensils, would be made a part of the scene, and the hashers would adopt the argot relevant to the situation enacted. For example, the "bit" for one work session staged the kitchen and dining room as a hell ship, with the hashers cast as the mutineers, the girls as "Powdered Pirates," and the cooks as "Ahab" and "Bly." Knives became "harpoons," the dinner meat became "salt horse," going out into the dining room was "walking the plank," one abundantly endowed sorority sister became the "treasure chest," and so on. In another session the kitchen was part of the Third Reich, with cooks "Goebbels" and "Goering" sending the hasher "Pots and Pans Panzer Corps" out to face the girls, who were now cast as "Storm Troopers" and "Girdled Gestapo." Serving the food was making a "Blitzkrieg," chicken was a "Luftwaffe Loser," and "bravery under fire" while in the dining room was rewarded with lettuce leaf medals at an "awards ceremony." "Bits," if contagious enough, would go on for more than one work session or even more than one day. Often the same "bit" would be recurrent, returning for replay every few months and year after year (e.g., the science fiction or horror movie "bit," the gangster "bit," and the western hero-villain "bit").

It would appear that the "bit" serves a number of functions for the hashers. It is, not unlike the therapeutic applications of **psychodrama** and **role playing**, an opportunity for a more or less legitimized expression of hostility. It serves also as a distraction from the repetitive drudgery and potential boredom of the hasher's work tasks, allowing him, in effect, to be more creative and expressive while on the job. Furthermore, the "bit," while affecting the hashers' enactment of an interconnecting and interdependent set of fantasy roles, serves to tighten the cohesion of the informal work group. As one hasher said, not without pride, "When we've got our own laughs going for us, this job is no sweat." Lastly, it would seem that the hasher welcomes the relatively clearly defined and uncomplicated roles of the "bit." Even if the play-acting roles are acknowledged fancy and are ephemeral, they are less ambiguous, less conflict-ridden, and less distasteful than his actual work role.

Other forms of symbolic withdrawal from the hasher work situation are also common. In the subject sorority house, the threats to quit, to leave the field, ran about 20 per week. Rarely did any hasher go through the entire week without stating his intention to quit the next week. Each new work day brought with it a new challenge to "finish up faster than yesterday, and get the hell out of here."

In the kitchen, stories of the "I am a great lover" variety are daily bantered about by the hashers, expressed in a fashion that seems to insist "away from here, I really do manipulate and dominate the coeds." Many joking references and comic routines concerning homosexuality are observed, the hashers themselves using a falsetto voice or feigning homosexual characteristics. The homosexual routine does, in fact, at times represent itself with the elaborateness of a "bit." Such behavior is often seen in social environments where the masculine role is perceived by males to be threatened. Elkin, for example, describes clinically the need for overt erotic expression manifest among members of Army barracks.[25] Zurcher describes the "salty language" and "sea stories" of sexual conquest among recruits isolated in the Naval Training Center.[26] Following Blauner's lead mentioned above, it may be that the emphasis on sexual topics during the work sessions is an effective means whereby the hashers can put some of their sex role expectations back into the job.

On those nights when the girls bring male guests to the sorority house, the hashers are especially belligerent. Venomously, the hashers comment about the dates the girls have—"I wonder if she's paying him a flat fee, or by the hour." "God, she must have robbed a grave to get him!" On such occasions, the role conflict of the hasher is exacerbated, since he must wait on college *couples*. Some hashers flatly refuse to work at these times. Others will agree to work in the kitchen, but refuse to wait on tables.

The conflicts and resultant reactions thus far reported are seen, as indicated by the interview material, to be typical of the hasher-in-sorority situation, though the degree of conflict and defense varies from house to house. The interview material also revealed that two hasher groups would enter intramural athletic contests as representatives of their sororities, but the remaining six groups steadfastly refused to do so. The key variable influencing the degree to which the hashers would thus agree to identify with the sorority appeared to be the degree of status differentiation in the house—those with more rigid "class" lines, thus with a situation that emphasized the hasher-college man conflict, are not identified with and are not represented. The two sorority houses represented in intramural sports by their hasher groups are more informal and relaxed in

---

[25]H. Elkin, "Aggressive and Erotic Tendencies in Army Life," *The American Journal of Sociology*, 51 (March 1946), pp. 408–413.

[26]Louis A. Zurcher, "The Naval Recruit Training Center: A Study of Role Behavior in a Total Institution," *Sociological Inquiry*, in press.

hasher-member interaction.

It appears that the degree of **social distance** between hashers and members is less a function of the size of the house than a function of its relative status on the campus. The "'loser" sororities apparently have greater need to maintain class lines within their houses than do the "top" sororities. This relationship was difficult to assess and is cautiously presented, considering the techniques used in this study and the fact that the work setting of the hasher is affected by other variables—e.g., the managerial styles of the house mothers and the cooks. The significant point is that, in *all* the houses considered here, there was evidence of some degree of social distance between the hashers and the girls, of hasher role conflict, and of the hashers' need to abate that conflict.

Most of the sororities permit a yearly "turn-about" day, during which the girls wait on the hashers. Such role reversals are seen in other social groups that have a sharp status differential and restricted social interaction—e.g., Naval vessels (enlisted men take over the ship for a few hours when it crosses the Equator);[27] military academies (lower classmen are allowed to command the upper classmen for a day),[28] asylums and prisons (skits in which patients and inmates mimic the staff members).[29] Such behavior can be taken to be a clear indicator of the awareness of and resentment of status inferiority.

---

[27] Louis A. Zurcher, "The Sailor Aboard Ship: A Study of Role Behavior in a Total Institution," *Social Forces*, 43 (March 1965), pp. 389–400.

[28] Sanford Dornbusch, "The Military Academy as an Assimilating Institution." *Social Forces*, 33 (May 1955), pp. 316–321.

[29] E. Goffman, *Asylums* (New York: Doubleday & Co., 1961).

Conclusion

The role conflict experienced by the individual who must enact both the roles of hasher in a sorority and college man is seen to be accompanied by a pattern of defense mechanisms that serve to abate the conflict. The defense pattern consists of: (1) rationalization (the job is only temporary); (2) denial (reluctance to identify with the job); (3) projection (the girls are "low born"); (4) aggression (verbal and mitigated physical hostility toward the girls); (5) withdrawal (horseplay, general zaniness on the job, and threats to quit); (6) compensation (emphasis on discussions of sexual dominance). These defense mechanisms are, however, clearly seen to be expectations of the informal organization of the hasher group. Like the "Rate Buster" of Mayo,[30] a hasher who works too hard, who tries to please the girls, or who does not join in the horseplay is branded as a "brown noser," and suffers group ostracism. This seldom happens, though, since on the first day of his job as a hasher, the individual experiences role conflict, and has need of some means for resolution of that conflict. Thus he is quite willing, in fact, eager, to accept the defense system that has become institutionalized in the informal work group. By enactment of these behaviors he not only implements functional defenses, but he gains the security of membership in the informal organization.

In summary, then, the role of hasher in a sorority house demands that the incumbent behave in a manner inconsistent with the expectations for a college man. The individual who must enact both of these

---

[30] F. J. Roethlisberger and William J. Dickson, *Management and the Worker* (New York: John Wiley & Sons, 1964), p. 522.

roles must resolve the dissonance in the best way he can. He is aided in this resolution by an institutionalized defense pattern which is part of the expectations of the hasher informal organization. Thus in this case of perpetuated role conflict, defense mechanisms, though they are implemented by individuals, are socially delimited by and within the conflict engendering social situation.

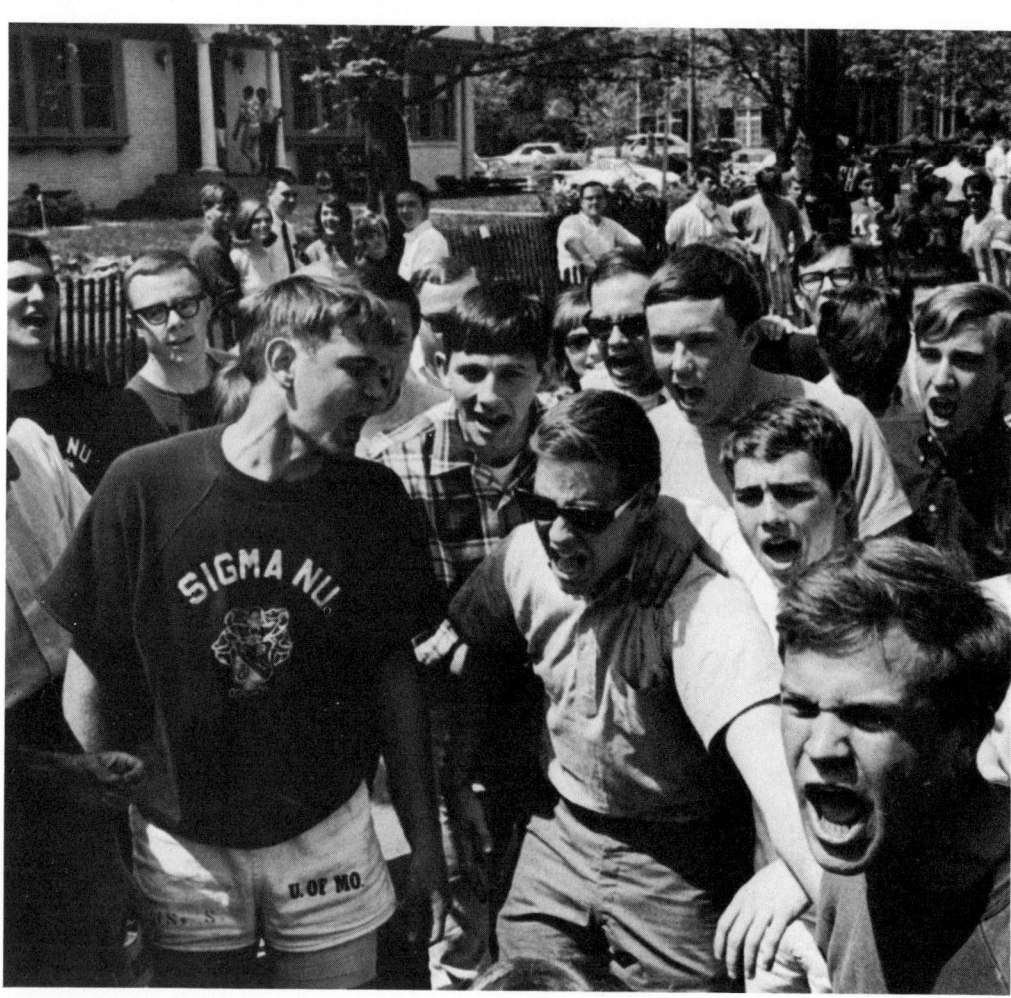

SOCIAL STRATIFICATION

Social Class and Campus Dating

IRA L. REISS

General Background of the Research Area

About 30 years ago, there began to appear in the sociological literature accounts of dating practices on college campuses. Although earlier writers had mentioned the same phenomenon, it was a 1937 journal article by Willard Waller that has come to epitomize this early literature on campus dating customs.[1] Waller reported that the older accepted code of a courtship system that led to formal engagement and marriage in a predictable fashion had decayed and was being replaced by a thrill seeking and exploitive type of relationship which was not integrated with marriage. This new type of relationship was a dalliance relationship, needed to fill in the time it took to get a college education and establish oneself financially. Connected with this type of dating was the "rating-dating complex" which was a set of customs that established one's prestige on campus and which in turn determined one's dating desirability. The key prestige variables were things like popularity, access to cars and money, and belonging to the best Greek organizations. Serious, marriage oriented dating did not involve these prestige ratings. Thus, such prestige rating-and-dating was not viewed as "true" courtship. This campus dating system was discerned by Waller at the Pennsylvania State Univer-

---

[1] Willard Waller, "The Rating and Dating Complex," *American Sociological Review*, 2 (October, 1937), pp. 727–734. Joseph K. Folsom was one of the sociologists who presented similar ideas before Waller's article.

sity in the early 1930's and was documented by discussion and interviews with students.

In order to clarify the place of my research, it may be well to recount very briefly a few of the relevant studies that followed the Waller article. In the 1940's Hollingshead brought forth considerable evidence indicating the social behavior of adolescents was functionally related to the social class of their parents.[2] Particularly relevant here was Hollingshead's finding that dating among high school students was heavily controlled by social class background. Then shortly after the war Harold Christensen, Robert Blood, and William Smith, in separate research work, tested college students to see if the sort of rating factors (cars, money, dancing ability, etc.) which Waller found to hold at Penn State would also hold true in their samples.[3] They each found that the students in their sample largely rejected the "competitive-materialistic" items that Waller reported and instead favored "personality" factors such as "sense of humor, cheerful, good sport, natural and considerate."[4] Blood found that the type of **value system** Waller was speaking of was most likely to be found among the Greeks on campus but that even there it was not supported unanimously by any means. These findings brought into question Waller's own views.[5] Nevertheless, it must be borne in mind that Waller's observations may have been correct for the time and place they were made.

In 1960 Everett Rogers and Eugene Havens published a study done on Iowa State College students.[6] They had 11 judges rank the Greek organizations and the major residence on campus and then, by interviews with a random sample of 725 students and by checking the student newspapers, they gathered evidence regarding the relation of prestige to dating of various types. They found a high probability for people to date those who are ranked similar to themselves. They concluded from this:

Therefore, Waller's hypothesis that prestige ranking governs casual campus dating but not more serious mate selection is not substantiated to any great degree by the present findings. Instead, these finding indicate that students follow prestige lines at all stages of the mate selection process.[7]

A study of fraternity pledging at an East-

---

[2] August B. Hollingshead, *Elmtown's Youth*, New York: John Wiley and Son, 1949.
[3] Harold T. Christensen, *Marriage Analysis*, New York: Ronald Press, 1958, 2nd edition, esp. pp. 235–243, 261–264; Robert O. Blood, Jr., "A Retest of Waller's Rating Complex," *Marriage and Family Living*, 17 (February, 1955), pp. 41–47; William M. Smith, Jr., "Rating and Dating: A Restudy," *Marriage and Family Living*, 14 (November, 1952), pp. 312–317.
[4] See in particular Robert O. Blood, Jr., "Uniformities and Diversities in Campus Dating Preferences," *Marriage and Family Living*, 18 (February, 1956), pp. 37–45. An interesting report of a similar research project on a Negro campus can be found in Charles S. Anderson and Joseph S. Himes, "Dating Values and Norms on a Negro College Campus," *Marriage and Family Living*, 21 (August, 1959), pp. 227–229.

[5] At about this same time an article by Samuel H. Lowrie had questioned Waller's characterization of campus dating. See "Dating Theories and Student Responses," *American Sociological Review*, 16 (June, 1951), pp. 334–340. A more recent discussion of this point can be found in Jack Delora, "Social Systems of Dating on a College Campus," *Marriage and Family Living*, 25 (February, 1963), pp. 81–84.
[6] Everett M. Rogers and A. Eugene Havens, "Prestige Rating and Mate Selection on a College Campus," *Marriage and Family Living*, 22 (February, 1960), pp. 55–59.
[7] Rogers and Havens, *ibid.*, p. 59.

ern college by Gene Levine and Leila Sussmann lent support to the Rogers and Havens findings on prestige factors in dating.[8] Levine and Sussmann found that it was the wealthier students who more often pledged and who more often were accepted into fraternities and who in addition had the "proper" attitudes toward fraternities. Thus, there seemed to be a class factor not only in campus ratings but in parental background that distinguished the Greek and non-Greek student.

In effect, these findings on campus dating radically revamped much of Waller's position. The "competitive-materialistic" system of values that Waller described seems to be present on college campuses today mainly as a **sub-cultural** element, most likely to be found among the Greek organizations. But the more recent findings on class prestige factors in dating are even more important theoretically. Waller's view of the prestige system at Penn State was not a view of people of different parental social classes dating along those class lines. Rather, Waller explicitly stated that he did not believe there were any basic social class background differences among the students:

The students of this college are predominantly taken from the lower half of the middle classes, and constitute a remarkable homogeneous group. Numerous censuses of the occupation of fathers and of living expenses seem to establish this fact definitely.[9]

---

[8]Gene N. Levine and Leila A. Sussmann, "Social Change and Sociability in Fraternity Pledging," *The American Journal of Sociology*, 65 (January, 1960), pp. 391–399.

[9]Waller, *op. cit.*, p. 729.

Social Class and Campus Dating 161

The prestige that Waller spoke of was obtained by success in dating the highest ranked girls and boys. The rating-dating system was a popularity system in which having a good line, knowing how to dance, dressing nicely, all had a part. It was, to Waller, based predominantly on dating desirability, and social class in any fundamental sense was not the basis of it. The system produced a sort of superficial rating-dating class of its own rather than depending on any more basic class system. Thus, one important question now is, is there a more fundamental class system both on and off campus with which the campus dating system is integrated and which Waller has overlooked? The Levine and Sussmann study of fraternities lends support to a positive answer to this question as does the Rogers and Havens study. Research on social class homogamy in marriage and engagement also strongly supports the view of the importance of social class in mating.[10] Careful research of this sort has not often been done on the college campus. In fact, some writers stress the democratization effects of college life and the homogeneity of social class on campuses.[11] Nevertheless, I am suggesting that the social classes on campus are not simple "popularity" classes but that they are stable class structures based on many campus values and that they reflect parental social class and affect serious as well as casual dating.

Theory and Hypotheses

In its broadest sense the orientation of my research embodies the well tested theory that *the dating patterns of a group will follow the social class lines of that group and thereby encourage class endogamous dat-*

---

[10] The classic study establishing homogamy in mating is Ernest W. Burgess and Paul Wallin, *Engagement and Marriage,* New York: Lippincott, 1953. There is an excellent account of the relation of parental class and student dating in Winston W. Ehrmann, *Premarital Dating Behavior,* New York: Henry Holt, 1959, pp. 144–169. For interesting evidence that sorority and fraternity people marry each other, see A. Philip Sundal and Thomas C. McCormic, "Age at Marriage and Mate Selection: Madison, Wisconsin, 1937–1943," *American Sociological Review,* 16 (February, 1951), pp. 37–48, esp. p. 47. Sixty-one per cent of the sorority girls married fraternity boys. A recent study reporting class homogamy in campus marriages and showing parental influence is Robert H. Coombs, "Reinforcement of Values in the Parental Home as a Factor in Mate Selection," *Marriage and Family Living,* 24 (May, 1962), pp. 155–157. For a much older statement along these lines see Alan Bates, "Parental Roles in Courtship," *Social Forces,* 20 (May, 1942), pp. 483–486. For evidence on the continued importance of social class in mate selection in general, see Simon Dinitz, Franklin Banks, and Benjamin Pasamanick, "Mate Selection and Social Class: Changes During the Past Quarter Century," *Marriage and Family Living,* 22 (November, 1960), pp. 348–351; J. Daniel Ray, "Dating Behavior as Related to Organizational Prestige," (M.A. Thesis), Indiana University, 1942; Ernest A. Smith, "Dating and Courtship at Pioneer College," *Sociology and Social Research,* 40, 1955, pp. 92–98. Marvin Sussman has shown the ways parents control marriage in a New Haven study: "Parental Participation in Mate Selection and Its Effect Upon Family Continuity," *Social Forces,* 32 (October, 1953), pp. 76–81.

[11] Listed below is one such study that tested for class homogamy in campus marriages and found little evidence of it. These authors believe that the campus is a democratizing influence which *reduces* class endogamy. Clark R. Leslie and Arthur H. Richardson, "Family Versus Campus Influences in Relation to Mate Selection," *Social Problems,* 4 (October, 1956), pp. 117–121. The literature on intermarriage also mentions that the campus breaks through traditional barriers. See Albert I. Gordon, *Intermarriage,* Boston: Beacon Press, 1964. However, there could be a democratization concerning interfaith marriage, without affecting class endogamy.

ing and mating.[12] The implications of this theory have only rarely been tested on college campuses although it is often spoken about.[13] It follows from this theory that one should expect to find a stratified dating system on any campus, except those campuses where, due to extremely small size and homogeneity, there is no class distinction among the students. It also follows from our knowledge that student behavior reflects parental class, that the social class differences among students should reflect class differences among the parental adult population.[14] It is of theoretical value to know not only whether or not the campus is stratified but to know whether the class system tends to reflect in some ways the parental class lines. If it does, then one latent consequence of such a system may be to maintain some remnant of adult control over mating via the promotion of class endogamous marriages which parents generally seem to favor.

The Waller approach to campus dating focused on specific date-rating factors and took them to be the essence of the dating system. It is my contention that the rating factors are merely symptoms of basic campus and parental class distinctions and that the entire system can best be understood from this social class perspective. The rating-dating system of any sort, competitive or personality based, is believed to be a direct reflection of the campus and parental class system and a way of clarifying and identifying class differences. Such clarification is viewed as part of a serious mate-selection system. Thus, Waller's view that rating-dating is a dalliance system and not integrated with serious dating or mating is questioned.

In summary, I am proposing to test two hypotheses related to the basic "class-dating" theory: (1) serious dating on campus will be in line with an existing campus stratification system, and (2) campus dating will reflect the parental class system.

Methodology

The data on campus dating were gathered at a coeducational liberal arts college in Virginia. The 19 Greek organizations (ten fraternities and nine sororities) had 840 members and 151 pledges out of a total student body of 1800 single students. There were 809 single independent students. There was a relatively even sex ratio in both Greek and independent groupings. It was decided that full information on Greek serious dating practices would be obtained as one test of the stratification-dating theory. If in 19 highly organized fraternities and sororities there was no indication of the relation of social class and serious dating, then the theory and its derivative hypotheses would be brought into question. In addition to the sample of all seriously dating Greeks, I drew a **random sample** which I could use to rank all campus groups, to obtain information on pa-

---

[12]The references in footnote 10 are relevant here. Also, the role of stratification in love relations has been dealt with in William J. Goode, "The Theoretical Importance of Love," *American Sociological Review*, 24 (February, 1959), pp. 38–47.

[13]For a relatively early statement in this area and an interesting test of courtship among college men see Robert F. Winch, "Interrelations Between Certain Social Backgrounds and Parent-Son Factors in A Study of Courtship Among College Men," *American Sociological Review*, 11 (June, 1946), pp. 333–341, esp. p. 338. For a study showing similarities and changes in basic values see Robert McGinnis, "Campus Views in Mate Selection: A Repeat Study," *Social Forces*, 36 (May, 1958), pp. 368–373.

[14]Hollingshead had found considerable evidence that the social class of one's parent was a good predictor of adolescent behavior. Hollingshead, *op. cit.*

rental social class, and to further test on a representative sample the relation of campus class to dating patterns in both independent and Greek student groups. The random sample was an important group since it represented the entire campus. The all Greek sample was used to give a fuller and more detailed picture of the serious dating patterns of the Greeks.

The Greek organizations all met on Monday nights and usually had over 90% attendance at meetings. I sent one student assistant to each Greek organization to obtain information regarding all "serious" dating relationships.[15] A serious dating relation was defined as a relatively exclusive dating relation such as going steady, being pinned or engaged. All such relations were reported to my informants together with information on the Greek, independent, or off-campus status of the dating partner. If class-dating were found in these serious relations it would be evidenced that serious dating relationships were not *just* based on "**personality factors**" but that these very personality factors could possibly be viewed as influenced by stratification factors.[16] Finally, if one wanted to check on the relation of mating to stratification then serious dating and not just casual dating must be checked.

The check of all 19 Greek organizations yielded 133 serious dating relations for sorority girls and 112 such relations for fraternity boys. About 30% of the Greek members were involved in serious relations. Sixty-two of these relations were between a sorority girl and a fraternity boy. (These figures are for members only, not pledges. Pledges were also investigated

and they will be reported on later.) The 62 couples consisting entirely of Greeks on campus afforded a check on the reliability of our information. If our data were accurate the sororities and fraternities should each report 62 matched serious relations. This was the case.[17]

In addition to this all-Greek sample, a random sample of all single students on the campus was drawn and given a questionnaire. One hundred forty-four questionnaires were obtained.[18] There were 25 non-responses who were mostly students who were not located by my research assistants. Questionnaires were given out and picked up within a few hours by my 19 assistants. The questionnaire asked the respondent to rank each of the 10 fraternities as high, medium, or low, and to do the same for the 9 sororities, and to give reasons for the rankings assigned. In addition, questions were asked concerning the students' background including income and occupation of father, their own dating behavior, and the relative rank they would give to male and female independents and Greeks.

The all-Greek sample containing all 245 seriously dating Greeks was used as one test of Hypothesis One concerning the congruence of the dating system with the campus class system. The random sample of the campus was used to further check this hypothesis for both Greeks and independents, to rank all campus groups, and also to check the second hypothesis concerning the relation of campus class to parental social class.

---

[15] The student assistants went back two more times to verify and check all information they had received the first time.
[16] Blood, *op. cit.*, Smith, *op. cit.*; both stress personality factors as crucial in dating.
[17] One additional couple broke up due to differences in the definition of their relationship that came to the foreground during the research.
[18] There were 16 pledges and 5 No Answers on organizational membership which were not included in the general analysis of Greeks and independents in this paper. This left 123 respondents to be used in the general analysis. The pledges were analyzed separately.

TABLE 1

*Percentage Distribution of Types of Serious Dating Partners Among Greeks in the All Greek Sample**

	Percentage of Each Type of Partner				Number of Serious Dating Relations**
	High Ranked Greeks	Low Ranked Greeks	Off-Campus	Independent	
High Ranked Fraternities	63	12	17	8	(86)
Low Ranked Fraternities	14	19	23	44	(47)
High Ranked Sororities	44	8	48	0	(60)
Low Ranked Sororities	15	21	45	19	(52)

*Significant differences exist between high and low ranked Greeks in their choice of a Greek dating partner and in the per cent dating Greeks and in the per cent dating independents. Also, a significant difference exists between fraternities and sororities in per cent dating off-campus.

**The per cent of total members involved in serious relations is not significantly different for these four groups. Going from top to bottom of the table the per cent is: 31, 27, 32, 25.

The Campus Stratification System

If the first hypothesis is correct there should be a significant **association** between the rank of the various campus segments and the serious dating patterns of these groups. Table 1 presents information on all the Greek students who were involved in serious dating. The fraternities and sororities were listed according to the ranking assigned by the random sample of campus students. The majority of students agreed on all rankings, although the rankings on sororities were more unanimous than the rankings on fraternities. The fraternities were divided into five high and five low ranked groups and the sororities into five high and four low ranked groups. It should be noted that many other cuts were tried on these data and the results were the same, i.e., there is a significant and strong relation between one's organizational rank and that of one's serious date. This is particularly true for the high ranked Greeks.

Table 1 also shows that although all Greek organizations have roughly the same per cent involved in serious dating, the high ranked Greek organizations (particularly the fraternities) have a significantly higher per cent involved in serious dating with members of Greek organizations rather than with off-campus or independents. Serious dating within the Greek system is dominated by the high ranked organizations. The low ranked Greeks, for the most part, obtain their serious dates outside the Greek system. It should be noted here that the Greek dating reported by our random sample was very similar and this is evidence of the representativeness of our random sample.

When we look in Table 1 at the relation of sorority ranking to the choice of dating an off-campus or an independent male, the results are rather striking. Of the high ranked sorority girls who are not dating within the Greek system, all of them are dating off-campus and not one is seriously dating an independent male on campus. Whereas, of the low ranked sorority girls, 19% seriously date independent males. Since there are an equal supply of Greeks and independents on campus and an equal sex ratio, this pattern seems to imply an avoidance of independents, perhaps due to a low ranking on campus. This avoidance is particularly pronounced for the high ranked sororities.

If we look at fraternity members in Table 1 to see their choice of off-campus or independent dates, we find a pattern somewhat similar to that of the sororities. Table 1 shows that the high ranked fraternity men prefer off-campus dates significantly more than the low ranked fraternity men. In fact, the low ranked fraternity men date independent females more than they date off-campus girls. Here too, then, is evidence that the independents are ranked low particularly by high ranked Greeks, but it would seem that the independent females are not avoided to the extent that the independent males are. Our double standard culture dictates that in a dating relation, if one person is to be higher in status than the other, it should be the male; and perhaps this is why independent females are not avoided as much as independent males.[19]

There is direct evidence of the relative ranking of campus groups from our random sample which can be compared with the above evidence from the Greek sample. We asked the random sample respondents to state their relative ranking of independent males and fraternity males and of independent females and sorority girls. Rankings were asked for in terms of one's personal views and not in terms of what one thought others would generally say. The results indicated that most individuals, except independent males, feel that independent males rank below fraternity males. The independent females were evenly divided regarding their own superiority, and the independent males closely agreed with them. However, most all the Greeks were convinced that sorority girls outranked the independent girls.[20]

It should be noted that this view of the independents is generally shared by both high and low ranked Greeks.[21] Thus, it would seem that when low ranked Greeks date independents, they believe they are dating "down" but are willing to do so for other compensatory reasons or, in the case of males, simply because they don't feel the distance is so great and that it is accepted for males to date down. Perhaps some of the low ranked fraternity males date independent females with sexual goals uppermost in mind. However, in serious dating relationships this is less likely to happen.[22]

---

[19]For evidence and elaboration on the double standard see Ira L. Reiss, *Premarital Sexual Standards in America,* Glencoe, Ill.: The Free Press, 1960, esp. ch. 4.

[20]Eighty per cent of the independent males thought they ranked higher than fraternity men but all other groups had over 80% who said the opposite. Fifty per cent of the independent females felt they ranked higher than sorority girls. Although the independent males agreed, over 80% of the Greeks disagreed.

[21]Low fraternity as compared to high fraternity men are somewhat kinder in their ratings of independents whereas low sorority girls are almost unanimous in giving low rank to independents. These differences were not quite significant.

[22]For data on this see Winston W. Ehrmann, *op. cit.,* chs. 4 and 5.

TABLE 2

Percentage of Those Who Date Greeks, Who Are Dating in High Ranked Greek Organizations, in the Random Sample

Group	Per cent Dating High Ranked Greeks
High Ranked Greeks	78₍₄₁₎*
Low Ranked Greeks	54₍₂₄₎
Independent Females	50₍₂₀₎
Independent Males	20₍₁₀₎

*The number to the right and below the percentage is the base for the percentage.

Additional evidence on this relative campus ranking comes from a further look at serious dating patterns of the independents in our random sample.[23] If independent males are ranked lower than the independent females, then it follows that the independent females in our random sample should report more serious relations with the upper classes, namely, the Greeks. This was the case—of 19 independent females with serious dates, 7 were with fraternity men. It should be noted that 5 of the 7 fraternity men dating independent females were from low ranking fraternities. This, too, would be expected. There were 11 independent males with serious dates, and only one was with a sorority girl and this was with a girl from the lowest ranking sorority on campus. Further, the independent females are more likely to have their serious dates on campus than are the independent males. Only one third of the serious dates were off campus for independent females, whereas two thirds of the serious dates of independent males were off campus. Finally, the independent females are involved with fraternity men about as much as the low ranked sorority girls, while the independent males are involved with sorority girls much less than low ranked fraternity males. The evidence on independents here is based on a small number of cases. However, since the results are consistent with several other checks, the confidence in the findings is increased.

In sum then, the stratification system which emerges at this point is one in which the Greeks are clearly at the top, but the low ranked Greeks are more likely to date seriously outside the Greek part of the system. In addition, the independents seem stratified by sex, with females ranked higher than males; and here too it is noted that the females have their serious dates more within the total campus system and the independent males have their serious dates predominantly outside the entire campus system.

Casual dating was also checked in the random sample and proved to follow stratification lines quite similar to serious dating. Many independents, especially males, do not date at all in Greek organizations. Table 2 shows the distribution of those students who do date Greeks. The same relations among high and low Greeks and

---

[23] The independent females reported the largest group of friends from the other three campus groups, thereby further showing their pivotal positions and their tendencies to date both independent and Greek boys.

male and female independents prevail in casual dating as prevailed in serious dating.[24] It may be argued that if casual dating and serious dating both show a similar relation to the campus rating system, then the rating system is integrated with serious dating and mating and is "true" courtship and not just a dalliance system as Waller contended.

An additional search was made via the questionnaire and campus records to see whether the above noted differences in campus prestige are related to differences in some key characteristics of the students in the four major campus groups. A comparison of age at which dating began among sorority and independent females revealed no significant differences. However, the same comparison of independent males and fraternity males revealed a moderately strong and almost significant difference.[25]

A stronger and a significant difference appeared between the fraternity and independent males when compared on whether they had been in love before. There was no significant difference among females.[26] Thus, it seems the fraternity males started dating earlier and had more love experiences. This "sociability" factor is one that was found to characterize fraternity men in the Levine and Sussmann study referred to above.[27] Such "sociability" background may well represent a social class difference in this sample as it did in the Levine and Sussmann sample.

A check of attitudes toward premarital intercourse was also undertaken. The independent males were the most conservative male group. This somewhat fits with their lack of dating and love experience. The low fraternity males were the most liberal group with high fraternity males falling in the middle. All females were about equally conservative.

The reasons for the relative ranking of the fraternities and sororities given by the total random sample were also examined to see if independents and Greeks differed here. All groups agreed that high ranking was given to a Greek organization for things such as sociability, intelligence and maturity, and campus activities. These were the most frequently mentioned ranking factors. There is evidence that these reasons are accurate perceptions of differences among the Greek organizations. A search of school records revealed that the high ranked Greeks control the student assembly and its officers. All but 7 of the 125 student assembly members during a three year period preceding the study were Greeks, and of the 118 Greeks, 87 were from high ranked Greek organizations. Of 63 Greek class officers, 53 were high

---

[24]Table 2 is composed of answers from those who do date in Greek organizations to the question, "In which Greek organizations have you dated the most?" Some respondents will include serious dating as well as casual. However, the bulk of the dating reported is casual. Further, when known serious dating is eliminated, the relationship still holds up the same as reported although a little weaker. Actually, the relation is understated since about 35% of the independent females and almost 60% of the independent males do not date Greeks at all. This fact supports the relation of social class and dating but is not presented in the table.

[25]Sorority girls had 74% who started dating by age 16 to the independent girls 66%. The percentages for fraternity and independent males were 65 and 41 respectively.

[26]Sorority girls had 84% who had been in love to the independent girls 94%. The percentages for fraternity and independent males were 96 and 60 respectively.

[27]Levine and Sussmann, op. cit.

ranked Greeks. This relation held up for sororities as well as fraternities.

Good looks and good grades were evaluated differently by Greek and independent males. The Greeks stressed good looks and the independents stressed good grades. Available evidence generally fits these rankings. In the three years preceding this study, 30 beauty queens were chosen. Five of them were low ranked Greeks; 25 were high ranked Greeks; none of the beauty queens were independents. In terms of academic grades, the high ranked sororities outdo the low ranked sororities. However, among males the situation is different and the high ranked fraternities do not outdo the low ranked fraternities in grades. The independent males are better than the fraternity males in grades; but the independent females are poorer than the sorority females. The academic grade records for a ten year period were checked and verified that this was a stable patterning of grades.

Finally, independent males valued dancing, sports, and parties less than fraternity males. The differences among sorority and independent females in rankings were fewer than those between fraternity and independent males. The sorority females gave more importance to such items as good manners, dress, and dancing ability, but otherwise there was general agreement. So here, too, the independent females are closer to the Greek females than the independent males are to the Greek males.

Some of the reasons for ranking Greek organizations are similar to the sort of factors about which Willard Waller wrote. In particular, this is true of such factors as "good dancer," "good dresser," "good looking." These factors were not the most frequently mentioned; nevertheless, here is evidence of the sort of rating-dating that Waller had in mind. However, and this is my major point here, to focus on these factors as the heart of the dating system and to conclude that the system is superficial and unintegrated with marriage is to miss the crux of the matter. I am suggesting that these factors are merely part of the complex of factors which defines what sort of organization the high ranked students on campus achieve. These prestige factors are some of the variables that go with belonging to a certain campus social class and serve to identify that class. They are merely symbols of campus class status, and it is that class status that is crucial, not the symbols.[28]

I should add here that an examination of the dating behavior of the 151 pledges in the Greek organizations revealed a very similar pattern to that of Greek members. This examination involved all pledges from all Greek organizations. Also, a study checking Greek rating and dating was done on this same campus in 1954 with quite similar results.[29] Thus, the stratification we are describing has roots in the past and our examination of pledges indicates that it is being extended into the future.

Campus Social Class and Parental Social Class

Although other studies have shown that parental social class affects dating and mating, there is very little data on the rela-

---

[28] For a discussion of how fashion in dress symbolizes status see Bernard Barber and Lyle S. Lobel, "Fashion in Women's Clothes and the American Social System," *Social Forces*, 31 (December, 1952), pp. 124–131.

[29] This unpublished study was done by two students: Withers Davis and Penny Hutchinson.

TABLE 3

Percentage of Fathers with High Status Occupations for Various Campus Groups in the Random Sample*

Groups	Per cent of Fathers in High Status Occupations
High Fraternity	69$_{(13)}$**
Low Fraternity	54$_{(13)}$
High Sorority	80$_{(25)}$
Low Sorority	60$_{(10)}$
Independent Female	42$_{(31)}$
Independent Male	41$_{(22)}$

*Differences within the three pairs in this table are not significant but the difference between all Greeks and all Independents is significant.
**The number to the right and below the percentage is the base for the percentage.

tion of campus social class to parental social class. Evidence from our own sample is relevant here, although our testing of this hypothesis is nowhere near as thorough as was our testing of Hypothesis One. We have shown above that the fraternity men are more socialized in terms of dating and love experience. There is also evidence showing that Greeks value elements such as dress, parties, dancing, sports, and drinking activities more than independents. Such values are again part of a "socialized" image of man which the Greeks promote and which Levine and Sussmann have identified as part of the middle classes.[30]

In the random sample, I also have information on fathers' income and occupation. Here too some differences appear among the campus strata. As can be seen in Table 3 the overall occupations of Greeks are significantly higher than those of the independents. High status occupation here is defined as executive or professional. There is also a difference in occupation of father between high and low fraternities and high and low sororities. However, these differences are not quite significant. The differences in Table 3 reflect the general rank of each campus group as discussed in this paper.[31]

The females in sororities are somewhat higher in class background than the independent females and are also somewhat above the fraternity men. Females in college often come from higher class backgrounds than males. Possibly this is due to females' college attendance being considered of secondary importance to males' college attendance and so those females that do go to college come from wealthier

---

[30]Levine and Sussmann, *op. cit*. Religious differences were also checked and the only religious difference discovered was that low fraternity men were highest on Catholic and Baptist members.

[31]An unpublished study by two of my students (Rusty Dietrich and Barbara Clarke) at this same college did show that, among Freshmen, independent females as compared to sorority girls had lower income, less church attendance, and fewer parents who had been in sororities. No test of males was done in this study.

homes.[32] This higher background may further explain the reluctance of sorority girls (particularly high ranked ones) to date independent males.

A check on income revealed one interesting relationship. Although the differences between high and low ranked Greeks and male and female independents were present, the difference between all independents and all Greeks disappeared.[33] Independent females in particular came out quite high on income. One might interpret these occupational and income results as indicating that although Greeks come from higher social classes as indicated by occupation, they do not come from wealthier homes. Thus, the overall campus class differences between Greeks and independents reflect the style of life of each group as related to occupational background more than income background. It may be argued that the occupation of a father affects male values more than female values. Thus, despite their wealth the independents, particularly the males, lack the values that go with the high occupational groupings and thus are ranked lower on campus. Although this *post factum* explanation does make sense of these findings, it must, of course, be tested in new research.

The question raised in Hypothesis Two asks how parental social class affects the relationship, found in Hypothesis One, between one's own campus class rating and the campus class rating of one's date. Unfortunately, the more crucial tests of Hypothesis Two cannot be made with the existing data I have available. Such tests would involve checking the various possible relations between parental social class and campus social class dating more directly. For example it is possible that, even though high campus class individuals are more likely to come from high parental classes (see Table 3), parental social class does not affect the campus class dating system. For example, even though the higher parental class boys join the higher ranking fraternities, the reasons why these boys most often date equally high campus ranked girls may well be fully independent of their parental social class. This possibility does *not* fit with Hypothesis Two. On the other hand, it is possible that parental class would fully explain the tendency of high campus ranked boys to date high campus ranked girls. If so, when one held parental social class constant and looked at only one parental social class at a time, the relation showing high campus ranked boys dating high campus ranked girls would disappear. If this happened, then one could conclude that parental class fully explained why boys and girls dated as they did within the campus class system. This would fit with Hypothesis Two.

Finally, there is another possible way that the parental social class system could influence the campus class dating system. It could be that one's campus social class acts as an intervening variable between one's parental social class and one's choice of a dating partner. Possibly it is because one has high parental social class that one gets involved in high campus class groups and these high campus class groups might develop a style of life which in turn would make one more likely to date others from

---

[32]Recent evidence of females' higher status on other specific campuses can be found in Leslie Richardson, *op. cit.,* p. 120, and Robert P. Bell and Leonard Blumberg, "Courtship Intimacy and Religious Background," *Marriage and Family Living,* 21 (November, 1959), pp. 356–360, esp. p. 357.

[33]The mean income based on questionnaire response of the random sample is estimated to be: High Fraternity, $12,400; Low Fraternity, $9,400; High Sorority, $12,600; Low Sorority, $11,100; Independent Females, $13,000; and Independent Males, $12,400.

similar high campus groups. This eventuality would also fit with Hypothesis Two for it would show the influence of parental class on the campus social class dating system. It is hoped that future research will test these several possibilities and thereby afford us a more precise test of Hypothesis Two.[34]

In sum then, this check of Hypothesis Two shows that there is some evidence to support the hypothesis that the stratification system on the college campus reflects the stratification system of the students' parents. However, the evidence is surely more suggestive than conclusive and is not nearly as complete as that supporting Hypothesis One.

Conclusions

The importance of this theoretical approach is its relevance for much of the past work on campus dating. In part, it tests ideas often verbalized but seldom tested, and tries to organize the many *ad hoc* findings in this area into one theory. The theory bears on Waller's position in that it defines his "materialistic-competitive" system as but one set of rating factors that can be used to symbolize the class differences among students. The rating-dating system (whether "competitive" or "personality" based) doesn't block mating; it is more an indication of the presence of an underlying campus stratification system than it is an indication of a thrill centered, exploitative dating system unintegrated with marriage or social class. As a matter of fact, the rating system operates not only on casual dating but in serious dating also and therefore seems well integrated with marriage. The manifest consequences of this dating system may well be involved with the establishment of one's rating, as Waller suggested, but the latent consequences are the support of campus and parental class endogamy. It may further be hypothesized that since parents usually favor matings within the same social class, then another latent consequence is to aid in achieving such parental goals. Awareness of such latent consequences is crucial to the understanding of the campus dating system. Without this awareness the system may appear to be merely an "irrational" system of dalliance.

There is need for several types of additional research. First it would be important to examine a more representative sample of American college students to see how this theory and its derivative hypotheses fare on different types of campuses. Stratification on campuses without Greek organizations needs investigation. My data indicate that independents do indeed have hierarchical divisions just as Greeks do, but more investigation is needed. Testing this theory on various size campuses with differing proportions of Greeks would also be valuable. In addition, how individual choice operates within the limits of a stratification system should be conceptualized more clearly. There is the important

---

[34] I did ask each person in the random student sample to give me information on his or her parental social class. However, in order to make the checks suggested it would be necessary to have parental social class information on *both* the boy and the girl involved in a dating relationship. My random sample consisted mostly of students who were seriously dating someone else *not* included in the sample and this left us with a lack of knowledge about the parental class of their dates. Because of this we could only perform the partial testing of Hypothesis Two which appears in the text and in Table 3.

problem of how such factors as propinquity, ideal mate image, parental images, basic values, and other variables operate in relation to social class and in relation to mate selection in general. Finally, the relation of other institutions such as the political, economic, and religious to campus dating and campus class should be explored.

It is particularly important in the analysis of a "free dating system," such as we possess, to keep in mind the ways in which the system is structured and the controls of a socio-cultural nature that are operative. It is all too easy to believe the cultural ideology that we have a "free" system. The theory put forth in this paper keeps the socio-cultural limitations of our dating system in the foreground. It is by focusing on such socio-cultural factors that we may obtain insight into the functional relations of mate-selection to the overall institutional structure of our society.

BUREAUCRACY

The Navy Disbursing Officer As A Bureaucrat

RALPH H. TURNER

Every administrative structure exists in order to achieve certain goals, which goals normally originate outside the structure and are imposed on it from the top. A bureaucratic administrative system is supposed to function as a nearly impersonal machine, individual discretion entering only when alternate procedures are compatible with the system. The ordinary official is expected to apply procedures with blind precision, irrespective of the degree to which they achieve or subvert the general goals.

Needless to say, actual administration often fails to adhere closely to the goals of the **organization**. Reasons for the divergence may be inadequacies of the procedural pattern and conflicting procedures, conflicting goals within the organization, inadequacies of the bureaucrats themselves, and, most important, the position of each functionary as not only a square on the organization chart but also as a focus of pressures applied by a number of informal structures not envisaged in the formal pattern.

The purpose of this paper is to describe a few of the sociologically relevant influences which bear on a certain type of bureaucratic official, namely, the Navy disbursing officer. Bureaucracy is conceived as defined by Max Weber.[1] Though certain types of influence are more clearly

---

[1] Cf. H. H. Gerth and C. Wright Mills, translators and editors, *From Max Weber: Essays in Sociology* (New York: Oxford University Press, 1946), pp. 196–244.

displayed in the position of the disbursing officer, most of what is said will also apply to any Supply Corps officer and, to a lesser degree to all naval officers. The findings are the result of participant observation by the writer, both as a disbursing officer during the war and as an observer of other officers in a similar position.

From the standpoint of the present analysis there are three characteristics which distinguish the disbursing officer in degree from the remainder of the naval organization. First, disbursing officers handle matters of immediate personal importance to their clients. Navigation, gunnery, etc., may be more vital to the lives of the men, but their problems are vague to those not directly concerned. An error in a pay account or a delay in pay day is more quickly recognized and more loudly protested by the rank and file than deficiencies in most other departments aboard ship. Consequently the disbursing officer and his staff are under constant bombardment for favors and incessant criticism for their mistakes—real or imagined—or failures to grant favors.

Second, the disbursing officer is a bureaucrat serving a larger bureaucracy of which he is an integral part. Robert Merton has noted the important fact that a government servant is usually superordinate to his clients,[2] not in any formal sense, but because the client has no direct authority over him and no effective access to anyone of superior authority. Superordination and subordination are clearly defined in the Navy by the label which each man carries on his uniform. Though most of the disbursing officer's clients are enlisted men and hence subordinate, a good many will be officers of senior rank who are thereby

empowered to reward or punish him in various ways. Thus in adhering to the formal patterns relating to disbursing the officer must often act counter to the larger formal pattern by defying a senior officer.

Finally, the disbursing officer, unlike most other bureaucrats, is personally accountable and financially liable for any deviation from regulations in the expenditure of government funds in spite of any contrary order from a superior officer.

Three characteristics of the social structure in which the disbursing officer finds himself which make it difficult for him to behave as the ideal bureaucrat will be discussed. First is the frequent conflict between regulations (as interpreted by the disbursing officer) and orders from superiors, both of which are supposed to be obeyed. Second is the subordination of the disbursing officer through rank to many of his clients. Third is the network of informal structures, which exert particular pressure on the disbursing officer because of the crucial services which he dispenses. The facilitating conditions for the operation of these influences include the following: the disbursing officer's incomplete command of voluminous and rapidly changing regulations; the ambiguousness or incompleteness of regulations with respect to many situations; acceptance of properly signed vouchers as proof of fact by the General Accounting Office in auditing disbursing accounts, so that certain documents can be falsified with impunity; those personality traits of the officer which resist strictly impersonal behavior.

Within the **formal structure** the distinctive problem of the disbursing officer is that of reconciling orders from superiors with regulations when they seem to conflict. Orders may be issued by senior officers in the supply department (of which disbursing is a part) or by the commanding

---

[2] "Bureaucratic Structure and Personality," *Social Forces*, 18: 567, May 1940.

and executive officers of the activity. Conflicts with superior officers in the supply department are usually reconciled fairly smoothly because the supply officer understands the problem of disbursing accountability, often from earlier experience as a disbursing officer, and because of fairly close relationships between them. Conflicts stemming from orders by the commanding and executive officers, who have little knowledge of and little patience with disbursing regulations, and who are generally not accustomed to being asked by a subordinate to discuss the advisability of an order they have issued, present a ticklish problem. If the order seems to be at all important to the officer in question, the senior supply officer can usually be expected to add his pressure, through threats and suggested devices for "getting around" the law. The subsequent careers of disbursing and supply officers can be materially affected by notations which the commanding officer may enter in "fitness reports" submitted periodically to the Bureau of Naval Personnel.

The conflict between regulations (as interpreted) and orders from superiors is not limited to the disbursing function or even to military organizations. The conflict is incipient in every bureaucratic structure because the rational type of **authority**, as Weber has indicated, involves recognition both of rules and the right of officials to issue orders.[3] Though the hierarchy of officials exists only to administer the rules, which in turn express the purposes of the organization, it is patent that official behavior and commands may often counter the rules. In the small informal organization of a business hiring only a handful of employees, rules may be largely unformulated and procedures passed verbally down the hierarchy as required, thereby eliminating the conflict by making orders supreme. Or the opposite extreme in which authority is expressed solely through a code of rules, each functionary being left to apply the rules without supervision, might be imagined but hardly realized in an actual situation. Because of the inadequacy of either rules or hierarchical authority alone to serve the purposes of bureaucratic administration, both must be present. Thus the ideal type, bureaucracy, is itself a compromise between two ideal extremes, utilizing and compromising two channels of authority which may be in conflict.

Bureaucracies differ, however, in the degree to which they emphasize chain of command or rules. Business organizations tend to vest greater authority in the chain of command, minimizing numbers of rules and winking at violations if the official achieves results. "Cutting through red tape," is the popular phrase for de-emphasizing rules. Government bureaucracies stress rules more strongly because of their different aims and because of fear of abuse of authority by officials, and through civil service regulations functionaries are given more authority to defy superiors in the application and interpretation of rules. Many a former business executive serving as a naval officer in charge of civilian employees in navy yards has been startled to find his orders called into question by subordinates, and to find himself powerless to enforce his orders. As businesses get larger the emphasis on rules to insure uniform practice reduces the contrast with government bureaucracy. Custodians of funds in business or government are more tightly bound by rules and less subject to arbitrary orders from superiors.

In the Navy, and probably in other bu-

---

[3] Max Weber, *Wirtschaft und Gesellschaft* (Tübingen: J. C. B. Mohr, 1925), p. 124.

reaucratic structures, the intensity of the conflict varies with different levels in the hierarchy. For the lower ranks of enlisted men the conflict hardly exists because they are explicitly denied the right to make decisions on their own.[4] At the higher levels the official is confronted with fewer and broader orders so that in the top ranks the conflict arises less frequently. Thus the conflict between orders and regulations is most acute at the intermediate levels, from ensign to lieutenant in particular.

In business and in most naval positions, this conflict is resolved in favor of the order, the functionary not being held responsible for violating a rule in compliance with an order from a superior official. As indicated previously, the personal accountability of the disbursing officer denies this way out. Consequently, the Navy, recognizing the possibility of conflict, has provided two procedures for its resolution. The disbursing officer is to point out the apparent discrepancy to the superior and, if no understanding is reached, an inquiry may be sent to the Bureau of Supplies and Accounts. Or, the matter may be referred to the commanding officer who may order the disbursing officer to make the expenditure "under protest," the commanding officer thereby assuming full financial liability. The former procedure was used often during the war for minor issues, but senior officers are often unwilling to wait several months for answers and a disbursing officer who frequently resorts to this tactic is soon in poor standing. A disbursing officer considering the second method invariably pictures himself being transferred to "amphibs" and suffering various awful fates at the hands of a wrathful commanding officer, so the method is seldom employed. However, the occasional disbursing officer who has courage enough to threaten its use usually finds the commanding officer unwilling to assume the personal risk involved in defying him.

The very training given the disbursing officer in the supply corps school teaches him that the above methods are not approved ways of handling such difficulties. The young officer is taught that he must be a "Can do paymaster," in contradistinction to the type of officer who is always ready to cite the paragraph in the *Manual* which prevents any particular action being taken. The "Can do" officer can almost always find a way to do anything he is ordered to do. This emphasis, of course, partly reflects a general de-emphasis of rules fostered by the war. But it further reinforces the tendency for the disbursing officer to find "informal" ways of dealing with matters and to deviate from the ideal pattern of a bureaucrat.

The second obstacle to impersonal functioning by the disbursing officer is the system of rank. As indicated by Weber, military officers are marked off by class distinction.[5] And Talcott Parson has observed that, "there is no legitimate order without a **charismatic** element."[6] It is the union of class distinctions with a strong element of "charisma of office" which gives the rank structure its peculiar and powerful nature. Senior officers are expected to be treated with deference irrespective of their actions. Because of "class" levels, senior officers are usually able to punish or reward a lesser officer indirectly. However, through their charisma officers are gen-

---

[4] Cf. United States Navy, *The Bluejackets' Manual* (Annapolis: U.S. Naval Institute, 1940), p. 32.

[5] Max Weber, *op. cit.*, p. 128.

[6] *The Structure of Social Action* (New York: McGraw-Hill, 1937), p. 665.

erally held in far greater awe than their actual powers or inclinations warrant, and a lesser officer is often afraid even to suggest to a superior that his request is not in keeping with regulations. One of the problems of military organization lies in the rather widespread fear of superiors which creates extra labor and ill-feeling on the part of men who feel that they must find some way to conform to an erroneous or careless order. Rank has been too widely discussed to need further elaboration here except to note that the disbursing officer, who is at once both a functionary with specified duties and a position in a system of levels, sometimes finds that he cannot act without violating one of these roles.

A third obstacle to bureaucratic impartiality is the system of informal social groupings. Philip Selznick's three characteristics of the informal structure as found in business and labor union bureaucracies, namely, spontaneity, network of personal relations, and orientation toward control,[7] apply equally to naval situations.

These informal structures are of three sorts. Relatively enduring *friendship patterns* weigh heavily where the disbursing officer belongs to the same primary associations as do many of his clients. Particularly aboard ship where a relatively small number of officers live, eat and play poker together in a small space is this true. "Say, 'Pay,' I sure could use about twenty dollars before payday," or, "Isn't there some way I can get flight pay this month?" is the sort of appeal which comes constantly from friends. As a human being the disbursing officer wants to help his friends, and the penalty for brusque disposal of such requests is social ostracism.

A second type of *simulated friendship* or, in Navy jargon, "earbanging," relationships includes less enduring and more uncertain influences. Nevertheless, these are in many cases sufficiently persistent and organized relations among persons to justify the term "structure." They take a multitude of well-known forms: an officer treats one of lesser rank as an equal, he compliments the disbursing officer on the good reputation of his office, he jokes and attempts to appear as an old friend. The aim is always, first, to be defined as a person rather than an applicant in the disbursing officer's eyes, and second, to be defined favorably.

The third and most extensive sort of informal structure is that which may be called an *exchange system*. The officer who assigns staterooms aboard ship finds it easy to get extra food from the galley. The ship's photographer who makes some personal pictures of the supply officer gets first choice when the next shipment of fountain pens reaches "ship's store." Such exchanges are not usually verbalized as such among officers, but the officer who does another a favor has no doubt that there will be a return. However, there also exist extensive and well-verbalized systems for distribution of favors and certain types of supplies, especially at shore stations. The exchange structures extend so far that it is often difficult for a man to secure those services and equipment which are essential to his job unless he can promise some return. Aboard a large ship one attempt was made in the ship's store to sell the limited stock of watches and cigarette lighters on the basis of impartial drawings.

---

[7] "An Approach to a Theory of Bureaucracy," *American Sociological Review*, 8: 47–54, 1943. Selznick uses a different definition of bureaucracy, referring to deviations from the Weber construct which become informally organized and routinized.

Complaints were so many and vigorous from persons who claimed they had been promised a watch or were owed one that thereafter the "spoils" system was used, with much less complaint. Even some enlisted men in key positions, such as the mail clerk and carpenter's mates, are able to exercise influence over officers because of the services at their disposal. Needless to remark, any resort to strictly formal procedure impairs the disbursing officer's potentially exceptionally good position in the system of mutual benefits. Denunciations of these exchange structures are periodically issued by some commands, but such pronouncements are read by only a few and are seldom implemented by more than one or two courts-martial for petty thievery. Furthermore, commanding officers are frequently among the beneficiaries of such systems.

To the participants these exchange systems are widely different from bribery. Bribery is impersonal and is recognized as contrary to law and morals. Favor exchange systems are eminently personal. As long as the system functions smoothly it is just one man doing a favor for a "buddy," and only when a return favor is not forthcoming will the idea of exchange be stressed. And secondly, the exchange system incorporates its own code of behavior. The individual who puts legal technicality ahead of reciprocity is reprehensible, is spoken of with almost moral indignation. The system is not "wrong" or "crooked"; it is a moral system of its own and anyone who puts legality first is a hypocrite. However, there is an ambivalence of attitude toward the system. The official who follows it deliberately and impersonally in order to acquire too great a quantity of goods is disliked, though with a mixture of envy. The system is supposed to operate in leisurely fashion, maintaining the appearance that the goods acquired are secondary to the friendships involved.

The three sorts of systems described operate not only to grant favors to some but to withhold fair consideration from others. Since disbursing officers generally are stereotyped as acting slowly, being tied up in red tape and giving unsatisfactory assistance, prompt careful attention to the business of a client is often defined as a favor. Persons not favorably placed in the informal structures may be deprived of pay because of inadequate attention to their accounts or may suffer undue delay in the handling of their business.

The influence of these systems is felt not only directly by the disbursing officer but also through the enlisted men in his office. Because of their lack of official status, enlisted men develop especially elaborate and powerful informal structures. A new disbursing officer, in the interest of fairness, stopped the dispensing of favors by his enlisted men. A serious morale problem ensued because the disbursing office personnel, no longer able to contribute services, were simply dropped from the status-producing structures, or, as they complained, they had lost their "drag."

Under the combined impact of the informal structures and his formal office, what solutions does the disbursing officer reach? Four types of disbursing officer will be suggested on the basis of their divergent resolutions of the conflicting forces at work. These will be ideal constructs, but have sufficient empirical validity that any disbursing officer should be able to recognize them as applying to other officers he has known and also to tendencies within himself.

The *Regulation* type approximates the true bureaucrat in that he remains impervious to rank, informal structures, and orders of his superiors, but goes further in employing the narrowest possible interpretation of every regulation. For fear of the General Accounting Office his rule is, "When in doubt, don't." He is the stereotyped disbursing officer and the stereotyped bureaucrat.[8] This type is not in a majority during wartime, and consists chiefly of "green" officers who have not yet felt the full pressure of the contrary influences or have not yet learned how easily regulations may be manipulated, and of "mustangs," former enlisted men who have secured commissions.

Opposite is the type who doubts the potency of the General Accounting Office and feels that, "They can't hold me," if money is expended loosely. He will do anything for a friend or superior without debate. This type is limited to a very few reserve officers who seldom last very long, though many officers have sought escape from the anxieties of their position in the assurance that after the war Congress will pass a "relieving act."

On a different axis, and also fairly infrequent, is the *Sincere* type. He fails to recognize conflicts between regulations and orders from superiors and is unaware of the importance of the informal systems. Apparent conflicts he attributes to his own incomplete understanding of regulations, and rules are seen less as controls than as tools for the execution of orders. He is 100 per cent "sold" on the Navy, is well liked by his superiors and will be assigned positions of favor and responsibility so long as he is a junior officer. His naiveté places him in less favor when he reaches higher levels.

The commonest type is the *Realist*. Regulations are seen as illogical concatenations of procedures, restrictions and interpretations, frequently ambiguous, sometimes contradictory, and often, when strictly applied, defeating the purpose for which they were constructed. Rules specify chiefly the papers which must be filed in support of expenditures, and these may be correct without the payment being correct. The most successful career men of the supply corps include many of this type. They assume the regulation facade when the client is not fortunately placed in the informal or rank structure, but know how any payment may be made "legally" if the request comes from an important enough source.

Many conscientious officials join this type when they come to recognize that strict interpretation of rules often works injustice in terms of the rules' obvious intent and that efforts at strict enforcement are frequently nullified because other people know how to prepare papers "in correct form." Such an official begins by helping a client whose claim is payable within the intent of the law but is invalidated by a technicality to give the "right" information to insure payment. Differential treatment of clients on this basis is hard to maintain, so the officer soon finds himself giving such aid without reference to justification, or more frequently, under varying pressures and moods, wavering between a regulation attitude and an opportunistic attitude.

Two general tendencies emerge among disbursing officers as the consequence of orders conflicting with regulations and the pressures of rank and informal structure. One is differential treatment of clientele. Because of the time consumed in extra-routine treatment of persons on the "in," others get summary treatment. The

---

[8]*Cf.* Ludwig Von Mises, *Bureaucracy* (New Haven: Yale University Press, 1944), p. 41.

second tendency is for loopholes in regulations to become tools in the hand of the disbursing officer to elevate his own status. Thus he may become more concerned with his own bargaining power than with correct application of rules.

In sum, what has been shown is that during this last war powerful influences were at work on the navy disbursing officer, diverting him from functioning as an ideal-typical bureaucrat. These influences move him, not in the direction of ultra-formalism so frequently observed for bureaucrats in other contexts,[9] but toward personal functioning within systems of power and status in which rules become of secondary importance.

---

[9] *Cf.* Robert Merton, *op. cit.*, pp. 560–568.

SOCIAL INSTITUTION

To Comfort and to Challenge

CHARLES GLOCK, BENJAMIN RINGER, AND CARL R. BABBIE

Like General Custer, the contemporary church finds itself encircled by angry critics. Church leaders have good reasons to believe that any action they take will produce a hostile reaction from some quarter. Such attacks may take the form of critical books and tracts, reduced pledges, empty pews or public demonstrations. Some churches have been picketed for favoring racial segregation while others have been bombed and burned for favoring integration. Churches and churchmen have been condemned for entering public controversies and damned for staying out. On every side, concerned men and women stand ready to tell the church what to do and where to go.

The present study has not avoided joining the critics, perhaps, but this was not its motivation. Whatever the church is to be, it seemed a prerequisite to gain a better understanding of what it is now. This essentially is what we have sought to discover. Having completed the examination, it seems appropriate to return to the criticism and to reconsider it in light of what has been learned. Given the source of our data, the conclusions can be said only to apply directly to the Protestant Episcopal Church and indeed, the Protestant Episcopal Church as it existed in 1952. We suspect, however, that the portrait to be drawn reasonably characterizes the church-at-large, then and now.

At the root of the criticism of the church, as well as our examination of it, is a problem as old as the church itself, namely, a definition of its role. What ought the church's role in society be? The answer, of course, is that the church has many roles. First, it has many specialized religious roles. It is the primary agency for providing the sacraments, the focus of ritual life. It carries the burden of responsibility for religious education. Its missionaries circle the globe winning converts to Christianity. From an eschatological perspective, the church's most important role lies with the preparation of its followers for the Final Judgement. However, the church has played many nonreligious or quasi-religious roles as well. Sociologists generally attribute to religious institutions a major share in the task of generating and perpetuating the general principles and values upon which societies are based. In some countries, the church has been the center of established political control—in others, the seat of revolution.

While a variety of societal roles have been and might be played by the church, there are two which are especially relevant to an understanding of the current criticism of the church in America. These two roles are responses to the imperfections of the temporal order and represent two distinct historical orientations. From the time of Christ, the church has sought both to comfort and to challenge; to care for the "halt, the lame, and the blind" and those who are "weary and heavy laden," but also to make the church meaningful and influential in daily life. The contemporary church still seems committed to serve both functions. Like its forebear, however, it finds itself on the horns of a dilemma as to how to do so effectively.

The church's dual commitment to these two functions makes it unique among social institutions. Its commitment to comfort distinguishes the church from the political party and the social reform movement. Its commitment to challenge, on the other hand, distinguishes it from the rest home and social club. Yet, it is the church's explicit commitment to both functions which has generated much of the controversy in which it is presently embroiled.

As regards comfort, the church is committed first of all to the belief that the Christian faith itself possesses the power to surmount the trials and tribulations of daily life. For many Christians, this is no doubt an accurate appraisal; the centrality of their commitment to Christ is sufficient to enable them to transcend the slings and arrows of earthly existence. At the same time, however, the church has recognized that faith alone is not enough for all men. Thus it has also rendered more worldly assistance through efforts to collect and distribute clothing and food to the poor, to minister to the sick and to extend pastoral counseling to the anguished.

At first glance, the church's role as comforter seems incontrovertible. Comfort for those in need of it has always been an integral part of Christian love and compassion. That the church continues to provide comfort today should, it would seem, come as no surprise, nor evoke a critical reaction. Yet, some of the church's contemporary critics do question the church's wisdom. In their eyes, the church has become so much a captive of its commitment to comfort as to overshadow and nearly overwhelm the exercise of its commitment to challenge.

This criticism of the church as comforter is important and should be understood for what it is. None of the critics would deny the church's obligation to ease the burdens of those who suffer; they uniformly agree the church *should* act on this obligation. However, the critics' demand is for the church to actively seek to abolish suffering, rather than simply to make it more bearable. By helping people to cope with an imperfect society, the critics charge, the church becomes an accomplice to the preservation of the injustice and inequality which constitute the imperfection.

Thus, when the church helps the impoverished to tolerate their deprivations, it implies that involuntary poverty itself is tolerable in Christian eyes. Or, while the church may have provided valuable spiritual support for Negroes in America, many observers feel it has done so at the cost of "keeping Negroes in their place." In teaching men to live with their worldly sufferings, then, the church has run the risk of preserving suffering itself.

There are two aspects of this criticism of the church's comforting function. First, comforting the oppressed may prevent them from seeking or demanding something better from themselves in this life. By helping to make this life bearable through promising a greater reward "across Jordan," the church may effectively quell protestations for social change from the bottom of the social structure. Second, the critics fear that the values of social harmony and tranquility which make the "comfortable pew" so comfortable will have the effect of preventing movements toward social justice from originating at the top of the social structure. Thus, when the more fortunate parishioners feel they have helped to make life more tolerable for the suffering, they may be less zealous in bringing down the structures which foster suffering. In this sense, the church may ease the guilt and soothe the consciences of its more socially esteemed (hence, more influential) members, and prevent or inhibit them from acting on any natural inclinations to strive for social justice.

The data examined in the present study permit an empirical test of many of the critics' observations and assertions. First, the contention that the contemporary church is largely a comforting institution seems to be confirmed by the facts. . . . [I]t was discovered that parishioners whose personal attributes were the most devalued by the secular society were the most likely to become deeply involved in the church. Women, the elderly, the famililess, and parishioners of relatively low social status were all found to be more involved than their more esteemed counterparts. It was concluded, therefore, that parishioners deprived of status gratification in the secular society turned to the church for alternative rewards, for comfort and consolation. In short, dispensing comfort seems a major function of the contemporary church.

Furthermore, the critics are at least partly correct in their assessments of the church's attempt to challenge. . . . [I]t was observed that involved parishioners were no more or less likely to favor such efforts on the church's part. They did not differ significantly from the less involved in their support for having the church actively challenge the values and practices of the secular society. At the very least, it was evident that social concern was not a motivation to deep commitment to the church. Furthermore, degree of involvement was not related to agreement with those social and economic positions which the church did take. On the whole, what the church had to say seemed irrelevant to parishioners' social values.

Thus, the critics are not wholly correct. Involvement does not make parishioners less politically permissive. It simply has no effect. However, this observation does not rule out the possibility that a positive relationship between involvement and permissiveness might exist if the church did not emphasize its comforting function. On balance, the arguments made to support this notion still seem quite reasonable, although the present data do not permit an empirical test.

The analysis . . . does permit a further elaboration of the church's failure to challenge, however. If anything, church involvement seems to go hand-in-hand with a narrowly religious perspective. By their **religiocentric** commitment, involved parishioners appear to have defined more direct social action by the church as irrelevant or superfluous. Having asserted that religious instruction could prevent war, they are not especially concerned, on religious grounds, with the possible value of a United Nations. Having expressed their belief that religion should be taught to children in schools, they do not feel their religious commitment entails support for a politically active church among adults. Having participated in religiously sponsored charities, they do not feel religiously constrained to support other, secular, charitable activities.

This belief in the miraculous power of faith, then, constitutes an alternative to social action as a means for dealing with the problem of suffering. It is not necessary to deal directly with injustice in society. Win men to Christ, and injustice and suffering will automatically disappear. From this viewpoint, if all men truly subscribed to the teachings of the Christian faith, there would be no need for civil rights demonstrations, for there would be no discrimination. There would be no need for peace protests, for there would be no war. In the minds of many churchmen then, the solution to all social problems lies in spreading the Christian faith.

That Christian faith has the power to transform individual lives is evidenced by Christian saints and martyrs of the past and present. There is less evidence, however, that it applies wholesale and that the vast body of persons calling themselves Christians have been so transformed. Nonetheless, this is the orientation which many parishioners feel the church should take in confronting the problems of secular society.

Perhaps this is all the church can or ought to do. Perhaps more active and partisan efforts to challenge its followers should be abjured, and it should concentrate even more on its task of alleviating human misery, thereby winning men to Christ. This would be one solution to the church's present dilemma. Nevertheless, if the church were to withdraw from direct social action and concentrate its energies on providing comfort, the probable changes in the nature of the church would be severe. Surely there will always be suffering in the world, and the church would never want for people to comfort. However, a church limited exclusively to such concerns would differ little from a rest home. Furthermore, this orientation would, in effect, deny a traditional Christian commitment. Those clergymen and parishioners who feel their church must challenge the imperfections of society would probably desert.

To adopt the alternative route, to become exclusively an institution devoted to social protest and social reform, would be equally disastrous. It, too, would require an explicit denial of a traditional Christian concern, in this case, the commitment to comfort. Moreover, were the church to follow this course, it could not even count on the support of its most committed members—those who have turned to the church for relief. We have already seen that moderate efforts at challenge are largely ineffective. For the church to even hope to be influential, its stands on issues would have to be much stronger and its demands on parishioners much more persistent.

Past experience already sounds a warning against this orientation. Where the church has become actively engaged in controversial and unpopular issues, it has all too often alienated its membership, losing their moral and economic support. When the church has been critical of the abuses of capitalism, it has alienated the businessmen among its constituency. When it has pointed to inconsistencies in the practices of unions, it has lost the loyalty of union members. The condemnation of racial **segregation** estranges the prejudiced, and a strong pacifist position might produce apostasy among defense workers in the church. In short, when the church calls for specific social change, it must face the fact that it will lose support among those who are living comfortably within the existing conditions.

While some may feel that this is the price which the church must expect to pay, this orientation represents a losing proposition ultimately. First, while church leaders with strong social consciences may justifiably resent being supported financially by hypocritical parishioners, the complete withdrawal of such finances could render the church wholly impotent. While a destitute church might know in its heart that it was right, it would be forced to admit in its head that it could accomplish nothing.

Second, an uncompromising reorientation of the church to work exclusively for social justice would represent a denial of the church's responsibility for those who would leave the church. In facing hypocrisy among its members, the church must decide whether it is to rid itself of the hypocrites or attempt to make them less hypocritical. Those most impatient with hypocrisy will surely answer that it is better to know one's enemies than to be deceived with half-way friends. Others, however, would argue that by losing its audience the church would lose effectively its potential to communicate.

A final problem is the old one of obtaining consensus about the constitution of a Christian society. The New Testament affords room for a variety of interpretations. Feudal societies and communal ones, democracies and dictatorships, socialism and capitalism have at different times and places all been espoused as reflecting the Christian ideal. Walter Rauschenbusch, not so long ago, thought that he had discovered the true social meaning of the Gospels; and the contemporary critics feel that they have rediscovered it for the modern age. The fact of the matter is that there are no systematic prescriptions in the New Testament for the organization of society. There are clues, of course, and it is these which have inspired men to ponder their meaning. But history has not demonstrated that a consistent interpretation is possible. It seems wishful thinking at best to conceive that an interpretation about which all men can agree can still be attained.

In sum, for the church to opt for either comfort or challenge as its principal task seems unreasonable. One might suggest, then, that the church seek to redress the balance between the two functions. Since the church's performance of a comforting role now overshadows its efforts to challenge, why not try to put a little more backbone in the latter, while maintaining a commitment to the former? That there is a receptivity to having the church become more active in challenging its constituency and the society is evident in the response to the contemporary critics of the church. One sign is the sale of the critics' books and the generally favorable reception these have received in the religious press. Another is the inspiration these writings have given to a spate of new experimental programs in the churches. Still another is the greater active involvement of clergy and laity alike in social protest.

Nonetheless, redressing the balance is no simple solution. First, the attempt to strengthen the church's challenge would probably engender many of the same problems discussed in connection with an exclusive concern for social change. The second difficulty lies with the incompatibility of the two functions. If making life more bearable for the deprived can prevent them from achieving more just conditions, the converse also seems true. To some extent, certainly, the open turmoil which would be produced by more intensive efforts to challenge would work against the church's continuing efforts to afford comfort. Those who come to the church in search of relief and tranquility are not likely to find it by embroiling themselves in demands for social change. Challenging social imperfections requires the taking of unpopular stands and those who would march with the church would have to anticipate ridicule and reprisals.

This fact is nowhere clearer than in the history of the Negro civil rights movement in the South. Negroes who have learned to survive in the past by a shuffle and a spiritual hymn now discover that standing fast with the radical church and with the Movement is anything but comfortable. Furthermore, to the extent that greater efforts to challenge would alienate the support of more prosperous parishioners, their paternalistic efforts—and these do provide a modicum of comfort—would have to be written off. In sum, redressing the balance between the church as comforter and as challenger seems a difficult solution at best.

Thus far we have dwelt on the gloomy aspects of the church's dilemma. The discussion has been aimed at elaborating the severe difficulties which confront the church as it seeks to meet its commitment to the two functions of comfort and challenge. However, in the belief that the ultimate hope for the church lies in a greater balance between the functions, we shall turn now to some of the positive solutions which are suggested by the data and by the preceding discussion. There are three proposals which the church might well consider.

A Reevaluation of Deprivation

Despite the heated criticism of the church's support for the status quo, there are many ways in which the church extends comfort to its followers which are acceptable even to its harshest critics. The comfort afforded by the church to those who have lost a beloved parent, for example, is a case in point. The need for comfort in this instance is inevitable, and no amount of **social change** can abolish the problem. Similarly, it seems likely that the elderly will always be disadvantaged, and although their lot can be improved through financial assistance, the special, spiritual support which the church can offer seems of continued importance. A similar defense can be made for comforting the physically and mentally handicapped.

It should be clear then that many of the deprivations which the church seeks to alleviate cannot easily be abolished by social change. Many of man's sorrows are inherent in his being. Others are based on more or less rational grounds. If the elderly and the physically handicapped are denied the status afforded the young and the well, there seems little the church can do other than ease the pain. Whether comfort in these circumstances supports the status quo seems irrelevant.

On the other hand, many of the deprivations of social life are notably irrational. Attaching more prestige to a white skin than a black one is a classic example. The belief that the impoverished deserve to live in poverty is another. For the church to condone and perpetuate the status quo in these regards is indeed unacceptable. Not only are such deprivations as these irrational at base, but it is evident that they are subject to abolition through programs of social change. What is called for here is challenge, not comfort.

The church must decide when to comfort and when to challenge. The church—and its critics—must admit that some of the circumstances which plague man cannot be changed, but must be lived with. Others, however, can be changed and should not be lived with in any society which is informed by Christian principles. The current problem of the church is that it has indiscriminantly meted out its comfort without an informed consideration of whether its action would be beneficial or detrimental in the long run.

We should not be misled to think that the reevaluation of the many forms of deprivation provides an easy solution to the problem. Not the least of the difficulties to be faced is that of reaching agreement as to the forms of deprivation which ought to be comforted primarily and those which should be challenged and abolished. With regard to aging for example, while there are inherent disadvantages to being elderly, many irrational deprivations are often added to the burden. It might be deemed necessary by some to seek to generate more respect for the elderly in society, or to break down discrimination against the aged in hiring. Similarly, while being female entails a number of inherent disadvantages in secular life, some members of the church might feel it important to whittle away at the less reasonable restrictions which women face. There is no clear scheme for ultimately classifying all forms of deprivations into those to be comforted and those to be challenged. Nevertheless, an overt attempt at such a rethinking of the church's comforting activities can at least single out the less ambiguous instances and clarify the choices for the more ambiguous ones.

Another difficulty, of course, is that it cannot be assumed that all individuals who are deprived on irrational grounds would want their situations changed. As difficult as it may be to accept ideologically, there are those who are content to live with their deprivations within the status quo and who would prefer the comfort which the church now offers over the strife and turmoil which social change would require. Ultimately it would seem necessary for the church to be willing to continue providing comfort in such instances, even though the bulk of its efforts is given to helping abolish the source of the deprivation.

In sum, what seems called for is that the church become more self-conscious about the implications of its actions—both manifest and latent. If its response to deprivation were informed by a more sophisticated understanding of the nature of human suffering, it is even possible that the church might be able to take considerably more pride in what it does both to comfort and to challenge. One senses a certain embarrassment on the part of churchmen when confronted with assertions that the church is the society's principal agent for providing comfort. Insofar as the comfort provided may help perpetuate the existence of intolerable social conditions, embarrassment is probably the appropriate response. However, pride rather than embarrassment should attend on the church helping people to live with unfortunate circumstances which cannot be changed.

A Dual Structure for the Church

There are grounds for suggesting that the attempt to achieve a more effective balance between the two commitments might also call for a consideration, at least, of some modification in the organizational structure of the church. Through personal and continuing contacts, clergy and lay leaders in the local parish can best appreciate the idiosyncratic needs of parishioners. Moreover, the parish priest is in an excellent position to render spiritual first aid to those who face immediate and personal problems. In these situations where comfort is called for, it seems best provided through the familiar network of friends and clergy within the parish.[1]

The parish might not be the most effective setting for mobilizing parishioner support on social issues, however. The parish priest . . . has little success in winning parishioners to his views on social issues. This function could be better served perhaps by non-parish organizations—voluntary and/or interfaith.

First, a voluntary social action group can clearly be more effective in mobilizing its members than could ever be the case of the parish church whose ultimate aims are primarily religious. Thus a church-sponsored civil rights group can reach agreement on a program of action much more readily than would be possible in the parish. It is not surprising, then, to find increasing numbers of clergy and laymen (perhaps out of despair) forming and joining problem-oriented groups which deal with issues such as civil rights, peace, slums, homosexuality, labor relations, and so forth. Just as the parish priest can perhaps best determine the idiosyncratic needs of his own parishioners, these groups seem better equipped to form and carry out a challenging program to abolish the forms of deprivations which concern them.

From the church's point of view, interdenominational and interfaith groups are perhaps the most appropriate vehicle for meeting its commitment to challenge. The social problems which ought to be challenged and abolished are not the unique possession of any religious group. While each church might comfort its own members, the broader social issues carry a moral responsibility for all the churches. The formation of an Episcopal solution, a Presbyterian solution, a Congregational solution and a Lutheran solution to the problem of poverty would probably end in no solution. In this regard, interfaith cooperation seems essential. Such cooperation provides greater financial and intellectual resources and, by its representativeness, commands broader public attention and respect.

Although the data do not show that parishioners unanimously support such interfaith groups, it was evident that substantial support does exist. Furthermore, to the extent that support for such organizations—though not necessarily personal participation—can be presented as a religious act, parishioner response might be enhanced.

---

[1] Peter Berger and others have suggested that the parish church is in a particularly advantageous position to comfort. See, for example, Berger's discussion of Christian diaconate in *The Noise of Solemn Assemblies* (Garden City, N.Y.: Doubleday, 1961), pp. 140–143.

Broadening Religious Horizons

The proposal to make the parish the church's primary instrument of comfort is not intended also to mean the abdication of challenge at the parish level. On the contrary, even with a parallel institutional structure oriented to challenge, the potential would exist for doing more at the parish level than is currently being done. As we have already seen, parishioners generally, and the involved particularly, stand ready to carry out what they consider "religious" work. Most parishioners would support the church in speaking out on prayers in school; church involvement is an effective mobilizing factor in obtaining gifts to the Presiding Bishop's Fund and to Church World Service. Even in regard to less clearly religious matters, parishioners tend to favor "religious" action such as prayers and moral instruction.

This narrowness of perspective has probably generated the greatest impatience among the critics of the church. Many actions in daily life have important moral and ethical implications which should be informed by religious faith, yet the church has not succeeded in bringing the faithful to recognize this. For most parishioners, issues such as race relations, poverty, war and immigration still are purely secular, to be decided on other than religious grounds.

The church's past program of challenge, it would seem, has helped to perpetuate this myopic view of the implications of faith. While church leaders have often recognized the need for Christian action on social issues, their attempt to challenge church members has been directed, at once, at both a too abstract and a too concrete level. The church proclaims "Peace on Earth" as a Christian ideal and encourages churchmen to support the United Nations, but the links between the two messages are all too often not elaborated. The painful result is that while church members may applaud the church's abstract position, many feel no constraint to accept the concrete proposals. Thus, for many parishioners, the road from "Peace on Earth" to the United Nations is not immediately clear, and the church has not been successful in showing the way. By not specifying the links which connect the general with the specific, the church has failed to generate support for its concrete proposals and has, thereby, endangered the realization of its principles.

Three measures seem called for. First, the church should continue to seek consensus on general Christian principles. As suggested earlier, this represents a hopeful beginning, although it is not a sufficient accomplishment. Second, the church must undertake a conscious educational program through which to point out the ethical implications of daily actions in secular life. A simple concern for peace is not sufficient. All parishioners ought to realize, for example, that the Christian ideal of peace may often conflict with nationalistic and economic interests. The reasons for and instances of such conflicts should be understood. Furthermore, church members should be encouraged to examine the ways in which their own personal interests are at stake in the issue, and they should be led to realize the many ways in which their daily actions may influence the ultimate achievement of peace. In short, the church must convince its members that although secular factors are introduced into the consideration of social issues, religious concerns do not become any less relevant.

Third, we feel that an educational program which would enhance parishioners' understanding of the religious implications of their daily lives would be more successful if partisan positions were not taken by the church.[2] The basis of any educational program ought to be the presentation of both sides of an issue. Past experience has shown, moreover, that when the church has taken a strong and unequivocal position on an issue, it has alienated members whose nonreligious interests are threatened and has led them to suspect the motives, logic and wisdom of the church's actions. There is no evidence that taking an unpopular stand has changed the thinking of many parishioners. Forcing them to recognize that the Christian principles which they profess are involved in the stand which they themselves take, however, seems potentially more fruitful.

To many, we suspect, such an approach will appear compromising and to beg the question. For them, the moral urgency of some of today's problems demands a more forthright response from the church and in their eyes, there is no question about what that response should be. The church's task, however, seems to be not so much one of reinforcing those who are now morally sensitive as making morally sensitive those who now are not. This is more likely to be accomplished, we would aver, through the church helping its followers to analyze and interpret the values which undergird both sides of a controversial issue than by stumping for one side in an unequivocal way.

A case in point is the problem of gaining equality for Negroes in our society. This is one of those morally urgent questions which seem to call for no other than a partisan stand. By and large, this is the stand which American churches have adopted, but with what effect? Seventy million church members devoted to the Negroes' cause, it would seem, ought to be able to move mountains. But, of course, mountains are not being moved, only hills and at a much slower pace than many would like.

Whether or not the church has the capacity to play this special kind of educational role is, of course, an open question. It would call upon churchmen to transcend their own partisan commitments in the interests of the larger cause. Moreover, it would require on their part a sensitivity to not only the values of both sides but an understanding of how these values came into being. Here, perhaps, we are counting on the possibility of another kind of miracle. Still, in the long run, this route seems more promising than any other for the church's commitment of challenge at the parish level.

---

[2] The logic of my co-authors on this matter seems compelling; however, I feel impelled to take exception to the conclusions drawn. In my estimation, the church, even on the parish level, should take partisan stands on the more morally urgent issues of the day. If it avoids doing so merely because many of its parishioners hold a contrary view, it would then be less than true to the fulfillment of one of its major missions in society: namely that of exhorting man to act in accordance with basic moral and other ideals, and it would thereby deprive mankind of a major agency for motivating people to do what they should do instead of merely doing what is expedient or what they want to do.

To paraphrase the eminent sociologist Vilfredo Pareto, no one expects a person to act only in reference to his ideals, but the absence of a clear-cut statement of these ideals would result in the person's failure to take even a step in the direction of their fulfillment. And so may it well be with the church. An explicit statement of its convictions may have little immediate influence on the secular behavior of its parishioners, but it nevertheless reminds them of the disparity between their behavior and the ideals that represent the moral conscience of the religious community.

Benjamin B. Ringer

DEVIANCE

Stripteasers: The Anatomy and Career Contingencies of A Deviant Occupation

JAMES K. SKIPPER, JR.
AND CHARLES H. McCAGHY

Social scientists have frequently sought explanations of deviant behavior in terms of either the characteristics of individuals who become deviant, or the processes by which deviant behavior develops. Cohen (1966:41–45) classifies the most common research strategies as those which: 1) emphasize the "kinds" of persons who become deviant and the developmental process by which they become that "kind;" 2) focus on the situation or single pivotal episode which transformed individuals from normal to deviant; 3) use a combination of 1) and 2) wherein certain "kinds" of persons are assumed to be relatively vulnerable to deviant-producing situations; and 4) make the "interaction" process the salient variable, involving stages in which each is contingent upon the outcome of a previous stage.

Only the fourth strategy, the interaction process, incorporates the consideration that although it may be possible to delineate prime candidates for deviance, their initiation into the process of becoming deviant and their eventual emergence as full-blown systematic deviants are both problematic. Becker (1963:22–39) has suggested that a sequential model as embodied in the notion of "career" would be useful in understanding many forms of deviant behavior. Such a model would take into account both a sequence of steps and the factors or "career contingencies" on which the steps depend.

This is not to deny the efficacy of other research strategies in contributing to an understanding of deviants, but it is evident

that some, if not most, deviant behavior can be viewed in terms of order in time and space. In Cohen's (1966:103) succinct description: "It grows, it develops, it has a history." In the interaction strategy the kinds of individuals and circumstances are handled as components of a process. In other words, the background characteristics and situational variables are career contingencies—neither being considered as exclusive causes of the resulting behavior.

The purpose of this paper is to present the data on stripteasers who, to our knowledge, have rarely been the subjects of systematic social scientific research.[1] Strippers were initially of interest to us less because of the dearth of studies about them, than because of their involvement in a deviant occupation which is highly visible. The intent of the study was to discover variables relevant to the process or career sequence of becoming a stripper.

Traditionally, in American society, the human body has been considered relatively private and sacred. This has been especially true of females. Generally an adult woman is not expected to expose her nudity to any male not her spouse, with the exception of a physician and then only under highly structured circumstances involving health reasons. Over the past 20 years the amount of female skin which may be uncovered in the presence of males and the situations where it may be properly displayed have rapidly become more liberal.[2] Despite liberalization, stripping remains a deviant or at best marginal occupation. A large segment of the society probably considers being paid to take off one's clothes for no other purpose than to allow others to stare and ogle an unusual and low status, if not outright promiscuous, occupation. In a survey of 75 college students, we discovered a definite negative public image of strippers. In answer to the question, "What type of women do you think make their living by stripping?" the following words and phrases were representative of the replies: "hard women," "dumb," "stupid," "uneducated," "lower class," "can't do anything else for a living," "oversexed," "immoral," and "prostitutes."[3]

Our data leave little doubt that the strippers feel the impact of negative public sentiment. Almost every girl in our sample firmly believed that most people's conception of stripping was that it was dirty and immoral. This belief affects their behavior in public. For example, many of the girls avoid identifying themselves in public as strippers, preferring to call themselves dancers, entertainers, and the like. In this way they felt they were able to steer clear of a pariah label.

To date, few studies on the process of becoming deviant have included background characteristics of subjects as important variables; rather, the emphases have been upon the structure and steps involved in the relatively immediate learn-

---

[1] We were able to discover only one study concerning stripteasers, D'Andre (1965) and this is unpublished. However, there are interesting descriptions of the American burlesque scene. For example: Dressler (1937), Zeidman (1967), and Corio and DiMona (1968).

[2] One of the most recent and tangible indications of this liberalization is the use of nude actors and actresses in the New York City productions of "Hair" and "Oh! Calcutta!"

[3] In a study concerning nudity in art training, Jesser and Donovan (1965) provide data from 155 non-art university students and 122 of their parents showing that stripteasers were given a lower occupational ranking than such traditionally low status types of work as: janitor, artist's model and professional gambler. They also report that few respondents believed even a small percentage of female college students would model in the nude even for the sake of art.

ing and identification experiences.[4] In this research we were also concerned with locating factors which make persons differentially vulnerable to becoming involved in the process. To this end we attempted to delineate the salient social, psychological, and physical characteristics of our subjects as well as the crucial situations and events contingent to entering the occupation.

Procedure

The research can be properly called a field study. Data were collected utilizing both observational and interviewing techniques. While the focus of the study centered on a theater in one midwestern city, performances in clubs and theaters were viewed in ten major cities from Honolulu to New York, and from New Orleans to Chicago. Casual contacts and informal interviews were held with approximately 75 performers in the course of observing activities in the dressing room area backstage before, during, and after the shows. Formal, semistructured interviews lasting on the average of one and one-half hours were taken with 35 strippers.[5] Interviews were also taken with others, both male and female, whose work activities brought them in close contact with the girls. The interviews were conducted either in the backstage dressing room or at one of a series of bars in the vicinity of the theater. In all but one case, two researchers were present at each interview.

Anatomy of the Occupation

There are an estimated 7,000 women in this country who earn their living by removing their clothes in a titillating fashion before paying audiences (Jones, 1967). They are referred to variously as exotic dancers, burlesque queens, ecdysiasts, stripteasers, and strippers. Some form of the practice of stripping is legal in most sections of the United States. In fact, it is an institutionalized feature of many urban areas.

Stripping is limited primarily to four types of work settings: night clubs, theaters, carnivals, and an occasional private showing or "stag show" which may take place almost anywhere. The strippers interviewed in this study were working the eastern theater circuit sometimes called the "eastern wheel." It consists of 11 theaters in ten cities east of the Mississippi River. The theaters are operated by a firm located in New York City. Through a central booking agency, also located in New York City, the girls sign contracts to work the circuit for specified periods of time, usually several months. Three or four girls, with

---

[4] An exception is Wallace's (1965:163–202) study of skid row. Even among researchers interested in occupational socialization few have investigated the relationship between characteristics of individuals and their association with a particular occupation. Exceptions include: Mauksch (1960), Ladinsky (1963), Sherlock and Cohen (1966), and Colombotos (1969).

[5] In studies of deviant behavior sample size is often determined by the availability of cooperative respondents. Characteristically, this has kept the size relatively small. However, our N of 35 was not due to a scarcity of subjects, since during a year approximately 110–120 girls performed in the theater where the research took place. A decision to stop formal interviews at 35 was made because at about the 25th interview we were receiving no new information of theoretical significance. By the final interview we were convinced we had reached the point of "saturation." "Saturation means that no additional data are being found whereby the sociologist can develop properties of the category. As he sees similar instances over and over again, the researcher becomes empirically confident that a category is saturated." (Glaser and Strauss, 1967:61).

two or three comics, travel as a show and spend seven days in major cities and less time in smaller cities. However, there is considerable intermixing of girls so that one group is seldom together for long periods of time. Each theater has its own local manager, but with the exception of the "headliner" or star feature, he has little control over which strippers will be sent to him and at what time. The strippers are required to belong to a union, the American Guild of Variety Artists. The minimum wage on the theater tour is $175 per seven day week. The strippers also receive traveling expenses (train fare) but not room and board. The booking agency automatically receives five percent of each stripper's wages.

The enforcement of obscenity laws in the state where the strippers were interviewed is usually left up to local officials. This results in considerable variation in interpretation of what is obscene among the cities which have burlesque theaters. The city which was the prime site of the research is more permissive than most in its interpretation of the law. In the argot of the occupation, it is known as a "strong" city. Performers are allowed to bare their breasts completely and are permitted to "flash." Flashing consists of lowering the G-string so that the pubic area is displayed. Although the G-string may be lowered to the knees or ankles its complete removal is apparently considered obscene.[6]

Physical, Social, and Psychological Characteristics of Strippers

Since stripping involves displaying the body, the physical characteristics and ap-

---

[6]Yet, this does occur on occasion. Removal of the G-string is an integral part of the performance of two of the headliners included in the sample.

196 *Sociology*

pearance of the performers are of utmost importance. All of the women interviewed were Caucasian. Of the total of 110 strippers with whom we came in contact only two were Negro and none was Oriental. While the vast majority were natural brunettes, the actual hair coloring on stage was about equally divided among blonds, brunettes and redheads. The girls ranged in age from 19–45. However, 60 percent were between the ages of 20 and 30.

In terms of body type the strippers' measurements showed considerable variation. However, compared to the average American woman between the ages of 20 and 30, and even Playboy Playmates of the Month, the strippers were taller, heavier, with larger hips, and had extremely well-developed busts, several approaching astronomical proportions.[7]

Five foreign countries (Brazil, Cuba, France, Germany, and Iran) and 16 American states were given as homes of origin. Of the girls born in the United States, all sections of the country were represented with the exception of the deep South. Four of the strippers came from rural backgrounds; the rest were born and/or raised in standard metropolitan areas of over 100,000 inhabitants.

The socioeconomic class standings of the strippers' families of orientation indicate that many of the girls are not recruited from the lowest strata of the society. Using the Hollingshead (1957) two-factor index of social position ten of the strippers came from families in classes I and II, nine from class III, and 12 from classes IV and V. (Social class data were not available for four cases). Thus, for many of the girls stripping cannot be considered an avenue of upward intergenerational social mobility. The formal educational background of the strippers was also higher than we had anticipated. The range of schooling was from 7–16 years. Twenty-two of the girls had graduated from high school; of these seven had attended at least one year of college and another had achieved a B.A. degree. Four of the strippers stated they were raised in Jewish homes, 14 in Catholic and 12 in Protestant. There were also a Mormon and a Seventh-day Adventist. Three girls claimed their parents had no religious preference. While several of the strippers indicated they still attempted to practice their religion, only four man-

---

[7] Comparison of Mean Body Measurements: Strippers, Playboy Playmates, and the Average American Woman (Age 20–30)

Strippers N = 35

Height	Weight	Bust	Waist	Hips
5:7	130	38	25	38¼

Playmates N = 179

Height	Weight	Bust	Waist	Hips
5:5	117	36¼	22	35½

Average Woman N = 355

Height	Weight	Bust	Waist	Hips
5:4	126.2	34	25.8	36.9

The range of measurements were: height 5–6 feet, weight 110–150 pounds, bust 32–50 inches, waist 21–30 inches, hips 35–40 inches. It must be noted that these figures are based on the respondents' claims. We did not conduct the measurements ourselves. However, we have confidence in their relative validity. For example, many of the strippers admitted, and sometimes apologized for, less generous endowment than was publicly advertised.

In 1968 a scientific anthropometric survey of women between the ages of 20 and 30 was conducted for the apparel industry to provide information on which to base garment sizes. The data on the average American women used above are derived from this study (*Cleveland Plain Dealer*, 1968).

The data presented above are based on the first 179 Playboy Playmates of the Month (*Playboy*, 1969).

aged to participate in religious activities with any regularity. Eleven of the girls had never been married. Of the 24 girls who had ever been married, two were widowed, two were still married to their first husband, while the other 20 girls had all experienced at least one divorce. Fifteen of the strippers had children, six of them having more than one.

Several patterns are found in the early life of the strippers. They are: first ordinal position in the family; early physical maturation; early coital experience; absence of the father from the home by adolescence; and early independence and departure from home. Perhaps the most significant trait common to the strippers interviewed is also one of the most difficult to explain and understand. Thirty-one of the 35 strippers (89 percent) were first born in their family of orientation and, of these, just five were only children.[8] Moreover, one of the four later-born strippers was 15 years younger than the next oldest child in the family and from age two she was the only child left living with the parents.

While there is general agreement among behavioral scientists that birth order is an important factor in influencing personality and behavior, there is little consensus on exactly what its influence is. The psychological literature on the subject is voluminous, conflicting, and inconsistent. Sampson (1965:220), after reviewing over 150 studies, found only enough evidence to support the following conclusions about the first born:

As compared with the later-born individual, it appears that the first-born or the only child (1) is more likely to attain a position of intellectual eminence, particularly in the more scientific fields, (2) is less likely to express overtly aggressive feelings, (3) is more likely to seek the company of others when he is anxious, and to benefit from such affiliative activity, yet (4) is less likely to be a sociable, outgoing highly rated individual, one who is empathic and sympathetic. In addition it is probable that, as compared with the later-born child, the first-born is (1) more likely to experience a sudden shift in the centrality of his family role, particularly with respect to attention and affection, and (2) more likely to experience a conflict over the issue of dependence *versus* independence.

Before examining the possible influence of first ordinal position on the personality and behavior of the girls who became strippers, it is necessary to discuss several other patterns in their family situations. Although our data are not complete in all cases, there is a clear indication that at least 60 percent of the girls came from broken and unstable homes, where they received little attention and affection. A characteristic feature was the absence of the father from the home, or if he was present, his disintegrating influence on family relationships.[9] In four cases the girl's father had passed away before she reached school age. In 14 others the parents were divorced or separated, the children staying with their mothers during adolescence. There were two instances where the father was in the home but was alcoholic, and another where the father committed in-

---

[8]We were unable to ascertain the actual percentage of first born children in the general population. However, it appears that of those families which had children in the home under 18 years of age in 1967, approximately 35 percent of the children were first born (Current Population Reports, June 25, 1968:3).

[9]We were not able to determine the actual percentage of first born females in the general population whose biological fathers were not in their home at the start of adolescence. However, based on divorce and mortality rates we would estimate the figure to be between 20 and 30 percent.

cest with the child. It was not uncommon for the girls to have closer relationships with maternal grandparents than with either their mother or father.

Perhaps the lack of attention and affection in the home can be best illustrated by the case of the girl who was raped at the age of nine while walking through a park at night. She stated that although the man hurt her during the act, afterwards he held her in his arms and "loved" her. He told her, "It hurts now, but later you will appreciate it." At the time the girl's parents were divorced and she was living with her mother, who was seldom home. She never reported the incident to her mother. A few days later when the pain had subsided, she said she had a craving to be "held and loved," and she went out looking for boys. Due to her early physical development, she had little difficulty finding them. Her first child was born at age 11, and a second at age 13.

It is important to note that almost all the strippers reached puberty at an early age.[10] This alone, of course, may cause emotional and social stress. But for these girls, physical maturity also brought great sexual attractiveness. When these combine with the lack of both affection and parental understanding, the possibilities of severe stress occurring are increased significantly. We believe that in order to meet love and affectional needs, these girls began to use and display their bodies as a means of gaining attention and recognition they did not receive at home.

Sure, after I bloomed I always dressed so people could see how big my breasts were. After all, a pair of 48's can make a girl feel like a real person. Everybody pays attention.

A need for attention, exhibitionistic behavior, and a natural curiosity about sex led many of the girls to early coital experiences.[11] For example, two girls claimed to have been raped before the age of 15. Later in the interviews, however, they admitted that while legally it might have been rape, in fact they had not resisted assault but courted it. As one girl put it:

I was looking for it; curious, you know. I wanted to know what it was like. I guess you might say I kind of led them on.

In a second case:

I was just budding and becoming aware that men were paying attention to me by the whistling and comments. I was picked up at a drug store by a man who promised to take me to a company fair. I knew what was going to happen.

The final important pattern concerns the regularity with which these girls broke family ties by or before age 18 and became independent.[12] Usually, but not always,

---

[10]Kinsey, et al. (1953:123–124) report that the median age of breast development for women in their sample was 12.4 years and first menstruation 13.0 years. The strippers on the average appear to develop one to two years earlier than the women in Kinsey's sample.

[11]Kinsey, et al. (1963:287–288) note that in their sample of females "pre-marital coitus was relatively rare in the early teens." They also report that irrespective of age at marriage only three percent of the females had coital experience by age 15 and only 20 percent by age 20. While our data on strippers are not complete, we do have evidence that at least 25 percent had sexual intercourse before age 15 and at least 75 percent before age 20.

[12]Duvall (1962:14) estimates the average woman breaks away from her family of orientation in her 20th year. Thus the strippers in our sample left home two to three years earlier than the average woman.

marriage was the vehicle used.

I left home when I was 12 years old, and got a job as a nude model. I was a big girl, no one guessed I was under age.

I got married while I was still in high school and had to quit.

I decided to marry this guy right after I left high school. That's when I left home for good.

At this point we can assess the possible relationship between the girls' ordinal position in the family and their personality and behavior. There is no doubt that the strippers had experienced little parental attention and affection. However, we have no direct evidence that this resulted from a shift in centrality of position with the birth of siblings. On the contrary, from what we know of the family situation, we speculate that the later-born did not fare much better than the first-born. Nevertheless, we do have some evidence that their resulting behavior was not the same: First, the later-born siblings remained or are remaining in the home longer than did the strippers. Second, in no case did we discover a brother entering or pursuing a deviant career. Finally, of the 14 strippers who had younger sisters (a total of 32 female siblings) in only one instance did the later-born follow in her sister's footsteps and become a stripper.

It appears consistent with the pattern of the first-born that the girls did seek the company of others outside the family to meet their need for affection. In the short run, their relationships with men outside the home were pleasing and satisfying. But we have no evidence of causal linkage between these activities and ordinal position.

The entrance into any occupation, be it stripping or plumbing, is not explainable solely in terms of particular personality and physical traits or family characteristics and experiences. Obviously there are girls whose backgrounds match the type discussed above who do not become strippers. Nevertheless, these described factors may make it easier for girls to view stripping as an acceptable occupational choice when other social factors converge making stripping a behavioral alternative.

Occupational Choice of Stripping

Sherlock and Cohen (1966) describe two important approaches to occupational choice: The first is termed "purposive" in which the choice is made on the basis of reward and access. The individual rationally considers reward preferences and his chances for access to various occupations. Final choice is usually a compromise between rewards and access and is based on a series of previous choices. The second approach is "adventitious" in that occupational choice is characterized as spontaneous, non-rational, fortuitous, and based on situational pressure and contingencies. Rational considerations play a minor role, if any. Sherlock and Cohen suggest:

The adventitious approach as we have called it, perhaps best describes recruitment to unskilled or semi-skilled occupations. The purposive approach seems to fit the case of skilled occupations including the professions.

With but one exception in our sample, it is the adventitious approach which better describes the occupational choice process of strippers. Furthermore, stripping qualifies as an unskilled occupation requiring little talent and almost no formal training. However, in the area of economics, rationality does play a key role in choosing to strip.

Economic considerations play such an important part in the girls' motivation to become and to remain strippers that it deserves special consideration. Perhaps the most forceful way to put it is to say that of the 35 girls interviewed only one had the talent, training, or education to make more money at any other legal occupation than stripping. As mentioned previously, the union minimum wage per seven day week for strippers is $175. However, we did not find any stripper who was being paid less than $200 per week. There are three levels of strippers: 1) Headliners, that is feature attractions, the stars of the show, 2) co-features, girls who are just under headliner status, and 3) line girls, all strippers who have not achieved the title of headliner or co-feature. The weekly pay of the line girls we interviewed ranged from $200–$250, co-features $275–$350, and headliners $275 to in excess of $1,500 with a median of $450. The girls also receive extra pay for any special shows. Usually the theaters have a special midnight show on Saturday nights, for which the girls receive the equivalent of a half day's pay. In addition, stripping offers easy access to moonlighting for those who choose to supplement their income as prostitutes. While prostitution is practiced more among strippers in the club setting than in the theater, some of the girls do turn tricks while on the road. At $35–$100 a trick,[13] one girl even claimed to make more money at prostitution than stripping. In comparison to the wages which women are paid in other occupations (clerks, secretaries, waitresses, nurses, teachers, etc.), strippers receive very high incomes.

---

[13] We did not meet any girls who would admit to prostitution for less than $35 a trick.

Although only a handful will ever become wealthy directly from stripping, those who do are visible enough to serve as symbols to other girls of what just might happen to them some day.

One of the more surprising aspects in the process of becoming a stripper is the lack of anticipatory socialization and formal training which the girls receive before entering the occupation. Although the age when the girls began stripping ranged from 14 to 29, over 50 percent of them were disrobing for a living before they were old enough to vote, and 80 percent before their 25th birthday. Only two of the girls reported having any desire to become strippers in the sense that someone might desire to become a teacher or a nurse, or even considered it a possibility much before the time they actually became strippers. The two exceptions are rather unique. One girl started stripping at age 14 and claimed she had never thought seriously about any other legal occupation. The second, a transsexual, was a male prostitute and a female impersonator while still in high school. She stated that this was what she wanted to do with her life—but not as a male. After the operation she became a stripper and a female prostitute. These cases are unusual. For the other girls the decision to become a stripper and their first performance were separated in time by only a few days and, in several cases, by less than an hour. Only one of the girls admitted to having another stripper as a role model, and only five related that they had even asked someone, "What do you do when you get on stage?" before their first professional performance. Besides the transsexual, who had experience performing as a female impersonator, none of the girls had any formal preparation for stripping. In fact, several of the girls had never even seen a strip show before they became professional performers themselves.[14]

Fourteen of the girls had received training as dancers and some had performed professionally. At first glance this would appear to be a type of indirect preparation for stripping, and it is to the extent that it provides experience in performing before an audience. Today, however, very few strippers use dance steps as part of their act. In fact, the word dance does not even appear in Libby Jones' how-to-do-it book *Striptease* (1967). As one of the headliners told us:

Dancing is not a requisite to stripping. Actually, any girl should certainly be able to walk to music or have a sense of timing or indication of their 'move-walk.' Dancing is basically removed from the essence of what you are supposed to be doing in the first place, which is being provocative. If you are dancing around on stage you really are not being provocative. You might be talented, but you are missing the point of stripping.

In the argot of the occupation, almost all strippers are not dancers but: 1) posers, girls who take a few steps, turn, and pose while disrobing; 2) walkers, girls who strip while walking to music; and 3) pacers, girls who remove their clothers while walking double time to slow music. The lack of anticipatory socialization and any type of prior association with the occupation, much less a training period, is in sharp contrast to the process of induction reported for other deviant occupations. For example, consider the case of the jazz musician (Becker, 1963), the pool hustler (Polsky, 1967), or the professional criminal

---

[14]There is at least one "school" which purports to "training" strippers, but none of the girls in the sample had attended it.

(Sutherland, 1937); even some types of prostitutes must serve an apprenticeship (Bryan, 1965).

Despite the lack of an apprenticeship period there is evidence of congruence between the content of previous jobs and stripping. An analysis of the occupational history of the subjects revealed that over 70 percent held jobs prior to stripping in which the display of their physical attributes was an integral part. Fifteen of the girls were in show business as dancers, singers, go-go girls, jugglers, and "gimmick" girls. Four others were employed as artists' models and another six made their living as waitress-bar maids or show-type hat check girls in night clubs. Thus a pattern of exhibitionism is apparent in the career choices of the future strippers as well as in their early social relationships. We do not wish to imply that stripping is the next logical step in a history of exhibitionistic behavior. We do suggest, however, that when an opportunity to strip arises, such past job experiences make it easier for girls to view stripping as an acceptable occupational alternative.

This proposition assumes greater significance when one understands the nature of the girls' social situations when they make the decision to earn their living by stripping. With the exception of the two girls who had always wanted to be strippers, the rest entered the business under what can best be termed varying patterns of fortuitous circumstances. Consistent with the "adventitious" model of occupational choice, they became strippers more by chance than design, more by drift than aspiration. In almost every case there were precipitating events which involved economic considerations. The most common pattern concerned the girls working in some form of show business as entertainers, who found themselves unable to obtain sufficient bookings. These girls liked and identified with the world of show business, but they were forced to consider other occupations as a means of support. At this point, the suggestion was made to them either by a friend or their agent that they could obtain plenty of work if they were willing to take off their clothes. Although at first the idea of stripping was not appealing to them (it was not so much the idea of taking off one's clothes in public which was repugnant, but the loss of social status both in show business and in the general society), they began to realize that it did offer them a chance to stay in show business and still meet their economic problems. As one girl put it, "It sure beats going out and working." Another stated:

I never thought about stripping, it just happened. I always wanted to be a great dancer, but I just couldn't make it. I couldn't get enough work. A friend suggested I could make a fortune just showing my breasts. I asked my agent and he agreed. So I did. I have been stripping for ten years now. It kept me in the business and I make more money than I ever would have in dancing.

Among the girls who were not recruited directly from show business, the precipitating events leading them to stripping also involved financial considerations. Three of the strippers had never held any full-time jobs save that of housewife. When their husbands left them with small children they were faced with an immediate need for employment. Not knowing quite what to do, they turned to friends for help. In each case, they were advised they could make a lot of money quickly as "show girls." All three answered ads in the newspaper for "exotic dancers," were surprised to learn it involved stripping, took the job anyway because of the money, and have been stripping ever since. Several of the other girls were working in establishments which featured stripping. In two cases when a scheduled stripper did not show up for work they were asked to substitute. They did, and found out "it was not so hard" and decided to take the better paying job. In a third case:

I was 18 years old and had a job as a hat-check girl in a night club which had strippers. I got to know some of the girls. When I found out that they were making two and three times as much money as I was; I decided to try it. After all, I figured I had just as big breasts as they did. I have a 39 inch bust line you know, and that's what counts in this business.

Another girl was working as a cocktail waitress and in need of money. She stripped the first time to win a bet from a customer and then decided it was a lot easier than waiting on tables. A girl with a long history of various deviant acts claimed she was continually fired from jobs, especially waitressing, because of her physical beauty. Finally, in frustration, she decided to take advantage of her attractiveness, went to a burlesque theater and asked for a tryout. She explained:

I could not get a job doing anything else. People said I was too attractive to have around their business. It was society that made me a "sinful" stripper. Everywhere I go, people stare at me and talk. When I go into a church, all the little old ladies turn aside and whisper behind their fans, talking about me. Doctors always have me strip and give a complete examination. Even a priest wants to hold me and kiss my feet. Both men and women view me as an animal who is oversexed, as simply a sex object.

The situations of the artists' models were similar to those of the girls in show business. They were not always able to get

Stripteasers: The Anatomy and Career Contingencies of A Deviant Occupation

sufficient work and were looking for an occupation which provided more stable employment. One girl answered an ad in the newspaper and entered a striptease contest; another got started when her agent suggested she could strip between modeling assignments; and a third had a friend connected with the business who told her she would make a good stripper.

The remaining girls also entered the occupation in equally fortuitous circumstances involving economic need. We interviewed a college student who had been told by her boy friend she could supplement her income during a summer vacation by moonlighting as a substitute stripper. She was unsure of how long she would continue in the business. We also talked to a former beautician who had dressed the hair of several strippers. When she learned the income they commanded, she decided she was in the wrong business. Finally, one stripper related that she had been a teacher. Her husband took her to see a strip show. She thought the performances were mediocre. When she later learned what the strippers earned, she decided to try out. She was offered double her teacher's salary to start.

Summary and Discussion

While women who strip for a living on the eastern burlesque circuit are recruited from a wide range of social classes and religions, they do have some common characteristics. As a group their physiques are larger than average for women of their age, particularly their bust size. They are usually Caucasian and were born and/or raised in large metropolitan areas. Almost all were first-born children who apparently received little affection from their parents, especially from the father who generally was absent from the home by the time the girls reached their teens.[15] Most developed secondary sex characteristics at a relatively early age and, typically, they had coital experiences by age 16. By age 18 they became independent and left their family of orientation, usually by marrying.

Rarely had the girls considered stripping as a means of making a living until shortly before their first performance; in fact, only a few knew anything about the occupation until they were involved in it. Although they began stripping with little or no training, in most cases their previous employment had involved jobs in which display of their bodies to the public was an important aspect. In many cases the decision to strip was made during a perceived financial crisis, but in other cases the girls were making an adequate though modest income. In either instance, the key precipitating factor was a sudden awareness that stripping would provide rapid access to relatively high earnings with little preparation or sacrifice.[16]

Any relationship between these general characteristics and the process of becoming a stripper is not completely evident since the data are obviously not definitive and exceptions exist even within our limited sample. Nevertheless, among the majority, a consistent pattern of these characteristics emerges which suggests a tentative sequential model. It appears that the career sequence for most of the strippers involved three contingencies: 1) a tend-

---

[15] Kammeyer (1966) and others have argued that ordinal position for women may be related to an orientation toward the traditional feminine sex role. The first born in this study do not lend support to that hypothesis.

[16] It is interesting to note that the heroine Iris Hartford, a stripper in Burton Wohl's novel *A Cold Wind in August*, (1960) closely approximates both the background characteristics and experiences of the strippers in our sample.

ency toward exhibitionistic behavior for gain, 2) an opportunity structure making stripping an accessible occupational alternative, and 3) a sudden awareness of the easy economic rewards in stripping.

Exhibitionistic behavior for gain. In the age of micro-mini skirts, "see through" blouses and "teeny weeny" bikinis, it is difficult to formulate a specific definition of what now constitutes "exhibitionistic" behavior for women. Given the rigors of law enforcement in some cities there is little question that many customers of burlesque theaters see little more on the stage than they do on the street, in stores, and at the beach. Thus it can be argued that even when on stage, strippers are not necessarily any more "exhibitionistic" than a sizeable proportion of the female population. There is, however, a consistent pattern among our subjects of using their physical attributes for affectional and economic advantage prior to their entrance into the occupation.

As discussed above, most of the girls reached physical maturity and an awareness of their own sexual attractiveness at a relatively early age. These were concomitant with early sexual experiences which appear to have resulted from a striving for attention and affection lacking in their home. This utilization of their sexual attractiveness carried over into their selection of work experiences prior to stripping. We speculate, then, that by the time an opportunity for stripping arose most of the subjects, because of their adolescent and early employment experiences, were predisposed to view *any* occupation involving the display of their bodies as an acceptable economic alternative.

Opportunity structure. Three factors involving opportunity were important for our subjects during the process of becoming strippers: First, they all were living in a large metropolitan area with clubs and/or a theater employing strippers. Second, they were all reasonably attractive or possessed a physical anomaly, usually large breasts, which ensured they would be considered by a booking agency or employer. Third, in nearly all instances they learned they had qualifications for being strippers from friends, employers, agents, or other acquaintances. Usually these individuals also provided specific information on persons to contact who were hiring strippers. Although we have only limited data, we suspect that these differential associations were important in providing support as well as information for a career in stripping. The girls relied upon the advice of individuals who defined stripping as a legitimate occupational choice in view of the girls' economic circumstances.

Awareness of easy economic gain. At first glance it would seem that the process of becoming a stripper seems to fit almost perfectly the adventitious model of occupational choice. Stripping is unskilled work and for all but two subjects entry into the occupation was spontaneous, fortuitous, and based on situational contingencies with little regard for long-range career goals. However, from either the subjective view of the strippers, or from our perhaps less subjective view, their decision does not fit the adventitious model criterion of being a non-rational decision. The most important reward preference for every girl in the sample was monetary. Although there were a few cases in which secondary goals existed, usually a desire to stay in some form of show business, the decision to enter the occupation was made primarily on the basis of a perceived financial crisis or by a comparison with a current low paying job. Given the salience of the economic goal, the recognition that stripping requires little or no training period, and the realization that stripping will provide prompt financial reward greater than any other available legitimate occupation, the decision was a reasonable and purposive one.

While this sequence of career contingencies for becoming a stripper is based on data from subjects employed by the eastern wheel, it probably applies to most strippers on the western theater circuit and in clubs, since a large proportion of the sample had worked in both settings. Furthermore, it appears that regardless of the work setting, entrance requirements, performance, and pay are roughly equivalent.

The purpose of this study was to identify contingencies for entering the occupation. Further research may reveal others which distinguish those girls who continue in the occupation over a relatively long period, and still others which distinguish those who become more successful economically.

Such a sequence, if valid, has implications beyond the study of strippers. It indicates that limiting investigations to "kinds" of persons and situations as separate entities may result in a relatively static conception of deviant behavior. Since decisions to engage in, and probably continue in, deviant behavior involve an interaction process between the characteristics of individuals, their past experiences, and a number of situational conditions, it is imperative that greater research efforts be made in the direction of formulating sequential models incorporating these factors. From our experience, this research strategy may be particularly relevant to those deviant careers requiring specific attributes and limited entrance opportunities such as professional criminals, hustlers, and professional gamblers. In addition, the sequential model may be extremely helpful in casting light on the whole problem of occupational choice outside the area of deviancy.

References

Becker, Howard
   1963 Outsiders: Studies in the Sociology of Deviance. London: Collier-Macmillan.

Blau, P. et al.
   1956 "Occupational choice: A conceptual framework." Industrial and Labor Relations Review. 9:531–543.

Bryan, J.
   1965 "Apprenticeships in prostitution." Social Problems 12:287–297.

Cleveland Plain Dealer
   November 10, 1968.

Cohen, Albert K.
   1966 Deviance and Social Control. Englewood Cliffs, New Jersey: Prentice-Hall.

Colombotos, J.
   1969 "Social origins and ideology of physicians: A study of the effects of early socialization." Journal of Health and Social Behavior. 10:16–29.

Corio, Ann, and Joe DiMona
   1968 This Was Burlesque. New York: Grossett and Dunlap.

Current Population Reports
   June 25, 1968 Population Characteristics: Household and Family Characteristics, March 1967.

D'Andre, A.
   1965 "An occupational study of the strip-dance-career." Paper read at the Pacific Sociological Association Meetings, Salt Lake City, Utah.

Dressler, David
   1937 Burlesque As A Cultural Phenomenon. New York University: Unpublished doctoral dissertation.

Duvall, Evelyn
   1962 Family Development. Philadelphia: Lippincott.

Glaser, Barney and Anselm Strauss
  1967 The Discovery of Grounded Theory: Strategies for Qualitative Research. Chicago: Aldine.
Hollingshead, A.
  1957 "Two factor index of social position." New Haven: Yale University (mimeograph).
Jesser, C., and L. Donovan
  1969 "Nudity in the art training process." Sociological Quarterly 10:355–371.
Jones, Libby
  1967 Striptease. New York: Simon and Schuster.
Kammeyer, K.
  1966 "Birth order and the feminine sex role among college women." American Sociological Review 31:508–515.
Katz, F. and H. Martin
  1962 "Career choice processes." Social Forces 41:47–54.
Kinsey, Alfred, Wardell Pomeroy, Clyde Martin, and Paul Gebhard
  1953 Sexual Behavior in the Human Female. Philadelphia: W. B. Saunders.
Ladinsky, J.
  1963 "Careers of lawyers, law practice and legal institutions," American Sociological Review 28:47–54.
Mauksch, H.
  1960 A Sociological Analysis of the Nurse Role. University of Chicago: Unpublished doctoral dissertation.
Playboy
  January, 1969
Sampson, C.
  1965 The Study of Ordinal Position: Antecedents and Outcomes. Pp. 176–228 in Brendan Maher (ed.) Progress in Experimental Personality Research. New York: Academic Press.
Sherlock, B.
  1969 "The second profession: Parallel mobilities of the dental profession and its recruits." Journal of Health and Social Behavior 10:41–51

Sherlock, B., and A. Cohen
  1966 "The strategy of occupational choice: Recruitment to dentistry." Social Forces 44:303–313.
Sutherland, Edwin (ed.)
  1937 The Professional Thief. Chicago: University of Chicago Press.
Wallace, Samuel
  1965 Skid Row As A Way of Life. New York: Harper and Row.
Wohl, Burton
  1960 A Cold Wind in August. New York: Dell.
Zeidman, Irving
  1967 The American Burlesque Show. New York: Hawthorne Books Inc.

SOCIAL DISORGANIZATION

Wincanton: The Politics of Corruption

JOHN A. GARDINER, WITH THE ASSISTANCE OF DAVID J. OLSON

In general, Wincanton represents a city that has toyed with the problem of corruption for many years. No mayor in the history of the city of Wincanton has ever succeeded himself in office. Some mayors have been corrupt and have allowed the city to become a wide-open center for gambling and prostitution; Wincanton voters have regularly rejected those corrupt mayors who dared to seek reelection. Some mayors have been scrupulously honest and have closed down all vice operations in the city; these men have been generally disliked for being too straitlaced. Other mayors, fearing one form of resentment or the other, have chosen quietly to retire from public life. The questions of official corruption and policy toward vice and gambling, it seems, have been paramount issues in Wincanton elections since the days of Prohibition. Any mayor who is known to be controlled by the gambling syndicates will lose office, but so will any mayor who tries completely to clean up the city. The people of Wincanton apparently want both easily accessible gambling and freedom from racket domination.

Probably more than most cities in the United States, Wincanton has known a high degree of gambling, vice (sexual immorality, including prostitution), and corruption (official malfeasance, misfeasance and nonfeasance of duties). With the exception of two reform administrations, one in the early 1950's and the one elected in the early 1960's, Wincanton has been wide open since the 1920's. Bookies taking bets on horses took in several millions of dollars each year. With writers at most newsstands, cigar counters, and corner grocery stores, a numbers bank did an annual business in excess of $1,300,000 during some years. Over 200 pinball machines, equipped to pay off like slot machines, bore $250 Federal gambling stamps. A high stakes dice game attracted professional gamblers from more than 100 miles away; $25,000 was found on the table during one Federal raid. For a short period of time in the 1950's (until raided by U.S. Treasury Department agents), a still, capable of manufacturing $1 million in illegal alcohol each year, operated on the banks of the Wincanton River. Finally, prostitution flourished openly in the city, with at least 5 large houses (about 10 girls apiece) and countless smaller houses catering to men from a large portion of the state.

As in all cities in which gambling and vice had flourished openly, these illegal activities were protected by local officials. Mayors, police chiefs, and many lesser officials were on the payroll of the gambling syndicate, while others received periodic "gifts" or aid during political campaigns. A number of Wincanton officials added to their revenue from the syndicate by extorting kickbacks on the sale or purchase of city equipment or by selling licenses, permits, zoning variances, etc. As the city officials made possible the operations of the racketeers, so frequently the racketeers facilitated the corrupt endeavors of officials by providing liaison men to arrange the deals or "enforcers" to insure that the deals were carried out. . . .

To understand law enforcement in Wincanton, it is necessary to look at the activities of local, county, State, and Federal agencies. State law requires that each mayor select his police chief and officers "from the force" and "exercise a constant supervision and control over their conduct." Applicants for the police force are chosen on the basis of a civil service examination and have tenure "during good behavior," but promotions and demotions are entirely at the discretion of the mayor and council. Each new administration in Wincanton has made wholesale changes in police ranks—patrolmen have been named chief, and former chiefs have been reduced to walking a beat. (When one period of reform came to an end in the mid-1950's, the incoming mayor summoned the old chief into his office, "You can stay on as an officer," the mayor said, "but you'll have to go along with my policies regarding gambling." "Mr. Mayor," the chief said, "I'm going to keep on arresting gamblers no matter where you put me." The mayor assigned the former chief to the position of "Keeper of the Lockup," permanently stationed in the basement of police headquarters.) Promotions must be made from within the department. This policy has continued even though the present reform mayor created the post of police commissioner and brought in an outsider to take command. For cities of its size, Wincanton police salaries have been quite low—the top pay for patrolmen was $4,856—in the lowest quartile of middle-sized cities in the Nation. Since 1964 the commissioner has received $10,200 and patrolmen $5,400 each year.

While the police department is the prime law enforcement agency within Wincanton, it receives help (and occasional embarrassment) from other groups. Three county detectives work under the district attorney, primarily in rural parts of Alsace County, but they are occasionally called upon to assist in city investigations. The State Police, working out of a barracks in suburban Wincanton Hills, have generally taken a "hands off" or "local option" attitude toward city crime, working only in rural areas unless invited into a city by the mayor, district attorney, or county judge. Reform mayors have welcomed the superior manpower and investigative powers of the State officers; corrupt mayors have usually been able to thumb their noses at State policemen trying to uncover Wincanton gambling. Agents of the State's Alcoholic Beverages Commission suffer from no such limitations and enter Wincanton at will in search of liquor violations. They have seldom been a serious threat to Wincanton corruption, however, since their numbers are quite limited (and thus the agents are dependent upon the local police for information and assistance in making arrests). Their mandate extends to gambling and prostitution only when encountered in the course of a liquor investigation.

Under most circumstances, the operative level of law enforcement in Wincanton has been set by local political decisions, and the local police (acting under instructions from the mayor) have been able to determine whether or not Wincanton should have open gambling and prostitution. The State Police, with their "hands off" policy, have simply reenforced the local decision. From time to time, however, Federal agencies have become interested in conditions in Wincanton and, as will be seen throughout this study, have played as important a role as the local police in cleaning up the city. Internal Revenue Service agents have succeeded in prosecuting Wincanton gamblers for failure to hold gambling occupation stamps, pay the special excise taxes on gambling receipts, or report income. Federal Bureau of Investigation agents have acted against violations of the Federal laws against extortion and interstate gambling. Finally, special attorneys from the Organized Crime and Racketeering Section of the Justice Department were able to convict leading members of the syndicate controlling Wincanton gambling. While Federal prosecutions in Wincanton have often been spectacular, it should also be noted that they have been somewhat sporadic and limited in scope. The Internal Revenue Service, for example, was quite successful in seizing gambling devices and gamblers lacking the Federal gambling occupation stamps, but it was helpless after Wincantonites began to purchase the stamps, since local officials refused to prosecute them for violations of the State antigambling laws.

The court system in Wincanton, as in all cities in the State, still has many of the 18th century features which have been rejected in other States. At the lowest level, elected magistrates (without legal training) hear petty civil and criminal cases in each ward of the city. The magistrates also issue warrants and decide whether persons arrested by the police shall be held for trial. Magistrates are paid only by fees, usually at the expense of convicted defendants. All serious criminal cases, and all contested petty cases, are tried in the county court. The three judges of the Alsace County court are elected (on a partisan ballot) for 10-year terms, and receive an annual salary of $25,000.

Gambling and Corruption: The Insiders

THE STERN EMPIRE

The history of Wincanton gambling and corruption since World War II centers around the career of Irving Stern. Stern is an immigrant who came to the United States and settled in Wincanton at the turn of the century. He started as a fruit peddler, but when Prohibition came along, Stern became a bootlegger for Heinz Glickman, then the beer baron of the State.

When Glickman was murdered in the waning days of Prohibition, Stern took over Glickman's business and continued to sell untaxed liquor after repeal of Prohibition in 1933. Several times during the 1930's, Stern was convicted in Federal court on liquor charges and spent over a year in Federal prison.

Around 1940, Stern announced to the world that he had reformed and went into his family's wholesale produce business. While Stern was in fact leaving the bootlegging trade, he was also moving into the field of gambling, for even at that time Wincanton had a "wide-open" reputation, and the police were ignoring gamblers. With the technical assistance of his bootlegging friends, Stern started with a numbers bank and soon added horse betting, a dice game, and slot machines to his organization. During World War II, officers from a nearby Army training base insisted that all brothels be closed, but this did not affect Stern. He had already concluded that public hostility and violence, caused by the horses, were, as a side effect, threatening his more profitable gambling operations. Although Irv Stern controlled the lion's share of Wincanton gambling throughout the 1940's, he had to share the slot machine trade with Klaus Braun. Braun, unlike Stern, was a Wincanton native and a Gentile, and thus had easier access to the frequently anti-Semitic club stewards, restaurant owners, and bartenders who decided which machines would be placed in their buildings. Legislative investigations in the early 1950's estimated that Wincanton gambling was an industry with gross receipts of $5 million each year; at that time Stern was receiving $40,000 per week from bookmaking, and Braun took in $75,000 to $100,000 per year from slot machines alone.

Irv Stern's empire in Wincanton collapsed abruptly when legislative investigations brought about the election of a reform Republican administration. Mayor Hal Craig decided to seek what he termed "pearl gray purity" to tolerate isolated prostitutes, bookies, and numbers writers but to drive out all forms of organized crime, all activities lucrative enough to make it worth someone's while to try bribing Craig's police officials. Within 6 weeks after taking office, Craig and District Attorney Henry Weiss had raided enough of Stern's gambling parlors and seized enough of Braun's slot machines to convince both men that business was over for 4 years at least. The Internal Revenue Service was able to convict Braun and Stern's nephew, Dave Feinman, on tax evasion charges; both were sent to jail. From 1952 to 1955 it was still possible to place a bet or find a girl. But you had to know someone to do it, and no one was getting very rich in the process.

By 1955 it was apparent to everyone that reform sentiment was dead and that the Democrats would soon be back in office. In the summer of that year, Stern met with representatives of the east coast syndicates and arranged for the rebuilding of his empire. He decided to change his method of operations in several ways; one way was by centralizing all Wincanton vice and gambling under his control. But he also decided to turn the actual operation of most enterprises over to others. From the mid-1950's until the next wave of reform hit Wincanton after elections in the early 1960's, Irv Stern generally succeeded in reaching these goals.

The financial keystone of Stern's gambling empire was numbers betting. Records seized by the Internal Revenue Service in the late 1950's and early 1960's indicated that gross receipts from numbers amounted to more than $100,000 each month, or

$1.3 million annually. Since the numbers are a poor man's form of gambling (bets range from a penny to a dime or quarter), a large number of men and a high degree of organization are required. The organizational goals are three; have the maximum possible number of men on the streets seeking bettors, be sure that they are reporting honestly, and yet strive so to decentralize the organization that no one, if arrested, will be able to identify many of the others. During the "pearl gray purity" of Hal Craig, numbers writing was completely unorganized, many isolated writers took bets from their friends and frequently had to renege if an unusually popular number came up; no one writer was big enough to guard against such possibilities. When a new mayor took office in the mid-1950's, however, Stern's lieutenants notified each of the small writers that they were now working for Stern or else. Those who objected were "persuaded" by Stern's men, or else arrested by the police, as were any of the others who were suspected of holding out on their receipts. Few objected for very long. After Stern completed the reorganization of the numbers business, its structure was roughly something like this; 11 subbanks reported to Stern's central accounting office. Each subbank employed from 5 to 30 numbers writers. Thirty-five percent of the gross receipts went to the writers. After deducting for winnings and expenses (mostly protection payoffs), Stern divided the net profits equally with the operators of the subbanks. In return for his cut, Stern provided protection from the police and "laid off" the subbanks, covering winnings whenever a popular number "broke" one of the smaller operators.

Stern also shared with out-of-State syndicates in the profits and operation of two enterprises, a large dice game and the largest still found by the Treasury Department since Prohibition. The dice game employed over 50 men drivers to "lug" players into town from as far as 100 miles away, doormen to check players' identities, loan sharks who "faded" the losers, croupiers, food servers, guards, etc. The 1960 payroll for these employees was over $350,000. While no estimate of the gross receipts from the game is available, some indication of its size can be obtained from the fact that $50,000 was found on the tables and in the safe when the FBI raided the game in 1962. Over 100 players were arrested during the raid; one businessman had lost over $75,000 at the tables. Stern received a share of the game's profits plus a $1,000 weekly fee to provide protection from the police.

Stern also provided protection (for a fee) and shared in the profits of a still, erected in an old warehouse on the banks of the Wincanton River and tied into the city's water and sewer systems. Stern arranged for clearance by the city council and provided protection from the local police after the $200,000 worth of equipment was set up. The still was capable of producing $4 million worth of alcohol each year, and served a five-State area, until Treasury agents raided it after it had been in operation for less than 1 year.

The dice game and the still raise questions regarding the relationship of Irv Stern to out-of-State syndicates. Republican politicians in Wincanton frequently claimed that Stern was simply the local agent of the Cosa Nostra. While Stern was regularly sending money to the syndicates, the evidence suggests that Stern was much more than an agent for outsiders. It would be more accurate to regard these payments as profit-sharing with coinvestors and as charges for services rendered. The east coasters provided technical services in the operation of the dice game and still and "enforcement" service for the Wincanton gambling operation. When deviants had to be persuaded to accept Stern's domination, Stern called upon outsiders for "muscle"—strong-arm men who could not be traced by local police if the victim chose to protest. In the early 1940's, for example, Stern asked for help in destroying a competing dice game; six gunmen came in and held it up, robbing and terrifying the players. While a few murders took place in the struggle for supremacy in the 1930's and 1940's, only a few people were roughed up in the 1950's and no one was killed.

After the mid-1950's, Irv Stern controlled prostitution and several forms of gambling on a "franchise" basis. Stern took no part in the conduct of these businesses and received no share of the profits, but exacted a fee for protection from the police. Several horse books, for example, operated regularly; the largest of these paid Stern $600 per week. While slot machines had permanently disappeared from the Wincanton scene after the legislative investigations of the early 1950's, a number of men began to distribute pinball machines, which paid off players for games won. As was the case with numbers writers, these pinball distributors had been unorganized during the Craig administration. When Democratic Mayor Gene Donnelly succeeded Craig, he immediately announced that all pinball machines were illegal and would be confiscated by the police. A Stern agent then contacted the pinball distributors and notified them that if they employed Dave Feinman (Irv Stern's nephew) as a "public relations consultant," there would be no interference from the police. Several rebellious distributors formed an Alsace County Amusement Operators Association, only to see Feinman appear with two thugs from New York. After the association president was roughed up, all resistance collapsed, and Feinman collected $2,000 each week to promote the "public relations" of the distributors. (Stern, of course, was able to offer no protection against Federal action. After the Internal Revenue Service began seizing the pinball machines in 1956, the owners were forced to purchase the $250 Federal gambling stamps as well as paying Feinman. Over 200 Wincanton machines bore these stamps in the early 1960's, and thus were secure from Federal as well as local action.) In the 1950's, Irv Stern was able to establish a centralized empire which he alone determined which rackets would operate and who would operate them (he never, it might be noted, permitted narcotics traffic in the city while he controlled it). What were the bases of his control within the criminal world? Basically, they were three: First, as a business matter, Stern controlled access to several very lucrative operations, and could quickly deprive an uncooperative gambler or numbers writer of his source of income. Second, since he controlled the police department he could arrest any gamblers or bookies who were not paying tribute. (Some of the local gambling and prostitution arrests which took place during the Stern era served another purpose—to placate newspaper demands for a crackdown. As one police chief from this era phrased it, "Hollywood should have given us an Oscar for some of our performances when we had to pull a phony raid to keep the papers happy.") Finally, if the mechanisms of fear of financial loss and fear of police arrest failed to command obedience, Stern was always able to keep alive a fear of physical violence. As we have seen, numbers writers, pinball distributors and competing gamblers were brought into line after outside enforcers put in an appearance. Stern's regular collection agent, a local tough who had been convicted of murder in the 1940's, was a constant reminder of the virtues of cooperation. Several witnesses who told grand juries or Federal agents of extortion attempts by Stern, received visits from Stern enforcers and tended to "forget" when called to testify against the boss.

Protection. An essential ingredient in Irv Stern's Wincanton operations was protection against law enforcement agencies. While he was never able to arrange freedom from Federal intervention (although, as in the case of purchasing excise stamps for the pinball machines, he was occasionally able to satisfy Federal requirements without disrupting his activities), Stern was able in the 1940's and again from the mid-1950's through the early 1960's to secure freedom from State and local action. The precise extent of Stern's network of protection payments is unknown, but the method of operations can be reconstructed.

Two basic principles were involved in the Wincanton protection system—pay top personnel as much as necessary to keep them happy (and quiet), and pay something to as many others as possible to implicate them in the system and to keep them from talking. The range of payoffs thus went from a weekly salary for some public officials to a Christmas turkey for the patrolman on the beat. Records from the numbers bank listed payments totaling $2,400 each week to some local elected officials, State legislators, the police chief, a captain in charge of detectives, and persons mysteriously labeled "county" and "State." While the list of persons to be paid remained fairly constant the amounts varied according to the activities in operation at the time; pay-off figures dropped sharply when the FBI put the dice game out of business. When the dice game was running, one official was receiving $750 per week, the chief $100, and a few captains, lieutenants, and detectives lesser amounts.

While the number of officials receiving regular "salary" payoffs was quite restricted (only 15 names were on the payroll found at the numbers bank), many other officials were paid off in different ways. (Some men were also silenced without charge—low-ranking policemen, for example, kept quiet after they learned that men who reported gambling or prostitution were ignored or transferred to the midnight shift; they didn't have to be paid.) Stern was a major (if undisclosed) contributor during political campaigns—sometimes giving money to all candidates, not caring who won, sometimes supporting a "regular" to defeat a possible reformer, sometimes paying a candidate not to oppose a preferred man. Since there were few legitimate sources of large contributions for Democratic candidates, Stern's money was frequently regarded as essential for victory, for the costs of buying radio and television time and paying pollwatchers were high. When popular sentiment was running strongly in favor of reform, however, even Stern's contributions could not guarantee victory. Bob Walasek, later to be as corrupt as any Wincanton mayor, ran as a reform candidate in the Democratic primary and defeated Stern-financed incumbent Gene Donnelly. Never a man to bear grudges, Stern financed Walasek in the general election that year and put him on the "payroll" when he took office.

Even when local officials were not on the regular payroll, Stern was careful to remind them of his friendship (and their debts). A legislative investigating committee found that Stern had given mortgage loans to a police lieutenant and the police chief's son. County Court Judge Ralph Vaughan recalled that shortly after being elected (with Stern support), he received a call from Dave Feinman, Stern's nephew, "Congratulations, judge. When do you think you and your wife would like a vacation in Florida?"

"Florida? Why on earth would I want to go there?"

"But all the other judges and the guys in City Hall—Irv takes them all to Florida whenever they want to get away."

"Thanks anyway, but I'm not interested."

"Well, how about a mink coat instead. What size coat does your wife wear?"

In another instance an assistant district attorney told of Feinman's arriving at his front door with a large basket from Stern's supermarket just before Christmas. "My minister suggested a needy family that could use the food," the assistant district attorney recalled, "but I returned the liquor to Feinman. How could I ask a minister if he knew someone that could use three bottles of scotch?"

Campaign contributions, regular payments to higher officials, holiday and birthday gifts—these were the bases of the system by which Irv Stern bought protection from the law. The campaign contributions usually ensured that complacent mayors, councilmen, district attorneys, and judges were elected; payoffs in some instances usually kept their loyalty. In a number of ways, Stern was also able to reward the corrupt officials at no financial cost to himself. Just as the officials, being in control of the instruments of law enforcement, were able to facilitate Stern's gambling enterprises, so Stern, in control of a network of men operating outside the law, was able to facilitate the officials' corrupt enterprises. As will be seen later, many local officials were not satisfied with their legal salaries from the city and their illegal salaries from Stern and decided to demand payments from prostitutes, kickbacks from salesmen, etc. Stern, while seldom receiving any money from these transactions, became a broker; bringing politicians into contact with salesmen, merchants, and lawyers willing to offer bribes to get city business; setting up middlemen who could handle the money without jeopardizing the officials' reputations; and providing enforcers who could bring delinquents into line.

From the corrupt activities of Wincanton officials, Irv Stern received little in contrast to his receipts from his gambling operations. Why then did he get involved in them? The major virtue, from Stern's point of view, of the system of extortion that flourished in Wincanton was that it kept down the officials' demands for payoffs directly from Stern. If a councilman was able to pick up $1,000 on the purchase of city equipment, he would demand a lower payment for the protection of gambling. Furthermore, since Stern knew the facts of extortion in each instance, the officials would be further implicated in the system and less able to back out on the arrangements regarding gambling. Finally, as Stern discovered to his chagrin, it became necessary to supervise official extortion to protect the officials against their own stupidity. Mayor Gene Donnelly was cooperative and remained satisfied with his regular "salary." Bob Walasek, however, was a greedy man, and seized every opportunity to profit from a city contract. Soon Stern found himself supervising many of Walasek's deals to keep the mayor from blowing the whole arrangement wide open. When Walasek tried to double the "take" on a purchase of parking meters, Stern had to step in and set the contract price, provide an untraceable middleman, and see the deal through to completion. "I told Irv," Police Chief Phillips later testified, "that Walasek wanted $12 on each meter instead of the $6 we got on the last meter deal. He became furious. He said, 'Walasek is going to fool around and wind up in jail. You come and see me. I'll tell Walasek what he's going to buy.' "

Protection, it was stated earlier, was an essential ingredient in Irv Stern's gambling empire. In the end, Stern's downfall came not from a flaw in the organization of the gambling enterprises but from public exposure of the corruption of Mayor Walasek and other officials. In the early 1960's Stern was sent to jail for 4 years on tax evasion charges, but the gambling empire continued to operate smoothly in his absence. A year later, however, Chief Phillips was caught perjuring himself in grand jury testimony concerning kickbacks on city towing contracts. Phillips "blew the whistle" on Stern, Walasek, and members of the city council, and a reform administration was swept into office. Irv Stern's gambling empire had been worth several million dollars each year; kickbacks on the towing contracts brought Bob Walasek a paltry $50 to $75 each week.

Official Corruption

Textbooks on municipal corporation law speak of at least three varieties of official corruption. The major categories are nonfeasance (failing to perform a required duty at all), malfeasance (the commission of some act which is positively unlawful), and misfeasance (the improper performance of some act which a man may properly do). During the years in which Irv Stern was running his gambling operations, Wincanton officials were guilty of all of these. Some residents say that Bob Walasek came to regard the mayor's office as a brokerage, levying a tariff on every item that came across his desk. Sometimes a request for simple municipal services turned into a game of cat and mouse, with Walasek sitting on the request, waiting to see how much would be offered, and the petitioner waiting to see if he could obtain his rights without having to pay for them. Corruption was not as lucrative an enterprise as gambling, but it offered a tempting supplement to low official salaries.

NONFEASANCE

As was detailed earlier, Irv Stern saw to it that Wincanton officials would ignore at least one of their statutory duties, enforcement of the State's gambling laws. Bob Walasek and his cohorts also agreed to overlook other illegal activities. Stern, we noted earlier, preferred not to get directly involved in prostitution; Walasek and Police Chief Dave Phillips tolerated all prostitutes who kept up their protection payments. One madam, controlling more than 20 girls, gave Phillips et al. $500 each week; one woman employing only one girl paid $75 each week that she was in business. Operators of a carnival in rural Alsace County paid a public official $5,000 for the privilege of operating gambling tents for 5 nights each summer. A burlesque theater manager, under attack by high school teachers, was ordered to pay $25 each week for the privilege of keeping his strip show open.

Many other city and county officials must be termed guilty of nonfeasance, although there is no evidence that they received payoffs, and although they could present reasonable excuses for their inaction. Most policemen, as we have noted earlier, began to ignore prostitution and gambling completely after their reports of offenses were ignored or superior officers told them to mind their own business. State policemen, well informed about city vice and gambling conditions, did nothing unless called upon to act by local officials. Finally, the judges of the Alsace County Court failed to exercise their power to call for State Police investigations. In 1957, following Federal raids on horse bookies, the judges did request an investigation by the State Attorney General, but refused to approve his suggestion that a grand jury be convened to continue the investigation. For each of these instances of inaction, a tenable excuse might be offered—the beat patrolman should not be expected to endure harassment from his superior officers, State police gambling raids in a hostile city might jeopardize State-local cooperation on more serious crimes, and a grand jury probe might easily be turned into a "whitewash" in the hands of a corrupt district attorney. In any event, powers available to these law enforcement agencies for the prevention of gambling and corruption were not utilized.

MALFEASANCE

In fixing parking and speeding tickets, Wincanton politicians and policemen committed malfeasance, or committed an act they were forbidden to do, by illegally compromising valid civil and criminal actions. Similarly, while State law provides no particular standards by which the mayor is to make promotions within his police department, it was obviously improper for Mayor Walasek to demand a "political contribution" of $10,000 from Dave Phillips before he was appointed chief in 1960.

The term "political contribution" raises a serious legal and analytical problem in classifying the malfeasance of Wincanton officials, and indeed of politicians in many cities. Political campaigns cost money; citizens have a right to support the candidates of their choice; and officials have a right to appoint their backers to noncivil service positions. At some point, however, threats or oppression convert legitimate requests for political contributions into extortion. Shortly after taking office in the mid-1950's, Mayor Gene Donnelly notified city hall employees that they would be expected "voluntarily" to contribute 2 percent of their salary to the Democratic Party. (It might be noted that Donnelly never forwarded any of these "political contributions" to the party treasurer.) A number of salesmen doing business with the city were notified that companies which had supported the party would receive favored treatment; Donnelly notified one salesman that in light of a proposed $31,000 contract for the purchase of fire engines, a "political contribution" of $2,000 might not be inappropriate. While neither the city hall employees nor the salesmen had rights to their positions or their contracts, the "voluntary" quality of their contributions seems questionable.

One final, in the end almost ludicrous, example of malfeasance came with Mayor Donnelly's abortive "War on the Press." Following a series of gambling raids by the Internal Revenue Service, the newspapers began asking why the local police had not participated in the raids. The mayor lost his temper and threw a reporter in jail. Policemen were instructed to harass newspaper delivery trucks, and 73 tickets were written over a 48-hour period for supposed parking and traffic violations. Donnelly soon backed down after national news services picked up the story, since press coverage made him look ridiculous. Charges against the reporter were dropped, and the newspapers continued to expose gambling and corruption.

MISFEASANCE

Misfeasance in office, says the common law, is the improper performance of some act which a man may properly do. City officials must buy and sell equipment, contract for services, and allocate licenses, privileges, etc. These actions can be improperly performed if either the results are improper (e.g., if a building inspector were to approve a home with defective wiring or a zoning board to authorize a variance which had no justification in terms of land usage) or a result is achieved by improper procedures (e.g., if the city purchased an acceptable automobile in consideration of a bribe paid to the purchasing agent). In the latter case, we can usually assume an improper result as well—while the automobile will be satisfactory, the bribe giver will probably have inflated the sale price to cover the costs of the bribe.

In Wincanton, it was rather easy for city officials to demand kickbacks, for State law frequently does not demand competitive bidding or permits the city to ignore the lowest bid. The city council is not required to advertise or take bids on purchases under $1,000, contracts for maintenance of streets and other public works, personal or professional services, or patented or copyrighted products. Even when bids must be sought, the council is only required to award the contract to the lowest responsible bidder. Given these permissive provisions, it was relatively easy for council members to justify or disguise contracts in fact based upon bribes. The exemption for patented products facilitated bribe taking on the purchase of two emergency trucks for the police department (with a $500 campaign contribution on a $7,500 deal), three fire engines ($2,000 was allegedly paid on an $81,000 contract), and 1,500 parking meters (involving payments of $10,500 plus an $880 clock for Mayor Walasek's home). Similar fees were allegedly exacted in connection with the purchase of a city fire alarm system and police uniforms and firearms. A former mayor and other officials also profited on the sale of city property, allegedly dividing $500 on the sale of a crane and $20,000 for approving the sale, for $22,000, of a piece of land immediately resold for $75,000.

When contracts involved services to the city, the provisions in the State law regarding the lowest responsible bidder and excluding "professional services" from competitive bidding provided convenient loopholes. One internationally known engineering firm refused to agree to kickback in order to secure a contract to design a $15 million sewage disposal plant for the city; a local firm was then appointed, which paid $10,700 of its $225,000 fee to an associate of Irv Stern and Mayor Donnelly as a "finder's fee." Since the State law also excludes public works maintenance contracts from the competitive bidding requirements, many city paving and street repair contracts during the Donnelly-Walasek era were given to a contributor to the Democratic Party. Finally, the franchise for towing illegally parked cars and cars involved in accidents was awarded to two garages which were then required to kickback $1 for each car towed.

The handling of graft on the towing contracts illustrates the way in which minor violence and the "lowest responsible bidder" clause could be used to keep the bribe payers in line. After Federal investigators began to look into Wincanton corruption, the owner of one of the garages with a towing franchise testified before the grand jury. Mayor Walasek immediately withdrew his franchise, citing "health violations" at the garage. The garageman was also "encouraged" not to testify by a series of "accidents"—wheels would fall off towtrucks on the highway, steering cables were cut, and so forth. Newspaper satirization of the "health violations" forced the restoration of the towing franchise, and the "accidents" ceased.

Lest the reader infer that the "lowest responsible bidder" clause was used as an escape valve only for corrupt purposes, one incident might be noted which took place under the present reform administration. In 1964, the Wincanton School Board sought bids for the renovation of an athletic field. The lowest bid came from a construction company owned by Dave Phillips, the corrupt police chief who had served formerly under Mayor Walasek. While the company was presumably competent to carry out the assignment, the board rejected Phillips' bid "because of a question as to his moral responsibility." The board did not specify whether this referred to his poor corruption as chief or his present status as an informer in testifying against Walasek and Stern.

One final area of city power, which was abused by Walasek et al., covered discretionary acts, such as granting permits and allowing zoning variances. On taking office, Walasek took the unusual step of asking that the bureaus of building and plumbing inspection be put under the mayor's control. With this power to approve or deny building permits, Walasek "sat on" applications, waiting until the petitioner contributed $50 or $75, or threatened to sue to get his permit. Some building designs were not approved until a favored architect was retained as a "consultant." (It is not known whether this involved kickbacks to Walasek or simply patronage for a friend.) At least three instances are known in which developers were forced to pay for zoning variances before apartment buildings or supermarkets could be erected. Businessmen who wanted to encourage rapid turnover of the curb space in front of their stores were told to pay a police sergeant to erect "10-minute parking" signs. To repeat a caveat stated earlier, it is impossible to tell whether these kickbacks were demanded to expedite legitimate requests or to approve improper demands, such as a variance that would hurt a neighborhood or a certificate approving improper electrical work.

All of the activities detailed thus far involve fairly clear violations of the law. To complete the picture of the abuse of office by Wincanton officials, we might briefly mention "honest graft." This term was best defined by one of its earlier practitioners, State Senator George Washington Plunkitt who loyally served Tammany Hall at the turn of the century.

There's all the difference in the world between [honest and dishonest graft]. Yes, many of our men have grown rich in politics. I have myself.

I've made a big fortune out of the game, and I'm gettin' richer every day, but I've not gone in for dishonest graft—blackmailin' gamblers, saloonkeepers, disorderly people, etc.—and neither has any of the men who have made big fortunes in politics.

There's an honest graft, and I'm an example of how it works. I might sum up the whole thing by saying: "I seen my opportunities and I took 'em."

Let me explain by examples. My party's in power in the city, and it's goin' to undertake a lot of public improvements. Well, I'm tipped off, say, that they're going to lay out a new park at a certain place.

I see my opportunity and I take it. I go to that

place, and I buy up all the land I can in the neighborhood. Then the board of this or that makes its plan public, and there is a rush to get my land, which nobody cared particular for before.

Ain't it perfectly honest to charge a good price and make a profit on my investment and foresight? Of course, it is. Well, that's honest graft.

While there was little in the way of land purchasing—either honest or dishonest—going on in Wincanton during this period, several officials who carried on their own businesses while in office were able to pick up some "honest graft." One city councilman with an accounting office served as bookkeeper for Irv Stern and the major bookies and prostitutes in the city.

Police Chief Phillips' construction firm received a contract to remodel the exterior of the largest brothel in town. Finally one councilman serving in the present reform administration received a contract to construct all gasoline stations built in the city by a major petroleum company; skeptics say that the contract was the quid pro quo for the councilman's vote to give the company the contract to sell gasoline to the city. . . .

THE FUTURE OF REFORM IN WINCANTON

When Wincantonites are asked what kind of law enforcement they want, they are likely to say that it is all right to tolerate petty gambling and prostitution, but that "you've got to keep out racketeers and corrupt politicians." Whenever they come to feel that the city is being controlled by these racketeers, they "throw the rascals out." This policy of "throwing the rascals out," however, illustrates the dilemma facing reformers in Wincanton. Irv Stern, recently released from Federal prison, has

probably, in fact, retired from the rackets; he is ill and plans to move to Arizona. Bob Walasek, having been twice convicted on extortion charges, is finished politically. Therefore? Therefore, the people of Wincanton firmly believe that "the problem" has been solved—"the rascals" have been thrown out. When asked, recently, what issues would be important in the next local elections, only 9 of 183 respondents felt that clean government or keeping out vice and gambling might be an issue. (Fifty-five percent had no opinion, 15 percent felt that the ban on bingo might be an issue, and 12 percent cited urban renewal, a subject frequently mentioned in the papers preceding the survey.) Since, under Ed Whitton, the city is being honestly run and is free from gambling and prostitution, there is no problem to worry about.

On balance, it seems far more likely to conclude that gambling and corruption will soon return to Wincanton (although possibly in less blatant forms) for two reasons—first, a significant number of people want to be able to gamble or make improper deals with the city government. (This assumes, of course, that racketeers will be available to provide gambling if a complacent city administration permits it.) Second, and numerically far more important, most voters think that the problem has been permanently solved, and thus they will not be choosing candidates based on these issues, in future elections.

Throughout this report, a number of specific recommendations have been made to minimize opportunities for wide open gambling and corruption—active State Police intervention in city affairs, modification of the city's contract bidding policies, extending civil service protection to police officers, etc. On balance, we could probably also state that the commission form

Wincanton: The Politics of Corruption   221

of government has been a hindrance to progressive government; a "strong mayor" form of government would probably handle the city's affairs more efficiently. Fundamentally, however, all of these suggestions are irrelevant. When the voters have called for clean government, they have gotten it, in spite of loose bidding laws, limited civil service, etc. The critical factor has been voter preference. Until the voters of Wincanton come to believe that illegal gambling produces the corruption they have known, the type of government we have documented will continue. Four-year periods of reform do little to change the habits instilled over 40 years of gambling and corruption.

Anthropology

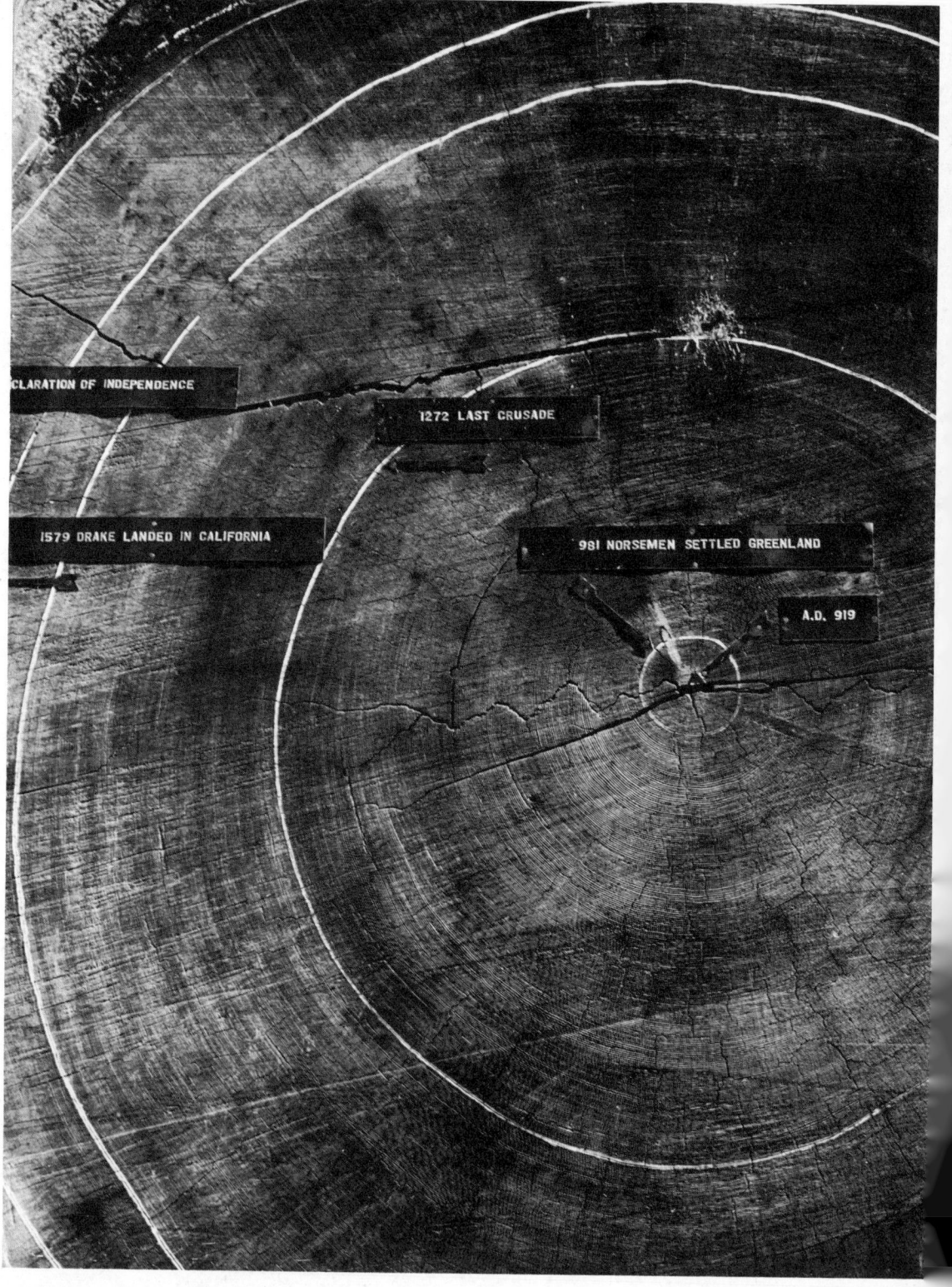

Anthropology

Introduction to Anthropology

Concepts:

Race
The Study of Race, S. L. Washburn

Chronology
Tree Rings—The Archaeologist's Time-Piece, Emil W. Haury

Socio-Linguistics
The Logic of Nonstandard English, William Labov

Life Cycle
A Yoruba Market-Woman's Life, Janheinz Jahn

Socialization
Maternal Care and Infant Behavior in Japan and America, William Caudill and Helen Weinstein

Practices
The Sexual Life of Savages: in North-Western Melanesia, Bronislaw Malinowski

Culture Relativity
Shakespeare in the Bush, Laura Bohannan

Culture Change
Fathoms and Feet, Acres and Tons: An Appraisal, Keith Gordon Irwin

Introduction to Anthropology

Anthropology and sociology are often difficult to distinguish from each other. Both are concerned with how individuals interact in **social relationships**. Indeed, many concepts are the same for both disciplines. Both, for example, consider **groups** as a critical point of departure for their work. And, many of the perspectives that guide research in the two fields are drawn from shared viewpoints of **social structures**, of **communities**, and of **society**. For example, both fields are intensely interested in **social stratification** and **social classes**.

The two fields differ first of all in the methods of research used and second, in the kinds of **groups** and **societies** studied. While generalization is risky, anthropologists usually make use of **participant** and **semi-participant observation** data and are less concerned with quantitative methods and statistics. But the field is changing and at least in American anthropology there is increased use of statistical procedures and samples which serve as a substitute or supplement to the more old-fashioned method of research by living with people.

Traditionally anthropologists have studied a single **tribe** or **society**. The anthropologist conceives of a **tribe** as being made up of individuals but does not look at them primarily as individuals, as the psychologist or, as **groups**, as the sociologist. Rather, he underplays individual characteristics and group life to focus on the broader mosaic of **society**. Anthropologists have tried to study primitive or isolated **societies** where **kinship** is the primary determinant of **social relationships**. But some anthropologists try to understand social life in terms of individual psychological characteristics to a larger extent than others while some emphasize the intensive study of self-cultures or **groups**, as the sociologist refers to **group**.

However, that which most distinguishes anthropology from the other **social sciences** is the concept of **culture** and the sense of history with which anthropologists view **social behavior** and the development of **communities** and **societies**.

Indeed, certain anthropologists interest themselves almost exclusively in trying to understand the **evolution** of people into their present state. This branch of anthropology, **physical anthropology**, will be illustrated by a reading in this section that discusses **race** from a bio-anthropological viewpoint. Naturally, there are other physical characteristics including the common ones of height and body structure that the anthropologist is interested in understanding from an evolutionary viewpoint.

Closely related to **physical anthropology** is the field of **archaeology**. Archaeologists are concerned with constructing the history of people and the way they lived prior to the time of written records. The archaeologist works primarily by discovering artifacts of past civilizations, the manufactured products of people, and by making sense of the social lives of those who lived in the past from knowledge about the physical environment that they created for themselves. The concept of **chronology** is chosen here to represent the field of **archaeology**.

A third field in which anthropologists work is **linguistics**. **Linguistics** is the study of **language**. It is interested in how each **language** is structured and in the relationships between **languages**. The physical **evolution** of people from an archaeological standpoint and from a linguistic standpoint are of course closely related. Anthropologists often work in teams or are themselves experts individually in several of these areas. We have included a reading on **socio-linguistics** to illustrate this field.

While each of these areas is of importance and is illustrated by a reading, the weight of this section is on **cultural anthropology**. In part this is because the field of **cultural anthropology** is by far the largest. Also **cultural anthropology** most frequently and most closely links anthropological work to the interests of other social scientists. It is the branch of anthropology most relevant to understanding people and the social scene. The concept of **cultural anthropology** is the complex whole which includes knowledge, **beliefs**, art, morals, law, customs, and habits acquired socially by people. It is clearly relevant to all other **social sciences** and it guides any effort to understand our social concepts.

The perspective of cultural anthropologists is critical to an understanding of differences in behavior and **values** in the United States. This perspective is also critical in trying to relate to what goes on in other parts of the world. Community members everywhere need to understand that many of our actions and **attitudes**, indeed most of them, are derived from the regularities and peculiarities of the **cultures** in which we live. Our standards of beauty, our ideas of appropriate conduct, our edifices and our relationships with each other are dependent on our **culture**—**culture** determines the shape and form of all our behavior and thought. Moreover, any judgments of other **groups** need to be made with a view to how what they do and what they believe fits within the fabric of their social system—within the cultural framework of their **society**. This cultural perspective has helped make sense out of the way medical doctors in large city hospitals and medicine men in isolated African **tribes** undertake their craft; how land is used and structures built in our cities and in small fishing villages in South America; and how sexual encounters are arranged in mid-western towns and on the plush resorts of the Riviera. Without this understanding of **cultures** it would be difficult for alien **cultures** to understand each other.

Physical Anthropology

Physical anthropology deals primarily with the **evolution** of people into their present state and with the varieties of **races** that exist today as a result of this **evolution**. In this sense, **physical anthropology** clearly overlaps and is related to other scientific fields, particularly biology. Since the subject of **evolution** is so well-developed and specialized, we have included in this section only one reading on **evolution**.

RACE

The major product of **evolution** relevant to human beings is the variety of **races** that exist among human beings. The reading by S. L. Washburn on *The Study of Race* not only provides a superb background and perspective on the whole subject of **race** but also points out many of the important implications of **race** in terms of our current **society** and **culture**. For instance, he emphasizes the fact that people must be studied as both biological and social organisms; that there is no sense in studying the process of race formation without studying human **culture**. For instance, in the United States, one can think of discrimination as a culture pattern.

In the American **community** considerable interest exists in the consequences of discrimination on both the sociological and psychological processes. In our discussion of **poverty** in the introduction to this book we noted the effect that **race** and **poverty** have on access to a reasonable diet and medical care. The Washburn article presents data on the relationship between **race** and learning. He notes that while early discussions of racial inferiority were centered on a biological interpretation of intelligence, the whole intellectual climate has changed. Learning and behavior have been proved to be much more affected by the environment. This reading is significantly related to the reading in the psychology section on the effects of race and social class on responsiveness, and the cognitive learning process. The findings of the Rosenhan study suggest that **social class** tends to be more important than **race** in terms of experimental learning.

Archaeology

The field of **archaeology** is concerned with reconstructing the history of people and the way they lived prior to the time of written records. For this reason, **archaeology** is frequently referred to as pre–history. Until a few years ago, the major tools of **archaeology** consisted primarily of digging tools such as shovels, since the archaeologist's method was to dig up the ruins of previous **societies**. From these the archaeologist attempted to infer the **culture** of previous **societies**. Recently, the study of **archaeology** has become much more sophisticated and specialized. The archaeologist now draws on several highly-technical fields to make increasingly precise dates and inferences about the sites that he studies. For instance, most people are aware of the fact that there is a naturally occurring isotope called carbon 14 which has a known half–life. Utilizing these facts, modern archaeologists are able to date organic material utilizing the carbon 14 method. This dating method is extremely helpful to the archaeologist in unravelling the history of people.

CHRONOLOGY

The reading on **chronology** gives a single sample of one method archaeologists have been using for dating items in the past: tree ring dating. The archaeologist gets most excited when he can find new ways to get better estimates on how old the artifacts are that he finds. Haury, in his discussion of dating by tree rings, captures and illustrates the excitement of the archaeologist when he makes new discoveries that enable him to date his material with ever-increasing precision. His discussion of the discovery and use of tree rings as a method of dating is an excellent example of an important archaeological tool.

Linguistics

From any reasonable point of view **language** is clearly a part of **culture**. However, the study of **language** has been so popular and so widespread that within anthropology there is a whole field called **linguistics. Linguistics** addresses itself purely to the study of **language**—both to the internal structure of individual **languages** and to the comparative study of the relationships among **languages**.

Without **language**, of course, social life would be impossible. It is the shared meanings that we have of different acts, gestures and sounds that allow members of a **community** to interact with each other and join together in collective activities. It is **language** that provides continuity to the **culture** of a **society**.

The important relationship between psychology and anthropology is emhasized by a comparison of **linguistics** and **schema**. The concept of **schema** was introduced in the section on psychology to refer to the abstract representation of experience, i.e., the psychological consequences that build up from different experiences. **Linguistics** shows that how one communicates depends upon the collective experiences of the **community**. In a sense, **language** depends also upon shared abstractions of experience which are gained from experience. In fact, several structures of **schema**, **concept** and **motives** concern themselves with **linguistics**. While **linguistics** is often regarded as a field of anthropology, at the level of structures, **linguistics** is a field of psychology. For example, problems of word recognition and memory, as discussed in the article by Shepard in the psychology section, are critical to the understanding of the process of communication.

A problem which has occupied linguists in the past has been the meaning or "semantics" of language. With the advent of computers many linguists became increasingly interested not only in the structure of languages but in the meaning of languages and the way in which different languages express similar ideas with different linguistic structures—the semantics of languages. For example, millions of dollars were spent to program computers to translate Russian and type it out in English in the 1950's and '60's. As one might expect, this attempt met with failure; no one ever succeeded in getting automatic machine or computer translation. This failure was brought about not because of a lack of knowledge of the structure of language but because of a lack of knowledge of semantics or meaning.

Like the computer, white middle-class America does not generally have a knowledge of the semantics of the languages used by various ethnic groups in the community. The article on socio-linguistics points out some of these semantic differences.

SOCIO-LINGUISTICS

Within cultures, the notion has been advanced that language competence is differently distributed by social groups. It is widely-held, for example, that the school problems of Black children are related to their verbal deficit. Such a view has been behind many recent theories on Black-White differences and behind many efforts at social action in the ghetto. The article by Labov argues differently. It is his position that Blacks merely use a "nonstandard" English. He argues that this language is no less complex or "worse" than standard English used by middle-class whites. He argues strongly that an understanding of this position is crucial to our ideas and views on race. The deficit theory needs to be critically challenged in the same way that Professor Washburn in his article on race discusses other ideas on racial differences.

This article on nonstandard English is included to illustrate the concept of socio-linguistics—the study of the relationship between characteristics of the social structure and the language of a society. Clearly, who we are, where we live, and what we experience are reflected in our language. This area of socio-linguistics is critical to the understanding of the social scene.

Cultural Anthropology

From the point of view of the social sciences, cultural anthropology is the branch of anthropology that is most "relevant." Cultural anthropology takes as its unique and characteristic area of study the subject of culture. Thus, in order to understand cultural anthropology, we must first define what we mean by culture; for it has many different meanings for different people.

What is Culture?

At the simplest level, *one could define* **culture** *as the collection of all the customs that characterize a given* **society** *or* **group**. *Traditionally,* **culture** *has been defined as that complex whole which includes knowledge,* **belief**, *art, morals, law, customs and any other capabilities and habits acquired by people as members of a* **society**. Customs can be learned and transmitted from one **generation** to another, so that a more precise definition of **culture** is the sum total of customs. This definition also corresponds to the definition of **culture** as "the way of life of a **society**." Not too many years ago one could have said that it was part of the **"culture"** of the United States for women to wear skirts and for men to wear pants or for women to wear long hair and for men to wear short hair. Clearly, as a descriptive observation, this is not necessarily true any more. This observation, however, makes it possible for us to illustrate several aspects of the concept of **culture**. In the first place, the fact that observations were true several years ago and are not true now illustrates the very important fact that various aspects of **culture** may change rapidly, a notion which we will be concerned with in more detail when we discuss the concept of **culture change**. It also illustrates the notion that there is some degree of sharedness about the aspect of **culture** or a **cultural trait**, which we shall see when we consider the concept of **culture relativity**. The wearing of pants by males may be thought of as a **cultural trait**, or hair style may be thought of as a **cultural trait**. This illustration shows that the boundaries of a **culture** are not necessarily extremely well-defined. For example, it leads us to talk about such things as whether or not **culture** is homogeneous; or whether the total **society** shares the same **cultural trait**. When we say that there is a "youth **culture**" we are referring to items or traits that youth share among themselves; an item that is not shared by an adult. For example, current hair length might distinguish youth **culture** from a **culture** that is not a youth **culture**. This notion of "subcultures" indicates that there are only certain parts of **society** that may share a given **cultural trait**. This problem of parameters is a very complex one. If one attaches a **culture** to a given **society**, then one might talk about a **group** of specific people in **social relationships**, namely "youth," and separate them out as a separate **society** from, say, older people.

The **traits** that make up a **culture** are not randomly organized; they form a system. These subsystems within a **society** can also be thought of as culture patterns, or large areas of **culture** that are organized into a system where there are clear-cut relationships among the various **traits** or elements of the **culture**. For example, various religions might constitute culture patterns. Or, our whole technological system might be thought of as a culture pattern.

The study of **culture** is still very much at the descriptive stage. It relies on description and intuitive interpretation, rather than experimentation, for its analysis. It is much easier to give examples of what we mean by **culture**—culture elements and culture patterns—than it is to give formal definitions.

LIFE CYCLE

In recent years anthropologists have used the method of obtaining lengthy personal documents or detailed life histories from members of the **societies** which were being studied. By integrating these life histories with the other kinds of knowledge anthropologists have about a **culture**, they are often able to obtain a coherent overview of the **culture**. The selection by Janheinz Jahn is a very sensitive life history of a Yoruba market woman's life—the Yoruba being a **tribe** that live in Nigeria who practice **polygamy**. The concept of **life cycle** in this **culture** is very neatly illustrated and conveyed by the author.

It is important to note here also that **role**, which was defined in the sociology section as patterned behavior that marks an individual's position in the **social structure**, is linked to the concept of **life cycle**. One's place in the **life cycle** is usually related to his **role**. For example, in the adolescent stage of the **life cycle**, an individual is generally a student. Or, young adults usually adopt the **role** of lovers. Conversely, in the **life cycle** stage of old age, one rarely assumes the **role** of a student. Focus on the concept of **life cycle** also makes it possible and convenient to look at the major transition points during the life of an individual, like birth, **marriage**, divorce, death. **Societies** everywhere mark these major transition points with elaborate **rituals** and ceremonies. **Rituals** are usually also opportunities for the expression of **emotion**. In the section on psychology, the emphasis was on the negative aspects of **emotion**. These negative forms of **ritual** and consequent **emotion** are usually found in institutionalized forms, such as the ceremonies pursuant to a death. However, **emotions** may be gratifying, instead of painful. Typically those ceremonial aspects of socialized life, such as **marriages** or religious **rituals**, are gratifying, thus involving **social institutions** in **rituals**.

SOCIALIZATION

The concept of **socialization** refers to the process by which persons acquire the **culture** of a given **society**. Sometimes anthropologists are concerned with ways in which a **society** socializes the young as well as the adult. The reading by two cultural anthropologists, Caudill and Weinstein, is a study of the different conceptions and behaviors Japanese and American mothers display with their three-month-old infants. Clearly, **culture** and behavior patterns are mainly transmitted by the mothers in a **society**, as mothers spend the most time with infants and children in their formative years.

PRACTICE

Two very prominent concepts in anthropology which continually arise in conjunction with one another are **belief** and **practice**. The anthropologist doing empirical research generally makes a simple distinction between the two by defining **belief** *as what people say and* **practice** *as what people do.* **Belief** *includes knowledge and ideals;* **practice** *includes customs, habits, and cultural behavior.* Of course it is not possible to completely separate belief and practice. Since we have not been able to include two readings to illustrate these significant concepts we have chosen an article on the way in which a society deals with courtship and **marriage** to illustrate the concept of **practices**.

The article by Malinowski emphasizes **practices** among the Trobriand Islanders. Malinowski was an anthropologist who happened to be in the Trobriand Islands when World War I broke out, and was interned there by the Germans. Malinowski was fortunate enough to be one of the first anthropologists to live among the natives over a long period of time, and he became intimately acquainted with the Trobriand **culture** and customs. In his article he talks about the courtship stage among the youth of the Trobriand Islands, and points out that the **culture** molds the way in which these youth act out their courtship behavior. In his opinion there is a narrower range of behavior that is appropriate among the Trobriands than among our own **society**.

The relationships among **beliefs**, **practices** and concepts in sociology and psychology are formidable. For example, in sociology, the term **norm** was used to refer to generally-agreed-upon standards of proper conduct. The sociologist classifies **norms** at the level of generally-accepted **ideology** and common behaviors. Behavioral **norms** are not necessarily consistent with ideological **norms**; **beliefs** and **practices** are not necessarily congruent either. For example, it is the **norm** that people should not steal, yet people steal. Or, it is the **norm** that there should be chastity on the part of the female before **marriage**, but in **practice** this is not usually the case.

Practices also are tied to the different **roles** that people occupy, although, naturally, not all individuals follow prescribed **practices** in acting out their **roles**. Sometimes, **groups** of individuals who are identified by their particular **practices** depart from these **practices** in their behavior. We have seen in the section on sociology how stripteasers depart from the **practices** of **society** and exhibit what is considered **deviant behavior**.

Psychologists are interested in the effects that **beliefs** can have on behavior, particularly **avoidance behavior. Fears** and anxiety in children are not necessarily based upon negative experiences, but rather can be based on **beliefs** that are transmitted by persons or the mass media. Oftentimes, experience and a familiarity with the **practices** of **society** operate to reduce anxiety and **avoidance behavior** which has built up through the unchallenged acceptance of **beliefs**.

CULTURE RELATIVITY

The concept of **culture relativity** refers to the fact that the interpretation of human behavior is relative to the cultural perspective from which it is viewed. Many anthropologists stress the concept because the problem of relativity leads to misunderstandings frequently between people of different **cultures**. For example, in our own **society**, black is a color associated with funerals and mourning; among the Chinese white has such connotations. An interesting example of **culture relativity**, or the lack of it, is found in the delightful article by Laura Bohannan. She describes in detail the reaction of the Tiv, a West African tribe, to Shakespeare's *Hamlet*. Her preconceptions that certain types of human situations were universal and so obvious and dramatic in their impact that people everywhere would interpret them in the same way were dissolved. In her article she describes her shock and dismay at the totally different interpretation the Tiv gave to *Hamlet*.

CULTURE CHANGE

Culture change refers to the process of timely change in **cultures**. **Culture change** is a dramatically more difficult process than the process of **diffusion** or of simple borrowing. In the article by Irwin on measurement we have a very interesting example of a **culture's** slowness in accepting new systems of measurement. He describes this situation as one of the most dramatic instances of one **culture** dragging its feet, as it were, concerning the adoption of a system that is clearly superior to its own.

In fact, **culture change** is an important and timely concept, and points up the vital relationship between **social institutions**, and consequently those in positions of power and authority, and their resistance to **culture change**. In fact, much of the unrest on college campuses today is related to the schism between what students view as a vital **culture change**, and the reluctance of **social institutions** or those in power to change accordingly. The next section on economics contains a selection by Charles Reich from his book, *The Greening of America*. This article reinforces the increasing pressures for change and the recalcitrant attitude of those in power concerning change.

We have noted throughout this introduction the continuing interrelation among the concepts of psychology, sociology and anthropology. The next two sections on economics and political science should contribute two other valuable perspectives on the disciplines we have already discussed.

RACE

The Study of Race

S. L. WASHBURN

... Discussion of the races of man seems to generate endless emotion and confusion. I am under no illusion that this paper can do much to dispel the confusion; it may add to the emotion. The latest information available supports the traditional findings of anthropologists and other social scientists—that there is no scientific basis of any kind for racial discrimination. I think that the way this conclusion has been reached needs to be restated. The continuation of antiquated biological notions in anthropology and the oversimplification of facts weakens the anthropological position. We must realize that great changes have taken place in the study of race over the last 20 years and it is up to us to bring our profession into the forefront of the newer understandings, so that our statements will be authoritative and useful.

This paper will be concerned with three topics—the modern concept of race, the interpretation of racial differences, and the social significances of race. And, again, I have no illusion that these things can be treated briefly; I shall merely say a few things which are on my mind and which you may amplify by turning to the literature, and especially to Dobzhansky's book, *Mankind Evolving*. This book states the relations between culture and genetics in a way which is useful to social scientists. In my opinion it is a great book which puts the interrelations of biology and culture in proper perspective and avoids the oversimplifications which come from overemphasis on either one alone.

The races of man are the result of human evolution, of the evolution of our species. The races are open parts of the species, and the species is a closed system. If we look, then, upon long-term human evolution, our first problem must be the species and the things which have caused the evolution of all mankind, not the races, which are the results of local forces and which are minor in terms of the evolution of the whole species. (A contrary view has recently been expressed by Coon in *The Origin of Races*. I think that great antiquity of human races is supported neither by the record nor by evolutionary theory.)

The evolution of races is due, according to modern genetics, to **mutation**, selection, **migration**, and **genetic drift**. It is easy to shift from this statement of genetic theory to complications of hemoglobin, blood groups or other technical information. But the point I want to stress is that the primary implication of genetics for anthropology is that it affirms the relation of culture and biology in a far firmer and more important way than ever in our history before. Selection is for reproductive success, and in man reproductive success is primarily determined by the social system and by culture. Effective behavior is the question, not something else.

Drift depends on the size of population, and population size, again, is dependent upon culture, not upon genetic factors as such. Obviously, migration depends on clothes, transportation, economy, and warfare and is reflected in the archeological record. Even mutation rates are now affected by technology.

Genetic theory forces the consideration of culture as the major factor in the evolution of man. It thus reaffirms the fundamental belief of anthropologists that we must study man both as a biological and as a social organism. This is no longer a question of something that might be desirable; it must be done if genetic theory is correct.

We have, then, on the one hand the history of genetic systems, and on the other hand the history of cultural systems, and, finally, the interrelation between these two. There is no evolution in the traditional anthropological sense. What Boas referred to as evolution was orthogenesis—which receives no support from modern genetic theory. What the geneticist sees as evolution is far closer to what Boas called history than to what he called evolution, and some anthropologists are still fighting a nineteenth-century battle in their presentation of evolution. We have, then, the history of cultural systems, which you may call history; and the history of genetic systems, which you may call evolution if you want to, but if you use this word remember that it means selection, migration, drift—it is real history that you are talking about and not some mystic force which constrains mankind to evolve according to some orthogenetic principle.

There is, then, no possibility of studying human raciation, the process of race formation, without studying human culture. Archaeology is as important in the study of the origin of races as is genetics; all we can do is reconstruct as best we can the long-term past, and this is going to be very difficult.

Now let me contrast this point of view with the one which has been common in much of anthropology. In the first place, anthropology's main subject, the subject of race, disregarded to an amazing degree the evolution of the human species. Anthropologists were so concerned with the subdivisions within our species and with minor detailed differences between small parts of the species that the physical anthropologists largely forgot that mankind is a species and that the important thing is the evolution of this whole group, not the minor differences between its parts.

If we look back to the time when I was educated, races were regarded as types. We were taught to go to a population and divide it into a series of types and to re-create history out of this artificial arrangement. Those of you who have read *Current Anthropology* will realize that this kind of anthropology is still alive, amazingly, and in full force in some countries; relics of it are still alive in our teaching today.

Genetics shows us that typology must be completely removed from our thinking if we are to progress. For example, let us take the case of the Bushmen. The Bushmen have been described as the result of a mixture between Negro and Mongoloid. Such a statement could only be put in the literature without any possible consideration of migration routes, of numbers of people, of cultures, of any way that such a mixing could actually take place. The fact is that the Bushmen had a substantial record in South Africa and in East Africa and there is no evidence that they ever were anywhere else except in these areas. In other words, they are a race which belongs exactly where they are.

If we are concerned with history let us consider, on the one hand, the ancestors of these Bushmen 15,000 years ago and the area available to them, to their way of life, and, on the other hand, the ancestors of Europeans at the same time in the area available to them, with their way of life. We will find that the area available to the Bushmen was at least twice that available to the Europeans. The Bushmen were living in a land of optimum game; the Europeans were living close to an ice sheet. There were perhaps from three to five times as many Bushmen ancestors as there were European ancestors only 15,000 years ago.

If one were to name a major race, or a primary race, the Bushmen have a far better claim in terms of the archaeological record than the Europeans. During the time of glacial advance more than half of the Old World available to man for life was in Africa. The numbers and distributions that we think of as normal and the races whose last results we see today are relics of an earlier and far different time in human history.

There are no three primary races, no three major groups. The idea of three primary races stems from nineteenth-century typology; it is totally misleading to put the black-skinned people of the world together—to put the Australian in the same grouping with the inhabitants of Africa. And there are certainly at least three independent origins of the small, dark people, the Pygmies, and probably more than that. There is no single Pygmy race.

If we look to real history we will always find more than three races, because there are more than three major areas in which the raciation of our species was taking place.

If we attempt to preserve the notion of three races, we make pseudo-typological problems. Take for example, again, the problem of the aboriginal Australian. If we have only three races, either they must be put with the people of Africa, with which they have nothing in common, or they must be accounted for by mixture, and in books appearing even as late as 1950, a part of the aboriginal Australian population is described as European, and listed with the Europeans, and the residue is listed with the Africans and left there.

The concept of race is fundamentally changed if we actually look for selection, migration, and study people as they are (who they are, where they are, how many they are); and the majority of anthropological textbooks need substantial revision along these lines.

Since races are open systems which are intergrading, the number of races will depend on the purpose of the classification. This is, I think, a tremendously important point. It is significant that as I was reviewing classifications in preparing this lecture, I found that almost none of them mentioned any purpose for which people were being classified. Race isn't very important biologically. If we are classifying races in order to understand human history, there aren't many human races, and there is very substantial agreement as to what they are. There are from six to nine races, and this difference in number is very largely a matter of definition. These races occupied the major separate geographical areas in the Old World.

If one has no purpose for classification, the number of races can be multiplied almost indefinitely, and it seems to me that the erratically varying number of races is a source of confusion to student, to layman, and to specialist. I think we should require people who propose a classification of races to state in the first place why they wish to divide the human species and to give in detail the important reasons for subdividing our whole species. If important reasons for such classification are given, I think you will find that the number of races is always exceedingly small.

If we consider these six or nine geographical races and the factors which produced them, I think the first thing we want to stress is migration.

All through human history, where we have any evidence of that history, people have migrated. In a recent *Anthropologist* there is a suggestion that it took 400,000 years for a gene that mutated in China to reach Europe. We know, historically, that Alexander the Great went from Greece into Northern India. We know that Mongol tribes migrated from Asia into Europe. Only a person seeking to believe that the races are very separate could possibly believe such a figure as that cited.

Migration has always been important in human history and there is no such thing as human populations which are completely separated from other human populations. And migration necessarily brings in new genes, necessarily reduces the differences between the races. For raciation to take place, then, there must be other factors operating which create difference. Under certain circumstances, in very small populations, differences may be created by genetic drift, or because the founders are for chance reasons very different from other members of the species.

However, the primary factor in the creation of racial differences in the long term is selection. This means that the origin of races must depend on adaptation and that the differences between the races which we see must in times past have been adaptive. I stress the question of time here, because it is perfectly logical to maintain that in time past a shovel-shaped incisor, for example, was more efficient than an incisor of other forms and that selection would have been for this, and at the same time to assert that today this dental difference is of absolutely no social importance. It is important to make this point because people generally take the view that something is always adaptive or never adaptive, and this is a fundamental oversimplification of the facts.

Adaptation is always within a given situation. There is no such thing as a gene which has a particular adaptive value; it has this value only under set circumstances. For example, the sickle-cell gene, if Allison and others are right, protects against malaria. This is adaptive if there is malaria, but if there is not malaria it is not adaptive. The adaptive value of the gene, then, is dependent on the state of medicine and has no absolute value. The same is true of the other characteristics associated with race.

I would like to go over some of the suggestions which have been made about the adaptive values of various structures in human beings, because I think these need to be looked at again.

I have stressed that the concept of race which comes from population genetics is compatible with what anthropologists have thought. I think that this concept represents great progress. But when I read the descriptions of the importance of adaptive characteristics, I am not sure that there has been any progress since the nineteenth century.

In this connection I should like to speak for a moment on the notion that the Mongoloids are a race which are adapted to live in the cold, that these are arctic-adapted people.

In the first place, in marked contrast to animals which are adapted to live in the arctic, large numbers of Mongoloids are living in the hot, moist tropics. Altogether unlike animal adaptation, then, the people who are supposed to be adapted to the cold aren't living under cold conditions, and I think we should stress this. For thousands of years the majority of this group have not been living under the conditions which are supposed to have produced them. They are presumed, as an arctic-adapted group following various laws, to have short extremities, flat noses, and to be stocky in build. They are, we might say, as stocky as the Scotch, as flat-nosed as the Norwegians, and as blonde as the Eskimos. Actually, there is no correlation, that is, none that has been well worked out, to support the notion that any of these racial groups is cold-adapted.

Let me say a few more words on this lack of correlation. If one follows the form of the nose, in Europe, as one moves north, narrow noses are correlated with cold climate; in Eastern Asia low noses are correlated with cold climate. In neither case is there the slightest evidence that the difference in the form of the nose has anything whatsoever to do with warming the air that comes into the face. Further, if we look at these differences expressed in this way, we see that they are posed in terms of nineteenth-century notions of what a face is all about.

Let us look at it differently. The nose is the center of a face. Most of a face is concerned with teeth, and bones, and muscles that have to do with chewing. The Mongoloid face is primarily the result of large masseter muscles and the bones from which these muscles arise (malar and gonial angles). This is a complex structural pattern related to the teeth, and a superficially very similar pattern may be seen in the Bushman, whose facial form can hardly be attributed to adaptation to cold.

The face of the Neanderthal man has recently been described also as cold-adapted, though it does not have the characteristics of the Mongoloid face. We are told that the blood supply to the Neanderthal face was greatly increased because the infraorbital foramen was large, bringing more blood to the front of the face. In actual fact, most of the blood to our face does not go through that artery. The artery that carries most of the blood to the face comes along the outside, and even our arteries are far too large to go through the mental or infraorbital foramen of Neanderthal man. This kind of statement, as well as the statement that the maxillary sinus warmed the air and that the function of a large orbit was to keep the eyes from freezing, seems to me an extraordinary retrogression to the worst kind of evolutionary speculation—speculation that antedates genetics and reveals a lack of any kind of reasonable understanding of the structure of the human face.

The point I wish to stress is that those who have spoken of the cold-adaptation of the Mongoloid face and of the Neanderthal face do not know the structure of the human face. We have people writing about human faces who are anatomically illiterate. I am genetically illiterate; I do not know about the hemoglobins. I am not asserting that all of us should be required to be literate in all branches of physical anthropology. As Stanley Garn points out, the field has become complicated, but people who are writing about the structure of the human face should learn the elements of anatomy.

The adaptive value of skin color has been repeatedly claimed, but recently Blum has indicated that the situation is more complicated than it appeared. In the first place, he points out that the melanin in the skin doesn't do what anthropologists have said it has done. The part of the skin which mainly stops ultraviolet light, the short-wave length light, is a thickened *stratum corneum*, rather than melanin.

Again, the chimpanzee and the gorilla live in precisely the same climatic conditions in Uganda, but the gorilla has one of the blackest, most deeply pigmented skins of the primates and the chimpanzee has a very light skin. It simply is not true that skin color closely parallels climate. The point here is that racial classification tells us very little. The classification poses problems; it does not solve them.

In scientific method, as I see it, one looks at relevant data and when these data are laid out, as in, say, the classification of races, one may then find a correlation which is helpful. But after that, one has to do an experiment; one has to do something that shows that the correlation has validity. And it's no use continuing to correlate nose-form or skin color with climate. The crude correlations were made many years ago, and to advance the study of race requires new methods and more sophisticated analyses.

When I was a student, there were naive racial interpretations based on the metrical data. When these became unacceptable politically the same people used naive constitutional correlations to reach the same conclusions of social importance. Today we have naive concepts of adaptation, taking the place of the earlier interpretations, and a recrudescence of the racial thinking.

All along the line there have been valid problems in race, valid problems in constitution, and valid problems in adaptation. What I am protesting against strongly is the notion that one can simply take a factor, such as a high cheekbone, think that it might be related to climate, and then jump to this conclusion without any kind of connecting link between the two elements—without any kind of experimental verification of the sort of material that is being dealt with. If we took really seriously this notion that a flat face with large maxillary sinuses, deep orbits, and big brow ridges is cold-adapted, it is clear that the most cold-adapted animal in the primates is the gorilla.

Race, then, is a useful concept only if one is concerned with the kind of anatomical, genetic, and structural differences which were in time past important in the origin of races. Race in human thinking is a very minor concept. It is entirely worth while to have a small number of specialists, such as myself, who are concerned with

the origin of gonial angles, the form of the nose, the origin of dental patterns, changes in blood-group frequencies, and so on. But this is a very minor, specialized kind of knowledge.

If classification is to have a purpose, we may look backward to the explanation of the differences between people—structural, anatomical, physiological differences —and then the concept of race is useful, but it is useful under no other circumstances, as far as I can see.

When the meaning of skin color and structure is fully understood, it will help us to understand the origin of races, but this is not the same thing as understanding the origin of our species. It will help in the understanding of why color was important in time long past, but it will have no meaning to modern technical society.

I turn now to a brief statement on the influence of culture upon race. Beginning with agriculture and continuing at an ever-increasing rate, human customs have been interposed between the organism and the environment. The increase of our species from perhaps as few as five million before agriculture to three billion today is the result of new technology, not of biological evolution. The conditions under which the races evolved are mainly gone, and there are new causes of mutation, new kinds of selection, and vast migration. Today the numbers and distribution of the peoples of the world are due primarily to culture. Some people think the new conditions are so different that it is better no longer to use the word race or the word evolution, but I personally think this confuses more than it clarifies.

All this does not mean that evolution has stopped, because the new conditions will change gene frequencies, but the conditions which produced the old races are

The Study of Race 241

gone. In this crowded world of civilization and science, the claim has been made repeatedly that one or another of the races is superior to the others. Obviously, this argument cannot be based on the past; because something was useful in times past and was selected for under conditions which are now gone, does not mean that it will be useful in the present or in the future.

The essential point at issue is whether the abilities of large populations are so different that their capacity to participate in modern technical culture is affected. Remember in the first place that no race has evolved to fit the selective pressures of the modern world. Technical civilization is new and the races are old. Remember also that all the species of *Homo* have been adapting to the human way of life for many thousands of years. Tools even antedate our **genus**, and our human biological adaptation is the result of culture. Man and his capacity for culture have evolved together, as Dr. Dobzhansky has pointed out. All men are adapted to learn language—any language; to perform skillful tasks—a fabulous variety of tasks; to cooperate; to enjoy art; to practice religion, philosophy, and science.

Our species only survives in culture, and, in a profound sense, we are the product of the new selection pressures that came with culture.

Infinitely more is known about the language and culture of all the groups of mankind than is known about the biology of racial differences. We know that the members of every racial group have learned a vast variety of languages and ways of life. The interaction of genes and custom over the millenia has produced a species whose populations can learn to live in an amazing variety of complex cultural ways.

Racism is based on a profound misunderstanding of culture, of learning, and of the biology of the human species. The study of cultures should give a profound respect for the biology of man's capacity to learn. Much of the earlier discussion of racial inferiority centered on the discussion of intelligence; or, to put the matter more accurately, usually on that small part of biological intelligence which is measured by the IQ. In the earlier days of intelligence testing, there was a widespread belief that the tests revealed something which was genetically fixed within a rather narrow range. The whole climate of opinion that fostered this point of view has changed. At that time animals were regarded as primarily instinctive in their behavior, and the genes were supposed to exert their effects in an almost mechanical way, regardless of the environment. All this intellectual climate has changed. Learning has proved to be far more important in the behavior of many animal species, and the action of the complexes of genes is now known to be affected by the environment, as is, to a great degree, the performance that results from them. For example, Harlow has shown that monkeys learn to learn. Monkeys become test wise. They become skillful in the solution of tests —so monkeys in Dr. Harlow's laboratories are spoken of as naive or as experienced in the use of tests. To suppose that humans cannot learn to take tests is to suppose that humans are rather less intelligent than monkeys.

Krech and Rosenzweig have shown that rats raised in an enriched environment are much more intelligent and efficient as maze-solvers than rats that have been given no opportunity to learn and to practice before the testing. To suppose that man would not learn through education to take tests more efficiently, is to suppose that our learning capacities are rather less than those of rats.

The human is born with less than a third of the adult brain capacity, and there is tremendous growth of the cortex after birth. There is possibly no mammalian species in which the environment has a longer and more direct effect on the central nervous system than man. We should expect, then, that test results are going to be more affected by the environment of man than in the case of any other animal. Deprivation studies of monkeys and chimpanzees and clinical investigations of man show that the lack of a normal interpersonal environment may be devastating to the developing individual.

Today one approaches the study of intelligence expecting to find that environment is important. The intellectual background is very different from that of the '20's. The general results on testing may be briefly summarized as follows:

The average IQ of large groups is raised by education. I believe the most important data on this are the comparisons of the soldiers of World War I and of World War II. More than 80 per cent of the soldiers tested in World War II were above the mean of those tested in World War I. This means a wholesale massive improvement, judged by these tests, in the sons of the people who fought in World War I.

In the states where the least educational effort is made, the IQ is the lowest. In fact, as one looks at the review in Anastasi, it is exceedingly difficult to see why anyone ever thought that the IQ measured innate intelligence, and not the genetic constitution as modified in the family, in the schools, and by the general intellectual environment.

I would suggest that if the intelligence quotients of Negroes and Whites in this country are compared, the same rules be used for these comparisons as would be used for comparisons of the data between two groups of Whites. This may not seem a very extreme thing to suggest, but if you look at the literature, you will find that when two groups of Whites differ in their IQ's, the explanation of the difference is immediately sought in schooling, environment, economic positions of parents, and so on, but that when Negroes and Whites differ in precisely the same way the difference is said to be genetic.

Let me give you but one example of this. Klineberg showed years ago in excellent studies that the mean test scores of many Northern Negro groups were higher than those of certain groups of Southern Whites. When these findings were published, it was immediately suggested that there had been a differential migration and the more intelligent Negroes had moved to the North. But the mean of Northern Whites test results is above that of Southern Whites. Are we to believe that the intelligent Whites also moved to the North?

There is no way of telling what the IQ would be if equal opportunity were given to all racial and social groups. The group which is sociologically classified as Negro in the United States, about one-third of whose genes are of European origin, might well test ahead of the Whites. I am sometimes surprised to hear it stated that if Negroes were given an equal opportunity, their IQ would be the same as the Whites'. If one looks at the degree of social discrimination against Negroes and their lack of education, and also takes into account the tremendous amount of overlapping between the observed IQ's of both, one can make an equally good case that, given a comparable chance to that of the Whites, their IQ's would test out ahead. Of course, it would be absolutely unimportant in a democratic society if this were to be true, because the vast majority of individuals of both groups would be of comparable intelligence, whatever the mean of these intelligence tests would show.

We can generalize this point. All kinds of human performance—whether social, athletic, intellectual—are built on genetic and environmental elements. The level of all kinds of performance can be increased by improving the environmental situation so that every genetic constitution may be developed to its full capacity. Any kind of social discrimination against groups of people, whether these are races, castes, or classes, reduces the achievements of our species, of mankind.

The cost of discrimination is reflected in length of life. The Founding Fathers were wise to join life, liberty, and the pursuit of happiness, because these are intimately linked in the social and cultural system. Just as the restriction of social and economic opportunity reduces intelligence so it reduces length of life.

In 1900 the life expectancy of White males in the United States was 48 years, and in that same year the expectancy of a Negro male was 32 years; that is a difference of 50 per cent, or 16 years. By 1940 the difference had been reduced to ten years, and by 1958 to six. As the life ex-

pectancy of the Whites increased from 48 to 62 to 67 years, that of the Negroes increased from 32 to 52 to 61 years. They died of the same causes, but they died at different rates.

Discrimination, by denying equal social opportunity to the Negro, made his progress lag approximately 20 years behind that of the White. Somebody said to me, "Well, 61, 67, that's only six years." But it depends on whose six years it is. There are about 19 million people in this country sociologically classified as Negroes. If they die according to the death rate given above, approximately 100 million years of life will be lost owing to discrimination.

In 1958 the death rate for Negroes in the first year of life was 52 per thousand and for Whites 26. Thousands of Negro infants died unnecessarily. The social conscience is an extraordinary thing. A lynching stirs the whole community to action, yet only a single life is lost. Discrimination, through denying education, medical care, and economic progress, kills at a far higher rate. A ghetto of hatred kills more surely than a concentration camp, because it kills by accepted custom, and it kills every day in the year.

A few years ago in South Africa, the expectation of life for a Black man was 40 years, but it was 60 at the same time for a White man. At that same time a White woman could expect 25 more years of life than a Black woman. Among the Blacks the women lived no longer than the men. People speak of the greater longevity of women, but this is only because of modern medicine. High birth rates, high infant mortality, high maternal mortality—these are the hallmarks of the history of mankind.

Of course there are biological differences between male and female, but whether a woman is allowed to vote, or the rate that she must die in childbirth, these are a matter of medical knowledge and of custom. Biological difference only expresses itself through the social system.

Who may live longer in the future—Whites or Negroes? There's no way of telling. Who may live longer in the future—males or females? There is no way of telling. These things are dependent on the progress in medical science and on the degree to which this progress is made available to all races and to both sexes.

When environment is important, the only way genetic difference may be determined is by equalizing the environment. If you believe in mankind, then you will want mankind to live on in an enriched environment. No one can tell what may be the ultimate length of life, but we do know that many people could live much longer if given a chance.

Whether we consider intelligence, or length of life, or happiness the genetic potential of a population is only realized in a social system. It is that system which gives life or death to its members, and in so doing changes the gene frequencies. We know of no society which has begun to realize the genetic potential of its members. We are the primitives living by antiquated customs in the midst of scientific progress. Races are products of the past. They are relics of times and conditions which have long ceased to exist.

Racism is equally a relic supported by no phase of modern science. We may not know how to interpret the form of the Mongoloid face, or why $Rh^°$ is of high incidence in Africa, but we do know the benefits of education and of economic progress. We know the price of discrimination is death, frustration, and hatred. We know that the roots of happiness lie in the biology of the whole species and that the potential of the species can only be realized in a culture, in a social system. It is knowledge and the social system which give life or take it away, and in so doing change the gene frequencies and continue the million-year-old interaction of culture and biology. Human biology finds its realization in a culturally determined way of life, and the infinite variety of genetic combinations can only express themselves efficiently in a free and open society.

References

Anastasi, Anne
    1958 Differential psychology: Individual and group differences in behavior. New York, The Macmillan Company.

Blum, Harold F.
    1961 Does the melanin pigment of human skin have adaptive value? The Quarterly Review of Biology 36:50–63.

Coon, Carleton S.
    1962 The origin of races. New York, Alfred A. Knopf.

Dobzhansky, Theodosius
    1962 Mankind evolving: The evolution of the human species. New Haven and London, Yale University Press.

Dublin, Louis I., Alfred J. Lotka, and Mortimer Spiegelman
    1949 Length of life: A study of the life table. (Revised Edition.) New York, The Ronald Press Company.

Klineberg, Otto
    1935 Race differences. New York and London, Harper & Brothers.

Krech, David, Mark R. Rosenzweig, and Edward L. Bennett
    1962 Relations between brain chemistry and problem-solving among rats raised in enriched and impoverished environments. Journal of Comparative and Physiological Psychology: 55:801–807.

CHRONOLOGY

Tree Rings—The Archaeologist's Time-Piece

EMIL W. HAURY

Since 1929 Southwestern archaeology has stood on a much surer footing than at any other time in the history of its development. This stabilization is due to the research of Dr. A. E. Douglass of Tucson, Arizona, whose inquiries into the reaction of trees to weather, from an astronomic standpoint, led, as a ramification, to the use of the annual growth rings in trees in dating the pre-Spanish remains of man in the Southwest. From the standpoint of the archaeologist, the most significant progress date in Dr. Douglass' study was June 22, 1929. On that day ended a long search for a particular sequence of rings needed to complete the ring record. This sequence was found in a log in the Showlow ruin, and united two chronologies then extant, the one a floating series of five hundred and eighty years, the other an historic series extending from 1929 to about 1280 A.D. The great value of the joining of these two series lay in the fact that it became possible, for the first time, to speak of the age of the Southwest's foremost ruins in terms of the Christian calendar. By this one step, forty old villages, occupied by the Pueblo Indians before the arrival of Europeans, were placed historically. That this achievement was possible where written records were not kept seemed unbelievable; that the discovery was made by an astronomer who utilized material thought worthless by the archaeologist seemed still more incredible. But, in the brief six years which have elapsed since the Showlow log was found, the Southwestern student has come to take **dendrochronology**, or "tree time," as a matter of course, giving data gained through this medium precedence over knowledge gleaned in any other way. In fact, it may be stated without equivocation that the tree-ring approach has been the greatest single contribution ever made to American archaeology. In the regimentation of facts it has taken priority over typological and associational studies, even over **stratigraphy** which heretofore had proven itself the most valuable control. Tree rings and stratigraphy have shown themselves to be complementary and have combined to build a chronology which shall endure. The whole-hearted acceptance and the continued use of the tree-ring approach by the Southwesternist will be an undying tribute to Dr. A. E. Douglass, the inventor of the system.

Since the finding of the first date ever to be derived from a pre-Spanish ruin, Kawiakuh in the Jeddito Valley, in 1928, many ruins, large and small, aggregating well over two hundred, have been dated by Dr. Douglass and his students. Impressive as this figure is, it is nevertheless admittedly small and forms but a very meager percentage of the ruins for which a potential date is possible.

The locality now affected by tree-ring dating in the Southwest may be limited by Mesa Verde on the north, Prescott on the west, Globe on the south, and Pecos on the east; thus including practically all of the plateau and mountain area. In the main, this area includes the sections where Basket Maker and Pueblo remains are the most dense. It is not too much to hope that extensions will be made from this region to include other cultures whose position in time can now be determined only by less satisfactory means. Especially bright are the prospects of carrying the system to other archaeological areas, as, for example, the Mississippi Valley.

Through painstaking research and the application of a rigorous procedure in the study of tree rings, Dr. Douglass has been able to establish a chronology for the Southwest extending in an unbroken line from the present almost to the time of Christ. Quoting from the Annual Report of the Chairman of the Division of Plant Biology of the Carnegie Institution, Dr. Douglass writes:

"The long southwestern tree-ring records . . . have given a rainfall history, back to about 650 A.D. Two earlier sequences of 'Basket Maker' age, secured by Earl H. Morris, were joined together in March 1933, making a total length of about 800 years. Since January 1932, a definite relationship of the more recent of these to modern chronology has been under consideration. This connection was found in a superb specimen from Chetro Ketl collected and dated by Miss Florence M. Hawley in December 1931. This has been supported by many others, and has enabled us to carry a well-established chronology back to about 200 A.D. and a somewhat complacent record to 11 A.D. A few excellent charcoal sections of prehistoric beams collected in 1927 by Mr. Morris have been identified as dating near 350 A.D."

This chronology has a two-fold value for the archaeologist. First, it holds the key for dating countless other ruins that fall within its span, for wood which has not yet been excavated may be compared with this ring record at any time in the future; second, it offers a weather record, a story of years of drought and of plenty, which opens a large field for study along ecological lines. Owing to local variations in the ring patterns, the master plot or chart of the rings which we now possess does not operate over the entire Southwest. Rapid strides are being made annually to remedy this by the construction of new chronologies. The net result of these studies will bring an even wider area into the picture where dates may be obtained from ruins. In that section where the chronology has functioned with the most success, we find that ruins have yielded dates which fall into a span of more than thirteen centuries, beginning with about the year 1700 for the latest, and extending to about 350 A.D. for the earliest. It may be fairly stated that the lower limit has not yet been reached. The significance of this naturally is that, where so great a span of time is involved, a new means is supplied for arranging antiquities into stages without the need of cumbersome and often inexact nomenclatures. But more than this, the span of years into which we now know that Basketmaker III and Pueblo IV ruins fall has been an eye-opener as to the rate of culture growth. The ages estimated for some of the major and late ruins on purely empirical grounds were shown to be somewhat too high by the actual dates, but the discrepancy was not inordinately large. Further, the order of periods was unchanged, which in itself is an excellent commentary on the reliability of the methods developed in local research prior to the addition of dendrochronology. For the earlier stages in Basketmaker-Pueblo growth, however, the estimates were considerably in excess of the actual dates. To be specific, dates for those Basketmakers who possessed pottery, which were generally placed before Christ, can now be carried forward to at least 700 A.D. As a consequence, the periods following Basketmaker III are later than heretofore supposed, Pueblo I, for example, dating from the late 700's to approximately 900, and Pueblo III at its zenith dates about 1100. The evident fact is that the development from primitive beginnings to the peak of achievement was a swift one, and did not require the centuries of laborious evolution generally imagined. In this point, then, dendrochronology has brought about perhaps the most revolutionary single element in archaeological thought. We have also learned that the development did not progress equally over a wide area; in marginal areas a Pueblo II stage had been reached when at other points Pueblo III was already in full flower.

Reviewing the distribution of dated ruins within the present time scale, we find that sites placed culturally in Pueblo III and IV, dating from 1000 to 1350, are most numerous, thus giving us the fullest data on those stages. With the exception of the Flagstaff area, Pueblo II is practically undated and, for Pueblo I, dates are available for both the eastern and western variants. From this point back, the information is very sketchy.

As I see it, there are three angles in the tree-ring-archaeological relationship which must be considered. These are: the field angle, covering the collecting of the beam material; the laboratory angle, embracing the dating of the wood or charcoal samples; and the interpretative angle, in which the facts discovered in the preceding step are integrated and fitted into the background.

For the first of these, it is unnecessary to go into detail, as the field man is already acquainted with the general methods and requirements.[1] Sampling in standing ruins requires specialized equipment, and should be done with due regard for the antiquities involved. The recovery of charcoal and decayed wood from open sites is also beset with special problems which must be met as they arise. Success or failure in getting satisfactory dates, i.e., the final growth layer of the tree, may depend upon the method of handling the beam material in

---

[1] McGregor, J. C., Tree Ring Dating; Museum Notes, Museum of Northern Arizona, Vol. 3, No. 4, 1930.

the field by the field technician, for neglect or improper treatment may cause a partial loss of outer rings on fragile specimens.

Looking at the problem from the angle of one who dates the wood, I believe it cannot be too strongly urged that the excavator himself should have a fundamental knowledge of woods, and the utility of ring types. With such knowledge, laboratory work could be reduced to a minimum. However, a wise policy to pursue at all times, whether conversant with the subject or not, is to save all material about which there may be any doubt. The excavator's task does not stop with the selection and care of the material, for, if improperly recorded, certain desired information will assuredly be lost. Wood should receive the same careful attention that is accorded to all other types of specimens. The fullness of the results will depend to a degree upon the thoroughness and wideness of the sampling. The more rooms giving beam material, the better the growth changes of the structure and the history of the culture will be understood.

The second phase, the dating of the wood, is beyond a doubt the most important and crucial step of the three, for inaccuracies will inevitably lead to chaos in the third step, the interpretation. This is to say that to express the cutting date of a log as 1100 A.D. definitely places it; the quantity is unchanging; it is either right or wrong. The weight of the decision naturally rests upon the individual who undertakes the dating, and his responsibility is therefore very great. This dictates that he should proceed with sound and discerning judgment based upon substantial facts. By common consent, it was decided at the tree-ring conference at Flagstaff in 1934 that at least two competent individuals should agree on any date before such a date is published, thus verifying its accuracy.

Some misunderstanding has been created in the past by the failure to specify whether a published date was the bark date[2] or that of the innermost ring of the log. For the archaeologist, the bark date only has real or primary value. On the other hand, the innermost ring and those intervening are of interest to the student concerned with chronology-building and cycle studies. It is therefore the further duty of the examiner of the wood to state the true condition of the date, whether derived from the final ring or from the last ring on a specimen with an indeterminate number missing. All these points must be seriously considered in the interpretative angle.

A few words may be said at this point in connection with the release of tree-ring data. It is naturally desirable that dates be released as soon as possible after they have been determined. It is realized, however, that the reports in which they should properly be published may be years in preparation, and that their immediate publication through normal channels may not be feasible. To meet this contingency and others, the idea of issuing a tree-ring bulletin was conceived less than a year ago by those vitally interested in dendrochronology. It was felt that the long delay in the issuance of dates might retard the advancement of the study, especially in chronology building, and at the same time withhold vital information from the archaeologist. The publication of the dates in a small quarterly in no way detracts from their value in the final published form. To endow such information with maximum value, it is desirable that together with data as to the origin of the wood, the sap-heart date, bark date, etc., the culture affiliation should also be stated as clearly as possible. Without this the

---

[2]Denoting the final layer of woody tissue grown by the tree, occurring beneath the bark.

dates have little or no meaning to the archaeologist. If, in the tabular form of presentation, the lack of space demands the use of Pueblo I, Pueblo II, etc., the variants of these periods should be explicitly stated. For the benefit of those concerned with the dating of wood, a combined chronology reproduced in a line cut would also be invaluable, for, by this means, information as to local differences in the ring records could be uniformly and inexpensively disseminated. I should like to emphasize the fact that, since the student's reliance on or rejection of tree-ring data will depend largely upon its fullness and the form of publication, this step should be carefully planned.

We now come to the third consideration, namely the interpretation of tree-ring facts from the standpoint of archaeology. We may ask at once, are there any standards of correlation which may be offered for general acceptance? While to answer this question requires some discussion, it may be admitted from the start that each case in which tree-ring dates have contributed to our knowledge of ruins, special circumstances demanded special consideration in the interpretation, and that a formula or group of standards cannot be absolutely set down. To restate the query put a moment ago, to what extent can we rely upon wood from a room in order to date the masonry and the associated artifacts? An answer can be given only after a careful inspection of the related facts, as wholly different explanations may be controlled by these.

One of the first points to be considered is the question of cutting date, versus deadwood date. This is to say, does the bark date on a log represent the actual time of cutting by the people who built it into their dwelling, or does it represent the last year of the life of the tree which died through natural causes and stood or lay in the forest for a long period before being selected by man? It is generally believed that deadwood or wind-fallen trees were infrequently utilized, first, because this type of wood is much more resistant to the axe than green or live wood, and secondly, in the case of pine and most woods in the local forests, it soon decays and becomes unfit for use. If used, however, it must have been rarely, since the task of hunting out proper deadwood in the forest would probably exceed that of cutting fresh logs. An occasional piece thus incorporated into a structure in which the beams were dominantly live wood, would give an earlier date. It could be largely discounted since precedence, in most instances, must be given to the most recent dates. Exceptions to this would be cases of remodeling or replacements, i.e., fresh logs built into an existing building. Further support for the use of live wood is obtained in cases where a series of logs from a single room terminate with the same ring, representing the same year. In one instance with which I am acquainted, twenty-four logs from a pithouse gave the same terminal date. The probability of the occurrence of this condition, if deadwood has been selected for the structural beams, is extremely small. Repetitions of this case call for a generalization to the effect that live wood was generally used, and that the final ring be accepted as representing the construction time. One condition that may introduce error is the possibility that beams once cut were not immediately used, but were allowed to season in order to avoid sagging. Although seasoning of logs is practised by the Pueblos to some extent, it cannot be positively asserted that this procedure obtained in ancient times. A variation of a year or two in the dates of logs of a given house may suggest this. If seasoning prevailed, house-building was definitely planned a year or two in advance, a condition which was probably not general. Emergency situations must also have arisen which demanded immediate construction. Admitting that a year or two elapsed between cutting and construction time, the factor is so small as to be trivial, and the problem resolves itself into a very minor one.

While wood found within a room is most apt to be related to it structurally, several other conditions may also prevail which might prove to be disturbing factors in the interpretation. For example, charcoal from the fireplace might conceivably give far more recent dates than the roof beams. Where the structure has been burned, it may not always be possible to segregate wood from the two sources. A further confusing situation might be created by the dumping of discarded wood into an abandoned room which was being filled with rubbish; however, here the nature of the wood and its position in the fill will usually give some clue as to its origin. Logs found as an integral part of the house, i.e., built into the walls or lying on the floor in such a position as to indicate clearly that they were once in the roof, are naturally the most convincing in offering construction dates. Let us take an ideal case to see what possibilities might arise where definite structural wood is being dealt with. Say that six major logs supporting a roof give, in each case, the same bark date of 1300. Little leeway is possible here in interpretation, for the odds overwhelmingly favor that date as the time of construction, or within a year or two in case of seasoning. Should one of the logs give a date of 1150, the obvious discrepancy of 150 years can best be explained by supposing that that particular log was salvaged from an older structure. This situation is known to have occurred in the past, as witness the log taken from a house in Oraibi a few years ago which was cut in the late 14th century.[4] Or we may find that one or more of the logs gives a reading of 1350, fifty years later than the remaining five. In this event, a repair or replacement may be indicated. It is further conceivable that each of the six logs will give different dates, probably indicating a heterogeneous collection of beams, in which event only the latest date will be of any particular value. Such a condition must be rated as highly unsatisfactory. It will be readily seen that the various situations thus outlined will, in one way or another, affect the interpretation. Each set of circumstances presents a particular problem, the solution of which cannot be reached by pre-arranged standards.

A similar set of conditions may be visualized in working out the relationship of the dates of a room to those of the artifacts contained within. To put this as a question: Are the artifacts within a house approximately the same age as the house itself? Generally speaking, they are; however, in some instances they may be more recent. This is said with full recognition of the possibility of finding old pottery and the like in recent rooms, and recent materials in rooms which have been occupied for a long time. In this case judgment must be influenced by the archaeological conditions. The best form of proof for dating artifacts in this manner lies in the consistent appearance of a trait or traits within rooms of the same general age. This is to say that group data became the decisive factor. For example, the Canyon Creek cliff

[4] Douglass, A. E., The Secret of the Southwest Solved by Talkative Tree-Rings; National Geographic Magazine, December 1929, p. 754.

ruin,[5] located on the Fort Apache Indian Reservation, offered eighteen datable rooms out of a total of about sixty. These rooms are scattered throughout the length and breadth of the structure in both the first and second stories. The artifacts from all rooms were uniformly of the same generic kind, reflecting no period changes, and the range of dates from the eighteen rooms was between 1326 and 1348. From this it may be concluded that the material culture is of comparable age, or perhaps a little later. It can be unerringly dated to the 14th century. This angle of tree rings and archaeology is one of the most vital, and, because of its admitted importance, a correlation should not be attempted without full comprehension of all related information.

Once material culture has been satisfactorily dated in a region, objects native to that place, but alien to another, become valuable time indicators. In such cases tree rings are directly responsible for ordering the data in the primary area, and indirectly in the adjoining area. The value of this approach is particularly high in such regions where, owing to physiographic and other conditions, tree rings may never be utilized. The time status of the Hohokam of the Gila Basin has been worked out chiefly by this method. The same principle will doubtless be brought into play in the study of Mexican and Mississippian cultures.

Exact as a date may be, it is not possible to value each one equally. Distinctions arise which are governed to a certain extent by conditions already outlined, and by others which will be mentioned presently. We need to consider the value of a single date versus many dates, first, from a one-type site, i.e., one in which the occupation was short and the material culture all of one phase, and second, from a site long occupied, in which growth changes are apparent. An individual date from a one-type ruin can be more rigidly interpreted than one from a large complex site, since, in the former, there was little opportunity for old beams to be re-used and for other disturbing factors to creep in. Single dates may be strengthened by dates from other sites of approximately the same age and cultural association. As an example, two dates from Gila Pueblo, a one-type ruin, are 1345 and 1385. While these are indicative of the age, there is of course room for error. However, with dates ranging from 1326 to 1348 in the Canyon Creek ruin, and with a terminal date of 1383 for the Showlow ruin, both of which manifest cultural ties with Gila Pueblo, the dates procured at Gila Pueblo may be admitted as valid.

In the case of a site giving several stages, group data only will give satisfactory results, for individual dates offer too great an opportunity for misinterpretation owing to the possibility of re-used beams. One important case of this character is now before us. The earliest date from a ruin in the Southwest is about 350 A.D. This was obtained from a log found by Mr. Earl H. Morris in Mummy Cave, Canyon del Muerto. Archaeologically, it is known that this cave was occupied from Basketmaker II times, but the conditions were so confused that the association of the beam in question could not be positively determined. No matter how strong the temptation may be to date the culture on the strength of this log, it cannot legitimately be done until further dates or relevant facts have been gathered.

While we have been concerned so far

---

[5] Haury, E. W., The Canyon Creek Ruin and the Cliff Dwellings of the Sierra Ancha; Medallion Papers XIV, Gila Pueblo, Globe, Arizona, 1934.

mainly with dates from structural wood, Dr. Florence M. Hawley has also demonstrated the utility of charcoal fragments from rubbish heaps in the case of Chetro Ketl.[6] The value of pottery sequences obtained from the study of daily sweepings of broken pottery and charcoal, as a check against information obtained in the building itself, needs hardly to be pointed out. This study also helps in solving the problem of the length of time involved in the accumulating of rubbish mounds.

So far, the climatic angle of tree rings and archaeology has only been mentioned. Yet here lies a very fertile field, for past weather and human activity are intimately related. In the present chronology, which just falls short of 2000 years, one extended drought and several short ones are recorded. We suspect that the most severe of these, the drought lasting from 1276 to 1299, profoundly affected certain of the Southwestern peoples, and was responsible in the main for shifts in the population at about that time. But so far we have done little more than look at the raw and isolated facts. Here the archaeologist must cooperate with the climatologist whose interpretation of the tree-ring calendar from the weather angle is needed before it is possible to carry the study forward along strictly archaeological lines.

We would do well to ask ourselves at this point whether or not the tree-ring data we now have conflicts with the archaeological evidence. It has already been intimated that, before the benefits of dendrochronology were available, the error of age estimates of culture stages increased progressively from recent to remote times. However, since this adjustment has been made in the minds of students of Southwestern archaeology, it can be said that no glaring conflicts, such as radically differing dates for the same cultural stage, have occurred. Indeed, should a violent disagreement occur, it would be well to look into the possibility of irregular conditions in the archaeological evidence. Improper release of dates and too rigid an interpretation, may tend to throw the facts out of alignment. On this last point, it is well to remember that, while a date may generally place a developmental stage, it does not delimit it. A problem relating to this part of the discussion has recently been raised by Mr. John C. McGregor, who, in dating wood from pit-houses excavated by the Museum of Northern Arizona, found a span of 150 years in bark dates from the wood of a single pit-house. Upon first consideration, one might say that the house was occupied for this period, and that towards the end of the occupancy, log replacements were made, thus accounting for the great difference in time. The improbability of a 150-year life for an underground house, and the lack of change in the material culture associated with it, in view of the more rapid changes general over the Southwest, tend to temper this idea. But the problem is not easily solved. A likely explanation is that, in the construction of the house, the builders robbed an old dwelling for useful beams, adding to them others cut currently, and consequently of much later date.

Much, very much indeed, has been accomplished in the few years that dendrochronology and archaeology have joined hands, but the work has literally only begun. Some ramifications of the subject have been almost entirely neglected. Along lines of basic research more work is necessary. For example, master plots covering zones or more restricted areas than we

---

[6]The Significance of the Dated Prehistory of Chetro Ketl, Chaco Canyon, New Mexico. The University of New Mexico Bulletin, Vol. I, No. 1, 1934.

now possess, would be invaluable in hastening the dating in marginal areas, as in the Mimbres, where certain fundamentals shown in the Flagstaff chronology were apparently not repeated. Fortunately Dr. Douglass and Mr. H. S. Gladwin are now at work on this problem and results may soon be expected. Research on woods other than those now used should lead to worthwhile results.

Extension of tree-ring dating to other areas is a challenge which cannot be overlooked. First steps outside of the nuclear area in the Flagstaff-Chaco Canyon sector, were made to the east in the Rio Grande where Mr. W. S. Stallings, of the Laboratory of Anthropology, has succeeded in the difficult task of building up a basic chronology extending to 1100 A.D.[7] In the Tennessee Valley, Dr. Hawley has obtained significant results from wood found in Mound-builder remains. Northern Mexico and possibly parts of South America may similarly prove to be rich fields. For the tropics, the outlook is not bright, although not altogether hopeless. In my opinion, illuminating work might well be done in Egypt where an abundance of useful wood of dynastic times is available. While the Egyptian chronology has been worked out with reliability on astronomic and historic ground, I believe it is not unlikely that tree rings might well substantiate and possibly amplify this.

The degree to which success will come in the relationship of American archaeology and dendrochronology will depend largely upon the degree of coöperation among those vitally concerned in the study. Due to its involved nature, the welfare of the subject depends upon coördinated efforts. Lacking this, the most unique check yet discovered on the changing quality of human culture cannot bear its richest fruit.

---

[7] A Tree-Ring Chronology for the Rio Grande Drainage in Northern New Mexico; Proceedings of the National Academy of Sciences, Vol. 19, No. 9, pp. 803–806; 1933.

SOCIO-LINGUISTICS

The Logic of Nonstandard English

WILLIAM LABOV

In the past decade, a great deal of federally sponsored research has been devoted to the educational problems of children in ghetto schools. In order to account for the poor performance of children in these schools, educational psychologists have attempted to discover what kind of disadvantage or defect they are suffering from. The viewpoint that has been widely accepted and used as the basis for large scale intervention programs is that the children show a cultural deficit as a result of an impoverished environment in their early years. Considerable attention has been given to language. In this area the deficit theory appears as the concept of verbal deprivation. Negro children from the ghetto area are said to receive little verbal stimulation, to hear very little well-formed language, and as a result are impoverished in their means of verbal expression. They cannot speak complete sentences, do not know the names of common objects, cannot form concepts or convey logical thoughts.

Unfortunately, these notions are based upon the work of educational psychologists who know very little about language and even less about Negro children. The concept of **verbal deprivation** has no basis in social reality. In fact, Negro children in the urban ghettos receive a great deal of verbal stimulation, hear more well-formed sentences than middle-class children, and participate fully in a highly verbal culture. They have the same basic vocabulary, possess the same capacity for conceptual learning, and use the same logic as anyone else who learns to speak and understand English.

The notion of verbal deprivation is a part of the modern mythology of educational psychology, typical of the unfounded notions which tend to expand rapidly in our educational system. In past decades linguists have been as guilty as others in promoting such intellectual fashions at the expense of both teachers and children. But the **myth** of verbal deprivation is particularly dangerous, because it diverts attention from real defects of our educational system to imaginary defects of the child. As we shall see, it leads its sponsors inevitably to the hypothesis of the genetic inferiority of Negro children that it was originally designed to avoid.

The most useful service which linguists can perform today is to clear away the illusion of verbal deprivation and to provide a more adequate notion of the relations between standard and nonstandard **dialects**. In the writings of many prominent educational psychologists, we find very poor understanding of the nature of language. Children are treated as if they have no language of their own in the preschool programs put forward by Bereiter and Engelmann (1966). The linguistic behavior of ghetto children in test situations is the principal evidence of genetic inferiority in the view of Jensen (1969). In this paper, we will examine critically both of these approaches to the language and intelligence of the populations labeled "verbally deprived" and "culturally deprived" and attempt to explain how the myth of verbal deprivation has arisen, bringing to bear the methodological findings of sociolinguistic work and some substantive facts about language which are known to all linguists. Of particular concern is the relation between concept formation on the one hand, and dialect differences on the other, since it in this area that the most dangerous misunderstandings are to be found.

Verbality

The general setting in which the deficit theory arises consists of a number of facts which are known to all of us. One is that Negro children in the central urban ghettos do badly in all school subjects, including arithmetic and reading. In reading, they average more than two years behind the national norm (see *New York Times*, December 3, 1968). Furthermore, this lag is cumulative, so that they do worse comparatively in the fifth grade than in the first grade. Reports in the literature show that this poor performance is correlated most closely with socioeconomic status. Segregated ethnic groups seem to do worse than others—in particular, Indian, Mexican-American, and Negro children. Our own work in New York City confirms that most Negro children read very poorly; however, studies in the speech community show that the situation is even worse than has been reported. If one separates the isolated and peripheral individuals from members of central peer groups, the peer-group members show even worse reading records, and to all intents and purposes are not learning to read at all during the time they spend in school (see Labov et al. 1968).

In speaking of children in the urban ghetto areas, the term *lower class* frequently is used, as opposed to *middle class*. In the several sociolinguistic studies we have carried out, and in many parallel studies, it has been useful to distinguish a lower-class group from a working-class one. Lower-class families are typically female-based, or matrifocal, with no father present to provide steady economic support, whereas for the working-class there is typically an intact nuclear family with the father holding a semiskilled or skilled job. The educational problems of ghetto areas run across this important class distinction. There is no evidence, for example, that the father's presence or absence is closely correlated with educational achievement (e.g., Langer and Michaels 1963; Coleman, et al. 1966). The peer groups we have studied in south-central Harlem, representing the basic vernacular culture, include members from both family types. The attack against cultural deprivation in the ghetto is overtly directed at family structures typical of lower-class families, but the educational failure we have been discussing is characteristic of both working-class and lower-class children.

This paper, therefore, will refer to children from urban ghetto areas rather than lower-class children. The population we are concerned with comprises those who participate fully in the vernacular culture of the street and who have been alienated from the school system.[1] We are obviously dealing with the effects of the **caste** system of American society—essentially a color-marking system. Everyone recognizes this. The question is: By what mechanism does the color bar prevent children from learning to read? One answer is the notion of cultural deprivation put forward by Martin Deutsch and others (Deutsch and associates 1967; Deutsch, Katz, and Jensen 1968). Negro children are said to lack the favorable factors in their home environment which enable middle-class children to do well in school. These factors involve the development of various cognitive skills through verbal interaction with adults, including the ability to reason abstractly, speak fluently, and focus upon long-range goals. In their publications, these psychologists also recognize broader social factors.[2] However, the deficit theory does not focus upon the interaction of the Negro child with white society so much as on his failure to interact with his mother at home. In the literature we find very little direct observation of verbal interaction in the Negro home. Most typically, the investigators ask the child if he has dinner with his parents, if he engages in dinner-table conversation with them, if his family takes him on trips to museums and other cultural activities, and so on. This slender thread of evidence is used to explain and interpret the large body of tests carried out in the laboratory and in the school.

The most extreme view which proceeds from this orientation—and one that is now being widely accepted—is that lower-class Negro children have no language at all. The notion is first drawn from Basil Bernstein's writings that "much of lower-class language consists of a kind of incidental 'emotional' accompaniment to action here and now" (Jensen 1968, p. 118). Bernstein's views are filtered through a strong bias against all forms of working-class behavior, so that middle-class language is seen as superior in every respect—as "more abstract, and necessarily somewhat more flexible, detailed and subtle" (p. 119). One can proceed through a range of such views until he comes to the preschool programs of Bereiter and Engelmann (1966;

---

[1] The concept of nonstandard Negro English (NNE) and the vernacular culture in which it is embedded is presented in detail in Labov, et al. (1968, sections 1.2.3 and 4.1). See volume 2, section 4.3 for the linguistic traits which distinguish speakers who participate fully in the NNE culture from marginal and isolated individuals.

[2] For example, in Deutsch, Katz, and Jensen (1968) there is a section on Social and Psychological Perspectives which includes a chapter by Proshansky and Newton on "The Nature and Meaning of Negro Self-Identity," and one by Rosenthal and Jacobson on "Self-Fulfilling Prophecies in the Classroom."

Bereiter, et al. 1966). Bereiter's program for an academically oriented preschool is based upon the premise that Negro children must have a language with which they can learn and the empirical finding that these children come to school without such a language. In his work with four-year-old Negro children from Urbana, Bereiter (et al. 1966, pp. 113 ff.) reports that their communication was by gestures, single words, and "a series of badly connected words or phrases," such as *They mine* and *Me got juice*. He reports that Negro children could not ask questions, that "without exaggerating . . . these four-year-olds could make no statements of any kind." Furthermore, when these children were asked "Where is the book?" they did not know enough to look at the table where the book was lying in order to answer. Thus Bereiter concludes that these children's speech forms are nothing more than a series of emotional cries, and he decides to treat them "as if the children had no language at all." He identifies their speech with his interpretation of Bernstein's restricted code: "the language of culturally deprived children . . . is not merely an underdeveloped version of standard English, but is a basically non-logical mode of expressive behavior" (Bereiter, et al. 1966, pp. 112–13). The basic program of his preschool is to teach them a new language devised by Engelmann, which consists of a limited series of questions and answers such as "Where is the squirrel?" "The squirrel is in the tree." The children will not be punished if they use their vernacular speech on the playground, but they will not be allowed to use it in the schoolroom. If they should answer the question, "Where is the squirrel?" with the illogical vernacular form "In the tree" they will be reprehended by various means and made to say, "The squirrel is in the tree."

Linguists and psycholinguists who have worked with Negro children are apt to dismiss this view of their language as utter nonsense. Yet there is no reason to reject Bereiter's observations as spurious. They were certainly not made up. On the contrary, they give us a very clear view of the behavior of student and teacher which can be duplicated in any classroom. In our own work outside of adult-dominated environments of school and home, we have not observed Negro children behaving like this.[3] However, on many occasions we have been asked to help analyze the results of research into verbal deprivation conducted in such test situations.

Here, for example, is a complete interview with a Negro boy, one of hundreds carried out in a New York City school. The boy enters a room where there is a large, friendly, white interviewer, who puts on the table in front of him a toy and says: "Tell me everything you can about this." (The interviewer's further remarks are in parentheses.)

[12 seconds of silence]
(What would you say it looks like?)
[8 seconds of silence]
A space ship.
(Hmmmm.)
[13 seconds of silence]
Like a je-et.
[12 seconds of silence]
Like a plane.
[20 seconds of silence]
(What color is it?)

---

[3]The research cited here was carried out in south-central Harlem and other ghetto areas in 1965–1968 to describe the structural and **functional** differences between Negro nonstandard English and standard English in the classroom. It was supported by the Office of Education as Cooperative Research Projects 3091 and 3288. Detailed reports are given in Labov, et al. (1965), Labov (1967), and Labov, et al. (1968).

Orange. (2 seconds) An' whi-ite. (2 seconds) An' green.

[6 seconds of silence]

(An' what could you use it for?)

[8 seconds of silence]

A je-et.

[6 seconds of silence]

(If you had two of them, what would you do with them?)

[6 seconds of silence]

Give one to some-body.

(Hmmm. Who do you think would like to have it?)

[10 seconds of silence]

Cla-rence.

(Mm. Where do you think we could get another one of these?)

At the store.

(Oh ka-ay!)

We have here the same kind of defensive, **monosyllabic behavior** which is reported in Bereiter's work. What is the situation that produces it? The child is in an asymmetrical situation where anything he says can literally be held against him. He has learned a number of devices to avoid saying anything in this situation, and he works very hard to achieve this end. One may observe the **intonation patterns** of

$$\text{and} \quad a\ ^2\ \text{space}\ ^2\ \text{sh}\ ^3\ \text{ip}\quad\quad ^2 a\ ^3\ 'O'\ ^2\ \text{know}$$

which Negro children often use when they are asked a question to which the answer is obvious. The answer may be read as: "Will this satisfy you?"

If one takes this interview as a measure of the verbal capacity of the child, it must be as his capacity to defend himself in a hostile and threatening situation. But unfortunately, thousands of such interviews are used as evidence of the child's total verbal capacity, or more simply his verbality. It is argued that this lack of verbality explains his poor performance in school. Operation Head Start and other intervention programs have largely been based upon the deficit theory—the notions that such interviews give us a measure of the child's verbal capacity and that the verbal stimulation which he has been missing can be supplied in a preschool environment.

The verbal behavior which is shown by the child in the situation quoted above is not the result of the ineptness of the interviewer. It is rather the result of regular sociolinguistic factors operating upon adult and child in this asymmetrical situation. . . .

The view of the Negro speech community which we obtain from our work in the ghetto areas is precisely the opposite from that reported by Deutsch or by Bereiter and Engelmann. We see a child bathed in verbal stimulation from morning to night. We see many speech events which depend upon the competitive exhibition of verbal skills—sounding, singing, toasts, rifting, louding—a whole range of activities in which the individual gains status through his use of language (see Labov, et al. 1968, section 4.2). We see the younger child trying to acquire these skills from older children, hanging around on the outskirts of older peer groups, and imitating this behavior to the best of his ability. We see no connection between verbal skill in the speech events characteristic of the street culture and success in the schoolroom.

Verbosity

There are undoubtedly many verbal skills which children from ghetto areas must learn in order to do well in the school situation, and some of these are indeed characteristic of middle-class verbal behavior. Precision in spelling, practice in handling abstract symbols, the ability to state explicitly the meaning of words, and a richer knowledge of the Latinate vocabulary, may all be useful acquisitions. But is it true that all of the middle-class verbal habits are functional and desirable in the school situation? Before we impose middle-class verbal style upon children from other cultural groups, we should find out how much of this is useful for the main work of analyzing and generalizing, and how much is merely stylistic—or even **dysfunctional**. In high school and college, middle-class children spontaneously complicate their syntax to the point that instructors despair of getting them to make their language simpler and clearer. In every learned journal one can find examples of jargon and empty elaboration, as well as complaints about it. Is the elaborated code of Bernstein really so "flexible, detailed and subtle" as some psychologists (e.g., Jensen 1969, p. 119) believe? Isn't it also turgid, redundant, bombastic, and empty? Is it not simply an elaborated style, rather than a superior code or system?[4]

Our work in the speech community makes it painfully obvious that in many ways working-class speakers are more effective narrators, reasoners, and debaters than many middle-class speakers who temporize, qualify, and lose their argument in a mass of irrelevant detail. Many academic writers try to rid themselves of that part of middle-class style that is empty pretension, and keep that part that is needed for precision. But the average middle-class speaker that we encounter makes no such effort; he is enmeshed in verbiage, the victim of sociolinguistic factors beyond his control.

I will not attempt to support this argument here with systematic quantitative evidence, although it is possible to develop measures which show how far middle-class speakers can wander from the point. I would like to contrast two speakers dealing with roughly the same topic—matters of belief. The first is Larry H., a fifteen-year-old core member of the Jets, being interviewed by John Lewis. Larry is one of the loudest and roughest members of the Jets, one who gives the least recognition to the conventional rules of politeness.[5] For most readers of this paper, first contact with Larry would produce some fairly negative reactions on both sides. It is probable that you would not like him any more than his teachers do. Larry causes trouble in and out of school. He was put back from the eleventh grade to the ninth, and has been threatened with further action by the school authorities.

JL: What happens to you after you die? Do you know?
Larry: Yeah, I know. (What?) After they put you in the ground, your body turns into—ah—bones, an' shit.
JL: What happens to your spirit?
Larry: Your spirit—soon as you die, your spirit leaves you. (And where does the spirit go?)

---

[4]The term code is central in Bernstein's (1966) description of the differences between working-class and middle-class styles of speech. The restrictions and elaborations of speech observed are labeled as codes to indicate the principles governing selection from the range of possible English sentences. No rules or detailed description of the operation of such codes are provided as yet, so that this central concept remains to be specified.

[5]A direct view of Larry's verbal style in a hostile encounter is given in Labov, et al. (1968, volume 2, pp. 39–43). Gray's Oral Reading Test was being given to a group of Jets on the steps of a brownstone house in Harlem, and the landlord tried unsuccessfully to make the Jets move. Larry's verbal style in this encounter matches the reports he gives of himself in a number of narratives cited in section 4.8 of the foregoing report.

Well, it all depends . . . (On what?) You know, like some people say if you're good an' shit, your spirit goin' t'heaven . . . 'n' if you bad, your spirit goin' to hell. Well, bullshit! Your spirit goin' to hell anyway, good or bad.
JL: Why?
Larry: Why? I'll tell you why. 'Cause, you see, doesn' nobody really know that it's a God, y'know, 'cause I mean I have seen black gods, pink gods, white gods, all color gods, and don't nobody know it's really a God. An' when they be sayin' if you good, you goin' t'heaven, tha's bullshit, 'cause you ain't goin' to no heaven, 'cause it ain't no heaven for you to go to.

Larry is a paradigmatic speaker of nonstandard Negro English (NNE) as opposed to standard English. His grammar shows a high concentration of such characteristic NNE forms as negative inversion ("don't nobody know . . ."), negative concord ("you ain't goin' to no heaven . . ."), invariant *be* ("when they be sayin' . . ."), dummy *it* for standard *there* ("it ain't no heaven . . ."), optional copula deletion ("if you're good . . . if you bad . . .") and full forms of auxiliaries ("I have seen . . ."). The only standard English influence in this passage is the one case of "doesn't" instead of the invariant "don't" of NNE. Larry also provides a paradigmatic example of the rhetorical style of NNE: he can sum up a complex argument in a few words, and the full force of his opinions comes through without qualification or reservation. He is eminently quotable, and his interviews give us many concise statements of the NNE point of view. One can almost say that Larry speaks the NNE culture (see Labov, et al. 1968, vol. 2, pp. 38, 71–73, 291–92).

It is the logical form of this passage which is of particular interest here. Larry presents a complex set of interdependent propositions which can be explicated by setting out the standard English equivalents in

linear order. The basic argument is to deny the twin propositions:

(A) If you are good, (B) then your spirit will go to heaven.

(∼A) If you are bad, (C) then your spirit will go to hell.

Larry denies (B) and asserts that if (A) or (∼A), then (C). His argument may be outlined as follows:

1. Everyone has a different idea of what God is like.
2. Therefore nobody really knows that God exists.
3. If there is a heaven, it was made by God.
4. If God doesn't exist, he couldn't have made heaven.
5. Therefore heaven does not exist.
6. You can't go somewhere that doesn't exist.

(∼B) Therefore you can't go to heaven.
(C) Therefore you are going to hell.

The argument is presented in the order: (C), because (2) because (1), therefore (2), therefore (∼B) because (5) and (6). Part of the argument is implicit: the connection (2) therefore (∼B) leaves unstated the connecting links (3) and (4), and in this interval Larry strengthens the propositions from the form (2) "Nobody knows if there is . . ." to (5) "There is no . . . ." Otherwise, the case is presented explicitly as well as economically. The complex argument is summed up in Larry's last sentence, which shows formally the dependence of (∼B) on (5) and (6):

An' when they be sayin' if you good, you goin' t'heaven, (The proposition, if A, then B)
Tha's bullshit, (is absurd)
'cause you ain't goin' to no heaven (because B)
'cause it ain't no heaven for you to go to (because (5) and (6)).

This hypothetical argument is not carried on at a high level of seriousness. It is a game played with ideas as counters, in which opponents use a wide variety of verbal devices to win. There is no personal commitment to any of these propositions, and no reluctance to strengthen one's argument by bending the rules of logic as in the (2)-(5) sequence. But if the opponent invokes the rules of logic, they hold. In John Lewis's interviews, he often makes this move, and the force of his argument is always acknowledged and countered within the rules of logic. In this case, he pointed out the fallacy that the argument (2)-(3)-(4)-(5)-(6) leads to (∼C) as well as (∼B), so it cannot be used to support Larry's assertion (C):

JL: Well, if there's no heaven, how could there be a hell?
Larry: I mean—ye-eah. Well, let me tell you, it ain't no hell, 'cause this is hell right here, y'know! (This is hell?) Yeah, this is hell right here!

Larry's answer is quick, ingenious, and decisive. The application of the (3)-(4)-(5) argument to hell is denied, since hell is here, and therefore conclusion (C) stands. These are not ready-made or preconceived opinions, but new propositions devised to win the logical argument in the game being played. The reader will note the speed and precision of Larry's mental operations. He does not wander, or insert meaningless verbiage. The only repetition is (2), placed before and after (1) in his original statement. It is often said that the nonstandard vernacular is not suited for dealing with abstract or hypothetical questions, but in fact speakers from the NNE community take great delight in exercising their wit and logic on the most improbable

264   Anthropology

and problematical matters. Despite the fact that Larry H. does not believe in God, and has just denied all knowledge of him, John Lewis advances the following hypothetical question:

JL: ... but, just say that there is a God, what color is he? White or black?
Larry: Well, if it is a God ... I wouldn' know what color, I couldn' say,—couldn' nobody say what color he is or really *would* be.
JL: But now, jus' suppose there was a God—
Larry: Unless'n they say ...
JL: No, I was jus' sayin' jus' suppose there is a God, would he be white or black?
Larry: ... He'd be white, man.
JL: Why?
Larry: Why? I'll tell you why. 'Cause the average whitey out here got everything, you dig? And the nigger ain't got shit, y'know? Y'unnerstan'? So—um—for—in order for *that* to happen, you know it ain't no black God that's doin' that bullshit.

No one can hear Larry's answer to this question without being convinced that they are in the presence of a skilled speaker with great "verbal presence of mind," who can use the English language expertly for many purposes. Larry's answer to John Lewis is again a complex argument. The formulation is not standard English, but it is clear and effective even for those not familiar with the vernacular. The nearest standard English equivalent might be: "So you know that God isn't black, because if he was, he wouldn't have arranged things like that."

The reader will have noted that this analysis is being carried out in standard English, and the inevitable challenge is: why not write in NNE, then, or in your own nonstandard dialect? The fundamental reason is, of course, one of firmly fixed social conventions. All communities agree that standard English is the proper medium for formal writing and public communication. Furthermore, it seems likely that standard English has an advantage over NNE in explicit analysis of surface forms, which is what we are doing here. We will return to this opposition between explicitness and logical statement in subsequent sections on grammaticality and logic. First, however, it will be helpful to examine standard English in its primary natural setting, as the medium for informal spoken communication of middle-class speakers.

Let us now turn to the second speaker, an upper-middle-class, college-educated Negro man (Charles M.) being interviewed by Clarence Robins in our survey of adults in Central Harlem.

CR: Do you know of anything that someone can do, to have someone who has passed on visit him in a dream?
Charles: Well, I even heard my parents say that there is such a thing as something in dreams some things like that, and sometimes dreams do come true. I have personally never had a dream come true. I've never dreamt that somebody was dying and they actually died, (Mhm) or that I was going to have ten dollars the next day and somehow I got ten dollars in my pocket. (Mhm). I don't particularly believe in that, I don't think it's true. I do feel, though, that there is such a thing as—ah—**witchcraft**. I do feel that in certain cultures there is such a thing as witchcraft, or some sort of *science* of witchcraft; I don't think that it's just a matter of believing hard enough that there is such a thing as witchcraft. I do believe that there is such a thing that a person can put himself in a state of *mind* (Mhm), or that—er—something could be given them to intoxicate them in a certain—to a certain frame of mind—that—that could actually be considered witchcraft.

Charles M. is obviously a good speaker who strikes the listener as well-educated, intelligent, and sincere. He is a likeable and attractive person, the kind of person that middle-class listeners rate very high on a scale of job suitability and equally high as a potential friend.[6] His language is more moderate and tempered than Larry's; he makes every effort to qualify his opinions, and seems anxious to avoid any misstatements or overstatements. From these qualities emerge the primary characteristic of this passage—its verbosity. Words multiply, some modifying and qualifying, others repeating or padding the main argument. The first half of this extract is a response to the initial question on dreams, basically:

1. Some people say that dreams sometimes come true.
2. I have never had a dream come true.
3. Therefore I don't believe (1).

Some characteristic filler phrases appear here: *such a thing as, some things like that,* and *particularly.* Two examples of dreams given after (2) are afterthoughts that might have been given after (1). Proposition (3) is stated twice for no obvious reason. Nevertheless, this much of Charles M.'s response is well-directed to the point of the question. He then volunteers a statement of his beliefs about witchcraft which shows the difficulty of middle-class speakers who (a) want to express a belief in something but (b) want to show themselves as judicious, rational, and free from superstitions. The basic proposition can be stated simply in five words:

"But I believe in witchcraft."

However, the idea is enlarged to exactly 100 words, and it is difficult to see what else is being said. In the following quotations, padding which can be removed

---

[6]For a description of subjective reaction tests which utilize these evaluative dimensions see Labov, et al. (1968, section 4.6).

without change in meaning is shown in parentheses.

(1) "I (do) feel, though, that there is (such a thing as) witchcraft." *Feel* seems to be a euphemism for 'believe.'
(2) "(I do feel that) in certain cultures (there is such a thing as witchcraft)." This repetition seems designed only to introduce the word *culture,* which lets us know that the speaker knows about anthropology. Does *certain cultures* mean 'not in ours' or 'not in all'?
(3) "(or some sort of *science* of witchcraft.)" This addition seems to have no clear meaning at all. What is a "science" of witchcraft as opposed to just plain witchcraft?[7] The main function is to introduce the word *science,* though it seems to have no connection to what follows.
(4) "I don't think that it's just (a matter of) believing hard enough that (there is such a thing as) witchcraft." The speaker argues that witchcraft is not merely a belief; there is more to it.
(5) "I (do) believe that (there is such a thing that) a person can put himself in a state of mind . . . that (could actually be considered) witchcraft." Is witchcraft as a state of mind different from the state of belief, denied in (4)?
(6) "or that something could be given them to intoxicate them (to a certain frame of mind) . . . ." The third learned word, *intoxicate,* is introduced by this addition. The vacuity of this passage becomes more evident if we remove repetitions, fashionable words and stylistic decorations:

But I believe in witchcraft.
I don't think witchcraft is just a belief.

A person can put himself or be put in a state of mind that is witchcraft. Without the extra verbiage and the "OK" words like

---

[7]Several middle-class readers of this passage have suggested that *science* here refers to some form of control as opposed to belief. The science of witchcraft would then be a kind of engineering of mental states. Other interpretations can of course be provided. The fact remains that no such difficulties of interpretation are needed to understand Larry's remarks.

science, culture, and *intoxicate,* Charles M. appears as something less than a first-rate thinker. The initial impression of him as a good speaker is simply our long-conditioned reaction to middle-class verbosity. We know that people who use these stylistic devices are educated people, and we are inclined to credit them with saying something intelligent. Our reactions are accurate in one sense. Charles M. is more educated than Larry. But is he more rational, more logical, more intelligent? Is he any better at thinking out a problem to its solution? Does he deal more easily with abstractions? There is no reason to think so. Charles M. succeeds in letting us know that he is educated, but in the end we do not know what he is trying to say, and neither does he.

. . . I have attempted to explain the origin of the myth that lower-class Negro children are nonverbal. The examples just given may help to account for the corresponding myth that middle-class language is in itself better suited for dealing with abstract, logically complex, or hypothetical questions. These examples are intended to have a certain negative force. They are not controlled experiments. On the contrary, this and the preceding section are designed to convince the reader that the controlled experiments that have been offered in evidence are misleading. The only thing that is controlled is the superficial form of the stimulus. All children are asked "What do you think of capital punishment?" or "Tell me everything you can about this." But the speaker's interpretation of these requests, and the action he believes is appropriate in response is completely uncontrolled. One can view these test stimuli as requests for information, commands for action, threats of punishment, or meaningless sequences of words. They are probably intended as something altogether different—as requests for display,[8] but in any case the experimenter is normally unaware of the problem of interpretation. The methods of educational psychologists such as used by Deutsch, Jensen, and Bereiter follow the pattern designed for animal experiments where motivation is controlled by simple methods as withholding food until a certain weight reduction is reached. With human subjects, it is absurd to believe that identical stimuli are obtained by asking everyone the same question.

Since the crucial intervening variables of interpretation and motivation are uncontrolled, most of the literature on verbal deprivation tells us nothing about the capacities of children. They are only the trappings of science, approaches which substitute the formal procedures of the scientific method for the activity itself. With our present limited grasp of these problems, the best we can do to understand the verbal capacities of children is to study them within the cultural context in which they were developed. . . .

Logic

For many generations, American school teachers have devoted themselves to correcting a small number of nonstandard English rules to their standard equivalents, under the impression that they were teaching logic. This view has been reinforced and given theoretical justification by the claim that NNE lacks the means for the expression of logical thought.

Let us consider for a moment the possibility that Negro children do not operate with the same logic that middle-class adults

---

[8]The concept of a request for verbal display is here drawn from a treatment of the therapeutic interview given by Blum (in press).

display. This would inevitably mean that sentences of a certain grammatical form would have different truth values for the two types of speakers. One of the most obvious places to look for such a difference is in the handling of the negative, and here we encounter one of the nonstandard items which has been stigmatized as illogical by schoolteachers—the double negative, or as we term it, negative concord. A child who says "He don't know nothing" is often said to be making an illogical statement without knowing it. According to the teacher, the child wants to say "He knows nothing" but puts in an extra negative without realizing it, and so conveys the opposite meaning. "He does not know nothing," which reduces to "He knows something." I need not emphasize that this is an absurd interpretation. If a nonstandard speaker wishes to say that "He does not know *nothing*," he does so by simply placing contrastive stress on both negatives as I have done here ("He *don't* know *nothing*") indicating that they are derived from two underlying negatives in the deep structure. But note that the middle-class speaker does exactly the same thing when he wants to signal the existence of two underlying negatives: "He *doesn't* know *nothing*." In the standard form with one underlying negative ("He doesn't know anything"), the indefinite *anything* contains the same superficial reference to a preceding negative in the surface structure as the nonstandard *nothing* does. In the corresponding positive sentences, the indefinite *something* is used. The dialect difference, like most of the differences between the standard and nonstandard forms, is one of surface form, and has nothing to do with the underlying logic of the sentence.

We can summarize the ways in which the two dialects differ:

	Standard English, SE
Positive:	He knows something.
Negative:	He doesn't know anything.
Double Negative:	He *doesn't* know *nothing*.

	Nonstandard Negro English, NNE
Positive:	He know something.
Negative:	He don't know nothing.
Double Negative:	He *don't* know *nothing*.

This array makes it plain that the only difference between the two dialects is in superficial form. When a single negative is found in the deep structure, standard English converts *something* to the indefinite *anything*, NNE converts it to *nothing*. When speakers want to signal the presence of two negatives, they do it in the same way. No one would have any difficulty constructing the same table of truth values for both dialects. English is a rare language in its insistence that the negative particle be incorporated in the first indefinite only. The Anglo-Saxon authors of the Peterborough Chronicle were surely not illogical when they wrote *For ne waeren nan martyrs swa pined alse he waeron*, literally, "For never weren't no martyrs so tortured as these were." The "logical" forms of current standard English are simply the accepted conventions of our present-day formal style. Russian, Spanish, French, and Hungarian show the same negative concord as nonstandard English, and they are surely not illogical in this. What is termed "logical" in standard English is of course the conventions which are habitual. . . .

. . . The problems working-class children may have in handling logical operations are not to be blamed on the structure of their language. There is nothing in the vernacular which will interfere with the development of logical thought, for the logic of standard English cannot be distinguished from the logic of any other dialect of

English by any test that we can find.

What's Wrong With Being Wrong?

If there is a failure of logic involved here, it is surely in the approach of the verbal deprivation theorists, rather than in the mental abilities of the children concerned. We can isolate six distinct steps in the reasoning which has led to positions such as those of Deutsch, or Bereiter and Engelmann:

1. The lower-class child's verbal response to a formal and threatening situation is used to demonstrate his lack of verbal capacity, or verbal deficit.
2. This verbal deficit is declared to be a major cause of the lower-class child's poor performance in school.
3. Since middle-class children do better in school, middle-class speech habits are seen to be necessary for learning.
4. Class and ethnic differences in grammatical form are equated with differences in the capacity for logical analysis.
5. Teaching the child to mimic certain formal speech patterns used by middle-class teachers is seen as teaching him to think logically.
6. Children who learn these formal speech patterns are then said to be thinking logically and it is predicted that they will do much better in reading and arithmetic in the years to follow.

In the preceding sections of this paper I have tried to show that the above propositions are wrong, concentrating on 1, 4, and 5. Proposition 3 is the primary logical fallacy which illicitly identifies a form of speech as the cause of middle-class achievement in school. Proposition 6 is the one which is most easily shown to be wrong in fact, as we will note below.

However, it is not too naive to ask: "What is wrong with being wrong?" There is no competing educational theory which is being dismantled by this program, and there does not seem to be any great harm in having children repeat, "This is not a box" for twenty minutes a day. We have already conceded that NNE children need help in analyzing language into its surface components, and in being more explicit. But there are serious and damaging consequences of the verbal deprivation theory which may be considered under two headings: theoretical bias, and consequences of failure.

THEORETICAL BIAS

It is widely recognized that the teacher's attitude toward the child is an important factor in his success or failure. The work of Rosenthal and Jacobson (1968) on self-fulfilling prophecies shows that the progress of children in the early grades can be dramatically affected by a single random labeling of certain children as "intellectual bloomers." When the everyday language of Negro children is stigmatized as "not a language at all" and "not possessing the means for logical thought," the effect of such a labeling is repeated many times during each day of the school year. Every time that a child uses a form of NNE without the copula or with negative concord, he will be labeling himself for the teacher's benefit as "illogical," as a "nonconceptual thinker." Bereiter and Engelmann, Deutsch, and Jensen are giving teachers a ready-made, theoretical basis for the prejudice they already feel against the lower-class Negro child and his language (for example, see Williams, Chapter 18 in this volume). When teachers hear him say "I don't want none" or "They mine," they will be hearing through the bias provided by the verbal deprivation theory—not an English dialect different from theirs, but the "primitive mentality of the savage mind."

But what if the teacher succeeds in training the child to use the new language consistently? The verbal deprivation theory holds that this will lead to a whole chain of successes in school, and that the child will be drawn away from the vernacular culture into the middle-class world. Undoubtedly this will happen with a few isolated individuals, just as it happens for a few children in every school system today. But we are concerned not with the few but the many, and for the majority of Negro children the distance between them and the school is bound to widen under this approach.

Proponents of the deficit theory have a strange view of social organization outside of the classroom. They see the attraction of the peer group as a substitute for success and gratification normally provided by the school. For example, Whiteman and Deutsch (1968, pp. 86–87) introduce their account of the deprivation hypothesis with an eyewitness account of a child who accidentally dropped his school notebook into a puddle of water and walked away without picking it up: "A policeman who had been standing nearby walked over to the puddle and stared at the notebook with some degree of disbelief." The child's alienation from school is explained as the result of his coming to school without the "verbal, conceptual, attentional, and learning skills requisite to school success." The authors see the child as "suffering from feelings of inferiority because he is failing; he withdraws or becomes hostile, finding gratification elsewhere, such as in his peer group."

To view the peer group as a mere substitute for school shows an extraordinary lack of knowledge of adolescent culture. In our studies in south-central Harlem we have seen the reverse situation—the children who are rejected by the peer group are most likely to succeed in school. Although in middle-class suburban areas, many children do fail in school because of their personal deficiencies, in ghetto areas it is the healthy, vigorous, popular child with normal intelligence who cannot read and fails all along the line. It is not necessary to document here the influence of the peer group upon the behavior of youth in our society, but we may note that somewhere between the time that children first learn to talk and puberty, their language is restructured to fit the rules used by their peer group. From a linguistic viewpoint, the peer group is certainly a more powerful influence than the family (e.g., Gans 1962). Less directly, the pressures of peer-group activity are also felt within the school. Many children, particularly those who are not doing well in school, show a sudden sharp downward turn in the fourth and fifth grades, and children in the ghetto schools are no exception. It is at the same age, at nine or ten years old, that the influence of the vernacular peer group becomes predominant (see Wilmott 1966). Instead of dealing with isolated individuals, the school is then dealing with children who are integrated into groups of their own, with rewards and value systems which oppose those of the school. Those who know the sociolinguistic situation cannot doubt that reaction against the Bereiter-Engelmann approach in later years will be even more violent on the part of the students involved, and their rejection of the school system will be even more categorical.

The essential fallacy of the verbal deprivation theory lies in tracing the educational failure of the child to his personal deficiencies. At present, these deficiencies are said to be caused by his home environment. It is traditional to explain a child's failure in school by his inadequacy. But when failure reaches such massive proportions, it seems to us necessary to look at the social and cultural obstacles to learning, and the inability of the school to adjust to the social situation. Operation Head Start is designed to repair the child, rather than the school; to the extent that it is based upon this inverted logic, it is bound to fail.

CONSEQUENCES OF FAILURE

The second area in which the verbal deprivation theory is doing serious harm to our educational system is in the consequences of this failure, and the reaction to it. As failures are reported of Operation Head Start, the interpretations which we receive will be from the same educational psychologists who designed this program. The fault will be found not in the data, the theory, nor in the methods used, but rather in the children who have failed to respond to the opportunities offered to them. When Negro children fail to show the significant advance which the deprivation theory predicts, it will be taken as further proof of the profound gulf which separates their mental processes from those of "civilized," middle-class mankind.

A sense of the failure of Head Start is already in the air. Some prominent figures in the program are reacting to this situation by saying that intervention did not take place early enough. Caldwell (1967, p. 16) notes that:

. . . the research literature of the last decade dealing with social-class differences has made abundantly clear that all parents are not qualified to provide even the basic essentials of physical and psychological care to their children.

The deficit theory now begins to focus on the "long-standing patterns of parental deficit" which fill the literature. "There is, perhaps unfortunately," writes Caldwell (1967, p. 17), "no literacy test for motherhood." Failing such eugenic measures, she has proposed "educationally oriented day care for culturally deprived children between six months and three years of age." The children are returned home each evening to "maintain primary emotional relationships with their own families," but during the day they are removed to "hopefully prevent the deceleration in rate of development which seems to occur in many deprived children around the age of two to three years."

There are others who feel that even the best of the intervention programs, such as those of Bereiter and Engelmann, will not help the Negro child no matter when such programs are applied—that we are faced once again with the "inevitable hypothesis" of the genetic inferiority of the Negro people. Many readers of this paper are undoubtedly familiar with the paper of Arthur Jensen in the *Harvard Educational Review* (1969) which received immediate and widespread publicity. Jensen (p. 3) begins with the following quotation from the United States Commission on Civil Rights as evidence of the failure of compensatory education:

The fact remains, however, that none of the programs appear to have raised significantly the achievement of participating pupils, as a group, within the period evaluated by the Commission. (U.S. Commission on Civil Rights 1967, p. 138)

Jensen believes that the verbal-deprivation theorists with whom he had been associated—Deutsch, Whiteman, Katz, Bereiter—have been given every opportunity to prove their case, and have failed. This opinion is part of the argument which leads him to the overall conclusion (p. 82) that "the preponderance of the evidence is . . . less consistent with a strictly environmental

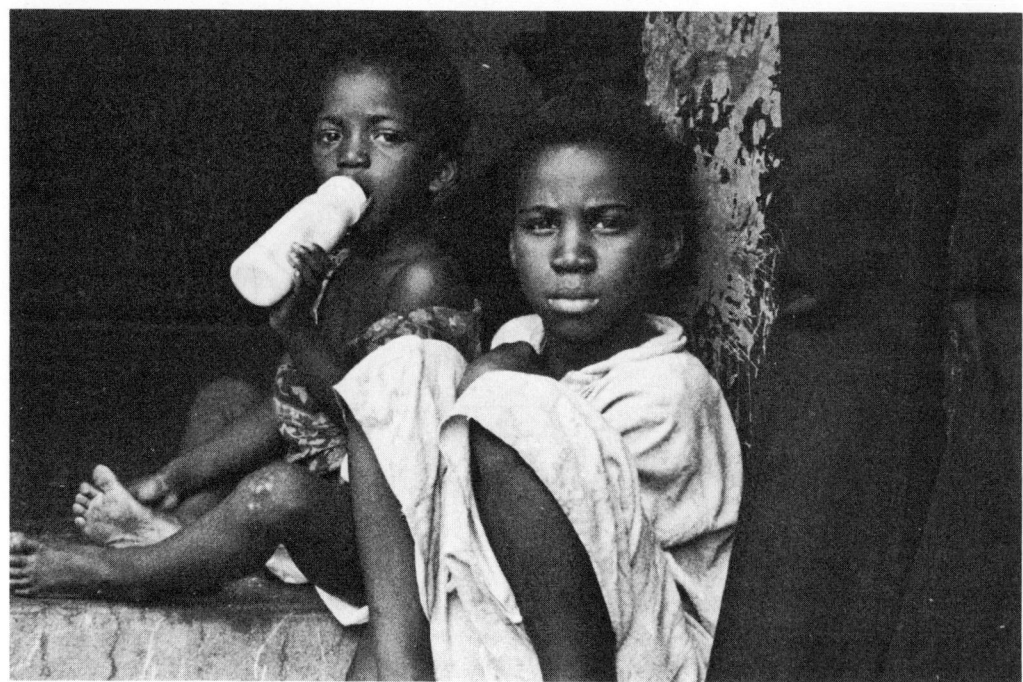

hypothesis than with the genetic hypothesis." In other words, racism—the belief in the genetic inferiority of Negroes—is the most correct view in the light of the present evidence.

Jensen argues that the middle-class white population is differentiated from the working-class white and Negro population in the ability for "cognitive or conceptual learning," which Jensen calls Level II intelligence as against mere "associative learning" or Level I intelligence:

> ... certain neural structures must also be available for Level II abilities to develop, and these are conceived of as being different from the neural structures underlying Level I. The genetic factors involved in each of these types of ability are presumed to have become differentially distributed in the population as a function of social class, since Level II has been most important for scholastic performance under the traditional methods of instruction. (Jensen 1969, p. 114)

Jensen found, for example, that one group of middle-class children were helped by their concept-forming ability to recall twenty familiar objects that could be classified into four categories: animals, furniture, clothing, or foods. Lower-class Negro children did just as well as middle-class children with a miscellaneous set, but showed no improvement with objects that could be so categorized.

The research of the educational psychologists cited here is presented by them in formal and objective style, and is widely received as impartial scientific evidence. Jensen's paper has been reported by Joseph Alsop and William F. Buckley, Jr. (*New York Post*, March 20, 1969) as "massive, apparently authoritative . . . ." It is not my intention to examine these materials in detail, but it is important to realize that we are dealing with special pleading by those who have a strong personal commitment. Jensen is concerned with class differences in cognitive style and verbal learning. His earlier papers incorporated the cultural deprivation theory which he now rejects as a basic explanation.[9] Jensen (1968 p. 167) classified the Negro children who fail in school as "slow learners" and "mentally retarded" and urged that we find out how much their retardation is due to environmental factors and how much is due to "more basic biological factors." His conviction that the problem must be located in the child leads him to accept and reprint some truly extraordinary data. To support the genetic hypothesis Jensen (1969, p. 83) cites the following percentage estimates by Heber (1968) of the racial distribution of mental retardation (based upon IQs below 75) in the general population.[10]

These estimates, that almost half of lower-class Negro children are mentally retarded, could be accepted only by someone who has no knowledge of the children or the community. If he had wished to, Jensen could easily have checked this against the records of any school in any urban ghetto area. Taking IQ tests at their face value, there is no correspondence between these figures and the communities we know. For example, among seventy-five boys we worked with in central Harlem who would fall into status categories 4 or 5 above, there were only three with IQs below 75. One spoke very little English; one could barely see; the third was emotionally disturbed. When the second was retested, he scored 91, and the third retested at 87.[11] There are of course hundreds of realistic reports available to Jensen. He simply selected one which would strengthen his case for the genetic inferiority of Negro children.

In so doing, Jensen was following a standing tradition among the psychologists who developed the deficit hypothesis. The core of Deutsch's environmental explanation of poor performance in school is the Deprivation Index, a numerical scale based on six dichotomized variables. One variable is "the educational aspirational level of the parent for the child." Most people would agree that a parent who did not care if a child finished high-school would be a disadvantageous factor in the child's educational career. In dichotomizing this vari-

[9] In Deutsch, et al. (1968), Jensen expounds the verbal deprivation theory in considerable detail, for example (p. 119): "During this 'labeling' period . . . some very important social-class differences may exert their effects on verbal learning. Lower-class parents engage in relatively little of this naming or 'labeling' play with their children . . . . That words are discrete labels for things seems to be better known by the middle-class child entering first grade than by the lower-class child. Much of this knowledge is gained in the parent-child interaction, as when the parent looks at a picture book with the child . . . ."

[10] Heber's (esp. 1968) studies of eighty-eight Negro mothers in Milwaukee are cited frequently throughout Jensen's paper. The estimates in this table are not given in relation to a particular Milwaukee sample, but for the general United States population. Heber's study was specifically designed to cover an area of Milwaukee which was known to contain a large concentration of retarded children, Negro and white, and he has stated that his findings were "grossly misinterpreted" by Jensen (*Milwaukee Sentinel*, June 11, 1969).

Socio-Economic Status	Percent of Whites	Percent of Negroes
1 (highest)	0.5	3.1
2	0.8	14.5
3	2.1	22.8
4	3.1	37.8
5 (lowest)	7.8	42.9

[11] The IQ scores given here are from group rather than individual tests and must therefore not be weighed heavily; the scores are from the Pintner-Cunningham test, usually given in the first grade in New York City schools in the 1950s.

able Deutsch was faced with the fact that the educational aspiration of Negro parents is in fact very high, higher than for the white population, as he shows in other papers.[12] In order to make the Deprivation Index work, he therefore set the cutting point for the deprived group as "college or less." (see Whiteman and Deutsch 1968, p. 100). Thus if a Negro child's father says that he wants his son to go all the way through college, the child will fall into the "deprived" class on this variable. In order to receive the two points given to the "less deprived" on the index, it would be necessary for the child's parent to insist on graduate school or medical school! This decision is not discussed by the author; it simply stands as a *fait accompli* in the tables. This is the type of data manipulation carried on by those who are strongly committed to a particular hypothesis.

No one can doubt that the reported inadequacy of Operation Head Start and of the verbal deprivation hypothesis has now become a crucial issue in our society.[13] The controversy which has arisen over Jensen's article typically assumes that programs such as Bereiter and Engelmann's have tested and measured the verbal capacity of the ghetto child. The cultural sociolinguistic obstacles to this intervention program are not considered, and the argument proceeds upon the data provided by the large, friendly interviewers whom we have seen at work in the extracts given above.

The Linguistic View

Linguists are in an excellent position to demonstrate the fallacies of the verbal deprivation theory. All linguists agree that nonstandard dialects are highly structured systems. They do not see these dialects as accumulations of errors caused by the failure of their speakers to master standard English. When linguists hear Negro children saying "He crazy" or "Her my friend," they do not hear a primitive language. Nor do they believe that the speech of working-class people is merely a form of emotional expression, incapable of expressing logical thought....

The exact nature and relative importance of the structural differences between NNE and standard English are not in question here. It is agreed that the teacher must approach the teaching of the standard through a knowledge of the child's own system. The methods used in teaching English as a foreign language are recommended, not to declare that NNE is a foreign language, but to underline the importance of studying the native dialect as a coherent system for communication. This is in fact the method that should be applied in any English class.

Linguists are also in an excellent position

---

[12]In Table 15-1 in Deutsch and associates (1967, p. 312), section C shows that some degree of college training was desired by 96, 97 and 100 percent of Negro parents in class levels I, II, and III, respectively. The corresponding figures for whites were 79, 95, and 97 percent.

[13]The negative report of the Westinghouse Learning Corporation and Ohio University on Operation Head Start was published in the *New York Times* (April 13, 1969). The evidence of the failure of the program is accepted by many, and it seems likely that the report's discouraging conclusions will be used by conservative Congressmen as a weapon against any kind of expenditure for disadvantaged children, especially Negroes. The two hypotheses mentioned to account for this failure are that the impact of Head Start is lost through poor teaching later on, and more recently, that poor children have been so badly damaged in infancy by their lower-class environment that Head Start cannot make much difference. The third "inevitable" hypothesis of Jensen is not reported here.

to assess Jensen's claim that the middle-class white population is superior to the working-class and Negro populations in the distribution of Level II, or conceptual, intelligence. The notion that large numbers of children have no capacity for conceptual thinking would inevitably mean that they speak a primitive language, for even the simplest linguistic rules we discussed above involve conceptual operations more complex than those used in the experiment Jensen cites. Let us consider what is involved in the use of the general English rule that incorporates the negative with the first indefinite. To learn and use this rule, one must first identify the class of indefinites involved—*any, one, ever*, which are formally quite diverse. How is this done? These indefinites share a number of common properties which can be expressed as the concepts "indefinite," "hypothetical," and "nonpartitive." One might argue that these indefinites are learned as a simple list, by association learning. But this is only one of the many syntactic rules involving indefinites—rules known to every speaker of English, which could not be learned except by an understanding of their common, abstract properties. For example, everyone knows, unconsciously, that *anyone* cannot be used with preterit verbs or progressives. One does not say, "Anyone went to the party" or "Anyone is going to the party." The rule which operates here is sensitive to the property [+ hypothetical] of the indefinites. Whenever the proposition is not inconsistent with this feature, *anyone* can be used. Everyone knows, therefore, that one can say "Anyone who was anyone went to the party" or "If anyone went to the party . . ." or "Before anyone went to the party . . . ." There is another property of *anyone* which is grasped unconsciously by all native speakers of English; it is [+ distributive]. Thus if we need one more man for a game of bridge or basketball, and there is a crowd outside, we ask, "Do any of you want to play?" not "Do some of you want to play?" In both cases, we are considering a plurality, but with *any*, we consider them one at a time, or distributively.

What are we then to make of Jensen's contention that Level I thinkers cannot make use of the concept *animal* to group together a miscellaneous set of toy animals? It is one thing to say that someone is not in the habit of using a certain skill. But to say that his failure to use it is genetically determined implies dramatic consequences for other forms of behavior, which are not found in experience. The knowledge of what people must do in order to learn language makes Jensen's theories seem more and more distant from the realities of human behavior. Like Bereiter and Engelmann, Jensen is handicapped by his ignorance of the most basic facts about human language and the people who speak it.

There is no reason to believe that any nonstandard vernacular is in itself an obstacle to learning. The chief problem is ignorance of language on the part of all concerned. Our job as linguists is to remedy this ignorance; but Bereiter and Engelmann want to reinforce it and justify it. Teachers are now being told to ignore the language of Negro children as unworthy of attention and useless for learning. They are being taught to hear every natural utterance of the child as evidence of his mental inferiority. As linguists we are unanimous in condemning this view as bad observation, bad theory, and bad practice.

That educational psychology should be strongly influenced by a theory so false to the facts of language is unfortunate; but that children should be the victims of this ignorance is intolerable. It may seem that the fallacies of the verbal deprivation theory are so obvious that they are hardly worth exposing. I have tried to show that such exposure is an important job for us to undertake. If linguists can contribute some of their available knowledge and energy toward this end, we will have done a great deal to justify the support that society has given to basic research in our field.

References

Alatis, J., ed. *Georgetown Monographs in Language and Linguistics, No. 22*. Washington, D.C.: Georgetown University Press, 1970.

Bereiter, C., and Engelmann, S. *Teaching Disadvantaged Children in the Preschool*. Englewood Cliffs, N.J.: Prentice-Hall, 1966.

Bereiter, C.; Engelmann, S.; Osborn, Jean; and Reidford, P. A. An academically oriented preschool for culturally deprived children. In F. Hechinger, ed., *Pre-school Education Today*. New York: Doubleday, 1966.

Bernstein, B. Elaborated and restricted codes: Their social origins and some consequences. In A. G. Smith, ed., *Communication and Culture*. New York: Holt, Rinehart & Winston, 1966.

Blum, A. The sociology of mental illness. In J. Douglas, ed., *Deviance and Respectability*. New York: Basic Books, (in press).

Caldwell, Bettye M. What is the optimal learning environment for the young child? *American J. Orthopsychiatry* 1967, 37:8–21.

Chomsky, N. *Aspects of the Theory of Syntax*. Cambridge, Mass.: M.I.T. Press, 1965.

Coleman, J. S., et al. *Equality of Educational Opportunity*. Washington, D.C.: U.S. Office of Education, 1966.

Deutsch, M., and associates. *The Disadvantaged Child*. New York: Basic Books, 1967.

Deutsch, M.; Katz, I.; and Jensen, A. R., eds., *Social Class, Race, and Psychological Development*. New York: Holt, Rinehart & Winston, 1968.

Gans, H. *The Urban Villagers*. New York: Free Press, 1962.

Heber, R. Research on education and habilitation of the mentally retarded. Paper read at Conference on Sociocultural Aspects of Mental Retardation, June 1968, Peabody College, Nashville, Tenn.

Jensen, A. R. Social class and verbal learning. In M. Deutsch, et al., eds., *Social Class, Race, and Psychological Development*. New York: Holt, Rinehart & Winston, 1968.

———. How much can we boost IQ and scholastic achievement? *Harvard Educational Review* 1969, 39:1–123.

Labov, W. On the grammaticality of everyday speech. Paper presented at the annual meeting of the Linguistic Society of America, December 1966, New York.

———. Some sources of reading problems for Negro speakers of nonstandard English. In A. Frazier, ed., *New Directions in Elementary English*. Champaign, Ill.: National Council of Teachers of English, 1967. Also reprinted in J. C. Baratz and R. W. Shuy, eds., *Teaching . Black Children to Read*. Washington, D.C.: Center for Applied Linguistics, 1969.

———. Negative attraction and negative concord in four English dialects. Paper presented at the annual meeting of the Linguistic Society of America, December 1968, New York.

———. Contraction, deletion, and inherent variability of the English copula. *Language* 1969, 45:715–62.

Labov, W.; Cohen, P.; Robins, C. A preliminary study of the structure of English used by Negro and Puerto Rican speakers in New York City. Final report, U.S. Office of Education Cooperative Research Project No. 3091, 1965.

Labov, W.; Cohen, P.; Robins, C.; and Lewis, J. A study of the nonstandard English of Negro and Puerto Rican speakers in New York City. Final report, U.S. Office of Education Cooperative Research Project No. 3288 Vols. 1, 2. Mimeographed. Columbia University, 1968.

Labov, W., and Robins, C. A note on the relation of reading failure to peer-group status in urban ghettos. *The Teachers College Record* 1969, 70:396–405.

Langer, T. S., and Michaels, S. T. *Life Stress and Mental Health.* New York: Free Press, 1963.

Rosenthal, R., and Jacobson, Lenore. Self-fulfilling prophecies in the class-room: teachers' expectations as unintended determinants of pupils' intellectual competence. In M. Deutsch, et al., eds., *Social Class, Race, and Psychological Development.* New York: Holt, Rinehart & Winston, 1968.

United States Commission of Civil Rights. *Racial Isolation in the Public Schools,* Vol. 1. Washington, D.C.: U.S. Government Printing Office, 1967.

Whiteman, M., and Deutsch, M. Social disadvantage as related to intellective and language development. In M. Deutsch, et al., eds., *Social Class, Race, and Psychological Development.* New York: Holt, Rinehart & Winston, 1968.

Wilmott, P. *Adolescent Boys of East London.* London: Routledge & Kegan Paul, 1966.

LIFE CYCLE

A Yoruba Market-Woman's Life

JANHEINZ JAHN

One topic that must be considered in the study of any society is the definition of the family unit. Does the family consist of a man and his wife and their children—sometimes called the **nuclear family**? Does the family consist of a nuclear family plus the parents of the husband or wife? In such an **extended family**, as it is called, a man might bring his bride to his home to live. This new nuclear family would then be a part of a larger family unit. Probably the most striking form of family unit to members of our culture is the polygamous family, in which one or more nuclear families are linked by one common spouse. Two varieties of polygamy are **polyandry**, where one woman is married to two or more men, and **polygyny**, where one man is married to two or more wives. Polyandry is quite rare (one example is the Toda of India), but polygyny is quite common. In fact polygyny is found all over the world. Our form of exclusively monogamous marriage is, in contrast, found in a minority of the world's cultures. (Some observers have facetiously suggested that with our divorce and remarriage procedures we in fact practice "serial" polygamy.) Not only are simultaneous plural marriages common, but the women involved are quite happy with the system. With our monogamous bias, it is difficult for us to envision a woman's content under such circumstances. For this reason, the following sketch of a Yoruba woman should prove of special interest.

One relatively new technique in gathering ethnographic data is the presentation of a life history of a particular individual in a society. Too often one reads monographs *which tell how "the Yoruba" do this or "the Ibo" do that. One can read an entire book without ever coming upon a flesh and blood individual. Life histories, to be sure, cannot be used in place of standard ethnographic techniques. Often important aspects of culture, e.g., religion, are only briefly mentioned by an informant, and thus the ethnographer's information on a certain point might be badly incomplete if he had to rely solely upon what was serendipitously collected in a life history. On the other hand, an informant in a life history may give important emotional attitudinal information about various aspects of his culture, information which the ethnographer might never have thought of eliciting or might never have obtained even if he had attempted to elicit it. The following life history is well written, and it was written by a literary man, not an anthropologist. (The author shows his amateur standing when he indicates that much of his information came from European friends rather than from the subject herself.)*

Anyone who tours West Africa with a camera will first seek out the markets in all the places he goes to: for the striking contrasts in color between all the fruits in their bright yellows and greens and reds; the shapes of the chicken-baskets, the pots, bowls and calabashes; and above all for the women in their cotton, velvet and tulle dresses, with gay and often daring patterns which emphasize the silky blackness of bare arms and shoulders; for the bold twisting of the headscarves and the immense numbers of elaborate 'hair-dos' in which the fuzzy hair is parted, tied up or plaited; for the dignified gait of the housewives as they carry home their purchases in calabashes filled to overflowing; for the lofty patience with which the market-women squat behind their wares, the tender grace and the lack of embarrassment with which they give their breasts to their babies, the flashing smile with which they coax likely customers, the beauty of the young women and the characterful faces of the old; for their quiet gestures and gliding steps, and the play of light and shade on the matte gloss of dark skin. At the markets Africa reveals itself as a continent of human beauty.

All West African markets are gay with color and vitality, but there are fine distinctions between different regions. The European manufacturers in Manchester, Birmingham, Rotterdam and Lyons, who produce the cheaper materials and print them with bright colors, cannot simply sell the same patterns and color combinations to Abidjan on the Ivory Coast and Ibadan in Nigeria. Every region has its stylistic traditions, which decide the local fashions; the manufacturer has the pattern for each market designed and tried out in the place where he hopes to sell it. Dakar is attuned to a medley of pastel shades, glittering with incrustations of polished bronze and bright silver tones. Freetown likes straight-line patterns and lines of dots in deeper colors, Abidjan goes in for harmonies of three colors with one dominant, such as green-yellow-white, white-yellow-brown, blue-black-white. Accra prefers earthy shades ranging from yellow to dark brown by way of ochre and red. In the markets of the Niger Delta, at Sapele and Warri, yellow and red check is worn, combined with violet, and with gay embroidered birds and elephants on it. Yoruba markets, on the other hand, have an overall blue appearance from the varied shades of blue in the women's dresses, combining materials of natural indigo batik with symbolical patterns or their commercial imitations.

The camera may capture the colors, the gestures, the shadows, the robes, the wares. It may carry the pictures across the oceans, turning them into exotic and erotic dreams. But for the women the markets are part of everyday life, the rhythms and conditions of which are more concealed than revealed by the whirl of surface gaiety. Consequently the life of the women receives strangely little attention in travellers' accounts. It is not easy to probe into, of course, and discloses itself to a foreigner only if he adds up his separate observations and connects them into a single whole. If he does this, a pattern emerges by which all these women live, women who cannot read or write and are therefore summarily dismissed by many European authors. Rolf Italiaander, for instance, in a book published in 1954, says they '. . . can neither read nor write, so they are not even half civilized, but are at a most primitive stage of development.'[1]

Just how 'primitive' these women are or are not, I hope to show by a particular example, a woman whom I will call Ewumi, born twenty-seven years ago in the town of Ede, which may be regarded as fairly typical of Nigeria. It is in Yoruba country, 150 miles from the coast and thus not directly exposed to the commercial influences of the ports. It is not too deep in the bush either, but on the main railway line from Lagos to Kano; and it has a good asphalt road leading to it. It is of medium size, with about 70,000 inhabitants; much of my information on Ewumi comes from European friends who live there.

Ewumi, then, was born in 1933. Her father, a respectable citizen of Ede, was like most other citizens a farmer, his land being a day's walk away from the town. He would be away from home for days, planting the yams, hoeing the round hillocks, weeding his land, tying up the beans, harvesting the maize, digging up the yams, and so on. With uncles, cousins and neighbors he marched out into the bush, where amidst much singing and also encouragement from the drummers[2] they would lend each other a hand in tilling their fields. Sometimes, but not often, baby Ewumi was there too, on the back of her mother, who might be helping to hoe, should there ever be a shortage of hands. But Ewumi's mother had her own field between her family's estates, which was usually looked after by her brothers.

In her first years Ewumi seldom saw her father, and he played no part in her life. Only the mother was ever present: Ewumi was strapped to her back, and it was from there that by degrees the girl came to take in her own little world. This included her brother, three years old, and her sister, six years older, who was already helping mother and was sometimes allowed to carry her little sister on her own back. Then there were the grandmother and aunts and their children. Ever since she could think, Ewumi's family provided a solid framework within which she could feel secure; but she was never away from her mother.

Her mother slept near Ewumi. She took Ewumi to market on her back (with the purchases stacked on her head) and to the seasonal dances of town or clan.[3] Ewumi would go to sleep there whenever she felt like it, whether her mother was going out to the fields, sitting at the market or dancing through the night at one of the religious festivals: practically before she could stand, Ewumi learnt the rhythms of the music for these. She sucked at her mother's

---

[1] Rolf Italiaander, *Wann reist du ab, weisser Mann?* (Hamburg, 1954), p. 25.

[2] Cf. Janheinz Jahn, *Muntu* (London, 1961), pp. 124ff.

[3] Cf. Ulli Beier, *A Year of Sacred Festivals in One Yoruba Town* (Lagos, 1959).

breasts whenever she wanted, she never had to cry in hunger or lie alone in the dark. 'Timetable-feeding is unheard of and self-regulation of the child is the absolute rule,' writes Beier. 'Moreover the child can get as much erotic pleasure from its mother's breast as it likes, as it will be allowed to play with the breast at any time. Weaning too is done most gently and carefully. In some cases, where a child is extremely difficult, it may even be allowed to come to its mother's breast (very occasionally) after the new child is born.'[4]

When Ewumi was three, her mother gave birth again, and this time it was a boy. By now Ewumi had grasped something of life, she was weaned and no longer so completely dependent on her mother. But so that she should not feel neglected, she was now treated by her mother with extra tenderness, a cock was sacrificed for her, and she was bathed in the same water as her baby brother to develop feelings of kinship with him. Three years later, when Ewumi was six, her mother had another baby, and now it was the three-year-old brother who was bathed with the baby.

It is no matter of chance that the mother has a child every three years, and there would be great disapproval in her family if things were any different. For as soon as a woman finds herself pregnant, she may not have any more intercourse with her husband until the child is weaned. Most mothers leave their husbands for quite a long time and return to their own mothers, so as to devote themselves wholly to the children. 'All this is only possible,' Beier remarks, 'in a society where men have many wives, because otherwise they would have to remain celibate for

---

[4] Ulli Beier, "The Position of Yoruba Women," *Présence Africaine*, I–II (1955), p 45.

stretches of nearly three years.'[5]

The three-year rhythm of births has many advantages for the child. In a European family the father may often feel the accidentally-born child as an intruder robbing him of his wife's attention, and conversely the child may feel neglected because of his father, which sometimes leads to an Oedipus complex; whereas here the father does not figure in the small child's existence at all. Moreover the baby's feeding is ensured in a country where the protective bodies contained in the mother's milk are essential defences against a whole series of dangerous diseases; cow's milk would provide no adequate substitute, even if cattle-breeding were possible in these areas infested by the tsetse fly. But there is of course no cow's milk, except for European tinned milk or milk powder, which is both far too expensive and also very hard to obtain, especially in the quantities that would be necessary if the native population were to depart from the three-year rhythm of births. Finally this also stops an elder child feeling too jealous on the birth of the next baby. It is natural for a child of less than two to feel neglected when the new baby arrives; a three-year-old is already more sensible and beginning to discover a world of his own. 'All these things may account for the balance and harmony we find in Yoruba children.'[6]

While her brother came under his father's care at seven, Ewumi, being a girl, stayed on with her mother, learning housework and having her own household duties, going to fetch water from the well in a calabash, which she had learnt to carry on her head, helping look after her small brother, now four, and minding him when her mother went to market; for her mother had grown older too and did not find it so easy now to have the four-year-old strapped to her hips, as well as the market goods on her head and the baby on her back. Yet Ewumi was by no means alone with her little brother, she was in the midst of her elder sisters and cousins, a whole troop of children going about their games and duties under the surveillance of relatives and neighbors.

She learnt to cook, and wash clothes, to grind pepper, and pound maize and dried yam slices in the mortar. On Sundays she went with her mother and sisters and brothers to the Baptist Mission church, and eagerly joined in the hymns she had learnt there. That did not stop her taking part in the town's old religious festivals,[7] especially in the four-day festival of the new yams in July in honor of the *Orishas*[8] (the gods) and the seven-day festival in honor of the god Shango at the end of the rainy season. Ewumi was an intelligent girl, and the Baptist minister thought she ought to go to the mission school; but since her parents couldn't afford to pay school fees for all the children, they decided to send only the two boys, who might thereby get an office job later on.

Ewumi grew up into a fine girl. At fifteen she was going to market on her own, her wares being matches, razor-blades and cigarettes; and this gave her a chance to talk to and flirt with young men while selling. When her mother had reached marriageable age, *her* parents had long chosen their daughter a mate, who had as little choice in the matter as the girl. Ewumi, however, could herself choose—of course within limits. She was shrewd enough to consider only the young men of whom her

---

[5] Ibid.
[6] Beier, "The Position of Yoruba Women," p. 45.
[7] Cf. Beier, *A Year of Sacred Festivals*. . . .
[8] Cf. Jahn, *Muntu*, pp. 65ff.

clan would approve; it would have been foolish for a young woman to throw away light-heartedly the support she needed from her family when married. Partly with her knowledge and partly without, contacts were made between families: a few young men were tipped off by their relatives to buy razor-blades or cigarettes from her, and between the three or four proposed candidates she could exercise a free choice.

The one she liked best was Dele from the Olabisi family, a merry fellow and a hard-working farmer, who besides the traditional crops grew cocoa on his land—the fashionable new crop from which you were supposed to get rich quick. When both were sure that their families approved the connection, Ewumi received expensive bridal gifts from her suitor, worth the equivalent of about £25. These belonged to her, they were the basic capital for her subsequent trading, and had nothing to do with the bride-price, which at Ede is fixed at £12. Dele found no difficulty in paying this price, for a marriage here is not so much a contract between two individuals as the symbol of two families being joined together. Every member of Dele's family contributed something to the sum needed, and Ewumi's father, who received the bride-price, had to distribute it among all the members of the family.[9]

So the day came when amidst the customary ceremonies and festivities she entered her husband's household. The young couple lived in an annex, a mud hut with a corrugated-iron roof and room for further expansion. At first she had much to order and arrange before she could settle down in the new clan. Being a true Yoruba woman, she could not let her husband keep her, and with the price of her bridal gifts she bought wares for sale; she set them out on a rough-hewn table outside the hut at a corner of the road, where there would be a lot of people passing. She offered sugar, tinned milk, tinned sardines, soap, matches, kerosene for lamps and refrigerators—all European articles which did not spoil.

When she became pregnant, the marriage had so far fulfilled its purpose, for marriage is not consummated by two people living together but by the begetting of children. Ewumi was proud of her fertility, and as she loved her husband, she brought him her friend Toro, who with Ewumi had for years excelled in the Baptist Church choir, as second wife—after thorough consultation with all the families concerned. Dele's hut got an extension, and Ewumi carried out her duties at the wedding of Dele and Toro, thereby showing herself a true *'iyali'*—mother of the house—as she could now call herself. Having welcomed her husband's guests in the prescribed way, and initiated Toro into her duties, she now returned with all her belongings into her parents' family.

She was now free to concentrate on her business. She got rid of the European wares, which were likely to bring only a small profit, and transferred her activity to the market. She was very good at making *ogi*, a maizemeal dish. Since both her own family and her husband's grew maize, she bought the raw material cheap direct from the producer. She had only to take the maize to the miller to be ground into meal, and then make *ogi* with it. So her profit came from the difference between the retail and wholesale price as well as from the work she put in. These profits were 'ploughed back' into wares that would not spoil.

Her confinement was properly cele-

---

[9] Cf. Beier, "The Position of Yoruba Women," p. 40.

brated: Dele was proud of Ewumi and buried the after-birth, the ceremony required to make him the legal father, the 'owner' of the child. It was a girl, and was given the name of Gbemi after a dead great-grandmother. Ewumi carried her baby daughter on her back, went to the market every day with fresh *ogi*, and increased her prosperity. The only snag was the miller's price for grinding, which was gradually going up.

Communication with her husband and Toro was confined to periodical friendly visits, going to church with them on Sundays, and taking part in the festivals of town and clan. Little Gbemi on her back grew bigger, and when she was beginning to wean her daughter, many a man at the market made her friendly offers—for she was beautiful, had shown she could bear healthy children and had enough milk for them. She was now nineteen.

But she only laughed at her suitors' advances; as soon as Gbemi was weaned, she returned to her husband's house. Toro had still not become pregnant, and Ewumi told her of all sorts of effective 'medicines' (charms), recommended prayers and sacrifices to Shango, the *Orisha* embodying reproduction powers, and to *Egungun* (the ancestors). As 'mother of the house' she organized communal living according to the prevailing custom: for five days she cooked the food for her husband and slept with him; then Toro cooked for him and slept with him for the next five days. Ewumi as *'iyale'* had to welcome guests when they came, but this is the only privilege she had. For a few months the two wives looked after their husband in turn, till Ewumi was sure she was pregnant again and returned once more to her family's farm.

At the market she had long had her fixed place among other women who also sold *ogi*; her two neighbors were old, and their *ogi* was not so good, but their clans saw to it that they also had their turnover. Their children were already grown up, so they no longer needed to earn such large amounts.

When Ewumi was delivered again, it was a boy, and they called him Adebayo. But great as was their joy, it was mixed with anxiety, for Adebayo was rather delicate, and also prone to fits. And when the worried parents brought him to the *Ifa* oracle,[10] it transpired that he was an *abiku*, a spirit-child, who only comes on earth to leave it again soon. Ewumi would have to make all possible efforts to see the child stayed on the earth and did not go back again to his spirit companions. An *abiku* has wonderful dreams, he has visions of his spirit companions and plays wonderful imaginary games with them.[11] And when his time comes, some time between the ages of four and ten, the spirits demand that the child returns to them. However attached he may be to his mother, if he is not strong enough, he must obey them. The mother will then pray that the child be restored to her, and there are women who maintain that they have given birth to the same child seven times. If the child is reborn, it can easily be recognized by a small mark which is scratched on a dead child's face or body; the scar will then appear on the new-born baby in the same place. Many grown-ups show such 'identification marks'; in one confirmed case, Beier notes, 'the parents expected a certain mark to appear, and described it before the baby

---

[10] Cf. Ulli Beier, *Sacred Wood Carvings from One Small Yoruba Town* (Lagos, 1957), p. 9. [For further discussion of the Ifa oracle, see William Bascom, "The Sanctions of Ifa Divination," *Journal of the Royal Anthropological Institute* 71 (1941), 43–54.—Ed. Note.]

[11] Cf. Beier, *A Year of Sacred Festivals* . . . , p. 26.

was born. The mark appeared as expected, and I saw it myself.'[12]

Ewumi would treat Adebayo with the greatest care, would never let him out of her sight, would satisfy his every want, put up with all his moods. If he was called away even so, she could be sure he would be born to her again and again, until one day he would stay alive and with her. But if her care for him never let up for a moment, the *abiku* might even stay with her the first time, and she would be able to have more children than if she had to give birth to the same one several times.

'The *abiku* is often a problem child,' says Beier. 'Many of those I have known are very temperamental and make great demands on their parents. If a wish is not fulfilled at once, they will threaten to die. The terrified parents will then all too often put up no resistance to the child and suffer its tyranny in the hope that it may be persuaded to live. The *abiku* is nearly always the unusual one, the out-of-the-ordinary child, in many cases it is the exceptionally brilliant child. Therefore the *abiku* is given exceptional treatment. But this does not offend the other children, who are treated much more sternly. Because after all, they know that these are not ordinary children like themselves. Thus Yoruba society has solved the educational problem of how to give the exceptional child the freedom it requires to develop its **personality**, while at the same time supplying the more rigid discipline which the average child must have to feel secure.'[13]

So Ewumi had given birth to a spirit-child, a problem child; but soon other worries were added. The price the miller demanded for grinding the maize had gone up so much that the women who sold ogi found their earnings seriously reduced. Ewumi discussed the matter with the other women at the main market, and they all agreed not to accept the price any longer; so Ewumi appealed to the *iyalode*, the woman chief of the town, who looked after the women's interests in their dealings with the men and the king: every town in Yoruba country has such a woman chief.

Ewumi was one of the delegation which conducted negotiations with the millers for the *iyalode*. But millers are men: they were adamant and refused to lower the grinding price. The *iyalode* began to threaten, and after a few days the millers said they were ready to come to terms; yet the negotiations trailed on, and the *iyalode* had the impression that the millers were dragging them out till the *ogi*-sellers' stores were used up and one or other of them would be forced to have more maize ground and pay the price demanded. Then the *iyalode* called all the *ogi*-sellers out on strike. She sent her messengers—and on the same day all the *ogi*-sellers began to grind their maize by hand. After a week the millers yielded and accepted unconditionally the price fixed by the *iyalode* according to the women's wishes.[14]

The *iyalode* and the *ogi*-sellers would scarcely have heard of such a thing as a trade union. Their strike was no imitation of European methods, no transference of modern European processes into Yoruba life; it was simply the way such conflicts were traditionally settled. As every clan has its chief and every professional group its spokesman, so the women too have their independence and their own organizations, which owe their impact above all to the traditional religious cults. In the Shango cult, which is the most important one at Ede, the high priest

---

[12]Beier, *A Year of Sacred Festivals* . . . , p. 92.

[13]Beier, *A Year of Sacred Festivals* . . . , p. 64.

[14]Cf. Beier, "The Position of Yoruba Women," p. 40.

A Yoruba Market-Woman's Life

is a woman, the *Iya Shango* (Mother of Shango), and it gives her tremendous influence. There are two male secret societies, the *egungun* (ancestors) society, which makes the bond between the living and the dead,[15] and the *oro* society, which has a secret executive power.[16] But the *ogboni* society, which controls both these and is a check on the king's power—it consists of all important tribal chiefs and priests—contains women members as well as men. Unlike Christian social life, that of the Yorubas has never been patriarchal; so the women have long been able to secure special economic monopolies for themselves. Pottery, dyeing, spinning and the batik process are exclusively women's business; no man may practice these trades. At the market women have a monopoly in most of the goods for sale. Men may sell meat and leather goods there, but almost everything else is in the hands of the women: yams and cassava, tomatoes and other vegetables, cola nuts, palm oil, cooked dishes, mats, baskets, skins, necklaces, jewelery, native 'medicines,'[17] and materials.

Ewumi was now earning well again at the market. Her attention to customers was often distracted, of course, by Adebayo, her spirit-child, but the customers were patient and understanding, for they knew the duties of a mother to an *abiku*. Dele often came to visit her either in the market or in her house, not only to see how Adebayo was going on. He was worried about

---

[15]Cf. Beier, *A Year of Sacred Festivals* . . . , p. 26.
[16]Cf. Geoffrey Parrinder, *West African Religion* (London, 1949), pp. 141ff., and Olumide Lucas, *The Religion of the Yoruba* (Lagos, 1948), pp. 120ff.

[17]Cf. Beier, "The Position of Yoruba Women," p. 41.

Toro, who had still not conceived, was unhappy over it and moody, now imploring Ewumi and Dele for new counsels and 'medicines', now accusing people of making her barren by witchcraft. Ewumi advised Dele to take a third wife, particularly as she herself had given birth to an *abiku*, did not know if he would stay in this world and how often she might have to bring him into it again. Dele had for some time been toying with the idea, and had already picked out a woman called Efuneye, a blacksmith's second wife, who had already borne her husband two healthy children and who sold cola nuts a few market alleys away. Dele had now and then bought cola nuts from her for years, but in the last weeks his need for them seemed to have increased enormously, and Efuneye had shown that she did not object to his wooing—Dele being ten years younger than her husband. So a meeting was arranged between Efuneye and Ewumi, the two women liked each other, and the rest was only a financial matter.

Since Efuneye had lived with her husband for over five years, she had to return only half the bride-price on divorce, and could keep the bridal gifts. Dele readily gave her further bridal gifts, and his family readily found the bride-price. The blacksmith was not exactly pleased, but had to admit that he sometimes beat Efuneye, so that grounds had been given for the divorce. After the usual formalities Efuneye entered Dele's household with her two children, a six-year-old boy and a three-year-old girl.

The coming of a new wife already blessed with children made Toro even more painfully aware of her failure. Her depressions alternated with fits of temper, and Dele's aunts and grandmother had to intervene to see that order was kept in his house. Efuneye, however, was very popular with all, which incensed Toro all the more. Ewumi watched the situation with distress; Efuneye often came and asked her to come home soon, as with two of them there Toro's tempers would be more easily controlled. Dele would have been glad to get rid of Toro, he beat her to give her grounds for divorce, dropped hints to friends about her beauty—she was certainly the most beautiful and also the youngest of his wives—yet no suitor would turn up. Dele had even got his family's permission to do without the return of the bride-price if need be, but Toro wanted to stay, so he just had to put up with her.

The nearer the time came when Ewumi had to wean her problem child, the more worried she became. She went on feeding him longer than usual, which in itself was good for an *abiku*, but because of this child she was afraid of going back into her husband's house. With a directness that was almost unseemly she pointed out to the men who flirted with her at the market that there was a fine shapely girl to be had in Dele's house; but they only laughed, they knew the situation and paid all the more compliments to Ewumi herself. She entreated Dele either to bring Toro somehow to her senses or else get rid of her. But neither the sacrifices to Shango and other *Orishas* nor prayers in the churches seemed to help. Even Toro's mother couldn't cope with her.

Ewumi began to listen more attentively to the friendly things said to her, and in particular she could not help thinking about the advances of a rich elderly merchant. He already had eight wives and a lot of children, all of whom lived together in harmony and comfort; and he offered most attractive bridal gifts.

When Dele learnt that the merchant's hopes were well founded, Ewumi and he had a long discussion. Dele would like to have kept her, but for the sake of her little *abiku* she refused to return into a house of strife. The air the child breathed there was poison, she said: a spirit-child had to have happiness round him and peace; if he saw Toro in one of her rages, he would die. Dele admitted she was right. He loved Ewumi, and she loved him, yet the child's welfare was decisive as ever. 'The child is the cornerstone of African society.'[18]

She gave him and his family half the bride-money back, neglect on the part of the husband was given as grounds for the divorce, and both wept on parting. The merchant was received formally but very politely by Ewumi's family; his gifts to the bride were in keeping with his wealth, but Ewumi did not seem particularly impressed and kept them with her own savings.

The *iyale* of her new home was an elderly, wise and kindly woman, who took great care over household arrangements and saw to it that the rota of wifely duties did not get out of hand. Some of the wives were already quite old, and only two were suckling children. Ewumi had to prepare her husband's food only five days every month. In such a well-off household there was no lack of assistance or space; she found the peace she had longed for in order to devote herself entirely to her little *abiku*. After she had carried out her wifely duties three times—she had to be passed over at her first turn because of menstruation—it transpired that she was again pregnant. But as she had learnt to appreciate the household's cheerful and harmonious atmosphere, she did not go back to her own family. Adebayo was thriving, and it really seemed as if he meant to stay with her; while Gbemi, now five, romped about with the other children as if they were her brothers and sisters.

With Dele, meanwhile, things were much less peaceful. When Efuneye became pregnant, Toro almost went out of her mind, and the two women came to blows. The relatives had to intervene, and Toro was sternly rebuked, but she only worked everybody up the more with her poisonous talk; and when Dele came home from his fields two days later, he beat her harder than ever. She cried the whole night, but next morning immediately started a new row. Dele's clan conferred, after which a delegation was sent off to Toro's clan, earnestly requesting them to take the misguided creature back. But she would not even listen to the remonstrances of her own relatives, and abused the clan elder so violently that they formally renounced her: the elder said that never in human memory had such a thing occurred in his clan. So Dele had to take her back home again. Divorce is easy for a woman, almost impossible for a man. For morals in Yoruba society, and the rules derived therefrom, are based on a simple but good principle: any arrangement which tends to ensure the production of many children and which guarantees that no women will be left to die as spinsters, is moral in this society.[19] Since nobody now wanted to have Toro, Dele was obliged to go to the last resort.

Having donned his ceremonial robes and taken some money, he seized Toro's hand, pulled her crying out of the house, and went with her into the palace of the king, the *Timi* of Ede. There he threw himself down before the king, gave him the money, and pointing to Toro said: 'Timi, I present her to you.' Then he told the king how things had come to this pass. The king could not

---

[18] Georges Balandier, *Zwielichtiges Afrika* (Stuttgart, 1959), p. 38.

[19] Cf. Beier, "The Position of Yoruba Women," p. 44.

refuse the present, but had to take her.

A 'town king' among the Yorubas has some privileges, of course, in the choice of wives: for instance, if a woman kneels on his carpet by mistake, he may claim her as his wife. But he has more duties than rights, he must marry the crippled and sick girls, all those who normally would have no chance of finding a husband, and must take the women nobody wants.[20]

When she heard what Dele had done, Ewumi did not stay much longer in the merchant's house. She discussed things with Dele and her family, gave the merchant the full bride-money back and all the rich personal gifts, for she had been with him less than a year. In order to marry her again, Dele had to make good half the bride-money which she returned. It was his right to hold it back three months, to make sure of her faithfulness and constancy; but he paid it at once, being sure of his Ewumi.

The celebrations for her re-entry into his house coincided with a farewell party; for Efuneye's eldest son was now seven and returned to his real father, the blacksmith, according to custom. Since both wives, Ewumi and Efuneye, were now pregnant again, they together looked for a third wife for Dele; their choice fell on Ewumi's youngest sister, with whom Ewumi had always got on extremely well.

Since then another three years have passed, Ewumi and Efuneye have had their babies, and their entire offspring, including the "problem child', Adebayo, have stayed alive. Ewumi's sister has also had a baby, but it died soon after it was born—infant mortality is still high. Ewumi and Efuneye have remained close friends, they mind the children alternately and also swap stalls at the market. Efuneye too now sells *ogi*, but Ewumi has spent her savings on hardware: lamps, bicycle-chains, clothes-hangers, alarm-clocks, aluminium pots and buckets. Her youngest brother, a lanky lad of seventeen, still single, who lives with a great-uncle, looks after her stall in the covered market at Onitsha. He is a reliable boy and hands over his profits every month, which she puts back into goods. If her businesses go on flourishing like this, she will soon have her own lorry (as her aunt has), will engage a good driver, and earn still more with haulage deals, which bring in good money. Adebayo will then one day be able to study in Europe.

---

[20]Cf. *Ibid.*, p. 43.

SOCIALIZATION

Maternal Care and Infant Behavior in Japan and America

WILLIAM CAUDILL
AND HELEN WEINSTEIN

Human behavior can be distinguished, in one sense, from that of other animals in the degree to which it is influenced by culture—that is, influenced by shared patterns of action, belief, feeling, and thinking that are transmitted knowingly and unknowingly from one generation to the next through learning. The influence of culture is universal in that in some respects a man learns to become like all men; and it is particular in that a man who is reared in one society learns to become in some respects like all men of his society and not like those of others. A general question underlying the investigation reported here concerns the degree of importance of particular cultural differences, as a variable in the understanding of human behavior.

We began the present longitudinal study of children over the first six years of life in Japan and America because we wished to explore how early in the lives of infants, and in what ways, cultural differences become manifest in behavior. Our focus on culture as a variable is in no way meant to deny the great, and interrelated, importance of other major sources of variation, such as genetic endowment and physiological functioning of the infant, psychological characteristics of the parents, and position of the family in the social structure. Rather, by either controlling for or randomizing the effect of these other sources of variation, we wished to estimate more clearly the amount of the total variance in our sample of human behavior which may be attributed to cultural differences.

In the present study, we selected a matched sample of 30 Japanese and 30

TABLE 1

	Distribution of Cases in Terms of Independent Variables			
	Japanese (30 cases) Father's Occupation		American (30 cases) Father's Occupation	
Sex of Infant	Salaried	Independent	Salaried	Independent
Male	9	9	10	5
Female	6	6	10	5

American three-to-four-month-old infants—equally divided by sex, all firstborn, and all from intact middle-class families living in urban settings—and carried out an observational study in the homes of these infants during 1961–64. This article gives the results of that study. Subsequently, we made observations in the homes of the first 20 of these same children in each culture at the time they became two-and-a-half years of age, and again when they became six years of age, but these data have not as yet been analyzed. . . .

On the basis of our previous work in Japan over the past fourteen years, coupled with a study of the literature, we have come to feel that the following differing emphases on what is valued in behavior are important when life in Japan is compared with life in America. These differing emphases seem to be particularly sharp in the areas of family life and general interpersonal relations with which we are most directly concerned here, and perhaps to be somewhat less evident in other areas of life such as business, the professions, or politics.[1] Japanese are more "group" oriented and interdependent in their relations with others, while Americans are more "individual" oriented and independent.[2] Going along with this, Japanese are more self-effacing and passive in contrast to Americans, who appear more self-assertive and aggressive. In matters requiring a decision, Japanese are more likely to rely on emotional feeling and intuition, whereas Americans will go to some pains to emphasize what they believe are the rational reasons for their action. And finally, Japanese are more sensitive to, and make conscious use of, many forms of nonverbal communication in human relations through the medium of gestures and physical proximity in comparison with Americans, who predominantly use verbal communication within a context of physical separateness.

---

[1] Even in the latter areas, however, the differences in emphasis are still evident. . . .

[2] These patterns of sleeping are not a function of "overcrowding" in the Japanese home, but rather are a matter of choice, as is shown in Caudill and Plath. Much the same point can be made concerning bathing. Starting at approximately the beginning of the second month of life, the Japanese infant is held in the arms of the mother or another adult while they bathe together in the deep bathtub (furo) at home or at the neighborhood public bath (sentó), and this pattern of shared bathing will continue for a Japanese child until he is about ten years of age, and often much longer . . . . In contrast, the American mother seldom bathes with an infant; rather, she gives him a bath from outside of the tub, and she communicates with him verbally and by positioning his body.

One particularly pertinent example of the latter point is that a Japanese child can expect to co-sleep with his parents until he is ten years of age, and that in general a person in Japan can expect to co-sleep in a two-generation group, first as a child and later as a parent and grandparent, over half of his life span; to sleep alone is considered somewhat pitiful because a person would, therefore, be lonely. In this regard, things are quite different in America, and the generations are usually separated in sleeping arrangements shortly after birth and remain so throughout the life cycle of the individual.[3]

---

[3]Although Japan is at one extreme in the length of time spent co-sleeping in a two-generation group, America is probably at the other extreme in this, and in many matters concerned with child rearing. Indeed, compared with the rest of the world, family life in the United States is in many ways rather peculiar. . . .

In summary, in normal family life in Japan there is an emphasis on interdependence and reliance on others, while in America the emphasis is on independence and self-assertion. The conception of the infant would seem to be somewhat different in the two cultures. In Japan, the infant is seen more as a separate biological organism who from the beginning, in order to develop, needs to be drawn into increasingly interdependent relations with others. In America, the infant is seen more as a dependent biological organism who, in order to develop, needs to be made increasingly independent of others. Our more specific hypotheses in this study came from this general background of family life and interpersonal relations in the two cultures.

As indicated earlier, we expected that our Japanese mothers would spend more time with their infants, would emphasize physical contact over verbal interaction, and would treat them as objects to be acted upon rather than as objects to be interacted with. But, more than this, we expected the quality of the interaction to be differently patterned in the two cultures, and in Japan for it to be a mutually dependent, even **symbiotic**, relation in which there was a blurring of the boundaries between mother and child.[4] In contrast, we expected that our American mothers would spend less time with their infants, would encourage their physical activity and chat with them more, and would treat them more as separate objects to be interacted with. And we expected the interaction in America to give evidence of the self-assertion of the child and his budding awareness of separateness from his mother. . . .

Design and Method

The design of our study called for 30 Japanese and 30 American normal infants, who at the time of observation would be between three and four months of age and would be matched as previously described. . . .

The Japanese families are of solely Japanese ancestry, and the American families are white and at least second-generation families of European ancestry. All of the Japanese families are nominally Buddhist, and the American families are divided among Protestant (18 cases), Catholic (9 cases), and Jewish (3 cases) affiliation. . . .

All of the families are residents of large cities. In the Japanese sample, we selected 20 cases from Tokyo and 10 from Kyoto because we wished also to take a look at the differences, if any, in child rearing in the two cities. The general way of life in Tokyo is thought of as more modern, and in Kyoto as more traditional. We did not find any significant differences between the two cities as measured by the dependent variables for infant and caretaker behavior, and have combined the cases from the

---

[4]This hypothesis concerning the greater mutual dependency of mother and child in Japan will become more pertinent as we analyze in the future our great wealth of data on children in the two countries at 2½ and 6 years of age. But it is symbolized at birth by the widespread custom in Japan for the hospital to present the infant's navel cord (*heso no o*) to the mother upon discharge. The cord is sprinkled with preservative powder, and placed in a neat wooden box which is tied with ribbon. This is, of course, not too different from the custom of some American parents of saving locks of hair, baby shoes, and other objects as mementos of their child's infancy. The difference lies in the "directness" of the relation of the symbol to its meaning in Japan, and to the history of the symbolic object thereafter. In Japan the cord of the new infant is only one of many such cords of other family members that may be kept in the home, either in the household Buddhist altar or in a safe place in a bureau drawer. Custom varies from region to region, and household to household, as to the subsequent disposition of the cord. If the infant is a girl, she may be given the cord to take with her to her husband's household upon marriage; or the mother may retain the cords of all of her children, and these may be placed with her body in the coffin upon her death. In our interviews with the 20 Japanese mothers whose children we followed up at 2½ years of age, we inquired about whether they had received their first child's navel cord and what meaning this had for them. We did not ask similar questions of our American mothers as it seemed inappropriate to do so. Of the 19 Japanese mothers from whom we have relevant information, 17 had received their cords from the hospital. Of the two mothers who had not, one was sad about this as she was keeping her own cord with that of her second child, which she had received since the second child was born in a different hospital. All of the 17 mothers who had received the cords kept them safely, and 8 mothers said the cord had real meaning for them; the other 9 mothers said that the cord only represented an old custom, but they usually added, ". . . but you can't just throw it away."

two cities. In the American sample, all cases were selected from the metropolitan area of Washington, D.C.

All of the families are middle class as measured by the occupation and education of the father and the education of the mother.[5] Although the Japanese sample is equally divided into 15 salaried and 15 independent business families, the American sample contains 20 salaried families and 10 independent business families because we had trouble in locating American cases in which the father was engaged in a small independent business. . . .

At the time of the initial contact with a mother we further explained our study, and told her that we wished to observe the ordinary daily life of her baby. We requested that during our observations she go about her normal routine in the home, including leaving the house if this was her usual activity. We received excellent cooperation from the mothers in both cultures, and in this regard it is important to note that we stressed that our focus was on the life of the baby, and not directly on the behavior of the mother. As explained to the mothers, our method of observation calls for the observer to be near the infant at all times, and if a mother (or other caretaker) leaves the room, the observer stays with the infant. . . .

We worked with each family for two days; usually these were consecutive days, and they were never separated by more than a few days. In general we spent about four hours on each day with a family, starting at nine in the morning on the first day, and at one in the afternoon on the second day. In planning our visits, we avoided days on which the mother or baby was ill, and in both cultures we spaced our work throughout all seasons of the year.

In making the observations we used a time-sampling procedure adapted from that originally developed by Rheingold. In this method, one observation of approximately one second in duration is made every fifteenth second in terms of a set of predetermined variables concerning the behavior of the infant and the caretaker. We designed an observation sheet that listed the variables down the side of the page, and provided columns for 40 observations across the page.[6] For each observation, a decision was made for all variables as to their occurrence or nonoccurrence, although only occurrences received a check mark on the observation sheet. Four observations were made each minute, and thus a single observation sheet covered a period of ten minutes, or 40 observations. Upon completion of an observation sheet, the observer took a five-minute break during which she clarified, if necessary, the data recorded on the completed sheet,

---

[5]In the Japanese sample, 12 of the fathers are college graduates in professional or managerial positions (8 are salaried, and 4 are independent), and 18 of the fathers are college or high school graduates in white-collar or highly skilled trade jobs (7 are salaried and 11 are independent). In the American sample, 14 of the fathers are college graduates in professional or managerial positions (10 are salaried, and 4 are independent), and 16 of the fathers are college or high school graduates in white-collar or highly skilled trade jobs (10 are salaried and 6 are independent). Of the Japanese mothers, 7 are college graduates, 19 are high school or technical school graduates, and 4 have less than a high school education. Of the American mothers, 9 are college graduates, 20 are high school or technical school graduates, and 1 has less than a high school education. . . .

[6]An illustration of the original observation sheet may be found in a preliminary report of this research, given at the Ninth International Seminar on Family Research in Tokyo in 1965. . . .

TABLE 2

Adjusted Mean Frequencies, in Total Observations, of Infant Behavior: by Culture, Father's Occupation, and Sex of Infant

Categories of Infant Behavior	Adjusted Mean Frequencies								
	Culture			Father's Occupation			Sex of Infant		
	Japanese	American	Correlation†	Salaried	Independent	Correlation†	Male	Female	Correlation†
Infant Awake	494	493	.01	474	521	.20	498	488	.04
Breast or Bottle	66	55	.11	59	62	.03	63	57	.06
All Food	68	74	.06	71	71	.00	74	68	.06
Finger or Pacifier	**69**	**172**	**.44****	116	127	.06	124	116	.04
Total Vocal	94	116	.25	100	112	.13	108	102	.07
Unhappy	**66**	**45**	**.33**	50	64	.21	55	57	.03
Happy	**30**	**59**	**.51***	45	44	.02	48	41	.14
Active	**51**	**95**	**.45***	73	74	.02	73	73	.00
Baby Plays	**83**	**170**	**.50***	129	124	.03	133	119	.09
Toy	48	82	.28	66	64	.01	76	52	.21
Hand	**14**	**27**	**.33**	21	20	.01	21	20	.01
Other Object	**22**	**57**	**.47***	41	38	.04	34	46	.18
Canonical Correlation‡			**.80***			.24			.38
Total Cases	30	30		35	25		33	27	

†This partial correlation is the square root of the ratio of (a) the sum of the squared deviations from the mean attributable to the independent variable in question, to (b) the total sum of the squared deviations minus the sum of the squared deviations attributable to the control variables and their interactions. When this partial correlation is squared, the result is a measure of the proportion of variance attributable to the independent variable in question. The means and partial correlations for all findings significant at $p < 0.05$ are printed in boldface. One asterisk (*) indicates $p < 0.01$, two asterisks (**) indicate $p < 0.001$.

‡The variables of "Total Vocal" and "Baby Plays" are not included in the canonical correlations because of linear dependency with their constituent variables "Unhappy" and "Happy," and "Toy," "Hand," and "Other Object." The means for the constituent variables do not, however, add exactly to the mean for the corresponding total variable because of rounding and the weights used to standardize frequencies of observations across cultures . . . The variable of "Infant Awake" is also omitted from the canonical correlations in this table to make them comparable with the canonical correlations in Tables 6, 8, and 9.

and also wrote descriptive notes concerning the context of the behavior that had just occurred. At the end of this five-minute break, another sheet of 40 observations was begun. . . .

As can be seen in Table 2, the types of infant behavior in which there are no differences between the two cultures are those clearly concerned with biological needs. Thus, there are no significant differences in the amount of time awake, sucking on breast or bottle, or intake of all food.[7] Technically, there also is no difference in the amount of total vocalization, but the correlation is .25, which is just short of being significant ($F = 3.7$, $df = 1/52$, $p < 0.058$). . . .

To generalize, the areas of similarity in both cultures point to the expression of biological needs by all of the infants, and the necessity for all of the mothers to care for these needs. Beyond this, however, the differences lie in the styles in which infants and mothers behave in the two cultures.

The American baby appears to be more physically active and happily vocal, and more involved in the exploration of his body and his environment than is the Japanese baby, who, in contrast, seems more subdued in all these respects. These differences can be seen in Table 2, which shows the American infant as more active,[8] more happily vocal (and quite possibly more totally vocal, as indicated earlier), more exploring of his body by greater sucking on his fingers (or by putting other parts of his body and objects into his

---

[7]As indicated earlier, there was very little breast feeding among the American mothers, and, hence, "breast" and "bottle" were combined. As is to be expected, the finding on the variable of "breast" considered separately shows the Japanese infant to be greater, with a mean of 30, compared to the American infant with a mean of 3 ($F = 10.1$, $df = 1/52$, $p < 0.01$). On the other hand, "bottle" considered separately is not significantly different, although the Japanese mean of 37 is lower than the American mean of 51 ($F = 1.0$, $df = 1/52$, $p < 0.32$). When semi-solid food is considered as a separate variable, the American infant is greater, with a mean of 19 compared to a Japanese mean of 2 ($F = 16.2$, $df = 1/52$, $p < 0.001$).

[8]We are particularly interested in the category of "active," and we thought that the greater occurrence of gross bodily movements among the American infants might be related to the difference in temperature in the homes, especially in the winter, in the two cultures. In general, we avoided doing observations during particularly hot or cold days—when the outside temperature was above 85 or below 45 degrees Fahrenheit. The temperature inside of the homes in Tokyo, Kyoto, and Washington, D.C., is about the same during the warmer months of May-October, but during the cooler months of November-April the temperature in the Japanese homes probably averages about five to ten degrees less than that maintained in the American homes. During the cooler months, Japanese infants wear more clothing and are under more covers than American infants. Fortunately, roughly half of the cases in each culture were observed during the warmer months. For the American infants, there is no difference between the active behavior of the cases observed during the cooler (a mean of 125 observations) and warmer (a mean of 128 observations) months (using a Mann-Whitney U test of the rank-order of the frequencies, $z = 0.18$, n.s.). For the Japanese infants, however, the cases observed during the warmer months (a mean of 65) are more active than those in the cooler months (a mean of 34) ($z = 2.1$, $p < 0.05$). Nevertheless, in the cross-cultural comparison of the infants observed only during the warmer months the American babies are still the more active ($z = 3.0$, $p < 0.01$). Naturally, then, the American infants are also the more active ($z = 3.8$, $p < 0.001$) in the comparison of cases observed during the cooler months. It appears, therefore, that temperature of the home and heavier clothing make some difference, but not enough to account for the greater activity of the American infant.

mouth),[9] and more exploring of his environment in playing with toys, hands, and other objects. The Japanese infant, on the other hand, is only greater in unhappy vocalization. . . .

The differences in styles of caretaking in the two cultures appear to be equally pronounced. The American mother seems to have a more lively and stimulating approach to her baby, as indicated in Table 3, which shows the American caretaker as positioning the infant's body more, and looking at and chatting to the infant more. The Japanese mother, in contrast, is present more with the baby, in general, and seems to have a more soothing and quieting approach, as indicated by greater lulling, and by more carrying in arms, and rocking. . . .

In summary, then, of the analyses by culture of the total observations, the expression of the infant's biological needs, and the mother's basic caretaking of these needs, are the same in both cultures; but beyond this, the styles of the infant's behavior and the mother's care are different. The Japanese baby seems passive, and he lies quietly with occasional unhappy vocalizations, while his mother, in her care, does more lulling, carrying, and rocking of her baby. She seems to try to soothe and quiet the child, and to communicate with him physically rather than verbally. On the other hand, the American infant is more active, happily vocal, and exploring of his environment, and his mother in her care does more looking at and chatting to her baby. She seems to stimulate the baby to activity and to vocal response. It is as if the American mother wanted to have a vocal, active baby, and the Japanese mother wanted to have a quiet, contented baby. In terms of the styles of caretaking of the mothers in the two cultures, they seem to get what they apparently want. That these two patterns do, indeed, discriminate between the cultures is indicated by the significant canonical correlations for infant behavior (.80) and for caretaker behavior (.79). . . .

Conclusion

In this report of work with Japanese and American middle-class mothers and their firstborn, three-to-four-month-old infants, our analysis quickly revealed that of the three independent variables considered, culture is by far the most important source

---

[9] The occurrence of behavior in the category of "finger or pacifier" appears to be related to breast versus bottle feeding in both cultures, although the Japanese infants are in general much lower in any sort of comparison. The clearest data on this question come from the comparison of those mothers who never breast fed versus those mothers who were feeding entirely by breast (no use of the bottle at all) at the time of observation. The 9 American infants who were never breast fed have an average of 196 observations in the category of "finger or pacifier," while the 4 American infants being fed entirely by breast have an average of 97 observations in this category. Among the Japanese cases, the 4 infants who were never breast fed have an average of 88 observations in the category of "finger or pacifier," while the 6 infants being entirely breast fed have an average of 42 observations in this category. Thus, there is roughly twice as much finger sucking by babies who have never been breast fed in both cultures, but the average for the Japanese babies fed entirely by bottle is lower than the average for the American babies fed entirely by breast. It seems unlikely, therefore, that the greater average number of observations for the American infant in the variable of "finger or pacifier" is due to differences in methods of feeding. It may be due, however, to the greater use of a pacifier by the American mother, who often puts this device into her child's mouth as she leaves the room. The Japanese mother, in contrast, makes very little use of a pacifier.

of difference in the behavior of these infants and caretakers. This is followed by father's occupation, which is important in the Japanese situation but not in the American. Sex of infant, at least at three-to-four months of age, is of little relevance.

Reviewing our findings in reverse order of importance, there is a hint, stemming from the intra-cultural analyses, that American mothers may give somewhat more attention, particularly of an affectionate sort, to their boy babies, but this is a tenuous

TABLE 3

Adjusted Mean Frequencies, in Total Observations, of Caretaker Behavior: by Culture, Father's Occupation, and Sex of Infant

	Adjusted Mean Frequencies								
	Culture			Father's Occupation			Sex of Infant		
Categories of Caretaker Behavior	Japanese	American	Correlation†	Salaried	Independent	Correlation†	Male	Female	Correlation†
Caretaker Present	541	421	.37*	437	543	.33	471	494	.08
Feeds	74	71	.03	71	74	.04	78	65	.13
Diapers	23	17	.24	19	21	.08	20	20	.02
Dresses	12	13	.03	12	14	.11	13	12	.05
Positions	8	19	.49**	13	14	.02	15	12	.17
Pats or Touches	34	47	.23	38	43	.08	41	39	.04
Other Care	17	23	.15	21	19	.05	19	22	.10
Plays with	39	24	.25	29	35	.10	34	28	.10
Affections	7	9	.09	7	10	.17	9	7	.20
Looks at	242	299	.27	247	302	.26	278	260	.09
Talks to	101	123	.21	101	127	.24	116	107	.09
Chats	79	120	.42**	94	108	.25	102	96	.06
Lulls	22	3	.44**	8	20	.28	14	11	.09
In Arms	197	139	.27	133	217	.36*	163	175	.06
Rocks	46	20	.35*	22	47	.34	39	25	.19
Canonical Correlation‡			.79**			.52			.51
Total Cases	30	30		35	25		33	27	

†See footnote in Table 2 for explanation of this partial correlation. The means and correlations for all findings significant at $p < 0.05$ are printed in boldface. One asterisk (*) indicates $p < 0.01$, two asterisks (**) indicate $p < 0.001$.

‡Canonical correlations do not include the variable of "Talks to" because of linear dependency with the constituent variables "Chats" and "Lulls"; the means of the constituent variables do not, however, add exactly to the mean for the total variable because of rounding and the weights used to standardize frequencies of observations across cultures . . .

finding in the American data, and there are no findings by sex of infant in the Japanese data.

The analysis by father's occupation produced more results, but all of these, upon further examination, proved to be important only for the Japanese data. In the Japanese independent business families the infant is awake more, and the caretaker is present more, and talks to, lulls, carries, and rocks the infant more than in the salaried families. In contrast, the caretaker in the salaried families is only greater in looking at the infant when compared with the caretaker in the independent business families.

In the single matter of looking at her infant more frequently, the mother in the salaried Japanese family seems more like the American mother, who, in the general cross-cultural analysis, looks at her infant more often. But the American mother also chats with her infant frequently, whereas the Japanese salaried mother is more silent than the Japanese independent business mother. If, as is reasonable, we consider the salaried mother in Japan to be more "modern," then, in her move toward modernity, she seems to have subtracted from traditional ways of caretaking rather than to have added anything new. If anything, the independent business mother in Japan is closer to the American mother in the extent of her direct involvement with her infant. Thus, with regard to the relation of child care to social change, there would not seem to be any simple connection between a move toward modernity for the family in general and a shift toward Western patterns of child care.

The preceding findings, although of interest, become pale in the light of the strong findings of cultural differences. American infants are more happily vocal, more active, and more exploratory of their bodies and their physical environment, than are Japanese infants. Directly related to these findings, the American mother is in greater vocal interaction with her infant, and stimulates him to greater physical activity and exploration. The Japanese mother, in contrast, is in greater bodily contact with her infant, and soothes him toward physical quiescence, and passivity with regard to his environment. Moreover, these patterns of behavior, so early learned by the infant, are in line with the differing expectations for later behavior in the two cultures as the child grows to be an adult.

For now, we believe we have arrived at distinctive patterns of learned behavior for infants in Japan and America. Analysis of our data for the first 20 of the same cases in each culture at two-and-a-half and six years of age will establish whether these patterns persist and jell in the behavior of the children we are studying. Our prediction is that this will happen, because of the strong external pressures for conformity and the strong internal pressures toward being accepted favorably by one's fellows, in any culture.

If these distinctive patterns of behavior are well on the way to being learned by three-to-four months of age, and if they continue over the life span of the person, then there are very likely to be important areas of difference in emotional response in people in one culture when compared with those in another. Such differences are not easily subject to conscious control and, largely out of awareness, they accent and color human behavior. These differences add a zest to life and interpersonal encounters, but they can also add to bewilderment and antagonism when people try to communicate across the emotional barriers of cultures.

We hope that our analysis helps to illuminate the reasons for some of these difficulties in cross-cultural communication despite the seeming increase in similarity between countries in the modern world. One may wish, on moral and practical grounds, for greater real understanding by people of each other across cultures, but it is a moot point whether the world would be a better place in which to live if such cultural differences were to be obliterated.

PRACTICES

The Sexual Life of Savages: in North-Western Melanesia

BRONISLAW MALINOWSKI

Beauty, Color, and Scent in Love-making

We know by now how a Trobriand girl and boy are first attracted to each other, how they come together, how their intrigue develops, leading to separation or marriage; but we know little as yet of the way in which two lovers spend their time together and enjoy each other's presence.

In this as in all other aspects of Melanesian tribal life, custom and convention dictate to a large extent even the details of behavior. Individual deviations always exist, but they fall within a relatively narrow range; much narrower unquestionably than at our own culture level. A lover does not expect from his or her partner the improvisation of a love rhapsody, but rather a properly executed repetition of traditional routine. The places in which it is desirable to make love, the manner of making it, the very types of caress, are defined by tradition. Independent informants would describe exactly the same procedure almost in the same words.

The word *kwakwadu* is a technical term which signifies something like "amorous transactions" or "being together for purposes of love." It would be easier perhaps to express it in German, as *erotisches Beisammensein*, or by the American colloquialism "petting party" or "petting session." English speech habits are, unfortunately, refractory to stereotyped terminology, except in matters of morality. The *kwakwadu* has a wide meaning. It signifies a collective excursion, or party of several couples setting out on a love picnic; the being together of two people who are in love with each other—a sort of erotic *tête-à-tête;* the caresses and approaches before the final union. It is never used euphemistically to designate the sexual act. At a collective picnic some of the games . . . are first played in common, and afterwards the lovers seek solitude two by two. We shall attempt to reconstruct the behavior of a pair who have left such a party, or else started off alone in order to enjoy each other's company in some favorite spot.

The scrub surrounding the village, which is periodically cut for gardens, grows in a dense underbrush and does not everywhere offer a desirable resting place. Here and there, however, a large tree, such as the *butia,* is left behind for the sake of its perfumed flowers, or there may be a group of pandanus trees. Pleasant shady places, too, can be found under an old tree in one of the groves which often mark the site of a deserted village, whose fruit trees, coconut palms, and big banyans make an oasis within the stunted tropical undergrowth of recent cultivation. On the coral ridge (*raybwag*) many spots invite a picnic party. Cavities and hollows in the coral, rocks of queer or attractive shape, giant trees, thickets of fern, flowering hibiscus make the *raybwag* a mysterious and attractive region. Especially delightful is the part which overlooks the open sea towards the east, towards the islands of Kitava, Iwa, and Gawa. The roar of the breakers on the fringing reef, the dazzling sand and foam and the blue sea, provide the favorite surroundings for native love-making, and also constitute the scene in which the mythical drama of incestuous love has been laid by native imagination.

In such places the lovers enjoy the scent and color of the flowers, they watch the birds and insects, and go down to the beach to bathe. In the heat of the day, or during the hot seasons, they search for shady spots on the coral ridge, for waterholes and for bathing places. As the cool of the evening approaches they warm themselves on the hot sand, or kindle a fire, or find shelter in some nook among the coral rocks. They amuse themselves by collecting shells and picking flowers or scented herbs, to adorn themselves. Also they smoke tobacco, chew betelnut, and, when they are thirsty, look for a coconut palm, the green nut of which yields a cooling drink. They inspect each other's hair for lice and eat them—a practice disgusting to us and ill associated with love-making, but to the natives a natural and pleasant occupation between two who are fond of each other, and a favorite pastime with children. On the other hand, they would never eat heavy food on such occasions and especially would never carry it with them from the village. To them the idea of European boys and girls going out for a picnic with a knapsack full of eatables is as disgusting and indecent as their *kwakwadu* would be to a Puritan in our society.

All such pleasures—the enjoyment of landscape, of color and scent in the open air, of wide views and of intimate corners of nature—are essential features in their love-making. For hours, sometimes for days, lovers will go out together gathering fruits and berries for food and enjoying each other's company in beautiful surroundings. I made a point of confirming these particulars from a number of concrete instances; for, in connection with the question of romantic love already discussed, I was interested to know whether love-making had direct satisfaction only for its object, or whether it embraced a wider sensory and aesthetic enjoyment. Many of the pleasures which enter into general games, amusements, and festivities, also form part of personal *kwakwadu.*

Of course, love is not made only in the

open air; there are also special occasions for bringing lovers together in the village. ... [T]he special institution of the *bukumatula* and the more provisional arrangements of younger people have been mentioned. In the village, however, privacy is almost impossible except at night, and the activities of lovers are much more curtailed. They lie next to each other on a bunk and talk, and when they are tired of this, proceed to make love.

The Conversation of Two Lovers

It is not easy to reconstruct personal conversations which in their nature take place under very intimate conditions and without witnesses. A question couched in such general terms as "What do a boy and a girl talk to each other about at a *kwakwadu*?" is likely to be answered by a grin, or, if the man is familiar with the ethnographer, by the standard reply to all difficult questions: *Tonagowa yoku*, "you fool"; in other words, "Don't ask silly questions."

From the spontaneous confidences of some of my friends, however, I obtained some glimpses into what passes during these *tête-à-têtes*. A boy would often repeat, for the sake of impressing me or just to give me some definite news, what a girl told him and what he replied, or vice versa. There is no doubt that the Trobriand lover boasts freely to his sweetheart and expects a sympathetic listener and an enthusiastic response. I have already mentioned how Monakewo used to tell me of the great impression he had made on Dabugera and how greatly she admired his exploits and virtues. Mekala'i was equally certain that Bodulela was deeply impressed by any achievements which he related to her. Gomaya, a young chief of Sinaketa and an incurable braggart, would tell me how his betrothed, to whom he was plighted in infancy, would wonder at his stories of personal excellence, of magical knowledge and of overseas adventure. In fact, whenever a Trobriander went into details about his love affairs, the impression made on his mistress would never be absent from his account, and would be related to me, in native fashion, as fragments of an actual conversation.

Gossip about other people's business, and especially about their love affairs, is also a common subject of conversation between two lovers; and on many occasions much of it ultimately came my way, in that a boy would repeat what he had heard from his sweetheart. For the rest, they talk of what they are doing at that moment, the beauties of nature, and of the things they like or do not like. Sometimes, too, a boy will vaunt his exploits in those pursuits in which women do not usually participate, such as *kula* expeditions, fishing, bird-snaring, or hunting.

Thus a love affair may be set in a rich context of general interest, as regards both mutual activity and conversation; but this varies with the intelligence and the personality of the partners. Ambitious, imaginative people would not be content with mere sensuous pleasure; but the obtuse and limited would proceed no doubt, directly to the cruder stages—the usual caresses and the sexual act.

Erotic Approaches

The place occupied by the kiss in South Sea communities is of general and perennial interest. It is a widely prevalent opinion that kissing is not practised outside the Indo-European horizon. Students of anthropology, as well as frequenters of comic opera, know that even in such high civilizations as those of China and Japan the kiss as a gesture in the art of love is unknown.

A European shudders at the idea of such cultural deficiency. For his comfort, it may be said at once that things are not so black as they look.

To get at the facts and to see these in their right perspective, the question must first be put more precisely. If we ask whether lip-activities play any part in love-making, the answer is that they certainly do. As we shall see, both in the preliminary caresses and in the later stages, the mouth is busy. On the other hand, if we define kissing more precisely as a prolonged pressing of mouth against mouth with slight intermittent movements—and I think that all competent authorities would agree with such a definition and with the proposition that this is the main erotic preliminary in Europe and the United States—then the kiss is not used in Trobriand love-making. Certainly it never forms a self-contained independent source of pleasure, nor is it a definite preliminary stage of love-making, as is the case with us. This caress was never spontaneously mentioned by the natives, and, to direct inquiries, I always received a negative answer. The natives know, however, that white people "will sit, will press mouth against mouth—they are pleased with it." But they regard it as a rather insipid and silly form of amusement.

Kissing in the narrow sense is also absent as a cultural symbol, whether as a greeting, an expression of affection, or a magical or ritual act. The rubbing of noses (*vayauli*) as an act of greeting is rare, and never done except between very near relatives; it is said that parents and children or husband and wife would thus celebrate their reunion after long separation. A mother who is constantly petting her small child, will frequently touch it with her cheek or her lips; she will breathe upon it, or, putting her open mouth against its skin, caress it gently. But the exact technique of kissing is not used between mother and child, and in no form is it so conspicuous with them as with us.

The absence of kissing in the narrower sense brings us to a deeper difference in love-making. The natives, I am convinced, never indulge in erotic caresses as a self-sufficient activity; that is, as a stage in love-making which covers a long period of time before full bodily union is accomplished. This is a local and not a racial character, for I am equally convinced (see above) that among other Melanesians, in Dobu and probably among the Motu, in the Sinaugolo and Mailu tribes, engaged couples do meet, lie together, and caress each other without cohabitation.

The comparison, however, cannot be satisfactory, for my knowledge of the latter tribes is much less complete than in the case of the Trobriands, and so I can only suggest a subject for further research. It is extremely important to know whether the nature of preliminary love is correlated with the level of culture, or with the social regulation of it—above all, with the moral restrictions condemning prenuptial intercourse.

We have spoken rather fully about kissing, to satisfy a general curiosity on this point. Let us now observe the behavior of two lovers alone on their bunk in the *bukumatula*, or in a secluded spot in the *raybwag* or jungle. A mat is usually spread on the boards or on the earth, and, when they are sure of not being observed, skirt and pubic leaf are removed. They may at first sit or lie side by side, caressing each other, their hands roaming over the surface of the skin. Sometimes they will lie close together, their arms and legs enlaced. In such a position they may talk for a long time, confessing their love with endearing phrases, or teasing each other (*katudabuma*). So near to each other, they will rub noses. But though there is a good deal of nose-rubbing, cheek is also rubbed against cheek, and mouth against mouth. Gradually the caress becomes more passionate, and then the mouth is predominantly active; the tongue is sucked, and tongue is rubbed against tongue; they suck each other's lower lips, and the lips will be bitten till blood comes; the saliva is allowed to flow from mouth to mouth. The teeth are used freely, to bite the cheek, to snap at the nose and chin. Or the lovers plunge their hands into the thick mop of each other's hair and tease it or even tear it. In the formulae of love magic, which here as elsewhere abound in over-graphic exaggeration, the expressions, "drink my blood" and "pull out my hair" are frequently used. This sentence, volunteered by a girl's sweetheart, describes his erotic passion:

Binunu vivila dubilibaloda, bigadi;
She sucks woman lower lip (ours), she bites;
tagiyu bimwam
we spit, she drinks.

Erotic scratches are an even more direct way of hurting and of drawing blood. We have already spoken of these as the conventional invitation of a girl to a boy. We also described their place in tribal festivities. But they are also a part of intimate love-making, and a mutual expression of passion:

Tayobobu, tavayauli, takenu deli;
We embrace, we rub noses, we lie together;
bikimali vivila otubwaloda,
she scratches woman on back (ours),
ovilavada
on shoulders (ours);
sene bwoyna, tanukwali, bitagwalayda
very much good, we know, she loves us
senela.
very much indeed.

On the whole, I think that in the rough usage of passion the woman is the more active. I have seen far larger scratches and marks on men than on women; and only women may actually lacerate their lovers . . . The scratching is carried even into the passionate phases of intercourse. It is a great jest in the Trobriands to look at the back of a man or a girl for the hall-marks of success in amorous life. Nor have I ever seen a comely girl or boy without some traces of *kimali* in the proper places. Subject to general rules of good taste and specific **taboo**, the *kimali* marks are a favorite subject for jokes; but there is also much secret pride in their possession.

Another element in love-making, for which the average European would show even less understanding than for the *kimali*, is the *mitakuku*, the biting off of eyelashes. As far as I could judge from descriptions and demonstrations, a lover will tenderly or passionately bend over his mistress's eyes and bite off the tip of her eyelashes. This, I was told, is done in orgasm as well as in the less passionate preliminary stages. I was never quite able to grasp either the mechanism or the sensuous value of this caress. I have no doubt, however, as to its reality, for I have not seen one boy or girl in the Trobriands with the long eyelashes to which they are entitled by nature. In any case, it shows that the eye to them is an object of active bodily interest. Still less enthusiasm will probably be felt by the romantic European towards the already mentioned custom of catching each other's lice and eating them. To the natives, however, it is a pastime, which, while pleasant in itself, also establishes an exquisite sense of intimacy.

The Act of Sex

The following is a condensed description

of the whole process of love-making, with several characteristic incidents, given me by my friend Monakewo:

Takwakwadu: dakova,   kadiyaguma,
We make love: our fire, our lime gourd,
kaditapwaki: kada   gala,   mwasila.
our tobacco;   food (ours)   no,   shame.
Bitala,   tala   kaytala   ka'i
We go,   we go   (for)   one (wood)   tree
kayviava;   tasisu,   takakakutu;
tree big,   we sit,   we louse and eat;
taluki   vivila:
we tell to   woman:
"takayta."   Biwokwo,
"we copulate" (let us copulate).   It is finished,
bitala   ovalu;   ovalu   tala
we go   to village; in village   we go
obukumatula,   takenu tabigatona.
to bachelors' house,   we lie, we chatter.
Kidama   kadumwaleta,   taliku
Supposing   we are alone,   we undo
yavida,   biliku   dabela
pubic leaf ours   she undoes   skirt (hers)
tamasisi.
we sleep.

This may be freely rendered: "When we go on a love-making expedition we light our fire; we take our lime gourd (and chew betel-nut), we take our tobacco (and smoke it). Food we do not take, we would be ashamed to do so. We walk, we arrive at a large tree, we sit down, we search each other's heads and consume the lice, we tell the woman that we want to copulate. After it is over we return to the village. In the village we go to the bachelors' house, lie down, and chatter. When we are alone he takes off the pubic leaf, she takes off her fibre skirt: we go to sleep."

With regard to the act itself, perhaps the most noteworthy feature is the position.

The woman lies on her back, the legs spread and raised, and the knees flexed. The man kneels against her buttocks, her legs resting on his hips. The more usual position, however, is for the man to squat in front of the woman and, with his hands resting on the ground, to move towards her or, taking hold of her legs, to pull her towards him. When the sexual organs are close to each other the insertion takes place. Again the woman may stretch her legs and place them directly on the man's hips, with his arms outside them, but the far more usual position is with her legs embracing the man's arms, and resting on the elbows.

An interesting text gives the description of both methods:

Kidama   vivila   sitana
Supposing   woman   a little bit
ikanupwagega;   kaykela   bima
she lies open (-legged);   legs hers   it comes
ogipomada.   Kidama   ikanupwagega
on our hips. Supposing she lies open (-legged)
senela,   ikanubeyaya,
very much indeed,   she lies right open,
kaykela   bima   o   mitutugu kaylavasi.
leg hers   it comes   on   end mine elbow.

Which may be rendered:

"When the woman opens her legs only a little, her legs come (i.e., rest) on my hips; when she lies with legs spread out very much, lies right open, her legs rest on my elbows."

Congress is sometimes effected in a reclining position. Lying side by side, with the lower limbs pressed against each other, the woman places her upper leg on top of the man, and the insertion is made. This mode, which is less popular, is used at night in the *bukumatula* (bachelors' house). It is less noisy, as the natives say, and requires less space; and is done in order not to wake up the other inmates of the house.

No other positions are used. Above all, the natives despise the European position and consider it unpractical and improper.

The natives, of course, know it, because white men frequently cohabit with native women, some even being married to them. But, as they say: "The man overlies heavily the woman; he presses her heavily downwards, she cannot respond (*ibilamapu*)."

Altogether the natives are certain that white men do not know how to carry out intercourse effectively. As a matter of fact, it is one of the special accomplishments of native cook-boys and servants who have been for some time in the employ of white traders, planters, or officials, to imitate the copulatory methods of their masters. In the Trobriands, Gomaya was perhaps the best actor in this respect. He still remembered a famous Greek buccaneer (Nicholas Minister was the name he went by among other beachcombers), who had lived in the islands even before the establishment of the government station. Gomaya's performance consisted in the imitation of a very clumsy reclining position, and in the execution of a few sketchy and flabby movements. In this the brevity and lack of vigor of the European performance were caricatured. Indeed, to the native idea, the white man achieves orgasm far too quickly; and there seems to be no doubt that the Melanesian takes a much longer time and employs a much greater amount of mechanical energy to reach the same result. This, together with the handicap of the unfamiliar position, probably accounts for the complaints of white men that native girls are not responsive. Many a white informant has spoken to me about perhaps the only word in the native language which he ever learned, *kubilabala* ("move on horizontally"), repeated to him with some intensity during the sexual act. This verb defines the horizontal motion during sexual intercourse, which should be mutual. The noun *bilabala*, originally means a horizontally lying log; and *bala* as a root or prefix, conveys a general sense of the horizontal. But the verb, *bilabala*, does not convey the immobility of a log; on the contrary, it gives the idea of horizontal motion. The natives regard the squatting position as more advantageous, both because the man is freer to move than when kneeling, and because the woman is less hampered in her responsive movements—*bilamapu*—a compound of *bila*, from *bala*, horizontal, and *mapu*, repay or respond. Also in the squatting position the man can perform the treading motion (*mtumuta*), which is a useful dynamic element in successful copulation. Another word, *korikikila*, implies at the same time rubbing and pushing, a copulatory motion.

As the act proceeds and the movements become more energetic, the man, I was told, waits until the woman is ready for orgasm. Then he presses his face to the woman's, embraces her body and raises it towards him, she putting her arms round him at the same time and, as a rule, digging her nails into his skin. The expression for orgasm is *ipipisi momona* = the seminal fluid discharges. The word *momona* signifies both the male and the female discharge; as we know, the natives do not make any sharp distinction between male semen and the glandular secretions of a woman, at least, not as regards their respective functions. The same expression *ipipisi momona* is also applied to (male or female) nocturnal pollution. The word for onanistic ejaculation is *isulumomoni*, "it boils over sexual fluid." Male masturbation is called *ikivayli kwila*—"he manipulates penis"; female masturbation is described in concrete phrases and has no specific name.

An interesting personal account was given to me by Monakewo and illustrates some of the points just mentioned. It was hardly discreet of him to speak of his mistress by name; but the ethnographer's love for the concrete instance may excuse my not emending it.

Bamasisi deli   Dabugera;   bayobobu,
I sleep together   Dabugera;   I embrace,
bavakayla   bavayauli.
I hug all length, I rub noses.
Tanunu dubilibaloda,
We suck lower lips ours,
pela   bi'ulugwalayda;   mayela   tanunu;
because we feel excited;   tongue his we suck;
tagadi   kabulula;   tagadi   kala   gabula;
we bite   nose his;   we bite   his   chin;
tagadi   kimwala;   takabi
we bite   jaw (cheek) his; we take hold (caress)
posigala,   visiyala.   Bilivala   minana:
armpit his,   groin his.   She says   this woman:
"*O didakwani,   lubaygu,   senela;*
"O it itches,   lover mine, very much indeed;
kworikikila   tuvayla,   bilukwali
rub and push   again,   it feels pleasant
wowogu—   kwopinaviyaka,   nanakwa
body mine—   do it vigorously, quick
                 bipipisi   momona:—
(so that)   it squirts   sexual fluid:—
kwalimtumutu   tuvayla   bilukwali
tread   again   it feels pleasant
wowogu."
body mine."

FREE TRANSLATION

"When I sleep with Dabugera I embrace her, I hug her with my whole body, I rub noses with her. We suck each other's lower lip, so that we are stirred to passion. We suck each other's tongues, we bite each other's noses, we bite each other's chins, we bite cheeks and caress the armpit and the groin. Then she will say: 'O my lover, it itches very much . . . push on again, my whole body melts with pleasure . . . do it vigorously, be quick, so that the fluids may discharge . . . tread on again, my body feels so pleasant.'"

The same informant gave me the following samples of a conversation which would occur after the act, when the two rested in each other's arms:

"Kayne   tombwaylim   yaygu?"
"Whether   sweetheart thine   I?"
"Mtage!   nabwayligu   yoku—   sene
"Yes!   sweetheart mine thou—   very much
magigu;   tuta, tuta, bitakayta;
desire mine;   time, time, we copulate;
sene   migimbwayligu
very much   face yours beloved by me
migim   tabuda!"
face thine   cross-cousins!"
"Gala   magigu   bukuyousi
"No   desire mine   you get hold
nata   vivila   nava'u;
one   woman   new woman;
yoku wala,   yaygu."
thou indeed, I."

"Am I thy sweetheart?" "Yes, thou art my sweetheart; I love thee very much; always, we shall cohabit. I love thy face very much; it is that of a cross-cousin (the right woman for me)." "I do not desire that thou shouldst take a new woman; just thou and I."

I was informed that sexual relations between married people would be on the same lines, but, from the following text, it is clear that passion ebbs with time:

Vigilava'u   imasisisi   kwaytanidesi
Married newly   they sleep   single one
kabasi;   bimugo   vayva'i
bed theirs;   it matures   matrimony
bikwaybogwo, kwayta kabala,   kwayta
it is old,   one   bed her,   one
kabada.   Bisala'u   uwasi,
bed ours.   It is energetic   body theirs,
magisi   bikaytasi,   bikenusi
desire theirs   they copulate,   they lie
deli   bikamitakukusi   bivayaulasi
together   they bite eyelashes   they rub noses,
bigedasi.
they bite.

"Newly married people sleep together in one bed. When matrimony has matured, when it has become old, she sleeps in one bed, and we (i.e., husband) sleep in another. When they feel sexually vigorous they want to cohabit; then they lie together, they bite their eyelashes, they rub their noses, they bite each other."

Here my informant, Tokulubakiki, a married man, tries to convey the idea that even long-married persons can behave at times as lovers.

In conclusion,[1] I should like to draw the attention of the reader to the data supplied by Dr. W. E. Roth and other informants concerning the sexual life of the aborigines of Australia.[2] The subject is of considerable importance as the mechanism is very characteristic of the whole nature of erotic approach. The manner in which the Queensland aborigines copulate closely resembles that described ... In both regions the act can be so carried out that there is the minimum of bodily contact. I think that this to a great extent accounts for the undiscriminating way in which young and handsome boys will sometimes fornicate with old and repulsive women. On the other hand, where love exists, the man can bend over the woman or the woman raise herself to meet him and contact can be as full and intimate as is desired.

---

[1] Compare also what has been said about native ideas concerning the anatomy and physiology of procreation and the psycho-physiological mechanism of falling in love ...

[2] Dr. W. E. Roth, *Ethnological Studies Among the North-West Central Queensland Aborigines*, 1897, and H. Basedow, in *J.R.A.I.*, 1927, on "Subincision and Kindred Rites of the Australian Aboriginal," pp. 151–6.

CULTURE RELATIVITY

Shakespeare in the Bush

LAURA BOHANNAN

One of the by-products of anthropological fieldwork is that the ethnographer is afforded an opportunity to see his own culture from a different perspective. The self-evident and the commonplace become terribly difficult to explain and justify when one discusses them with a member of another culture. (Just try explaining the American game of baseball, or even just the concept of a "strike," to someone not from the United States and see what happens.) Moreover, the way in which members of another culture understand or misunderstand materials from the ethnographer's culture may prove extremely illuminating.

In theory, a thorough comparative study of two cultures should provide sufficient data to predict with some accuracy what misunderstandings are likely to occur when a member of culture A discusses a given topic with a member of culture B. Perhaps an analogy from comparative linguistics will illustrate this point. A native speaker of French will normally not be able to articulate the initial consonantal **phonemes** in the English words "thigh" and "thy." The "th" sounds, both voiced (with the vocal cords vibrating) and voiceless, simply do not occur in the French inventory of phonemes (linguistic units of sound). To understand the difference between voiced and voiceless sounds in English, try to whisper the word "thy." It can't be done. If you whisper "thy," you get "thigh" because the initial phoneme in "thigh" is the voiceless [θ]. Try dip/tip or zip/sip, other pairs of words which reflect the same voiced/voiceless distinction.

A knowledge of French phonology would show not only that neither "th" sound occurs, but also that the nearest sounds in French are the [s] and [z] phonemes. Thus one could predict that for the English voiced "th" sound [ð], the French native will substitute the voiced sound [z]. "This'll" becomes "Zees'll," while the voiceless substitution transforms "thistle" into "seesle." (Since French does not have the vowel [i] as in "this," the substitution of [i] results in "thees," as it also does when a native speaker of Spanish speaks English.) The point is that these substitutions are predictable, recurrent phenomena and this insight is by no means limited to problems of language learning. Mistakes in any aspect of culture resulting when a member of one culture attempts to employ an element of another culture are often predictable. This has important implications for the comparative study of politics with respect to international diplomacy. Possibly, one could predict how the policy of nation A would be misunderstood by the citizens of nation B and moreover one could explain why it was thus misunderstood!

When Laura Bohannan introduced Shakespeare's Hamlet to the Tiv of West Africa, she found that they interpreted it in the light of their own culture. Obviously, this is what all peoples do the world over, that is, interpret new ideas in the light of their own culture. This is why it is the height of naïveté for an anthropologically uninformed do-gooder or a governmental representative (the categories are not mutually exclusive) to think that merely introducing a new "helpful" element to a particular group will cause it to "take" in this group. It never occurs to some that perhaps democracy, Christianity, and the capitalist ethic are not for export. But even if they are for export, such ideas are bound to be interpreted in ways different from the ways they are interpreted in the United States. Note the use of the plural, ways, for each culture may interpret these ideas differently. The question is thus not just what Hamlet means to the Tiv, but what does Hamlet mean to a Hindu, to an Arab, or to a Trobriand Islander? In the study of culture it is not enough to know the native elements of the other culture and to interpret their culture, e.g., their literature (folklore); we must also know how members of other cultures interpret our literature and culture. For this reason, Laura Bohannan's essay is a most interesting one. . . .

Just before I left Oxford for the Tiv in West Africa, conversation turned to the season at Stratford. "You Americans," said a friend, "often have difficulty with Shakespeare. He was, after all, a very English poet, and one can easily misinterpret the universal by misunderstanding the particular."

I protested that human nature is pretty much the same the whole world over; at least the general plot and motivation of the greater tragedies would always be clear—everywhere—although some details of custom might have to be explained and difficulties of translation might produce other slight changes. To end an argument we could not conclude, my friend gave me a copy of Hamlet to study in the African bush: it would, he hoped, lift my mind above its primitive surroundings, and possibly I might, by prolonged meditation, achieve the grace of correct interpretation.

It was my second field trip to the African tribe, and I thought myself ready to live in one of its remote sections—an area difficult to cross even on foot. I eventually settled on the hillock of a very knowledgeable old man, the head of a homestead of some hundred and forty people, all of whom were either his close relatives or their wives and children. Like the other elders of the vicinity, the old man spent most of his time performing ceremonies seldom seen these days in the more accessible parts of the tribe. I was delighted. Soon there would be three months of enforced isolation and leisure, between the harvest that takes place just before the rising of the swamps and the clearing of new farms when the water goes down. Then, I thought, they would have even more time to perform ceremonies and explain them to me.

I was quite mistaken. Most of the ceremonies demanded the presence of elders from several homesteads. As the swamps rose, the old men found it too difficult to walk from one homestead to the next, and the ceremonies gradually ceased. As the swamps rose even higher, all activities but one came to an end. The women brewed beer from maize and millet. Men, women, and children sat on their hillocks and drank it.

People began to drink at dawn. By midmorning the whole homestead was singing, dancing, and drumming. When it rained, people had to sit inside their huts: there they drank and sang or they drank and told stories. In any case, by noon or before, I either had to join the party or retire to my own hut and my books. "One does not discuss serious matters when there is beer. Come, drink with us." Since I lacked their capacity for the thick native beer, I spent more and more time with *Hamlet*. Before the end of the second month, grace descended on me. I was quite sure that *Hamlet* had only one possible interpretation, and that one universally obvious.

Early every morning, in the hope of having some serious talk before the beer party, I used to call on the old man at his reception hut—a circle of posts supporting a thatched roof above a low mud wall to keep out wind and rain. One day I crawled through the low doorway and found most of the men of the homestead sitting huddled in their ragged cloths on stools, low plank beds, and reclining chairs, warming themselves against the chill of the rain around a smoky fire. In the center were three pots of beer. The party had started.

The old man greeted me cordially. "Sit down and drink." I accepted a large calabash full of beer, poured some into a small drinking gourd, and tossed it down. Then I poured some more into the same gourd for the man second in seniority to my host before I handed my calabash over to a young man for further distribution. Important people shouldn't ladle beer themselves.

"It is better like this," the old man said, looking at me approvingly and plucking at the thatch that had caught in my hair. "You should sit and drink with us more often. Your servants tell me that when you are not with us, you sit inside your hut looking at a paper."

The old man was acquainted with four kinds of "papers": tax receipts, bride price receipts, court fee receipts, and letters. The messenger who brought him letters from the chief used them mainly as a badge of office, for he always knew what was in them and told the old man. Personal letters for the few who had relatives in the government or mission stations were kept until someone went to a large market where there was a letter writer and reader. Since my arrival, letters were brought to me to be read. A few men also brought me bride price receipts, privately, with requests to change the figures to a higher sum. I found moral arguments were of no avail, since in-laws are fair game, and the technical hazards of forgery difficult to explain to an illiterate people. I did not wish them to think me silly enough to look at any such papers for days on end, and I hastily explained that my "paper" was one of the "things of long ago" of my country.

"Ah," said the old man. "Tell us."

I protested that I was not a storyteller. Storytelling is a skilled art among them; their standards are high, and the audiences critical—and vocal in their criticism. I protested in vain. This morning they wanted to hear a story while they drank. They threatened to tell me no more stories until I told them one of mine. Finally, the old man promised that no one would criticize my style "for we know you are struggling with our language." "But," put in one of the elders, "you must explain what we do not understand, as we do when we tell you our stories." Realizing that here was my chance to prove *Hamlet* universally intelligible, I agreed.

The old man handed me some more beer to help me on with my storytelling. Men filled their long wooden pipes and knocked coals from the fire to place in the pipe bowls; then, puffing contentedly, they sat back to listen. I began in the proper style, "Not yesterday, not yesterday, but long ago, a thing occurred. One night three men were keeping watch outside the homestead of the great chief, when suddenly they saw the former chief approach them."

"Why was he no longer their chief?"

"He was dead," I explained. "That is why they were troubled and afraid when they saw him."

"Impossible," began one of the elders, handing his pipe on to his neighbor, who interrupted, "Of course it wasn't the dead chief. It was an omen sent by a witch. Go on."

Slightly shaken, I continued. "One of these three was a man who knew things"—the closest translation for scholar, but unfortunately it also meant witch. The second elder looked triumphantly at the first. "So he spoke to the dead chief saying, 'Tell us what we must do so you may rest in your grave,' but the dead chief did not answer. He vanished, and they could see him no more. Then the man who knew things—his name was Horatio—said this event was the affair of the dead chief's son, Hamlet."

There was a general shaking of heads round the circle. "Had the dead chief no living brothers? Or was this son the chief?"

"No," I replied. "That is, he had one living brother who became the chief when the elder brother died."

The old man muttered: such omens were matters for chiefs and elders, not for youngsters; no good could come of going behind a chief's back; clearly Horatio was not a man who knew things.

"Yes, he was," I insisted, shooing a chicken away from my beer. "In our country the son is next to the father. The dead chief's younger brother had become the great chief. He had also married his elder brother's widow only about a month after the funeral."

"He did well," the old man beamed and announced to the others, "I told you that if we knew more about Europeans, we would find they really were very like us. In our country also," he added to me, "the younger brother marries the elder brother's widow and becomes the father of his children. Now, if your uncle, who married your widowed mother, is your father's full brother, then he will be a real father to you. Did Hamlet's father and uncle have one mother?"

His question barely penetrated my mind; I was too upset and thrown too far off balance by having one of the most important elements of *Hamlet* knocked straight out of the picture. Rather uncertainly I said that I thought they had the same

Shakespeare in the Bush   313

mother, but I wasn't sure—the story didn't say. The old man told me severely that these genealogical details made all the difference and that when I got home I must ask the elders about it. He shouted out the door to one of his younger wives to bring his goatskin bag.

Determined to save what I could of the mother motif, I took a deep breath and began again. "The son Hamlet was very sad because his mother had married again so quickly. There was no need for her to do so, and it is our custom for a widow not to go to her next husband until she has mourned for two years."

"Two years is too long," objected the wife, who had appeared with the old man's battered goatskin bag. "Who will hoe your farms for you while you have no husband?"

"Hamlet," I retorted without thinking, "was old enough to hoe his mother's farms himself. There was no need for her to remarry." No one looked convinced. I gave up. "His mother and the great chief told Hamlet not to be sad, for the great chief himself would be a father to Hamlet. Furthermore, Hamlet would be the next chief: therefore he must stay to learn the things of a chief. Hamlet agreed to remain, and all the rest went off to drink beer."

While I paused, perplexed at how to render Hamlet's disgusted soliloquy to an audience convinced that Claudius and Gertrude had behaved in the best possible manner, one of the younger men asked me who had married the other wives of the dead chief.

"He had no other wives," I told him.

"But a chief must have many wives! How else can he brew beer and prepare food for all his guests?"

I said firmly that in our country even chiefs had only one wife, that they had servants to do their work, and that they paid them from tax money.

It was better, they returned, for a chief to have many wives and sons who would help him hoe his farms and feed his people; then everyone loved the chief who gave much and took nothing—taxes were a bad thing.

I agreed with the last comment, but for the rest fell back on their favorite way of fobbing off my questions: "That is the way it is done, so that is how we do it."

I decided to skip the soliloquy. Even if Claudius was here thought quite right to marry his brother's widow, there remained the poison motif, and I knew they would disapprove of fratricide. More hopefully I resumed, "That night Hamlet kept watch with the three who had seen his dead father. The dead chief again appeared, and although the others were afraid, Hamlet followed his dead father off to one side. When they were alone, Hamlet's dead father spoke."

"Omens can't talk!" The old man was emphatic.

"Hamlet's dead father wasn't an omen. Seeing him might have been an omen, but he was not." My audience looked as confused as I sounded. "It *was* Hamlet's dead father. It was a thing we call a 'ghost.'" I had to use the English word, for unlike many of the neighboring tribes, these people didn't believe in the survival after death of any individuating part of the personality.

"What is a 'ghost?' An omen?"

"No, a 'ghost' is someone who is dead but who walks around and can talk, and people can hear him and see him but not touch him."

They objected. "One can touch zombis."

"No, no! It was not a dead body the witches had animated to sacrifice and eat. No one else made Hamlet's dead father walk. He did it himself."

"Dead men can't walk," protested my audience as one man.

I was quite willing to compromise. "A 'ghost' is the dead man's shadow."

But again they objected. "Dead men cast no shadows."

"They do in my country," I snapped.

The old man quelled the babble of disbelief that arose immediately and told me with that insincere, but courteous, agreement one extends to the fancies of the young, ignorant, and superstitious, "No doubt in your country the dead can also walk without being zombis." From the depths of his bag he produced a withered fragment of kola nut, bit off one end to show it wasn't poisoned, and handed me the rest as a peace offering.

"Anyhow," I resumed, "Hamlet's dead father said that his own brother, the one who became chief, had poisoned him. He wanted Hamlet to avenge him. Hamlet believed this in his heart, for he did not like his father's brother." I took another swallow of beer. "In the country of the great chief, living in the same homestead, for it was a very large one, was an important elder who was often with the chief to advise and help him. His name was Polonius. Hamlet was courting his daughter, but her father and her brother . . . [I cast hastily about for some tribal analogy] warned her not to let Hamlet visit her when she was alone on her farm, for he would be a great chief and so could not marry her."

"Why not?" asked the wife, who had settled down on the edge of the old man's chair. He frowned at her for asking stupid questions and growled, "They lived in the same homestead."

"That was not the reason," I informed them. "Polonius was a stranger who lived in the homestead because he helped the chief, not because he was a relative."

"Then why couldn't Hamlet marry her?"

"He could have," I explained, "but Polonius didn't think he would. After all, Hamlet was a man of great importance who ought to marry a chief's daughter, for in his country a man could have only one wife. Polonius was afraid that if Hamlet made love to his daughter, then no one else would give a high price for her."

"That might be true," remarked one of the shrewder elders, "but a chief's son would give his mistress's father enough presents and patronage to more than make up the difference. Polonius sounds like a fool to me."

"Many people think he was," I agreed. "Meanwhile Polonius sent his son Laertes off to Paris to learn the things of that country, for it was the homestead of a very great chief indeed. Because he was afraid that Laertes might waste a lot of money on beer and women and gambling, or get into trouble by fighting, he sent one of his servants to Paris secretly, to spy out what Laertes was doing. One day Hamlet came upon Polonius's daughter Ophelia. He behaved so oddly he frightened her. Indeed"—I was fumbling for words to express the dubious quality of Hamlet's madness—"the chief and many others had also noticed that when Hamlet talked one could understand the words but not what they meant. Many people thought that he had become mad." My audience suddenly became much more attentive. "The great chief wanted to know what was wrong with Hamlet, so he sent for two of Hamlet's age mates [school friends would have taken long explanation] to talk to Hamlet and find out what troubled his heart. Hamlet, seeing that they had been bribed by the chief to betray him, told them nothing. Polonius, however, insisted that Hamlet was mad because he had been forbidden to see Ophelia, whom he loved."

"Why," inquired a bewildered voice, "should anyone bewitch Hamlet on that account?"

"Bewitch him?"

"Yes, only witchcraft can make anyone mad, unless, of course, one sees the beings that lurk in the forest."

I stopped being a storyteller, took out my notebook and demanded to be told more about these two causes of madness. Even while they spoke and I jotted notes, I tried to calculate the effect of this new factor on the plot. Hamlet had not been exposed to the beings that lurk in the forests. Only his relatives in the male line could bewitch him. Barring relatives not mentioned by Shakespeare, it had to be Claudius who was attempting to harm him. And, of course, it was.

For the moment I staved off questions by saying that the great chief also refused to believe that Hamlet was mad for the love of Ophelia and nothing else. "He was sure that something much more important was troubling Hamlet's heart."

"Now Hamlet's age mates," I continued, "had brought with them a famous storyteller. Hamlet decided to have this man tell the chief and all his homestead a story about a man who had poisoned his brother because he desired his brother's wife and wished to be chief himself. Hamlet was sure the great chief could not hear the story without making a sign if he was indeed guilty, and then he would discover whether his dead father had told him the truth."

The old man interrupted, with deep cunning, "Why should a father lie to his son?" he asked.

I hedged: "Hamlet wasn't sure that it really was his dead father." It was impossible to say anything, in that language, about devil-inspired visions.

"You mean," he said, "it actually was an omen, and he knew witches sometimes send false ones. Hamlet was a fool not to go to one skilled in reading omens and divining the truth in the first place. A man-who-sees-the-truth could have told him how his father died, if he really had been poisoned, and if there was witchcraft in it; then Hamlet could have called the elders to settle the matter."

The shrewd elder ventured to disagree. "Because his father's brother was a great chief, one-who-sees-the-truth might therefore have been afraid to tell it. I think it was for that reason that a friend of Hamlet's father—a witch and an elder—sent an omen so his friend's son would know. Was the omen true?"

"Yes," I said, abandoning ghosts and the devil; a witch-sent omen it would have to be. "It was true, for when the storyteller was telling his tale before all the homestead, the great chief rose in fear. Afraid that Hamlet knew his secret he planned to have him killed."

The stage set of the next bit presented some difficulties of translation. I began cautiously. "The great chief told Hamlet's mother to find out from her son what he knew. But because a woman's children are always first in her heart, he had the important elder Polonius hide behind a cloth that hung against the wall of Hamlet's mother's sleeping hut. Hamlet started to scold his mother for what she had done."

There was a shocked murmur from everyone. A man should never scold his mother.

"She called out in fear, and Polonius moved behind the cloth. Shouting, 'A rat!' Hamlet took his machete and slashed through the cloth." I paused for dramatic effect. "He had killed Polonius!"

The old men looked at each other in supreme disgust. "That Polonius truly was a fool and a man who knew nothing! What child would not know enough to shout, 'It's me!'" With a pang, I remembered that these people are ardent hunters, always armed with bow, arrow, and machete; at the first rustle in the grass an arrow is aimed and ready, and the hunter shouts "Game!" If no human voice answers immediately, the arrow speeds on its way. Like a good hunter Hamlet had shouted, "A rat!"

I rushed in to save Polonius's reputation. "Polonius did speak. Hamlet heard him. But he thought it was the chief and wished to kill him to avenge his father. He had meant to kill him earlier that evening. . . ." I broke down, unable to describe to these pagans, who had no belief in individual afterlife, the difference between dying at one's prayers and dying "unhousell'd, disappointed, unaneled."

This time I had shocked my audience seriously. "For a man to raise his hand against his father's brother and the one who has become his father—that is a terrible thing. The elders ought to let such a man be bewitched."

I nibbled at my kola nut in some perplexity, then pointed out that after all the man had killed Hamlet's father.

"No," pronounced the old man, speaking less to me than to the young men sitting behind the elders. "If your father's brother has killed your father, you must appeal to your father's age mates; *they* may avenge him. No man may use violence against his senior relatives." Another thought struck him. "But if his father's brother had indeed been wicked enough to bewitch Hamlet and make him mad that would be a good story indeed, for it would be his fault that Hamlet, being mad, no longer had any sense and thus was ready to kill his father's brother."

There was a murmur of applause. *Hamlet* was again a good story to them, but it no longer seemed quite the same story to me. As I thought over the coming complications of plot and motive, I lost courage and decided to skim over dangerous ground quickly.

"The great chief," I went on, "was not sorry that Hamlet had killed Polonius. It gave him a reason to send Hamlet away, with his two treacherous age mates, with letters to a chief of a far country, saying that Hamlet should be killed. But Hamlet changed the writing on their papers, so that the chief killed his age mates instead." I encountered a reproachful glare from one of the men whom I had told undetectable forgery was not merely immoral but beyond human skill. I looked the other way.

"Before Hamlet could return, Laertes came back for his father's funeral. The great chief told him Hamlet had killed Polonius. Laertes swore to kill Hamlet because of this, and because his sister Ophelia, hearing her father had been killed by the man she loved, went mad and drowned in the river."

"Have you already forgotten what we told you?" The old man was reproachful. "One cannot take vengeance on a madman; Hamlet killed Polonius in his madness. As for the girl, she not only went mad, she was drowned. Only witches can make people drown. Water itself can't hurt anything. It is merely something one drinks and bathes in."

I began to get cross. "If you don't like the story, I'll stop."

The old man made soothing noises and himself poured me some more beer. "You tell the story well, and we are listening. But it is clear that the elders of your country have never told you what the story really means. No, don't interrupt! We believe you when you say your marriage customs are different, or your clothes and weapons. But people are the same everywhere; therefore, there are always witches and it is we, the elders, who know how witches work. We told you it was the great

Shakespeare in the Bush

chief who wished to kill Hamlet, and now your own words have proved us right. Who were Ophelia's male relatives?"

"There were only her father and her brother." Hamlet was clearly out of my hands.

"There must have been many more; this also you must ask of your elders when you get back to your country. From what you tell us, since Polonius was dead, it must have been Laertes who killed Ophelia, although I do not see the reason for it."

We had emptied one pot of beer, and the old men argued the point with slightly tipsy interest. Finally one of them demanded of me, "What did the servant of Polonius say on his return?"

With difficulty I recollected Reynaldo and his mission. "I don't think he did return before Polonius was killed."

"Listen," said the elder, "and I will tell you how it was and how your story will go, then you may tell me if I am right. Polonius knew his son would get into trouble, and so he did. He had many fines to pay for fighting, and debts from gambling. But he had only two ways of getting money quickly. One was to marry off his sister at once, but it is difficult to find a man who will marry a woman desired by the son of a chief. For if the chief's heir commits adultery with your wife, what can you do? Only a fool calls a case against a man who will someday be his judge. Therefore Laertes had to take the second way: he killed his sister by witchcraft, drowning her so he could secretly sell her body to the witches."

I raised an objection. "They found her body and buried it. Indeed Laertes jumped into the grave to see his sister once more —so, you see, the body was truly there. Hamlet, who had just come back, jumped in after him."

"What did I tell you?" The elder appealed to the others. "Laertes was up to no good with his sister's body. Hamlet prevented him, because the chief's heir, like a chief, does not wish any other man to grow rich and powerful. Laertes would be angry, because he would have killed his sister without benefit to himself. In our country he would try to kill Hamlet for that reason. Is this not what happened?"

"More or less," I admitted. "When the great chief found Hamlet was still alive, he encouraged Laertes to try to kill Hamlet and arranged a fight with machetes between them. In the fight both the young men were wounded to death. Hamlet's mother drank the poisoned beer that the chief meant for Hamlet in case he won the fight. When he saw his mother die of poison, Hamlet, dying, managed to kill his father's brother with his machete."

"You see, I was right!" exclaimed the elder.

"That was a very good story," added the old man, "and you told it with very few mistakes. There was just one more error, at the very end. The poison Hamlet's mother drank was obviously meant for the survivor of the fight, whichever it was. If Laertes had won, the great chief would have poisoned him, for no one would know that he arranged Hamlet's death. Then, too, he need not fear Laertes' witchcraft; it takes a strong heart to kill one's only sister by witchcraft.

"Sometime," concluded the old man, gathering his ragged toga about him, "you must tell us some more stories of your country. We, who are elders, will instruct you in their true meaning, so that when you return to your own land your elders will see that you have not been sitting in the bush, but among those who know things and who have taught you wisdom."

CULTURE CHANGE

Fathoms and Feet, Acres and Tons: An Appraisal

KEITH GORDON IRWIN

Who has not heard—and, hearing, perhaps believed—that our foot rule's length was set for all time by the boot length of an early English king? And that the size of the nose of another early monarch played, somehow, a part in setting the dimensions of our yardstick? And who has not read—and, reading, perhaps believed—that an acre's length was the furrow-long strip that a certain mythical yoke of oxen was able to plow between restings? And that the acre itself was the land that these oxen could turn over with the plow in a day's time? And who has not been told—and, listening, perhaps believed—that the entire system of weights and measures in common use in this country is but a hodgepodge of diverse units, in a plan that is without logic and with little merit?

It has long been recognized that historical facts may not square with the origins suggested in legendary tales. In the case of the common measures, there is convincing evidence that arrogant and whimsical kings and robust oxen were not the prime actors that the stories have implied. Nor is there truth behind the allegation that the common units were illogical in their nature or in their interrelationships. But is one to be condemned as a believer of fairy tales if he is inclined toward disturbing thoughts as to whether these age-old measures are either adequate or desirable for a modern world, and whether a proper and wholly defensible procedure might not be to discard the old system and start anew on a more modern one? Such thoughts need not be considered either irrelevant or inconsequential. Their consideration justifies the presentation of our common system against a background of history.

The Common Measures of Length and Farm Areas against the Background of History

Our present system of measures for distances on land and sea is a direct heritage from the half-forgotten measures brought to England by the Anglo-Saxons of fifteen centuries ago. The plan they used was so remarkable for its simplicity and high practicality that we might be pardoned for seeking to credit it to Saxon genius. But the plan itself antedated by at least half a thousand years the Saxon landing on British soil, for Greek literature left an ample record of its use along the shores and waterways of southeastern Europe even in early classical times.

The basic unit of this old plan was the arm stretch, or the distance spanned by the outstretched arms. The Greeks called this the *orguia*. In Europe it became the *toise* of the French, the *faedm* of the Danes, the *fathom* of the Saxons. Races of people differ in stature. So the actual length of this basic unit varied somewhat from one racial group to another. The classical metrologists report that the Greek arm stretch in Solon's time was equal to 72.90 of our inches. In medieval Europe its length in the Rhineland was equal to 79.08 inches. With the long-armed Saxons it reached 79.20 inches. But throughout Europe the same decimal plan was used for the smaller and larger units. The nature of the completely decimalized arrangement was worked out by the scholars first of all for the classical plan, for which Greek literature gave abundant clues. Under the name of the Greek Itinerary System this plan may be found listed among the measures of antiquity. The entirely comparable old English plan as developed by England's eminent metrologist, the late W. M. F. Petrie, was worked out from such source material as old maps, old itineraries, old laws, and the measurements of ancient buildings. In words of today the Saxon arrangement becomes:

10 finger widths	=1 doublehand
10 doublehands	=1 Saxofathom
10 Saxofathoms	=1 chain
10 chains	=1 furlong (for land measures) or 1 cablelength (for offshore measures)
1,000 Saxofathoms	=1 "thousand" (the old English sea-and-land mile)

Farm lands were laid out in a similar simple way:

A block of land 100 Saxofathoms wide by 100 Saxofathoms long	=10 acres
As this land would be plowed lengthwise, A strip of land 10 Saxofathoms wide by 100 Saxofathoms long	=1 acre

The Saxofathom, as a unit of length, has long since disappeared, being outlawed six centuries ago in favor of a shorter fathom. Yet that ghostly arm stretch is still the basic measure for the farm lands of an English-speaking world. A modern contrivance for measuring small acreages has, perhaps unwittingly, restored for the moment the old Saxon measures and the simplicity of the old plan. Because it has done so, the contrivance is worth describing. Made of light material and triangular in form, it has a waist high handle for the apex of the triangle and a strip of wood for the base. At either end of the strip, and jutting down a few inches, is a rounded peg. From center to center the pegs are 79.20 inches apart. This number is important, for it is the exact length of the old Saxofathom. The main measure is divided, on the baseboard, into 10 equal parts, and each of these, again, into 10 equal parts. These divisions correspond to the doublehand and finger-width units of the old plan. When in use the device is given a whirling, end-for-end motion as the operator walks down the boundary of the field he is measuring. For a square 10-acre field the count should be 100 Saxofathoms for width and the same for length, and the report is that even an inexperienced operator will not miss these results by more than an inch or so. For fractional acreages or plots of ground not dimensioned in any exact Saxofathom manner, the scale upon the base of the device is called into play, any part of the main unit being represented as a decimal fraction. For fields laid out with square corners the acreage is found in all cases by multiplying together the length and width, as measured in Saxofathoms, and dividing the result by 1,000. The plan is that of the Saxons. The use of the decimal point, if one is needed, is the only part of the plan that is modern.

Had the men of that long-ago time in England not been such tall men, with such a great reach of arm and long stride, a second development in English measures would certainly have followed a different course and a simpler one. In the year 1066 Saxon England was conquered by the Normans from across the English Channel. In the following centuries Norman castles took the place of the simple fortified homes of the Saxon thanes, and abbeys and Gothic cathedrals were reared on the sites of earlier church structures. Skilled workers were needed for this construction—workers in carved wood and fashioned stone, forged metal and shaped glass, embossed leather and embroidered tapestry. Such craftsmen, brought to England from the continent, were, in general, shorter in stature than the fair-haired, blue-eyed Saxons. As the Saxofathom was too long a distance for their outstretched arms to span, their measures, of necessity, were based upon shorter lengths. At first the units adopted by one craft may have had no close agreement with those of other crafts. And there must have been trouble between the various craft groups, between the hewers of wood and shapers of stone who knew only Saxon measures. A compromise plan was imperative if confusion was to be avoided.

About the year 1250 such a compromise plan was developed; by 1350 it was in virtually universal use in all but the most rural districts of England. This plan set up a *new fathom* exactly 10/11 as long as the old Saxofathom. This new unit was divided in half to get the clothmaker's *yard*, and into 6 parts for the craftsman's *foot*.

The new fathom met with no special objection from those who held the lands of England. The acre, of course, was no longer to be referred to as 10 fathoms by 100 fathoms in size, for the fathom itself had changed. It was now 11 new fathoms by 110 new fathoms. The plan had lost part of its decimal simplicity, but the boundaries of the acre were intact. And the rod—a common measuring stick of 2½ Saxofathoms—was not changed in length, though new notches were to be cut on it to mark off its length into sixteen ½ feet. The furlong was also intact. But for some reason the old mile of 10 furlongs was discarded. For it there was substituted a *statute* mile of 8-furlong length. This meant for the square mile of farm land a drop from 1,000 acres to 640 acres.

Of the subordinate units of the old plan, a few had to be forced out of existence to prevent confusion. Thus the old yard was legally abolished to make way for the new one, which was 10/11 as long. The finger width also gave way to the inch. For the hand—as a twentieth of the Saxofathom—there was a different fate. By a mere 1 per cent increase in size it was to fit into the new plan as a 4-inch measure. Thus only a few changes were made in bringing the craftsman units into accord with those of old England, and none of these affected land areas or invaded property rights. Yet the full consummation of the shift of measures, small as it was, stretched almost across two centuries.

In 1624 an attempt was made to restore the simplicity of the Saxon plan for farm measurement. Edmund Gunter, a practical English mathematician, proposed in that year an arrangement of measures that bypassed the old Saxofathom and reintroduced the old double hand under the name of link. If we include the finger width as the smallest unit, we may write the Gunter plan as:

10 finger widths	= 1 link
100 links	= 1 chain
10 chains	= 1 furlong
10 square chains	= 1 acre
1 square furlong	= 10 acres

On the practical side, Gunter devised for the surveyor a skillfully constructed chain with 100 equal links. With the aid of such a chain the surveyor could measure farm areas rapidly and accurately and report the result in simple, decimalized units. George Washington, as a young man, used Gunter's equipment and plan, as did all American surveyors from Washington's time almost to our own.

The Gunter measures did not gain common acceptance among farm people, for the plan neglected that versatile measuring unit of the farm, the rod. To the surveyor an acre would be 10 square chains of land; to the farm user it would be a block of land 4 rods wide by 40 rods long, or its equivalent. To that extent, the Gunter attempt to restore the decimal simplicity of the old measures fell short of accomplishment.

In Saxon days there had been no difference between the length-measure plan as used for distances on land and for distances out from the shore except that the furlong of the landsman was the cable length of the seaman. The sea and land plans were to diverge, however, when the new fathom was adopted. The men of the sea were to retain the old system in its entirety, cutting all units to 10/11 their former size, in keeping with the change in the fathom. This meant that the sea mile of 1,000 new fathoms was, after this, considerably longer than the 8-furlong statute mile used for land measurement.

Some centuries later, a small but highly important change was made in the sea mile's length. By that time the ocean navigators had discovered that the length of a minute of arc on a great circle of the earth was slightly more than 1,000 fathoms. By increasing the sea mile to 1013.4 fathoms, the two would be brought into coincidence. In time this change was adopted officially, the new length becoming the *nautical mile* of the seaman, or the *geographical mile* of the cartographer.

As the result of these several stages of development, each entirely logical in itself, the English system of length and surface measures came to be not a single plan but a composite of three interwoven designs. The old English part had given the English-speaking nations their farmland unit of the acre and the statute mile. The craftsman part had contributed the yard, the foot, and the inch. The distance-at-sea part had furnished the nautical mile. And the units so developed may not readily be changed. The farms of the British nations and the United States would seem to have imposed an unbreakable rigidity upon the size of the acre. The foot that received its length when there were few crafts has, today, embroidered around it the workday measures of a thousand occupations. The size of the nautical mile is fixed by the very earth itself.

The Metric Measures against the Background of History

We shall now need to turn our attention to a modern plan that was devised to eliminate the more pronounced disadvantages inherent in such older systems as that of England.

In the decade that followed the American Revolution the use of decimal fractions took on practical importance. In the money system devised for our newly established country these fractions when used with decimalized money units made a combination that was startling in simplicity and usefulness. To carry this same idea to the whole field of measurement became the dream of scientists and others the world over.

Only a French Revolution could have brought such scientific dreams so swiftly to fruition, for that period was one of those rare times in history when old standards were swept away, without a word of protest, to make room for new ones carried on a wave of high idealism. There was no compromising, no counting of costs. Many of the plans pressed so urgently by the savants and accepted so enthusiastically by the revolutionary assembly were not, however, to become a permanent part of the structure of French measurement. The ten-day week ran too counter to human requirements to gain more than a transitory existence. The decimalized plan for the hours of the day and the new form in which the year's calendar was cast met a like fate. And so did the plan for measuring the earth in a new kind of degree—though the failure here was related to the international scope of the plan and the puny effect that the decisions of a revolutionary assembly of France would have in dictating the measures of a world. The plan itself proposed that the old method of dividing a quadrant of the earth into 90 degrees, with each degree marked off into 60 minutes of arc, be changed to give each quadrant 100 new-sized degrees and each of these, 100 new-sized minutes of arc. Although this novel plan soon passed into oblivion, it was to leave a permanent imprint on another part of the over-all plan, as we shall see.

The plan developed for the handling of measures and weights, unlike most of the others, was to outlast the French Revolution. It was intended to be ideal both for land and for sea, and its final form was a modernized version of the English nautical mile plan and that of the old Saxon-Teutonic sea-and-land system dovetailed to give a single composite. For all its attempt at high practicality, this French, or metric, plan was to fail at a point where success seemed most certain. And a chance factor was to prove of outstanding importance in its acceptance.

In the sea part of the plan, there is a close basic relationship between the metric measures and those of England. The nautical mile, as has been pointed out, matches the length of a minute of arc on a great circle of the earth. The "metric mile" was devised along the same line of reasoning. It was to match the length of a hundredth of a hundredth of the earth's quadrant, following the idea of the new-sized degree and new-sized minute of arc, whose existence in a sort of blueprint stage we have already mentioned. Just as a thousandth of the nautical mile was (very nearly) a fathom, so a thousandth of the "metric mile" was to be (exactly) the length of the new French basic measure to be known as the meter.

This "metric mile" (later christened the kilometer) was, by nature of its relation to the size of the earth's quadrant, 540/1000 as long as the English nautical mile. That it failed as a useful sea measure may not be charged to any gross error in the measurement of that part of the earth that this unit was to represent. It came, instead, from the evanescent nature of the new-sized degree upon which its length had depended. Today in metric countries the same nautical mile is in use as in the rest of the world, this length of a minute of arc on a great circle appearing, quite awkwardly, as 1,852 meters.

The newly devised measures were, however, successful as land units. This was not through design. It was due to a chance relationship, to the fact that the meter was half as long as the old north-Europe fathom. This ancient arm-stretch unit, which, among the Saxons, was the basis for all measurements on land and waterways, had its counterpart in the measures used by the Teutonic tribes that invaded the continental Roman provinces with the collapse of the Western Roman Empire. It was in terms of these fathoms that the captured Roman lands were laid out anew. There was, it is true, a little variation from tribe to tribe in the length of this almost universal measure. The Saxofathom was a little longer than most of the others. Its length, as mentioned previously, was that of 79.20 present-day inches. For the districts along the Rhine the corresponding length was 79.08; for some parts of France it was 78.24, and for Spain 78.98. Strike an average of the last three and you have 78.77. Double the length of the meter and you have 78.74. The similarity is startling. It seems much too close to be the result of chance. But upon that accidental relationship was to rest much of the acceptance of the metric system as a land measure for continental Europe.

The importance of that relationship may, perhaps, best be shown by placing the metric plan of length beside the well-decimalized Saxon system. Had the meter been *exactly* half as long as the Saxofathom it would necessarily follow that every Saxon unit of length from the finger width to the old English mile would be matched, unit for unit, by a metric measure of half its size. Extended to farm land, a block of ground that measured 100 Saxofathoms by 100 Saxofathoms would be 200 meters by 200 meters. In Saxon terms that much land would be 10 acres, in metric 4 hectares. Even the English statute mile, though not a part of the original Saxon plan, would fit into the simple scheme of relationships. Its length of 8 furlongs, or 800 Saxofathoms, would be equal to 1,600 meters.

In the average American the relation of Saxon and metric measures that we have pointed out will arouse no particular interest. Propose to him that we could secure international uniformity in the matter of land areas by cutting down our 10-acre fields to 4-hectare size and our miles to 1,600-meter lengths, and he may but shrug his shoulders. He wants to know how much would have to be pared off. Tell him that it would amount to but 3.83 feet for each dimension of the 10-acre block and about 30 feet for the mile, and he may reply that 30 feet is almost as wide as a country road. You argue that this small change would make our measurements agree with those of continental Europe and the Americas to the south of us, and he responds,

"If they really want unity that much, let them up the meter a bit to match what we have to offer." He does not consider himself a reactionist or a blockader of progress. His answer represents, to him, simply common sense.

The Background for the Common and Metric Units of Weight

Up to this point we have followed only the story of the development of measures of length and surface. We should speak somewhat briefly of other units as well.

It has often been implied that the plan used by the founders of the metric system in arriving at weight units was unique. On the contrary, all comprehensive systems of measurement and weight from the time of Solon in ancient Athens down to the present appear to have used it. It would be more logical to stress the point that in the metric plan the relation of small weights to each other or to large weights was in every case a decimal one.

How the gram-weight of the metric system was to represent the weight of a cubic centimeter of pure water at a temperature of 4 degrees Centigrade is doubtless familiar to everyone who has studied the physical sciences. How the English craftsman obtained the weight of the pound is seldom told. This weight unit came into general use in England in the relatively brief period between the years 1300 and 1333. As may be judged from internal evidence and from a knowledge of similar methods used elsewhere in Europe, the English plan was to set the weight of a cubic foot of water equal to 1,000 "ounces," that of 16 cubic feet of water equal to 1,000 "pounds." The metric plan was to parallel the other, but with a more complete decimalization, when it set the weight of a cubic decimeter of water equal to 1,000 "grams," and the weight of a cubic meter of water equal to 1,000 "kilograms."

It is always far easier to prepare accurate replicas of a standard weight than to develop the standard itself from volume measurements, a fact that has been recognized since Solon's time. The original standard establishing the legal size of the pound was placed in the English Exchequer in the time of Edward III. A new standard, conforming to the original one, was prepared in the reign of Queen Elizabeth. Although neither of these is in existence now, close replicas of Elizabeth's pound constitute the standards of today in England and the United States. Whatever may have been the case in the earlier standards, those of today are too heavy by half a drop of water per ounce, if the cubic foot of water used in checking the weights is measured under the same refinement of conditions specified for metric weights. The error, which amounts to 8 parts in 6.992, or 11/100 of 1 per cent, may have been introduced in connection with Elizabeth's standard. It appears reasonably certain that her advisory committee suggested that the weight of the pound should, for commercial convenience, be made equal to 7,000 troy grains. For pure water at a temperature of 4 degrees Centigrade, the correct value is exactly 6,992 grains.

The similarity in basic plan between the cubic foot of water and the ounce, on the one hand, and the cubic decimeter (or liter) and the gram, on the other, explains certain relationships between English and metric measures that have been noted by technical and scientific workers. Thus, the weight of a liter of a gas as given in grams matches in number value that of a cubic foot of the gas as recorded in ounces. Also, the specific gravity of a solid or liquid has a numerical value that is the same as the weight of the solid or liquid in grams per cubic decimeter, or the weight in ounces per cubic foot, if these weights are divided by 1,000. For example, the specific gravity of mercury is 13.6; a cubic decimeter of it weighs 13,600 grams; a cubic foot will weigh 13,600 ounces. Or the weight of moisture present in a sample of air will be expressed by the same number whether given in grams per cubic meter or in ounces per thousand cubic feet. Or a solution of a certain strength may be made either by adding the required number of grams of the material to make up a liter of solution or by using the same number of ounces in making up a cubic foot of solution. Such similarities can be almost endlessly extended, but always, it should be noted, the results will match only to three figures, for there is an inherent error in the English plan of 8 parts in a total of 7,000.

Our Wine Measures

The pint and gallon that we use for liquid measures are not, by their nature, comparable either to the cubic foot or to such metric measures as the liter. They represent wine measures set up under legislation for the wine-handling trade. The tun, a large unit not mentioned in a direct way in the early English laws, was the quantity of wine that in a vat measuring 4 feet by 4 feet on the inside would fill it to a depth of 25 inches. This much wine was considered to weigh 2,000 pounds. Since wine has an average specific gravity very close to 0.96 for wine-cellar temperatures, the results were always close to the 2,000-pound estimate. The basic small unit of this wine plan was the pint, a measure that was 1/2000 of a tun and so would hold a pound of wine.

In later times many commodities other than wine were, at one time or another, measured out in "pints"—that is, in capacity vessels of an assortment of sizes each designed to hold a pound of a certain kind of commodity. The Queen Anne bushel, which has been in use with us since colonial times, is an example of a 64-pint measure set up for grain.

During the nineteenth century the British Empire, plagued with a multiplicity of such "pints," swept away the wine measures, the Queen Anne bushel, and a variety of other capacity devices, replacing them by a single system in which the imperial gallon, a new unit, was to have the volume of 10 pounds of water and the new bushel was to be 8 imperial gallons in size. The plan stopped short, however, of being adequate from a modern point of view. It failed to make the pint the volume of a pound of water, with the pint divided decimally into smaller units. These two points were important.

Our pint and gallon are not adapted to general work with liquids to the extent that the British imperial gallon and the metric liter are. It should be noted, however, that our pint is basically defined in terms of water, for it was to be a vessel holding one pound of a liquid whose weight (as indicated by the specific gravity) would be 96/100 that of water. It would follow then that 96 pints (12 gallons) of water would weigh exactly 100 pounds, and a sixteenth as much, or 6 pints of water, would weigh exactly 100 ounces. These values are completely correct for temperatures close to 60 degrees Fahrenheit, or wine-cellar conditions. Even the Queen Anne bushel is not so bizarre in its capacity as the legal content of 2150.42 cubic inches would imply. It is exactly 56/45 of a cubic foot in size; so 45 bushels of grain will just fill a bin whose inside measurements are 7 feet by 8 feet by 1 foot.

The tun of wine as a liquid capacity measure seems always to have been matched in the early days of the wine measures by the idea of a tun weight of 2,000 pounds, which is what such a quantity of wine would weigh. Given a more modern spelling and now applied to commodities in general, this weight unit is our 2,000-pound ton. And tunnage, or the number of tuns of wine that a boat might carry, is now tonnage and represents any load or cargo measured in tons.

Another tun-weight idea was in use, from the beginning, among seamen. It was a gross weight taking in the weight of the tun of wine and the containers for the wine. Whether the liquid was handled in barrels or casks, 12 pounds of container weight was estimated as being required for each 100 pounds of wine, or 240 pounds for each 2,000 pounds of wine. This gross ton of 2,240 pounds soon became fixed for all commodities carried by ships. Its continued use has long resulted in a moderate amount of confusion.

Troy and Apothecary Weights

Not long before the development of the English weight plan, the thriving Italian cities of Venice, Florence, Genoa, and Milan had set up an integrated plan of a similar nature to fit their commercial needs. And the same had been true of the group of federated cities along the Rhine, the North Sea, and the Baltic known as the Hanseatic League. For all three—England, the Italian communes, and the Hansa cities —the weight units were derived from the weight of a cubic foot of water. England, as we have noted, divided the weight of their cubic foot into 1,000 ounces. The Hanseatic League split the weight of its somewhat larger cubic foot into 1,000 onzen. The Italian cities with a still larger basic cubic foot divided it into 1,333 1/3 onzia. The result was an English ounce of 437.5 grains, a Hansa onze of 480.0 grains, and an Italian onzia of 436.2 grains.

The *Oxford Historical Dictionary* suggests that the abbreviation "oz.," as used for the common ounce, is, in reality, that of the Italian onzia. The difference between 437.5 and 436.2 grains was evidently so slight that the two weights must have been considered commercially equivalent for ordinary weighing.

The Hansa onze, nearly 10 per cent heavier than the other two, was known in England as the troy ounce. This weight unit dominated the commercial dealings of Western Europe during the ascendency of the Hanseatic League, for the weighing of silver and gold, as well as for drugs and luxury items which, coming from the East, were distributed by the merchants of the Rhineland cities. By the close of the reign of Elizabeth of England the prime importance of the Rhineland onze and its companion weights of the drug trade was dwindling. Bitter religious wars had obliterated old trade routes. The products of India, China, and the Spice Islands were reaching Europe by cargo ships that ran directly to the cities that faced out on the Atlantic. There were new sources for silver and gold, and new weight systems for their handling.

By the end of the nineteenth century the troy and apothecary weights which, in an earlier day, had been raised by the Hansa cities to a position of international importance had vanished in all countries but our own. The metric countries had built their pharmacopoeia around metric units. The British had abolished all the old weight units of these two systems except the troy ounce, using it only in the minting of coins. Even in the United States there has been a gradual shift away from the old apothecary weights to metric ones in the filling of prescriptions and the compounding of medicines, and to common weights in wholesale drug handling. It is not improbable that another decade may see the end of the scruple and the drachm. Perhaps the "fine ounce" may be gone as well. They have all outlived their usefulness.

Modernizing Changes of the Past Three Quarters of a Century

This brings the story of the development of the English and metric units down to the year 1870. The English system was, by that time, half a thousand years old; the metric system had not yet spanned a century. But neither had as yet reached a condition of immobility. Thus in the decade following 1870 we find the metric system being improved for scientific purposes through the concerted efforts of an international group of scientists. New definitions were set for the meter, kilogram, and liter, and smaller units were added to the original plan. It was in this period that the meter changed its status from a French measure to an international one.

From that same period of time modernizing changes began to be applied to the common units, most of the modifications being along the line of decimal-fraction handling of the foot, inch, and pound. Thus the new engineer's chain, supplanting Gunter's chain for surveying and land measurement, was 100 feet long, with the foot divided decimally. Before the turn of the century the micrometer, a device that could be used to measure the parts of a machine to the hundredth or even thousandth of an inch, had been added to the mechanic's list of indispensable tools.

The shift to decimal dimensioning has been largest in the metal trades. In this connection we have the report of S. B. Elrod, of Purdue University, at the 1948 meeting of the American Society for Engineering Education:

Fractional dimensions are giving way to decimal dimensions. The two place decimal system inaugurated by the late Carl E. Johanssen, in the Ford Motor Company plants, has gained ground rapidly and is used by most of the automotive industry and over 80 percent of the aircraft industry. The system has the advantages of the metric system without requiring a re-educational and re-tooling program. Surveys conducted periodically show the shift to decimal dimensions continues steadily.

With us another movement has also been under way that is directly related to the idea of modernization. By the turn of the century, or shortly after, many devices had been perfected that could measure or weigh in an automatic and highly accurate manner, the results being reported to decimal-fraction parts of the unit used. There were odometers to measure the length of trips, chronometers to read time intervals, and vending machines to report on gasoline supplied and its cost. All were practical, all were illustrative of the ease with which decimally divided units can be handled in measurement and in calculation.

But something more than decimal dimensioning and mechanical devices is needed to give a real modernization to the common plan. As in the metric system, well-named large and small units are needed within the framework of the decimalized main measures of length and weight. Strangely enough, the know-how needed to design a machine that automatically measures liquids to thousandths of a pint, determines to the nearest pound the weight of a load of coal, or carries out the thousand and one things demanded of weighing and measuring devices does not include the know-how for the production of a modernized plan built about the common units. Nor have the engineering schools or industry itself presented a program that might effect such a plan, though each has made some contribution to the emerging pattern of modernization. Considering the present status of our capacity measures and the difference in such measures as used in this country from those of other English-speaking countries, it may be considered surprising that the more thoughtful representatives of engineering and industry have given but nominal approval to the proposed substitution of the "pound-pint," or volume of a pound of water, for all other pints. By replacing our present wine pint and grain pint with such a pound-pint, and fitting it into the framework of the imperial gallon and British bushel, we could achieve a capacity plan having both logic and practicality. With such a plan we may envision a day when the kilopint and millipint of the English-speaking world would become the useful measures that the kiloliter and milliliter are for the metric countries.

The Possibility of World Unity in the Matter of Measures and Weights

Even a well-modernized treatment of the common units cannot be expected to result in a plan that would equal that of the metric system. As a younger system, the metric units had a greater over-all simplicity of relationships. The weight standards were more accurately constructed. Each main unit was the center of a decimalized arrangement of both large and small secondary units, for which a simple and consistent naming plan had been developed. These things made it the best that the human mind could conceive and the human hand construct.

In 1866, by act of Congress, the use of metric units was legally sanctioned in this country. This meant that a duality of measures would, after that date, be permitted. And it was freely predicted that the meter, liter, hectare, and kilogram would soon supplant, in a competitive way, the foot, pint, acre, and pound of the older system. This prediction was based upon two premises: the appeal that an international system of measures and weights might be expected to have for the liberal-minded thinkers of America, and the practical advantages of the metric system itself.

The results were highly disappointing. America was definitely not international-minded. And the practical advantages were considered nebulous by a people whose life activities had been geared to the common units. Thus the farm population could see no advantage in the use of the hectare and kilometer over the acre and the mile that would justify the effort involved in making the change. Within the home a somewhat similar condition existed. Such craftsman units as the yard and foot had been built about the height, the arm-stretch, and the stride of men. And the American home, reflecting the life of the people who lived there, had used these units for the sizes of rugs, the heights of ceilings, and the dimensions of furniture and other equipment. It was quite understandable, then, that the housewife would discover no advantage in substituting the unfamiliar and awkwardly long meter for the homely, useful units about which her home and its life had been developed. Likewise in the shop the American worker discovered no advantage in the centimeter over the inch, as a small unit of length, that would justify the redesigning of the machinery in the shop to give whole-number dimensions in centimeters or millimeters for such things as bolts, steel thickness, gears, and shafting.

None of the population groups that we

have mentioned—the farm people, the housewives, and the workers in the shops—had considered the metric system as a whole. Each group condemned the new system as impractical because it failed to offer advantages in some limited field. There is a reverse side to the picture. Gains have been made for metric units in such special areas as the scientific laboratory, where the handling of small lengths, volumes, and weights is almost universally done in such units. Even operational plants that handle raw materials by the ton or gallon may have a laboratory equipped only with metrically calibrated apparatus. In the field of machinery manufacture, the producer of scientific equipment normally makes products fitting whole-number metric dimensions. Those producing general equipment intended for metric countries may follow the same policy. But for the vast majority of the factories which, in this country, are producing tools and machine products for the American public only common-unit dimensioning will be used. To do otherwise would lose a hundred customers for one that might be gained. And the same general idea extends to all the major fields of human endeavor in the United States.

For many of us it is with reluctance that we acknowledge that our dream of world uniformity in weights and measures is, after all, but a dream. To be sure, England, centuries ago, shifted from the agrarian measures of the Saxons to the industrial measures of the craftsmen, and did it without devastating effects. But the units of the old plan and the new were fully commensurate, no property lines were affected, and the industrial workers were convinced of the need for the change. Any attempt to install the metric system in present-day America, supplanting the common units in a legal way, would be favored by none of the factors that supported the change to craftsman units. We may, of course, point out that France made such a shift and emerged successfully. But our present situation does not parallel that of France toward the close of the eighteenth century. Previous to the adoption of the metric plan that country was without any unified, national system. Several length standards were in use, each supreme in its own area. The weight units, though quite uniform throughout France, needed drastic redesigning. They represented the thousand-year-old coinage weights of Charlemagne, for which some worn coins of old Byzantium had been the model. For this peculiar combination of measurement ills the introduction of metric values could have the desirable effect of a compromise plan, not far out of line with old measures, yet capable of sweeping away all the old outmoded or conflicting standards. A somewhat similar set of conditions was present at the time of the establishment of the German Empire in 1871. The somewhat variant measure and weight standards of the numerous kingdoms, principalities, and duchies that were combined in empire formation were brushed aside, the meter and kilogram, as compromise units, taking their place.

For the system of common units found in this country and other English-speaking nations there is present no mixture of rival measures that would call for eradication, no desperate need of a compromise proposal whose forceful adoption could bring order to a chaotic situation. No parallel to a France or a Germany exists.

In an indirect way the adoption of the metric system by continental Europe was to improve the situation for those countries which, like our own, use the foot, the

acre, and the pound. By eliminating the older measures of that continent that went by the name of foot and acre and pound, the widespread metric adoption left the world with but one foot and one meter, one acre and one hectare, one pound and one kilogram.

Thus we conclude our report on the origin and development of the English and metric systems. With such a background we should be able to make some rather reliable predictions as to the future.

The history of the past would seem to justify with certainty the following aspect of the future. These two systems—English and metric—that today dominate so completely the industrial world will continue, side by side, as the giants of the world of tomorrow. Neither has been able to absorb the other—a situation that will not change in any foreseeable future.

On a second point there would seem to be equal certainty. The common system is still in the process of change, with the future offering ample opportunity for further modernization.

Economics

Economics

Introduction to Economics

Concepts:

Scarcity
Scarcity, Competitive Behavior, and Economics, Alchian and Allen

Exchange
The Economic Organization of a P.O.W. Camp, R. A. Radford

Poverty
The Merchant and the Low-Income Consumer: The Poor Pay More, David Caplovitz

Capitalism
Litton Industries: Big Brother as a Holding Company, David Horowitz and Reese Erlich

Property
Pollution, Property and Prices, J. H. Dale

Socialism
Ujamaa—The Basis of African Socialism, Julius Nyerere

The Corporate State
The Greening of America, Charles Reich

Introduction to Economics

Economics can be defined as the study of how people organize themselves for the purpose of collectively utilizing the earth's resources to meet human needs. In this sense, economics is closely related to political science, which often determines who gets what, when, how.

Economics is also a difficult discipline to define simply because it encompasses many fields and overlaps with many other specialties. For instance, one of the domains of economics—using the earth's resources to satisfy man's material wants—is also considered to be the domain of agriculture, engineering and business. However, economics, unlike these other fields, is less concerned with the *technical* aspects of problems and more concerned with providing analyses and alternatives for output, allocation and resources.

Economics deals fundamentally with questions of **social organization**. It proceeds from three assumptions: (1) that mankind has an endless number of wants, (2) that the total resources available to the society are insufficient to satisfy these wants, and (3) that the scale of preferences for these wants is not identical for every individual.

Economics and Power

Economics can be more specifically defined then as the organization of a system which will utilize the available resources in a fashion which will maximally satisfy the human wants of the members of the **society** in accordance with some prescribed priority ranking—how the total production or **GNP (Gross National Product)** is to be structured and how it is to be distributed. Strictly speaking, this determination of the structure or composition of the **GNP**, as well as the determination of how it is to be distributed, falls within the provinces of both economics and political science. The setting of priorities is intimately tied to the question of power and to politics. The **group** which has superior power will inevitably see to it that **society** is organized in such a way that the largest possible share of the available resources will be allocated to it. For instance, in a slave-holding **society**, the slaves, because they are powerless, are permitted only enough goods and leisure time to enable them to survive and reproduce themselves. The free individuals in such a **society** reserve for themselves both the bulk of the production and the bulk of the leisure (i.e., they contribute proportionately less to the productive process while consuming proportionately more).

In most societies, power groups are more rationalized than in slave-holding societies. Blood (i.e., royalty), superstition, religion, wisdom, and property are examples of bases other than naked power which at various times and places have served to rationalize the emergence of privileged classes. Closer inspection of each of these bases, however, is likely to reveal that the favored group achieved its position of privilege as a direct result of the power which it could wield over the rest of the society. Thus, power seems to be the ultimate arbiter of the allocation of resources.

In Europe, where the term "political economy" has been far more common than the narrower term "economics," it is generally felt that the study of how society allocates its resources must inescapably involve a study of the power relationships in that society. To study resource allocation in isolation from power relationships, as has been the traditional practice in America, is considered by Europeans—and by a growing number of Americans—to be a sterile exercise at best. It certainly seems to be one which can have neither predictive nor policy value.

Concepts and Ideologies

The readings chosen to illustrate economic concepts in this section have political as well as economic aspects. The list of concepts selected is neither exhaustive nor homogeneous. For instance, some of the major subfields of economics, such as international trade and finance, labor and collective bargaining, production theory, public finance, banking, economic growth and stability have been omitted due to lack of space. The diverse nature of the topics chosen is illustrated by the fact that some of the concepts are physical, such as scarcity; some are operational, such as exchange; and some are systemic, such as socialism. The reading on the military-industrial complex and on the ghetto marketplace describe in specific detail the day-to-day operation of two vastly important and contrasting segments of the giant U.S. economy. Viewed collectively, however, the readings should provide the student with some sense of the conceptual foundations and social innovations upon which the discipline of economics has been built. At the same time the readings should focus the student's attention on some of the problem areas in the contemporary national economy.

Because we are living in an era of bitter contention between two differing economic ideologies—the private enterprise, or capitalist system versus some form of socialist organization—almost any in-depth discussion of economics can easily become enmeshed in ideological crossfire. This Introduction will, however, include a brief comparison of capitalism and socialism. Since the focus of the material is on the American economy, capitalist production and distribution practices, rather than socialist ones, are focal points for most of the readings. To balance off this bias in favor of the free enterprise approach to socioeconomic organization and also because the editor felt it to be important for American students to have at least a passing familiarity with the thinking behind the other major form of socio-economic organization prevalent in the modern world, a brief article on socialism was included. An article on African socialism, rather than a classical Marxist statement or a report on the Soviet or Chinese economies, was chosen as an interesting example of an alternative way for people to organize their society.

SCARCITY

The concept of scarcity is fundamental to economics because the resources which are available to satisfy people's wants are clearly limited. We shall be concerned with *how* limited in our discussion of pollution. These resources generally fall into three categories: land, labor, and capital.[1] According to this taxonomy, land includes all non-human items of value, in their natural state; labor refers to the human potential for performing work (physical or mental); and capital refers to natural resources which have been transformed from their natural state to a more useable form by the application of labor to them. More recently, the term "capital" has included the human factor when it has undergone transformation from its natural state. People who have received education, training, or skills are coming to be viewed as embodying a capital component within themselves as well as a pure labor component. The term human capital has become fashionable in describing this condition. It can refer to the years of training which distinguish the surgeon from the day laborer, but it can also refer to the distinction between the semi-skilled and the unskilled worker.

Since the supply of resources is limited, the economist must determine whose wants and what wants are to be satisfied, in what order, and what items are to be produced; in what quantity they are to be produced; and who is going to get them. The first two questions are generally termed the problems of *production*; the third question is called the problem of *distribution*. Several closely-related problems to production and distribution are efficiency of the use of resources, and a concern for the exhaustibility of their supply in relationship to the needs of future generations.[2] The search for the best way to deal with these problems, and their ramifications, constitutes the core matter of economics.

---

[1] Adam Smith, *The Wealth of Nations*, London, 1776.

[2] The student is probably well aware of the first and third of these problem areas, under the popular labels of "full employment" and "ecology/conservation." The second problem area, efficiency, may be less familiar to him. Efficiency, to the economist, means the achievement of a desired end with the minimum utilization of society's scarce resources. In simple terms this usually means producing goods and services in the cheapest possible manner. The determination of "cheapest," however, is not always easy because the proper frame of reference is the entire society, not merely the entity which is engaged in the production operation. See the readings on Pollution Rights for further elaboration of the problems of measuring and allocating costs.

The reading by Alchian and Allen shows how the concept of **scarcity** pervades all economic analysis. It also illustrates some of the ways which people have chosen to deal with the problem of allocating limited resources among competitive demands. At this level, the economic problem is clearly one of the most familiar of all human problems—one which every student encounters when he attempts to budget his inadequate funds.

Although beginning students often "tune out" or skip over graphs, tables and charts which are introduced to assist him, apparently in disbelief of the saying that "a picture is worth a thousand words," for better or for worse Alchian and Allen's essay employs graphic material. The **production possibility curve**, which they introduce at the beginning of their essay, is an indispensable device for illustrating the concept of **scarcity** and the related topics of choice and **competition**. Using "guns and butter" as symbolic representations of war-related and peace-related goods which a **society** can utilize its resources to produce, the **production possibility curve** defines the maximum production boundary which lies within the productive capabilities of the economy in question. In this theoretical abstraction, a peaceful nation would produce butter and no guns and a war-loving nation would produce the opposite. Most nations would fall somewhere between these extremes, and the possible trade-offs as one sacrifices butter to produce guns traces out the **production possibility curve**.

This trade-off between two objectives competing for the same resources also provides the basis for the economist's conception of **cost**. Whereas the layman tends to calculate the **cost** of an item in terms of dollars-and-cents, the economist recognizes that money is merely a tool introduced to aid us in comparing the real goods and services which the **society** produces. It is not the sheckels of the affluent which can feed and clothe the poor; for this noble purpose, food and clothing are necessary. So the economist often ignores the "dollar cost" of an item and seeks to go behind the dollar figure to discover the *real* **cost** of producing a good. This real **cost** he measures in terms of another good whose production one must forego in order to produce the item in question. Thus, in terms of the guns vs. butter example, the real **cost** (sometimes called the **opportunity cost**) of producing guns may usefully be viewed as the amount of butter which the economy must forego in order to produce guns. In understanding this principle, it is often helpful to envision the **cost** of building a $10 million bomber plane as the equivalent of a 400 bed hospital, or of five moderately-sized elementary schools, which the economy would have to forego building in order to release resources to build the plane.

Economists, then, have very special ways of looking at everyday matters, and this sometimes makes for confusion in **communication**. In the selection on **scarcity**, for example, Alchian and Allen introduce the idea of **competition** by using the example of the production of two goods, guns and butter, which are in **competition** with each other for the economy's scarce factors of production. But the authors quickly shift their discussion to another, and equally important, manifestation of **competition**—that of **competition** between individuals, and subsequently between **groups** of individuals. The underlying concepts of **scarcity** and **competition** are identical, of course, in the three types of manifestations.

It is also interesting to note here that violence is one form of **competition** for scarce resources. The same form of behavior, here the matter of violence of behavior, may be regarded as appropriate and at other times it may be classified as **deviant**. Individuals who practice it may be regarded as psychopaths or in other ways as emotionally disturbed. Both the concepts of **deviance** and **psychopathology** have been considered earlier in this book—the former in the section on sociology and the latter in the section on psychology.

EXCHANGE

The practice of trading seems to be universal to all people. Some of the earliest known records of civilization show that people bartered with their neighbors. A characteristic of primitive societies is that the **family** unit is frequently self-sufficient, each **family** hunting or raising its own food, building its own shelter, and providing its own clothing. However, **specialization** develops with civilization and specific individuals, **families**, or **groups** gradually emerge as the suppliers of certain products or services for the entire **community**. This **specialization** makes trading necessary. The farmer exchanges his surplus food to the shoemaker for shoes, to the doctor (or medicine man) for health care, to the carriage-maker for a wagon. Eventually the act of trading itself becomes a specialty, and merchants of various sorts begin to appear. A class of individuals arises who produce no tangible product but who earn their living exclusively from buying and selling the output of others.

The form of **exchange** in a particular country is found to be congruent with the **social structure** of that country and with the various **beliefs** and **practices** of individuals living in a particular **community**. Indeed, trading in itself is one of the **practices** that anthropologists have spent considerable time trying to study and to understand.

Money facilitates this process of trading, thereby relieving both buyer and seller of the need to have to search for someone who not only has what they want but who also wants what they have. By trading goods for some convenient, widely-acceptable **commodity** of limited availability but of wide desirability the act of buying is separated from the act of selling. Indeed, it is fair to state that the complex industrial society which we know today would have been impossible without the use of money. Non-monetary **societies** may still survive in a few isolated enclaves of New Guinea or Brazil, and there are certainly rural areas within many countries where **families** are virtually self-sufficient or trade primarily on a barter basis. Such places are, however, fast disappearing as their inhabitants get glimpses of the outside world and begin to want products which they cannot produce.

As the **society** becomes ever more sophisticated, the nature of the monetary unit becomes more abstract. The need for a monetary unit with an intrinsic value (e.g., gold) succumbs, first to the use of mere pieces of paper (bank notes); these initially may be promises of a government or of a bank to redeem them for a substance of intrinsic value. Later the monetary unit becomes a promise of a bank to provide paper money or credit (checking accounts). Most recently the checking account, which is in large part merely a contractual agreement to shift bookkeeping credits among various customers, is giving way to the credit card which is an even more ephemeral method of shuttling numbers among offices to facilitate the trading process.

Although the use of money greatly facilitates the operation of an economy, it is not an unmixed blessing. Once introduced, money, far from remaining a passive aid to the **exchange** process, quickly assumes a life of its own and begins to exert a direct influence on the economy's operation. If a substance of intrinsic value, such as gold, is used for money, then prices of goods will be affected not only by the relative intensity with which various goods are desired but also by the **value** which is currently placed on gold as a **commodity** and the extent to which gold is scarce or plentiful (i.e., on the demand for and supply of gold.) If paper money is used, the price level of goods is going to be heavily affected by the amount of such money which is issued, with higher prices being associated with a larger volume of money and lower prices with a smaller volume. Governments generally reserve for themselves the exclusive authority to issue money, so the government's monetary policy inescapably exerts a considerable influence over the price level, and ultimately over the stability of the economy. The implications of this power are especially vivid if one reflects on the possibility which the government has, through its control of the money supply, to buy whatever it wishes merely by printing new money rather than by commandeering, via taxation, existing money from the pockets of its citizens. This highly tempting route to public expenditures can quickly lead to rapidly rising prices, known as **inflation**, and to serious strains in the total society. To the extent that the banking system has the power to issue credit, it too can stimulate or depress the economy by the looseness or tightness of its credit policies. The entire area of money and banking is a fascinating and vital aspect of the study of economics.

The selection on *The Economic Organization of a POW Camp* by R. A. Radford effectively capsulizes the development and operation of a typical market (**exchange**) economy. One can actually observe the process of **exchange** developing from its primitive beginning into a sophisticated market **society** using money, credit, and advertising, and even exhibiting such market pathologies as **inflation, deflation** and the institution of price controls. The operation of the miniature market economy of a single prison camp dramatically illustrates interrelationships between the concepts of **scarcity, exchange,** and **value. Value** in this situation clearly refers to the intensity with which a good is demanded, as reflected in the amount of some other good which a buyer is willing to give up to obtain the good in question. This is much like **cost**, which is really a way of *measuring value*.

It is important to note here that systems of **exchange** work only if there are substantial agreements between the parties involved regarding what constitutes right and proper modes of conduct. In the process of **exchange** the **norms** that the individuals who are buyers and sellers hold become critical for the successful conduct of economic transactions.

Another important aspect of any exchange relationship is the **value** placed upon what the buyers and sellers or the traders place on different goods and **commodities**. The article on the economic organization of a POW camp illustrates this point. In this camp, various types of food had different **values** and these changed as either they became more abundant or more scarce. For example, the price of margarine in a POW camp increased when the packages of Canadian butter decreased. Oftentimes changes in resource levels led to differences in the way things were valued and to changes in **beliefs** and behaviors.

Supply and Demand

The operation of the market mechanism provides the basic underpinning to a capitalist, or market, economy and the principles which underlie it are probably not unrelated to the operation of a planned, non-market economy. The father of modern economics, the Scotch philosopher Adam Smith, set out the basic outline of the market mechanism in his classic work, *The Wealth of Nations* (1776) and it has been refined by a number of later writers, most notably the 19th century British economist Alfred Marshall.

The capitalistic market system works on the principle of supply and demand. Each buyer helps to determine the demand for the good, and is interested in purchasing the good for the lowest expenditure of money. Each seller helps to determine the supply and is interested in obtaining the highest possible price for his goods. From the haggling of these two conflicting interests a mutually satisfactory price is determined and a sale can then be consummated, objectively and with maximum efficiency.

The impersonal efficiency with which the market allocates goods and resources is, however, the subject of some severe criticism. Critics of the market system argue that the **market** is impersonal only among persons who have sufficient funds to be "in the market," but that the **market** ignores those whose income is so low that they cannot even enter the **market** in any effective way. The bidding in the **market** may register an effective demand for thousands of summer homes for the wealthy while it indicates no effective demand for inexpensive housing (at prices which will attract such housing to be built). Those who need shelter are often too poor to bid the resources (bricks, glass, carpenters, architects, etc.) away from the more lucrative "summer home" industry. Whether in fact this result can better be attributed to the operation of the market or to the inequity in the distribution of income is currently a matter of some debate within the economics profession.

POVERTY

Another serious criticism of the "market" system, at least in a modern industrial society, is that the seller is usually in a considerably stronger bargaining position than the buyer. This gives the seller an unfair advantage in the marketplace.

David Caplovitz' reading on *The Merchant and the Low-Income Consumer* describes one type of market reality in American society. It contrasts rather sharply not only with the idealistic theoretical market of Adam Smith and Alfred Marshall but also with the POW camp market and with the general market situation in less disadvantaged communities of the U.S.

The "ideal" market assumes perfect knowledge on the part of both buyer and seller regarding the quality and availability of the goods being bargained for. It assumes knowledge regarding the availability of similar or substitute goods and all aspects of conditions surrounding the transaction (credit, delivery, warranties, etc.) It also assumes relative equality in bargaining strength between the two parties. In Caplovitz' world these conditions are not realized with the result that the market proves to be far from objective or efficient, and works continually to the disadvantage of the poor, who have no mobility and are not therefore able to "shop around."

The ramifications of poverty are many. Poverty is related to concepts in sociology, psychology and political science. Poverty is related to justice, a concept that will be discussed in the section on political science, in that the poor clearly are manipulated and cheated in their negotiations as buyers.

Poverty is also related to the concept of race. It is unnecessary of course to point out that discriminatory practices that have existed and persist in the United States have continued to keep many Black people in poverty. The economic consequences of this discrimination lead in many cases to the poor, that is, Blacks, paying more.

Poverty and its consequences are related also to the concept of social disorganization. In this sense the concept means that poor people, by the very way in which society is structured, necessarily live together in areas where problems of crime, drunkenness and the general malaise of the environment reduce the likelihood of merchants settling or remaining. Thus, competition invariably is reduced among sellers. Those merchants who do remain are likely to be themselves disreputable and perfectly comfortable in conning and cheating the family on welfare or the family living in poverty or at the margins of poverty. These unfair consumer practices to which the poor are exposed are symptomatic of social disorganization.

Poverty is also related to the psychology concept of emotion. The roots of emotions are many. Individuals differ in their biophysical makeups. Of course, their outlooks are greatly determined by the **socialization** process with which their lives are intertwined. This **socialization** process is determined, to a considerable extent, by the economic **status** of individuals and their **families**. Economic deprivation has its consequences in the feelings of insecurity throughout childhood and adolescence; in terms of diet; in the deprivation of physical things; in the differences that result in social interaction; and in the ability to participate in social events; in the discriminatory allocation of resources for schools and other public goods; and so on. Thus, **poverty** has severe consequences on the emotional as well as the physical constitutions of individuals.

CAPITALISM

Whereas the article by Caplovitz illustrates the inequities of the marketplace from the perspective of the poor and ill-informed ghetto-based consumer, the article by Horowitz and Erlich, *Litton Industries: Big Brother as a Holding Company* describes the operation of the **market** from the perspective of one of the giants of American industry. The United States has had a history of excessive concentration of industry in the hands of a single or a very few firms. These "**trusts**" which sprang up after the Civil War led to the passage of the Sherman Anti-Trust Act (1890) and to the colorful "**trust** busting" activities of President Theodore Roosevelt. Their malpractices provided some of the earlier publicized manifestations of inequity in the American marketplace. The attempt to create a free and competitive market system through legislation also proved unsuccessful. 80 years after the passage of the Sherman Anit-Trust Act we still find greater concentration in more industries than before the Act was passed. There are many factors now operating to make it more rather than less difficult to maintain a competitive situation on the supply side of the **market**. These are: the greater scale on which industry now operates; the tremendous investment required in plant and equipment; and the widespread use of advertising, especially on such expensive mass media as television.

This trend toward concentration has gone through three distinct stages. "**Trusts**" were the products of "horizontal combination"—of the actions of several firms in the same industry, e.g., steel industries collaborating together to rig prices or otherwise cheat the consumer, or of a giant firm buying out (or forcing out) its competitors so that it could enjoy a **monopoly**. The next era saw a period of "vertical combination," where a firm bought out the previous stage of production (such as a steel mill purchasing its own iron mines) or a later stage of production (such as a steel mill purchasing a metal furniture company which could use its steel). Today we find ourselves in the third era of industrial concentration—the "**conglomerate**"—where a firm grows by taking over other firms in unrelated industries in octopus-like fashion.

The violence which the giant **conglomerate** does to the idealized concept of a free, competitive **market** is self-evident. After World War II, the government itself entered the market as the underwriter of a number of our giant corporations. Government contracts (usually military procurement of one sort or another) to favored corporations has had devastating effects on the free competitive market. Really, the government and the corporate giants have allied themselves together in open opposition to the competitive market concept which underlies the free capitalistic model. Increasingly, a form of state capitalism is becoming the order of the day, under the title of the "military-industrial complex."

Capitalism is more than a particular style or posture regarding the production and consumption of resources in society. It determines, and is responsive to, a particular ranking of what is important. The term social stratification was introduced as a concept in the sociology section. There a relatively microscopic example was employed, namely the evaluation of dating on a college campus. However, the politico-economic system of the country in many ways influences the criteria that one holds important. In peoples' experience all societies have had a social stratification system. In our society the acceptability of the style of economic life identified by Litton Industries clearly makes money and the sheer accumulation of wealth a critical if not the critical criterion for one's status in the community. Capitalism is not only expressed at a macroscopic level in terms of size and tactics within the business world but it is reflected on a microscopic level in the rankings that exist among people.

PROPERTY

The right of American citizens to own unlimited amounts of all types of goods, including land, natural resources, and the physical means of production (including, until 1863, even human beings), and to have this property protected by law, remains a cornerstone of American capitalism, differentiating our society from the various forms of socialism which currently flourish in the world.

Nevertheless, despite the general acceptance in America of the concept of private ownership of the nation's goods and resources, air and a portion of the nation's terrain and water supplies have traditionally been excluded from private ownership. For example, our highways, city streets, and public parks fall into the category termed "public goods"; they are owned by no one and by everyone. Their maintenance is usually borne from tax revenues.

However, limitations on the free use of public goods have been necessary, such as restrictions on the actions of individuals to maximize the usefulness of the public resources for the entire community. For instance, parking meters along the curbs of a busy thoroughfare maximize the usefulness of a scarce public good—curb parking space—by spreading it among a number of people.

Thus, the practice of regulating as well as of charging for the use of public goods is an established tradition. In recent years, however, the increasingly visible deterioration of the living environment in the more industrialized areas of the world has created a surge of interest in the whole topic of public goods and the way in which such goods are being used. Indeed, at the very heart of the environmental or ecological crisis lies this basic question: To what extent does Mr. A. have a right to utilize a public good in a way that diminishes Mr. B's ability to enjoy the same good? This question is also closely tied to the concept of **scarcity** which, as we have seen, is concerned with the fact that the resources of people are clearly limited.

This question is by no means new. Economists have long recognized its existence (although they have usually treated it as merely an interesting theoretical excursion, called "externalities," rather than as a major topic of study). The real world has gone blithely on with little appreciation of its profound implications until a series of ecological disasters occurred in the late sixties with such rapidity that the "environmental crisis" suddenly emerged as a major issue. After some people had actually died from polluted air during temperature inversions in London and New York; after the despoliation of beaches in California and New England by oil spills; after repeated scares of possible mercury poisoning from eating fish caught in polluted streams; after four of the five Great Lakes were declared to be seriously polluted; after the Cuyahoga River in the Cleveland area had actually caught fire because of the pollutants which it contained did the American public begin to challenge the right of industry to destroy the nation's irreplaceable natural resources and to poison and kill innocent people in the pursuit of profit maximization. The realization began to take shape in the public mind that the disposal of industrial wastes was properly a **cost** of doing business, like a firm's other **costs**, and that it was not fair to charge the public for these **costs** in the form of higher medical expenses, higher cleaning bills, impaired health, less accessible recreation sites, and other direct and indirect charges.

Good **cost accounting**, as well as economic efficiency and proper pricing, would all require that any meaningful computation of the **cost** of producing an item must necessarily include *all* inputs, or **costs** of production. This would include such indirect **costs** as the payment necessary to restore the environment to its condition prior to the beginning of the production cycle. Succinctly put, an attitude has begun to emerge which says that industry should either be prohibited from polluting or else be made to pay for its transgressions. The article on *Pollution, Property and Prices* represents an attempt to devise a means for measuring and levying such charges. Our **society** is only in its infancy in explaining how this can be done.

SOCIALISM

The only significant operating alternative to the capitalist model to which we can turn is **socialism**. **Socialism** is in operation in various forms in countries such as the Soviet Union and much of Eastern Europe, in Cuba, China,

North Korea, North Vietnam, Burma, Tanzania, Guinea, and perhaps a few other nations. In some places it may be called **communism**. In reality there are no countries which claim to have communist economic systems at this time. For most communist countries **socialism** is viewed as merely a stage in their **evolution** toward a system of pure **communism**, although it is the stage in which the so-called communist countries all find themselves today.

A brief comparison of **capitalism** and **socialism** reveals that under **capitalism** the means of production are privately owned and under **socialism** the non-human factors (**land** and **capital**) are owned collectively (usually this means owned by the state). Under **capitalism** the motive or incentive for production is profit; under **socialism** the motive for production is use (this merely means that priority is given to the producing of objects which the public needs rather than to those items for which the public is most willing to pay.) Under **capitalism** the **national income** is divided on the basis of bidding in the marketplace using money earned from work or from property income; under **socialism** a significant hunk of the pie is shared equally among all the citizens on the basis of need, although the largest piece of the **national income** continues to be allocated on an individual market-type basis which differs only slightly from a capitalist economy. (Under **communism**, money would become largely unnecessary because the national income would be freely available to all on the basis of need.)

However, perhaps the principal difference between the two systems lies in the differing attitude toward life upon which **socialism** and **capitalism** are predicated. The capitalist ethic is one of individualism and self-advancement, with little or no care taken for the well-being of one's fellowman. The socialist ethic, however, is one of **collectivism**, of subservience of the individual good to the good of the total **community**. The essay by Julius Nyerere, the President of Tanzania, eloquently captures this ethical **attitude** which underlies the true socialist philosophy, wherever it may be found.

The article on African **socialism** is also a valuable illustration of the concept of **cultural relativity**. Julius Nyerere provides us with an understanding of the meaning of **socialism** within the context of an African nation and within the **norms**, **beliefs** and **practices** that structure that type of **society**. His plea is that the economic system of his country be viewed in relation to the **social structure** and **values** of Tanzania. He is elaborating the same point as the article *Shakespeare in the Bush*—the illustration of **cultural relativity** in the anthropology section—that not all peoples would attach the same meaning to the same set of actions and behaviors.

THE CORPORATE STATE

The affluence which American **capitalism** has produced in many ways has not proved to be the ultimate accomplishment or the harbinger of happiness which an earlier **generation** of social theorists might have projected. As America entered the 1970's her economy was rapidly approaching the trillion dollar mark. The income of the average American was more than twice that of most other industrialized nations, and several times as great as the world average. Americans had more cars (and more auto accidents), more refrigerators, more children in school, and consumed (and wasted) more food than any people in recorded history. The transport of **humans** to the surface of the moon and back was merely the most spectacular of a series of post World War II American technological achievements.

Even as the world's wealthiest, most technologically advanced, and most powerful nation rode on the crest of its glory, internal murmurs of disaffection and dissatisfaction with the structure of American **society** were swiftly expanding into distinctly audible rumblings and in some cases into fatally destructive explosions. The Viet Nam war forced millions of Americans to take an honest look at the nature of their **society**. A nucleus of the American people, largely consisting of middle-class college students and their young teachers, began raising probing questions about the structure, operation, and **values** of their **society**. They looked askance at the maldistribution of income and wealth—at the **poverty** which persisted among unprecedented wealth. They decried the lack of human warmth and compassion in the impersonal attitude of the giant corporation, of the welfare state, of the split-level suburb, and of the mass production assembly line. They noted with horror the despoliation of the national ecology as the upper-middle class fled from the smog-laden cities to the polluted and eroded countryside. They observed their parents driving themselves at heart-attack pace—for what purpose no one was quite sure. They asked the government why they were being ordered to go to Asia to kill defenseless people who had done them no harm and when the government could provide no answer, they concluded that the imperatives of the system were to blame.

This questioning of the **values** and life style of American **society**, although too new to permit prediction, may prove to be a major factor in shaping American **society** for the balance of the 20th century. Although it is not a phenomenon which is tied uniquely to the economic aspects of American **society**, it seems fair to say that the basis of the disaffection centers more on the economic manifestations of American life than on any other aspect. This argues in favor of the school of thought that the economic structure and relationships in every **society** determine all other relationships in that **society**.

Thus, there is ample indication that American **society** is currently either on the verge or in the midst of an unprecedented refashioning of its **values** and **norms**, a refashioning which will transform the economic structure and institutions as well as the rest of American **society**. Charles Reich's piece from *The Greening of America*, while not telling us exactly where the **society** may be heading, helps us to pinpoint some major pathologies which are demanding **attention**.

In many ways the problems that are being discussed in *The Greening of America* are a consequence of the fact that our **social institutions** are not working well and are not being responsive to the needs and demands of the people, of **society**, and of the pressures from within and without for social and **cultural change**. In many ways when Reich is damning the administration and hierarchy in the United States from the standpoint of sociology and the perspective of the sociologist he is actually being critical of our intra- and inter-institutional arrangements. The administrative and hierarchical arrangements that exist are supported and nurtured because of the acceptability of our **social institutions**. Change is required by **social institutions** as well as by individuals. In these times, the **beliefs** of social scientists focus on the need for institutional change as the potential solution to America's problems. Some social scientists are skeptical whether individual modifications and personal changes will have much of an impact. The comments made about the welfare system in the United States in the next section on political science are an illuminating illustration of the difficulties within contemporary **social institutions**.

SCARCITY

Scarcity, Competitive Behavior, and Economics

ALCHIAN AND ALLEN

Scarcity

Two villains—nature and the rest of us people—dominate your life and prevent you from having all you want. Nature is niggardly: it provides fewer resources than we could use, and much of what is available is made useful only by hard work. As for the rest of us people, the problem stems not from malevolence; your wants and ours simply exceed what is available. Do not suppose that if we were less greedy, more would be within your grasp. For greed impels us to produce more, not only for ourselves, but, miraculously, more for you too—provided that productivity-inducing institutional arrangements exist.

Man wants more than is available and more than there is any prospect of obtaining. Some assert that we *could* satisfy our "needs" if only we were more efficient or worked harder or both. As a former government official has put it: "We have not had enough of anything, because we have not used fully the fantastic productive power which could provide us with enough of everything." "Enough" of *everything*? To satisfy *every* conceivable whim and desire? Of *every* person? It is a frustrating fact that the world is a poor place. Despite religious and philosophical exhortations to abandon natural desires for "more," our wants evidently are boundless: as soon as we have more of this, we want still more of it and also more of that . . . and that . . . and that . . . To say that we always want more is to say that man lives, even in the most affluent societies, in a state of scarcity.

An alternative explanation of man's material dilemma is that we *do* produce "enough" stuff in the aggregate, but—because of selfishness, inept planning, and poor taste—we turn out the wrong things: silly gadgets and cosmetics and over-large and too frequently remodeled automobiles instead of more symphony orchestras, better housing, art museums, and lunar explorations. But this expresses merely a preference for one collection of output *instead of* another basket. Planning would not avoid or vitiate scarcity. Indeed, in the blissful absence of scarcity, there would be no occasion to plan; with non-scarce resources, there would be no necessity to decide if productive services should be shifted between "silly" output and "wholesome" output. (What's in a name? Is it possible that the puritan would label as "silly" a product which the debonair would consider "wholesome"?)

A simple diagram dealing with two commodities, "guns" and "butter," can illustrate some features of scarcity. In Figure 1-1, society could produce a maximum quantity of $0P_1$ of guns if all available resources were directed to that end; alternatively, $0P_2$ of butter could be produced if there is no output of guns; and any combination of the commodities could be produced along line P_1P_2. Society can achieve a production point *on* or *inside* the P_1P_2 boundary line, but it cannot get *outside* that boundary, given its present productive powers and tastes for leisure. (1) A problem to be solved, somehow, by the socioeconomic organization is determining at what *point* to be on that boundary—that is, determining the total output *mix*. Point *A* has more guns; *B*, more butter. Which will be chosen? (2) Will society produce an output combination as large as feasible? Or will it underproduce at a point *inside* the bounded area. Being inside may be the result of two kinds of inefficiency: (a) un-

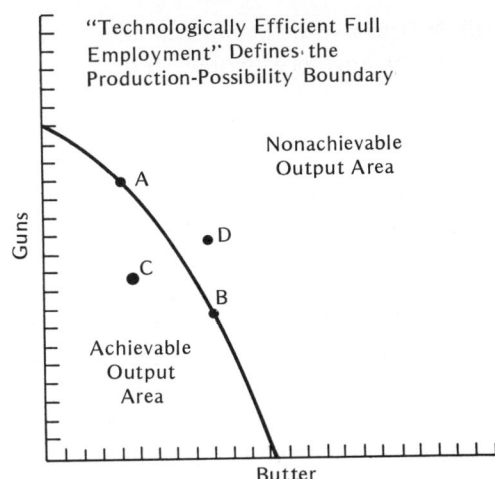

Figure 1-1
Scarcity, Efficiency, and Choice Illustrated by Production-Possibility Boundary

The curved line portrays largest combinations of amounts of guns and butter producible in the economy. Any point on the line (e.g., A or B) can be produced. No combination of guns and butter outside the curved line (e.g., point D) can be achieved by the economy given its productive powers and preference for leisure. Less would be produced if the productive resources were unemployed or used inefficiently—as, for example, indicated by point C. In some manner society selects a point on the boundary or inside it. The closer to full efficiency that the economy operates, the closer, by definition, it is to the production boundary. We shall be studying later the means for determining the output combination and efficiency of production.

necessarily idle, unused resources or (b) misdirected, though fully employed, resources. (3) Growth is indicated in Figure 1-2 by an outward *shift* of the production-possibility boundary. This means society has become richer by acquiring improved technology or by more productive resources or both.

Even more is involved in the problem of scarcity. What determines how much *each* person produces and gets of that total? And what determines the particular *mix* of goods *he* consumes? These and more subtle issues, to be elaborated later, constitute the area of economic study.

Competition

Competition always exists where there is scarcity. With scarcity there is only a choice among limited options, and we compete with each other for those options. Hence, in a society of more than one person, *scarcity implies competition*. There is only one way to avoid competition: according to the renowned practical philosopher, Arnold Palmer, "If you aren't competing, you're dead." And conversely.

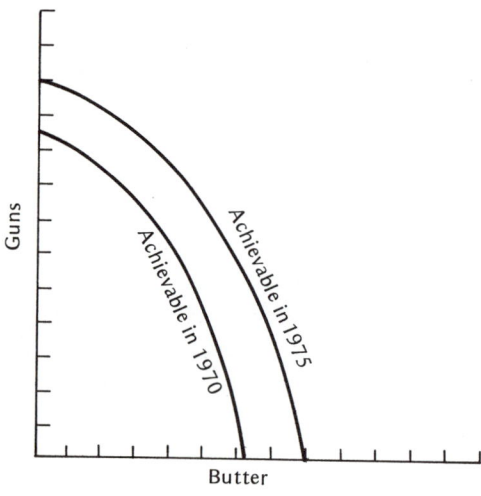

Figure 1-2
Growth of Economic Productive Powers of the Economy

A richer, more productive economy is represented by a production-possibility boundary that is higher and more to the right, as for 1975 compared to 1970. Growth can occur in several ways. A greater production-possibility boundary is usually induced by a larger labor force. (But does the output per person increase? That cannot be indicated by this diagram, which gives only the social totals.) Moving the frontier outward involves restricting consumption by saving either to create more productive goods or to invest in knowledge and inventions. (Problem: Suppose the two boundaries intersected. Which would represent greater productive power?)

You may have heard: "The free-enterprise, private-property system, because it is competitive, promotes antisocial, jungle behavior. It induces cheating, conformity, discrimination, and the dominance of the lowest quality, while discouraging humane behavior toward one's fellow men." But *competition*—whether it does, or necessarily must, yield dire consequences—is not unique to the free-enterprise, private-property system. *Competition exists in every social system.* It is a result of conflicts of interest in a world of scarcity—not of the social, cultural, or economic system within which we live. However, there are many forms of competition. We have some choice, even as individuals, about which form to rely on more heavily. Consider some, though it may seem like thinking of the unthinkable.

VIOLENCE AS A FORM OF COMPETITION

Violence is an important mode of competition—that is, of resolving interpersonal conflicts of interests. Before rejecting violence as a means of competition, observe that it is highly respected and widely practiced—at least when applied successfully on a nationwide scale. When Caesar conquered Egypt, he was praised and honored by the Romans; had he instead roughed up a few people in Rome, he might have been damned as a ruffian and thief. When Alexander conquered the Near East, he was not regarded by the West as a gangster; neither was Charlemagne after he had conquered Europe. The white man acquired America from the native inhabitants by force. Lenin and his successors are not universally regarded in Russia as a line of gangsters. Nor is Franco regarded by all in Spain as merely a successful gangster who seized power by force. Nor Castro in Cuba, nor Nasser in Egypt.

This method is so effective that the application of violence or force is a jealously guarded monopoly of the national government. But we shall see that in certain areas of activity within a nation, violence or force is an accepted method of eliminating competitors—always, of course, for the good of the people as a whole, according to those who use it. Our street demonstrations and riots are sometimes regarded—even by college students—as appropriate forms of competition for access to political power and economic goods.

OFFERS OF EXCHANGE AS A FORM OF COMPETITION

As an alternative to violence, mutual exchange is available as a solution—even though it, too, is sometimes classed as improper. As a matter of fact, a free-enterprise economic system—a system in which the bulk of property is privately owned—is a commonly used basis of competition. But let Adam Smith, the eighteenth-century British economist, comment:

> Man has almost constant occasion for the help of his brethren, and it is in vain for him to expect it from their benevolence only. He will be more likely to prevail if he can interest their self-love in his favor, and show them that it is for their own advantage to do for him what he requires of them. Whoever offers to another a bargain of any kind, proposes to do this: Give me that which I want, and you shall have this which you want, is the meaning of every such offer; and it is in this manner that we obtain from one another the far greater part of those good offices which we stand in need of. It is not from the benevolence of the butcher, the brewer, or the baker, that we expect our dinner, but from their regard to their own interest. We address ourselves not to their humanity but to their self-love.

[We] will investigate this kind of competition in great detail, but [we] will investigate the others, too, with possibly surprising implications.

OTHER TYPES OF COMPETITION

Violence and exchange are only two of an enormous variety of interpersonal competitive techniques. The range of other common techniques can be suggested by a few examples.

Suppose you had to distribute 200 tickets to the Rose Bowl football game without selling them to the highest bidders. What forms of competition would you use in assigning priorities for deciding to whom to award the tickets? That is, what system of rationing or allocation would you use? If the authors could set the rules, we would ask all applicants to send pictures, preferably in bathing suits. (Males need not apply.) We would select the prettiest 300—using our own standards of "prettiness"—and ask them to appear in our offices for interviews. Of these we would then select the most personable 200—using our own standards of "personality."

Certainly this pleasant system is discriminatory. *All* competition is discriminatory. That, indeed, is its purpose: to discriminate among the various claimants in deciding who gets what. Beauty and personality as competitive, discriminatory factors are generally accepted and applied widely every day. Men and women select mates, in part at least, according to beauty and personality. You and I allocate our money to the prettiest women for letting us see them perform in the movies. In fact, it is difficult to find many situations in which beauty is not a source of competitive advantage.

If you think beauty is an improper criterion, you might use the "first come, first served" method. For instance, you could insist that all the applicants run a race and give the tickets to the first 200 to arrive at the finish line. Sounds silly. If you simply replace the words "finish line" by "box office at the Rose Bowl," it is now realistic, but is it less silly? The only difference is that for Rose Bowl tickets there is no uniform starting time or place, so that some people start out a lot earlier and then camp right at the finish line. In any case, economic theory does *not* say that any particular form of competition is silly.

But is it fair? That depends on the circumstances and on what you mean by "fair"—it depends on the kind of competition *you* prefer. If you think "fair" means giving everyone an equal chance, would you want to give everyone an equal chance to operate on you for appendicitis, or to sing for you at a concert, or to teach you, or to be your wife, or to be the person you had to hire in your restaurant—or to whom you give Rose Bowl tickets? An equal chance could be provided by putting everyone's name (even those who did not take the time to apply for a ticket) on cards, then drawing 200 at random. That would be as equal a chance as possible, and nondiscriminatory. But, again, do you want to pick your mate that way? Do you want men selected for the armed forces that way? Obviously, "fair" or "preferred" does not mean "equal chance."

Before we leave this sampling of modes of competition, note a difficulty. After the goods (Rose Bowl tickets in this example) are initially distributed and rationed, what is to stop your selected recipients from handing the tickets on to other people, according to other preferred criteria? What is to prevent the prettiest girls from handing the tickets to the handsomest boys? It is extremely difficult to ensure that one's competitive selective criterion will in fact be the only criterion followed. Of course, he *might* tell all persons to whom he initially gives the tickets that they must go to the game themselves and not re-allocate the tickets in exchange for money or love. How he might enforce that condition, we leave to you.

Competitive Criteria and Survival Traits

Nothing in economic theory suggests that any particular form of competition is "absurd." That evaluation rests on cultural and personal preferences. The first-come, first-served race to the box-office window, if used to parcel out food, would mean that the people best able to camp out or withstand the rigors of waiting in line would have the best prospects of survival and prosperity. In accordance with the classic theory of selective survival of the fittest, that type of person would prevail. And the institution of "camping out" would be characteristic of the economy. Instead, if food were parceled out to the tallest people, with short people getting the least, you can understand why the average height of the population would increase over time. And, alternatively, if beauty were rewarded, the beauty of women would increase—because women would make deliberate, conscious efforts to improve their beauty, and because the more beautiful would be more likely to survive. Or one might propose to allocate goods on the basis of forensics and personality, somewhat as we compete for political office. Under that system, the society would become noted for its articulate and personable people. Or resources could be given to those with the most talent for deception and misrepresentation; the reader can imagine the mores and dominant types that would evolve in that society. Or resources could go mainly to those who are best able to create goods and services. In that kind of society the more productive would be the wealthier and the dominant group.

Scarcity, Productive Activity, and Culture

In the wide gamut of economic problems of every society, there is, then, a pervasive, inescapable, inevitable pair: *scarcity and competition*. That is the starting point of our analysis, and behavioral consequences stemming directly or indirectly from it are our subject matter.

Since the fiasco in the Garden of Eden, most of what we want must be acquired through sweat, strain, and anxiety. Since we cannot have *all* of *everything* we want, we must *choose* how best to use available resources. What things shall we make and in what proportions? Under what institutions and laws? How and with what resources? Who will consume which goods and how much? How much shall we direct from current to future consumption?

These questions leave open the matter of precisely *who* is to make the decisions of what and how much to produce, how the production is to be done, and what goods to allocate to each person. To say simply that "we" do so does not identify who makes those detailed decisions, under what circumstances, and in response to what incentives and penalties. How is the diverse information about every person, his capabilities and preferences, to be collected and coordinated into decisions guiding *each* person? Is it to be done under the direction of an all-powerful economic czar with central planning? Is there any feasible alternative?

Not all systems for organizing production lead to equally efficient or productive results. *Appropriate* specialization in production combined with rational exchange of goods leads to a larger output and wealth than nonspecialization (self-sufficiency) or inappropriate specialization. What are the characteristics of "appropriate" production, or efficient production (as it is called in economic jargon)? What institutional arrangements encourage that kind of productive activity? Kinds of property rights, rights of access to markets and rights to exchange goods and services, kind of money system used—all these are influential.

Whatever type of societal organization is used, what are the kinds of social and cultural behavior it will foster in people? Not many know much about these questions. Even a former President of the United States admitted that he felt unable to evaluate and refute charges that the private-property, open-market exchange (capitalist) system for organizing production and distribution was not only less efficient, but also bred more materialistic, less humanitarian, and inferior cultural traits than did socialism.

Economics, it is apparent, is concerned with fundamental, pervasive issues of society: What goods shall be produced? In what proportions? By whom and in what manner? For whose consumption? How much of current income shall be saved for the future? Who will suffer the losses of bad decisions? And to each of these questions should be appended, "According to *whose* preferences and by *whose* authority?" Finally, what are the social and cultural effects of the ways in which those questions are answered? Economics is a social science—a study of society.

Our Economic Activities

Consider the awesome dimensions of the American community: a population of over 200,000,000 includes a labor force of 80,000,000 (one third of whom are women) and, through 11,000,000 business units (including 9,000,000 single proprietorships, 1,000,000 partnerships, and 1,000,000 corporations), annually produces goods and services worth almost $1,000,000,000,000—some 30 percent of the world total. Who designed and who now directs this vast production-and-distribution machine? In small and intimate matters, willy-nilly individual decision making may be tolerable, but to resolve the vital, over-all, aggregate problems, it seems that someone must be in charge.

But American economic activity is *not* directed, planned, or controlled by any economic czar—governmental or private. No person or group poses detailed questions of how the community is to use its resources, and no one imposes comprehensive answers to the questions. Yet such problems—large and small—somehow *are* solved daily. No particular person has been appointed to ensure that adequate food reaches every city each day and is allocated among competing claimants—and yet the people eat. No "big brother" oversees the multitudinous and infinitely varied operations of the economy and ensures that the essential functions are performed. The alternative to "big brother" evidently is not chaos and anarchy. An economic order does exist; some sort of control and direction does operate. Moreover, this mysterious system allows individuals and businesses to be essentially autonomous—and self-interested—agents (though subject to the constraints that define private property arrangements) and, at the same time, yields a viable and enviable degree of economic efficiency.

The individual, far from wrestling with grandiose problems of the universe, decides how much of his own wealth and income to expend for this or that, what kind of work to do to increase his wealth, and how much of his income to save. No farmer adds up the total demands for food in a city, comparing the total with the amount being shipped to the city, to make sure (because of his compassion) that adequate supplies will be available. Instead, with his individual interest and perspective, he asks, "Would I personally be richer or poorer if I shipped more or less?" No commission resolves issues of the "big picture" of the economy; instead, millions of us make decisions on our own "little pictures."

Although many of us successfully solve our personal problems, we may still be grossly ignorant about how our actions and laws affect the solutions to large problems that every society must solve. Comprehension of these larger problems requires understanding of economic theory, even if virtually no economic theory is required for our individual economic decisions. We can be sure that economic analysis is being ignored when any of the following incorrect assertions are proposed: the rationale of the capitalistic system requires a "harmony of interests"; customers must take what producers offer them; automation reduces available jobs; tariffs protect domestic wage earners from foreign labor; our otherwise unlimited productive capacity is curtailed by monopolistic capitalists who arbitrarily set prices high, unions protect workers from greedy employers; inflation hurts the wage earner and benefits the employer; social-security payments contributed by employers to their employees are paid for by the employers; private firms serve private interests while publicly owned agencies serve public interests; social conscience and civic sensitivity are or should be the main guides to business corporate behavior; unemployment occurs because not enough jobs are available or because some people are too shiftless and lazy; or American agriculture produces a surplus of wheat because it is so productive. And that is only a tiny sample!

Three Attributes of Economic Analysis

To help understand what economics is, three of its methodological attributes should be clarified.

(1) Economic theory is "positive" or "non-normative." It does not give criteria for determining which consequence or type of behavior or economic policy is a good or better one—any more than physics tells whether gases are a "better" state of being than solids, or any more than medicine can tell whether you "ought" not to smoke and drink. Economics can tell only the consequences of certain conditions, policies, or choices. It is scarcely the proper role of the economist to sit on Mt. Olympus and decree what consequence is desirable or preferable to another.

(2) Economics explains what conditions will lead to what consequences. Economics yields conditional "if-A-then-B" propositions; it does not forecast that the A will occur—although some *economists* (as opposed to economics) may hazard such forecasts.

(3) A valid core of economic theory exists and is applicable to *all* economic systems and countries. There is *not* one special economic theory for capitalism and another for communism, although significant differences exist in the institutions and legal frameworks to which the theory is applied. For the present, it is sufficiently accurate to define capitalism as a system of exchangeable, private-property rights in goods and services, with the central government protecting and enforcing these rights. **Private-property rights**, in turn, can be defined as the rights of owners to choose the use of their goods and resources (including labor and time) as they see fit. If a rock is said to be my property and a piece of glass is yours, I have control over only the rock, and you over only the glass; for me to throw my rock through your glass without your permission would violate your rights to use only your property as you see fit. In socialism, at the other extreme, rights to the uses of a good are not assigned to specified individuals but instead are divided among various people in government agencies, who decide about uses and consequences to be borne. This is a system of "government ownership."

Market exchange of property rights is applicable to a wider class of activity in a capitalistic private-property economy than it is in a socialistic society. This does not mean there is no market exchange in the latter; there is, of course, a great deal. However, the extent of and reliance on interpersonal market exchange is greater in a capitalistic system. In a socialist system, on the other hand, political power and exchange of *non*-privately held rights are used much more widely to solve the economic questions. If we were to devote primary attention to socialist systems, we would investigate much more fully political exchange, political decision making, and political competition.

Although applicable to all economic systems, historically economic theory has been more extensively applied to the analysis of capitalistic systems. More recently it has been applied to socialistic institutions.

In sum, economics studies the competitive and cooperative behavior of people in resolving conflicts of interest that arise because wants exceed what is available.

Introductory comments cannot adequately reveal what economics is or the richness of applications of economic theory. Only a study of economics can do that. Free societies and the open markets characterizing them *have* grown and prospered in the face of almost universal illiteracy about economic theory, so there *are* limits to the significance and usefulness of the formal study of economics. But give it a fair try, anyway. Economics does deal with things important on both a private and a social level; and attention to the principles of analysis can provide valuable experience in analyzing problems and utilizing evidence. Unless you fight it assiduously, it may well even be quite interesting.

EXCHANGE

The Economic Organization of a P.O.W. Camp

R. A. RADFORD

Introduction

After allowance has been made for abnormal circumstances, the social institutions, ideas and habits of groups in the outside world are to be found reflected in a Prisoner of War Camp. It is an unusual but a vital society.

One aspect of social organization is to be found in economic activity, and this, along with other manifestations of a group existence, is to be found in any P.O.W. camp. True, a prisoner is not dependent on his exertions for the provision of the necessities, or even the luxuries of life, but through his economic activity, the exchange of goods and services, his standard of material comfort is considerably enhanced. And this is a serious matter to the prisoner: he is not "playing at shops" even though the small scale of the transactions and the simple expression of comfort and wants in terms of cigarettes and jam, razor blades and writing paper, make the urgency of those needs difficult to appreciate, even by an ex-prisoner of some three months' standing.

Nevertheless, it cannot be too strongly emphasized that economic activities do not bulk so large in prison society as they do in the larger world. There can be little production; as has been said the prisoner is independent of his exertions for the provision of the necessities and luxuries of life; the emphasis lies in exchange and the media of exchange.

Everyone receives a roughly equal share of essentials; it is by trade that individual preferences are given expression and comfort increased. All at some time, and most people regularly, make exchanges of one sort or another.

Although a P.O.W. camp provides a living example of a simple economy which might be used as an alternative to the Robinson Crusoe economy beloved by the textbooks, and its simplicity renders the demonstration of certain economic hypotheses both amusing and instructive, it is suggested that the principal significance is sociological. True, there is interest in observing the growth of economic institutions and customs in a brand new society, small and simple enough to prevent detail from obscuring the basic pattern and disequilibrium from obscuring the working of the system. But the essential interest lies in the universality and the spontaneity of this economic life; it came into existence not by conscious imitation but as a response to the immediate needs and circumstances. Any similarity between prison organization and outside organization arises from similar stimuli evoking similar responses.

The following is as brief an account of the essential data as may render the narrative intelligible. The camps of which the writer had experience were Oflags and consequently the economy was not complicated by payments for work by the detaining power. They consisted normally of between 1,200 and 2,500 people, housed in a number of separate but intercommunicating bungalows, one company of 200 or so to a building. Each company formed a group within the main organization and inside the company the room and the messing syndicate, a voluntary and spontaneous group who fed together, formed the constituent units.

Between individuals there was active trading in all **consumer goods** and in some services. Most trading was for food against cigarettes or other foodstuffs, but cigarettes rose from the status of a normal commodity to that of currency. RMk.s existed but had no circulation save for gambling debts, as few articles could be purchased with them from the canteen.

Our supplies consisted of rations provided by the detaining power and (principally) the contents of Red Cross food parcels—tinned milk, jam, butter, biscuits, bully, chocolate, sugar, etc., and cigarettes. So far the supplies to each person were equal and regular. Private parcels of clothing, toilet requisites and cigarettes were also received, and here equality ceased owing to the different numbers dispatched and the vagaries of the post. All these articles were the subject of trade and exchange.

The Development and Organization of the Market

Very soon after capture people realized that it was both undesirable and unnecessary, in view of the limited size and the equality of supplies, to give away or to accept gifts of cigarettes or food. "Goodwill" developed into trading as a more equitable means of maximizing individual satisfaction.

We reached a transit camp in Italy about a fortnight after capture and received ¼ of a Red Cross food parcel each a week later. At once exchanges, already established, multiplied in volume. Starting with simple direct barter, such as a non-smoker giving a smoker friend his cigarette issue in exchange for a chocolate ration, more complex exchanges soon became an accepted custom. Stories circulated of a padre who started off round the camp with a tin of cheese and five cigarettes and returned to his bed with a complete parcel in addition to his original cheese and cigarettes; the market was not yet perfect. Within a week or two, as the volume of trade grew, rough scales of exchange values came into existence. Sikhs, who had at first exchanged tinned beef for practically any other foodstuff, began to insist on jam and margarine. It was realised that a tin of jam was worth ½ lb. of margarine plus something else; that a cigarette issue was worth several chocolates issues, and a tin of diced carrots was worth practically nothing.

In this camp we did not visit other bungalows very much and prices varied from place to place; hence the germ of truth in the story of the itinerant priest. By the end of a month, when we reached our permanent camp, there was a lively trade in all commodities and their relative values were well known, and expressed not in terms of one another—one didn't quote bully in terms of sugar—but in terms of cigarettes. The cigarette became the standard of value. In the permanent camp people started by wandering through the bungalows calling their offers—"cheese for seven" (cigarettes)—and the hours after parcel issue were Bedlam. The inconveniences of this system soon led to its replacement by an Exchange and Mart notice board in every bungalow, where under the headings "name," "room number," "wanted" and "offered" sales and wants were advertized. When a deal went through, it was crossed off the board. The public and semipermanent records of transactions led to cigarette prices being well known and thus tending to equality throughout the camp, although there were always opportunities for an astute trader to make a profit from arbitrage. With this development everyone, including nonsmokers, was willing to sell for cigarettes, using them to buy at another time and place. Cigarettes became the normal currency, though, of course, barter was never extinguished.

The unity of the market and the prevalence of a single price varied directly with the general level of organization and comfort in the camp. A transit camp was always chaotic and uncomfortable: people were overcrowded, no one knew where anyone else was living, and few took the trouble to find out. Organization was too slender to include an Exchange and Mart board, and private advertisements were the most that appeared. Consequently a transit camp was not one market but many. The price of a tin of salmon is known to have varied by two cigarettes in 20 between one end of a hut and the other. Despite a high level of organization in Italy, the market was morcellated in this manner at the first transit camp we reached after our removal to Germany in the autumn of 1943. In this camp—Stalag VIIA at Moosburg in Bavaria—there were up to 50,000 prisoners of all nationalities. French, Russians, Italians, Jugo-Slavs were free to move about within the camp; British and Americans were confined to their compounds, although a few cigarettes given to a sentry would always procure permission for one or two men to visit other compounds. The people who first visited the highly organized French trading center with its stalls and known prices found coffee extract—relatively cheap among the tea-drinking English—commanding a fancy price in biscuits or cigarettes, and some enterprising people made small fortunes that way. (Incidentally we found out later that much of the coffee went "over the wire" and sold for phenomenal prices at black market cafes in Munich: some of the French prisoners were said to have made substantial sums in RMk.s. This was one of the few occasions on which our normally closed economy came into contact with other economic worlds.)

Eventually public opinion grew hostile to these monopoly profits—not everyone could make contact with the French—and trading with them was put on a regulated basis. Each group of beds was given a quota of articles to offer and the transaction was carried out by accredited representatives from the British compound, with monopoly rights. The same method was used for trading with sentries elsewhere, as in this trade secrecy and reasonable prices had a peculiar importance, but as is ever the case with regulated companies, the interloper proved too strong.

The permanent camps in Germany saw the highest level of commercial organization. In addition to the Exchange and Mart notice boards, a shop was organized as a public utility, controlled by representatives of the Senior British Officer, on a no profit basis. People left their surplus clothing, toilet requisites and food there until they were sold at a fixed price in cigarettes. Only sales in cigarettes were accepted—there was no barter—there was no haggling. For food at least there were standard prices: clothing is less homogeneous and the price was decided around a norm by the seller and the shop manager in agreement; shirts would average say 80, ranging from 60 to 120 according to quality and age. Of food, the shop carried small stocks for convenience; the capital was provided by a loan from the bulk store of Red Cross cigarettes and repaid by a small commission taken on the first transactions. Thus the cigarette attained its fullest currency status, and the market was almost completely unified.

It is thus to be seen that a market came into existence without labor or production. The B.R.C.S. may be considered as "Nature" of the textbook, and the articles of trade—food, clothing and cigarettes—as free gifts—land of manna. Despite this, and despite a roughly equal distribution of resources, a market came into spontaneous operation, and prices were fixed by the operation of supply and demand. It is difficult to reconcile this fact with the labor theory of value.

Actually there was an embryo labor market. Even when cigarettes were not scarce, there was usually some unlucky person willing to perform services for them. Laundrymen advertised at two cigarettes a garment. Battle-dress was scrubbed and pressed and a pair of trousers lent for the interim period for twelve. A good pastel portrait cost thirty or a tin of "Kam." Odd tailoring and other jobs similarly had their prices.

There were also entrepreneurial services. There was a coffee stall owner who sold tea, coffee or cocoa at two cigarettes a cup, buying his raw materials at market prices and hiring labor to gather fuel and to stoke; he actually enjoyed the services of a chartered accountant at one stage. After a period of great prosperity he overreached himself and failed disastrously for several hundred cigarettes. Such large-scale private enterprise was rare but several middlemen or professional traders existed. The padre in Italy, or the men at Moosburg who opened trading relations with the French, are examples: the more subdivided the market, the less perfect the advertizement of prices, and the less stable the prices, the greater was the scope for these operators. One man capitalized his knowledge of Urdu by buying meat from the Sikhs and selling butter and jam in return: as his operations became better known more and more people entered this trade, prices in the Indian Wing approximated more nearly to those elsewhere, though to the end a "contact" among the Indians was valuable, as linguistic difficulties prevented the trade from being quite free. Some were specialists in the Indian trade, the food, clothing or even the watch trade. Middlemen traded on their own account or on commission. Price rings and agreements were suspected and the traders certainly co-operated. Nor did they welcome newcomers. Unfortunately, the writer knows little of the workings of these people: public opinion was hostile and the professionals were usually of a retiring disposition.

One trader in food and cigarettes, operating in a period of dearth, enjoyed a high reputation. His capital, carefully saved, was originally about 50 cigarettes, with which he bought rations on issue days and held them until the price rose just before the next issue. He also picked up a little by **arbitrage**; several times a day he visited every exchange or Mart notice board and took advantage of every discrepancy between prices of goods offered and wanted. His knowledge of prices, markets and names of those who had received cigarette parcels was phenomenal. By these means he kept himself smoking steadily—his profits—while his capital remained intact.

Sugar was issued on Saturday. About Tuesday two of us used to visit Sam and make a deal; as old customers he would advance as much of the price as he could spare us, and entered the transaction in a book. On Saturday morning he left cocoa tins on our beds for the ration, and picked them up on Saturday afternoon. We were hoping for a calendar at Christmas, but Sam failed too. He was left holding a big black treacle issue when the price fell, and in this weakened state was unable to withstand an unexpected arrival of parcels and the consequent price fluctuations. He paid in full, but from his capital. The next Tuesday, when I paid my usual visit, he was out of business.

Credit entered into many, perhaps into most, transactions, in one form or another. Sam paid in advance as a rule for his purchases of future deliveries of sugar, but many buyers asked for credit, whether the **commodity** was sold **spot** or **future**. Naturally **prices** varied according to the terms of sale. A treacle ration might be advertized for four cigarettes now or five next week. And in the future market "bread now" was a vastly different thing from "bread Thursday." Bread was issued on Thursday and Monday, four and three days' rations respectively, and by Wednesday and Sunday night it had risen at least one cigarette per ration, from seven to eight, by supper time. One man always saved a ration to sell then at the peak price: his offer of "bread now" stood out on the board among a number of "bread Monday's" fetching one or two less, or not selling at all—and he always smoked on Sunday night.

The Cigarette Currency

Although cigarettes as currency exhibited certain peculiarities, they performed all the functions of a metallic currency as a unit of account, as a measure of value and as a store of value, and shared most of its characteristics. They were homogeneous, reasonably durable, and of convenient size for the smallest or, in packets, for the largest transactions. Incidentally, they could be clipped or sweated by rolling them between the fingers so that tobacco fell out.

Cigarettes were also subject to the working of **Gresham's Law**. Certain brands were more popular than others as smokes, but for currency purposes a cigarette was a cigarette. Consequently buyers used the poorer qualities and the Shop rarely saw the more popular brands: cigarettes such as Churchman's No. 1 were rarely used for trading. At one time cigarettes hand-rolled from pipe tobacco began to circulate. Pipe tobacco was issued in lieu of cigarettes by the Red Cross at a rate of 25 cigarettes to the ounce and this rate was standard in exchanges, but an ounce would produce 30 home-made cigarettes. Naturally, people with machine-made cigarettes broke them down and re-rolled the tobacco, and the real cigarette virtually disappeared from the market. Hand-rolled cigarettes were not homogeneous and prices could no longer be quoted in them with safety: each cigarette was examined before it was accepted and thin ones were rejected, or extra demanded as a makeweight. For a time we suffered all the inconveniences of a debased currency.

Machine-made cigarettes were always universally acceptable, both for what they would buy and for themselves. It was this intrinsic value which gave rise to their principal disadvantage as currency, a disadvantage which exists, but to a far smaller extent in the case of metallic currency;— that is, a strong demand for non-monetary purposes. Consequently our economy was repeatedly subject to deflation and to periods of monetary stringency. While the Red Cross issue of 50 or 25 cigarettes per man per week came in regularly, and while there were fair stocks held, the cigarette currency suited its purpose admirably. But when the issue was interrupted, stocks soon ran out, prices fell, trading declined in volume and became increasingly a matter of barter. This deflationary tendency was periodically offset by the sudden injection of new currency. Private cigarette parcels arrived in a trickle throughout the year, but the big numbers came in quarterly when the Red Cross received its allocation of transport. Several hundred thousand cigarettes might arrive in the space of a fortnight. Prices soared, and then began to fall, slowly at first but with increasing rapidity as stocks ran out, until the next big delivery. Most of our economic troubles could be attributed to this fundamental instability.

Price Movements

Many factors affected prices, the strongest and most noticeable being the periodical currency inflation and deflation described in the last paragraphs. The periodicity of this price cycle depended on cigarette and, to a far lesser extent, on food deliveries. At one time in the early days, before any private parcels had arrived and when there were no individual stocks, the weekly issue of cigarettes and food parcels occurred on a Monday. The non-monetary demand for cigarettes was great, and less elastic than the demand for food: consequently prices fluctuated weekly, falling towards Sunday night and rising sharply on Monday morning. Later, when many people held reserves, the weekly issue had no such effect, being too small a portion of the total available. Credit allowed people with no reserves to meet their non-monetary demand over the weekend.

The general price level was affected by other factors. An influx of new prisoners, proverbially hungry, raised it. Heavy air raids in the vicinity of the camp probably increased the non-monetary demand for cigarettes and accentuated deflation. Good and bad war news certainly had its effect, and the general waves of optimism and pessimism which swept the camp were reflected in prices. Before breakfast one morning in March of this year, a rumor of the arrival of parcels and cigarettes was circulated. Within ten minutes I sold a treacle ration, for four cigarettes (hitherto offered in vain for three), and many similar deals went through. By 10 o'clock the rumor was denied, and treacle that day found no more buyers even at two cigarettes.

More interesting than changes in the general price level were changes in the **price structure**. Changes in the supply of a commodity, in the German ration scale or in the make-up of Red Cross parcels, would raise the price of one commodity relative to others. Tins of oatmeal, once a rare and much sought after luxury in the parcels, became a commonplace in 1943, and the price fell. In hot weather the demand for cocoa fell, and that for soap rose. A new recipe would be reflected in the price level: the discovery that raisins and sugar could be turned into an alcoholic liquor of remarkable potency reacted permanently on the dried fruit market. The invention of electric immersion heaters run off the power points made tea, a drag on the market in Italy, a certain seller in Germany.

In August, 1944, the supplies of parcels and cigarettes were both halved. Since both sides of the equation were changed in the same degree, changes in prices were not anticipated. But this was not the case: the non-monetary demand for cigarettes was less elastic than the demand for food, and food prices fell a little. More important however were the changes in the price structure. German margarine and jam, hitherto valueless owing to adequate supplies of Canadian butter and marmalade, acquired a new value. Chocolate, popular and a certain seller, and sugar, fell. Bread rose; several standing contracts of bread for cigarettes were broken, especially when the bread ration was reduced a few weeks later.

In February, 1945, the German soldier who drove the ration wagon was found to be willing to exchange loaves of bread at the rate of one loaf for a bar of chocolate. Those in the know began selling bread and buying chocolate, by then almost unsaleable in a period of serious deflation. Bread, at about 40, fell slightly; chocolate rose from 15; the supply of bread was not enough for the two commodities to reach parity, but the tendency was unmistakable.

The substitution of German margarine for Canadian butter when parcels were halved naturally affected their relative values, margarine appreciating at the expense of butter. Similarly, two brands of dried milk, hitherto differing in quality and therefore in price by five cigarettes a tin, came together in price as the wider substitution of the cheaper raised its relative value.

Enough has been cited to show that any change in conditions affected both the general price level and the price structure. It was this latter phenomenon which wrecked our planned economy.

Paper Currency—Bully Marks

Around D-Day, food and cigarettes were plentiful, business was brisk and the camp in an optimistic mood. Consequently the Entertainments Committee felt the moment opportune to launch a restaurant, where food and hot drinks were sold while a band and variety turns performed. Earlier experiments, both public and private, had pointed the way, and the scheme was a great success. Food was bought at market prices to provide the meals and the small profits were devoted to a reserve fund and used to bribe Germans to provide grease paints and other necessities for the camp theatre. Originally meals were sold for cigarettes but this meant that the whole scheme was vulnerable to the periodic deflationary waves, and furthermore heavy smokers were unlikely to attend much. The whole success of the scheme depended on an adequate amount of food being offered for sale in the normal manner.

To increase and facilitate trade, and to stimulate supplies and customers therefore, and secondarily to avoid the worst effects of deflation when it should come, a paper currency was organized by the Restaurant and the Shop. The Shop bought food on behalf of the Restaurant with paper notes and the paper was accepted equally with the cigarettes in the Restaurant or Shop, and passed back to the Shop to purchase more food. The Shop acted as a bank of issue. The paper money was backed 100 per cent by food; hence its name, the Bully Mark. The BMk. was backed 100 per cent by food: there could be no over-issues, as is permissible with a normal bank of issue, since the eventual dispersal of the camp and consequent redemption of all BMk.s was anticipated in the near future.

Originally one BMk. was worth one cigarette and for a short time both circulated freely inside and outside the Restaurant. Prices were quoted in BMk.s and cigarettes with equal freedom—and for a short time the BMk. showed signs of replacing the cigarette as currency. The BMk. was tied to food, but not to cigarettes: as it was issued against food, say 45 for a tin of milk and so on, any reduction in the BMk. prices of food would have meant that there were unbacked BMk.s in circulation. But the price of both food and BMk.s could and did fluctuate with the supply of cigarettes.

While the Restaurant flourished, the scheme was a success: the Restaurant bought heavily, all foods were saleable and prices were stable.

In August parcels and cigarettes were halved and the Camp was bombed. The Restaurant closed for a short while and sales of food became difficult. Even when the Restaurant reopened, the food and cigarette shortage became increasingly acute and people were unwilling to convert such valuable goods into paper and to hold them for luxuries like snacks and tea. Less of the right kinds of food for the Restaurant were sold, and the Shop became glutted with dried fruit, chocolate, sugar, etc., which the Restaurant could not buy. The price level and the price structure changed. The BMk. fell to four-fifths of a cigarette and eventually farther still, and it became unacceptable save in the Restaurant. There was a flight from the BMk., no longer convertible into cigarettes or popular foods. The cigarette reestablished itself.

But the BMk. was sound! The Restaurant closed in the New Year with a progressive food shortage and the long evenings without lights due to intensified Allied air raids, and the BMk.s could only be spent in the Coffee Bar—relict of the Restaurant—or on the few unpopular foods in the Shop, the owners of which were prepared to accept them. In the end all holders of BMk.s were paid in full, in cups of coffee or in prunes. People who had bought BMk.s for cigarettes or valuable jam or biscuits in their heyday were aggrieved that they should have stood the loss involved in their restricted choice, but they suffered no actual loss of market value.

Price Fixing

Along with this scheme came a determined attempt at a **planned economy**, at price fixing. The Medical Officer had long been anxious to control food sales, for fear of some people selling too much, to the detriment of their health. The deflationary waves and their effects on prices were inconvenient to all and would be dangerous to the Restaurant which had to carry stocks. Furthermore, unless the BMk. was convertible into cigarettes at about par it had little chance of gaining confidence and of succeeding as a currency. As has been explained, the BMk. was tied to food but could not be tied to cigarettes, which fluctuated in value. Hence, while BMk. prices of food were fixed for all time, cigarette prices of food and BMk.s varied.

The Shop, backed by the Senior British Officer, was now in a position to enforce price control both inside and outside its walls. Hitherto a standard price had been fixed for food left for sale in the Shop, and prices outside were roughly in conformity with this scale, which was recommended as a "guide" to sellers, but fluctuated a good deal around it. Sales in the Shop at recommended prices were apt to be slow though a good price might be obtained: sales outside could be made more quickly at lower prices. (If sales outside were to be at higher prices, goods were withdrawn from the Shop until the recommended price rose: but the recommended price was sluggish and could not follow the market closely by reason of its very purpose, which was stability.) The Exchange and Mart notice boards came under the control of the Shop: advertizements which exceeded a 5 per cent. departure from the recommended scale were liable to be crossed out by authority: unauthorized sales were discouraged by authority and also by public opinion, strongly in favor of a just and stable price. (Recommended prices were fixed partly from market data, partly on the advice of the M.O.)

At first the recommended scale was a success: the Restaurant, a big buyer, kept prices stable around this level: opinion and the 5 per cent tolerance helped. But when the price level fell with the August cuts and the price structure changed, the recommended scale was too rigid. Unchanged at first, as no deflation was expected, the scale was tardily lowered, but the prices of goods on the new scale remained in the same relation to one another, owing to the BMk., while on the market the price structure had changed. And the modifying influence of the Restaurant had gone. The scale was moved up and down several times, slowly following the inflationary and deflationary waves, but it was rarely adjusted to changes in the price structure. More and more advertizements were crossed off the board, and black market sales at unauthorized prices increased: eventually public opinion turned against the recommended scale and authority gave up the struggle. In the last few weeks, with unparalleled deflation, prices fell with alarming rapidity, no scales existed, and supply and demand, alone and unmellowed, determined prices.

Public Opinion

Public opinion on the subject of trading was vocal if confused and changeable, and generalizations as to its direction are difficult and dangerous. A tiny minority held that all trading was undesirable as it engendered an unsavory atmosphere; occasional frauds and sharp practices were cited as proof. Certain forms of trading were more generally condemned; trade with the Germans was criticized by many. Red Cross toilet articles, which were in short supply and only issued in cases of actual need, were excluded from trade by law and opinion working in unshakable harmony. At one time, when there had been several cases of malnutrition reported among the more devoted smokers, no trade in German rations was permitted, as the victims became an additional burden on the depleted food reserves of the Hospital. But while certain activities were condemned as antisocial, trade itself was practiced, and its utility appreciated, by almost everyone in the camp.

More interesting was opinion on middlemen and prices. Taken as a whole, opinion was hostile to the **middleman**. His function, and his hard work in bringing buyer and seller together, were ignored; profits were not regarded as a reward for labor, but as the result of sharp practices. Despite the fact that his very existence was proof to the contrary, the middleman was held to be redundant in view of the existence of an official Shop and the Exchange and Mart. Appreciation only came his way when he was willing to advance the price of a sugar ration, or to buy goods spot and carry them against a future sale. In these cases the element of risk was obvious to all, and the convenience of the service was felt to merit some reward. Particularly unpopular was the middleman with an element of monopoly, the man who contacted the ration wagon driver, or the man who utilized his knowledge of Urdu. And middlemen as a group were blamed for reducing prices. Opinion notwithstanding, most people dealt with a middleman, whether consciously or unconsciously, at some time or another.

There was a strong feeling that everything had its "just price" in cigarettes. While the assessment of the just price, which incidentally varied between camps, was impossible of explanation, this price was nevertheless pretty closely known. It can best be defined as the price usually fetched by an article in good times when cigarettes were plentiful. The "just price" changed slowly; it was unaffected by short-term variations in supply, and while opinion might be resigned to departures from the "just price," a strong feeling of resentment persisted. A more satisfactory definition of the "just price" is impossible. Everyone knew what it was, though no one could explain why it should be so.

As soon as prices began to fall with a cigarette shortage, a clamor arose, particularly against those who held reserves and who bought at reduced prices. Sellers at cut prices were criticized and their activities referred to as the black market. In every period of dearth the explosive question of "should non-smokers receive a cigarette ration?" was discussed to profitless length. Unfortunately, it was the non-smoker, or the light smoker with his reserves, along with the hated middleman, who weathered the storm most easily.

The popularity of the price-fixing scheme, and such success as it enjoyed, were undoubtedly the result of this body of opinion. On several occasions the fall of prices was delayed by the general support given to the recommended scale. The onset of deflation was marked by a period of sluggish trade; prices stayed up but no one bought. Then prices fell on the black market, and the volume of trade revived in that quarter. Even when the recommended scale was revised, the volume of trade in the Shop would remain low. Opinion was always overruled by the hard facts of the market.

Curious arguments were advanced to justify price fixing. The recommended prices were in some way related to the calorific values of the foods offered: hence some were overvalued and never sold at these prices. One argument ran as follows: —not everyone has private cigarette parcels: thus, when prices were high and trade good in the summer of 1944, only the lucky rich could buy. This was unfair to the man with few cigarettes. When prices fell in the following winter, prices should be pegged high so that the rich, who had enjoyed life in the summer, should put many cigarettes into circulation. The fact that those who sold to the rich in the summer had also enjoyed life then, and the fact that in the winter there was always someone willing to sell at low prices were ignored. Such arguments were hotly debated each night after the approach of Allied aircraft extinguished all lights at 8 p.m. But prices moved with the supply of cigarettes, and refused to stay fixed in accordance with a theory of ethics.

Conclusion

The economic organization described was both elaborate and smooth-working in the summer of 1944. Then came the August cuts and deflation. Prices fell, rallied with deliveries of cigarette parcels in September and December, and fell again. In January, 1945, supplies of Red Cross cigarettes ran out: and prices slumped still further: in February the supplies of food parcels were exhausted and the depression became a blizzard. Food, itself scarce, was almost given away in order to meet the non-monetary demand for cigarettes. Laundries ceased to operate, or worked for £s or RMk.s: food and cigarettes sold for fancy prices in £s, hitherto unheard of. The Restaurant was a memory and the BMk. a joke. The Shop was empty and the Exchange and Mart notices were full of unaccepted offers for cigarettes. Barter increased in volume, becoming a larger proportion of a smaller volume of trade. This, the first serious and prolonged food shortage in the writer's experience, caused the price structure to change again, partly because German rations were not easily divisible. A margarine ration gradually sank in value until it exchanged directly for a treacle ration. Sugar slumped sadly. Only bread retained its value. Several thousand cigarettes, the capital of the Shop, were distributed without any noticeable effect. A few fractional parcel and cigarette issues, such as one-sixth of a parcel and twelve cigarettes each, led to monetary price recoveries and feverish trade, especially when they coincided with good news from the Western Front, but the general position remained unaltered.

By April, 1945, chaos had replaced order in the economic sphere: sales were difficult, prices lacked stability. *Economics has been defined as the science of distributing limited means among unlimited and competing ends*. On 12th April, with the arrival of elements of the 30th U.S. Infantry Division, the ushering in of an age of plenty demonstrated the hypothesis that with infinite means economic organization and activity would be redundant, as every want could be satisfied without effort.

POVERTY

The Merchant and the Low-Income Consumer: The Poor Pay More

DAVID CAPLOVITZ

The visitor to East Harlem cannot fail to notice the sixty or so furniture and appliance stores that mark the area, mostly around Third Avenue and 125th Street. At first this may seem surprising. After all, this is obviously a low-income area. Many of the residents are on relief. Many are employed in seasonal work and in marginal industries, such as the garment industry, which are the first to feel the effects of a recession in the economy. On the face of it, residents of the area would seem unable to afford the merchandise offered for sale in these stores.

That merchants nevertheless find it profitable to locate in these areas attests to a commonly overlooked fact: low-income families, like those of higher income, are consumers of many major durables. The popular image of the American as striving for the material possessions which bestow upon him both comfort and prestige in the eyes of his fellows does not hold only for the ever-increasing middle class. The cultural pressures to buy major durables reach low- as well as middle-income families. In some ways, consumption may take on even more significance for low-income families than for those in higher classes. Since many have small prospect of greatly improving their low social standing through occupational mobility, they are apt to turn to consumption as at least one sphere in which they can make some progress toward the American dream of success. If the upper strata that were observed by Veblen engaged in conspicuous consumption to symbolize their social superiority, it might be said that the lower classes today are apt to engage in *compensatory consumption*. Appliances, automobiles, and the dream of a home of their own can become compensations for blocked social mobility.¹

The dilemma of the low-income consumer lies in these facts. He is trained by society (and his position in it) to want the symbols and appurtenances of the "good life" at the same time that he lacks the means needed to fulfill these socially induced wants. People with small incomes lack not only the ready cash for consuming major durables but are also poorly qualified for that growing substitute for available cash—credit. Their low income, their negligible savings, their job insecurity all contribute to their being poor credit risks. Moreover, many low-income families in New York City are fairly recent migrants from the South or from Puerto Rico and so do not have other requisites of good credit, such as long-term residence at the same address and friends who meet the credit requirements and are willing to vouch for them.²

Not having enough cash and credit would seem to create a sufficient problem for low-income consumers. But they have other limitations as well. They tend to lack the information and training needed to be effective consumers in a bureaucratic society. Partly because of their limited education and partly because as migrants from more traditional societies they are unfamiliar with urban culture, they are not apt to follow the announcements of sales in the newspapers, to engage in comparative shopping, to know their way around the major department stores and bargain

---

¹I am indebted to Robert K. Merton for suggesting the apt phrase, "compensatory consumption." The idea expressed by this term figures prominently in the writings of Robert S. Lynd. Observing the workers in Middletown, Lynd noted that their declining opportunities for occupational advancement and even the depression did not make them class-conscious. Instead, their aspirations shifted to the realm of consumption.

> Fascinated by a rising standard of living offered them on every hand on the installment plan, they [the working class] do not readily segregate themselves from the rest of the city. They want what Middletown wants, so long as it gives them their great symbol of advancement–an automobile. Car ownership stands to them for a large share of the "American dream"; they cling to it as they cling to self respect, and it was not unusual to see a family drive up to the relief commissary in 1935 to stand in line for its four or five dollar weekly food dole. [The Lynds go on to quote a union official:] It's easy to see why our workers don't think much about joining unions. So long as they have a car and can borrow or steal a gallon of gas, they'll ride around and pay no attention to labor organization. . . . [Robert S. Lynd and Helen Merrill Lynd, *Middletown in Transition* (New York: Har-

court, Brace and Co., 1937), p. 26. See also pp. 447–448.]

It should be noted that the Lynds identify the installment plan as the mechanism through which workers are able to realize their consumption aspirations. Similar observations are to be found in *Knowledge for What?* (Princeton University Press: 1939), pp. 91, 198. Lynd's student, Eli Chinoy, also makes use of the idea of compensatory consumption in his study of automobile workers. He found that when confronted with the impossibility of rising to the ranks of management, workers shifted their aspirations from the occupational to the consumption sphere. "With their wants constantly stimulated by high powered advertising, they measure their success by what they are able to buy." Eli Chinoy, "Aspirations of Automobile Workers," *American Journal of Sociology*, 57 (1952), 453–459. For further discussion of the political implications of this process, see Daniel Bell, "Work and its Discontents" in *The End of Ideology* (New York: The Free Press of Glencoe, 1960), pp. 246 ff.

²A frequent practice in extending credit to poor risks is to have cosigners who will make good the debt should the original borrower default. The new arrivals are apt to be disadvantaged by their greater difficulty in finding cosigners.

centers, to know how to evaluate the advice of salesmen—practices necessary for some degree of sophistication in the realm of consumption. The institution of credit introduces special complex requirements for intelligent consumption. Because of the diverse and frequently misleading ways in which charges for credit are stated, even the highly-educated consumer has difficulty knowing which set of terms is most economical.[3]

These characteristics of the low-income consumer—his socially supported want for major durables, his small funds, his poor credit position, his lack of shopping sophistication—constitute the conditions under which durables are marketed in low-income areas. To understand the paradox set by the many stores selling high-cost durables in these areas it is necessary to know how the merchants adapt to these conditions. Clearly the normal marketing arrangements, based on a model of the "adequate" consumer(the consumer with

---

[3]Professor Samuel S. Myers of Morgan State College has studied the credit terms of major department stores and appliance outlets in Baltimore. Visiting the ten most popular stores, he priced the same model of TV set and gathered information on down-payments and credit terms. He found that the cash price was practically the same in the various stores, but that there were wide variations in the credit terms leading to sizeable differences in the final cost to the consumer. (Based on personal communication with Professor Myers.)

In his statement to the Douglas Committee considering the "Truth in Interest" bill, George Katona presented findings from the consumer surveys carried out by the Survey Research Center of the University of Michigan. These studies show that people with high income and substantial education are no better informed about the costs of credit than people of low income and little education. See *Consumer Credit Labeling Bill, op. cit.*, p. 806.

funds, credit, and shopping sophistication), cannot prevail if these merchants are to stay in business.

On the basis of interviews with fourteen of these merchants, the broad outlines of this marketing system can be described. This picture, in turn, provides a backdrop for the more detailed examination in later chapters of the marketing relationship from the viewpoint of the consumer.

Merchandising in a Low-Income Area

The key to the marketing system in low-income areas lies in special adaptations of the institution of credit. The many merchants who locate in these areas and find it profitable to do so are prepared to offer credit in spite of the high risks involved. Moreover, their credit is tailored to the particular needs of the low-income consumer. All kinds of durable goods can be obtained in this market at terms not too different from the slogan, "a dollar down, a dollar a week." The consumer can buy furniture, a TV set, a stereophonic phonograph, or, if he is so minded, a combination phonograph-TV set, if not for a dollar a week then for only a few dollars a week. In practically every one of these stores, the availability of "easy credit" is announced to the customer in both English and Spanish by large signs in the windows and sometimes by neon signs over the doorways. Of the fourteen merchants interviewed, twelve claimed that from 75 to 90 per cent of their business consisted of credit and the other two said that credit made up half their business. That these merchants extend credit to their customers does not, of course, explain how they stay in business. They still face the problem of dealing with their risks.

THE MARKUP AND QUALITY OF GOODS

It might at first seem that the merchant would solve his problem by charging high rates of interest on the credit he extends. But the law in New York State now regulates the amount that can be charged for credit, and most of these merchants claim they use **installment contracts** which conform to the law. The fact is that they do not always use these contracts. Some merchants will give customers only a card on which payments are noted. In these transactions the cost of credit and the cash price are not specified as the law requires. The customer peddlers, whom we shall soon meet, seldom use installment contracts. In all these cases the consumer has no idea of how much he is paying for credit, for the cost of credit is not differentiated from the cost of the product.

Although credit charges are now regulated by law, no law regulates the merchant's markup on his goods. East Harlem is known to the merchants of furniture and appliances in New York City as the area in which pricing is done by "numbers." We first heard of the "number" system from a woman who had been employed as a bookkeeper in such a store. She illustrated a "one number" item by writing down a hypothetical wholesale price and then adding the same figure to it, a 100 per cent markup. Her frequent references to "two number" and "three number" prices indicated that prices are never less than "one number," and are often more.

The system of pricing in the low-income market differs from that in the bureaucratic market of the downtown stores in another respect: in East Harlem there are hardly any "one price" stores. In keeping with a multi-price policy, price tags are conspicuously absent from the merchandise. The customer has to ask, "how much?," and the answer he gets will depend on several things. If the merchant considers him a poor risk, if he thinks the customer is naive, or if the customer was referred to him by another merchant or a peddler to whom he must pay a commission, the price will be higher. The fact that prices can be affected by "referrals" calls attention to another peculiarity of the low-income market, what the merchants call the "T.O." system.

Anyone closely familiar with sales practices in a large retailing establishment probably understands the meaning of "T.O." When a salesman is confronted with a customer who is not responding to the "sales pitch," he will call over another salesman, signal the nature of the situation by whispering, "this is a T.O.," and then introduce him to the customer as the "assistant manager."[4] In East Harlem, as the interviewers learned, T.O.s extend beyond the store. When a merchant finds himself with a customer who seems to be a greater risk than he is prepared to accept, he does not send the customer away. Instead, he will tell the customer that he happens to be out of the item he wants, but that it can be obtained at the store of his "friend" or "cousin," just a few blocks away. The merchant will then take the customer to a storekeeper with a less conservative credit

---

[4]The initials stand for "turn over." The "assistant manager" is ready to make a small concession to the customer, who is usually so flattered by this gesture that he offers no further resistance to the sale. For further descriptions of the "T.O.," see Cecil L. French, "Correlates of Success in Retail Selling," *American Journal of Sociology*, 66 (September, 1960), 128–134; and Erving Goffman, *Presentation of Self in Everyday Life* (New York: Doubleday, Anchor Books, 1959), pp. 178–180.

policy.[5] The second merchant fully understands that his colleague expects a commission and takes this into account in fixing the price.[6] As a result, the customer who happens to walk into the "wrong" store ends up paying more. In essence, he is being charged for the service of having his credit potential matched with the risk policy of a merchant.

As for the merchandise sold in these stores, the interviewers noticed that the furniture on display was of obviously poor quality. Most of all, they were struck by the absence of well-known brands of appliances in most of the stores. To find out about the sales of better-known brands, they initially asked about the volume of sales of "high-*price* lines." But this question had little meaning for the merchants, because high prices were being charged for the low-quality goods in evidence. The question had to be rephrased in terms of "high *quality*" merchandise or, as the merchants themselves refer to such goods, "custom lines." To quote from the report of these interviews:

It became apparent that the question raised a problem of communication. We were familiar with the prices generally charged for high quality lines and began to notice that the same prices were charged for much lower quality merchandise. The markup was obviously quite different from that in other areas. The local merchants said that the sale of "custom" merchandise was limited by a slow turnover. In fact, a comparable markup on the higher quality lines would make the final price so prohibitively high that they could not be moved at all. A lower markup would be inconsistent with the risk and would result in such small profits that the business could not be continued.

The high markup on low-quality goods is thus a major device used by the merchants to protect themselves against the risks of their credit business. This policy represents a marked departure from the "normal" marketing situation. In the "normal" market, competition between merchants results in a pricing policy roughly commensurate with the quality of the goods. It is apparent, then, that these merchants do not see themselves competing with stores outside the neighborhood. This results in the irony that the people who can least afford the goods they buy are required to pay high prices relative to quality, thus receiving a comparatively low return for their consumer dollar.

In large part, these merchants have a "captive" market because their customers do not meet the economic requirements of consumers in the larger, bureaucratic marketplace. But also, they can sell inferior goods at high prices because, in their own words, the customers are not "price and quality conscious." Interviews found that the merchants perceive their customers as unsophisticated shoppers. One merchant rather cynically explained that the amount of goods sold a customer depends not on the customer but on the merchant's willingness to extend him credit. If the merchant is willing to accept great risk, he can

---

[5] The interviewers found that the stores closer to the main shopping area of 125th Street generally had more conservative credit policies than those somewhat farther away. This was indicated by the percentage of credit sales the merchants reported as defaults. The higher-rental stores near 125th Street reported default rates of 5 and 6 per cent, those six or seven blocks away, as high as 20 per cent.

[6] The referring merchant does not receive his commission right away. Whether he gets it at all depends upon the customer's payment record. He will keep a record of his referrals and check on them after several months. When the merchant who has made the sale has received a certain percentage of the payments, he will give the referring merchant his commission.

sell the customer almost as much as he cares to. Another merchant, commenting on the buying habits of the customer, said, "People do not shop in this area. Each person who comes into the store wants to buy something and is a potential customer. It is just up to who catches him."

The notion of "who catches him" is rather important in this economy. Merchants compete not so much in price or quality, but in getting customers to the store on other grounds. (Some of these gathering techniques will shortly be described.)

Another merchant commented rather grudgingly that the Negroes were beginning to show signs of greater sophistication by "shopping around." Presumably this practice is not followed by the newer migrants to the area.

But although the merchants are ready to exploit the naiveté of their traditionalistic customers, it is important to point out that they also cater to the customer's traditionalism. As a result of the heavy influx of Puerto Ricans into the area, many of these stores now employ Puerto Rican salesmen. The customers who enter these stores need not be concerned about possible embarrassment because of their broken English or their poor dress. On the contrary, these merchants are adept at making the customer feel at ease, as a personal experience will testify.

Visiting the area and stopping occasionally to read the ads in the windows, I happened to pause before an appliance store. A salesman promptly emerged and said, "I know, I bet you're looking for a nice TV set. Come inside. We've got lots of nice ones." Finding myself thrust into the role of customer, I followed him into the store and listened to his sales-pitch. Part way through his talk, he asked my name. I hesitated a moment and then provided him with a fictitious last name, at which point he said, "No, no—no last names. What's your first name? . . . Ah, Dave; I'm Irv. We only care about first names here." When I was ready to leave after making some excuse about having to think things over, he handed me his card. Like most business cards of employees, this one had the name and address of the enterprise in large type and in small type the name of the salesman. But instead of his full name, there appeared only the amiable, "Irv."

As this episode indicates, the merchants in this low-income area are ready to personalize their services. To consumers from a more traditional society, unaccustomed to the impersonality of the bureaucratic market, this may be no small matter.

So far, we have reviewed the elements of the system of exchange that comprise the low-income market. For the consumer, these are the availability of merchandise, the "easy" installments, and the reassurance of dealing with merchants who make them feel at home. In return, the merchant reserves for himself the right to sell low-quality merchandise at exorbitant prices.

But the high markup on goods does not insure that the business will be profitable. No matter what he charges, the merchant can remain in business only if customers actually pay. In this market, the customer's intention and ability to pay—the assumptions underlying any credit system—cannot be taken for granted. Techniques for insuring continuity of payments are a fundamental part of this distinctive economy.

FORMAL CONTROLS

When the merchant uses an installment contract, he has recourse to legal controls over his customers. But as we shall see, legal controls are not sufficient to cope with the merchant's problem and they are seldom used.

Repossession.—The merchant who offers credit can always repossess his merchandise should the customer default on payments. But repossession, according to the merchants, is rare. They claim that the merchandise receives such heavy use as to become practically worthless in a short time. And no doubt the shoddy merchandise will not stand much use, heavy or light. One merchant said that he will occasionally repossess an item, not to regain his equity, but to punish a customer he feels is trying to cheat him.

Liens *Against Property and Wages.*—The merchant can, of course, sue the defaulting customer. By winning a court judgment, he can have the customer's property attached. Should this fail to satisfy the debt, he can take the further step of having the customer's salary garnisheed.[7] But these devices are not fully adequate for several reasons. Not all customers have property of value or regular jobs. Furthermore, their employers will not hesitate to fire them rather than submit to the nuisance of a **garnishment**. But since the customer knows he may lose his job if he is garnisheed, the mere threat of garnishment is sometimes enough to insure regularity of payments.[8] The main limitation with legal controls, however, is that the merchant who uses them repeatedly runs the risk of forfeiting good will in the neighborhood.

---

[7] It is of some interest that the low-income families we interviewed were all familiar with the word "garnishee." This may well be one word in the language that the poorly educated are more likely to know than the better educated.

[8] Welfare families cannot, of course, be garnisheed, and more than half the merchants reported that they sell to them. But the merchants can threaten to disclose the credit purchase to the welfare authorities. Since recipients of welfare funds are not supposed to buy on credit, this threat exerts powerful pressure on the family.

Discounting Paper.—The concern with good will places a limitation on the use of another legal practice open to merchants for minimizing their risk: the sale of their contracts to a credit agency at a discount. By selling his contracts to one of the licensed finance companies, the merchant can realize an immediate return on his investment. The problem with this technique is that the merchant loses control over his customer. As an impersonal, bureaucratic organization, the credit agency has recourse only to legal controls. Should the customer miss a payment, the credit agency will take the matter to court. But in the customer's mind, his contract exists with the merchant, not with the credit agency. Consequently, the legal actions taken against him reflect upon the merchant, and so good will is not preserved after all.

For this reason, the merchant is reluctant to "sell his paper," particularly if he has reason to believe that the customer will miss some payments. When he does sell some of his contracts at a **discount**, his motive is not to reduce risk, but rather to obtain working capital. Since so much of his capital is tied up in credit transactions, he frequently finds it necessary to make such sales. Oddly enough, he is apt to sell his better "paper," that is, the contracts of customers who pay regularly, for he wants to avoid incurring the ill will of customers. This practice also has its drawbacks for the merchant. Competitors can find out from the credit agencies which customers pay regularly and then try to lure them away from the original merchant. Some merchants reported that in order to retain control over their customers, they will buy back contracts from credit agencies they suspect are giving information to competitors.[9]

Credit Association Ratings.—All credit merchants report their bad debtors to the credit association to which they belong. The merchants interviewed said that they always consult the "skip lists" of their association before extending credit to a new customer. In this way they can avoid at least the customers known to be bad risks. This form of control tends to be effective in the long run because the customers find that they are unable to obtain credit until they have made good on their past debts. During the interviews with them, some consumers mentioned this need to restore their credit rating as the reason why they were paying off debts in spite of their belief that they had been cheated.

But these various formal techniques of control are not sufficient to cope with the merchant's problem of risk. He also depends heavily on informal and personal techniques of control.

INFORMAL CONTROLS

The merchant starts from the premise that most of his customers are honest people who intend to pay but have difficulty managing their money. Missed payments are seen as more often due to poor management and to emergencies than to dishonesty. The merchants anticipate that their customers will miss some payments and they rely on informal controls to insure that payments are eventually made.

All the merchants described their credit business as operating on a "fifteen-month year." This means that they expect the customer to miss about one of every four payments and they compute the markup accordingly. Unlike the credit companies, which insist upon regular payments and add service charges for late payments, the neighborhood merchant is prepared to extend "flexible" credit. Should the customer miss an occasional payment or should he be short on another, the merchant considers this a normal part of his business.

To insure the close personal control necessary for this system of credit, the merchant frequently draws up a contract calling for weekly payments which the customer usually brings to the store. This serves several functions for the merchant. To begin with, the sum of money represented by a weekly payment is relatively small and so helps to create the illusion of "easy credit." Customers are apt to think more of the size of the payments than of the cost of the item or the length of the contract.

More importantly, the frequent contact of a weekly-payment system enables the merchant to get to know his customer. He learns when the customer receives his pay check, when his rent is due, who his friends are, when job layoffs, illnesses, and other emergencies occur—in short, all sorts of information which allow him to interpret the reason for a missed payment. Some merchants reported that when they know the customer has missed a payment for a legitimate reason such as illness or a job layoff, they will send a sympathetic note and offer the customer a gift (an inexpensive lamp or wall picture) when

---

[9] Not all merchants are particularly concerned with good will. A few specialize in extending credit to the worst risks, customers turned away by most other merchants. These men will try to collect as much as they can on their accounts during the year and then will sell all their outstanding accounts to a finance company. As a result, the most inadequate consumers are apt to meet with the bureaucratic controls employed by the finance company. For a description of how bill collectors operate, see Hillel Black, *Buy Now, Pay Later* (New York: William Morrow and Co., 1961), chap. 4.

payments are resumed. This procedure, they say, frequently brings the customer back with his missed payments.

The short interval between payments also functions to give the merchant an early warning when something is amiss. His chances of locating the delinquent customer are that much greater. Furthermore, the merchant can keep tabs on a delinquent customer through his knowledge of the latter's friends, relatives, neighbors, and associates, who are also apt to be customers of his. In this way, still another informal device, the existing network of social relations, is utilized by the neighborhood merchant in conducting his business.[10]

The weekly-payment system also provides the merchant with the opportunity to sell other items to the customer. When the first purchase is almost paid for, the merchant will try to persuade the customer to make another. Having the customer in the store, where he can look at the merchandise, makes the next sale that much easier. This system of successive sales is, of course, an ideal arrangement—for the merchant. As a result, the customer remains continuously in debt to him. The pattern is somewhat reminiscent of the Southern sharecropper's relation to the company store. And since a number of customers grew up in more traditional environments with just such economies, they may find the arrangement acceptable. The practice of buying from peddlers, found to be common in these low-income areas, also involves the principle of continuous indebtedness. The urban low-income economy, then, is in some respects like the sharecropper system; it might almost be called an "urban sharecropper system."[11]

The Customer Peddlers

Characteristic of the comparatively traditional and personal form of the low-income economy is the important role played in it by the door-to-door credit salesman, the customer peddler. The study of merchants found that these peddlers are not necessarily competitors of the store-owners. Almost all merchants make use of peddlers in the great competition for customers. The merchants tend to regard peddlers as necessary evils who add greatly to the final cost of purchases. But they need them because in their view, customers are too ignorant, frightened, or lazy to come to the stores themselves. Thus, the merchants' apparent contempt for peddlers does not bar them from employing outdoor salesmen (or "canvassers," as they describe the peddlers who work for one store or another). Even the merchants who are themselves reluctant to hire canvassers find they must do so in order to meet the competition. The peddler's main function for the merchant, then, is getting the customer to the store, and if he will not come, getting the store to the customer. But this is not his only function.

---

[10] The merchant's access to these networks of social relations is not entirely independent of economic considerations. Just as merchants who refer customers receive commissions, so customers who recommend others are often given commissions. Frequently, this is why a customer will urge his friends to deal with a particular merchant.

[11] The local merchants are not the only ones promoting continuous debt. The coupon books issued by banks and finance companies which underwrite installment contracts contain notices in the middle announcing that the consumer can, if he wishes, refinance the loan. The consumer is told, in effect, that he is a good risk because presumably he has regularly paid half the installments and that he need not wait until he has made the last payment before borrowing more money.

Much more than the storekeeper, the peddler operates on the basis of a personal relationship with the customer. By going to the customer's home, he gets to know the entire family; he sees the condition of the home and he comes to know the family's habits and wants. From this vantage point he is better able than the merchant to evaluate the customer as a credit risk. Since many of the merchant's potential customers lack the standard credentials of credit, such as having a permanent job, the merchant needs some other basis for discriminating between good and bad risks. If the peddler, who has come to know the family, is ready to vouch for the customer, the merchant will be ready to make the transaction. In short, the peddler acts as a fiduciary agent, a Dun and Bradstreet for the poor, telling the merchant which family is likely to meet its obligations and which is not.

Not all peddlers are employed by stores. Many are independent enterprisers (who may have started as canvassers for stores).[12] A number of the independent peddlers have accumulated enough capital to supply their customers with major durables. These are the elite peddlers, known as "dealers," who buy appliances and furniture from local merchants at a "wholesale" price, and then sell them on credit to their customers. In these transactions, the peddler either takes the customer to the store or sends the customer to the store with his card on which he has written some such message as "Please give Mr. Jones a TV set."[13] The merchant then sells the customer the TV set at a price much higher than he would ordinarily charge. The "dealer" is generally given two months to pay the merchant the "wholesale" price, and meanwhile he takes over the responsibility of collecting from his customer. Some "dealers" are so successful that they employ canvassers in their own right.[14] And some merchants do so much business with "dealers" that they come to think of themselves as "wholesalers" even though they are fully prepared to do their own retail business.

Independent peddlers without much capital also have economic relations with local merchants. They act as brokers, directing their customers to neighborhood stores that will extend them credit. And for this service they of course receive a commission. In these transactions, it is the merchant who accepts the risks and assumes the responsibility for collecting payments. The peddler who acts as a broker performs the same function as the merchant in the T.O. system. He knows which merchants will accept great risk and which will not, and directs his customers accordingly.

---

[12] A systematic study of local merchants and peddlers would probably find that a typical career pattern is to start as a canvasser, become a self-employed peddler, and finally a storekeeper.

[13] According to a former customer peddler, now in the furniture business, the peddler's message will either read "Please *give* Mr. Jones . . ." or "Please let Mr. Jones *pick out* . . ." In the former case, the customer is given the merchandise right away; in the latter, it is set aside for him until the peddler says that it is all right to let the customer have it. The peddler uses the second form when his customer is already heavily in debt to him and he wants to be certain that the customer will agree to the higher weekly payments that will be necessary.

[14] One tiny store in the area, with little merchandise in evidence, is reported to employ over a hundred canvassers. The owner would not consent to an interview, but the student-observers did notice that this apparently small merchant kept some four or five bookkeepers at work in a back room. The owner is obviously a "dealer" whose store is his office. As a "dealer," he has no interest in maintaining stock and displays for street trade.

There are, then, three kinds of customer peddlers operating in these low-income neighborhoods who cooperate with local merchants: the canvassers who are employed directly by the stores; the small entrepreneurs who act as brokers; and the more successful entrepreneurs who operate as "dealers." A fourth type of peddler consists of salesmen representing large companies not necessarily located in the neighborhood. These men are, for the most part, canvassers for firms specializing in a particular commodity, e.g., encyclopedias, vacuum cleaners, or pots and pans. They differ from the other peddlers by specializing in what they sell and by depending more on contracts and legal controls. They are also less interested in developing continuous relationships with their customers.

Peddlers thus aid the local merchants by finding customers, evaluating them as credit risks, and helping in the collection of payments. And as the merchants themselves point out, these services add greatly to the cost of the goods. One storekeeper said that peddlers are apt to charge five and six times the amount the store charges for relatively inexpensive purchases. Pointing to a religious picture which he sells for $5, he maintained that peddlers sell it for as much as $30. And he estimated that the peddler adds 30 to 50 per cent to the final sales price of appliances and furniture.

Unethical and Illegal Practices

The interviewers uncovered some evidence that some local merchants engage in the illegal practice of selling reconditioned furniture and appliances as new. Of course, no merchant would admit that he did this himself, but five of them hinted that their competitors engaged in this practice.[15]

---

[15]Events are sometimes more telling than words. During an interview with a merchant, the inter-

we shall see, several of the consumers we interviewed were quite certain that they had been victimized in this way.

One unethical, if not illegal, activity widely practiced by stores is "bait" advertising with its concomitant, the "switch sale." In the competition for customers, merchants depend heavily upon advertising displays in their windows which announce furniture or appliances at unusually low prices. The customer may enter the store assuming that the low offer in the window signifies a reasonably low price line. Under severe pressure, the storekeeper may even be prepared to sell the merchandise at the advertised price, for not to do so would be against the law. What most often happens, however, is that the unsuspecting customer is convinced by the salesman that he doesn't really want the goods advertised in the window and is then persuaded to buy a smaller amount of more expensive goods. Generally, not much persuasion is necessary. The most popular "bait ad" is the announcement of three rooms of furniture for "only $149" or "only $199." The customer who inquires about this bargain is shown a bedroom set consisting of two cheap and (sometimes deliberately) chipped bureaus and one bed frame. He learns that the spring and mattress are not included in the advertised price, but can be had for another $75 or $100. The living-room set in these "specials" consists of a fragile-looking sofa and one unmatching chair.[16]

The frequent success of this kind of exploitation, known in the trade as the

---

viewer volunteered to help several men who were carrying bed frames into the store. The owner excitedly told him not to help because he might get paint on his hands.

[16]In one store in which I inspected this special offer, I was told by the salesman that he would find a chair that was a "fairly close match."

"switch sale," is reflected in this comment by one merchant: "I don't know how they do it. They advertise three rooms of furniture for $149 and the customers swarm in. *They end up buying a $400 bedroom set for $600 and none of us can believe how easy it is to make these sales.*"

In sum, a fairly intricate system of sales-and-credit has evolved in response to the distinctive situation of the low-income consumer and the local merchant. It is a system heavily slanted in the direction of a traditional economy in which informal, personal ties play a major part in the transaction. At the same time it is connected to impersonal bureaucratic agencies through the instrument of the installment contract. Should the informal system break down, credit companies, courts of law, and agencies of law enforcement come to play a part.

The system is not only different from the larger, more formal economy; in some respects it is a *deviant* system in which practices that violate prevailing moral standards are commonplace. As Merton has pointed out in his analysis of the political machine, the persistence of deviant social structures can only be understood when their social functions (as well as dysfunctions) are taken into account.[17] The basic function of the low-income marketing system is to provide consumer goods to people who fail to meet the requirements of the more legitimate, bureaucratic market, or who choose to exclude themselves from the larger market because they do not feel comfortable in it. As we have seen, the system is extraordinarily flexible. Almost no one—however great a risk—is turned away. Various mechanisms sift and sort customers according to their credit risk and match them with merchants ready to sell them the goods they want. Even the family on welfare is permitted to maintain its self-respect by consuming in much the same way as do its social peers who happen not to be on welfare. Whether the system, with its patently exploitative features, can be seriously altered without the emergence of more legitimate institutions to perform its functions, is a question to be considered at length . . .

. . . It appears, for example, that there are enough consumers of these goods to support the many stores. But to what extent are low-income families oriented toward major durables? Which types of families are heavy consumers and which are not? What proportions of low-income families buy from neighborhood stores and from peddlers? How do the families with broader shopping horizons differ from those who buy only in the neighborhood? What prices do low-income families pay for their appliances and how do their shopping decisions affect the prices they pay? Since credit is the mainstay of the neighborhood merchant, which types of families make use of credit? And how do the consumers experience the pressures exerted upon them by the merchants? What sales gimmicks have resulted in the purchase of initially unwanted goods, and which families are particularly vulnerable to these gimmicks? What do low-income families do when they get into trouble as consumers? To what extent are they aware of community agencies that can help them with their problems as consumers, and how often do they make use of them? In short, we must still find out how the system of sales-and-credit is experienced by the consumers.

---

[17] Robert K. Merton, *Social Theory and Social Structure*, rev. ed. (New York: The Free Press of Glencoe, 1957), pp. 71–82.

CAPITALISM

Litton Industries: Big Brother as a Holding Company

DAVID HOROWITZ
AND REESE ERLICH

"According to our computer," says Robert Allan Jr., head of Litton Industries' Greek project, "there's less than 800 weeks before the present trend will be irreversible. . . . The need for food and the lack of capacity of technology in . . . underdeveloped nations will be overwhelming. . . . It's time that we got to work on it." To listen to Litton executives and to read their annual reports, one might suppose that Litton was some enormous social welfare agency rather than a multibillion-dollar defense contractor. In reality, it is both of these and more.

Litton Industries produces S&H Green Stamps and Stouffer Foods, missile guidance systems and nuclear attack submarines. It runs important programs of the War on Poverty at home. And abroad it recently secured an $800 million contract—to which Mr. Allan's statement referred—with the Greek military junta for the economic development of the whole geographical region of Western Peloponnesus and Crete. Litton is the perfect example of the new corporation extending itself beyond the limits that have divided the private oligarchies of business from the realms of responsibility traditionally reserved to government.

Already a new crop of names has appeared to describe this development, among them "New Industrial State" and "Contract State," as well as the older and more restricted term, "Military-Industrial Complex." The shape of the new social and economic system that is emerging from behind these labels is as distant from the

383

classical image of "free enterprise" capitalism as is Allan's statement from anything that one might expect to hear from a Calvin Coolidge, much less a Henry Ford.

Among the corporate bearers of this brave new American future, Litton stands out as something of a paradigm and archetype foreshadowing the shape of things to come. It is not just the new corporation, but the Now Corporation. It has gathered about itself the full mystique of modernity: advanced technology, the "systems engineering" approach (a product of military contracting), electronics and space. And the mystique has paid off phenomenally well, with a corporate growth rate which Business Week says may well be the fastest in the history of U.S. business.

In 1953, when a group headed by Charles "Tex" Thornton bought Litton, then a small electronics firm, for $1.5 million, the company showed $3 million in sales. This year its worth has grown to a fantastic $1.8 *billion* level, making it the 44th largest industrial corporation in the U.S., ranking ahead of such traditional giants as Alcoa Aluminum, Coca-Cola and Dow Chemical. The aura of futuristic competence that surrounds and powers Litton's conglomerate explosion is reinforced by the higher circles of the business world: *Fortune*, the Social Register of the business establishment, describes Litton as "the very symbol of all that is modern in U.S. management" and calls its guiding captains "as brilliant a group as can be found at the head of any corporation in the world."

It is perhaps natural that the guiding forces of American society, frustrated by the nation's stubborn social ills which appear to be insoluble by traditional means, should turn to the methodology of military-space development as the Way to Get Things Done. Unable to confront the real moral and political dimensions of its economic and social crisis, the American leadership defines the crisis as basically a technical problem and is immensely comforted thereby: the technical problem is large, to be sure, but it is one that can be handled without any serious reassessment of American values and institutions—and without the social upheaval that might be necessary to restructure them. If engineers employed by private corporations on contract to the government can put men on the moon, it is reasoned, surely they can cure the social and economic crisis at home.

The social engineering approach to race and poverty is merely the logical extension of the pervasive liberal doctrine of pragmatic America and the "end of ideology." As John F. Kennedy, whom many look on as the last national statesman to bear the torch of idealism, affirmed in his famous Yale address in 1962: "What is at stake is not some grand warfare of rival ideologies which will sweep the country with passion, but the practical management of a modern economy. What we need is . . . more basic discussion of the sophisticated and technical issues involved in keeping a great economic machinery moving ahead."

The domestic upheavals in the years following President Kennedy's address have torn to shreds the mythology of the crisis-free welfare state. But the mythology of salvation through the application of technology by the Great Partnership between government and the private corporations has not only survived, it has risen to a new intensity of apocalyptic promise. The theme recurs across the political spectrum, though Democrats may call it a domestic Marshall Plan while Republicans and Wallacites more candidly emphasize Incentives to Business. And if the extension of the contract state means further entrance of a military-social-industrial complex into governance of American society, maybe it is just the right outfit for the job.

Litton Industries was the first corporation to take over one of the poverty program's multimillion-dollar job corps camps—whose large urban centers are now run completely by private enterprise—and was an early promoter of the "military systems" approach for other areas of national policy. As the idea has caught on, proposals have proliferated. General Bernard Adolph Schriever, special Administration consultant on housing and urban development programs, has already suggested that aerospace's management process be applied to these programs, and aerospace industrial teams have begun pushing for contracts in such areas as urban traffic management and water conservation (California's waste disposal program is in the process of being handed over to Aerojet-General). Litton, for its part, has offered to contract whole local school systems, promising to put them on a sound footing and to run them smoothly and economically—a logical step since it is already a major textbook publisher and runs a college of its own in Michigan. It is a proposal that may well appeal to harried parents and tax-ridden homeowners.

Litton Industries has been *the* corporate success story of the postwar period just because it is the perfect product of the times, custom-made to fit the outlines of the new order. For the same reason, it is a perfect image of the economic developments of this period: the vast expansion of the military budget during the Cold War and the largest corporate merger wave in U.S. history.

While the notion of a military-industrial complex has gained currency in recent years, the *technological* underpinning of the new intimacy between government and business has gone largely unnoticed. Yet fully 70 percent of all research and development being done in the United States today (about $16 billion worth), is paid for by the federal government, whereas a little more than 20 years ago it supported almost none at all. The significance of this for the civilian economy was spelled out recently by Litton's number two man, Roy Ash, in explaining his company's relation to the military sector. Since "almost all new products have their first application in military uses," said Ash, "we always want at least 25 percent of our business in defense and space."

Ash's statement and the facts behind it reflect the final collapse of the cornerstone of old-fashioned capitalism. In the old days private corporations would develop technological innovations at their own expense, risking the outlay with a view to being rewarded by future returns from the competitive marketplace. This was the very essence of entrepreneurship. However, technical research has now become extremely expensive, and because of the gentlemanly pace of competition among the monopolistic giants of the American economy, these corporations are no longer forced by fear of rivals to risk such investments. So they have become accustomed to getting the government to pick up the tab before they move. These corporations have grown economically lazy, in part because *they* really *can* live better on the largess of the so-called welfare state. One of the factors that has made it possible for them to pry such huge sums of research money out of the government has been the unprecedented increase in the concentration of economic—and with it, political—power in the last decade.

This tremendous concentration movement in the economy has been spearheaded by the advance of the "conglomerate" corporations, formed by the acquisition of companies operating in diverse markets. Litton is the star of this movement, with enterprises in 18 distinct industrial categories.

To an uninitiated observer of the conglomerate phenomenon, Litton's fantastic rise has a distinctly mystifying air about it, like some kind of psychic levitation. For despite all the hullabaloo about new technologies and go-go management, Litton can point to no revolutionary innovation which has benefited the civilian economy and represents a tangible basis for its surging nonmilitary growth (about two-thirds of Litton's present sales, according to Roy Ash, are in civilian fields). One has only to think of Xerox and Polaroid, where jet-powered corporate growth and revolutionizing technology have gone hand in hand, to bring the contrast into focus. It is not that Litton produces nothing innovative or useful (if inertial guidance systems for missiles and fighter planes can be considered useful), but rather that nothing Litton has marketed seems to warrant its unparalleled record of corporate expansion. Indeed, most of Litton's technological innovations were already being developed in the 70 and more businesses which Litton has acquired—*before* they became part of the parent firm.

Yet to be mystified by this is merely to confuse what Thorstein Veblen called the "business system" with the industrial system—that is, to mistake the system of developing and implementing technologies to meet human needs for the system of making a buck off them. Litton's success is a function almost entirely of a brilliant, if sleight of hand, business strategy, with the U.S. government as silent partner. If the constituents of its success seem somewhat insubstantial to the ordinary man, the cash it has made is real. And in the "business system," it is the cash that counts.

. . .

When Tex Thornton and company took over Litton, it was essentially a laboratory production office, a very modest enterprise. After four years under the new management, Litton's annual sales had risen from $3 million to $100 million—and that was just the beginning.

The traditional conception of the growth of a business brings to mind images of the firm selling more of its products, creating new ones, and building new plants to produce more to sell. Only a fraction of Litton's growth, in fact, was achieved in this way. Of the $97 million increase during Tex's first four years, for example, sales from Charlie Litton's original firm accounted for only $11 million. The rest of the increase in sales resulted from the acquisition of some 17 previously existing companies and their incorporation into a new overall financial superstructure: "Litton Industries, Inc." As Thornton explains, "We had to grow fast. There wasn't time to learn a business, train people, develop markets. . . . We bought time, a market, a product line, plant, research team, sales force. It would have taken years to duplicate this from scratch."

Buying, not building, was the formula of Litton's growth. To understand how a small firm with limited resources *can* buy itself into bigness, one must understand how corporate growth can feed on itself. For the very act of **merger** creates new power to merge on an even larger scale through its effect on the value of the corporation's stock.

The value of the stock and therefore of the corporation is not determined by adding up the values of tangible assets: cash reserves, inventories, equipment, plant and so forth. The value of the stock is determined by what people are willing to pay for it, and they will pay more now if they expect its value to rise in the future. Of course these are not just expectations of expectations, but are ultimately derived from an assessment of the potential for real growth of corporate assets and earnings.

Expectations, however, are by nature intuitive, and intuition can be influenced by all kinds of intangible factors. Jack Dreyfus, head of one of the biggest mutual funds on Wall Street, once commented wryly on the subjective "glamour" factors which have gone into making the stock of corporations like Litton highly valued on the market, by offering his own prescription for such a success: "Take a nice little company that's been making shoelaces for 40 years and sells at a respectable six-times-earnings ratio. Change the name from Shoelaces Inc. to Electronics and Silicon Furth-Burners. In today's market, the words 'electronics' and 'silicon' are worth 15 times earnings. However, the real play comes from the word 'furth-burners,' which no one understands. A word that no one understands entitles you to double your entire score. Therefore, we have six times earnings for the shoelace business and 15 times earnings for electronics and silicon, or a total of 21 times earnings. Multiply this by two for furth-burners and we now have a score of 42 times earnings for the new company."

The key to conglomerate growth is the fact that a company's stock can be—and ordinarily is—the "money" that is used to purchase another corporation. So a smart businessman can make the process come full circle. By successfully creating a glamorous "growth image" on the stock market that excites expectations of real future growth, he can drive the value of his stock up. This then gives him new "money" with which to buy *real* assets in the form of another corporation: in other words, his business can grow in fact and not just on paper, thereby confirming the expectations he aroused and further strengthening the image. And so the circle becomes a spiral of increasing growth.

It it small wonder, then, that creating a glamour image is a major preoccupation of conglomerate managements like Litton's. Indeed, Litton was a pioneer in converting the traditionally staid Annual Report to Stockholders into a high-class Advertisement for Myself. Litton's reports look more like catalogues from Pasadena's Huntington Museum of Art than informational materials from a major industrial corporation. Abraham J. Briloff described it in the Financial Analysts Journal: "Litton's 1967 report is, as you undoubtedly know, a most beautiful document . . . which symbolizes the ethics of 20th century commercial life in the New Industrial State . . . distorted in my view is the series of graphs most beautifully set to type at page 55 of the annual report. . . . The curves which the eye is invited to make are optical illusions capable of inducing inappropriate investment decisions."

Another art which is employed in the production of a glamour image is creative accounting. This important technique of the Big Growth game is made possible by the looseness of the principles under which firms are audited. The usual methods are not as crude as those that were used at Hughes Aircraft, but their effects can be pretty significant.

As the pseudonymous "Adam Smith" notes in *The Money Game*, "Numbers imply precision, so it's a bit hard to get used to the idea that a company's net profit could vary by 100 percent depending on which bunch of accountants you call in, especially when the market is going to take that earnings number and create trends, growth rates, and little flashing lights in computers from it. And all this without any kind of skulduggery you could get sent to jail for." An explanation for this legal generosity was given by the real Adam Smith, the 18th century prophet of the free enterprise system. The very purpose of government, he wrote, was "to secure wealth, and to defend the rich from the poor."

The spread between one set of figures and another can be the difference between a real glamour stock and a merely good performer, as evidenced by Litton's 1967 report, which with one flick of the accounting wrist boosted the figure for the increase in the corporation's earnings over the previous year from 15 to 26 percent. This was accomplished by ignoring the pre-merger earnings of newly-acquired companies when estimating the increase. And this is only one of the gambits available to merger oriented firms. As "Adam Smith" observes, "If you are busy buying and selling companies, every time they pass through your accounting firm you get the chance to try to describe artistically some of the assets as earnings, to capitalize costs that have previously been expensed, and in general to create what Wall Street is looking for, which is a neat pattern of constantly growing earnings."

Conglomerates are so obviously based on highly speculative, not to say shady, principles that even the *Wall Street Journal* has been prompted to take off its gold-rimmed rose-colored glasses for an instant and ask a few probing questions about them: how much of their growth is based on improved products and efficiencies and how much reflects the attractive arithmetic of acquisition and the temptations of empire building? . . . Can they be managed efficiently?

This last question has an especially poignant ring for Litton's supermanagers. In 1968, Litton's second quarter report admitted a disastrous 30 percent earnings drop (Litton's stock price plummeted nearly 50 percent at the news), reflecting managerial errors so gross that not even the most creative accounting techniques could cover them up.

The mistakes affected several of Litton's divisions, including its business furniture, Royfax duplicators, Monroe calculators, and its Royal typewriter line. But the biggest error of all provided the clue to the overall pattern of Litton's debacle. The Litton shipyard, which had been accustomed to a rich diet of cost-plus contracts at the government trough ("Your chances of losing money" under such contracts, admits a Litton executive, "are not too great"), had for the first time bid competitively on a package basis for the construction of automated merchant vessels—a *civilian* contract under which you don't get to come back for more money if you can't make it at the agreed-upon price. The result of this market test was that Litton underestimated the costs, submitted a bid that was too low, and instead of netting a profit, had to write off a loss of $8 million.

In what must rank as the understatement of the year, *Fortune*, after noting that the key to Litton's setback was its inability to stand the test of the relatively competitive civilian market, observed: "The requirements for profitability in government work are less exacting than those of the private marketplace." They certainly are.

Under government contracts there is a decided lack of competitive strictures. Little or no capital is risked by the corporation. If it makes errors of judgment, timing, cost analysis and so forth, there are no competitors to take advantage of its mistakes. And it has an enormously understanding buyer. If costs are underestimated, they can always be adjusted up through contract renegotiation. One former Litton executive with responsibilities in this area estimated that as a matter of *normal* practice, Litton in the course of production and development renegotiated its contracts to one and a half times the original price—a nice margin for inept planning and mismanagement.

In short, its vulnerable, soap-bubble growth strategy could never have carried Litton so far had it not possessed the ability, though a small firm at the outset, to get a front-line position in the prime military contract game and latch on to that secret fuel which alone can launch space age corporations towards the moon: the financial largess of the state.

. . .

But political strings are only half the story. More than anything else, it is the defense contracting system itself, as it evolved after World War II, which has created the new and sinister relationship between the giant corporations and the state.

Following the profiteering scandals of World War I, which revealed that American business had milked the American taxpayer by "sliding" price policies on military contracts, and had spent the lives of many American soldiers by producing cheap, shoddy equipment, the practice of competitive bidding on government contracts was instituted to simulate the open market. The two armed services developed their own "in-house" design and production capabilities which served to measure and check outside performances. Under the pressures of the Second World War, contracting procedures on aircraft, ordnance and ammunition reverted to the cost-plus basis which had inspired the earlier scandals. Then a series of developments after the war produced the current unprecedented state of affairs.

First, as part of a movement heralded as a return to "free enterprise," plants, factories and facilities built by the government during the war were either sold to private corporations, usually at a fraction of their original cost, or were leased at nominal fees to contractors, to use for military contracts. This largely deprived the government of the performance "yardstick" of its in-house facilities.

Second, the Air Force was established as an independent military service. Naturally, it did not have the already built in-house capabilities of the other two services, so it hired out the entire process of designing, producing and even maintaining weapons systems, instead of presenting its own designs to contractors for production. This necessitated a cost-plus contractual basis, since no prearranged price could be fixed for so indeterminate a process. In addition, the Air Force's prime contracting corporations, now responsible for complete weapons systems, had to establish, in the words of one Congressional Report, "procurement organizations and methods which proximate those of the government." These prime contractors were thus in a position to force subcontracting small companies out of business, acquire their proprietary information, make or break geographical regions and decide a host of other critical issues of national import, without even the quasi-democratic checks imposed on the federal bureaucracy. No wonder H. L. Nieburg has warned of the ominous erosion of public control by the giant aerospace companies and has dubbed the whole relationship "the contract state."

Once established, prime systems contracting quickly spread to the other services. A losing battle with the Air Force for responsibility for missile program development taught the Army that its extensive in-house capabilities and technical independence were a distinct disadvantage. For in the political struggle over missile development, the Air Force's corporate prime contractors constituted a powerful lobby in Congress against which all the in-house expertise of the Army was of no avail. A quick learner when the future of its bureaucracy is at stake, the Army began to disband its in-house facilities and to surrender its jurisdictional and discretionary capacities to private industry and the latter's impressive political power. For any corporation in advanced technologies on the way up, prime contracting soon became the indispensable order of the day.

From the outset, the new Tex Thornton team at Litton had its eyes on the really big electronic equipment and systems markets. They were determined not to be pikers and they knew their way up the federal escalator, but they needed a break. In 1954, a team of Litton scientists headed by Dr. Henry Singleton appeared ready to give them one. He outlined a project for miniaturizing an inertial navigator and guidance system. Perfecting such a system was of paramount importance to the military, for it would be the only kind of navigational system that could not be electronically jammed. Further, a missile guided by such a navigator would not emit signals that would disclose its whereabouts. The military had already set out the objectives of such a system and various working devices had been produced, but they all weighed from 500 to 1000 pounds, too heavy for aircraft and missiles. Thus, Singleton was proposing an innovation that would revolutionize the field.

All that was needed to attempt to develop the system was capital. Of course the Litton management, well oriented towards the new age, had no intention of putting up their own money, or of raising it through old-fashioned loans or investors. For to raise capital in that way would entail risks and obligations. What Litton really needed was a banker who would not seek repayment of capital (with interest) if the investment bore no fruit, and if the project should come through, who would not insist on reaping any return on his investment. Could there *be* such a banker? Litton thought so.

With nothing but a wooden mock-up of the proposed navigator and a ten-cents-a-mile expense account for its station wagon, the Litton sales team set out to sell a miniaturized inertial navigation system to the Army Air Corps. In 1956, they finally convinced the purchasing agents at Fort Huachuca, Arizona, to finance the development of a prototype. For its proposal, Litton got a fixed price redeterminable contract for $214,902.

With the Fort Huachuca contract safely tucked away in their display kits, Litton salesmen then made the rounds of various other government agencies and aerospace firms, stressing the advantages of getting in on the ground floor with contracts for the navigators while the opportunity lasted. In 1957, Litton contracted to produce for Grumman, the chief Navy aircraft supplier, 68 of the navigators for Navy planes. By 1959, this contract was worth some $7,400,000. In subsequent months, Litton used its new foot in the door with Grumman to sell them additional items, until their total contracts amounted to a full $10 million.

According to the Steele case testimony of John McDonald, then head of Litton's electronics division's contract negotiations, Litton's engineers did successfully achieve the new revolutionary design. But Litton never delivered the prototype navigator to the Army, which had originally paid for it; instead, it used the design to fulfill its contract with Grumman Aircraft. All the Army got was a bagful of disassembled parts. In 1960, the Army purchasing officials canceled Litton's contract "for the convenience of the government."

As for Litton, it had won for itself a tremendous future contracting position for electronics and guidance systems in missiles, planes and even ships, on which all the federal give-away on costs and profits would be multiplied a thousandfold. No longer a little laboratory but a real comer in the field, Litton was now ready for a really golden opportunity: a major subcontract for the guidance system of the F-104 Starfighter jet. And when Germany decided to incorporate 700 F-104's into its postwar *Luftwaffe*, Litton bought two German companies just to produce the guidance systems for their version of the plane. Unfortunately, the *Luftwaffe's* Starfighter turned out to be, in the words of *Business Week*, "an essentially American product that now bears the blackest name in the history of German aviation." At least 83 of the planes crashed, killing 42 pilots and forcing Litton to modify the guidance system. Some time later a further modified version of Litton's navigator was installed in America's newest fighter plane, the ill-fated F-111, McNamara's notorious pet project and one of the costliest boondoggles of all time. The prime Navy contractor for that plane: Grumman Aircraft.

. . .

Titans and Olympians

While most eyes were focused on the presidential elections, an unprecedented humiliation was being visited upon one of the dinosaurs of the American corporate community. The United Fruit Company—whose board directors and presidents were accustomed to serving the nation as secretaries of State and directors of the CIA, and whose divisional branches exercised unchallenged supremacy over sovereign republics in the banana belt of Central America—found that it was the target of a series of takeover bids. Who would have the nerve?

Twenty-five years ago Textron, Incorporated, was only a diminutive manufacturer of textiles. Since then, however, the firm has acquired a new name and scores of companies spanning 27 industrial categories, and has taken a prominent place in the military-industrial complex. On election eve Textron announced that it was adding United Fruit to its family.

This was not the biggest merger of the year, but it dramatically symbolized the tremendous upheaval that is shifting the corporate foundations of American society. The U.S. is currently in the midst of the largest merger wave in its history, already twice the magnitude of any previous wave and still on the upswing, with no sign of peaking. The main action in this incredible concentration of economic power, accounting for about 90 percent of all acquisitions in 1968, is going to a new species of corporate organization: the conglomerate. Led by such aerospace giants as Litton Industries, Ling-Temco-Vought (L-T-V) and Textron, the conglomerates are already regarded by many as the heirs apparent to American corporate power. With their feet solidly planted in the military-industrial complex, each has managed to absorb close to a hundred other corporations and to create a composite giant whose scope of industrial enterprise is truly awesome.

This explosive velocity of conglomerate expansion makes the most fantastic projections seem plausible. Litton Industries provides a typical case in point. Fifteen years ago Litton was a $1.5 million electronics firm. Today, employing about 100,000 people in 28 countries, it is worth more than a thousand times as much. The record of L-T-V is equally spectacular. Twenty-two years ago, James J. Ling invested $3000 in an electronics shop in Dallas. Today the successor of that firm, L-T-V, is even bigger than Litton, with $1 billion in assets and $2 billion in sales. Moreover, the expansion of these conglomerates over whole empires seems to have no natural limit, unless it is the economic system itself. Indeed, one enthusiastic reporter of the L-T-V octopus has already run his story under the headline: "It is Theoretically Possible for the Entire United States to Become ONE VAST CONGLOMERATE Presided Over by Mr. James J. Ling." Nor is the prospect one from which Mr. Ling would shrink.

The Technology of Profit

The vast accretion of power in the last decade to military-based conglomerates like Litton and L-T-V has caused remarkably little public concern, considering the implications for an ostensibly free society. There are many factors behind this default, but probably the most important one is the least conspicuous. It is the universal conviction that bigness and even monopolistic concentration are inevitable, being the natural and necessary consequences of technological modernity. To protest therefore seems merely to stand in the way of progress, mindlessly repudiating the bounty of the age in favor of nostalgic illusions.

John Kenneth Galbraith, the New Monopolistic State's most urbane, unabashed and best-selling apologist, has expressed the wisdom of the times most eloquently: "By all but the pathologically romantic, it is now recognized that this is not the age of the small man." Is it the quest for monopoly profits that has resulted in the gargantuan enterprises which now dominate the American economy? Certainly not, says Galbraith: "Size is the general servant of technology, not the special servant of profits. The small firm cannot be restored by breaking the power of the larger ones. It would require, rather, the rejection of the technology which since earliest consciousness we are taught to applaud." Modern technology, says Galbraith, requires "planning, specialization and organization," and these require that the market be "superseded," "controlled" or "suspended," which is accomplished primarily by monopolistic concentration.

These statements, exuding all the natural plausibility of conventional wisdom, are wholly seductive. To offer empirical support for the generalizations seems almost superfluous. Yet the actual empirical studies that have been made provide no substantive basis for the thesis that technology requires monopoly—indeed they point strongly in the opposite direction.

Thus, the authoritative study in the field (Joe S. Bain's *Industrial Organization*) concludes that for 80 to 90 percent of the industries investigated, there is no need for high concentration to make production and distribution efficient. On the other hand, many of the new technologies have a decidedly decentralizing thrust, and as Dr. John M. Blair, chief economist for the Senate antitrust subcommittee, has pointed out, highly monopolistic industries like steel have been decentralizing their assembly plants at the same time that another model of monopolistic concentration, General Electric, has "shut down its huge Schenectady factory while making a veritable religion of decentralization."

If relatively high concentration is not technologically justified for single industry firms, it is hardly justified for the conglomerates, which are made up of randomly acquired companies encompassing diverse product lines and categories.

For that reason among others, the heads of Litton, like all conglomerate managements, don't like to admit that they are such an enterprise (although their more than 80 companies operate in 18 distinct industrial categories). According to number two man, Roy Ash, Litton's acquisitions have been in fields where its technological capabilities give it a competitive edge. "In truth," comments Fortune, "considerable mental agility is required to perceive an impending technological revolution in some of the businesses Litton has bought —e.g., office furniture."

Litton Industries cannot in fact seriously claim to provide any benefits of integrated production to its jumble of sub-units. And if they are sometimes inclined to invoke the salutary but mysterious influence of their mode of central management, when they get down to it the feature of their organization about which they are proudest is just how decentralized it is—with each division manager given his head and acquired companies remaining autonomous and even rivals of their sibling subunits. So the occult potency of Litton's management is like that of the magician who claims to be twice as good as any other because he can conjure a rabbit in a hat *and* make it disappear, all faster than the eye can see. The idea of some arcane technology of management—a notion drawn from military and space prime contracting activities—is Litton's stock in trade. The alternative, that central ownership is just that, that its prime function is to own—i.e., to concentrate financial, industrial and political power—is of course unthinkable.

But the *Wall Street Journal* did manage to think of it when they interviewed officials of Textron, and they got a rather candid response. Asked the Journal "How can any group of executives maintain control over such dizzyingly varied businesses in most of which they can have had no experience? The answer to the question, say Textron men, is simple. The company has acquired unrelated businesses to make money."

Office furniture aside, Ash's claim that Litton's size facilitates technological innovation reflects another major technological myth of our age: that the giant corporation is a necessary agent for *creating* new technologies. As Galbraith puts it: "A benign providence who, so far, has loved us for our worries, has made the modern industry of a few large firms an almost perfect instrument for inducing technical change. It is admirably equipped for financing technical development. Its organization provides strong incentives for undertaking development and for putting it into use. . . . There is no more pleasant fiction than that technical change is the product of the matchless ingenuity of the small man forced by competition to employ his wits to better his neighbor. Unhappily, it is a fiction. Technical development has long since become the preserve of the scientist and the engineer. Most of the cheap and simple inventions have, to put it bluntly, been made." Once again the record indicates that the "perfect instrument" must somehow be too sublime to do the job.

In an authoritative study of 61 "major contemporary inventions," it was found that only 12 of these could be attributed to the laboratories of large corporations. The jet engine was originated independently in England and Germany by individuals who were unable to interest the aircraft producers in it (the Englishman even allowed his patent to lapse). Kodachrome arose from the experiments of two musicians, "sometimes working in their kitchen sinks between concerts." Other examples of products of individual inventors—often working with primitive equipment—were the first computer (ENIAC), air conditioning, the modern self-winding watch (which was rejected by the Swiss watch companies when it was first offered to them), stereophonic sound reproduction, the syncromesh transmission, neomycin, frequency modulation (FM; it was opposed by RCA) and xerography. In military technology, individuals without organizational support were either responsible for, or played a crucial role in the development of, the gyrocompass, the helicopter, the atomic submarine and the sidewinder missile.

A closer look at the inventions that do come out of the laboratories of the industrial giants should quickly dispel Galbraith's "perfect instrument" idea. Arthur K. Watson, the head of IBM, the very symbol of modern technology in business, pointed out to an International Congress of Accountants in 1962, "The disk memory unit, the heart of today's random access computer, is not the logical outcome of a decision made by IBM management. It was developed in one of our laboratories as a bootleg project—over the stern warning from management that the project had to be dropped because of budget difficulties. A handful of men ignored the warning. They broke the rules. They risked their jobs to work on a project they believed in."

Can it be that the supercorporation of the space age is really all that shortsighted and tightfisted about seeking new technologies? Private industry does after all spend $9 billion a year on research and development (four per cent on basic research, the rest largely on altering, refining, packaging and marketing existing technologies). And of that, the larger firms, those with more than 5000 employees, certainly carry their share. Though they make up only three per cent of the companies doing research, they spend 85 per cent of the total. That looks like pretty extravagant entrepreneurial daring. Of course this investment in the future is made considerably easier for them by the fact that the government puts up 60 cents of every R&D dollar that private industry spends. Moreover, two-thirds of the rest is ultimately charged off as overhead on government contracts.

So it seems that the real **entrepreneur** is the government, who is not only extraordinarily openhanded about putting up the investment, but agreeably lighthearted about not reaping the profits on it. So agreeable, in fact, that it goes on to buy the product that it financed, at a healthy profit to the surrogate developer. Like buying the Brooklyn Bridge, this must be looked on as an act of peculiar generosity. It is a game where the roles of politician, general, corporate manager and government official are shifted around so rapidly that an embarrassed player can even forget if he is to be the donor or the recipient.

But then again it's not their money. If the corporation is spending the government's money, the government is spending the taxpayer's. If he had a very clear idea of it, the taxpayer might frown on this happy arrangement and spoil all the fun, but his attention is turned toward the welfare pennies allegedly squandered on people who don't work. Whereas the men on the board at Litton have very good jobs indeed.

Litton Industries is a **holding company** for its decentrally managed subsidiaries. But Litton is not merely a Beverly Hills address where worldwide profits are mailed to be figured by accountants into grand totals. It is a focal point for an empire's growing economic power which it applies with consummate skill to the great financial and political levers on Wall Street and Washington.

Litton is a new lord of the corporate realm; it has ascended to an order of nobility that had seemed at the time of World War II to be virtually closed by a stable system of fiefdoms which each of the major corporations had carved out of the Industrial Revolution, leaving no unclaimed ground on which a new economic power could be built. And in fact, although Litton has achieved sufficient financial strength—by playing an inflated stock market for all it is worth—to acquire properties in the economic heartland inhabited by the older corporations, the original and indispensable basis of Litton's strength was not successful competition in already allocated markets. Litton is first of all lord of a newly opened virgin territory. That is to say, Litton is not an industrial pioneer in traditional markets in the sense that one might characterize Polaroid or Xerox, whose spectacular growths have been based on new products which people have found highly useful. Litton is more the master of a "land grant dominion," dispensed and continuously subsidized by the federal government as part of the unbelievable largesse of the postwar contract state.

The form which these grants take is the military prime "systems" contract, and the region is electronics. A good example is Litton's contract to design, plan, produce and maintain, in accordance with broad requirements, a worldwide fleet of floating military bases. Since the price of a system not yet designed cannot be fixed in advance, in systems contracting the government in effect agrees to pay the corporation back whatever it spends, plus profits. The prime contractor is expected to turn around and subcontract whatever it can't do itself and the government advances funds to cover outlays by the contractor. So you don't really need investment capital or competence to get the job—or the profits.

Obviously it's nice work if you can get it. But who gets it and how? Since the criteria of cash and competence are consigned by government contracting policies to roles of distinctly secondary importance, the importance of a corporation's influence in the federal bureaucracies naturally looms inordinately large. For a long time, corporate political strategy had its focus on military decision makers, whether generals or civilians. However, as the military budget has become a permanent factor of major proportions in the economy as a whole, the ramifications of its spending policies have grown more and more extensive. From its contract to build the floating base system, for example, Litton gained facilities and expertise—at taxpayers' expense—which have given it the inside track on the civilian shipbuilding industry as well. More importantly, neither military policy nor the Defense bureaucracy is divorced from the rest of the national political structure, and the political power gained by the successful prime contractors in the military field has become an important basis for extending their field of operation to other areas where the federal government exercises responsibility and allocates its huge budget.

With an eye to the immense dominions of largesse still to be granted by the sovereign power, Litton has been careful to keep its representatives at court and to keep a foot in every available political door. Among its executives and directors are Defense Department secretaries and military generals, highly influential Democrats and equally important Republicans, liberal Humphrey supporters and the chief financial backer of Ronald Reagan—in short, the whole spectrum of legitimized political power (and potential contract dispensation). With its expansive political network as a foundation, Litton has been in the forefront of the move to extend systems contracting to nonmilitary fields. Litton was the first private contractor to take over responsibility for a War on Poverty Job Corps project and the first corporation to apply the systems approach to the economic development program of an entire geographical region (in Greece), and its distinctive mode of operation in these instances provides an ominous portent of things to come. Litton's career follows what may turn out to be the most natural line of development for the huge and continuously growing conglomerate corporations as they overflow the traditional limits which have contained them.

PROPERTY

Pollution, Property and Prices

J. H. DALE

... I have argued that whether we approach pollution problems from the standpoint of economics (**benefit-cost analysis**) or the standpoint of law (property rights) we can find no best solution to them; and that any anti-pollution policy is therefore bound to be in the nature of a social experiment that is neither right nor wrong, but only more or less successful in leading to wise and socially agreed-upon patterns of use of our air and water resources. ... I shall begin by sketching out one possible policy (or social experiment), and then discuss, in much greater detail, its implementation. ... I shall refer only to water-pollution problems; but the argument should apply equally well to air-pollution problems.

A Policy

I would have the Ontario government set up a Water Control Board, which I shall call the W C B for short. The legislative function of the W C B would be to decide what the quality of all natural waters in Ontario should be; its executive function would be to implement its decisions. Both functions would, of course, be subject to over-riding review and veto by the government of the day; but the intent of the legislation establishing the W C B, like the intent of legislation establishing all such boards, would be to insulate it from party politics. Being largely ignorant of the principles of public administration, I shall sidestep the important questions of how many Board members there should be, how long each should serve, and what their qualifications should be. (On the latter question, though, I don't think the members should all be experts or all amateurs; a mixture would be more to my liking. *None* of them should be a party hack.)

At its first meeting, the Board members will unanimously agree that their terms of reference, "to decide what the quality of all natural waters in Ontario should be," are quite absurd if interpreted literally. I would advise them to divide Ontario into "regions" and then try to set an "average" water quality for each region. Suppose they adopt this strategy. After long discussions about whether they should define regions as "watersheds" or "population clusters" or "groups of municipalities," or some combination of these and other criteria, they *do*, however, succeed in drawing a map that divides the province into "water control regions." Their major policy task is now to decide what the average water quality in each region should be.

They run into one dismaying difficulty right away; there is no measure of water quality! Scientists talk about water quality in terms of "suspended solids," "B O D," "dissolved oxygen," "nutrient content," "pesticide residues," and half a dozen other things. But there is no over-all measure of quality; it turns out that even "pure" unpolluted waters differ greatly in terms of most of these measures so that it is impossible to define "pure" water and therefore impossible to define "impure" water or to measure "the degree of pollution."

Well, there is no use arguing with science. But there is no use, either, in arguing with several millions of people who insist that there *is* pollution and that the W C B do something about it. The Board therefore tries a new line of attack. "Suppose," some members say, "we look at the problem the other way around. If we can't measure water quality we can at least measure the amount of waste that is dumped into natural waters; and that, after all, is what people mean by pollution." The experts agree that, at least in principle, the number of tons of waste that are put into the water *can* indeed be measured. They raise two sorts of difficulties, however, that the Board must consider before they try to set their policy in terms of "tons of waste."

The first is that people are not interested in tons of waste but in the damage done by wastes; a ton of pulp liquor does different *sorts* of damage, and probably a different *amount* of damage, than a ton of untreated sewage. To get around this problem, the Board agrees that it will have to draw up a "table of equivalents" for different types of wastes, so that they may be expressed in some common denominator as it were. But it is immediately pointed out that a ton of any particular kind of waste will do much more damage in some places than in others; the damage done will depend on the particular character of the water, since some rivers and lakes have a greater capacity for absorbing wastes than others, and on the particular uses people make, or would like to make, of the water in question. A tentative way around this difficulty seems to be for the W C B, in consultation with its engineers, to draw up a *different* table of equivalents for each region, so that regional differences both in water and in water use can be allowed for, at least in a very rough and ready way. This solution will also enable the Board to make some allowance for the phenomena of counteracting and escalating combinations of waste. Wastes that counteract one another in one area may be given low damage ratings, though each is given a higher rating in areas where the other is not present; the reverse allowance may be made for escalating wastes. So far, the procedure seems practicable, if not very precise.

The second difficulty, the experts report, is that they can measure without too much difficulty the amounts of waste at identifiable "waste outfalls"—where pipes enter the water—but they really cannot measure with any accuracy the amount of wastes that enter water systems from surface run-off or from fallout from the air. However, the experts agree that, in water pollution at least, most wastes come from identifiable sources, and the Board therefore decides to defer the run-off problem, and to deal initially only with pollution from waste outfalls.

The W C B can now, I think, feel that it has made some progress toward enunciating a policy; or, rather, it has found a way in which its policy, when formed, can be enunciated. True, much remains to be done. A table of equivalents has to be drawn up for each water control region; this work will have to go forward in consultation with scientists who know their wastes and their waters, and with local interests who know the uses that people make of the water in their areas. There then remains the crux of the matter: How many "equivalent tons" of waste will the Board allow to be dumped in the water in each region? That is where the crunch comes. We have already seen that there is no "correct" answer to the problem; there is certainly going to be no unanimity to whatever answer is given; but the Board's main function is, precisely, to answer it.

Suppose the Board, after long deliberation, finally makes the following announcement: "The W C B has decided on a water quality control policy for a trial period of five years. During each of the next five years the equivalent tons of waste injected into the water in each water control region must not exceed the equivalent tonnage of wastes that were injected into the water last year. The Board will announce shortly how it intends to implement this policy. During the five-year trial period the policy will be subjected to continuous study and appraisal, and at the end of five years a new policy announcement will be made."

And so we have a brand new water-pollution policy! But how will it work? Vacationers may wonder whether the policy will permit new cottages to be built at the lake during the next five years. New cottages could be built if they were equipped with septic tanks, or if present cottagers built a small sewage treatment plant, reduced the present inflow of wastes entering the lake, and thus "made room" for newcomers. The same would be true for industry or urban housing; by treating present wastes more fully, growth in population and production could be allowed for without exceeding the present inflow of wastes to natural water systems. To that extent, at least, the policy sounds practicable. It will not, of course, do anything to *reduce* pollution (though the policy sets a maximum waste discharge, and there is nothing to prevent people from discharging less than this maximum) but it should help stop the *growth* of pollution (except that part of the problem that derives from run-off and fall-out). The policy therefore seems to be helpful—if it works. It is to the interesting question of implementing their policy that the W C B, and we, now turn.

Three Possible Ways of Implementing a Policy

To an economist, there are only three basically different ways of implementing the Board's policy. The first we shall call "regulation." The W C B can issue a regulation requiring all factories and municipalities to reduce their discharges by, say, 5 per cent (to allow for growth) or it can set an allowable quota of waste, expressed in equivalent tons, to each outfall, and simply decree that that quota shall not be exceeded. In the latter case, of course, it must make sure that the sum of the individual quotas is no greater than the over-all figure it has established for the region.

The second technique can be called "subsidization." We suppose that the W C B has direct access to "unlimited" provincial funds, raised either by taxation or by borrowing. The Board could, then, decide to subsidize whatever expenditures were necessary to keep the amount of wastes down to the figure it has chosen for each region. It could subsidize municipalities by building sewage treatment plants for their use; where factories discharge their wastes directly into water systems (rather than indirectly through municipal sewers) the Board could pay the cost of linking them up to municipal sewers or of installing waste treatment systems in the factory. The Board would then have direct control over the measures (and expenditures) required to ensure that its own policy objective was achieved.

The third technique we shall call "pollution charges." The Board, under this system, announces that it is going to levy a "disposal fee" on all those who dispose of their wastes into natural water systems. The fee per ton of waste may vary at different outfalls, and the charge may also increase as the number of tons of discharge increases. This technique is based on the principle that if you charge a person for disposing of his wastes he will find ways to reduce the amount of wastes he disposes of, and that the more you charge him the stronger the incentive he will have to find some less damaging method of disposing of his wastes. The Board, however, may have to do quite a bit of "trial-and-error pricing" before it hits on a system of charges that results in the total amount of wastes that are discharged into water systems being equal to, or slightly less than, its target figure.

There are many fascinating and important comparisons and contrasts to be made between these three broad methods of enforcing our water-pollution policy. What is especially interesting is that both the techniques themselves and the analysis of them that follows apply to *most* social problems and are by no means confined to pollution problems. We cannot here discuss other social problems; but perhaps the reader might entertain himself by applying this kind of analysis to, say, aircraft safety standards, traffic problems, or building codes. It is interesting to note that the parking meter, as a solution to parking problems, exemplifies our third technique: a fee is levied for the right to park on public property, and different fees are levied on different streets. Traffic problems are controlled mainly by regulation and partly by charges (fines), and many educational problems are dealt with by subsidies. But, in principle at least, the technique that is actually used in each case could be replaced by either of the other two.

Note, first, that even though we have referred to our three techniques as "basically different" they in fact appear to amount to much the same thing. The W C B's policy can be met by a particular set of regulations, a particular set of subsidies, or a particular set of charges. "But who pays?" you will ask. Actually, we answered that question . . . when we were discussing the cost of the English system of "property rights in fishing" to the fishermen and the municipal or industrial polluters. If people are divided into groups, different control techniques have different results; under a subsidy scheme the polluter receives money (or equipment) while under a charging scheme he pays out money. However, if we carry the analysis a step further, we see that in a charging scheme producers and municipalities will recoup the money they pay out by charging higher prices and higher taxes for their goods and services; the same will be true of the higher costs industries and municipalities will be forced to bear if the W C B uses regulations rather than charges. If subsidies are used, prices of goods and municipal services will not go up, but provincial taxes will. In the end, the costs will be spread around, and the general population will pay for pollution control. This is why, when we are dealing with a large population and a large area such as Ontario, it seems more realistic to deal with society as a whole, rather than with groups. If we were dealing with, say, a pollution problem caused by one factory in a dormitory suburb, it would make sense to distinguish the factory group from the residents, and such problems are of course important. Here, however, we are dealing with what economists call "general equilibrium" situations, in which we are all simultaneously producers *and* consumers, polluters *and* pollutees. It is then true that, no matter who passes the money to whom in the first place, we all pay in the end. (Whether we pay *equally* depends on a host of factors, such as the taxation system, individual consumption habits, and so on; but there will be individual discrepancies in the burden of pollution control no matter how the control is implemented.)

Astonishingly, therefore, whether you pay industries (and people) not to pollute, or charge them for the right to pollute, or simply tell them that they must pollute only so much and no more, the outcome is still much the same. Pollution can be kept to the same amount by any one of the techniques, and everyone pays for keeping it to that amount. It is largely a waste of time for the pot to call the kettle black where pollution problems are concerned; everyone pollutes and everyone pays for not polluting.

Does it, then, make no difference which technique the W C B uses to enforce its policy? It certainly *does* make a difference, an enormous difference; even though the costs of getting the benefit are shared, the amount of cost (and also the type of cost) differs greatly from one scheme to another. Consider a simpler case for a moment. Suppose that we wanted to decrease the number of high-school drop-outs by, say, 90 per cent. We could do so by paying prospective drop-outs whatever price would lead nine out of ten of them *not* to dropout; or by charging them a fee for the right to drop out that would result in only one out of ten prospects deciding to do so; or by passing a law forbidding drop-outs (but allowing kick-outs). The paying scheme would be very costly to the taxpayer in terms of money because every student worth his salt would think of dropping out in order to collect his payment for deciding not to! The law forbidding drop-outs would, I think, be worse; those who wanted to drop out badly enough would have to do enough damage or otherwise make enough of a nuisance of themselves to be kicked out. The taxpayer would have to pay for the damage, or for controlling the nuisance. Much more serious, though, would be the feelings of resentment at being forced to stay in school by those who would otherwise have dropped out, and even by those who would like to think they *could* drop out if they wanted to; the cost in terms of educational morale might be high. The *charging* scheme would cost practically nothing to administer; those who still decided to drop out would actually be a small source of revenue to taxpayers; and there would probably be a lot less idle talk among students about dropping out than there is now—those who wanted to drop out badly enough would simply pay their exit fee and leave. A rather similar analysis applies to our three techniques of pollution control, though here there are many more things to consider.

Two Variants of the Basic Techniques

Whether regulations, subsidies, or charges are used to implement a pollution policy, there is a choice between what I shall call "across-the-board" schemes and "point-by-point" schemes. By the former I mean regulations, or subsidies, or charges, that are applied uniformly to all polluters or all sewage outfalls; by the latter I mean schemes in which regulations (subsidies, charges) are adjusted to suit the circumstances of each individual polluter or outfall. In practice there are some across-the-board schemes that blend into point-by-point schemes, so that there is really a whole spectrum of ways to implement a policy. Our classification of all possible schemes into six types is designed to illuminate the main features of a variety of techniques actually used by pollution control agencies. Throughout, we shall suppose that the immediate goal of the W C B is to reduce the number of equivalent tons of waste currently being discharged into water systems by 5 per cent.

Across-the-board regulation would be most unfair. It would also be inefficient in the economic sense, i.e., the same result could be achieved at lower cost by some other scheme. Suppose that the W C B issues a regulation saying simply that "All existing factories and municipalities must reduce the amount of waste they discharge into water systems by 5 per cent next year." Those factories and municipalities which were *already* spending a good deal of money to treat their wastes would be justifiably annoyed; they would argue that those who now did *nothing* about their wastes should be the ones to carry the main burden of the over-all reduction in waste discharge, and that only when everyone is in the same position should everyone be treated in the same way. Moreover, municipalities on large fast-flowing rivers will want to know why they should have to reduce their waste output as much as municipalities on small, sluggish streams where the pollution problem is much greater. Again, there may be two factories, a furniture factory and a cannery, side by side, each of which dumps the same number of equivalent tons of waste into a river. Yet it may be much cheaper for the furniture factory to reduce its waste discharge by 10 per cent than for the cannery to reduce its discharge by 5 per cent. What does justice demand here? It is at least clear that the total cost of reducing waste inflow into the river from these two plants by 5 per cent would be less if the furniture plant alone were required to introduce anti-pollution measures than if both plants were required to do so.

On the other hand, if the W C B were to attempt point-by-point regulation it would have a massive administrative problem on its hands. A separate regulation would have to be drafted for each outfall, or perhaps for each polluter, each regulation taking into account the condition of the water into which the waste is discharged, and the cost to different polluters of reducing their pollution; it would also be desirable on purely economic grounds to try to minimize the total costs to all polluters of achieving a given reduction in over-all waste discharge, but to do this would require a fantastic amount of information that in practice would be very difficult and expensive to get. In any event a large bureaucracy would be required to gather all the information and undertake all the interviews that would be necessary before the thousands of individual regulations could be drafted. The administrative costs of point-by-point regulation would be enormous.

Control by regulation, then, does not seem to be a very attractive way to enforce our pollution policy. If it is of the across-the-board type it is likely to be unfair and inefficient (i.e., more costly to the polluters than some other scheme that would achieve the same reduction in pollution). If it is point-by-point regulation the whole thing seems, quite simply, impracticable. And yet the first recourse of governments when electorates demand that they "do something" about a problem is nearly always to pass laws and issue regulations about it. In Ontario, at present, most waste treatment expenditures result from laws or regulations, or from the recognition by municipalities and factories that if they don't do something about their wastes on their own initiative they will soon be forced to do so by provincial regulation. Some of the unfairness and inefficiency that we have identified as being inherent in control by regulation is reduced in practice by measures that fall between across-the-board and point-by-point schemes; regulations are applied to industries, instead of single firms, and to groups of municipalities of a certain size, or in a certain area, instead of single municipalities. For the most part, though, these compromise techniques do more to camouflage the difficulties inherent in regulatory schemes than to reduce them.

Industries and municipalities show a certain fondness for the subsidy method of controlling pollution, because they then don't have to raise *their* prices, or *their* taxes, to the consumer; it is only *provincial* taxes that are increased. This is a rather silly attitude, but it seems very hard for people to learn that *everyone* must pay to reduce pollution, and that the important question is not *who* lays out the money in the first place, but *how much* is paid to achieve what benefits. Subsidy schemes are prey to all the difficulties inherent in regulatory schemes. If an annual subsidy of so much per ton of waste withheld from the water system is given to each polluter in order to reduce his waste discharge by 5 per cent, the scheme will be unfair and also inefficient—and therefore very costly to the Treasury, because as we have seen it costs different industries and different municipalities different amounts to reduce their wastes by 5 per cent. Some will make money on the deal, others will lose. Moreover the scheme is an open invitation to blackmail, just like the scheme for paying students not to drop out of school. Once the subsidy is announced every large waste-producing industry in the country that can reduce its wastes at a cost per ton that is less than the subsidy per ton it earns by doing so will converge on the area in order to engage in the profitable industry of producing wastes and then treating them. Some of these problems could be avoided if the government subsidized everyone equally in the sense that polluters were paid, not a fixed subsidy per ton of waste reduced, but whatever subsidy was required by each polluter to reduce his waste discharge by 5 per cent. Special precautions would have to be taken to avoid fraud, but there would be no "blackmail" problem and no problem of some gaining while others lost; the scheme, however would be very inefficient, and therefore needlessly costly. If on the other hand, an attempt were made to apply the subsidy technique selectively, so that the bulk of the subsidy went to industries and municipalities that could process their wastes most cheaply, the scheme would be somewhat less inefficient in the economic sense but would run into all the problems inherent in the point-by-point regulatory scheme, namely, high costs of administration, a large bureaucracy, and long and complicated negotiations between the control agency and thousands of individual polluters.

There remains the technique of pollution charges. An across-the-board charge of so much per equivalent ton of waste discharged, levied on all municipalities and factories in a given water control region would avoid one of the major disadvantages of the other two schemes; not *all* polluters would be required to reduce their pollution by a fixed percentage, and each could decide for himself how much it would pay him to reduce his waste discharge in light of the charge that is levied. To gain this advantage, however, the W C B would have to experiment a bit with different levels of charges in order to find the one that would result in the total amount of pollution being reduced by approximately 5 per cent. However, the scheme might still be considered inefficient in that it made no allowance, at least *within* a water control region, for different intensities of existing pollution in different parts of the water system, i.e., it would make no allowance for the different waste-handling capacities of different rivers and lakes. Point-by-point charges would involve virtually all the costs, both political and economic, associated with point-by-point regulatory or subsidization schemes. It should be noted, however, that theoretical economists tend to favor the point-by-point charging scheme. Like the other point-by-point schemes it could, in principle, be completely efficient in the economic sense —though, as I hope I have made clear, I am confident that none of them could be completely efficient in practice. The point-by-point charging scheme does have some slight advantage over the others in that it requires less information to put it into effect (although it requires more trial-and-error experimentation in order to get along with the smaller amount of information); as compared with subsidization schemes it also has the "advantage" that it reduces financial problems for the government (though it increases financial problems for the polluters).

As you can see, I have tried in this section to apply a rough version of "cost-benefit" analysis to different control techniques in order to find out which is the least costly way of achieving a given benefit—or, to put it the other way around, which scheme returns the greatest benefit for a given administrative cost. And so far, the only control technique that seems to have any significant advantage over the others is the scheme of across-the-board pollution charges. So let us work on it a bit more.

A Digression on Region-Wide Pricing

All of our across-the-board schemes, we have said, suffer from the disadvantage that they fail to differentiate between different locations within a given water control region. I have so far accepted the argument put forward by factory-owners, and usually accepted by economists, that of two factories discharging the same amounts of the same wastes, the one that does less damage (because it is located on a fast-flowing or very large or thinly populated body of water where the pollution problem is not

serious) should pay less for pollution control than the one that does more damage (because it is located on a slow-flowing, or small, or heavily populated body of water where the pollution problem *is* serious).

On second thought, I reject that argument. If it were accepted, we would be led to favor pollution control schemes that tended to even out pollution geographically and make pollution levels the same everywhere. It is true that if we could somehow equalize water pollution at, say, Belleville and Toronto, we would in some sense equalize Toronto's and Belleville's pollution damage; and it is also true that for a given average water quality (in this case the average of the quality at Belleville and at Toronto), more waste could be discharged into Lake Ontario if industry were equally divided between Toronto and Belleville than if it were unequally divided, as it now is. But I don't think people *want* pollution to be the same everywhere. As a Torontonian I sometimes go to Presqu'ile, near Belleville, to swim, and I dont *want* the swimming near Belleville to be as bad (or good) as it is near Toronto; I very much fear that if pollution levels were equalized between the two areas I couldn't swim in either. It is not because I live in Toronto that I want unequal pollution; I would feel exactly the same way if I lived in Belleville. As a matter of fact, if I valued swimming more highly than I do I would probably live in Belleville. And if a resident of Belleville valued big-city life more than he did swimming he would probably move to Toronto. The point is that we *all* benefit from variety, and that in the age of the motor car our variety doesn't have to be where we live—it can be a couple of hundred miles away. Therefore, if one of the W C B's water control regions extends from, say Toronto to Belleville, I think that it is desirable that pollution charges at Belleville should be just as high as they are at Toronto, even though Belleville has less of a pollution problem than Toronto, and thus has more "unused pollution capacity" than Toronto. That is the way I want to keep it; I want to keep Belleville less populated and less industrialized than Toronto; and I think that people in Belleville (those born there who haven't moved to Toronto, and those born in Toronto who have moved to Belleville) will agree.

The point at issue is so important that we must look at it again. The W C B, through its pollution charges, has the power to influence the location of industry. (It has a similar power to influence the location of populations; but we shall conduct the argument purely in terms of industry.) If it charges the same rates throughout an area it will have no effect on the location of industry within that area, but if there are rate differentials between cities, or different rivers, within the area, the pollution charges will have a "location effect," and the larger the differentials the larger the effect. If the Board charges less where pollution is less (Belleville) it will create a tendency for industry to move from highly polluted areas (Toronto) to less-polluted areas, and thus to spread both industry and pollution more evenly over the area. If it establishes the opposite differential, so that pollution charges are lower in highly polluted areas (Toronto), it will create a tendency to centralize both pollution and industry. Which tendency should the Board favor? Or should it adopt the neutral position of charging the same rates over an entire water control region?

We saw . . . that urbanization and concentration of economic activities increased pollution; on this line of thought, a policy that tends to decentralize industry seems desirable. Such a policy is sound, I think, so long as waste disposal and recreation are compatible uses of water, and up to a certain level of waste disposal the two uses *are* compatible. . . . if it were possible to spread the existing population and production evenly over Ontario there would probably be no pollution problem in the province.

However, the economics of concentrated production are apparently so great, and the desire to live in cities so strong, that waste disposal in urbanized areas is likely to be far greater than the amount that is compatible with at least some recreational uses of the water. At some point, then, the two uses become competitive, and as pollution grows beyond this point some recreational uses (e.g., swimming) are precluded. The effect of this development, in terms of our example, is to increase the value of the recreational uses of the water at Belleville and reduce their value at Toronto. It is therefore no longer correct to argue that industry at Belleville does less damage than it does at Toronto; this conclusion would be correct if recreation were valued at the same figure in both areas, as was reasonable so long as a full range of recreational activities was possible in both areas. But *because* of serious pollution at Toronto the recreational value of Belleville water increases and becomes greater than that of Toronto water. Thus there can be no presumption that an industry would do less damage if it located at Belleville than if it located at Toronto; it might do more.

In general, then, I do not think that region-wide pricing of pollution rights can be shown to be economically inefficient. The rather common conclusion that pollution charges should be lower in less populated and less polluted areas of a region because less damage is done in such areas seems to be based on the assumption that the fewer the people there are to be damaged in an area the less the damage that will be done. This argument overlooks the elementary point that people are mobile and do not stay at home every hour of the year. In fact, most of the damages done by pollution in lightly populated sections of Ontario are likely to be suffered, not by the residents of those areas, but by city people, who place higher and higher values on unpolluted areas within easy driving distances of their homes as their urban environments become more and more polluted.

As you may have realized, we have now come, by a rather roundabout route, to the . . . conclusion . . . that a "separate facilities" solution to conflicting interests—such as pollution versus recreation—is often desirable. Residents of East Toronto and West Toronto cannot separate the water they use, and they must come to a *common* decision about what the quality of water at Toronto is going to be (or accept the decision of some higher-level government). But there is no necessity for the quality of water at Belleville to be the same as the quality of water along the Toronto beaches. There is every reason, it seems to me, to try to keep it different. Let us hope that provincial control of pollution will not result in province-wide pollution! We have argued our point in terms of different areas within one water control region. But exactly the same argument applies to the question of pollution charges as between the regions themselves.

We cannot presume to advise the real authorities, but we can issue directives to our imaginary W C B. I suggest that we tell the Board that it must never adopt a system of pollution charges that will tend to decentralize industry and spread pollution around; pollution in one region must never be reduced by increasing pollution in another. The Board may adopt a locationally neutral pricing policy—which implies the same price per ton of waste discharged throughout the whole province; or it may charge different rates in different water control regions, so long as the lower rates are in the *more* polluted areas and the higher rates in the *less* polluted areas. The locational effect of the differential charges will then be to concentrate industry and pollution even further in the areas where they are now concentrated, and to create a greater contrast in pollution levels between different areas than now exists. These are strong directives, and we may wish to modify them at some later date in the light of experience. At the moment, however, we opt for a pricing system that favors differential pollution between areas and regions rather than one that tends to equalize pollution everywhere.

The Best Way

Once we drop the charge of economic inefficiency against regionwide pricing, the across-the-board pollution-charges technique of implementing our pollution policy looks even better. We have already seen that it is efficient as between different firms and municipalities because each polluter decides for himself by how much, if at all, he should reduce his wastes. The burden of pollution control is thus shared in exactly the right way, without the W C B's having to agonize over the question of how to find a just and reasonable sharing of the cost of the scheme. Since every polluter adjusts to the charges in whatever way minimizes *his* cost, the social cost of achieving the target amount of waste discharge–which is the sum of the costs borne by all polluters (and, of course, by the consumers of their products, in the case of industries)—will also be automatically minimized. There can be no doubt that this scheme is by far the most efficient, i.e., the least costly, way for the W C B to implement its policy. It has the great additional advantage, as compared with any of the point-by-point schemes, that its administrative costs are very low. The main thing the Board has to do to put the scheme into effect is to declare the fee that everyone must pay for the right to discharge one equivalent ton of waste into natural waters anywhere in a water control region. . . .

Run-Off Pollution

Wastes that enter water and air systems not at identifiable outfalls or "emission points," but at hundreds of thousands, or millions, of points, pose special problems. We are not yet sure how important run-off wastes are in causing water pollution, but there is ample evidence that private automobiles are a major source of air pollution in cities.

I shall not comment extensively on these problems. . . . Across-the-board regulatory schemes (which involve a change in property rights) seem attractive where they can be easily enforced, as is the case in proposals to require automobile producers to equip their products with emission-control devices. (It is quite another matter, however, to police the effectiveness of such devices that have been in use for several years.) Farmers located along lakes or rivers might be required to take measures to prevent excessive run-off from their land. Excise taxes—a form of across-the-board system of charges—might be used to increase the cost of, and therefore to encourage a more efficient use of, fertilizers and insecticides; a license fee for automobiles that was more steeply graduated with respect to horsepower than is now the case might very well do more to reduce air pollution than regulations requiring emission-control devices. Subsidies may be justifiable in some cases, as where a farmer has a run-off problem that is particularly difficult to correct.

In giving such brief attention to "diffuse" pollution, I do not imply in any way that it is unimportant. It is often very important, and in my opinion ought to be attacked vigorously. A number of problems are involved, and no doubt it will be desirable to utilize a variety of techniques for controlling them.

Summary

A pollution control policy, in the commonly accepted sense of the phrase, must control pollution. Someone, somehow, has to come up with some sort of limitation on the dumping of wastes into the water and the air. Or, to put it another way, whoever "owns" the air and the water must establish rules about their use or . . . "property rights" in their use. There are an infinite number of such policies or rules about property rights. In this chapter we have arbitrarily chosen one water-pollution control policy for discussion purposes. The policy consists simply of dividing up a large piece of geography, Ontario, into several smaller pieces of geography, which we called water control regions (I haven't said how many water control regions there should be because I don't *know* how many there should be) and having an authority, a water control board, decide the maximum number of equivalent tons of waste that can be dumped in the waters of each region in each year.

The main purpose of this chapter has been to show that economic analysis, which is all but useless in helping us to decide on a policy, is all but indispensable in helping us to decide on the best way of implementing a policy once it has been chosen. The criterion is simply that the best way of implementing a policy is the least costly way, counting *all* costs: costs to individuals as provincial taxpayers (including the very important cost of administering the scheme); costs to individuals as municipal taxpayers; and costs to individuals as consumers of goods and services.

On this criterion, the system of charging a uniform amount for the right to discharge wastes into the natural water system (so much per equivalent ton of waste per year to every polluter at any location in the region) was found to be far superior to any of the other half-dozen schemes considered. It was efficient in the sense that the total direct cost of implementing the policy was distributed amongst waste-dischargers in the fairest and least costly possible way; each polluter decided for himself how he could minimize his costs of waste disposal—to what extent it would be profitable for him to reduce his wastes and to what extent it would be profitable to continue to discharge them into the natural water system even after paying the discharge fees or pollution charges of doing so. It was the most efficient scheme also in the sense that its administrative costs appeared to be lower than those of any other scheme. . . .

SOCIALISM

Ujamaa—The Basis of African Socialism

JULIUS NYERERE

Socialism, like democracy, is an attitude of mind. In a socialist society it is the socialist attitude of mind, and not the rigid adherence to a standard political pattern, which is needed to ensure that the people care for each other's welfare.

The purpose of this paper is to examine that attitude. It is not intended to define the institutions which may be required to embody it in a modern society.

In the individual, as in the society, it is an attitude of mind which distinguishes the socialist from the non-socialist. It has nothing to do with the possession or non-possession of wealth. Destitute people can be potential capitalists—exploiters of their fellow human beings. A millionaire can equally well be a socialist; he may value his wealth only because it can be used in the service of his fellow men. But the man who uses wealth for the purpose of dominating any of his fellows is a capitalist. So is the man who would if he could!

I have said that a millionaire can be a good socialist. But a socialist millionaire is a rare phenomenon. Indeed he is almost a contradiction in terms. The appearance of millionaires in any society is no proof of its affluence; they can be produced by very poor countries like Tanganyika just as well as by rich countries like the United States of America. For it is not efficiency of production, nor the amount of wealth in a country, which makes millionaires; it is the uneven distribution of what is produced. The basic difference between a socialist society and a capitalist society does not lie in their methods of producing wealth, but in the way that wealth is distributed.

While, therefore, a millionaire could be a good socialist, he could hardly be the product of a socialist society.

Since the appearance of millionaires in a society does not depend on its affluence, sociologists may find it interesting to try and find out why our societies in Africa did not, in fact, produce any millionaires—for we certainly had enough wealth to create a few. I think they would discover that it was because the organization of traditional African society—its distribution of the wealth it produced—was such that there was hardly any room for parasitism. They might also say, of course, that as a result of this Africa could not produce a leisured class of landowners, and therefore there was nobody to produce the works of art or science which capitalist societies can boast. But works of art and the achievements of science are products of the intellect—which, like land, is one of God's gifts to man. And I cannot believe that God is so careless as to have made the use of one of His gifts depend on the misuse of another!

Defenders of capitalism claim that the millionaire's wealth is the just reward for his ability or enterprise. But this claim is not borne out by the facts. The wealth of the millionaire depends as little on the enterprise or abilities of the millionaire himself as the power of a feudal monarch depended on his own efforts, enterprise or brain. Both are users, exploiters, of the abilities and enterprise of other people. Even when you have an exceptionally intelligent and hard-working millionaire, the difference between his intelligence, his enterprise, his hard work, and those of other members of society, cannot possibly be proportionate to the difference between their 'rewards.' There must be something wrong in a society where one man, however hard-working or clever he may be, can acquire as great a 'reward' as a thousand of his fellows can acquire between them.

Acquisitiveness for the purpose of gaining power and prestige is unsocialist. In an acquisitive society wealth tends to corrupt those who possess it. It tends to breed in them a desire to live more comfortably than their fellows, to dress better, and in every way to outdo them. They begin to feel they must climb as far above their neighbors as they can. The visible contrast between their own comfort and the comparative discomfort of the rest of society becomes almost essential to the enjoyment of their wealth, and this sets off the spiral of personal competition—which is then anti-social.

Apart from the anti-social effects of the accumulation of personal wealth, the very desire to accumulate it must be interpreted as a vote of 'no confidence' in the social system. For when a society is so organized that it cares about its individuals, then, provided he is willing to work, no individual within that society should worry about what will happen to him tomorrow if he does not hoard wealth today. Society itself should look after him, or his widow, or his orphans. This is exactly what traditional African society succeeded in doing. Both the 'rich' and the 'poor' individual were completely secure in African society. Natural catastrophe brought famine, but it brought famine to everybody—'poor' or 'rich'. Nobody starved, either of food or of human dignity, because he lacked personal wealth; he could depend on the wealth possessed by the community of which he was a member. That was socialism. That is socialism. There can be no such thing as acquisitive socialism, for that would be another contradiction in terms. Socialism is essentially distributive. Its concern is to see that those who sow reap a fair share of what they sow.

The production of wealth, whether by primitive or modern methods, requires three things. First, land. God has given us the land, and it is from the land that we get the raw materials which we reshape to meet our needs. Secondly, tools. We have found by simple experience that tools do help! So we make the hoe, the axe, or the modern factory or tractor, to help us to produce wealth—the goods we need. And thirdly, human exertion—or labor. We don't need to read Karl Marx or Adam Smith to find out that neither the land nor the hoe actually produces wealth. And we don't need to take degrees in Economics to know that neither the worker nor the landlord produces land. Land is God's gift to man—it is always there. But we do know, still without degrees in economics, that the axe and the plough were produced by the laborer. Some of our more sophisticated friends apparently have to undergo the most rigorous intellectual training simply in order to discover that stone axes were produced by that ancient gentleman 'Early Man' to make it easier for him to skin the impala he had just killed with a club, which he had also made for himself!

In traditional African society everybody was a worker. There was no other way of earning a living for the community. Even the Elder, who appeared to be enjoying himself without doing any work and for whom everybody else appeared to be working, had, in fact, worked hard all his younger days. The wealth he now appeared to possess was not his, personally; it was only 'his' as the Elder of the group which had produced it. He was its guardian. The wealth itself gave him neither power nor prestige. The respect paid to him by the young was his because he was older than they, and had served his community longer; and the 'poor' Elder enjoyed as much respect in our society as the 'rich' Elder.

When I say that in traditional African society everybody was a worker, I do not use the word 'worker' simply as opposed to 'employer' but also as opposed to 'loiterer' or 'idler'. One of the most socialistic achievements of our society was the sense of security it gave to its members, and the universal hospitality on which they could rely. But it is too often forgotten, nowadays, that the basis of this great socialistic achievement was this: that it was taken for granted that every member of society—barring only the children and the infirm—contributed his fair share of effort towards the production of its wealth. Not only was the capitalist, or the landed exploiter, unknown to traditional African society, but we did not have that other form of modern parasite—the loiterer, or idler, who accepts the hospitality of society as his 'right' but gives nothing in return! Capitalistic exploitation was impossible. Loitering was an unthinkable disgrace.

Those of us who talk about the African way of life, and, quite rightly, take a pride in maintaining the tradition of hospitality which is so great a part of it, might do well to remember the Swahili saying: '*Mgeni siku mbili; siku ya tatu mpe jembe*'—or, in English, 'Treat your guest as a guest for two days; on the third day give him a hoe!' In actual fact, the guest was likely to ask for the hoe even before his host had to give him one—for he knew what was expected of him, and would have been ashamed to remain idle any longer. Thus, working was part and parcel, was indeed the very basis and justification of this socialist achievement of which we are so justly proud.

There is no such thing as socialism without work. A society which fails to give its individuals the means to work, or, having given them the means to work, prevents them from getting a fair share of the products of their own sweat and toil, needs putting right. Similarly, an individual who can work—and is provided by society with the means to work—but does not do so, is equally wrong. He has no right to expect anything from society because he contributes nothing to society.

The other use of the word 'worker', in its specialized sense of 'employee' as opposed to 'employer', reflects a capitalist attitude of mind which was introduced into Africa with the coming of **colonialism** and is totally foreign to our own way of thinking. In the old days the African had never aspired to the possession of personal wealth for the purpose of dominating any of his fellows. He had never had laborers or 'factory hands' to do his work for him. But then came the foreign capitalists. They were wealthy. They were powerful. And the African naturally started wanting to be wealthy too. There is nothing wrong in our wanting to be wealthy; nor is it a bad thing for us to want to acquire the power which wealth brings with it. But it most certainly is wrong if we want the wealth and the power so that we can dominate somebody else. Unfortunately there are some of us who have already learnt to covet wealth for that purpose, and who would like to use the methods which the capitalist uses in acquiring it. That is to say, some of us would like to use, or exploit, our brothers for the purpose of building up our own personal power and prestige. This is completely foreign to us, and it is incompatible with the socialist society we want to build here.

Our first step, therefore, must be to re-educate ourselves; to regain our former attitude of mind. In our traditional African society we were individuals within a community. We took care of the community, and the community took care of us. We neither needed nor wished to exploit our fellow men.

And in rejecting the capitalist attitude of mind which colonialism brought into Africa, we must reject also the capitalist methods which go with it. One of these is the individual ownership of land. To us in Africa land was always recognized as belonging to the community. Each individual within our society had a right to the use of land, because otherwise he could not earn his living and one cannot have the right to life without also having the right to some means of maintaining life. But the African's right to land was simply the right to use it: he had no other right to it, nor did it occur to him to try and claim one.

The foreigner introduced a completely different concept, the concept of land as a marketable commodity. According to this system, a person could claim a piece of land as his own private property whether he intended to use it or not. I could take a few square miles of land, call them 'mine', and then go off to the moon. All I had to do to gain a living from 'my' land was to charge a rent to the people who wanted to use it. If this piece of land was in an urban area I had no need to develop it at all; I could leave it to the fools who were prepared to develop all the other pieces of land surrounding 'my' piece, and in doing so automatically to raise the market value of mine. Then I could come down from the moon and demand that these fools pay me through their noses for the high value of 'my' land; a value which they themselves had created for me while I was enjoying myself on the moon! Such a system is not only foreign to us, it is completely wrong. Landlords, in a society which recognizes individual ownership of land, can be, and usually are, in the same class as the loiterers I was talking about: the class of parasites.

We must not allow the growth of parasites here in Tanganyika. The TANU Government must go back to the traditional African custom of land holding. That is to say, a member of society will be entitled to a piece of land on condition that he uses it. Unconditional, or 'freehold', ownership of land (which leads to speculation and parasitism) must be abolished. We must, as I have said, regain our former attitude of mind—our traditional African socialism—and apply it to the new societies we are building today. TANU has pledged itself to make socialism the basis of its policy in every field. The people of Tanganyika have given us their mandate to carry out that policy, by electing a TANU government to lead them. So the Government can be relied upon to introduce only legislation which is in harmony with socialist principles.

But, as I said at the beginning, true socialism is an attitude of mind. It is therefore up to the people of Tanganyika—the peasants, the wage-earners, the students, the leaders, all of us—to make sure that this socialist attitude of mind is not lost through the temptations to personal gain (or to the abuse of positions of authority) which may come our way as individuals, or through the temptation to look on the good of the whole community as of secondary importance to the interests of our own particular group.

Just as the Elder, in our former society, was respected for his age and his service to the community, so, in our modern society, this respect for age and service will be preserved. And in the same way as the 'rich' Elder's apparent wealth was really only held by him in trust for his people, so, today, the apparent extra wealth which certain positions of leadership may bring to the individuals who fill them, can be theirs only in so far as it is a necessary aid to the carrying out of their duties. It is a 'tool' entrusted to them for the benefit of the people they serve. It is not 'theirs' personally; and they may not use any part of it as a means of accumulating more for their own benefit, nor as an 'insurance' against the day when they no longer hold the same positions. That would be to betray the people who entrusted it to them. If they serve the community while they can, the community must look after them when they are no longer able to do so.

In tribal society, the individuals or the families within a tribe were 'rich' or 'poor' according to whether the whole tribe was rich or poor. If the tribe prospered, all the members of the tribe shared in its prosperity. Tanganyika, today, is a poor country. The standard of living of the masses of our people is shamefully low. But if every man and woman in the country takes up the challenge and works to the limit of his or her ability for the good of the whole society, Tanganyika will prosper; and that prosperity will be shared by all her people.

But it must be shared. The true socialist may not exploit his fellows. So that if the members of any group within our society are going to argue that, because they happen to be contributing more to the national income than some other groups, they must therefore take for themselves a greater share of the profits of their own industry than they actually need; and if they insist on this in spite of the fact that it would mean reducing their group's contribution to the general income and thus slowing down the rate at which the whole community can benefit, then that group is exploiting (or trying to exploit) its fellow human beings. It is displaying a capitalist attitude of mind.

There are bound to be certain groups which, by virtue of the 'market value' of their particular industry's products, will contribute more to the nation's income than others. But the others may actually be producing goods or services which are of equal, or greater, intrinsic value although they do not happen to command such a high artificial value. For example, the food produced by the peasant farmer is of greater social value than the diamonds mined at Mwadui. But the mine-workers of Mwadui could claim, quite correctly, that their labor was yielding greater financial profits to the community than that of the farmers. If, however, they went on to demand that they should therefore be given most of that extra profit for themselves, and that no share of it should be spent on helping the farmers, they would be potential capitalists!

This is exactly where the attitude of mind comes in. It is one of the purposes of Trade Unions to ensure for the workers a fair share of the profits of their labor. But a 'fair' share must be fair in relation to the whole society. If it is greater than the country can afford without having to penalize some other section of society, then it is not a fair share. Trade Union leaders and their followers, as long as they are true socialists, will not need to be coerced by the government into keeping their demands within the limits imposed by the needs of society as a whole. Only if there are potential capitalists amongst them will the socialist government have to step in and prevent them from putting their capitalist ideas into practice!

As with groups, so with individuals. There are certain skills, certain qualifications, which, for good reasons, command a higher rate of salary for their possessors than others. But, here again, the true socialist will demand only that return for his skilled work which he knows to be a fair one in proportion to the wealth or poverty of the whole society to which he belongs. He will not, unless he is a would-be capitalist attempt to blackmail the community by demanding a salary equal to that paid to his counterpart in some far wealthier society.

European socialism was born of the Agrarian Revolution and the Industrial Revolution which followed it. The former created the 'landed' and the 'landless' classes in society; the latter produced the modern capitalist and the industrial proletariat.

These two revolutions planted the seeds of conflict within society, and not only was European socialism born of that conflict, but its apostles sanctified the conflict itself into a philosophy. Civil war was no longer looked upon as something evil, or something unfortunate, but as something good and necessary. As prayer is to Christianity or to Islam, so civil war (which they call 'class war') is to the European version of socialism—a means inseparable from the end. Each becomes the basis of a whole way of life. The European socialist cannot think of his socialism without its father—capitalism!

Brought up in tribal socialism, I must say I find this contradiction quite intolerable. It gives capitalism a philosophical status which capitalism neither claims nor deserves. For it virtually says 'Without capitalism, and the conflict which capitalism creates within society, there can be no socialism!' This glorification of capitalism by the doctrinaire European socialists, I repeat, I find intolerable.

African socialism, on the other hand, did not have the 'benefit' of the Agrarian Revolution or the Industrial Revolution. It did not start from the existence of conflicting 'classes' in society. Indeed I doubt if the equivalent for the word 'class' exists in any indigenous African language; for language describes the ideas of those who speak it, and the idea of 'class' or 'caste' was nonexistent in African society.

The foundation, and the objective, of African socialism is the extended family. The true African socialist does not look on one class of men as his brethren and another as his natural enemies. He does not form an alliance with the 'brethren' for the extermination of the 'non-brethren'. He rather regards all men as his brethren—as members of his ever extending family. That is why the first article of TANU's creed is: '*Binadamu wote ni ndugu zangu, na Afrika ni moja.*' If this had been originally put in English, it could have been: 'I believe in Human Brotherhood and the Unity of Africa.'

'*Ujamaa*', then, or 'familyhood', describes our socialism. It is opposed to capitalism, which seeks to build a happy society on the basis of the exploitation of man by man; and it is equally opposed to doctrinaire socialism which seeks to build its happy society on a philosophy of inevitable conflict between man and man.

We, in Africa, have no more need of being 'converted' to socialism than we have of being 'taught' democracy. Both are rooted in our own past—in the traditional society which produced us. Modern African socialism can draw from its traditional heritage the recognition of 'society' as an extension of the basic family unit. But it can no longer confine the idea of the social family within the limits of the tribe, nor, indeed, of the nation. For no true African socialist can look at a line drawn on a map and say 'The people on this side of that line are my brothers, but those who happen to live on the other side of it can have no claim on me'; every individual on this continent is his brother.

It was in the struggle to break the grip of colonialism that we learned the need for unity. We came to recognize that the same socialist attitude of mind which, in the tribal days, gave to every individual the security that comes of belonging to a widely extended family, must be preserved within the still wider society of the nation. But we should not stop there. Our recognition of the family to which we all belong must be extended yet further—beyond the tribe, the community, the nation, or even the continent—to embrace the whole society of mankind. This is the only logical conclusion for true socialism.

THE CORPORATE STATE

The Greening of America

CHARLES REICH

There is a revolution under way. It is not like revolutions of the past. It has originated with the individual and with culture, and if it succeeds it will change the political structure only as its final act. It will not require violence to succeed, and it cannot be successfully resisted by violence. It is now spreading with amazing rapidity, and already our laws, institutions, and social structure are changing in consequence. Its ultimate creation could be a higher reason, a more human community, and a new and liberated individual.

This is the revolution of the new generation. It is a transformation that seems both necessary and inevitable, and in time it may turn out to include not only youth but the entire American people. The logic of the new generation's rebellion must be understood in light of the rise of the corporate state and the way in which the state dominates, exploits, and ultimately destroys both nature and man. Americans have lost control of the machinery of their society, and only new values and a new culture can restore control. At the heart of everything is what must be called a change of consciousness. This means a new way of living—almost a new man. This is what the new generation has been searching for, and what it has started to achieve. Industrialism produced a new man, too—one adapted to the demands of the machine. In contrast, today's emerging consciousness seeks a new knowledge of what it means to be human, in order that the machine, having been built, may now be turned to human ends.

Most of us see the nature of the present American crisis as a collection of problems, not necessarily related to each other, and, although profoundly troubling, nevertheless within the reach of reason and reform. Yet if we list these problems, not according to topic but as elements of larger issues concerning the structure of our society itself, we can see that the present crisis is an organic one, that it arises out of the basic premises by which we live, and that no mere reform can touch it in any way.

(1) *Disorder, corruption, hypocrisy, war.* The front pages of newspapers tell of the disintegration of the social fabric, and of the resulting atmosphere of anxiety and terror in which we all live. Lawlessness is most often associated with crime and riots, but there is lawlessness and corruption in all the major institutions of our society—matched by an indifference to responsibility and consequences, and a pervasive hypocrisy that refuses to acknowledge the facts that are everywhere visible. Both lawlessness and evasion find their ultimate expression in the Vietnam war, with its unprincipled destruction of everything human, and its random, indifferent, technological cruelty.

(2) *Poverty, distorted priorities, and legislation by power.* America presents a picture of drastic poverty amid affluence. There is a superabundance of some goods and activities, such as defense manufacture, while other needs, such as education and medical care, are at a starvation level for many. These closely related kinds of inequality are not the accidents of a free economy; they are intentionally and rigidly built into the laws and institutions of our society. An example is the tax structure, which subsidizes private wealth and production of luxuries and weapons at the direct expense of impoverished people and impoverished services. The nation has a planned economy, but the planning is done by the exercise of sheer private power, without concern for the general good.

(3) *Uncontrolled technology and the destruction of environment.* Technology and production can be great benefactors of man, but they are mindless instruments, and if undirected they career along with a momentum of their own. In our country, they pulverize everything in their path—the landscape, the natural environment, history and tradition, the amenities and civilities, the privacy and spaciousness of life, much beauty, and the fragile, slow-growing social structures that bind us together. Organization and bureaucracy, which are an application of technology to social institutions, increasingly dictate how we shall live our lives, with the logic of organization taking precedence over any other values.

(4) *Decline of democracy and liberty, powerlessness.* The Constitution and Bill of Rights have steadily been weakened. The nation has gradually become a rigid managerial hierarchy, with a small élite and a great mass of disenfranchised. Democracy has rapidly lost ground as power has been increasingly captured by giant managerial institutions and industrial corporations, and decisions have come to be made by experts, specialists, and professionals safely insulated from the feelings of the people. Most governmental power has shifted from Congress to administrative agencies, and corporate power is free to ignore both stockholders and consumers. As regulation and administration have grown, liberty has been eroded and bureaucratic discretion has taken the place of the rule of law. The pervasiveness of police, security men, the military, and compulsory military service show the changed character of American liberty.

(5) *The artificiality of work and culture.* Both work and living have become more and more pointless and empty. There is no lack of meaningful things that cry out to

be done, but our working days are used up in what lacks meaning: making useless or harmful products, or servicing the bureaucratic structures. For most Americans, work is mindless, exhausting, boring, servile, and hateful—something to be endured—while "life" is confined to "time off." At the same time, our culture has been reduced to the grossly commercial; all cultural values are for sale, and those that fail to make a profit tend to be destroyed. Our life activities have become vicarious and false to our genuine needs—activities fabricated by others and forced upon us.

(6) *Absence of community.* America is one vast, terrifying anti-community. The great organizations to which most people give their working day and the apartments and suburbs to which they return at night are equally places of loneliness and alienation. Modern living has obliterated place, locality, and neighborhood, and given us an anonymous separateness of existence. The family, the most basic social system, has been stripped to its functional essentials. Friendship has been coated over with a layer of impenetrable artificiality as men strive to live roles designed for them. Protocol, competition, hostility, and fear have replaced the warmth of the circle of affection that might sustain man against a hostile universe.

(7) *Loss of self.* Of all the forms of impoverishment that can be seen or felt in America, loss of self—a sort of death-in-life—is surely the most devastating. It is, even more than the draft and the Vietnam war, the source of discontent and rage in the new generation. Beginning with school, if not before, an individual is systematically stripped of his imagination, his creativity, his heritage, his dreams, and his personal uniqueness, in order to fit him to be a productive unit in a mass technological society. Instinct, feeling, and spontaneity are suppressed by overwhelming forces. As the individual is drawn into the meritocracy, his working life is split from his home life, and both suffer from a lack of wholeness. In the end, people virtually *become* their occupations and their other roles, and are strangers to themselves. Blacks long ago felt their deprivation of identity and potential for life. But white "soul" and blues are just emerging. A segment of our young people are articulately aware that they, too, suffer an enforced loss of self—that they, too, are losing the lives that could be theirs.

We seem to be living in a society that no one created and that no one wants. The feeling of powerlessness extends even to the inhabitants of executive offices. Yet, paradoxically, it is also a fact that we have available to us the means to begin coping with virtually all the problems that beset us. Most people would initially deny this, but reflection shows how true it is. We know what causes crime and social disorder and what can be done to eliminate those causes. We know the steps than can be taken to create greater economic equality. We are in possession of techniques for fashioning and preserving more livable cities and environments. Our problems are vast, but so is our store of techniques. It is simply not being put to use.

The American crisis, then, seems clearly to be related to an inability to act. But what is the cause of this paralysis? Why, in the face of every warning, have we been unable to act? Why have we not used our resources more wisely and justly? We tell ourselves that social failure gets down to individual moral failure: we must have the will to act; we must first find concern and compassion in our hearts. But this diagnosis is not good enough. It is contradicted by the experience of powerlessness that is encountered by so many people. Today, a majority of the people, as moral individuals, certainly want peace, but they cannot turn their individual wills into action by society. It is not that we do not will action but that we are unable to act, unable to put existing knowledge to use. The machinery of our society apparently no longer works, or we no longer know how to make it work.

The corporate state in which we live is an immensely powerful machine—ordered, legalistic, rational, yet utterly out of human control and indifferent to human values. It is hard to say exactly when our society assumed this shape. The major symptoms of change started appearing after the Second World War, and especially in the nineteen-fifties. The expenditure of a trillion dollars for defense, the destruction of the environment, the production of unneeded goods—these were not merely extensions of the familiar blunders and corruption of America's past; they were of a different order of magnitude. And although they were all an integral part of a legal and seemingly rational system, they were surrounded by a growing atmosphere of unreality. The stupidities and thefts of the Grant era were not insane; they were human departures from a reasonably human standard. In the nineteen-fifties, the norm itself—the system itself—became deranged.

Our present system has gone beyond anything that could properly be called the creation of capitalism or **imperialism** or a **power élite**. That would at least be a human shape. Of course, a power élite does exist, and is made rich by the system, but the members of the élite are no longer in control; they are now merely taking advantage of forces that have a life of their own. Other societies have had bad systems, but endured because a part of human enterprise went on outside the system. We have turned over everything to what can be thought of as a single vast corporation. It consists primarily of large industrial organizations, plus non-profit institutions such as foundations and the educational system, all related to the whole as divisions to a business corporation. Government, providing coördination and a variety of needed services, is only a part of this corporate state, which represents a complete reversal of the original American ideal and plan. The corporate state, and not the market or the people or any abstract economic laws, determines what shall be produced, what shall be consumed, and how it shall all be allocated. The corporate state determines, for example, that railroads shall decay while highways flourish, that coal miners shall be poor and advertising executives rich. The state is subject neither to democratic controls nor to Constitutional limits nor to legal regulation. Instead, the organizations that make up the corporate state are motivated primarily by the demands of technology and of their own internal structure. Technology has imperatives such as these: if computers have been developed, they must be put to use; if faster planes can be produced, they must be put into service; if there is a more efficient way of organizing an office staff, it must be adopted; if a psychological test provides added information for personnel directors, it must be used on prospective employees. The commanding officer of the California National Guard described the use of a helicopter at Berkeley for attacking students with chemicals as "logical." As for business organizations, their imperative is to grow. They need stability, freedom from outside interference, constantly increasing profits. Everyone in the organization wants more and better personnel, more functions, increased status and prestige—in a word, growth. The medium through which these imperatives operate is law. The legal system acts as an instrument of corporate-state domination, and it acts to prevent the intervention of human values or individual choice. Although the forces driving the state are impersonal rather than evil, they are wholly indifferent to man's needs, and tend to have the same consequences as would a system expressly designed for the purpose of destroying human beings and their society.

The essence of the corporate state is that it is relentlessly single-minded; it has just one value, the value of technology as represented by organization, efficiency, growth, progress. No other value is allowed to interfere with this one—not amenity, not beauty, not community, not even the supreme value of life itself. Thus, the state is essentially mindless; it has only one idea, and it merely rolls along, never stopping to think, consider, balance, judge. Only such single-valued mindlessness would cut the last redwoods, pollute the most beautiful beaches, invent devices to injure and destroy plant and human life. To have just one value is to be a machine.

In the following attempt to outline the main features of the corporate state, the description is meant to be cumulative, for it is the interrelationship of the several elements that gives the state its extraordinary form. In the case of the corporate state, the whole is more than the sum of the parts, and the truth is in the whole, not the parts.

Amalgamation and Integration

We normally consider the units of the corporate state—such as the federal government, an automobile company, a private foundation—as if they were separate from each other. This, however, is not the case. In the first place, there is a marked tendency for supposedly separate units to follow parallel policies, so that an entire industry makes identical decisions as to pricing, kind of product, method of distribution; the automobile and the air-travel industries show this. Second, very different companies are coming under combined management through the device of forming conglomerates, which place vast and diverse empires under unified control. But even more significant is the disappearance of the line between "public" and "private." In the corporate state, most of the "public" functions of government are actually performed by the "private" sector of the economy. And most "government" functions are services performed for the "private" sector.

Let us consider first how government operations are "privately" performed. To a substantial degree, this relationship is formalized. The government hires private firms to build national-defense systems, to supply the space program, to construct the interstate highway system, and even to do its thinking for it. An enormous portion of the federal budget is spent in simply hiring out government functions. This much is obvious, although many people do not seem to be aware of it. What is less obvious is the "deputizing" system by which a far larger sector of the private economy is enlisted in government service. For example, a college teacher may receive a form from the Civil Service Commission asking him for certain information about an individual who is applying for a government job. When the teacher fills out the form, he is acting as if he had been "deputized" by the government; that is, he is performing a service for the government—one for which he might even feel himself entitled to compensation. Now consider a foundation that is granted special nontaxable status. The foundation is in this favored position because it is engaged in activities that are deemed to be of "public benefit." That is, it is the judgment of the government that some types of activity are public services although performed under private auspices. The government itself could do what private foundations now do—aid education, sponsor research, and carry out other projects that do not command a profit in the commercial sense—but the government has decided that these functions are better performed by foundations. This is the same judgment that the government makes when it hires Boeing to build bombers, or a private construction firm to build an interstate highway. Public utilities—airlines, railroads, truck carriers, taxicabs, oil pipelines, telephones—are all "deputized" in this fashion. They carry on *public* functions—functions that in other societies might be taken on by the government itself.

This summer, it was reported that the broadcasting industry was participating in a "crusade" against drug use. At the urging of President Nixon to "get the message across" to young people that drug use is "weakening the character" of the United States, television and radio responded in such diverse ways as adding a drug-addiction problem to the plot line of a daytime serial, delivering editorials against drugs, devoting news programs to the drug "crisis," cancelling all programs for an entire day to present twenty-four hours devoted exclusively to the subject of drug abuse, and inserting subtle anti-drug messages amid programs of rock music. Since broadcasters get their licenses from the federal government, there may be some question whether this concerted campaign was the purely voluntary action of private businesses. And the fact that the campaign was not limited to announcements but was also incorporated into supposedly neutral entertainment programs shows the extent to which the entire content of broadcasting can become political in nature, and serve to carry out policies of government. Even the most ordinary family or adventure program shows only an approved attitude toward government. If the "Mission Impossible" team undertook an anti-Vietnam-war mission, or a comedian made some serious jokes about patriotism, the broadcasters involved would surely feel that they had reason to worry about the loss of their licenses.

Let us now look at the other side of the coin: government as the servant of the private sector. Once again, the relationship is sometimes formal and obvious. The government spends huge amounts for research and development, and private companies are often able to get the benefits of this. Airports are built at public expense for private airlines to use. Highways are built for private trucking firms to use. The government pays all sorts of subsidies, direct and indirect, to various industries. It supplies credit services and financial aid to homeowners. It grows trees on public forest lands and sells them at cut-rate prices to private lumber companies. It builds roads to aid ski developments.

It is true that government has always existed to serve the society—police and fire departments help business, too, and so do wars that open up new markets. This is what government is and always has been all about. But today governmental activity in aid of the private sector is enormously greater, more pervasive, more immediately felt than ever before. The difference between the local public services provided in 1776 and the expenditure of millions of dollars in subsidies to the shipping industry is not only one of degree. In the difference between a highly autonomous, localized economy and a highly interdependent one, there is a difference of principle as well as one of degree. Government help today is an essential, not a luxury. The airlines could not operate without allocation of routes and regulation of landings and take-offs, nor could the television industry without corresponding regulation. The educational system, elementary school through high school, is necessary for the production of people able to work in today's industry. Thus, it may be said that everyone who operates "privately" really is aided and subsidized, in one degree or another, by the public. The sturdy independent rancher rides off into the sunset on land irrigated by government subsidy, past sheep whose grazing is subsidized and crops whose prices are artificially maintained by government action; he does not look like a welfare client, but he is on the dole nevertheless.

Regulation, originally an instrument of reform, has been remade into a service to industry. State and federal laws enable the oil industry to act as an *oligopoly*, closely controlling imports, production, and prices that otherwise might be subject to the wishes of consumers and to the other influences of "free enterprise." Without these convenient laws to eliminate competition and the free market, the oil industry might have to go to the trouble and expense of "regulating" itself. Thus, the motion-picture industry and the professional-sports industry have elaborate systems of private regulation, including "commissioners," a corpus of laws, and a scale of fines and other penalties, all designed to place the industry on the best and most united basis to sell its product. Such regulation as is performed by federal agencies like the F.C.C., S.E.C., F.T.C., and C.A.B. is remarkably similar in general effect, but it is a service rendered at taxpayers' expense.

Once the line between "public" and "private" becomes meaningless and is erased, the various units of the corporate state no longer appear to be parts of a diverse and pluralistic system in which one kind of power limits another kind of power. The various centers of power do not limit each other; they all weigh in on the same side of the scale, with only the individual on the other side. Once we realize that what is public and what is private have been merged, we can discern the real monolith of power, and see that there is nothing at all within the system to impose checks and balances, to offer competition, to raise even a voice of caution or doubt. We are all involuntary members, and there is no zone of the "private" to offer a retreat.

One way to appreciate the true nature of the public-private amalgamated state is to list a few of the kinds of power that can be found in the United States:

Power to make one publication available to airline passengers but not another.

Power to raise bank *interest rates*.

Power to forbid apartment dwellers to have pets or children.

Power to require peanut-butter eaters to choose either "creamy" or "chunky" peanut butter and to prevent them from buying real, unhydrogenated peanut butter.

Power to force all young people who want to go to college to take examinations requiring a certain standardized kind of mechanical problem-solving.

Power to popularize snowmobiles instead of snowshoes.

Power to dominate public consciousness through the mass media.

Power to induce lung cancer in thousands of persons by promoting the sale of cigarettes.

Power to turn off a man's telephone service.

Power to encourage or discourage various forms of scholarship, educational activity, philanthropy, and research.

Power to construct office buildings with windows that will not open, or without any windows at all.

Power to determine what life styles will not be acceptable for employees.

Power to make relatively large or relatively small investments in the

The Greening of America

safety of consumer products.

Power to change the culture of a foreign country.

Were we told that all this power was held by a single tyrannical ruler, we would find the prospect frightening indeed. As things are, however, we are likely to take comfort in the thought that although the power may exist, it is divided in many ways, held by many different entities, and subject to all sorts of checks, balances, and controls, and that for the most part it applies only to persons who subject themselves to it voluntarily—by taking a job with a corporation, for instance. But the power of the corporate state is not so easily escaped. The refugee from a job in one corporation will find a choice of other corporations all prepared to subject him to similar control as an employee. The television viewer who tires of one network finds the others even more tiresome. Can railroad passengers do anything about conditions they object to? Do they find alternative means of transportation readily available?

Editorials denouncing students often say that a student who does not like the way a university is run should leave. But society makes it all but mandatory for a young person to complete his education, and in their rules and practices most universities are extraordinarily alike. Moreover, the penalty for many young men who leave is to be drafted. Under these circumstances, it is hardly accurate to say that a student has submitted "voluntarily" to a university's rules. The student's case is the case of the railroad traveller, the peanut-butter eater, the man who wants a bank loan, the corporate employee, the apartment-house dweller who wants to keep a pet. The integration of the corporate state makes inescapable what was formerly voluntary, and powers that once were small and gentle become monstrous and terrifying.

The better organized, the more tightly administered, the more rational and inclusive the corporate state becomes, the more every organization turns into a government, and all forms of power take on the aspect of government decrees.

The Principle of Administration and Hierarchy

The decisions, policies, and activities of a society might theoretically be carried out by a variety of methods—voluntary coöperation by individuals, or the physical coercion of a military tyranny, or more subtle coercion of psychological conditioning. The corporate state has chosen to rely on hierarchical administration. The principle here is that the best way to conduct any activity is to subject it to rational control. A framework of organization is provided. Lines of authority, responsibility, and supervision are established as clearly as possible; everyone is arranged in a hierarchy. Rules are drawn for every imaginable contingency, so individual choice is minimized. Arrangements are made to check on what everyone does, to have reports and permanent records. The random, the irrational, and the alternative ways of doing things are banished.

It is worth recalling how this condition derived from classic liberalism, and, more proximately, from the New Deal and the welfare state. Liberalism adopted the basic principle that there is no need for management of society itself; the "unseen hand" is all that is needed. The New Deal modified this principle by requiring activities to be subject to "the public interest." Gradually, this came to mean ever-tightening regulation in directions fixed by the demands of a commercial, technological mass society. Gradually, it came to mean the replacement of a "political" state with an "administrative" state. (So pervasive, indeed, is the principle of administration that in many ways the corporate state is in its essence an administrative state.) A political state, in our present meaning, is one in which all sorts of differences in culture and opinion coexist, are represented in the political process, and contribute to the diversity and balance of the nation. This political model has also been called the "conflict" model. By either term, this resembles the original model on which our society was founded. Administration means a rejection of the idea of conflict as a desirable element in society. Administration wants extremes adjusted; it wants differences settled; it wants to find out which way is best and use that way exclusively. Whatever refuses to be adjusted is considered by administration to be "deviance," a departure from the norm that must be treated and cured. It is a therapeutic model of society, in which variety is compromised and smoothed over in an effort to make everything conform to "the public interest." Political radicals are expected to be "responsible"; blacks are expected to be "integrated." The state "knows what is best" for everyone; its massive energies, power, and apparatus are focused on making sure that everyone accepts "what is best."

The structure of the administrative state is that of a hierarchy in which every person has a place in a table of organization, a vertical position in which he is subordinate to someone and superior to someone else. This is the structure of any bureaucracy; it represents a "rationalization" of organization ideals. When an entire society is subjected to this principle, it creates a small ruling élite and a large group of workers who play no significant part in the making of decisions. Though they continue to vote in political elections, they are offered little choice among the candidates; all the major decisions about what is produced, what is consumed, how resources are allocated, the conditions of work, and so forth, are made administratively.

Hierarchy takes on particular importance in the organizations where most people work. It declares that, as workers, most men and women must accept the absolute authority and superiority of someone "above" them. For the boss to be empowered to tell a worker how to perform his work is one thing, but all too often the boss is treated as a higher form of human being. We have frequently heard criticism of the "childishness" of the average adult American; in many instances, hierarchy not only encourages but demands childishness—the wholesale turning over of responsibility and self-respect to someone in authority. One of the key points in the rebellion of the new generation is rejection of such authority and insistence upon personal responsibility and true personal equality.

Administration seeks to remove decision-making from the area of politics to the area of "science." Democratic or popular choice is rejected in favor of a "rational" weighing of all the factors by experts. Procedures are set up by which decision-making is channelled, and care is taken to define exactly which institution shall make which decisions. For each type of decision, there is someone "best" qualified to decide; administration avoids participation in decisions by the "less qualified." If followed, these procedures usually produce a decision that is a compromise or balance and that rejects any particular choice in its pure, uncompromised form. Choice takes place within narrow limits. A weighing of all the factors produces a decision somewhere in between, rather than at one or another "extreme."

Administration has no values of its own, except the institutional ones just described.

Theoretically, it could accept any values. In practice, however, it is strongly conservative. Things go most smoothly when the status quo is maintained, when change is slow, cautious, and evolutionary. The more elaborate the machinery of administration is, the less ready it is for new, disquieting values. And "rationality" finds some values easier to understand, to justify, to put into verbal terms than other values. It can understand quantity better than quality. Administration is neutral in favor of present policy.

Public welfare offers an example of the administrative model of society. The theoretical object of public welfare is to protect people from the hazards of forces in an industrial society that are beyond their control and from the other hazards of life against which neither family nor local community any longer offers help—to provide every person with a minimum standard of security, well-being, and dignity. With the introduction of administration as the means for carrying out public welfare, the emphasis shifts to regulation of exactly who is qualified for welfare, how much is allotted, how it is spent, whether rules are being followed. A large apparatus is developed for checking up, for keeping records, for making and enforcing rules, for punishing infractions. Some of this may save money, but the saving is minimized by the costs of administration. Some of this may also serve the purpose of punishing the poor for not working, even though many are unable to work. But the "accomplishments" of administration are almost secondary; after a while, what it does ceases to have an outside reference and it acquires a life of its own.

While the tendency of administration may appear to be benign and peaceful, as opposed to the turbulence of conflict, it is actually violent. For the very idea of imposed order is violent. It demands compliance; nothing less than compliance will do; and it must obtain compliance, by persuasion or management if possible, by repression if necessary. It is convinced that it has "the best way" and that all other ways are wrong; it cannot understand those who do not accept the rightness of its views. A growing tension and anger develop against those who would question what is so carefully designed to be "best" —for them as well as for everybody else. Thus, it is not uncommon for public-school administrators to engage in repression of independent thinking by students, although the ability to think independently is presumably an important objective of education. At the Del Valle High School in Walnut Creek, California, the students produced a "controversial" yearbook last spring. It included a poem by Robert Danielson, a seventeen-year-old star of the school baseball team, poking fun at school athletes who "don't reason" and "don't ask questions." Because of the poem, young Danielson was told by his coach that he would not receive a team letter and was not welcome at the presentation-awards dinner. The coach sought to mitigate this punishment by telling the faculty, "I like the kid. . . . I think he's pathetic, but I like him. If I hadn't, he wouldn't have played baseball for me for two years." Meanwhile, the principal threatened the faculty adviser of the yearbook, Mrs. Hildegarde Buckette, with dismissal; however, the principal and Mrs. Buckette reached an understanding whereby the yearbook would be subject in the future to "guidelines" established by a faculty committee. Administration wants the best for everybody, and all it asks is that individuals make their lives conform to the framework established by the state.

Political Science

Political Science

Introduction to Political Science

Concepts:

Sovereign Power
Stability and Change in Africa, Julius Nyerere

Legitimacy
"Hell, No, We Won't Go!", John Cooney and Dana Spitzer

Representation
We Will Exercise Our Rights, Steve Wasserman

Interest Groups
The Food and Drug Administration and the Pill, Alice J. Wolfson and Philip E. Wolfson

Justice
If You Were On Welfare, Richard M. Elman

Liberty
Americans Betrayed, Morton Grodzins

Ideology
The Black Revolution: A Primer for White Liberals, Charles V. Hamilton

Revolution
A Double Deception: The Problem of Aggression, Howard Zinn

Introduction to Political Science

The political scientist investigates the ways in which people govern themselves; he is a continuing student of government and politics. Government, in the broadest sense, is a system of rules, regulations and controls which order human relationships. This general definition includes more than city halls, draft boards, or the politics of Washington, Moscow or Peking. A labor union, a civil rights group, a professional association, indeed, any social **group** is a government. These various informal "governments" are of interest to the political scientist because they help to shape the form of the political system by the ways in which they interact and by the demands they place on "the system." Most political scientists, however, are more interested in the more formal units of the overall political system, such as the constitutions, courts, politicians, administrators, elections, and so on. These are some of the units which comprise what is referred to as the "political structure," which exists to order and regulate **society**.

Thus, the *basic units* of a political system are its identifiable parts, such as the legislature, the judiciary or the executive. These *basic units*—in a smoothly functioning political system—have interdependent functional relationships with each other; each part influences and is influenced by all the other parts. The *structures* of a political system usually refer to the political **roles** that people hold, or to political **groups** in the system. The *processes* of the political system are the decision-making activities and the political actions which enforce the government's policies.

Different political systems have different kinds of structures or political institutions. For example, some systems have a two-chamber legislative structure wherein one "house" can **veto** the acts of the other; others, a political structure where only one "house" has ultimate political authority in the system. The courts in a few political systems are able to exercise **judicial review**, that is, to declare legislative acts unconstitutional. This is not the case in most political systems, however. A Council of Elders or a strong political party boss might be the major decision-making institution in some political systems; a tribal chief or military general might rule in another. Some systems might have a written constitution which sets forth various powers to be exercised and rights of the citizens; some systems might rely on custom to determine such powers and rights, or even on military force. All of these various mechanisms for governance constitute political institutions in the system, designed to make the system "work."

How a particular political system or government "works" is of course dependent on the **culture** it represents. Government is part of a broader **culture** by which it is influenced and sometimes changed. In the anthropology section, we defined "**culture**" as "the complex whole which includes knowledge, **belief**, art, morals, law, customs, and any other capabilities acquired by people as members of **society**." The concept of **culture change** illustrated that when social and political institutions do not respond to the needs and demands of individuals and **societies** for change, this may lead—as we shall see in our discussion on the concept of **revolution**—to attempts to overthrow the government by violent means.

As **culture** is transmitted from **generation** to **generation**, so, obviously, do political systems tend to perpetuate their own **values** and **practices**. Their members tend to share society's **norms** and **goals** and to follow society's **practices**. This process of **political socialization** also begins with the child in the **family** and continues into adulthood, where individuals enter new **groups** such as work groups on their jobs. These new **groups** may or may not introduce conflicting **values** or **norms** to the individual's conception of the political system.

The political scientist is concerned with government, politics and power. Government, as we have seen, establishes the rules of behavior which are set up to enforce and realize **group** and individual interests and **goals**. It may also refer to the set of formal governmental institutions, or the political structures, which enforce and regulate legal codes. Politics and the political system are generally thought to be synonymous with government in this latter sense. However, when one talks about political power, one is talking about those relationships among individuals and **groups** in a **society** where one individual or **group** is subordinate to another in terms of some activity. When an individual obtains a position of power in the political system he usually gains a **status** or position through which he is authorized to use his power on other subordinate individuals or **groups**. His **role** in terms of the political system can be defined, therefore, in terms of the expectations that other individuals or **groups** have as to how he should exercise his power.

In our readings, we will be concerned with several concepts of political science, one of which is **sovereign power** or ultimate decision-making authority beyond which there is no appeal. This concept is closely related to the concept of **legitimacy**, for a **sovereign power** should rule by the consent of those individuals it represents. **Representation**, therefore, is another concept of concern to the political scientist. Unless all persons in the political system speak and act on all occasions for themselves, they will need some form of **representation** to assure that their views are being heard. Of course, in the representative process, specific sub-groups within the system may organize to push for their particular self-interests; these are called **interest groups**, pressure groups or lobbies. Sometimes, **interest groups** may be motivated by a particular political philosophy or **ideology**.

This **ideology** might coincide with that of the political system in which they are operating. If not, there may be conflict which, if intense and persistent enough, may lead to an attempt to overthrow the established system by violent means, that is, by **revolution**. This kind of conflict usually signals that certain individuals or **groups** feel that their **liberty** as citizens of the existing political structure is being violated. These citizens may also feel that their interests are not being heeded; that the **sovereign power** of the political system is illegitimate and does not deserve their support.

As the readings in this section illustrate, the formation of a government presents numerous problems at any given time in history and in any given place. The governing process is a dynamic, not a static one. Whether the governing institutions are **legitimate** or not depends on how they are viewed by the citizens and others in terms of the **values** and aspirations of these citizens. The laws or "rules of the game" which should prevail, and the relationship of representatives and those they represent to those laws, are perennial problems in political science. The rights and responsibilities —or the leeway and limits—of **interest groups** and **ideologies** raise difficult questions of **consensus** and how one builds and maintains a **society** which is based on the **consensus** of its citizens.

Sovereign Power

We have seen that power concerns a relationship between individuals or **groups** where one is subordinate to the other. Political power may be based on psychological or on military and physical power; it may mean control over the minds of other people—such as the kind of psychological power which a **charismatic** leader holds over his followers, or it may mean physical power over the actions of other people, such as that wielded by military dictatorships.

Sovereign power is political power wielded by an ultimate decision-making person or **group**, beyond which there is no appeal. This kind of power is not to be confused with the power exercised by private, voluntary **groups** over their members. **Sovereign power**, in this essay, refers to that authority which adheres in political institutions and which makes decisions legally binding on the body politic, that is the members of the political system. A **sovereign** political **power** has authority over the life and death of its citizens. Thus, this power is to be distinguished from "influence" or power exercised, say, by a church or fraternity or labor union or business association over its members. In the sociology and economics sections, power is dealt with in a somewhat different way. The term usually includes the control and manipulation of people and the direction of collective efforts by a variety of formal and informal means. **Sovereign power** is a more specific concept referring to ultimate or final authority. In the political context, the sovereign entity might be elected by the constituents, gain position through inheritance, or even through the projection of his or her **charisma**, or by a **revolution**. In all but the latter two instances, there is usually a pre-existing, acceptable set of rules (written or unwritten constitution) determining the political process of succession to office.

It is important to point out that, by definition, **sovereign power** cannot be divided. In other words, *ultimate* authority to rule must rest *somewhere* —either by consent or by force.

In the United States, the Civil War was an example of a national **sovereign power** asserting itself forcefully vis-à-vis the southern slave states. These states had challenged the former's power to make final, binding decisions on the question of the extension of slavery. This notion of "**state sovereignty**" or the notion that the states held ultimate decision-making power over the federal government concerning some matters had persisted in this country among some elements since the establishment of the Constitution in 1787. The notion of "**divided sovereignty**," a situation in which several **groups** have overlapping decision-making power, had been allowed to persist, precisely because it was psychologically beneficial to permit it. But there came a point beyond which it was no longer possible to permit political preference to prevail over political reality.

The same is true of the history of Black people in the United States in relation to their treatment by the southern states after the Civil War. Relying on the Tenth Amendment to the Constitution, the southern states insisted that they had sovereignty over local, public education and could therefore maintain racially segregated public schools within their borders. The Federal Supreme Court ruled otherwise in 1954, and three years later in 1957 in Little Rock, Arkansas, President Eisenhower had to use federal troops to force a local high school to admit Black students.

The point is, of course, that every overt challenge to sovereignty is a stress or strain on the political system. And a **sovereign power** prefers to avoid such challenges whenever possible. President Nyerere speaks to the necessity of **sovereign power** in his address to Canadians on problems of stability and change in African governments. The article, the second by Julius Nyerere in this volume, discusses a different type of political organization from that of the United States. The interrelationships between older governments and newer nations is well-illustrated by Nyerere's comments in this article. A traditionally serious problem in international politics is the extent to which small, new nations can maintain their **sovereign power** in the face of large, strong nations. One of the interesting dilemmas for countries such as the United States with their own particular private corporate system is whether or not they will respond to the challenges raised by the President of Tanzania in his article. The national government in the United States is sovereign over private corporations, as it is over the several states, but whether it chooses to exercise that sovereignty—and under what circumstances—is another matter.

Legitimacy

A **sovereign power** is generally considered to be politically stable when it is based on the consent of its citizens rather than on military force. Thus, sovereignty is very dependent upon **legitimacy**, which is the acceptance of the existing political institutions as right and proper by most of its citizens. **Legitimacy** depends upon how society's **values** fit with the existing political institutions and **ideology**. **Legitimacy** involves the capacity of the system to foster and maintain the **belief**, which may be mostly psychological, that the existing political institutions are the most appropriate ones for the **society**. In other words, there must be the feeling that the institutions have the right to make the decisions.

The article on desertions and draft dodgers by John Cooney and Dana Spitzer points up how intensely the Viet Nam conflict has divided American **society** and how many young Americans consider the present United States administration to be illegitimate. In a sense, the solution of the draft dodger is also illegitimate in the opinion of some other elements in the **society**. That is, refusing to serve in a war the draftee considers morally wrong or unjust is illegitimate as far as the military authorities or draft board is concerned. This only reinforces the fact that whether an act or a political system is legitimate or illegitimate is determined by the perspective of particular **groups** and whether the act or system fits their **values**.

In the United States today one hears a great deal about the "illegitimacy" of the political system. Lack of political **legitimacy**, i.e., **a crisis of legitimacy**, often means that the established political institutions must resort more and more to physical force to rule; the result can be said to be a challenge to sovereignty. It means that **consensus** is breaking down; that the rules of the game are no longer the solidifying, binding force. Lack of **legitimacy** means that new **interest groups**, holding fundamentally different political **ideologies** and **attitudes** towards "the law" are making themselves heard on the political scene. And all this is associated with major normative and structural changes in the **society**—or at least dynamic attempts at such changes.

Twentieth-century Americans are not accustomed to such political challenges on their own shores. And to a great extent, many **social institutions**—the school, the church, the **family**, the press, radio and television, literature, patriotic ceremonials—are experiencing new challenges to their **roles**. In the sociology section, the reading on **social institutions** concerned current **attitudes** within the church with respect to stands on discrimination and racism, and the role of the institution in creating a better social system. Here the argument is extended to other aspects of the social scene. In many ways, the **crisis of legitimacy** is also a crisis of **social institutions**.

These **social institutions** have presented a picture of an America free from the political turmoil of Latin American countries, and free from the political instabilities involved with new developing nations of Africa and Asia. They have stressed the strength of **consensus** in the United States, but this is changing drastically, as is revealed by the crisis in our slums and on our campuses and by repeated marches on the nation's capital. And precisely because the change is so dynamic, so unexpected by many in the establishment, both public and private, and so threatening to the known quantity of the status quo, many American social scientists have been either unable to accept the implications of the dynamic challenge to **legitimacy** or unable to agree with the premises of the challenge—i.e., the illegitimacy of the institutions.

Crises of legitimacy are often crises of change; they occur during a transition to a new **social structure**. The conditions for a **crisis of legitimacy** are usually: 1) if the **status** of major conservative institutions is threatened during the period of structural change; 2) if all the major **groups** in the **society** do not have access to the political system in the transitional period, or at least as soon as they develop political demands.

Most of the so-called "establishment" does not stop to question the **legitimacy** of doing what is "expected," although more and more young people are constantly questioning the **legitimacy** of their daily actions. A number of males who are about to be or have been drafted, not only challenge the **legitimacy** of participating in the Indo China conflict, but since the United States is willing to resort to force as a response to their challenge of **legitimacy**, have been forced to remove themselves to other countries. As we have seen, the article on draft dodgers in Sweden illustrates the consequences of challenging the structures and of being placed outside of them. It also serves as a useful illustration of the concept of **culture relativity** described in the anthropology section, and shows that how one's actions and challenges to authority are assessed depends upon the **norms**, **values** and **beliefs** of people in particular **cultures**.

Representation

A system of **representation** is necessary in **societies** which claim to be "democratic" or representative, and where all the people do not make all the political decisions all the time. While more efficient and rational than a system that does not provide for **representation**, this system has its dangers. **Interest groups** and power élites which tend to spring up under representative governments often ignore the interests of the excluded. Even within the system of **representation**, a representative may not be the "real" representative of his constituents. For example, one theory of **representation** and **practice** holds that a representative acts in the interest of his constituents as he sees it, even though this may be contrary to his constituents' preferences. Another theory of "real" **representation** holds that an elected representative acts conscientiously as a spokesman for the preferences of his constituency, following its mandate when making his decisions. Obviously, a representative who shares the **values** and **norms** of his constituents will automatically vote their preferences in acting in terms of his own preferences.

The question of **representation** is related to several constant problems.

What **attitudes** and actions will excluded **groups**—at least those who feel they are not properly represented in political decision-making—take? The fact is, of course, that frequently new **groups** seeking access to the political system must fight to restructure the decision-making processes in order to make a place for themselves. Essentially, this is the anti-establishment strategy of many high school and college students today.

The article on **representation** by a Berkeley high school student, Steve Wasserman, relates student efforts to obtain **representation** in the Berkeley schools through the formation of a Student Union. This Student Union is characterized as a more responsive and representative kind of government than the student government, which has to obtain faculty and administrative approval for leafletting or organizing. The **attitude** of the students is, of course, that students themselves are the only ones who can correctly represent themselves and their needs. Political science is always concerned with the question of the nature of **representation**. Should each and every person and/or **group** be represented on each and every decision-making body? That is, is it reasonable to assume that students, teachers, parents, taxpayers and non-taxpayers should be represented in the educational system? If so, should they be represented equally? Or should more weight be given to one **group** over another? What kinds of criteria should determine decisions to these questions?

The article also demonstrates the lack of power that adolescents in the United States have, and their inability to influence the course of political and social affairs. In terms of **social stratification**, age as well as sex and skin color may be powerful determinants of where one stands in relationship to others and how hard one has to struggle to voice his **beliefs** and points of view, factors that could possibly influence his fate and the fate of others.

Interest groups

In representative forms of government, **interest groups** develop to lobby for policies favorable to their self-interest. It is not to be expected that governments can equally represent all interests at all times—especially in a **pluralistic society**. The more varied, specialized and complex a **society** becomes, the more one is likely to see the development of these **groups** which function and gain power mainly by a process of shifting alliances. For instance, on one issue, a group may ally with another group which is concerned with this issue, and it may be competing with this same group on another issue.

Some **interest groups** are closer to the centers of political power and are able to exert more influence than others. Likewise, the less a group's **goals** and interests coincide with those of the government and other **groups** in the **society**, the less power that **group** will have. The article by the Wolfsons on "The Pill" demonstrates how various **interest groups** combine to lobby and exert influence at the federal level. In some form or another, such a process takes place wherever political decisions are made.

It is much easier for a **group** to identify with the political system when that **group** perceives that it has gained substantial benefits from the system, and when it does not feel it is a deliberate target for exploitation by the system. Thus, a farmer in Iowa, accustomed to having his interests protected by the American Farm Bureau Federation, or a businessman in Indiana, accustomed to getting political results from his membership in the National Association of Manufacturers, may find it quite difficult to accept the views, say, of members of The Black Panther Party or of the Weathermen, that the American political system is illegitimate. The fact is, of course, that in relation to *their* (the farmer and the businessman) interests, the system is quite **legitimate**.

It is possible, of course, for a **group** to perceive that no matter how hard it tries to achieve its goals through political persuasion, favorable results are not possible. It may then decide to pursue tactics not acceptable to other **groups** or to the government—such as the use of violence. When this happens, it is often said that that **group** is not "working within the system," that is, it has chosen tactics which do not abide by the "rules of the game": bargaining, negotiating, compromising. Such a situation frequently leads to the kind of **crisis of legitimacy** referred to earlier.

Justice

Early Greek natural law philosophers defined **justice** in terms of the natural superiority and inferiority of men. They believed that **justice** required that these differences be recognized in building a political society. Later political philosophers profoundly disagreed with the Greek view of **justice** and held that natural inequalities among men were *politically* irrelevant. They held that man's **justice** was mainly motivated by self-interest. Many political activists of the twentieth century hold different **attitudes** and see this later notion of **justice** and equality as basically elitist and aristocratic in their struggle against sociopolitical orders. They would reject both the notion of natural superiority and inferiority as well as the description of man as basically self-seeking. They would also reject the idea of a strong, absolute sovereign. For instance, **justice** in terms of the economic interpretation of a Marxist would suggest that people's nature is shaped by the modes of economic production in the **society**, that the ultimate just **society** (where eventually the state would wither away) would be constructed on the basis of "from each according to his ability, to each according to his needs." And as the mode of production changed from **capitalism** to **socialism, justice** would no longer be defined in terms of every man against every man, but would have each man receiving an equitable share of the collective wealth.

The article by Richard Elman on welfare indicates the concern of twentieth century Americans, mostly liberal, middle-class political activists, that the poor get an equal share of the available resources. In this sense, they are concerned that the state should provide the equitable share; this they consider only just. However, in reality, the present welfare system and the way poor Americans live is clearly unjust. The person on welfare is chained to a variety of requirements about what he cannot spend his money on and how he allocates the minimal resources provided. The poor not only clearly do not receive *justice*, but within the system in which they operate, they receive less for their dollar and do not have much choice in how they spend it.

Liberty

Most political *societies* have always been faced with the probem of trying to balance the requirements of national security and individual *liberty*. This balancing of prerequisites is not a particularly pressing problem for *societies* inclined toward *authoritarianism*, *totalitarianism* or *fascism*. And in some instances, one will find a justification made for suppressing individual *liberties* on the grounds that the collective security—i.e., the very continued existence—of the *society* required it. This position is put forth either when the decision-makers perceive a military threat from outside, as in war, or when it is decided that a highly disciplined, planned economic and sociopolitical structure is necessary for development. This latter view is normally associated with developing *societies* where economic resources are relatively scarce. There is also the situation where the authorities decide that in order to protect the system against potential adversaries within its boundaries, it is necessary to rule against individual *liberties*. Many protesters of American foreign policy and of racial practices in the 1960's and 1970's have concluded that the United States has already gone too far in suppressing their legitimate protests.

Morton Grodzins' study of the evacuation and confinement of Americans of Japanese ancestry during World War II presents this problem in very sharp focus. It is an event in recent American history which is often forgotten or suppressed. Grodzins concludes that public policy in that instance was more a function of the politics of prejudice and panic than of any judicious attempt to weigh the requirements of national security on the one hand against the individual *liberties* of American citizens of Japanese ancestry on the other. The article illustrates at a behavioral level one reaction of anger, *fear* and anxiety which resulted in the confinement, social degradation, and severe economic loss of extensive numbers of citizens.

Ideology

An *ideology* is a *society's* dominant set of *beliefs* about the right and proper *norms* and *goals* of people's political and economic institutions, and the means by which they can be attained. It embodies *society's* dominant

values, which are regarded as sacred, and justifies and explains the basic social order. Unlike a political philosophy, which discusses the nature of people, the nature of **society** and the "good life," a political **ideology** is more closely related to organizational activity calculated to obtain short-term as well as long-term **goals**.

Ideologies provide a general framework which is based on certain assumptions, **values**, resources and **goals** of a **society**, within which **societies** can judge the usefulness of short-term and long-term policies and programs. **Ideologies** reflect the general **ethical value system of a society**; the particular understanding of the historical development of institutions and processes in **societies**, the application of these phenomena to current conditions, and a projection of future **goals**, based on all of these. They provide a general perspective on the **community**, and help explain momentary and long-term changes in **societies**.

The same **ideologies** can exist in **societies** which have different types of political structures or governments. For example, **capitalism** in the United States is quite different from **capitalism** in England; **socialism** in Tanzania is different from **socialism** in Sweden. **Ideologies** surround not only formal and informal ways of dealing with social inequities and matters of **social disorganization**, but are involved with the different functional relationships among **social institutions**.

Thus **capitalism**, a matter discussed in the section on economics, is more than simply a particular set of monetary arrangements but is framed within an **ideology** that determines what one regards as important in evaluating an individual. Similarly, the same interrelationships can be gleaned from the discussion of **socialism** in an emerging country in Africa, in the economics section.

In discussing **ideologies**, it should be pointed out that the political **ideologies** held by individuals and **groups** do not necessarily develop instantaneously; rather they are frequently passed on from **generation** to **generation** through the long-term process of **political socialization**. This generally determines the different **beliefs** and **practices** in **societies**. While perhaps too much is made of one's early socialization in determining political **ideologies**, think back to the article in the section on anthropology describing the child-rearing differences in Japan and the United States. Many analysts would argue that there are at least some relationships to be traced from such early experiences which determine the ideological orientation of both persons and **groups**.

Ideology *attempts to link what is with what ought to be*, and this is not always easy when dealing with governments and political power structures. The article on *The Black Revolution: A Primer for White Liberals*, addresses this serious linkage problem in connection with the struggle for racial equality. This article expresses the concern of white liberals to extend the concepts of democracy—**egalitarianism** and **libertarianism**—to all races. As far as the Blacks are concerned, the "reality" is that years of alliances and cooperation with white liberals have only served to bring about a lack of improvement in their condition. In fact, many Black Power advocates maintain that they have steadily lost ground in relation to the progress of whites. The **ideology** of Black Power has been to start from a base of self-awareness and identity and to develop a viable political power from this base.

Revolution

We have noted that when it is not possible for contentious **groups** within a **society**, which may hold different political **ideologies** from the dominant **ideology** of the **society**, to reconcile their differences by peaceful, political means, they may resort to force and violence in an attempt to overthrow the government.

The American Declaration of Independence of 1776 reads: ". . . when a long train of abuses and usurpations, pursuing invariably the same object, evinces a design to reduce them (the people) under absolute despotism, it is their right, it is their duty, to throw off such government and to provide new guards for their future security."

Political **revolutions**, as referred to in this essay, are associated with the use of force and violence. The aim is to dislodge existing political power structures and to implement new ones. This need not have a particular ideological orientation—i.e., liberal, progressive, conservative—and one frequently finds that a **revolution** has really meant only a **coup d'état**, that is, one small **group** of leaders replaces another **group** in power. And this change may not result in substantially improved conditions for the masses of citizens.

There is an unfortunate tendency to classify virtually all mass political action as **revolution**. This is unfortunate, because what might be involved is the important phenomenon of **social change** whereby new **groups** come into the political system and share power with existing **groups**. This is more properly to be understood as sociopolitical reform, and not as **revolution**. Usually, both the excessively violent aspect and the complete displacement of older, existing power structures are absent from this process. In this connection, the article on the "Black Revolution" in the United States is a misnomer. What is happening racially should not be considered a **revolution**. It is an intense struggle for political sharing of power and for equal economic and educational opportunities.

One frequently hears the word "**revolution**" used to describe major revisions or changes in other spheres of activity. For example, we speak of a "**revolution**" in fashion designs, a "**revolution**" in educational techniques, and so forth. To a political scientist, however, the term has the particular meaning related to the transference (usually violent) of decision-making power, where the previous institutions and agents exercising power are completely displaced and a wholly new political system is instituted.

Revolutions are generated from a number of causes, but normally it is felt that masses of people are not basically prone to revolutionary action unless there is some state of mind that stems from the rising expectation that their economic, social and political conditions *can* be improved by such action. A people who are totally without hope or who must spend all their time merely trying to survive, physically, are not prospective candidates for revolutionary battle. Rather than becoming revolutionized, such people are likely to become **politically traumatized**—i.e., withdrawn, not active, immobilized politically, and of the opinion that regardless of the sort of activity that is pursued—voting or revolting—little change will occur in their lives. A revolutionary struggle comes not only out of a need to overcome deprivation and oppression, but also out of a feeling that such struggle, however difficult and protracted, will result in substantial positive changes.

Howard Zinn's article on Viet Nam attempts to show that the United States is intervening in a struggle that is essentially an internal nationalist-communist revolutionary struggle in Viet Nam. His article has relevance to the concept of **belief** discussed in the anthropology section, where it was noted that **beliefs**, in the **culture** of certain **societies**, operate to influence behavior. Here, in Professor Zinn's article, one finds that it is the **beliefs** held by individuals, rather than the "objective facts" that have determined the level and form of our participation in the Viet Nam conflict. **Beliefs** may be specific to particular social and biological behaviors or they may converge, and sometimes this is the definition of **ideology**—to form a pattern that leads to particular collective behavior on the part of **communities** and nations.

Summary

We have continued to point out the interrelationships of the social science disciplines in our discussion of political science. Political systems are composed of individuals who act in terms of basic units, structures, and processes, much like the political system itself. **Groups**, **roles** and **status** are as important to the political scientist as to the sociologist for they help him determine political activities, **interest groups**, and the **political socialization** process. The basic anthropological concept of **culture** is also basic to the political scientist since governments are dependent on and influenced by the **cultures** they represent. **Culture changes** in the face of intransigent political structures have been known to produce revolutionary situations. Political science is also dependent on economics, both ideologically and systemically. Many political **ideologies** are firmly based on an economic interpretation of the social order—especially **socialism**, **communism** and **capitalism**.

In more recent years, precisely because of the rapid development of technology and the growing **political socialization** of increasingly larger numbers of people throughout the world, the way people organize to govern themselves is becoming more and more a dynamic process. **Sovereign power** is being challenged from within and from without various systems; new institutions of **legitimacy** are being demanded. New forms of **representation** are the subject of constant demand and experimentation (such as more student power in schools or **community control** in urban areas); **interest groups** are becoming more prolific, thus broadening the base of political participation. Established, élite ruling **groups** are being challenged continuously. People are demanding wholly new definitions of **justice** to fit the modern political and economic conditions; individual **liberty** is becoming more and more a precious commodity around which people are building new **ideologies**. **Revolution** in various sections of the world is becoming a **norm**, not an exception.

The study of government and politics is not new. As long as people have grouped themselves into political **societies**, we have had those who have attempted to study this process. But as **societies** have grown and become more complex, the tools and techniques for studying this process have been changed. This essay has presented some concepts that have been perennially associated with the problems of governance. Political scientists attempt to understand these concepts in the difficult context of constantly changing demands of dynamic **societies**.

Hopefully, all the **social sciences** will continue to help people cope with their environment and at the same time help them to explore and to understand the complex world about them. By bringing all the **social sciences** into play in analyzing complex social problems, such as air, noise and water pollution, the ecological crisis, the economy, continuing international conflicts, **poverty** and so on, the **social sciences** are continuing to meet contemporary demands for "relevancy" and for "action."

SOVEREIGN POWER

Stability and Change in Africa

JULIUS NYERERE

Mr. President, Ladies and Gentlemen,

This is my first visit to the University of Toronto but it is very far from being my first contact with it. People from this University have worked at our University College in Dar es Salaam and in many different sectors of our Government; they have made great contributions to our progress. We have many old and valued friends here: people to whom we are indebted for good service gladly rendered.

Let me begin, therefore, by expressing to this University our appreciation for the co-operation and assistance we have received. You have released good people to work with us, and not just sent the people you could most gladly spare! Let me also say "thank you" to the individuals concerned. They have helped us to implement our policies; they have helped us to see and to understand the problems we are faced with; when we have asked, they have suggested alternative solutions to these problems—though I must hasten to add that they bear no responsibility for our failures. The decision to accept or reject their suggestions is one we have always reserved to ourselves!

This kind of technical assistance is very valuable to us. It also has a by-product which is, I believe, important to Canada as well. For not only have we learned something about Canada from these workers. As intelligent people who lived with us and worked with us, they have learned something about us. When they return to this country, they are therefore frequently able to spread an understanding of what we are trying to do. They can tell of our successes and our failures; more important, they can also put our actions into the context of our circumstances and our motives. I believe this to be important to both countries. For Tanzania's policy of self-reliance does not imply that we dream of isolating ourselves. We recognize that we are involved in the world and that the world is involved in us.

Involvement without understanding, however, can be embarrassing and even dangerous. And while the involvement is inevitable, a lack of understanding about Africa is only too easy. Our very existence as nations is exotic. And now our voices on the international scene are strident; we complain about things which others take for granted; we make demands on other nations of the world, which appear unreasonable to more traditional habits of thought. The reaction is natural. Our actions and our demands are looked upon with all the suspicion which is normally directed towards upstarts. And everything we do is judged in the light of attitudes which grew out of the aftermath of the second world war. In other words, every possible attempt is made to squeeze African events into the framework of the cold war or other big power conflicts.

The big question is always: "Is this or that African country pro-East or pro-West?"

These kinds of question are understandable because of the recent history of Europe and America. But they are the wrong questions for anyone who wishes to understand what is happening in Africa. They are based on a very fundamental mistake— and, I would add, an unwarranted degree of arrogance! They imply that Africa has no ideas of its own and no interests of its own. They assume the exclusive validity of the international conflicts which existed when we achieved nationhood. They are based on the belief that African actions must inevitably be determined by reference to either the Western liberal tradition or to communist theory or practice.

In fact, I hope that Africa has learned, and will continue to learn, from total human experience—from peoples in the West, East, North and South, whether we use these compass points as political or geographical terms! But what we are, in fact, trying to do is to solve the problems of Africa—and in our case, of Tanzania—as we experience them. And we are making this attempt as Africans and as Tanzanians: as people who have been shaped by a history which goes back further than the century or so of colonialism. Further, we look at the world as people who believe that they have something to contribute to mankind, as well as something to gain from it.

Our need for both change and stability

Yet we are new nations. Like every other people in the world we have always had a desire to be our own masters. We lost our freedom through defeat by the technically superior forces of Europe. Our first concern was to regain it, and our first priority now is to guard that freedom and to make it a reality.

When we did regain our freedom, however, we gained control over a different structure. In Tanzania it was more than one hundred tribal units which lost their freedom; it was one nation which regained it. By the forces of history we have been brought politically into this twentieth century world; our new freedom can only be maintained if we adopt other aspects of twentieth century life as well.

Another fundamental change makes other demands upon the national government which were not made on the traditional tribal governments. The Tanzanian people now know that our poverty, our ignorance, and our diseases, are not an inevitable part of the human condition. Once we accepted these things as the will of God; now they are recognized as being within the control of man. Political freedom is therefore no longer enough for us.

We in Tanzania are thus conscious of two overwhelming needs. We are determined to maintain our mastery over our own destiny—to defend our national freedom. We are also determined to change the condition of our lives. It is to meet these two needs that we must have both change and stability. Somehow these two must be combined, because in the circumstances of Tanzania, and indeed of Africa, neither is possible without the other.

Change to make freedom a reality

For although political and social stability is necessary to any real national or personal freedom, so too is change in our circumstances. At present our national freedom often exists on paper only, for our country is so poor, and so weak relative to other nations, that we do not play our rightful part in the human community. Decisions on matters which vitally concern us can be —and often are—made without any reference to us. And this is understandable. Even defending our national integrity against the intervention of foreign powers strains us to the utmost. A very great change in our economic well-being is necessary before we can meet these responsibilities of national freedom.

Nor is it only in national terms that real freedom is undermined by our poverty. What freedom has our subsistence farmer? He scratches a bare living from the soil provided the rains do not fail; his children work at his side without schooling, medical care, or even good feeding. Certainly he has freedom to vote and to speak as he wishes. But these freedoms are much less real to him than his freedom to be exploited. Only as his poverty is reduced will his existing political freedom become properly meaningful and his right to human dignity become a fact of human dignity.

This essential economic change will not, and cannot, take place in isolation. It depends upon, and it brings, social and political change. It is not even possible simply to expand the social and political organization which was introduced into the country by the colonial power. These were based on an individualistic philosophy which is contrary to both our traditions and our aspirations for human equality. And they were directed at the problems of imposing and maintaining an alien law and order, not at securing mobilization for the improvement in living conditions which our people now demand.

The need for stability

Yet stable government, and stability in the society, is also essential to our freedom. For without political stability African countries will remain the playthings of others. Without it, alien forces can influence our policies for their own benefit, and outside powers can wage their wars on our territories and with our peoples. It is perfectly true that many of us in Africa are in danger of getting a phobia about foreign plots, and of attributing to foreign machinations all the evils we suffer from. But although the original failures may be ours, no intelligent and knowledgeable person would deny that outside forces do take advantage of African division for their own benefit, or that they exacerbate our conflicts when this suits their purpose.

Quite apart from the defence of our

national integrity, however, stability is also essential for economic development. We cannot increase agricultural production, organize markets for home-produced goods, meet export orders, or arrange for the supply of essential investment goods, unless there is stability and security in the country. An effective administration, secure communications, and personal safety, are prerequisites for any attack on the poverty which now oppresses us.

In brief, change causes disturbance and thus upsets stability, but positive change is impossible without stability. And stability is itself impossible in Africa without change. Africa's task is therefore to achieve a difficult balance between the conflicting and complementary needs for change and stability.

Tanzania's internal policies

Tanzania is attempting to achieve change by deliberate policy, and to maintain stability by involving all the people in both the direction and the process of change. We are under no illusions about the difficulty of the task we have undertaken. With few socialists we are trying to build socialism; with few people conscious of the basic requirements of democracy we are trying to achieve change by democratic means; with few technicians we are trying to effect a fundamental transformation of our economy. And with an educational élite whose whole teaching encouraged motives of individualistic advancement, we are trying to create an egalitarian society!

It is not my intention to speak about these internal policies today. I will only say that so far we have retained our balance. But I am optimistic about our future, provided that factors outside our control do not prevent us from continuing with our efforts.

Change and stability in Southern Africa

For Tanzania is one small part of Africa, and our future is linked with that of the continent as a whole. Even if we wished, we could not be unaffected by what happens on this land mass. But in fact none of us in Africa has learned to think in exclusively nationalistic terms—we still think of ourselves as Africans. It is, of course, true that there are some conflicts between African states and within African states. Yet these are like the conflicts between the Provinces of Canada—important provided there is no overwhelming external challenge to the principles on which the existence of each state is based. Our part of Africa feels itself to be involved with all other parts. We are learning—indeed I think we have learned—that the people from one free state have no right or duty to intervene in the affairs of another free state. We recognize that each nation has to deal with the conflicting needs of stability and change in its own way. If we think other free peoples are wrong, or if they fail in their endeavors, we still have no choice but to adapt ourselves to deal with the problems that their policies create for us.

But the situation is very different in relation to Southern Africa and to the remaining Portuguese colonies in Africa. In Mozambique, Angola and Portuguese Guinea, the African peoples are being governed by an external power which categorically rejects the principle of self-determination. In Southern Rhodesia the colonial power claims to accept the principle of self-determination, but has utterly failed to assert its authority against a racialist minority which denies this principle. In South Africa the **apartheid** policy is imposed on the Africans and other non-white peoples, and maintained by the most ruthless suppression. And the United Nations has failed to take any effective steps to dislodge this same tyranny from South-West Africa. In all these cases, outside forces are suppressing Africans, and Africans are being humiliated and persecuted simply for being what they are—black or colored Africans.

In relation to all these areas of our continent, therefore, Africa as a whole recognizes a challenge from external forces and from a *racialism* which denies our rights as human beings. We cannot be uninvolved. Just one African state does not have a recent experience of colonialism—and for many years that was independent in name only. We have all suffered from some degree of racial discrimination. If we accept the continuation of such conditions in Southern Africa, we are denying our own moral right to freedom and human equality, and are forced to justify our existence on the grounds of an economic and military strength which we do not, in fact, possess. We cannot adopt this attitude.

But in any case, whatever the emotions may be, the fact is that Tanzania's freedom is itself in jeopardy while colonialism and racialism remain dominant on our borders. As long as we insist on making a reality of our freedom, and pursuing policies which uphold the dignity of African people, our existence is a threat to the colonialist and racialist states of Southern Africa. They would inevitably take steps to reduce the effectiveness of our policies and to control our actions. For just as their policy of racialism makes it daily more difficult for us to build a state on the basis of non-racialism, so they cannot secure their slave systems while the rest of Africa uses its freedom for the benefit of its people. The principles of freedom and equality have no validity unless they are of universal validity; and the principle of racial supremacy is invalid unless it is universally valid. Conflict between these two conceptions of humanity is inevitable. Where they meet, the conflict will become an active one.

Tanzania's concern with the situation in Southern Africa is thus not something which is extraneous to our other policies. It is a matter affecting our security. It is central to everything we try to do. It is not that we are great altruists who love freedom so much that we will fight for it everywhere and anywhere. We know our limitations. We also know that people can only free themselves—no one else can prevent them from trying to win their freedom, and no one else can do it for them. But in the case of Southern Africa, we and the other free states are all involved. We are all Africans; we all need to work together for the real development of any of us; and a continuing freedom struggle in one part of the continent affects the security of all other parts. This involvement is acutely realized in Tanzania because we are a border state between free Africa and colonial Africa; but the same considerations apply to a greater or lesser extent to all free African states. Very little can be understood about Africa until this is understood.

Let me therefore try to sum up our position on this matter. The common objective of the African people is self-determination for the peoples of Southern Africa and the other Portuguese colonies, and an end to the official propagation and practice of racialism in our continent. That is all. We are not anti-white terrorists wishing to impose a reverse racialism; we wish to uphold human equality and to give human dignity and non-racialism a chance to grow in our lands.

As far as the free states of Africa are concerned, what comes after freedom is an affair of the peoples of those territories.

It is not for us to decide what sort of government they will have or what sort of system they will adopt. Tanzania must support the struggle for freedom in these areas regardless of the political philosophy of those who are conducting the struggle. If they are capitalists, we must support them; if they are liberals, we must support them; if they are communists, we must support them; if they are socialists, we must support them. We support them as nationalists. Our own commitment to socialism in Tanzania is irrelevant to the right of the people of Mozambique (and the other areas) to choose their own government and their own political system. The right of a people to freedom from alien domination comes before socialism. The right of a man to stand upright as a human being in his own country comes before questions of the kind of society he will create once he has that right. Freedom is the only thing that matters until it is won. The support which is given to the freedom struggles by Tanzania and by other African states is neither a disguised form of new imperialism nor an evangelical mission for socialism or capitalism. It is a recognition of the oneness of Africa.

By peace or violence?

Yet there remains a big question. Is the freedom struggle to be waged by peaceful methods or by violence? Is Africa to support the freedom movement regardless of the methods used, or could we make our support conditional?

There are some people who appear to believe that there is virtue in violence and that only if a freedom struggle is conducted by war and bloodshed can it lead to real liberation. I am not one of these people; the Government of Tanzania does not accept this doctrine, and nor do any of the other free African Governments as far as I am aware. We know that war causes immense sufferings, that it is usually the most innocent who are the chief victims, and that the hatred and fear generated by war are dangerous to the very freedom and non-racialism it is our purpose to support. We have a deep desire for a peaceful transfer of power to the people. We believe that if a door is shut, attempts should be made to open it; if it is ajar, it should be pushed until it is open wide. In neither case should the door be blown up at the expense of those inside.

But if the door to freedom is locked and bolted, and the present guardians of the door have refused to turn the key or pull the bolts, the choice is very straightforward. Either you accept the lack of freedom or you break the door down.

That, unfortunately, is the present position in Southern Africa and, unless there is some new outside influence which forces a reversal of policy on those now in power, that is the choice now before us.

Portugal has proclaimed that its colonies in Africa are part of the metropolitan country and that self-determination for the peoples of these territories is therefore not a matter for discussion. Political organization is prohibited, all attempts at peaceful protest are suppressed, and change by negotiation is ruled out. In Rhodesia, the people's organizations have been banned and the leaders imprisoned. Even the British Government's absurd suggestion that the white minority should promise to bring discrimination to an end gradually has been answered by a clear statement of determination to maintain perpetual white supremacy. To the South African Government, discrimination on racial grounds is a basic article of faith which admits no argument.

In all these areas the demand for freedom has been rejected in principle. The door to progress is shut, bolted and barred.

In such a situation the only way the people can get freedom is by force. A peaceful end to oppression is impossible. The only choice before the people is organized or unorganized violence. But chaos will result, not freedom, from spontaneous uprisings when the frustrations get too great to be borne, or when some fresh turn of the screw goads the people to madness. Indeed, spontaneous uprisings in a modern and ruthless state are little more than mass suicide; they only achieve the release of death for many, and increased suffering for the others. When every avenue of peaceful change is blocked, then the only way forward to positive change is by channelling and directing the people's fury—that is, by organized violence, by a people's war against their government.

When this happens, Tanzania cannot deny support, for to do so would be to deny the validity of African freedom and African dignity. We are naturally and inevitably allies of the freedom fighters. We may decide, as we have decided, that no Tanzanian will take part in these wars; we may recognize the fact that we cannot arm the freedom fighters. But we cannot call for freedom in Southern Africa, and at the same time deny all assistance to those who are fighting for it, when we know, as well as they do, that every other means of achieving freedom has been excluded by those now in power.

The involvement of the West

But it is not only African states which are inevitably involved in this conflict. All the traditional friends and allies of the powers concerned are also involved. Portugal is a member of N.A.T.O. To say the very least—much less than we believe to be the case!—the resulting military support allows Portugal to devote a greater proportion of her men and resources to the occupation of her African colonies than would otherwise be the case. Further, Portugal is a member of E.F.T.A.; it derives great benefit from selling to its Western allies goods which originate in the African colonies. Such economic links are another factor in the ability of the poorest state in Europe to spend something like 47 per cent of its Budget on "overseas defence"—which really means on the maintenance of colonialism in Africa.

About South Africa's position, I am sure it is unnecessary for me to say very much. It has great wealth and economic strength derived in part from past foreign investment. Its continuing economic development also owes much to new investment and re-investment by Western firms, and its international trade links with the West are very important to both sides. Indeed, the size of the Western involvement in South Africa's economy can be gauged by the indignation with which African demands for an economic boycott are met.

The illegality of the Southern Rhodesian regime has led to an economic boycott being imposed on that country. Nonetheless, the refusal of the colonial power either to make the boycott a total and effective one, or to enforce its decisions by direct intervention, has a reason. It reflects a sense of involvement with that administration and the people it represents—in other words, the dominant minority.

But my real point is not the fact of the West's economic involvement with Southern Africa. My concern is with their ideological involvement. I am not accusing the Western powers of conscious racialism, but of a preoccupation with conflicts which are at present irrelevant to the situation in Africa.

N.A.T.O. is a Western military alliance against East European communism—perhaps against communism itself—and Portugal is a member of N.A.T.O. South Africa claims to be a bastion against communism in Africa. The regime in Rhodesia claims that it is defending its part of Africa against communist-inspired chaos. These states are all anxious that their struggle against the freedom movements should be interpreted in the West as part of a world-wide anti-communist struggle. The real danger which worries me is that the West will accept this interpretation, and that it will, in consequence, betray its own principles by supporting these Southern African regimes.

The principle of **self-determination** and of national freedom is part of the democratic ideal; it is enshrined in all the greatest philosophies and documents of the Western world. But will the West recognize that this is the question at issue in Southern Africa, or will it be confused by this talk of "Western civilization" fighting "Eastern communism"?

If the struggle in Southern Africa is seen as the freedom struggle which it in fact is, the policies of Western states—both governments and peoples—will be determined only by the degree of their willingness to sacrifice immediate economic interests to political principles. But if the West accepts the South African and Portuguese argument that they are fighting on behalf of the "free world" against communism, then I believe that in time this interpretation will become defensible—at least as regards their enemies. For if the West supports these racialist and fascist states, the freedom struggle will in reality become a part of the world ideological conflict—as it is now wrongly alleged to be. Further, I believe that if this is allowed to happen, we are liable to finish up with an even more disastrous conflict—a conflict of the races. For Africa and the West will be on opposite sides of the barricades; and Africa will have the support of Asia and large parts of Latin America.

Let me explain my fears and what I believe can be done by countries of the Western bloc to avoid such catastrophes.

Pressure for peaceful change

Africa is anxious for peace in Southern Africa. But the possibility of this depends upon the possibility of ending the present injustice without war. Neither free Africa nor the Western world has the right to ask the peoples of Southern Africa to accept indefinitely the present humiliation, oppression and foreign domination; and in any case they would not pay heed to any such demands. The only chance for peace in Southern Africa is if change can be secured without violence. If this is possible, no one will be happier than the people of Africa. But we have tried peaceful methods and we have failed. The people of Southern Africa are therefore resorting to war, and the free African states are supporting them. The only chance for peace now is if the allies of the Southern African states are willing and able to exert the kind of pressure which brings change with the minimum of violence.

Do the Western powers have the ability to exert such pressure? I believe that they have a great deal of power if they are willing to use it for this purpose. Both South Africa and Portugal gain great benefit from their association with the Western nations; they will not wish to lose that benefit.

It is possible that South Africa would refuse to make any concessions to the democratic sensibilities of its allies, even at the cost of complete international isolation. I say this is possible because many people in South Africa believe in apartheid as a religion and will defend their faith until death. But there are other South Africans who rejoice in, and who support, the segregationist policies of that Government because of the material benefit and the position of privilege it gives them. I believe this is the majority. Such people give a support which is conditional to the extent that it is not based on fear; there is a limit to the degree of international isolation they would be willing to accept rather than accept an organized move towards individual human equality. At the very least, therefore, strong Western pressure on South Africa could introduce a new uncertainty and new insecurity among the dominant group. The police state machine would thus lose the virtually total white support which it at present enjoys. In that case, the violence may not be of such long duration or of such bitterness.

But whatever the situation in South Africa, it is quite certain that Portugal could not withstand real pressures for change exerted by its N.A.T.O. allies. A nation can withstand pressures from outside when it is united in hostility to that pressure. But a poor nation cannot maintain its domination over territories twenty times its own size, and over populations 50 per cent greater than its own unless it has the support of more powerful countries. In relation to the Portuguese colonies at least, members of the Western alliance do have the power to secure peace in Africa. They have the power to make a continuation of their support conditional upon Portugal's accepting the principle of self-determination.

Thus, in one case certainly, and in the other case possibly, it is the West which makes the choice between peace and war in Southern Africa. The question is not whether the Western powers are able to exert pressure on Portugal and on South Africa, but whether they are willing to do so. It is the implications of that question which I hope the people of this and other countries will carefully consider.

For I must stress that the choice before the free states of the world—which includes both Canada and Tanzania—is not between peaceful change and no change. The choice is between peaceful change and conflict. In the absence of peaceful change and real prospects of it continuing, the African people will fight for their rights. They will destroy stability rather than suffer under the stability of oppression. They have already begun to do so. We are not at the eleventh hour; we are past the twelfth. Already peace has to be re-established and confidence regained—both of which are harder things to do than to prevent war or to retain trust. So what is the alternative to a change in Southern Africa which is combined with stability?

The implications of war

Portugal, South Africa and the regime in Southern Rhodesia are all heavily armed with modern weapons and they have access to more weapons. They even manufacture some. If the freedom fighters are to succeed in war, they too must have arms. Not even the most skilled guerrilla movement can fight machine guns with bows and arrows, or dig elephant traps across surfaced roads. Africa cannot supply these arms: we do not make them, and we have no money to buy them.

But if the Western powers will not put pressure on their friends to secure peaceful change, is it likely that they will supply arms to those who in desperation have decided to get change by force? We all know the answer. The freedom movements will therefore get their arms from the communist powers. And these communist powers will be their exclusive suppliers.

Stability and Change in Africa **451**

In these circumstances it is no use anyone telling the freedom fighters—or telling the free states of Africa—about the evils of communism, or about the possibility that the supplying states may present a bill for their support. We all know of that possibility; we do not imagine that communism makes great powers less subject to the temptations of greatness. But we are much less concerned about possible future dangers—which may never develop—than we are with present facts. And those facts are that Africa is occupied by an alien power now; its people are suffering under minority domination now. We have to fight these things. So, we accept arms from communist states, and say "thank you" for them.

On the same basis, the nationalists of Southern Africa get their training where they can and from whom they can. Sometimes free African states can help in this; sometimes they cannot. And when they cannot, it is again communist countries which offer to help, and again we accept with gratitude.

We know our own motives in these actions. We are not communists; we are nationalists desiring freedom. We recognize the possibility that those who are helping us may have different motives. That is what we are told and we have no proof that it is not so. But we do have proof of our existing need and of practical offers to help.

So the freedom fighters use communist arms and are trained in communist countries because they have no choice. This is happening now and it will continue. And then South Africa and Portugal will proclaim to their allies this 'proof' that they are fighting communism. They will show captured communist weapons and display some hapless prisoner-of-war (whom they will call a criminal) in order to persuade those opposed to communism to support their war against the freedom fighters. They will also show evidence of cruelties, and tell tales of fear and suffering experienced by non-combatants on their side. And they will argue that this is the kind of people their opponents are—communists and racialists. Some of this evidence will be forged, but some will be true. Wars are always ugly and brutal, and guerrilla warfare is no exception.

In the face of this kind of psychological pressure, I am afraid that Western states would strengthen their support for the Southern African regimes. They would argue that for their own protection it was necessary to prevent Africa from falling into the hands of communists. They will therefore strengthen their economic support, and then agree to sell arms—or to give them—to the regimes of Southern Africa. Even the democratic and liberal people of the Western states will lose sympathy for the freedom movements, because they will come to believe that these have been captured by the communists. And gradually this conflict will become the ideological conflict which at present it is not.

At that point, because Africa does not look at things through cold war spectacles, the nature of the conflict may change again: it may become a confrontation between the poor, colored world and the rich, white world. Only support for the freedom fighters from the Russian and East European communists would be breaking the color pattern, and perhaps saving the world from this disaster. Indeed, it may be that the liberal humanitarians of Western Europe and North America may find themselves grateful to the white communists!

I am talking of what seems to me to be a terrifying series of events unless some effort is made to break the chain of logic in African and Western bloc relations. Of course, I have grossly simplified what would really happen; but we in Africa are not very sophisticated people, and indeed I do not believe the masses in any country are politically sophisticated. Therefore, I think that the pattern I have outlined is the way things might well look to us from our different sides. The people in the West would be seeing us as communists who wish them ill; we would be seeing them as supporters of racialism and of tyranny.

The inevitable can be avoided

These possibilities are real. If they develop, the effect on Africa could be terrible, and Africa's freedom struggle will bring great trouble to the world instead of releasing new energies for human growth—which is what we would like to think will happen. Yet knowing all that, we cannot draw back. For these are dangers and, however inevitable they may appear in logic, they are possibilities only. Our oppression is real and present.

Yet I believe that the dangers I have outlined can still be avoided, or at least very greatly reduced, if the Western powers look at the Southern African question in its proper framework, and if they now take the necessary action to de-fuse the situation. I know that it is not easy for the Western states to put pressure on their allies; all developed states are reluctant to interfere in what they regard as the internal affairs of another developed state. I know too that international trade is of mutual benefit, and that—as far as the Western states are concerned—their partners' gain from this trade is incidental to their own. I know that the West has heavy investments in Southern Africa which they wish to protect. But I do not believe that these facts necessarily determine the issue, for I do not believe that the only thing which the West cares about is economics. I am neither a Marxist nor a Capitalist. I do not believe that every human value is, or need always be, sacrificed to economic interests. I believe that the basic philosophy of Western democracy has its own life and its own power, and that the people's concept of freedom can triumph over their materialism.

However, even if I did believe that economics was the only thing which mattered to the West, I would still ask myself whether short-term or long-term factors will determine the West's policies. For although South Africa may now be a bigger trading partner than all the rest of Africa put together—I do not know whether this is true for Canada—this will not always be the case. The population of South Africa is about 18 million; that of the rest of Africa is in the region of 250 million. However great the difference in wealth, these stark figures have their own logic—especially as the rest of us develop and become better markets because we are richer.

Further, the value of investments depends on their productivity. They are no use if the cost of protecting them is more than the return they give. And investments in areas of inevitable and foreseeable instability are surely of less value than investments where instability is a present but passing danger. For Southern Africa is still fighting for the right to begin change. Except to the extent that the kind of change develops out of the nature of the struggle, the real problems of African development in these areas will remain to be settled when freedom is won.

Conclusion

Mr. President, when you asked me to

speak at this University, it may be that you were expecting me to speak about the internal affairs of Tanzania or about the relevance of our experiment in socialism for other countries—though you were too kind to express your wishes. But I have chosen to talk of change as an essential element in the stability which we need, and to emphasize this in relation to Southern Africa. I have done this for a very particular reason.

This is a Canadian University, and we in Tanzania have very great respect and admiration for the people of Canada. We believe that this country has both the opportunity and the willingness to try to build bridges in the world, and in particular to build a bridge across the chasm of color. I therefore chose to discuss this question with you because I believe you will understand what I am trying to say, and will care about these matters.

I know, of course, that Canada has its own problems of cultural conflict, of peoples with different languages and different backgrounds living together. I know that within your own society you are now trying to work out new modes of co-operation, which allow a full expression of democracy without jeopardizing the special cultural interests of any minority: These are real problems for you; indeed your efforts in this matter are of world-wide interest. It would therefore not be surprising if such questions preoccupied the attention of the Canadian people. But the world is very small now. Canada's actions—or lack of them—in relation to Africa are also important to your future as well as to ours. For the questions are there; and the threat to peace is there. They will not go away because this large, wealthy and peace-loving state wishes to concentrate on its internal problems. You cannot escape giving an answer to the challenge of the freedom movements in Africa—even if it is only an answer by default.

Let me make it quite clear that I am not promising peace, stability, democracy, humanity or an absence of oppression in Africa, provided Canada (either alone or with its allies) recognizes the freedom struggle in Southern Africa for what it is, and adopts attitudes in conformity with its own principles. Africa has too many problems for that kind of optimism. When national freedom exists all over Africa, and when racial minorities cease to dominate any part of our continent, we will still have daunting difficulties to face and few resources with which to tackle them. We may still fail to make good use of our opportunities; we may be as slow to develop real individual freedom from both economic and political oppression as the worst states in the world. But we are determined to gain the chance to try to deal with these problems. And we can only give top priority to these questions of developing individual freedom and individual dignity when the whole of Africa is free.

The questions remain. Will Canada at least understand that freedom means as much to us in Africa as it does to any other people? And, if Canada cannot support our struggle, will it at least be able to refrain from giving comfort and help to those who would deny freedom and dignity to us? For the sake of Tanzania and Africa most of all, but also for the sake of future relations between men of different colors and different creeds, I hope that Canadians will be able to give attention to these problems. I hope that Universities like this one will help the people of this country to consider all the implications of their choice.

Mr. President, Ladies and Gentlemen: Thank you.

LEGITIMACY

"Hell, No, We Won't Go!"

JOHN COONEY
AND DANA SPITZER

Rather than have war, I would give up everything. I would give up my country.
Hynmahtu Yalat-keht (Chief Joseph)

What kinds of young men are defying their country by refusing to enter the military service or refusing to stay in once they have joined? Are they so disenchanted with their country that they don't care about not being able ever to return home without punishment? Why do they choose not to fight in a war that demands the presence of 500,000 American troops in Vietnam where 40,000 have already died? Are they heroes or cowards, or simply acting the way sane people should act when confronted with a government which says it wants to end the war but doesn't know how to do it?

Bruce Bell is 19 years old and for most of his life he has been everything his parents ever wanted in a son. A fair athlete, an active member of his Unitarian Church in Schenectady, New York, where his father is an engineer for General Electric, he was always among the top in his high school class. In matters of dress and manners his clothes followed the styles advertised in *Sports Illustrated* and his hair grew only to his ears. Unlike some students who received good grades, he never embarrassed his parents by taking to radical politics or other forms of controversy. The rules Bell broke were of the sort that kids all over the country disregarded in the latter half of the sixties; boozing, balling and smoking pot were things his parents were unlikely to find out about. When Stanford accepted him as a member of its freshman class in 1967 his parents were elated. When his name appeared on the Dean's list after a semester their pride grew. Then things began to change.

Bell found classroom lessons to be rather dull when compared to events outside. He developed interests in the war in Vietnam and in student politics. When students revolted at Stanford he sat in the administration building with hundreds of others. To Bell the sit-in was "beautiful" and the speeches by faculty and students more "relevant" than anything he had yet encountered at college.

Doubts set in about whether he needed the education one of America's most distinguished universities was offering him. When he returned to school in the fall of 1968 it was with the attitude that he would give it a try. He would try to make a go of it for his parents who were proud of him. But by Thanksgiving he realized it was no good. He dropped out of school and went home to think about what he was going to do with his life.

America in the late sixties does not allow its young men to leave college and ponder their futures. A few weeks after Bell went home he received a notice from his draft board that his student deferment had been suspended and that he was reclassified 1-A, meaning he had been placed in the prime category from which draftees are drawn. He appealed the ruling, asking to be reclassified as a conscientious objector. At Stanford he felt he had learned about the war in Vietnam. It was not the kind of war he wanted anything to do with.

Bell's hearing before Local Board 31 in Schenectady was very cordial but very short. He spoke for a few minutes, explaining why he should be allowed conscientious-objector status.

"I began by reminding them of Christ's teaching on nonviolence," he recalls. "I explained that the basis of all great religions was love, that war violated that spirit. I reminded them of Nuremberg—that it can be somebody's moral obligation to disobey orders from the state."

The eight men and one woman, whom Bell guessed to be anywhere from 50 to 70 years old, listened politely. When he finished, a man on the draft board spoke. "So you don't base your conscientious objection on any particular religious grounds," he said, part observation, part question.

"I knew then that I really hadn't gotten across. For me, I knew it would have to be jail or Canada."

As he told the story one evening last June in Toronto, Bell, a fuzzy-cheeked blond with hair now below his ears, spoke with a soft, eager voice.

"I couldn't have taken jail," he said. "I came to Canada a month after my hearing. It took me about a month to get landed and now I'm just living here. I suppose I'll get a job eventually, or maybe go to school. My parents don't agree with my decision to come up here. But they have been very understanding. They send me money, not much, but enough to get by."

Thousands of miles away, on the island-city of Stockholm, the thread of antiwar protest that is weaving through America's youth unites Bell with a young man who lacked Bell's bourgeois background and who, without Vietnam, probably would never have had anything in common with the thoughtful college boy.

John Woods is a 19-year-old high-school dropout whom the Pentagon would describe as someone who "could not adjust to Army life, and was a disciplinary problem." Chunky, dark-haired with deep-set, dark eyes, Woods bummed around the country working at odd jobs. His most significant possession was a Harley-Davidson motorcycle, "a big American machine," he says, grasping imaginary handlebars and revving up the engine.

With his job prospects at rock-bottom until he got his military service out of the way, Woods looked at some brochures that told him he could learn a trade in the Army and joined up in December, 1967. He soon realized the only trade he was learning was how to shoot a rifle. "You know," he muses now, "there isn't really too big a market for civilian killers in the States."

Almost a year elapsed and Woods still didn't have a trade. So he set out to get one. Woods became a journalist, helping to found *F.T.A.*, an anti-military underground newspaper at Fort Jackson, South Carolina. "It could mean Fun, Travel, Adventure," he says, referring to the Army enlistment slogan. "Or . . . it could mean Fuck The Army." But because of his new career, Woods found himself one day before his superiors who told him that he was being sent to Germany. "They got me orders in a couple of hours that normally take weeks," he says, still marveling at the efficiency the Army can show when it meets threats.

So Woods, who hails from Steubenville, Ohio, was shipped to Frankfurt, Germany. From his new station, he continued to distribute *F.T.A.* Then he was busted for distributing "subversive literature." Although this charge influenced his decision to desert, Woods made up his mind to go after talking with servicemen who had returned from Vietnam. "Some of them were broken up about what they had done. Some bragged about how many they killed. I'm not a pacifist, but I have to know who I'm shooting at and why."

In January of this year, Woods went to the Cologne chapter of Students for a Democratic Society and asked the members to help him escape to Sweden. From Cologne, S.D.S. sent him back to Frankfurt and two weeks later put him on a train for Hamburg.

"By then I was really shaking," he remembers. "It had been weeks that I was hiding out. They told me to go into a bar and sit two tables down on the left and be reading an American magazine. I had a copy of *Ramparts* with me and I was shaking and holding the magazine right below my eyes and looking over the top of it at everybody in the place. I was trying to let them know it was me: *I'm the guy you're helping out of here.*"

"Then this guy and girl who were sitting near me came over and asked me if I was the soldier, and I said yes. They took me to the Denmark border. They told me I was the 100th G.I. they helped this way. There was a border crossing about 800 yards wide that I had to run across. By now I'm shaking like a leaf and I'm all sweaty. It's night and the moon isn't very bright. I'm running across the field and a wire catches me waist high. I didn't know what it was at first and it really knocked me in the air. But I got up in a second and kept on running until I got to the other side. Another guy met me when I got there."

Traveling through Denmark wasn't difficult, Woods recalls. When he was on a boat from Copenhagen to southern Sweden, however, his nervousness caused a memory blackout concerning what he was to say when landing in Sweden. "I couldn't remember the words 'political asylum.' This guy was with me and I kept asking him what it was and he would tell me and then I'd forget. Things like 'insane asylum' and words like that were going through my mind and I thought 'My God to get all the way there and not to be able to get in because I can't remember the right words.' And then I'd turn to this guy again and ask him what the words were. But when I finally got there and needed to say them I remembered 'political asylum.' "

More and more young Americans are sharing Bell's and Wood's antipathy towards their government's involvement in Vietnam and are following their footsteps to foreign countries rather than fighting in an unpopular war. To the embarrassment of the United States, these young men are being granted refuge in Canada, Sweden and to a limited degree in other countries as well.

There is in both Canada and Sweden a strong anti-Americanism that makes it easier for the war resisters to cope once they arrive. Generally, those Canadians who resent the economic and cultural domination of their country by the United States are the ones most friendly to American exiles, often giving moral support and financial assistance. Most Canadians, however, including the government, have adopted a disinterested "live and let live" attitude. The only criterion for landed-immigrant status is that one pass a test based on age, job skills, education and other qualifications the Canadian government desires in immigrants. Once landed, an immigrant from the States must wait five years before applying for citizenship, but in the meantime he has most of the rights and obligations of citizenship, except voting.

The Swedish case is somewhat different. The anti-Americanism running through Swedish society is based on a widespread fear of the tremendous world power wielded by the United States. Such is the extent of this mistrust and hostility that often last year one heard Swedes bitterly joke that many other countries should participate in the election of the president of the United States, because he clearly controls the destinies of everyone, not just Americans. Moreover, the Swedish government, following public opinion, has opposed the United States in Vietnam, and this too gives support to American refugees' feelings that they made the right choice. Indeed, the title "deserter" often adds prestige to a youth in the eyes of the community.

The number of draft dodgers and deserters in Canada cannot be known exactly because the Canadian government has no way of finding out whether a young man entering the country is a dodger or an evader. There are no questions concerning such matters on the application to obtain landed-immigrant status.

Nevertheless, in 1967, the Royal Canadian Mounted Police, piecing together information from the Canadian Immigration Bureau, the United States Defense Department and the Federal Bureau of Investigation, estimated that there were 1,500 dodgers and deserters in Canada, a figure considerably higher than official U.S. estimates. If the R.C.M.P. estimate was reasonably accurate two years ago, then there are probably at least twice as many in Canada today. In a normal week, the Toronto Anti-Draft Programme, for example, helps about 20 dodgers or deserters find housing, jobs or other assistance. Since January, a spokesman says, the figure has doubled. *The Toronto Daily Telegram*, one of three daily newspapers in the city, claimed that 2,800 dodgers arrived in Canada in 1968, but the source of the figure was not given. The best estimate that can be made is that evaders number from 3,000 to 5,000, while deserters probably total less than 500.

In Sweden, accurate figures on the number of deserters living there are not available either. Representatives of the government, groups working with the deserters, and deserters themselves, however, estimate the number of American G.I.'s

DESERTION RATES PER 1000

	World War II 1944	
Army		63.00
Navy		3.00
Marines		6.90
	Korea 1953	
Army		19.50
Navy		8.70
Marines		29.60
	Vietnam 1968	
Army		29.10
Navy		8.50
Marines		22.40
Air Force		.44

who have sought refuge there at about 300. As of May 14, 1969, residence permits had been granted to 218 deserters, while another 39 had applied for them. But with the constant influx of servicemen and the occasional laxity in immediately applying for a permit, the actual number of deserters is higher.

There are fewer than 25 draft dodgers in Sweden and many of them work with the highly organized deserter movement there. They are reluctant to present their story, saying the deserters in Sweden are more important. For this reason there will be no details about the war resisters who fled to Sweden to avoid the draft. There are relatively few evaders in Sweden because most draftees, of course, receive their induction notices in the United States and it is much easier to get to Canada than to Sweden. Canada is also much better known as a haven for draft resisters than is Sweden. The large number of deserters in Sweden is due to the country's having spoken out against United States presence in Vietnam and its having granted soldiers humanitarian asylum during other wars.

The age of deserters living in Sweden ranges between 18 and 37, with most in their early 20's. They rank from private to captain; they came from Vietnam, Japan, Germany and the United States; and most of them had enlisted. The deserters estimate that 10 percent had served in Vietnam and that 50 percent were under immediate orders to report there. They represent all branches of the service, but the vast majority deserted from the Army. Although no racial data are available, government officials estimate that 10 percent of the deserters are black, which is below the percentage of blacks serving in the U.S. armed forces.

Since July, 1966, according to the Defense Department, there have been more than 53,000 desertions from all branches of the service, of which only 1,068 are thought to be in foreign countries. The comparatively small number of deserters living in Canada and Sweden, the Defense Department says, is because most deserters "go home or hide out someplace."

Draft dodgers and deserters in Canada, for the most part, are found in Toronto, Montreal and Vancouver, where there are well-established organizations to help them. In Sweden, the core of the deserter movement is in Stockholm, where more than half the refugees are settled. The rest are spread throughout the country.

Politically and organizationally, there is a major distinction between the draft dodgers and deserters in Canada and those in Sweden. In Canada, the draft dodgers are the center of radicalism among the exiles, while deserters tend not to see their act in a political context and, in fact, resent the radical war resisters' attempts to define their desertion in terms of a larger political view of the world. In Sweden, there is no division between dodgers and deserters. While there are many non-radical deserters, the most prominent deserter organization in the country holds radical viewpoints and many of its members consider themselves revolutionaries in the New Left mold.

In Toronto, two major organizations are available to help American war resisters. Both are staffed by evaders and deserters and are financially supported by sympathizers in Canada and the United States. The Toronto Anti-Draft Programme, headquartered in two sparsely furnished rooms in an office building at 2279 Younge Street, is primarily a counseling service. It will help an exile through the maze of Canadian law affecting immigrants, and once an émigré has attained landed status, it will refer him to employment agencies or a sympathetic business where he might find a job.

Although a few exiles live on money sent to them from home, most expect to find jobs once in Canada. But getting the job they expected when they left the states is sometimes difficult. Richard Kapp, a draft dodger who had just graduated from the University of Illinois with a masters degree in history, illustrated the dilemma of many college educated exiles.

Kapp, 27, well-groomed and wearing a brown business suit, discussed his job problems one day at the Anti-Draft Programme office:

"With a masters degree in history I've got no special skills," he explained. "On the other hand, when I tell these guys about my education, many of them feel I'm too educated for the jobs they have open." Because of a Canadian requirement that teachers complete a special one-year curriculum, his graduate degree was no help in getting him a teaching job which he had counted on when he left. After a week of interviewing through employment agencies, he had one solid prospect, a manager traineeship at $85 a week.

Kapp, who grew up in New Brunswick, N.J., the son, in his words, of a "lower middle-class racist," says he refused his draft call because "If I got killed in Vietnam, it wouldn't make any difference. So what's in it for me? I don't want to die. I've got a money hang-up and a lot of living to do."

The Toronto Anti-Draft Programme, in addition to job counseling, publishes a "Manual for Draft-Age Immigrants to Canada" that is a rich encyclopedia of information. Written by professors, lawyers, clergymen and businessmen, it is edited by Mark Satin, a Texas radical who founded the antidraft organization. The manual answers almost any question a young man might have about Canada. Since it was first published last year, more than 25,000 copies have been mailed out.

The Union of American Exiles at 44 St. George Street functions primarily as a housing service, but it also provides other sorts of "social action" for dodgers and deserters. Located on the campus of the University of Toronto, it is more attuned to the student movement and New Left ideology than is the Toronto Anti-Draft Programme, which concerns itself with the nuts and bolts of getting exiles settled. Charles Novogrodsky, press secretary of U.A.E., described the reasoning behind its political involvement. "The need for expanded services alone would never have been enough to generate the movement toward an organization of American exiles. Union members recognize the identity of social and political factors that have shaped and continue to shape their personal lives. For this reason, the Union is a place where talk, information, and action can be found that relates one's life in Canada to the broader, repressive aspects of North American society and politics in general." Yet both Toronto organizations work closely together, with a minimum of friction, despite the resistance of a large number of refugees to what they think of as "radicalization" efforts on the part of the leftist ideologues.

In contrast to the Toronto groups, the American Deserters Committee in Montreal is less cooperative with political radicals. Although founded by two politically active civilians, the A.D.C. is now completely in the hands of apolitical deserters. Located in a run-down French section along the St. Lawrence River, the A.D.C. office is bare and filthy. Two shabby couches face each other across a room. A fireplace mantel along one wall serves as a library. Vietnam and adventure stories are popular. Beside *Che Guevara Speaks* lies a copy of *The World's Greatest Dog Stories*.

That was the scene last June when about 30 deserters and a few wives and girlfriends gathered at the A.D.C. office. The meeting was a climax to several weeks of agitation among deserters who thought that the civilians who started the committee more than a year before and had been running it autocratically ever since, should step aside and allow the deserters to run the committee. The founders, Bill Hertzog and Jerry Bornstein, were not present, but the deserters were trying to be as kind to them as possible while firmly insisting that they must go.

Grant Fox, a 22-year-old deserter from Holbrook, Massachusetts, was more or less in charge. While he was explaining the issue, several young men were slugging each other playfully and wrestling. "God damn it, you guys, quit fucking around will you?" Fox yelled.

"Fuckin' around? Whose fuckin' around," giggled the errants, faces as scarlet as school boys caught by a teacher. Things settled down and Fox explained that most deserters were appreciative of everything Hertzog and Bornstein had done, but some resented their efforts to align the committee with radical politics.

"I mean it's whatever you guys want," Fox says. "Some of the guys don't think we should be messin' around with this politics shit. So whatever you guys decide, we should take a vote on it and stick to our decision." The vote ended formal ties with Bornstein and Hertzog, but there is a provision to consult with them periodically.

If the severance seems crude and thankless, that is not how Bornstein, a young sociologist from New York City, takes it. To him, a former CORE organizer and fund raiser, the rebellion was expected and natural. "They should run their own group now. There are enough of them to do it; and it will be better all the way around if they assume the responsibility for each other."

Fox, the ad hoc leader of the deserters, was sympathetic to Bornstein. "Jerry was around when we needed him. Without him a lot of guys up here would never have made it. He had the contacts we needed, for money, housing, the works. He was just too radical for most guys." But Fox did sense that the move by the deserters may have been a mistake.

"I don't know, frankly, whether we can keep the committee going without him, but the guys decided they wanted to go it alone. So here we are." Fox, who entered the Army in 1966 shortly after graduating from high school, seems well suited for the new task, which consists primarily of coordinating the wishes of the deserters with their sympathizers in Canada and the U.S. who provide both moral and economic support. Supporters, however, like Bornstein, tend to be "political," and their values often conflict with the deserters who are uninterested in getting "radicalized." Fox feels that differences in the educational backgrounds of many deserters and their supporters is a reason for the friction.

"Only a few of the deserters who come in have college educations," he says. "Sometimes the guys without much schooling get pissed off at the college boys for trying to take over. But shit, most of the time it's only the college guys or the guys who haven't gone to college but who are a little older who want to do anything for the committee."

The split that was formalized at the June Montreal meeting of the American Deserters Committee had already taken place in the Stockholm A.D.C. Two political factions had emerged, differing basically in their degree of radicalism. Far from backing off from politics as the deserter committee in Montreal has done, the A.D.C. in Stockholm is highly political, and many members are self-proclaimed revolutionaries. The second faction, which called itself the Underground Railway after breaking with the A.D.C., is also composed of very political people, but the U.R.'s members do not always agree with the often dogmatic stands of the A.D.C. Deserters who do not wish to become politically involved at all can bypass either organization.

John Toler is one of the key U.R. people. A founder of the A.D.C. when it was set up in 1968, Toler was instrumental in organizing a limited walkout of A.D.C. members a year later. A philosophy student at Stockholm University, he is one of three deserters in the city taking the most advanced language training available. "Initially, my decision to desert was moral. I now know it was political," he says, summing up the metamorphosis of the deserters who become political. The thin, blond, 23-year-old has "no regrets whatsoever" about his desertion. "I felt it was the only thing I could do."

Toler said the first six months are the

hardest in terms of adjustment. "You have to watch the death of much of your culture right down to your music and thoughts of mom. You've got to go on or stay in limbo." Toler said many deserters are living with girl friends. "And that makes it a lot easier." Toler lives with an attractive, politically active brunette, though whether it was her good looks or her politics that made it "easier," he didn't say.

Because of the difficulty Toler mentioned concerning the first six months after desertion, the A.D.C. helps new deserters learn the bureaucratic maze and also provides friendship. Just as important as these functions, however, is the attempt by radical members of the A.D.C. to orient new deserters towards their political philosophy. Of the estimated 180 deserters living in the Stockholm area, the A.D.C. claims the majority belong to the committee and this was supported by several deserter-connected groups. Many deserters devote their time and effort to the A.D.C. on a daily basis; others volunteer spare time to committee activities. The A.D.C. is the deserters' prime political forum and has steadily evolved into a revolutionary organization. Like radicals in the United States and elsewhere, many A.D.C. members see war, racism, poverty and American imperialism as springing from a corrupt system. As its radical horizons broadened, so did the A.D.C.'s affiliations. Last fall, it became an S.D.S. chapter.

Fighting for Home Far Away

The political activity of the radical deserters led to their breaking relations with the Swedish Vietnam Committee, one of 40 organizations in the country that are against the war in Vietnam and actively support the act of desertion. Composed of liberals supporting the Hanoi government and the aims of the National Liberation Front, the Swedish Vietnam Committee is the target of criticism from more leftist Swedish groups as well as radical deserters. Its opponents say it is afraid to let the deserters speak out because there might be economic boycotts by America against Swedish products.

Bertil Svahnstrom, executive secretary of the Swedish Vietnam Committee, while acknowledging a fear of boycotting denies that this is an influence on his group. He feels that the deserters should say anything they want. "The only thing we are against is deserters being pressured to become political when they do not want to be."

While most gave a moral reason as to why they deserted, those who became radicals felt that political activism gave more substance to the justification of desertion. For them, morality is secondary to the political reasons for opposing the war and United States domestic and foreign policy in general. They see themselves as true witnesses to the fact that there is a viable alternative to passive acceptance of what they call United States tyranny.

"If we were to become silent Swedes and not be involved in politics, then everything would be fine with Svahnstrom," says Bill Jones, a former co-chairman and founder of the A.D.C. before it became a leaderless S.D.S. chapter. Now a theoretician of the A.D.C.'s more revolutionary attitudes, Jones believes the radical Movement in the U.S. will reach an ultimate violent confrontation, with "the people" seizing control of the power structure from "those who oppress them." Paraphrasing Che Guevera, Jones hopes the revolution in America will be accomplished with a "minimum of bloodshed."

Jones views the deserters' position as "the most moral of all . . . and at least the most sane" when compared to those who fight a war they know nothing about and compared to people who profit from war. The war, he says, is the result of a "mass neurosis on the part of the American people." And he feels that working for change in the United States, albeit 3,000 miles away in Sweden, is a logical follow-through of the act of desertion.

"Ideally, if you want to effect change in the United States, you have to be there. But since we obviously are not in a position to do that, we have to do what we can from where we can . . . and that means here."

Jones bluntly says that complete assimilation into Swedish society on the part of the deserters would destroy the A.D.C.'s effectiveness. If they lose their identity as deserters, they will no longer be symbols of American resistance to the war. "We can still retain our own culture . . . we are a community apart from the Swedish. It is important that we do this to keep external pressure on the Army and the war effort."

A thin, bearded ex-seminarian, Jones joined the Army because his student deferment was a "cop out." Assigned to Germany as a medic, the 22-year-old youth deserted because he felt any position in the Army was giving at least passive support to U.S. presence in Vietnam. Although he does not believe amnesty will ever be granted, Jones gave one reason for wanting to return to the States—"to work for the Movement." Many deserters expressed the same desire and gave it as their chief reason for wanting to go home.

The Stockholm headquarters of the A.D.C. is at Upplandsgattan 18. There in the dank cellar of a massive gray apartment building, A.D.C. members work to increase desertion from the service. A newspaper, *The Second Front*, which is published from the poster-padded offices, is aimed at the Army. Another publication, *The Second Front Review*, is circulated among deserters in France, Canada and Sweden to keep them abreast of the deserter movement. Besides these enterprises, the deserters make radio tapes encouraging desertion which are transmitted from North Vietnam, East Germany and Cuba.

Though A.D.C. members have Swedish friends and many of them live with Swedish girls, their radicalism, focused on America, is a shield against being absorbed into the Swedish lifescape, and losing their identities as Americans. Even those who are fluent in the language and know Swedish customs, exist along with the others as an American colony working to "save America." As part of the radicalizing process, the A.D.C. holds closed-door meetings where theory and experiences are analyzed. Many of their ideas stem from the New Left literature that fills their bookshelves and is greedily read, often by people who said they previously had no desire to read. Underground newspapers and the radical weekly, *The Guardian*, supplement their literary diet. They feel they are treated more fairly by *The Guardian* than by established news media. Committee members are vitally interested in the most recent phases of the Movement in the United States and elsewhere, but particularly the United States. The effectiveness of the orientation can be seen in the fact that only two men interviewed in Sweden had been involved in peace, civil rights or radical movements prior to their military careers. Now many of them are aware of the most subtle nuances of leftist thought.

Yet, oddly, there is still much of the military about the A.D.C. members. Many still wear parts of their uniforms and their speech is salted with military references. This atmosphere and the holdover of military paraphernalia turn off some deserters.

Herb Rains is one of these. A 25-year-old photographer from Kaneohe, Hawaii, Rains differs from most deserters in that he was involved in peace and civil rights issues before his desertion. A reservist activated after the Pueblo affair, Rains deserted because many reservists were being sent to Vietnam.

With his thick, curly beard and long, dark-brown hair, dungarees and blue work shirt, Rains looks the part of the young radical. But he doesn't want to channel his energies into the A.D.C. because its "barracks atmosphere is part of what I was trying to get away from." Instead of working with the Americans, Rains wants to help the National Liberation Front Support Group, which is composed of Swedish radicals working for the aims of the N.L.F.

Like many deserters in Sweden, Rains is in a government-sponsored language school and living off the $20 a week paid unemployed deserters by the Swedish government. Besides this money, the deserters' rent is paid by the Social Bureau and they receive a small clothing allowance as well.

Again like many other deserters, Rains would consider going back to the United States, but not if a dishonorable discharge were the only way he could get there. Not one deserter interviewed said he would accept anything less than an honorable discharge, and few expressed regrets about the possibility of never being able to return home. One deserter summed up the prevailing sentiment concerning amnesty: "I'll go home if they admit that we were right and they were wrong . . . and I don't think that is going to happen."

While deserters in the Stockholm area have ample opportunity to express their opposition to the war, those living in the heavily wooded, rural areas do not. Ron Crow lives about 150 miles north of the city, on a farm that was donated to the deserters by a Swedish philanthropist. Tall, wiry and heavily bearded, Crow considers himself a radical but he also knows he is a farmer. His childhood was spent dirt-farming around Fort Worth, Texas, and his family was always on the brink of poverty. After dropping out of school in the ninth grade, Crow said he eventually joined the Army hoping to learn a trade so he could "get somewhere in the world."

Now 22, Crow first thought of opposing the war when he talked with returning Vietnam veterans. Their descriptions of what they had been through ("a lot of them just didn't think we had any business being over there") planted the seeds of desertion in his mind. He started listening more closely to talk about the war and reading about it. He concluded, "I just wouldn't go fight over there." So he deserted from Germany, but it took him two tries to make it.

"I was in a medical outfit and one day I got one of our trucks and just started driving north. Wouldn't you know that I ran out of gas right in the middle of an intersection in a city. All I could do was sit there and wait for them to take me away." Besides desertion, he was charged with theft and because of the medical supplies in the truck, narcotics and abortion charges were added to his crimes. After a stretch in the stockade, however, he was ready to try again.

"I was smarter the second time. I went down to the reenlistment station and signed up for another six years. I needed the $700 bonus pay to desert. This time I went to the train station and jumped on a train and they never caught me. There are a lot of people deserting on their bonus pay."

Crow is going to language school and is getting married shortly. After language training, he plans on working the farm full time and not returning to his job in a nearby steel mill. He was one of five deserters interviewed in Sweden who would not return to the United States under any conditions. "My life is here where I have everything I ever wanted," he says, "and it's away from the war and racism and a few rich people living off a lot of poor people. Why would I ever want to go back?"

Very few deserters or draft dodgers in either Canada or Sweden felt remorse at the prospect of not being able to return home. Most accepted their decision to leave the United States as final, although they would return if granted amnesty. But while amnesty is being spoken of in some liberal governmental circles in the United States, few deserters or dodgers believe it will become a reality. As one deserter in Sweden put it, "How can they dare to give us amnesty? If they did, nobody would fight in their next war. Everybody would just move to another country and wait for amnesty to be given again."

The deserters and evaders who are radicalized still believe the United States can be changed, either by violent revolution or less drastic internal and external pressures. Those who do not take an aggressive stance against their homeland's policies are more inclined to be less educated and more willing to lose their American identities. The radicals have ambivalent feelings about the United States. They believe it "must" be saved; at the same time, they loath what America is doing domestically and in foreign affairs. Those not radicalized put their act on either a moral plane or a more pragmatic, "Why should I get my ass shot off for nothing?"

As well as being an outlet for their thoughts and emotions, radicalism for many young exiles helps to make them feel still a part of what is happening in the United States. Though physically isolated, most are deeply committed to America and still want to play a part in whatever changes do take place here. They maintain their American identity in the hope of remolding America. It does not matter what country they are living in as long as they remain free to continue their efforts.

Graduate students and high school dropouts, Christians and nonbelievers, track stars and acid heads, radicals and hippies; they are all there, linked by a stubborn independence, a common revulsion against their country's war in Vietnam and by the 5-to-10-year prison sentences they face if they should ever return. Whether they come home is a question only the future can answer. Today, their ranks are swelling.

REPRESENTATION

We Will Exercise Our Rights

STEVE WASSERMAN

My name is Steve Wasserman. I am president of Berkeley High School in Berkeley, California. I have been in Berkeley since the sixth grade and have been involved in radical activity for the last five years. Since Berkeley has been the center of some of the most radical activity in the country, I naturally have been caught up in it. I have been through all the struggles: the Free Speech Movement, the Vietnam Day Committee, the Troop Train Demonstrations, the Eldridge Cleaver sit-ins, and the Peoples' Park demonstrations.

My first involvement was in the eighth grade when some friends and I organized an antiwar rally. We attempted to set up a Vietnam analysis committee which would be for political education, where kids could come and discuss the war and investigate its origins. The committee turned out to be very effective. We got a lot of student interest. We didn't know all that much about Vietnam, so it was helpful in that it motivated us to do a lot of reading and investigating.

Shortly after this, the hippie phenomenon emerged in the Bay Area. I was somewhat involved in that but not to a great extent. By the time I was in the tenth grade, the hippies were being suppressed and distorted by the media. In addition there was a political crackdown, which radicalized the hippies and led to a synthesis—at least in the Bay Area—between the hard politicos and people like the hippies who wanted a radical life style. To create a life style that is radical in a society which represses that life style is to become political. This synthesis of life style and politics turned out to be very beneficial to the Movement in the Bay Area, and consequently to the High School Movement.

High school students from all over the area began to question the way the schools were being run. They could see the similarities between the way the hippies were being repressed and the way the schools were forcing students to wear their hair a certain length, to comply with rigid dress codes, and not to question the school's authority. Students began to question; they began to question the school's authority to regulate their life styles and censor their political beliefs.

Students began to organize, and the first thing we did was create a Student Union. This is a union of students—black and white—designed to move for necessary changes in the school. It is an organization that students can relate to, one they can participate in. The Union is decentralized, each Union local formulates its own program independently of any central authority. Yet all schools support and aid each other. We feel that the kind of programs and projects that we will be embarking upon can specifically relate to and involve more students than ever before.

Previously, radicals have made the mistake of talking to students in abstract terms they can't understand or relate to. Like talking to kids about imperialism! Most kids don't even know what imperialism is; however, it is a concept which can be understood through specific examples, like the conditions in the schools that repress them. We can show how that relates to the general society, and what that society does. That's how we radicalize students. Not by telling them, "Here's what's happening man, don't you want to join in on it, don't you dig it," but by relating to them on the basis of their own oppressions.

What students want is action. Students were apathetic in the past because what happened was connected with bullshit student organizations. These organizations said there was a lot to do but never did anything. Students will participate if they have a chance.

For example, last year, during the Peoples' Park episode, we organized a sleep-in at the high school to protest the occupation of Berkeley by the military forces. We refused to leave the campus until peace was returned to the streets. Forty-three Berkeley High kids had been arrested the previous day, some kids had been shot, and it was dangerous just going to and from school. So we organized this sleep-in. We got a few hundred kids to participate: it was an action which they could identify with and believe in. It was a specific thing which related to them; it wasn't some abstract kind of thing which said: sign your name to this petition and that will do it. It was something they could do—something with their bodies. They could participate in an action which had meaning. The sleep-in was very crucial for the development of our kind of politics and how we think the Movement should relate to people. For example, we found that as a result of this repression we developed a great sense of community by just working together. It was really a beautiful thing. We woke up about 6:30 in the morning. The sun was up and we all sat around in a circle to have a communal breakfast and then go to school. It was really a beautiful thing, and the kind of togetherness that grew out of the sleep-in was really wonderful to behold. The alienation that students experience from the school system and from each other was overcome with their willingness to participate in a move that they could identify with.

As a result of this action and other events that occurred during the year, we developed over the summer a program which we feel speaks for the real needs of Berkeley High students. One of the basic points of the program concerns the exercise of our rights: the right of free speech, the right to leaflet, the right to have independent newspapers, the right to assemble and organize ourselves for our own needs, the right to take political action in our own interests without penalty, the right to do all of these things without administrative restrictions, interference, or approval.

Another point in our program concerns our commitment to struggle against racism. We will struggle against the racism that is institutionalized in the school system, in others, and in ourselves. Racism is used by big business, government, and school administrators to keep us divided and controlled. The competitive tracking and grading system, the daily classroom brainwash (American History, Civics, etc.), and disciplinary procedures are all examples of this racism. In addition there is the racism that is exercised against women.

High schools perpetuate the idea that women are inferior. They discourage girls from preparing for well-paying jobs, and channel them into Home Economics and Business classes. This does a great service to the business interests by supplying cheap office labor and unpaid household laborers. Schools prepare women to produce the next generation of workers and to buy expensive (status) products. Girls are taught to be docile, to be obedient to men, to be cute and stupid, in short, to "know their place." The oppression of women gives the guys a false sense of power. They don't mind being so powerless in the system as long as they have a woman to feel superior to. This is another form of divide-and-conquer by the system. We must all fight male supremacy and struggle for the equality of women.

Our program also calls for an end to the tracking system. The tracking system must be destroyed and replaced by education that has real meaning to us. The tracking system channels students into certain types of jobs. Blacks, Chicanos, and lower-income whites are put into classes that train them for factory jobs and the army. Women are trained for secretarial jobs and household work. Wealthy white kids are prepared for college, leading to professional and managerial positions. We must fight this system that keeps us competing against each other. Our education should not be based on the needs of employers or corporations, but on the needs of people.

We also plan to develop programs and activities that will appeal to students who are turned off the kind of hardline politics that don't integrate a life style with what they are doing. We want to have a joyous Movement. We have to create organizations which reflect the liberated society that we wish to achieve. These organizations can't be disguised in revolutionary rhetoric and merely reflect the class and authority that we oppose. In order to reflect that society which we want to achieve, we have this idea about having a joyous Movement. We want to create fairs, festivals, and centers of communication where students can meet for fun, for expression, and for communication. We will resist all puritanical restraints on what we can or cannot do, what we can say or cannot say, what we can think and what we cannot think. We will be open to a whole realm of things—like cultural fairs, like expressing our feelings about our art work and school work; in sum, we will do what we want, and resist all puritanical restraints.

And in relation to developing activities that are joyous, we intend to end oppressive Physical Education as it now exists.

We really resent the military regimentation of Physical Education, the drill sergeant mentality of gym teachers who train us to be submissive, unquestioning, and who try to instill in us an attitude that prepares us for the army. We will not tolerate it any longer. Physical Education has been one of the most overt physically repressive institutions in the modern school; it is indicative, to a large extent, of the medieval conditions in our schools. We believe that Physical Education is a good thing, but we believe that Physical Education doesn't have to subordinate the individual. We recognize the right of any student to refuse to participate in PE without academic penalty. At the present time you can complete all of your academic courses and get an F in gym for four years and not pass high school. They keep you in high school until you pass gym. We believe in Physical Education but feel it should be an open class where students can be free. I've seen kids who have flunked out of gym go all out and expend a hell of a lot of energy in an after-school game of soccer or something like that. After-school games are voluntarily entered into, not imposed from above. For example, as it is now, everyone has to wear the same kind of uniform with a gray sweatshirt. Well, we plan to organize a spontaneous demonstration where everyone will wear multi-colored sweatshirts. We envision mass refusals to run one more lap around the track, or a mass sit-down strike.

Our program also calls for an end to administrative control of student elections and organizations. We have to have student government that belongs to the students—that isn't manipulated by the administration and isn't a puppet or a rubber stamp for administration policies. We have to turn control of student elections and student activities over to students.

Similarly, we want to end suspensions and expulsions. The majority of suspensions and expulsions are for things like cutting. It seems ridiculous to suspend a student if he doesn't want to come to school in the first place. In addition, suspensions and expulsions serve to repress high school kids for political activities. They slap you with a suspension based on being disobedient to a teacher or interfering with a teacher in the performance of her duties. The definition of interference is left up to the administration. As they define it, it can cover anything. Talking back could be interference. We want to end suspensions and expulsions, and to develop human and humane means of dealing with disciplinary problems. And that means use of counselling and extensive sensitivity sessions with kids, parents, and teachers, where the whole problem can be talked out.

Basically, our program is one that students can relate to. Students can relate to getting screwed up by gym teachers, they can relate to having a good time in school, they can relate to an end to suspensions and expulsions, and they can relate to uniting with other people. They can relate to ending racism, and girls can relate to liberating themselves. Students can relate to having control over their own lives and control over their own activities, and they can relate to exercising their rights.

Part of the program that we have developed can't be put into practice within the existing system, since we would have to work on its terms: those terms are inherently repressive and bog us down in a lot of red tape. That is why we have formed a Student Union. The Student Union is inherently a more responsive and representative kind of government (if you wish to call it that) than is the student government.

Our means of communicating our program will be through the underground

press and the various programs and activities that I have outlined. There is no way of utilizing the official school newspaper, since it is under the control of the Journalism department and is subject to faculty review. All the articles that are submitted to school newspapers are subject to faculty approval, and if an article says something that doesn't deal with the school—like the war in Vietnam—it won't be printed.

Another point about our program is that we are not demanding it. We find that demands, in most instances, obfuscate the real nature of the struggle. And in most instances tend to co-opt it. We are not demanding any of our points because we don't recognize that the administration has the authority to give them to us. In a fundamental way the administration has no power to grant them. A lot of the things we want are against state law. The local school board and administration have no power to change state law. All they can say is, "Well, we are just carrying out state law, we are for you; as a matter of fact, we want to change those laws but can't do it." And that is why we have to carry out our program. We are not going to go to Reagan. We are not going to the state,, we're not going to the federal government. We are going to begin implementing the program —and begin breaking the law. Our actions will gain respect and support among students. Students know they have rights. If the authorities don't recognize that, well, fuck them. That will be our attitude. We are going to put this into practice and get students to come and support us by exercising our rights.

For example, after we print our program we're going to start leafletting it on campus. Exercising our rights. We are going to leaflet and we are not going to ask for permission. If the administration suspends us, we enter into another phase. We will call a rally for the next day. Students will clearly see that the administration had come down on us for merely exercising our rights, and we will gain their respect. This program cuts to the core of the system, and the administration, even if sympathetic to our goals, will be put in the unfortunate position of defending the status quo. By beginning to implement this program we will put the administration up against the wall. And even if they are sympathetic, the only thing that they will be able to do—because of pressure from above—is begin to repress our movement.

Obviously there will be a conflict between what we would like to see happen and what school officials themselves would like to see; what may finally emerge may be a compromise, or one side may win out. Ideally, if we are to preserve any kind of meaningful education, all courses should be made to relate to each other. Subjects should not be learned in a vacuum. Lots of kids say mathematics is irrelevant. Well, when you look closely, mathematics is not at all irrelevant. Society needs mathematics in the technology that runs our kind of society—it is a kind of circular relationship. What has to be demonstrated, though is the relationship between biology, history, and mathematics. All of these things have to be related.

I think a lot of the student revolt is a cry against specialization. Although specialization was once necessary for industrialization and technology, I think that there will be a return to the Renaissance Man: a man who not only knows a lot, but knows a lot about many things in depth, and can see the relationships between them. Like the relationships between people, government, society, nature, and wildlife. There has to be more emphasis on the sociological aspects of relationships. And that is what I think schools will have to involve themselves with. The fundamental questions concerning human and societal relations have to be explored and explained, and out of them has to grow a curriculum with course content which will involve and relate to people and their needs.

INTEREST GROUPS

The Food and Drug Administration and the Pill

ALICE J. WOLFSON AND
PHILIP E. WOLFSON

Further evidence of the crude experiment that has been played on over 8 million U.S. women and some 13 million women worldwide is the British and French withdrawals of high-estrogen oral contraceptives and strenuous warnings on the dangers of the pill to the women who continue to take the remaining oral contraceptives being sold in those countries. And finally, the Women's Liberation Movement has shown that the overwhelming number of American physicians neither scrupulously advise women of the dangers and side effects of the pill nor offer them a knowledgeable choice of other means of contraception.

In February, the Washington, D.C., Women's Liberation conducted a survey of women taking the pill. An analysis of the first 750 questionnaires returned from 35 states showed that over 40 percent of the respondents' doctors had never mentioned the possibility of side effects occurring from use of the pill. Of the 55 percent who were warned, usually only the mildest effects were mentioned, nausea and weight gain alone accounting for half of all side effect warnings. The possibility of cancer was revealed to only 2 percent of the women, and thrombo-embolism (blood clots), depression and infertility were rarely mentioned. With the protective curtain of medical secrecy thus drawn around the pill, it has been almost impossible for most women to exercise their right to informed consent to use of the pill.

The Pill Proponents

Despite mounting and incontestably damning evidence, organizations like the AMA and Planned Parenthood and the pill manufacturers and their research-supported physicians act as though it is their duty to give the pill a clean bill of health. The most common statistical game played by the Planned Parenthood people is to say that the dangers of pregnancy out-weigh the risks of the pill. It is important to clarify a few things with regard to this claim. Despite what pill proponents would like us to believe, oral contraceptives are not the only means of preventing pregnancy. The pill has not significantly lowered the birthrate and it has not become the panacea for population control. The lowest birthrate in this country occurred in the 1930s, long before the advent of the pill. It should also be noted that included in most statistics of maternal mortality from which pregnancy risks are compiled are the deaths from illegal abortions. Instead of advocating a sane and humane approach to birth control, the pill pushers apparently offer illegal abortion and the carcinogenic pill as our national policy of contraception.

Another argument often cited in favor of the pill is that what causes cancer in animals *may* not cause cancer in man. It is well known, however, that estrogens (one of the major components of the pill whatever the synthetic name given them) are carcinogenic in mice, rats, rabbits, hamsters and dogs, producing tumors of the breast, uterus, kidney, ovary, testicle, pituitary gland and bone marrow. All chemicals known to produce tumors in man produce tumors in animals, and frequently in the same site. It is a deadly game to propose that women be the guinea pigs in determining whether the reverse is true.

And finally, we are told that the pill is not as dangerous as crossing the street or taking aspirin. But we cross a street because we have to get to the other side, and we swallow aspirin and other potent drugs because we have a preexisting condition we want alleviated. The pill, however, is taken by healthy women to avoid pregnancy and, as our mothers knew very well, there are mechanical means that can do this almost as effectively and far more safely than oral contraceptives.

In spite of all this, the FDA resisted modifying its virtual blanket approval of the pill. American data on the dangers of the pill lagged far behind the British work. Original approval by the FDA for marketing of the drug was based on a study of 850 Puerto Rican and 132 U.S. women, during which five sudden deaths occurred among the Puerto Rican women. Since no autopsies were performed, no one will ever know if the FDA approved a drug that had already killed almost 1 percent of the women taking it. In any event, the example indicates the haste and sloppiness with which the pill was brought to the market before adequate assessment of its safety could be undertaken.

It was only during the Nelson Sub-committee hearings, as a result of the pressures of public clamor and the foreign withdrawal of oral contraceptives from the market, that the FDA appeared ready to take action. In public testimony Dr. Charles Edwards, FDA Commissioner, presented a 600-word statement, "What You Should Know About Birth Control Pills," which was to be included in the *Federal Register* as a compulsory package insert to all women on the pill.

The insert represented the first attempt in FDA history to communicate directly with the recipients of a medication. It warned of the symptoms and dangers of blood clots, and cautioned women who suffered from diabetes, epilepsy, migraine, high blood pressure, mental depression and other diseases about the need for special medical supervision. It described side effects and decreased fertility, and stated that though the pill had caused cancer in animals, it had not yet been proven to cause cancer in humans. Lastly, the insert stressed the right to individual consultation with the physician on risks and safety of the pill and the need for regular checkups. While the FDA did not propose withdrawal of the preparations which the British and French had taken off the market, they nonetheless had taken a major step toward allowing women to make an informed choice of contraceptive methods.

Twenty days had elapsed after publication of the insert when the then HEW secretary, Robert Finch, along with Dr. Edwards, suddenly announced the withdrawal of the original circular and its replacement by the following 96-word statement:

Oral contraceptives are powerful, effective drugs that should be taken only under the supervision of a physician. As with all effective drugs, they may cause side effects in some cases and should not be taken at all by some. *Rare instances of blood clotting are the most important known complication of the oral contraceptives.* These points were discussed with you when you chose this method of contraception.
While you are taking this drug, you should have periodic examinations at intervals set by your doctor and should report promptly any change in your state of health.

This statement was worse than no warning at all. It gave no information and minimized the hazards of blood clotting. Are 40 hospitalizations per 2,000 users "rare instances of blood clotting"? Is it a "rare instance" if you are one of the women killed or maimed because of lack of information?

In its coverage of the announcement that day, the Washington *Post* stated that the original insert had been withdrawn under pressure from the AMA, the drug companies, and Planned Parenthood-World Population. Later, in a stormy session with Women's Liberation members who were sitting-in in his office, Secretary Finch stated that the population-control people were after the FDA for scaring women off the pill. Commissioner Edwards, also present, denied that the original statement had been anything more than one of several versions to be decided upon for submission to the *Federal Register*. He was quickly taken to task by the women who had the transcript for the Senate Subcommittee hearings in which Edwards had cited the 600-word statement as the final version for the *Federal Register*.

Protecting The Producers

In the brief space of some 20 days, the FDA and its boss, Secretary Finch, had virtually reversed themselves by removing the only protection American women might have against ignorant use of a dangerous drug that permeates their entire bodies. Bowing to the supposedly external pressures of pill producers, the medical profession, and the population-control groups—during the Nelson hearings, the *AMA News* reported in front-page headlines: "Pill Hearings—Hazards Minimal"—the FDA indicated its real role to be that of protecting the producers from the consumers.

On April 1 the FDA Advisory Committee on Obstetrics and Gynecology met to discuss so-called secret British data that had sparked the removal of high-estrogen pills from the market in Britain and France, data that were published openly in the *British Medical Journal* two weeks later. They also met to discuss their position on the proposed 96-word warning.

The advisory committee does not have decision-making power in the FDA. It is exactly what its name implies: an advisory committee. Its value to the FDA and the HEW is increased or diminished according to what the latter two wish to hear. The committee had for years been the arbiter of information concerning the safety of the pill, had approved the pill's open sale in 1959, and until 1969 had lauded its use. Several of its members had given testimony adverse to the pill before the Nelson Subcommittee hearings. Would that testimony be retracted in the face of opposition from Finch and Edwards? Would the committee also respond to the political pressures from which they were supposed to be aloof?

The advisory committee is made up of gynecologists, some in research and some in clinical practice. Their bias runs from interest in population control to the concerns of the gynecologist in private practice. On the surface there appears to be little reason why they should be disturbed if interested consumers wished to sit in on their sessions.

Shortly after the meeting began—behind closed and locked doors—along with Judy Spelman we gained entrance to the conference room by a ruse. When the three uninvited guests appeared, the staid meeting broke into chaos. One of the doctors immediately took names and addresses, including zip codes, and asked for places of employment.

When told that the meeting was a closed session, we answered that where people's lives are at stake, there can be no closed sessions. We were particularly angry over the change from the 600-word "What You Should Know About Birth Control Pills" insert to the 96-word warning which had been arrived at in secret sessions.

Some of the doctors objected to discussing the British data in front of the group. "It's privileged information," they said. What appeared to be privileged information was not the British data, but what the American doctors would or would not do with it. One committee member, in commenting on the British data, said: "I see no reason to disagree with the data, but I wouldn't say it publicly."

At that point three plainclothesmen came up to us and asked us to step outside, but we told them to say anything they had to say in front of the committee. The security force then threatened us with physical ejection. This proposal met with approval from most of the members but with concern on the part of Drs. Philip Corfman, Roy Hertz, and Elsie Carrington, the only woman on the advisory committee. After a quick conference it was decided that instead of arresting us, the meeting would be adjourned if we did not leave. In turn, we proposed that we would leave for discussion of the British data if we could return for discussion of the package insert. This was agreed upon, although by no means unanimously, and we left.

Within an hour, Dr. Wolfson, who is in the Public Health Service and therefore under the jurisdiction of HEW, received a call from his immediate superior telling him that word had come down from Finch's office that he was *not* to go back to the meeting. What pressure could be applied to prohibit our return had immediately been used. The two women, however, not subject to such pressure, attended the afternoon session.

Can Consumers Read?

At the opening of the session, Dr. Edward Jennings, an FDA employee, explained that the 96-word warning had been recommended because the original 600-word insert was too complicated for most lay people to understand. He then read the 96-word statement, pointing out its subtle features for those who felt that the warning was worse than no warning at all. He noted that by including the statement, "when you chose this method of contraception," the warning, if read closely, suggested without seeming to do so that there were other forms of contraception. And with its statement, "these points were discussed with you," it offered the woman some guidelines as to how her doctor should behave.

Since most of the advisory committee acted as if the consumers cannot even read, it seemed absurd to be considering a warning, the subtleties of which had to be pointed out to a group of physicians.

A few of the doctors were upset that the FDA should be considering any kind of package insert. They felt that such a move cast doubt on the competence and integrity of the medical profession. Dr. Hertz, while agreeing with the general point, felt that the Senate hearings had made one thing very clear. Women did not know about the drug which 8½ million of them were taking. And it appeared that many doctors knew little about the medication either. The package insert was Hertz's version of "paying collectively for our sins."

When it was finally agreed upon that there would be no way to escape putting some kind of warning on the package, Dr. Hertz proposed a substitute for the 96-word statement. He suggested that since the warning was to be on the pill package, the most important thing was to tell women of the most dangerous symptoms so that they could get prompt treatment when necessary.

Dr. Hertz's proposal began another debate. One doctor was afraid that if the insert read "Call your doctor," too many people would call him at home and anger his wife. Others agreed, and a 15-minute discussion ensued on what word to substitute for "call." "Contact" was finally agreed upon.

With that important point settled, another doctor said that of the five symptoms (severe headache, blurred vision, pain in the legs, pain in the chest or cough, irregular or missed periods) only blurred vision actually warranted instant treatment. A woman could have any of the others and not be seriously ill.

The fact that any of the symptoms might be signaling an imminent stroke or blood clot seemed less important to him than the fact that he might get so many unnecessary phone calls. The more medically prudent doctors, however, carried the day on this particular issue and the five symptoms were retained in the warning.

The most liberal of the doctors balked at the suggestion that, in addition to the list of symptoms, something be put in to inform the patient that her doctor should have discussed things with her. "It would open us to a multitude of malpractice suits," he stated. All agreed and speedily discarded that section.

The final draft of Hertz's proposed insert reads as follows:

Do Not Take These Pills Without Your Doctor's Continued Supervision. Contact him if you experience these unexplained symptoms: (1) Severe Headache; (2) Blurred Vision; (3) Pain in the Chest or Cough; (5) Irregular or Missed Periods.

The last great debate of the day came over whether or not the 96-word warning had already been put into the *Federal Register*. This would make a difference as to whether the committee was acting as an advisory group to Secretary Finch, or whether they were responding, as an interested group of private citizens, to an established fact. Dr. Barnes, acting head of the advisory committee, said that the 96-word warning was the one that was to be entered in the *Federal Register* and that there would be no debate about that.

Since Miss Spelman and Mrs. Wolfson, along with other members of Women's Liberation, had met with Secretary Finch two days before and had been assured that the 96-word warning was not the final draft to go into the *Federal Register*, they challenged Commissioner Edwards. The Commissioner agreed that the Secretary was still open to suggestions. The advisory committee then voted to urgently request that Secretary Finch enter Dr. Hertz's warning into the *Federal Register* instead of the 96-word statement previously proposed.

The FDA Bows

Subsequently the completely political nature of the decisions of the FDA has been further demonstrated. In a statement on June 9 before the House Subcommittee on Intergovernmental Relations, Commissioner Edwards reported with respect to the proposed insert in the *Federal Register:*

We received a heavy response to this proposal. Most of it . . . from users expressing a desire and a need for much more information about these drugs. The letters demanded a public hearing to allow for an oral expression of their views and an opportunity to cross-examine the views of other interests.

Edwards stated that those opposed to an effective warning were population-control and family-planning groups, organized medicine, and the pharmaceutical companies. These interests won the day. Edwards denied a public hearing, and proposed a new warning even weaker, if possible, than the 96-word warning and leaving out the symptom-related addition proposed by Dr. Hertz. Thus, at the same time the FDA publicly admitted that women were struggling to gain the information about the pill necessary to make a decision on contraceptive choice, the FDA sided with the producers and denied women that right.

Experts could perhaps argue ad infinitum about the safety of the pill. A clearer issue is whether or not, in the presence of this controversy, women have the right to all of the information available about the drug so many of them are taking under the assumption that it is safe. Dr. Alan Guttmacher of Planned Parenthood and Dr. R. T. Ravenholt, head of the population-control program for the Agency for International Development, have deplored the fact that women are being "scared" off the pill. We contend that if women had been treated as thinking human beings instead of guinea pigs, none of the information disclosed in the Nelson hearings would have been new to them, and the "scare," which is actually the exercise of an informed choice, would not have occurred.

The advisory committee meeting and the revision of the warning statement offer a rare glimpse of how the medical profession closes ranks in time of crisis. The public may have the right to know, but the profession clings to its power and control. For 13 years the FDA failed the women of this country by allowing an untested drug to be marketed and promoted so recklessly. An effective insert encompassing all the known and suspected side effects of birth control pills is the least that the consumers should be able to expect from an agency whose declared purpose is to protect the public.

The Nelson Senate Subcommittee hearings last winter on oral contraceptives and the controversy that followed have raised doubts about the reliability and credibility of the government's consumer protection agency, the Food and Drug Administration.

No longer is there any question about the danger of the pill. Both American and European statistics have shown a six- to seven-fold increase in deaths due to blood clots among women on the pill. Estrogens have now been implicated as cancer-producing agents in five different animal species and have been found to cause over 50 different changes in human body chemistry, leading to the premature onset of diabetes, arteriosclerosis or hardening of the arteries, and hypertension. Many cancer experts predict large increases in the incidence of cancer of the breast, cervix and uterus as the latent period of 10 to 20 years of these tumors ends—the pill has now been on the market some 11 years.

JUSTICE

If You Were On Welfare

RICHARD M. ELMAN

I pity the young ones. They still want things. With me it's different. You know, it never seemed as if I had the right to expect anything. I remember when I wanted to visit my niece in Lake George. I had to ask them for the money, and they made it seem like they were doing me such a favor. Ever since then I have always felt that they have been doing me these favors, and I don't want to ask for anything more than I need. . . . At my age there isn't much you need; so I always say, "No, thanks," as nicely as I can. It's better that way because, if they can say yes, they can also say no. Why start trouble?

When I was young, people were talking then of eliminating poverty. It didn't do me any good. I've seen three big depressions in my life and three or four wars, and I've known a lot of people on Welfare. They are just like everybody else except they are different. You know what I mean? They don't have anything . . . anything at all except Welfare.

—*The Poorhouse State.*

In a fat, rich country such as this proposals about doing something for the welfare poor generally fall into two distinct categories: either hypocritical or else niggardly and grudging. The poor are believed to be a social problem. Something must be done about them, *for them, with them.* The poor exist. They demand sustenance. Will $1,600 a year sustain? To the urban black or Puerto Rican, or any of the declassed workers of the current recession, the proposed guaranteed sum of $1,600 a year simply guarantees that they will continue to be impoverished. In Alabama or Mississippi, on the other hand, such a sum may be a vast improvement over the absolute starvation amounts of $50 or $60 per family which is presently being doled out each month.

My mother gets $7.10 a month for gas and electricity. She pays about $30 [every two months]. You want to know why? I'll tell you why. We use the stove to heat the rooms. We burn the lights at night so the rats won't go near the baby. Also, it's dark where we live, even during the day. So if I am reading or sewing or studying from a book, I've got to burn the lights. The Welfare knows all this, and they are supposed to do something about it, but they never do. Every month we get this bill, and my mother pays it with the food money. Then she has to prove to the Welfare that she has used the food money to pay for the lights. . . .

I can remember the last time they turned off the lights. It was winter. My mother was so cold she started to cry. Then we all started to cry because it was so dark. We had to eat cold food out of tin cans until the Welfare called Con Edison and they turned the lights back on again. When he comes, my mother is angry with the man. "Pray to God you have not hurt these children. Believe me." Afterwards my little sister was sick for a week.

The poor suffer from our complete incapacity to imagine them. They are not us. They are not rich. Who are they?

One might presume to answer that they are ourselves with $1,600 a year or less. Imagine yourself living in a family with an income of $3,200. You will, of course, probably not be able to afford *Saturday Review*. You buy few books, not very many records (except, perhaps, for 45 rpms). You do not take vacations. The great questions of our time do not interest you.

A good part of your life is spent worrying. You have been afflicted with this terrible blight, and you wish to survive, make the most of it—that is, if you still feel human. Then you worry if there is enough food, if your children have the right clothing, about the rent, or the habits of your neighbors. You worry about the mail and if your check will arrive on time. Perhaps you worry what your children will be like ten years from now, or what you will be like. Or perhaps you are so far gone from a life of bare and bitter caring that you have begun to worry abstractly: about baseball averages, Diahann Carroll, or the problems of Mrs. Onassis.

At this point you may be saying it sounds just like my own life, just like me, myself, and when we are all finally alone together in one room, after a day at the office or spent in housewifery. There is this major difference: The administration proposes to pay the poor $1,600 to do what the Establishment pays off the middle classes to do at $7,000 or $10,000 or $15,000 or $20,000 or more a year, and we do not usually ask for ourselves, as a condition for such a benefice, that we worry about worrying ourselves out of our livelihoods.

I wish I could remember when I got this sickle-cell anemia. . . . I got two sick kids like me and another in the Kennedy homes in the Bronx . . . and sometimes you get pretty tired, but you just got to do certain things. After all, they say, if you don't take care of these kids, who will? They got a point.

But every time you want something extra from them it's a whole nuisance. Like carfare. Sometimes I got to spend 90 cents carfare for me and the kids to go off to Bellevue, because you can't leave them alone if you got to go there for some reason. And when I come back from Bellevue clinic I got to rush over here to Twenty-eighth Street for that carfare money or else I'm going to run short on food.

Well, even so, they don't just give you your money like that. Sometimes they want proof. Sometimes they say they will owe it to you. You got to be careful about the ones who say that. I learned you got to insist right then and there you want that carfare or else you don't get it. So you just got to sit there and wait for the man until he gives it to you. Sometimes I think I spend half my life waiting somewhere for 90 cents.

Nor do we ask ourselves to surrender the various "inalienable rights" of Americans that are foreign to the poor. Although Americans are "free" to cross state boundaries and choose residences to their liking, for example, special residency laws have been enacted by many states denying this guarantee to the person who applies for public assistance after coming from another state. And although all Americans are supposedly guaranteed freedom from fear of illegal searches and seizures or the arbitrary violation of their privacy, if you are on public assistance or living in a low-income public housing project, you can protect yourself against such actions only at the risk of disqualification or eviction. Large families are penalized with lower benefit levels; small families—such as a mother and one child—often are denied access to public housing.

For more than a hundred years all Americans presumably have been protected against "involuntary servitude," yet functionaries in city and state offices of "employment rehabilitation" do not interpret this to mean that their clients have the freedom to accept or reject work, even if they happen to be husbandless women with families. And if you as a beneficiary of a public assistance program appeal some violation of your rights, some new affront to your dignity, you are not guaranteed an impartial trial by a jury of peers but are brought before an **administrative tribunal** that can function with only the most perfunctory regard for **due process of law**.

You want to know how they close a case? I'll tell you. They know the mail is always late for people like us. If the investigator writes a letter to come for an appointment the day after tomorrow and he mails it tomorrow, you will not get the letter in time to come for the appointment. Then he closes your case just like that. It's punishment—you know. Sometimes it takes three months before they write all the papers again to put you back.

Fear dominates your life—fear that the check will be delayed in the mail, fear that your mailbox will be rifled, fear that your caseworker will be replaced (or that he won't be), fear that your landlord may harass you in any of hundreds of large or small ways, fear of violence, fear of life itself. You have no reason to hope for dramatic improvement. The reasons you are on welfare in the first place assure that. You have no education, or no mate, or poor health, or all of these handicaps. The concept of upward mobility is an abstraction. You may still hope your children can escape your fate, but not if you examine their situation with detachment.

The apartment was exploding with heat. It was so hot that one expected to see the thick paint bubbling against the moldings. As she escorted me down the hallway toward her sitting room, Mrs. Escobosa explained in a mixture of Spanish and English that others in the building had filed a complaint last year with the City Rent and Rehabilitation Administration when the building was on rent strike because there was no heat; now her landlord was getting even with her by refusing to turn off the valves, which he controlled from the cellar, even though it was midsummer.

"You see the things I have," Mrs. Escobosa said. She moved on to show me a bedroom with its stained mattresses on the dusty floor, where her children slept. Then she padded about in the heat toward her kitchen, showing me the darkened refrigerator, its door ajar because it no longer worked, the window box in which she kept a little food, the sweating copper pipe in the tin sink, which gushed cold running water over a half-filled bottle of milk. The kitchen was swarming with flies, which clung to the sweat on my face. I said, "You try to do your best, I see. . . ."

The poor do not always work. Most of the rest of us spend our time pretending that what we do with a day is work. We ask only that they pretend like us, and we punish them with more poverty when they don't. Perhaps we should stop kidding ourselves that their enforced leisure is at our expense. It may be that it is at *their* expense, if we truly believe in the value of work. It may be that *we* exist at *their* expense, if we truly do believe in the value of a human life.

One wonders what kind of brutes are prepared to pay out $1,600 a year in welfare to the so-called poor when, at the same time, they say they are perfectly satisfied if only 3.5 per cent—rising to 4 or 5 per cent—of the population is unemployed over the next decade? What sort of men are prepared to issue food stamps and order roast beef?

You and I are that sort of man, I'm afraid. We are as dissociated from the humanity of those we call the poor as we often are from our own humanities. If one could only imagine a President or a Congressional leader or an urban affairs adviser getting $1,600 a year, one could begin to believe that these proposals could do something. Then the poor themselves might be credible to us. But just as we and the governmental leaders of this era do not wish to live under terms of such enforced prudence, so, it seems, the poor do not also. They would like to be more beautiful, as in the Clairol ads; more mobile, with a Maverick; or more virile, with a large family. Ask yourself how much of this kind of behavior you can afford on $1,600 a year—$133 a month, $30 a week, $4.40 a day.

Two things I would like from the Welfare are the telephone and movies. I don't care for the TV, but I love movies. Now I know I am not supposed to spend the money [for the children] on such things; so I don't go very often, and when I do go, I worry. They ought to let us go to movies. If I had the right clothes, I could go sometime to see the mayor and tell him. . . . Maybe they ought to have a movie here for all the people on Welfare. It would be like the clinics. . . .
I would like the telephone to speak with my brother, who lives in Queens. Also, sometimes, when the children are sick, it would be nice to have a telephone because now I have to take them with me to a neighbor's house. . . . If it is late, I must send somebody to use the booth on the corner. If only they would put a [pay] telephone in our building it would be better, but the Welfare is the landlord, and they don't want to do it.

When I was writing *The Poorhouse State* in 1966, the welfare mothers of New York City were beginning to organize themselves to pressure a liberal bureaucracy into granting entitlements of approximately $100 a year to purchase sorely needed winter clothing for their schoolchildren. Some simply were hoping to use these extra stipends to help themselves to live. They were extremely successful. They exerted sufficient pressure, and winter coat checks began to pour through the mails. The response of the welfare bureaucracy was to cut back on the number of persons admitted to the welfare rolls, and to raise welfare budgets in general and cut out winter coat entitlements in particular. Since then, three years or more have skittered past; the cost of living for an urban family rises about one-half per cent a month.

Boondoggle, anybody?

I never knew anybody who made a living on Welfare. Some people say we cheat a lot. Maybe some people like to think they do, but they are poor just the same. Welfare is for poor people. It's not right to say those things about people because only the poor can collect it. You know what I mean? If it is for poor people, how can people say we are cheating?

We have dissociated ourselves as a responsible middle class when we are really in the same boat as the poor and do not care to know it. We tax them with loutishness for taxing us with their needs, though we tell those who are better off than we that they need to be where they are. I believe that any welfare reform that does not begin to address itself to the question of equalizing wealth in this country is simply a way of creating new poverty. It may be poverty at $3,200 a year; it will be poverty just the same.

If we are serious about reform, we should guarantee employment for life to those who must work. The questions of income maintenance and personality adjustment should be made entirely distinct before the law, and work should be considered an option, not a necessity, along with schooling, travel, or other leisure activities. What I am saying is that we ask the poor to join with us in helping to discover a good life for all of us, though I recognize that we do not trust them, nor they us; and that our lives in this country—on this planet—are threatened by problems larger than the poverty of a numerically small number of weakened and deprived persons. If I am being utopian, it is because realistic solutions have simply been the time-honored excuse for more and more brutalized prescriptions for the poor.

In those days I had this man for an investigator, and don't you think he didn't think so? You know what he asked me? He said, "Can't your wife help out?" So I thought I knew what he meant by that. I said, "You don't really mean that. You don't mean your wife peddle herself?" And this guy he just grinned at me. . . . Now what kind of a question is that to ask? My wife don't peddle anything. She got the kids to take care of. What kind of a question is that anyway?

The trouble with celebrating the fact that we may now be prepared to give an entitlement of $1,600 a year to every poor family is that it allows us to evade once again the question of what the good life should be. Unless we are prepared to face that question with the poor through the poor, we are dooming ourselves once again to suffer the rage of the poor; we are dooming ourselves, moreover, to visit our own rage on the poor. We are dooming ourselves to more of this same apartness through which we all suffer and rage on, and suffer others to suffer with us.

When I wrote *The Poorhouse State,* some 600,000 New Yorkers were on welfare, and, except for the aged and disabled, they were mostly all black or Spanish-speaking. All were poor, and none of them thought of it as a boondoggle. Today, I am told, more than a million are being subsidized poorly. The cry is that the rolls must be reduced. But perhaps our only hope is that the other seven million citizens also will be granted their entitlements so that the word welfare can become more than just an ironic way of referring to what we visit on some people at minimal expense to ourselves.

We have got to teach ourselves to share. If we don't, we will continue to destroy each other.

LIBERTY

Americans Betrayed

MORTON GRODZINS

The evacuation of Japanese Americans from the Pacific Coast in the spring and summer of 1942 was an act without precedent in American history. It was the first time that the United States government condemned a large group of people to barbed-wire inclosures. It was the first event in which danger to the nation's welfare was determined by group characteristics rather than by individual guilt. It was the first program in which race alone determined whether an American would remain free or become incarcerated.

Why did the evacuation take place? How did the national government determine that evacuation was necessary?

The single purpose of the following pages is to answer these questions. But the answers have more than a historical significance. The decision in favor of evacuation affected in the short run only a tiny minority of the nation's population; in the long run, it affects the whole people. The process of government is a continuing process; what it produced for Japanese Americans it can also produce for other Americans. The decision to evacuate was made in the face of emergency; but the Supreme Court has imbedded the principle of evacuation into the nation's constitutional system.

The evacuation, in short, is less important as a crisis program than as a permanent legacy of governmental action taken against the members of a minority group. It is less important as a historical incident than as a legal precedent. It is less important as a policy of government than as a demonstration of the policy-making process. It is less important for what it did to

Japanese Americans than for what it might do to all Americans.

One hundred and ten thousand Americans of Japanese ancestry were evacuated. Aliens and citizens, children and adults, males and females, were moved on short notice from their lifetime homes to concentration centers. No charges were ever filed against these persons, and no guilt was ever attributed to them. The test was ancestry, applied with the greatest rigidity. Evacuation swept into guarded camps orphans, foster-children in white homes, Japanese married to Caucasians, the offspring of such marriages, persons who were unaware of their Japanese ancestry, and American citizens "with as little as one-sixteenth Japanese blood."[1] Evacuation was not carried out by lawless vigilantes or by excited local officials. The program was instituted and executed by military forces of the United States with a full mandate of power from both the executive and the legislative branches of the national government.

The extraordinary mass movements were the product of an extraordinary situation. Of approximately 127,000 persons of Japanese ancestry residing in the United States (exclusive of Hawaii), more than 112,000 were concentrated in the three western states. Long before the war with Japan, resident Japanese were an unpopular and unwelcome group in the eyes of many residents of the West Coast. Their race and the semiclosed communities into which they were forced set them apart from the larger population. Their adherence to Old World culture patterns further served to emphasize their isolation and to make them the target of popular distaste. They were widely regarded as undesirable neighbors, as unfair competitors in many lines of business endeavor, and as residents of uncertain allegiance to America.

The war with Japan consequently turned grave suspicion upon the Japanese in America. The first weeks of the war were disastrously losing weeks for the United States and her allies. By their very concentration on the West Coast, American Japanese seemed in the best possible situation to aid the enemy. Threats of vigilantism and race riots were heard. Stories circulated about the treachery of Japanese residents at Pearl Harbor, and reports were made that Japanese in California, Oregon, and Washington were transmitting information to the enemy and preparing to undertake a program of mass sabotage.

Army officials charged with protecting the western combat area concluded that the inland movement of resident Japanese was essential to the national defense. The unprecedented program of mass evacuation was undertaken as a measure of grave "military necessity." . . .

The Evacuation Decision in Outline

1. On the plane of public discussion, the first weeks of the war were characterized by good will and cordiality shown resident Japanese on the West Coast. Within six weeks, however, demands for evacuation began to pyramid. Historical animosities were released by the increasing wartime tension. Race became synonymous with allegiance, and the American citizen of Japanese ancestry was identified with the Japanese enemy. The identification was furthered by the stories of treachery at Pearl Harbor (later proved false) and by the very nature of the enemy's attack there; and it was widely fostered by the historic foes of Japanese immigration, who capitalized on

---

[1] Western Defense Command and Fourth Army, *Final Report, Japanese Evacuation from the West Coast*, Government Printing Office, Washington, 1943, p. 145.

the crisis situation. Those friendly toward Japanese residents lacked precise information on the conduct of Japanese at Hawaii, were beset by fears of the then victorious Japanese enemy, and were completely ineffective in opposing mass evacuation. Significant opposition did not develop until after evacuation had become national policy.

The sincere patriotism of those demanding evacuation as a measure of immediate national defense can be accepted at full value. But it is clear that popular beliefs with respect to Japanese Americans were not based on actual fact. It is no less clear that those beliefs were used to support, and were supported by, deep-seated racial prejudice, the desire for economic gain, and the courtship of political favor. These last factors served to magnify the dangers of American Japanese, to minimize the danger of German and Italian alien enemy groups, and to impede consideration of any alternative to the wholesale exile of the Japanese. Under the guise of national defense, evacuation became an end in itself, a fortuitous wartime opportunity to rid the western states of their most unpopular minority group.

2. At the point that the War Department adopted evacuation as policy, the following factors were important:

Officers directly responsible for initiating the evacuation policy expressed vehement racial animosity. This racial animus was demonstrated in Lieutenant General DeWitt's original recommendation for mass movements, where the argument for complete rather than selective evacuation was expressed in the words, "The Japanese race is an enemy race and . . . the racial strains are undiluted." It was made clear at each step of the military control program which, progressively, bore harder on Japanese alien enemies and American citizens of Japanese ancestry while concomitantly becoming easier on German and Italian alien enemies. It was finally exprssed in General DeWitt's public statement that "a Jap's a Jap. . . . It makes no difference whether he is an American citizen, he is still a Japanese."

The regional pressures markedly influenced War Department policy. A significant time lag preceded both the regional demand for evacuation and the assumption of evacuation policy by the War Department; and military insistence on the drastic program came at a time of no increased national peril. Army justifications for mass evacuation paralleled, and in some cases copied verbatim, falsities and half-truths that characterized the regional demands. Military officers at first denied any necessity for evacuating Japanese from interior areas of California, then insisted upon that action in response to renewed regional pressure.

Military justifications for evacuation that were not directly traceable to racial theories or regional pressures failed to stand on their own merits. The fiction of dual citizenship was stretched to the point where Japanese with such status, but not Germans or Italians, became "half-and-half citizens." Military officers considered it suspicious that Japanese in America had *not* celebrated the emperor's birthday. The false charge that Japanese Americans failed to co-operate with federal intelligence agencies was cited as a reason for evacuation. Without apprehending a single person and without definitely establishing even the existence of shore-to-ship signaling, military officials presumed to determine the fact that Japanese Americans were aiding the enemy from shore. The three "most striking" illustrations of allegedly successful communication to enemy Japanese all took place *after* the recommendation for evacuation had been made; and two of those incidents occurred *after* all Japanese had actually been incarcerated. Yet, in his final report, the commanding general stated that these incidents, among others, led him "to conclude" that evacuation was a "military necessity."

General DeWitt's recommendation for mass evacuation was not subjected to critical review by the civilian heads of the War Department.

3. On the interdepartmental administrative planes, the Justice Department acceded to substantially every military request for a tightened program of internal security up to the point of the War Department's request that mass movements be undertaken. Justice Department officials based their opposition to evacuation on the arguments that (a) it was illegal; (b) it was administratively impossible for the Justice Department to undertake; and (c) it was unnecessary for the nation's defense. The legal impediments were soon brushed aside. The objection on the ground of administrative inexpediency was circumvented by the War Department's unexpected willingness to undertake the administrative task. The crucial issue remained: Was evacuation necessary? The Attorney-General, as the nation's leading law-enforcement officer, was not convinced that evacuation was a necessary measure of national safety. He believed that evacuation was a mistake. But War Department officials had defined evacuation as a measure of "military necessity," and the Attorney-General, conscious of his incomplete knowledge of the military situation, was unwilling to oppose Army judgment. Policy was set in the face of the fact that officials of the War and Justice departments achieved full and fundamental disagreement over the necessity of evacuation.

4. At the level of supplying criminal penalties for the Army's evacuation program, Congress accepted without question the War Department statement that evacuation was a "military necessity" and that immediate legislation was essential to the administration of the evacuation program. At no point did members of Congress exercise critical judgment on either of these points. There was no congressional examination of the basis of the military program and no congressional search for alternative methods of control. The little discussion that Congress gave to the harsh legislation was largely compounded of misunderstanding and irrelevancy. Congress abdicated its most important wartime role as a critic of the administration and validated the War Department's check without inspecting the amount for which it was drawn.

5. At the final stage of the policy-making process, evacuation was endowed with constitutional sanctity by the Supreme Court. In approving evacuation, the Court markedly relaxed its usual standards of review for civil liberties cases.

Region Versus Nation

The evacuation illustrated, more graphically than any other event in modern times, the gap in the federal system that results from its inevitable, if unwilling, encouragement of regional interests. The western proponents of evacuation, including their congressional representatives, insisted on the mass movements for reasons of regional advantage. The defense of the Pacific seaboard was, of course, also the defense of the nation. But every evidence has indicated that the national interest became lost in the desire of the region to dispose of its own economic and racial problem. The subordination of national to regional interests was illustrated at virtually every point of group pressure for evacuation: by the character of the arguments in favor of the movement; by the absence of any consideration of the effect that evacuation would have on the nation's other minority groups; and, perhaps most conclusively, by the attempts after evacuation to prevent for all time the return of Japanese to the Pacific Coast.

In historical perspective the evacuation was the second high point in the Pacific seaboard's dominance over national policy toward Japanese. The first great victory was the Oriental Exclusion Act of 1924; the second was the evacuation of 1942; a further attempt at a consistent third step—expulsion of Japanese from the nation or at least the western states—awaits a more opportune moment than attended the unsuccessful effort in that direction during the summer and winter of 1943.

The forces that brought about the evacuation were forces present for many years on the Pacific Coast. They were for long periods at least partially balanced and held in check by social pressures that favored equal treatment for all persons and that opposed programs built on racial classifications. But in 1942, as in 1924, this social equilibrium was completely disrupted. The racial viewpoint of the West Coast, representing only one segment of that area's population, established national policy.

In both instances the regional effort coincided with other propitious events: the famous Hanihara "grave consequences" note in 1924, for example; the war itself in 1942. The point, however, is that the western region originated, propagandized, and set in motion the policies both of exclusion and of evacuation. In both cases spokesmen of the West claimed greater public support than they actually possessed. And in both cases the western group was successful in having a program molded to its own immediate advantage made national policy without national discussion and without full consideration of the national interest.

Frailties of Governmental Process

The manner in which evacuation became governmental policy can be easily understood.

The war, at first, was a disastrous one. The Fourth Army Command had a limited wartime objective: protection of the West Coast. Its commanding general was a career officer without previous experience in civil affairs. He was subjected to many extreme pressures favoring evacuation. He was impressed with the possibility that Japanese Americans constituted a special danger, and he recommended evacuation in the firm conviction that it was demanded by military necessity.

Another commanding officer might certainly have rejected a policy of mass evacuation. This is indicated by both the policy that prevailed in Hawaii and the racial nature of the West Coast program. Nevertheless, the evacuation decision, however faulty it was, emerged intelligibly from the position of the commanding general on the West Coast and from the structure of political power in which he operated.

Once the military recommendation was sent to Washington, higher governmental officials validated and passed it on for a number of interrelated reasons: because they found it difficult to oppose a military leader in wartime; because they were impressed with the dangers of vigilantism and the popular discontent on the West Coast; because of the phenomenal success of the Japanese enemy in the South Pacific; because even harsh programs of excess caution seemed justified in the light of reports about fifth-column activities in Europe.

Finally, the Supreme Court found no difficulty in upholding the fullest freedom in the government's exercise of its war powers.

This explanation is no justification for the evacuation program. A true assessment of the policy was possible while it was being made, and a historian's hindsight was not needed to condemn it.

FACTS, FANCY, AND NATIONAL POLICY

One weakness of government that contributed to the evacuation policy was the failure on the part of the officials concerned to utilize available and essential information. The lack of information was crucial on two scores.

In the first place, no use was made of the techniques that existed to make an accurate estimate of the actual state of public opinion on the West Coast. Relatively exact data could have been collected on short notice with scientific survey techniques; and there were available within the federal government both the technical personnel and the administrative machinery to undertake the collection and interpretation of this information. A survey of opinion in California, covering only 102 individuals, was made by the Office of Facts and Figures late in January ,1942. This showed a much more balanced state of public attitudes than claimed by the proponents of evacuation. Yet there is nothing to indicate that this evidence, inadequate as the sample might have been, was ever brought before the officials who were responsible for the evacuation decision. No consistent attempt whatsoever was made to gather more inclusive data on the changing temper of the public.

The lack of such data sorely compromised the officials who opposed evacuation. At least some of those officials were not unaware of the activities of the organized pressure groups, and they had many doubts over the widespread claim that the population of the western states was "unanimously aroused" in favor of evacuation. But this partial insight did not encourage them to look for more exact information. Nor did it save them from the error of overestimating, in common with the proponents of the movement, the amount of mail received in support of evacuation. They were unable to prevent the complete success of those social groups and public officials who based their action, at least partially, on the assumption that public opinion was overwhelmingly in favor of evacuation.

Democratic government is not always justified in setting its policy completely in terms of a dominant national opinion. The justification becomes even more questionable when the dominant opinion is a momentary one or when it comes from a single region. The justification disappears entirely when the government acts as it did with respect to the Japanese evacuation. In this case, the skills for obtaining precise information on public attitudes were available. But policy was established in ignorance of this information.

A second type of knowledge, essential to policy-makers, concerned the Japanese American population itself. This minority group had been the subject of intensive scientific investigation for several decades before the evacuation. The result of this work was a large amount of exact information. Relatively precise data existed on everything from the significance of the Buddhist church to the meaning of dual citizenship; from the geographical distribution of resident Japanese to the social role of mutual aid societies.

These materials contained some corroboration for the fear that some resident Japanese were a danger in time of war;

they contained far more in refutation of the claim that the entire group was of special danger. But the library shelves were undisturbed, and the Japanese specialists were not consulted. The misinformation and falsity contained in the regional demands were accepted wholesale by the military officials on the West Coast, whose recommendations were accepted and transmitted into policy.

THE FEEBLENESS OF PROCEDURES

A related defect of government highlighted by the evacuation was the feebleness of procedures provided by the federal government for review of the policy decision.

Higher administrative officers and members of Congress had more inclusive responsibilities than the general commanding the western defenses. Their actions had to be fixed in consideration of national policy, in all its ramifications, and of the nation's position in the larger world community. Yet they acted without due regard for these considerations.

In one sense, it cannot be claimed that either administrative officials or members of Congress exercised vigilance that might normally have been expected from their respective offices in reviewing a policy of such fundamental importance. The War Department's acceptance of the policy without examination, the Justice Department's acquiescence without approval, and the Congress' sanction without understanding all contained elements of slothfulness.

Over and above the personal factor, institutional frailties contributed to the successive steps by which the evacuation policy was approved and passed upward without critical evaluation. The autonomy of commanding officers in such matters as the disposition and use of troops is an understandable administrative assumption in the military establishment. The transfer of this principle to human problems was as much the result of institutional defect as of intellectual error. The wholesale evacuation of population groups in an area in which civil courts were fully operating was a basically different problem from the training and disciplining of troops and their commitment to battle. Yet the War Department's review procedures were not altered when evacuation was considered. Civilian officials of the department accepted mass evacuation as "military necessity" because that decision was made by military men.

From the viewpoint of administrative organization, an even more important fault was the failure to resolve the Justice Department-War Department conflict over fundamentals. Policy by disagreement might have been avoided if the controversy had come before either the Bureau of the Budget, the cabinet, or the President himself. Actually, the dispute remained hidden. No further administrative review was given the basis of the policy, even though Justice Department officials believed it to be a policy of error. Executive Order 9066 was approved by the Bureau of the Budget on the very day it was presented. It was signed by the President a few hours after being laid on his desk. It was never discussed in cabinet meeting.

The apathy of Congress can be traced immediately to that body's general disposition to accede to the wartime demands of military leaders. In addition, members of the western states adhered to the regional line as a matter of course, while the absence of protest from the largely uninformed and uninterested nonwestern areas materially aided Congress' acceptance of the evacuation policy. But weaknesses in the structure of the Congress contributed to the disinterest of the vast majority of both houses. The Congress was simply not organized for criticism. Members of the

Congress were neither sufficiently aware of their responsibility as critics nor aware of the importance of that responsibility.

THE PRIMACY OF THE MILITARY

The control program of the Department of Justice (prior to February 14, 1942) failed to halt the public clamor for more drastic measures. This failure was not surprising, since the department's program was one of relative moderation, since a large portion of the public clamor was artificially inspired, and since successes of the Japanese in the South Pacific heightened public anxieties. But the shortcoming of the Department of Justice was on a subsidiary issue. The true measure of the department's program was in the results it achieved in the maintenance of internal security. And in this respect the program was eminently successful. Perhaps there was a need for the further strengthening of control measures, as a selective evacuation of individuals considered of particular danger. But, under the system as it existed, no known act of sabotage or espionage by resident Japanese aliens or Americans of Japanese ancestry took place. Success, however, was not sufficient. On the contrary, it was twisted into a positive argument in favor of evacuation: General DeWitt himself said in his final recommendation of February 14, 1942: "The very fact that no sabotage has taken place to date is a disturbing and confirming indication that such action will be taken."

That military officers were able to supersede civilian authorities on the basis of this type of reasoning was perhaps the fundamental weakness of government that led to the evacuation decision.

The evacuation policy was made during the tense, early days of the war. The apparent deadliness of the fifth column as it had operated in Europe was uppermost in the minds of many. The original blow at Pearl Harbor had been devastating. The war at first was a losing war. In view of the deep fears and uncertainties with respect to the final outcome of the struggle, it was understandably difficult for civilian officials to question and overrule the decisions of responsible military officers. But the very unwillingness of civilian authorities to review critically the military recommendation for evacuation was a fatal defect.

Once military officials were allowed to define the situation in military terms, the basic reasons for evacuation were submerged under the impenetrable slogan of "military necessity." It was precisely this fact that made public criticism of the policy ineffective; that induced civilian heads of the War Department to foster the evacuation; that forced Justice Department officials to an unwilling tolerance of the program; that turned aside the investigatory inclinations of Congress; and that fostered relaxation of the Supreme Court's usual standards of review.

The supremacy of military over civilian officials is in itself a negation of democratic principles. Military decisions are made without public discussion, are subject to no immediate criticism, and are calculated according to no rule of civil rights. Military rule, in effect, becomes one-man rule.

It is a fundamental axiom of democratic life that civilian authorities must retain their direction over the military establishment even in wartime. The proper balance between civil liberties and the larger public good is difficult to maintain, even in time of peace. That difficulty is compounded during war. Once military control is granted, the protection of civil liberties becomes virtually impossible.

The Negation of Political Rationality

Political rationality does not exist if rationality is defined as governmental policy decisions made solely through a process of objective deliberation by the people and their chosen representatives. The rationality of a given act can be judged only in the light of defined goals. If there were only one goal, there would be theoretically only one best way to achieve it: the rational way. But it is a gross error to assume that all people concerned with great policies of government strive toward a single purpose. Their motives are various and complex, and no single governmental action is "rational" in the sense that it naturally follows an enlightened discussion and best serves the immediate goals of all the people concerned.

A realistic definition of political rationality must therefore take into account all the conflicting group and individual interests, all the prejudices and provincialisms of various population segments, and all the conscious and unconscious motives that impel individuals and groups to take one course of action rather than another. Under these circumstances it is obvious that a single governmental program may be "rational" to one individual or group and entirely "irrational" to another. Where aims conflict, a single program can rarely satisfy all of them.

This is the normal situation; and the normal task of the national government is to formulate policy in the light of conflicting group interests but with a determination that the larger national interest must at all times be paramount. In this view, the activities of pressure groups are not a weakness of the governmental process. Those activities, on the contrary, are of the greatest potential usefulness. The self-interested groups supply the dynamic half-views out of which policy evolves. The administrative and legislative branches of government cannot achieve a rational policy either by accepting any single partial view or by placing the same value on all partial views and adopting their common ground. Democracy demands that the government establish policy with more than sensitivity to public pressures. The rational process of government presupposes not only free public discussion but also an independent appraisal of the available facts by governmental officials and their obligation to determine that a given policy promotes the national welfare.

The immediate goal presumably served by the Japanese evacuation was clear cut: protection of the West Coast as a war measure. But the national government, in addition to winning the war abroad, had an equal responsibility for maintaining democracy at home. The evacuation violated fundamental liberties of Americans. It was a significant new step for the American democracy, and, in Mr. Justice Murphy's terms, it bore a "melancholy resemblance" to the treatment accorded Jews in Nazi Germany. The civil liberties issue was inseparably linked to the evacuation decision. The very importance of personal liberties to the maintenance of democracy made the decision in favor of evacuation a historic decision of the American government.

Evacuation was a radical departure from traditional American ways and a disturbing model for the future. Yet full consideration of the merits of evacuation in terms of the national welfare was frustrated at each plane of the policy-making process. Regional considerations, emotional half-truths, and racial prejudice colored the public discussion and the original military decision in favor of evacuation. Neither at this point nor at any subsequent point in the entire history of evacuation policy-making did the necessity of evacuation receive full, impartial discussion. At no time in the entire process of decision-making was evacuation as a measure of national defense balanced against the facts available with respect to resident Japanese, against alternative methods of control, or against the implications for democracy in the incarceration of a racial group. The negation of political rationality marked each step in the process by which evacuation became public policy.

Americans in the past decade have held up to scorn the crudities of the Fascist regimes. Yet the history of the evacuation policy could be an episode from the totalitarian handbook. The resident Japanese minority became the scapegoat of military defeat at Hawaii. Racial prejudices, economic cupidity, and political fortune-hunting became intertwined with patriotic endeavor. In the face of exact knowledge to the contrary, military officials propounded the theory that race determined allegiance. Civil administrators and the national legislature were content to rubber-stamp the military fiat.

Americans in concentration centers at home provided a bitter irony at a time that Americans were fighting for the Four Freedoms abroad. Ideological issues were presented with bleak clarity in World War II. On the one hand, the nation's principal European enemy found energy in a doctrine of racial superiority, and the nation's Asiatic enemy propagandized its cause in terms of the colored races struggling against their white oppressors. On the other hand, the United States took leadership from a President who affirmed "Americanism is not, and never was, a matter of race or ancestry"; the strength of the country was conditioned by the unity of its diverse nationalities; millions of Chinese stood foremost among the nation's allies. The lines were clear cut, and the Japanese minority on the West Coast presented the United States with a magnificent opportunity to confound her enemies on both sides, to lend encouragement to her allies, and to build strength out of the diversity of her minority groups. No opportunity was more completely thwarted. The policy adopted was an affirmation of enemy principles.

The American Civil Liberties Union has called the Japanese evacuation "the worst single wholesale violation of civil rights of American citizens in our history." Later judgment will probably not lower that estimate, though it has already been tempered in historical perspective as abrogated rights have been restored and most Japanese in America have returned with full status to normal life.

Japanese Americans were the immediate victims of the evacuation. But larger consequences are carried by the American people as a whole. Their legacy is the lasting one of precedent and constitutional sanctity for a policy of mass incarceration under military auspices. This is the most important result of the process by which the evacuation decision was made. That process betrayed all Americans.

IDEOLOGY

The Black Revolution: A Primer for White Liberals

CHARLES V. HAMILTON

Among the Americans who have been most confused, distressed, and even disgusted by recent manifestations of the Black Revolution are many of those whites who have traditionally been known as liberals, and who have long been committed to the betterment of race relations and the attainment of civil rights in such fields as employment, education, and housing.

By word and deed, Black Power advocates—and I am one—have brought tension, uncertainty, and pain to the ranks of liberals. A few liberals have become active, outspoken opponents of the Black Revolution. Many are washing their hands entirely of "the race issue." Still others, while maintaining their commitment to civil rights, are plainly perplexed by the new issues raised by black militants.

It is an uncomfortable state of affairs, and one that is often depicted as dangerous to society. Yet I believe that the processes now at work can lead to constructive results—provided we are willing to examine those processes, understand them, and adapt ourselves to the changes that may be necessary.

In attempting to assess, briefly, some aspects of the Black Revolution that have proven so troublesome to white liberals, I will try not to repeat the points made by James Farmer in his article, "Are White Liberals Obsolete in the Black Struggle?" in *The Progressive* for January, 1968. I am in full agreement with those points. My comments will attempt to extend Mr. Farmer's discussion.

White liberals should recognize that their discomfort is well-founded: the Black

Revolution challenges—and, indeed, rejects—many of the values they hold dear. To an extent that even most liberals fail to recognize, these values have been broadly accepted by much (though not all) of American society. They are the values of individual freedom and equality, founded on John Locke's doctrine that man is basically rational, capable of knowing his self-interest and capable of reaching an accommodation based on that self-interest.

In the realm of race relations, these principles are articulated in terms of color-blindness. ("We don't hire on the basis of color; we hire on the basis of merit.") Racial integration is regarded as a highly desirable goal and one that is consciously sought.

Politics, in the liberal tradition, is seen as a protracted process. Men bargain, negotiate, and ultimately reach a compromise. Consensus is presumed, and political conflict is confined to certain predetermined rules of the game. Change is expected to be gradual, and the goal of objectivity is sought. Passion and subjectivity are eschewed. Considerable reliance is placed on discussion, debate—dialogue. There is an assumption that social problems can be resolved, especially if all parties are sincere and work "within the system."

There is an assumption, too, that "law" must be obeyed, and that "law" (meaning, of course, particular legal statutes) is made by legitimate processes. The authority of law-making bodies is not to be questioned; their particular decrees and statutes, perhaps, but not their fundamental authority to issue such decrees and statutes.

If one wishes to change the particular outputs, one does so "legally"—that is, by resort to the courts and the ballot box, primarily, and by pressure group lobbying in the legislature, although this last approach is suspect; it smacks of undue favors and "dirty politics." Liberal concern about "dirty politics" has led to a spate of reforms aimed at democratizing the political process: referendum, initiative, recall; party primaries; blue-ribbon reform candidates; anti-patronage measures. (It has been pointed out too infrequently that many of these liberal reforms have operated against the interests of masses of black people.)

All this is part of the liberal approach to politics in America. And black Americans have for years subscribed to this egalitarian, libertarian orientation. Their goal has been to enter the mainstream of the American polity by pursuing the liberal principle of legitimacy. But after years of fashioning alliances with liberals along these lines, the black masses find themselves confronted with the fact that they have not only failed to improve their condition, but that they have steadily lost ground in relation to the progress of whites.

The various educational systems, in the more liberal North as well as in the South, have failed to come to terms with the cultural (as well as the educational) needs of black children. Northern liberals showed no concern about the deficiencies in textbooks until black parents and students began to call this to their attention. The liberals had assumed the superior efficacy of *their* approach to education, and were convinced it would behoove black children to take advantage of it—even if they had to be bussed across town to do so. It never occurred to those white liberals that their standardized tests might be culturally biased. And even if they were, were not the little black children "culturally disadvantaged," "slow learners," "high risks"?

The liberals never gave much thought to the ultimate effect on black people of years of urban renewal; many were on the faculties of universities using urban renewal to relieve their "land-locked" condition. Some liberal professors raised their voices against the destruction of black neighborhoods. But most of the social scientists, more interested in their methodology and their correlations than in the social product (some call it value-free social science), took no interest in black community participation in urban renewal decision-making.

Today, some of these faculties are trying to rush to relevancy by adding courses dealing with black Americans to their curricula. They are groping to understand the demands of black student groups on the campuses, but many of the white liberal professors now find they are simply not relevant to a vast segment, an important segment, of this society—precisely because *their* (not just the students') education has been blindly incomplete.

Black people have been complaining about police brutality for years, but many white liberals did not get "up tight" about this issue until they began protesting against the war in Vietnam and experiencing the brutality themselves. Anti-war demonstrators have often described police tactics as "'unbelievable," but they have long been quite believable to black people. I would suggest that if those same white liberals were to start protesting this country's policies and practices toward South Africa, they would run up against the same firm billy clubs. (It is most instructive, incidentally, that white liberal America is not overly concerned about the economic support of South Africa's apartheid system offered by interests in this country. But this may become the next liberal fad when the Vietnam war is over.)

The point I want to make is that the white liberals' approach to problems of race in this country has not been as viable as many would like to think. Their agenda simply has not been as enlightened as a first glance would indicate. And this has been the case largely because they have been operating under a principle of legitimacy not particularly applicable to the development of black people. The liberal approach has specific relevance for a relatively secure, relatively "arrived" group, and it is capable of manipulating the system to permit a few to enter—as a few blacks have.

White liberals have never come to terms with the phenomenon of *institutional* racism in this country. It was Stokely Carmichael who broached this subject in the present-day context, and he was *followed* by the President's Commission on Civil Disorders (Kerner Commission). It is small wonder that few black people could get excited about the Commission's report. It merely articulated what many of us had been saying for years, and if many white liberals did not know it, then it is apparent they were operating on a different set of principles and premises.

I am suggesting that black people are pursuing a principle of legitimacy outside the traditional liberal framework—one that is concerned with *group* development, and that does not presume the existence of a consensus, especially on matters regarding race. This principle is very color-conscious. ("We want black principals to head schools in the black communities.") Racial integration is not regarded as a matter of immediate, high priority, because it is recognized that before any group can enter the open society it must first close ranks. Prolonged debate, discussion—dialogue—are luxuries which frequently cannot be afforded.

This principle is most usually associated with a society on the make, with a people coming out from under colonial rule into political independence and economic

development. In the present-day American context, it is manifested in demands for black community control of schools and law enforcement agencies; in such moves as black ownership of businesses in the black community.

Pursuing this principle, black people cannot assume the Lockeian notion of the rationality of man; in fact, in regards to race, they must assume that Western, Anglo-Saxon man might well be irreconcilably irrational. Politics as a protracted process becomes only a frustrating exercise, especially when one realizes the extent to which black people have been *systematically* excluded from decision-making.

The goal of the Black Revolution is development, and those institutions of society which put as much stock in procedure as in performance must be looked upon as obstacles to that goal. When people are excluded from participating, they see political delay in solving their problems as deliberate procrastination and unwillingness to act, not as inevitable, pluralist constraints on institutions.

Black people understand that the best way to pursue the fulfillment of their potentiality is to start from a firm base of self-awareness and identity. When liberals tell them to forget race and think of themselves only as Americans, they know that this is an invitation which only those in power can entertain—an invitation to cultural absorption. And such absorption will occur while other groups in the society protect and maintain their own cultural identity.

It is important to point out that in examining the contrast between liberal values and those of the Black Revolution, I am discussing two principles of *legitimacy:* one is not legitimate and the other illegitimate. Rather, one is more valid than the other for a previously colonized people set on rapid social change and development. The concerns and motivations of such people often simply do not coincide with those of people proceeding under an egalitarian, libertarian principle. Herein, I suggest, lies the major tension between white liberals and advocates of Black Power. Black Power groups must be viewed as new, relevant intermediary groups for a people who no longer trust the established, traditional, frequently liberal-oriented associations.

Should one conclude that black people have more in common with white conservatives than with liberals? Conservatives oppose bussing and are resistant to open housing; they see Black Power as a modern-day extension of Booker T. Washington—a misreading of both Mr. Washington and Black Power. At the same time, Black Power advocates push for community control of the schools (not for integration), and they call for consolidated, unified community groups (not dispersal).

A close examination will reveal, however, that ultimately the advocates of Black Power still have more in common with liberals than with conservatives. The former recognize, for example, the importance of the Federal government's role in the development of black communities—a role as crucial, in its way, as the in-put of external economic resources and technical assistance for the development of previously colonized countries. Conservatives, with their basically anti-centrist and anti-government views (i.e., anti-government for all but themselves), offer no useful partnership to the Black Revolution. They see Black Power as decentralist, when, in fact, it is an effort to build a more meaningful central relationship.

There is nothing irreconcilable about black people pursuing their own principle of legitimacy and subsequently taking their place as full-fledged members of the American pluralist society. This process, in itself, would lead to a vast transformation of the system. I see this process as comparable to new nations of Africa and Asia gaining their political independence, then adopting a particular principle of development and ultimately assuming their places as developed members of the society of nations.

The more dynamic the process of social change and the more we are personally involved in it, the more difficult it is to see such change in its overall, long-term developmental stages—and the easier it is to "lose our cool." But such is the challenge to those who would understand system transformation in a modern, industrial, heterogeneous society and who would create —during that delicate period of transformation—necessary and vital forms of communication and cooperation.

REVOLUTION

A Double Deception: The Problem of Aggression

HOWARD ZINN

This [essay] intends to examine the statement given most frequently by the United States government to the American public as the chief reason for our military action in Vietnam: that we are fighting to defeat "aggression from the North." I will try to show that (1) the conflict is not fundamentally due to "aggression from the North," and (2) the government itself does not believe that this is the reason the United States is in Vietnam. There are two official deceptions involved: the first as to the nature of the war, the second as to the nature of American foreign policy.

In his opening statement of January 28, 1966, before the Senate Foreign Relations Committee, Secretary of State Dean Rusk said: "The heart of the problem in South Vietnam is the effort of North Vietnam to impose its will by force. For that purpose Hanoi has infiltrated into South Vietnam large quantities of arms and tens of thousands of trained and armed men, including units of the North Vietnamese regular army. It is that external aggression, which the North has repeatedly escalated, that is responsible for the presence of United States combat forces." And again in that testimony: "The United States has a clear and direct commitment to the security of South Vietnam against external attack." And again: ". . . we shall do what is necessary to assist the South Vietnamese to repel the aggression against them."

Senator Fulbright was politely suspicious as he began one of those duels in which men of state speak to one another, elliptically, each knowing exactly what is on the other's mind, but never exposing the issue with such clarity that the mass public can really understand—a discussion, in other words, antithetical to democracy and typical of high-level diplomacy.

Fulbright: Could you tell us very briefly, when did we first become involved in Vietnam?

Rusk: That began 1949–1950, Mr. Chairman. . . .

Fullbright: Was France at that time trying to reassert her colonial domination of Vietnam? Was that her objective at that time?

Rusk replied, without answering that question, becoming more muddy as he went along. So that the reader can judge, here is his reply:

I think just at the conclusion of the war, in that part of the world, the first step that was taken was the restoration of the status quo ante bellum in the broadest sense in India, Burma, Malaysia, Indochina, Indonesia, and indeed in part in the Philippines, although the Philippines moved almost immediately for independence. In varying degrees each of these areas became independent from the former colonial country, and in different circumstances.

In the case of France, the first step that was made was to work out something like a commonwealth arrangement, associated states in which France would retain certain authority with respect to defense and foreign affairs. But there was never a firm basis of agreement among most of the Indochinese people themselves; and that moved—it proceeded inevitably and I think properly, toward a more clear independence.

Fulbright did not challenge in Rusk's evasion the false statement of fact on the "first step" of France. (Actually, the "first step" of France was to try a direct military recapture of her former colony, what Jean Lacouture calls "the colonial expedition"; only when this failed did she try a more indirect form of control through the puppet Bao Dai.) And Fulbright did not say bluntly to Rusk that he had not replied to the question; he simply *assumed* that Rusk had answered the question in the affirmative, and went on from there.

Fulbright: . . . but what moved the State Department of our government to assist France to retain her control of Vietnam . . . ?

Rusk: The problem there, sir, was—I am trying my best to remember something which happened quite a few years ago—the problem was not just that, or was not at all that really of assisting France and establishing and reinforcing a colonial position, but to give France a chance to work out its political settlement with these states on the basis of their own independence, and without having Communism as a basic—without giving to the Communists a basic position in Southeast Asia. . . .

Fulbright courteously refrained from a further discussion of France's aims—everybody in the world but Dean Rusk seemed to know that France's aim was precisely "establishing and reinforcing a colonial position." And he did not dissect the double American intention Rusk spoke of (independence *and* avoidance of Communism) by pointing out that this was at the time an impossible task since the leader of the independence movement in Vietnam was also the leader of the Vietnamese Communists: Ho Chi Minh. He went on instead to discuss the extent of United States aid ("I think it was approximately $2 billion," Rusk said) and other matters.

What was implicit in Fulbright's questioning was this: If "external aggression" was the reason for United States intervention, then why had the United States intervened (not with men, because France had 600,000 in Vietnam, but by bearing the main expenses of maintaining those 600,000 French troops) at a time when there was no North and South Vietnam, when there was clearly no "external" aggression, when it was the French vs. the Vietminh in a faintly disguised colonial war?

Rusk was, to put it in nonacademic language, "snowing" the American public, which in the main does not know the history of U.S. involvement in Indochina (indeed, Rusk himself was "trying my best to remember"), but millions of whom were watching the telecast of those hearings. And while there was some clever questioning of Rusk, there was not the kind of direct confrontation of falsehood with truth which people in a democracy deserve to have in the interrogation of government leaders.

Support for the French colonial war had started under Truman and continued under Eisenhower. Eisenhower, in a letter to Winston Churchill of April 4, 1954 (reproduced in Eisenhower's book *Mandate for Change*) wrote:

> Dear Winston: I am sure . . . you are following with the deepest interest and anxiety the daily reports of the gallant fight being put up by the French at Dien Bien Phu. . . . I fear that the French cannot alone see the thing through. . . . And if they do not see it through and Indochina passes into the hands of the Communists the ultimate effect on our and your global strategic position with the consequent shift in the power ratios throughout Asia and the Pacific could be disastrous, and, I know, unacceptable to you and me. . . .

Eisenhower was not talking to the public, but to an ally. He was explaining American support for the French not in any moral terms, like defeating "aggression," but in terms of "global strategic position" and "power ratios." Whatever the validity of Eisenhower's analysis he was candid. Shortly after this letter, Dulles proposed massive American military action to support the French.

It was very clear to all sides, in those years when the United States began its intervention in Indochina, that there was only one party engaging in "external aggression" and "external attack" in Vietnam: the French. And the United States was helping the French, massively, to reestablish control over a former colony. This simple fact of recent history—and this is what Fulbright was getting at in his opening questions—casts huge doubt, to put it moderately, on the administration's claims today that its major reason for being in Vietnam is to "repel the aggression."

From 1950 to 1954, the United States was giving aid to the aggressor in Vietnam. Can anyone with some recollection of recent history believe that if the Vietcong were about to win in South Vietnam—without *any* aid from anywhere else—the United States would keep hands off? Did we keep hands off in other cases where there was clearly no outside aggression—in Guatemala, in Cuba, in the Dominican Republic? Indeed, in Vietnam itself, as we shall see later, the United States had already landed 23,000 combat troops when the infiltration from the North was only a trickle and consisted almost entirely of Southerners.

But Rusk had an enormous television audience watching. And he said:

> If the infiltration of men and arms from the North were not in the picture, these troops of ours could come home; we have said that repeatedly. They went in there, the combat troops went in there because of infiltration of men and arms from the North, and that is the simple and elementary basis for the presence of American combat forces. . . .

Senator Frank Church of Idaho was not satisfied with Rusk's explanation. If it was only the presence of "foreign" soldiers (assuming the North Vietnamese to be "foreign") that caused the American military presence, then why were American troops stationed in South Korea? The following exchange took place:

Church: How many American troops are now stationed in South Korea?
Rusk: In South Korea, I think it is approximately 55,000.
Church: It has been twelve years now, roughly, since the truce, is that correct?
Rusk: Yes, sir, that is correct.
Church: How many Chinese combat troops are stationed in North Korea?
Rusk: I think there are no Chinese there at present. . . .
Church: Very well. We presently have 200,000 American troops in South Vietnam. Indications are that the buildup is going to continue. . . . Supposing that whatever the requirement may turn out to be, our military concentration, our American buildup of military forces in South Vietnam, is finally sufficient to suppress the Vietcong, and to pacify South Vietnam. Would you then think that it is likely to be any easier for us to withdraw from South Vietnam than it has been for us to withdraw from South Korea?
Rusk: . . . Indeed, the only reason for their presence is the infiltration of men and arms from North Vietnam. So the answer to your question would turn on what North Vietnam's conduct and attitude is.
Church: But North Korea hasn't been engaging in that kind of activity in South Korea for many years, has it?
Rusk: No, but you will recall—
Church: But our troops are still in South Korea.

Rusk then did not respond directly to what Church was saying. He simply went on for some length about the history of events in Korea, how a withdrawal there had led to a miscalculation, and then said: "I don't know what the future will hold on this particular point. It would depend a good deal on the general orientation, attitude, and posture of Peking. . . ."

What Church had succeeded in eliciting from Rusk was an indirect admission (but not easy for a television audience to follow carefully) that we maintained military forces in Asian countries *not* because of "aggression," but simply because of the *presence* of China on the Asian continent.

If, as Rusk said, "infiltration of men and arms from the North . . . is the simple and elementary basis for the presence of American combat forces," then it became important to determine how large a part men and arms "from the North" played in the Vietcong operations. Senator Pell questioned Rusk on this:

Pell: As I understand, there are about a quarter of a million Vietcong. What portion of those would be from North Vietnam?
Rusk: I would suppose that 80 percent of those who are called Vietcong are or have been Southerners. . . .
Pell: . . . but would it be a fact that the United States forces in South Vietnam would be about four times the number of those born in North Vietnam who are with the Vietcong and there would be no Chinese in South Vietnam?

Rusk did not respond to Pell's point about about the U.S. forces greatly outnumbering the North Vietnamese in South Vietnam; he confined his response to reiterating the point about no Chinese in South Vietnam. Pell did not press Rusk on this comparison of North Vietnamese and American "outsiders," but said:

This question of whether it is a Vietnamese war or an American war is one that concerns us here. . . . The more you read about it, the more you realize it is really one country, one people, one basic language with various divisions . . . so we have to determine how much of this is a civil war and how much is not.

Later on in the hearings, Senator Church rekindled this issue by pointing to the American Civil War, where the North did actually invade the South, and yet it was called a civil war. Then he said:

> ... Now, in Vietnam you can look at the war in Vietnam as a covert invasion of the South by the North or you can look at it as some other scholars do, as basically an indigenous war in which the North has given a growing measure of aid and abetment but either way you look at it it is a war between Vietnamese to determine what the ultimate kind of government is going to be for Vietnam. When I went to school, that was a civil war. ...

Senator Church's point is crucial, because if it is valid, then the entire government case on "aggression" is demolished. Civil wars and revolutionary wars always involve "aggression" by one side or the other. However, this may be morally justified, as in a revolution against an oppressive regime, or a civil war to end slavery. The use of the term "aggression" to capture American public support for the war in Vietnam invokes a moral principle which has had enormous appeal since the rise of Hitler: that no *nation* should cross the borders of another *nation* to try to take it over.

Vietnam is not only in fact "one country, one people," as Senator Pell said, but this unity was recognized in the Geneva Agreement of 1954, which the United States did not sign, but promised to uphold. The Final Declaration of the Geneva Accords, in Point 6, provided: "... the military demarcation line [the 17th parallel, the line dividing North and South Vietnam] is provisional and should not in any way be interpreted as constituting a political or territorial boundary." So we find the United States first backing Diem in his rejection of unification talks in 1956, and then using the continued separation of North and South as a basis for charging "aggression."

If Vietnam is one country, then no matter how many North Vietnamese are fighting in South Vietnam, they are still Vietnamese, whereas the Americans are not. That would make it a civil war, and not the kind of "aggression" officials have been talking about to justify the American military presence.

Even, however, if North Vietnam and South Vietnam are separate countries, the government has yet to prove its contention that North Vietnam is fundamentally responsible for what appears to be a revolution in the South against an unpopular regime, fighting for several years with local people and local weapons and only beginning to get aid from the North after the United States entered the war in force. On this question, the weight of evidence by scholars and observers is overwhelming:

1. Philippe Devillers, the French historian, author of the standard work on the early stages of the war. *Histoire du Vietnam 1945–1951* (writing in *The China Quarterly*, January-March 1962):

> The point of view of most foreign governments, in the West especially, is that the fighting going on in South Vietnam is simply a subversive campaign directed from Hanoi. The hypothesis is certainly a plausible one ... but it leaves out of account the fact that the insurrection existed before the Communists decided to take part, and that they were simply forced to join in. And even among the Communists, the initiative did not originate in Hanoi, but from the grass roots, where the people were literally driven by Diem to take up arms in self-defense.

2. Bernard Fall, in *The Two Viet-Nams*, referred to a speech by Walt Rostow in which Rostow said: "... the operation run from Hanoi against Viet-Nam is as certain a form of aggression as the violation of the 38th parallel by the North Korean armies in June, 1950." Fall commented:

> ... one might dismiss it as merely another one

of those commencement addresses that most speakers prefer history to forget. But it illustrates the muddled thinking of high Administration officials: The . . . assertion—that North Vietnamese infiltration into South Viet-Nam is the direct equivalent of the North Korean invasion of the ROK—omits the embarrassing fact that anti-Diem guerrillas were active long before infiltrated North Vietnamese elements joined the fray.

3. Jean Lacouture, in *Vietnam Between Two Truces*, writes:

. . . Hanoi claims that it is not intervening in the South, and Washington insists that the battle in the South is an invasion, while in reality it is a rebellion which originated locally but which Hanoi has increasingly supplied. The war originated in the South and is being waged and suffered by the South, although with growing participation by the North.

4. Donald S. Zagoria, a Columbia University specialist on Asian Communism, wrote (*Commentary*, February 1965):

Although the Vietcong does unquestionably get valuable help, training, and assistance from North Vietnam, it is reasonably clear that we are dealing with an indigenous insurrection in the South, and that this, not Northern assistance, is the main trouble.

5. David Halberstam, Vietnam correspondent for *The New York Times*, writing in that newspaper October 27, 1963:

Although much of the articulation for their war and their tactics and their trained cadres comes from Hanoi, this is primarily an indigenous war. The Vietcong manpower is locally recruited.

6. Robert Scigliano, who worked with Michigan State University's Vietnam Advisory Group, a government-connected project in South Vietnam, wrote in *South Vietnam: Nation Under Stress* (1964):

Only a small portion of the Communist military units and agents operating within the Republic of Vietnam has been sent from North Vietnam, and nearly all of these have been Southerners who withdrew to the North after the Geneva Agreements . . . The South Vietnamese government's claim of massive infiltration does not appear to be supported by the available evidence. . . . Similarly, most of the weapons and other supplies available to the Communist forces in the South have been obtained there. . . .

State Department "proof" of Northern aggression rests heavily on the fact that the creation of the National Liberation Front of South Vietnam was approved by the Third National Congress of the Lao Dong (Workers Party) of North Vietnam which met in Hanoi in September 1960. Scigliano talks about the revolt being "launched" and "directed" from North Vietnam, even while saying that Southern men and materials were the basic ingredients of this revolt. Political scientist Robert Scalapino, at the National Teach-In on May 15, 1965 in Washington, said that the Communist Party of South Vietnam, numbering 500, "could not be expected to dominate the 500,000-man Party of the North." (But it didn't have to *dominate* the Lao Dong; all it had to do was participate in the initiation of guerrilla action in the South.)

What the State Department omits from its account, Jean Lacouture reports in his book: that one year before the Hanoi Congress—that is, in 1959—as a result of fraudulent elections, witch-hunts, jailings under the Diem regime, "a guerrilla force began to operate which was probably the first sign of the reactivation of Communist organisms." This was in the northern provinces of South Vietnam. In other places, "at the periphery of the Plain of

Joncs, or in the Transbassac or in the Ben Cat region north of the capital, subversive groups fighting the regime had a primarily nationalist or religious orientation." Then, six months before the Hanoi Congress, in March 1960, there came "the actual birth of the National Liberation Front" when "a group of the old resistance fighters assembled in Zone D, issued a proclamation calling the prevailing situation 'intolerable' for the people as a result of Diem's actions, and called upon patriots to regroup with a view toward ultimate collective action."

Lacouture makes it clear that, far from the Hanoi government's having initiated the rebellion, it had problems of its own and wanted to keep things quiet for a while, but it was pressured by the Southern victims of the Diem regime to at least declare itself on the need for a revolt. The Party Congress in Hanoi did not issue its statement, Lacouture says, "except at the specific demand and under the moral pressure of the militants in the South, who criticized their Northern comrades' relative passivity in the face of the repression exercised against them by the Saigon authorities. . . ."

The historian Devillers goes into greater detail in his article "The Struggle for the Unification of Vietnam" in *The China Quarterly* (referred to above). He traces the revolt back to Diem's "manhunts" in 1957, roundups in 1958 ("A certain sequence of events became almost classical: denunciation, encirclement of villages, searches and raids, arrest of suspects, plundering, interrogations enlivened sometimes by torture . . ."), leading to the start of guerrilla warfare in 1959, and the official establishment of the NLF in December 1960 in the South. He makes it clear that not just Communists, but many non-Communist nationalist elements, were preparing for revolution against the Diem regime; he also refers to the *reluctance* of North Vietnam to become involved.

The United States government's charges of "aggression from the North" simply cannot stand up under examination, and only the general public's impatience with dates and figures enables the deception to be perpetuated for so long. According to the Department of State publication, *Aggression from the North*, 1800 men had infiltrated into South Vietnam from the North by 1960. At this time the United States already had 4000 military in South Vietnam. The State Department claims another 3700 infiltrated in 1961. But in that year, the United States added far more (6000, according to the Mansfield report; 11,000 according to Lacouture). And those "infiltrees" were not only Vietnamese, but they were mostly South Vietnamese returning home to join a revolution begun by fellow Southerners. In 1961 when, according to the State Department, there were a total of 4500 infiltrees from the North, President Kennedy accepted the General Staff recommendation to begin sending 40,000 troops to Vietnam.

Indeed, as late as the Spring of 1964, whatever infiltrees there were coming down were apparently still mainly or wholly Southerners, and most Vietcong weapons were still of local origin. On March 6, 1964, David Halberstam wrote in *The New York Times:* "the war is largely a conflict of Southerners fought on Southern land. No capture of North Vietnamese in the South has come to light, and it is generally believed that most Vietcong weapons have been seized from the South Vietnamese forces." At this time, the United States had at least 23,000 troops in South Vietnam. (The Geneva Accords limited the United States to 685 men, and Johnson in his 1965 State of the Union Address declared that the United States "would stand by the Geneva Agreements of 1954.")

In early 1965 the State Department issued a *White Paper* to document its charges of "aggression from the North." This was so quickly and thoroughly demolished by I. F. Stone's careful appraisal that it was hardly referred to again by administration spokesmen. Its charts and figures *looked* impressive, but when one did all the necessary counting, it turned out to have little substance. The White Paper claimed 19,550 infiltrees from 1959 to 1964, but it could only actually cite 23 infiltrees, and a check of the provinces these were born in indicates that only six were Northerners. Stone showed that the 179 captured Vietcong weapons listed by the White Paper as having come from Communist countries outside Vietnam were about 2 percent of the total number of weapons captured.

After Senator Mansfield's committee visited Vietnam it reported to the Committee on Foreign Relations in January 1966 that there were 14,000 North Vietnamese regular troops out of a total Vietcong strength of 230,000—that is, about 6 percent. At this time, there were 170,000 United States troops in Vietnam, or more than ten times the number of North Vietnamese. Indeed, there were in South Vietnam more troops from South Korea (21,000) than from North Vietnam, according to the Mansfield Report.

What was clear by 1966, when United States troops totaled 300,000, is that the United States had taken over the bulk of military operations from the South Vietnamese government, while the Vietcong, though receiving more help from North Vietnam, remained overwhelmingly a guerrilla army of Southerners. A *New York Times* dispatch of March 2, 1966, said that the flow of supplies to the Vietcong from North Vietnam had been averaging 12 to 30 tons a day, while the United States was moving, every day, 24,000 tons of supplies by ship alone "plus an undisclosed amount by air."

To use the relatively small amount of aid given the Vietcong by North Vietnam, or the weapons now increasingly coming to them from Communist countries, as evidence of "outside aggression" would be to deny the whole history of revolutions, which almost always have received help from the outside. Without French military aid, the American revolution might not have succeeded. Ninety percent of the gunpowder used by the colonists in the first few months of the war came from abroad. The culminating victory of the Revolutionary War at Yorktown was due in large part to the French fleet under Admiral de Grasse, and to 7800 French troops joining the 9000 Americans. On July 2, 1957, John F. Kennedy (speaking on the Senate floor about the revolution in Algeria) said: "Most political revolutions, including our own, have been buoyed by outside aid in men, weapons, and ideas."

The indigenous strength of the Vietcong is no longer open to serious dispute (the Mansfield Report shows that from 1962 to 1963, when 14,000 North Vietnamese joined the fray, over 100,000 men joined from the South). What is in doubt today is the indigenous nature of the force attempting to put down the Vietcong. During the Diem regime, and perhaps for two years after that, it could be said that South Vietnamese government forces, although equipped and financed almost entirely by the United States and augmented by American troops, were trying to defeat the Vietcong guerrillas. But they were failing. The hollowness of the South Vietnam government became more and more apparent. Its large conscripted army would not fight. A news dispatch of January 1965 indicated that 30 percent of the government's draftees deserted in six weeks. Over 100,000 deserted in the year 1965. The regime, unlike the guerrillas, did not have popular support.

By 1966, with American casualties exceeding South Vietnamese government casualties, with American planes filling the skies, with American equipment pouring in, with 300,000 United States troops engaging in most of the offensive operations, with $2 billion spent each month to conduct the war—and with the Ky regime tottering, able to stave off rebellion only in a brutal show of force abetted by the United States—this had become an American war. The South Vietnamese knew this. The demonstrations that took place in Saigon, Danang, Hué, were anti-American, with banners: "Americans Must Cease Interfering in Vietnamese Affairs" and "Stop Killing Our People." *The New York Times* reported on April 23, 1966 "resentment of the United States presence in many areas of South Vietnam."

The evidence points to a conclusion most Americans find distasteful: that the United States, by 1966, had taken on the French burden in Vietnam and, with a shadow government as a front, was putting down a nationalist-Communist revolution with the classic ferocity of a Western imperial power. Almost everybody in the world but Americans could see that, whatever the character of the Vietcong, they were Vietnamese, while the Americans, destroying land and people on a frightening scale, were the only ones who matched the accusation of "outside aggression."

Neither the history of events in South Vietnam nor the history of American policy outside South Vietnam supports the argument that the defeat of "aggression" is the reason for the U.S. military presence there. But it is an appealing one for presentation to mass television audiences. The administration does not really expect to deceive the informed minority in the country with this argument, just as it does not really expect them to believe that we are fighting for "freedom" in defending the Ky government, its predecessors and its successors. These are perimeter defenses, intended to discourage all but the truly obstinate questioners. When these are breached, then the officialdom falls back on the kind of argument that Dean Rusk gave to the House Foreign Affairs Committee, August 3, 1965: "The loss of Southeast Asia to the Communists would constitute a serious shift in the balance of power against the interests of the free world. And the loss of South Vietnam would make the defense of the rest of Southeast Asia much more costly and difficult." (Robert Scigliano reports, in *South Vietnam: Nation Under Stress:* "As American officials are wont to say in nonpublic pronouncements, Vietnam is a piece of real estate that must be held by the West.")

The United States government really doesn't care very much about "aggression from the North." It doesn't care deeply about "freedom" in South Vietnam. It doesn't care whether or not the revolution conducted by the guerrillas of the Vietcong is indigenous or not, idealistic or not, popular or not. What it does care about is that this revolution is a *Communist* revolution, which threatens to bring about, at the least, a Communist-dominated South Vietnam, or—more likely—a unified Communist Vietnam.

While the United States sometimes refers to this among other reasons, it does not like to put the problem so boldly and simply, even though almost all Americans are anti-Communist, because a fearful thing is implied: that wherever there is a Communist revolution imminent anywhere in

the world (and there are a number of countries where such a revolution could break out), the United States feels driven to take whatever action is necessary to prevent it or destroy it. And this makes of us what Rusk told the Foreign Relations Committee we would *not* be: "the gendarmes of the universe."

It is not just that 12 million more people would live under Communist rule. How serious a change can that be in a world where a billion people already live under such rule? And there is no persuasive evidence to indicate that the Vietnamese would be worse off under Ho Chi Minh than they have been under Diem or Ky; indeed, the lower classes—and most Vietnamese are peasants—would probably be better off. As Neil Sheehan, a troubled supporter of the American presence, wrote on returning from three years in Vietnam as a *New York Times* correspondent: "In Vietnam, only the Communists represent revolution and social change, for better or worse according to a man's politics."

The problem Rusk and Johnson and McNamara and both Bundys have said, is that a Communist Vietnam would (as Rusk put it) "constitute a serious shift in the balance of power." Not because of the shift in the tiny country of Vietnam. But because, as Johnson said at Johns Hopkins: "Let no one think for a moment that retreat from Vietnam would bring an end to conflict. The battle would be renewed in one country and then another." A Communist Vietnam would lead to a Communist Southeast Asia. A Communist Southeast Asia would lead to Communism developing in other parts of the world. And this would lead, as Rusk suggested in a speech of April 23, 1965, to the American Society of International Law, "to the eventual communization of the entire world."

This is the argument, often referred to as the "domino theory" or the "Munich analogy," that we need to examine now, because in one form or another it is accepted not only by Administration supporters; it is also accepted by many who believe we should halt our damaging offensive actions in Vietnam, while retaining our military presence there. It is, then, the chief argument against complete military withdrawal.

GLOSSARY*

Aboriginal (anthro.)—referring to the earliest known Homo sapiens inhabitants of a given area, or to the native population inhabiting a given area when European explorers and colonists first discovered it.

Adaptation (psych.) (anthro.)—the process of acquiring fitness to live in a given environment. Commonly, and most correctly, the term is applicable to changes in morphological traits of the physical body.

Adjustment (soc.)—the condition of being satisfied with one's social roles and statuses; the acceptance of conditions as they are.

Afferent nerves (psych.)—nerve fibers that carry impulses from the sense organs of the skin, viscera and muscles to the brain.

Analysis of (Co)variance (psych.)—a statistical technique which allows one to evaluate and control the relationship of one variable to another.

Anticipatory reinforcement (psych.)—the anticipation that a pleasant state of affairs will occur.

Apartheid (pol. sci.)—a policy of strict racial segregation and discrimination against the native Negroes and other colored peoples.

*The disciplines in parenthesis indicate those sections in which the concepts first appeared.

Arbitrage (econ.)—buying bills of exchange or stocks in one market and selling them at a profit in another market.

Archaeology (anthro.)—the systematic study of early or primitive cultures, especially as manifested by their artifacts, for the purpose of reconstructing and understanding their ways of life.

Assimilation (psych.)—the process by which people from different cultures who come into contact with each other lose their unique cultural identities and are merged into a homogeneous cultural unit different from any of the original components.

Association (soc.)—a process of interaction usually referring to the process whereby new groups are formed, or group cohesion is strengthened. A number of formally organized people who are bound together by the fact that they are seeking some objective.

Attention (psych.)—the focusing on one segment of experience while ignoring others.

Attitude (soc.)—a construct which refers to either a learned tendency to think or act in a certain evaluative way toward a specific object, person, idea or situation or a learned state of muscular readiness toward something before it is encountered.

Authoritarianism (pol. sci.)—the view that group interests are best achieved and

511

best served through the arbitrary and unlimited exercise of power by the agents of government.

Authority (soc.)—power or rule in a social or political gorup.

Autonomic activity (psych.)—referring to that part of the human organism which is concerned with carrying on the vital processes. It includes the viscera with their involuntary muscles and nervous system as distinct from the higher brain centers and striped muscles having to do with reasoning and movement.

Aversive stimuli (psych.)—unpleasant events that the organism wants to avoid.

Avoidance responses (Avoidance behavior) (psych.)—behavior aimed at avoiding or preventing unpleasant ends.

Behavior (individual and group) (soc.)—the acquired manner in which a human being acts in a given situation as a result of his previous individual or group association.

Behavioral inhibitions (psych.)—learned reactions that inhibit selected actions.

Behavioral sciences—the sciences concerned with the study of behavior. Often considered the same as Social Sciences.

Beliefs (anthro.)—those propositions which are accepted by a person as true.

Benefit-Cost Analysis (econ.)—evaluation of the desirability of a certain action by a careful comparison of all costs to be incurred with the benefits to be enjoyed.

Binary-choice (psych.)—a situation in which any two alternatives are available (e.g., yes-no, right-left).

Bureaucracy (soc.)—an organization that has a graded hierarchy of officials, each of whom is responsible to his superior; and where the various tasks and activities are allocated to individuals or groups on the basis of specialties and expertise.

Capital (econ.)—material objects used in the production of goods or the rendering of economic services; accumulated resources or skills available for use in the production process.

Capitalism (econ.)—an economic system of producing and distributing wealth in which the spirit of the system favors (1) the widespread private ownership of the means of production by individuals, or groups of individuals and (2) individual initiative in business enterprise primarily for private profit, and at private risk.

Caste(s) (anthro.)—rigid class distinction based on birth, wealth, or any arbitrary factor operating as a social system or principle.

Charismatic (soc.)—pertaining to a spiritual gift, designating extraordinary merit, grace, genius or power in a personality.

Chronology (anthro.)—the arrangement of events, dates, etc., in the order of occurrence. (Used mostly in archaeology.)

Class(es) (anthro.)—an aggregate of people who have the same status, rank, or common characteristic in a given society.

Cliques (soc.)—small, informal, often highly cohesive, non-kinship primary groups, whose members have about the same status.

Cognitive processes (psych.)—a general phrase indicating the components of thought and including memory, perception, reasoning and evaluation.

Cognitive transformations (psych.)—hypothetical processes in which a rule, concept, or idea is changed into a derivative cognitive construct.

Collective bargaining (econ.)—negotiations between an employer and representatives of workers organized into a union.

Collectivism (econ.)—the theory or practice of political and economic organization whereby all the people in a community collectively own the means of production and control the distribution of goods.

Colonialism (pol. sci.)—the system or policy whereby a country maintains foreign colonies for exploitative purposes.

Commodity (econ.)—an item commonly desired by consumers, or an item which serves as an input into the production of goods desired by consumers.

Communication (anthro.)—the process of making common or exchanging subjective states such as ideas, sentiments, beliefs, usually by means of language, though also by visual representation, imitation and suggestion.

Communism (econ.)—a socio-economic system based upon the principle of public ownership of and control of all capital and consumer goods, and no private property.

Community (soc.)—A sub-group with a territorial area, a degree of interpersonal acquaintance and contact, and some basis for coherence that separates it from neighboring groups. The totality of feelings and attitude that binds people into a group.

Competition (econ.)—the struggle for the possession or use of limited goods.

Concept (psych.)—the representation of a set of events or attributes that are common across a variety of experiences or objects.

Conditioned emotional responses (psych.)—a learned reaction involving the autonomic nervous system which has been conditioned to a stimulus.

Conditioned stimulus (psych.)—a stimulus that has gained the power to elicit a response through pairing the stimulus with the response.

Conglomerate (econ.)—a large corporation formed by the merger of a number of companies in unrelated, widely diversified industries.

Connotations (psych.)—indirect and metaphorical implications of a word (e.g., the connotations of "dictator" include ideas of power, cruelty and authority).

Consensus (pol. sci.)—an opinion or sentiment held by all or most of the people in a given group.

Consumer goods (econ.)—material objects used to satisfy immediately and/or directly some human want, need or desire.

Consumption (soc.) (econ.)—the use of goods or services in the satisfaction of human wants.

Contingencies (psych.)—the quality or condition of something that may or may not happen; being subject to accident or chance.

Corporate State (econ.)—a politico-economic organization whereby the state can be thought of as one large corporation, consisting primarily of large industrial organizations plus non-profit institutions like foundations, and the educational system, with government providing coordination and a variety of needed services.

Correlation (soc.)—the degree by which change in one variable is accompanied by corresponding change in another variable.

Cortical evoked potential (psych.)—a form of brain wave that is measured when a stimulus is presented.

Cost (econ.)—undesired actions or sacrifices which must be incurred if some objective is to be attained. (See **Opportunity Cost**.)

Cost accounting (econ.)—a system for recording, analyzing and allocating production and distribution costs.

Coup d'état (pol. sci.)—a sudden forceful stroke in politics, especially the sudden forceful overthrow of a government.

Covariation (psych.)—the degree to which two variables are related in a lawful way.

Crisis of legitimacy (pol. sci.)—a situation in which there is a lack of "political" legitimacy.

Critical period (moment) (psych.)—the period of time in development when certain events must occur if a physiological or psychological process is to develop normally.

Cue (psych.)—a stimulus that guides behavior often without entering consciousness.

Cultural anthropology (anthro.)—the branch of anthropology which studies the cultures of societies.

Cultural relativity (anthro.)—the point of view in which each cultural group is evaluated in terms of its own value system.

Culture (anthro.)—all of the socially meaningful conduct that is learned and shared in a particular society, such as customs, norms, language, economic and political beliefs, art, etc., plus all of the man-made material goods that have a social meaning.

Culture change (anthro.)—any modification in the modes of thinking or acting in a society.

Culture traits (anthro.)—a construct which refers to the simplest element in a culture: a way of using a culture object, a social norm, a social attitude and so on.

Curvilinear (psych.)—a relationship between two variables that is non-linear; usually a U or ∩ shape.

Defense mechanism (psych.)—a psychological device, usually unconscious, that is used by a person to justify his own behavior and avoid feelings of inadequacy.

Deflation (econ.)—the falling ratio between the available money supply and the available supply of goods, which serves to increase the purchasing power of money. Generally characterized by falling prices, usually accompanied by increased unemployment.

Dendrochronology (anthro.)—the technique of dating the age of archaeological items by use of tree rings.

Denotative (psych.)—the explicit or dictionary definition of a word or concept.

Desensitization therapy (psych.)—a form of psychotherapy in which anxiety, fears and inhibitions are extinguished through gradual presentation of the feared event or thing.

Deviant behavior (Deviance) (soc.)—a departure from or non-conformity with the norms of a society, or a given group within the society.

Deviant groups (soc.)—individuals who share behavior that departs from the norms of a society or group. These groups are often highly organized groups with deviant norms that are transmitted to other persons and which may result in stable deviant organizations.

Dialect (anthro.)—a specific variety of a language with sufficient differences in pronunciation, grammar and vocabulary to be considered a distinct entity, but not distinct enough from other dialects to constitute a separate language.

Diffusion (anthro.)—the spreading of culture traits, by borrowing or migration, from one cultural group to another.

Discount (econ.)—(1) a deduction from a stated price; (2) the bank's deduction of a certain amount of interest from a loan in advance of its use by the borrowers; (3) to take into present consideration the expected effects which future events will have on an item or action.

Discrepant (psych.)—an event that resembles but is not identical with some familiar event.

Disinhibitory (psych.)—the process by which an event temporarily interrupts an inhibitory process.

Divided sovereignty (pol. sci.)—a situation in which several groups have overlapping decision-making power.

Due process of law (pol. sci.)—the course of legal proceedings established by the legal system of a nation or state to protect individual rights and liberties.

Dysfunctional (psych.)—functioning abnormally or incompletely.

Economic indicators (econ.)—indicators of the current state of the economy, such as prices, wages, and unemployment figures.

Efficiency (econ.)—the ability to produce a desired effect, product, etc., with a minimum of effort, expense, or waste.

Egalitarianism (pol. sci.)—(1) the view that everyone, regardless of wealth, social status, race, nationality or sex should have the same political rights and (2) the view which assumes that each socio-economic class in a given society, and each race or ethnic group in the world, has the same relative proportions of genius, talent, mediocrity and defectiveness.

Eidetic (psych.)—mental images that are unusually vivid and almost photographically exact.

Electroencephalogram (psych.)—a tracing showing the changes in electrical potential produced by the brain.

Emotion (Emotional states) (psych.)—the interrelationship between distinctive external events and strong, salient, internal feelings.

Enervated (psych.)—deprived of strength; weakened physically, mentally or morally.

Entrepreneur (econ.)—a person who organizes and manages a business undertaking, assuming the risk for the sake of profit.

Epinephrine-induce (psych.)—a chemical produced by the body that is secreted during stress or excitement.

Ethical value system of a society (pol. sci.)—the group norms of a society which have to do with morals and standards of conduct.

Ethos (soc.)—beliefs and values about the conduct of persons and the general ways community life should be structured.

Evolution (anthro.)—the process of gradual change which carries the implication that each stage is dependent on the preceding stage.

Exchange (econ.)—a transaction in which

individuals voluntarily trade one or more items which they own (including money) for one or more items owned by others.

Expectations (soc.)—attitudes and beliefs about how individuals will behave in given roles.

Extended family (anthro.)—a large family unit of three or more generations related along the male or female line who live in a large single dwelling or a cluster of houses.

Family (anthro.) (soc.)—the basic social institution of one or more men living with one or more women in a socially-sanctioned and more or less enduring sex relationship with socially-recognized rights and obligations, together with their offspring.

Fascism (pol. sci.)—any of the related philosophies of political and economic organization which insist on a centralized, all-powerful and unimpeachable political authority which would have total control over the schools, the press, and other communications media, as well as commerce and all the important industries.

Fear (psych.)—a state marked by unpleasant feelings, usually elicited by expectations of harm or conflict.

Fixation time (psych.)—duration of time a person looks at a visual stimulus.

Formal structures (soc.)—the explicit pattern of relationships in a group or organization that outline the behavior and relationships of persons. These are often stated in laws, regulations, and other documents.

Functional (anthro.)—a special form of responsibility, which is the normal or characteristic action of a particular part of a whole, the performance of the particular activity being what distinguishes that part from other parts or the whole.

Futures price (econ.)—the price at which an item is expected to sell on a specified date in the future.

Ganglion potentials (psych.)—electrical potentials generated by a coherent collection of nerve cells.

Garnishment (econ.)—a notice ordering a person not to dispose of a defendant's property or money in his possession pending settlement of a lawsuit.

Generalization of extinction (psych.)—the tendency for classes of similar responses to decrease in occurrence to classes of similar stimuli.

Generation (anthro.)—a single state or degree in the succession of natural descent.

Genetic drift (anthro.)—the tendency for an isolated group of people to develop distinctive physical features over a period of generations, which would tend to make them physically different from other descendants of their ancestral progenitors.

Genus (anthro.)—a classification of plants or animals with common distinguishing characteristics: the main subgroup of the family; a small group of closely related species or a single species.

Goals (cultural goals) (anthro.)—an objective or purpose to be attained and toward the achievement of which policies and procedures are directed.

Gresham's Law (econ.)—in a bimetallic monetary system, it is the tendency for metallic money that is overvalued at the mint (compared to its open market value) to drive out of circulation the metallic money that is undervalued at the mint (compared to its open market value).

Gross National Product (GNP) (econ.)—the value of all the goods and services produced by the nation's labor force before deductions for depreciation, loss, obsolescence or use of capital.

Group (soc.)—two or more people between whom there is an established pattern of interaction; recognized as an entity by its own members and usually by others because of its particular type of collective behavior.

Holding company (econ.)—a corporation which controls enough of the stock of one or more other companies to control their business policies.

Human capital (econ.)—the skills and knowledge which an individual has acquired and which are useful in the production process.

Hypnotic regression (psych.)—the process by which a person is induced to think and act like a child during hypnotic trances.

Identification (psych.)—a psychological process in which a person believes that he or she shares psychological or physical similarities with another and experiences vicariously events that occur to the other.

Ideology (pol. sci.)—the aggregate of the ideas, beliefs, and modes of thinking characteristic of a group, such as a nation, class, caste, profession, religious sect or political party.

Imagery (psych.)—mental images as produced by memory or imagination or descriptions and figures of speech.

Imperialism (econ.)—a national policy and practice of expansion and control of foreign lands in order to exploit their natural resources, and to bind them politically and economically to the dominating country.

Impulse control (psych.)—restraining the tendency to act involuntarily and without reflection.

Incentive (psych.)—something that stimulates or encourages one to take action.

Inflation (econ.)—any upward movement of the price level.

Informal structure (soc.)—the pattern of relationships in a group or structure that is developed without reference to explicit, i.e., legal or otherwise formal agreements.

Installment contract (econ.)—an agreement of consumer credit allowing the buyer to have possession of an article by making a small initial payment and paying the remainder of the price in periodic payments until the sale price is entirely paid.

Institutions (soc.)—the social norms and standardized practices which are performed by special functionaries or by a permanently organized group of people to meet and fulfill continuous human and social needs.

Interest groups (pol. sci.)—a group of persons who are organized to realize certain goals.

Interest rate (econ.)—the amount of payment for the use of money.

Interpretation (psych.)—a person's conception of a subject.

Intonation pattern (anthro.)—the way in which words or phrases are stressed or accentuated by a speaker.

Judicial review (pol. sci.)—the power of a court to judge whether or not a given piece of legislation, or a given executive action, is consistent with the constitution.

Justice (pol. sci.)—the use of authority and power to uphold what is right, just, or lawful.

Kinship (soc.) (anthro.)—the relationship among people that exists because of genetic descent or marriage.

Labor (econ.)—(1) any skilled or unskilled work that is done for another person for a wage, as distinct from salaried employment, (2) any human effort to create an economic good or provide a service for the purpose of acquiring an income.

Land (econ.)—the natural resources of an area which exist with no expenditure of human labor.

Language (anthro.)—a system of sounds, symbols and concepts together with rules for their organization which permits communication about specific objects, actions, or ideas.

Legitimacy (pol. sci.)—the acceptance of the existing political institutions as right and proper by most of its citizens.

Leisure (soc.) (econ.)—free time that is not spent in working, eating, resting, illness, or idleness; a time of diversion from work and routine responsibilities.

Libertarianism (pol. sci.)—(1) the philosophical view that man has a free will and (2) the political philosophy which favors extending or liberalizing the political rights of individuals.

Liberty (pol. sci.)—the sum of rights and exemptions possessed in common by the people of a community or state.

Lien (econ.)—a claim on the property of another as security for the payment of a just debt.

Life cycle (anthro.)—the major transition points in all people's lives, for example, birth, marriage, and death.

Light-dark contrast (psych.)—the change in light flux produced by the border of light-dark areas or lines.

Linguistics (anthro.)—the study of the origins, structures, and changes of language.

Macroscopic studies (soc.)—studies of large-scale social organizations such as the community, societies, the military system, etc. as opposed to the study of small groups or of individuals.

Market (econ.)—a facility in which potential buyers and potential sellers are brought together to negotiate transactions.

Marriage (anthro.)—the legal partnership between a man and a woman.

Mean performance (psych.)—the average performance of a group or person.

Meaningless stimulus (psych.)—an event that has no meaning to a person.

Median (psych.)—the exact middle case in an odd number of cases; in an even number of cases, it is the point between two equal halves of the array.

Memory engram (psych.)—the constant that summarizes what is registered in memory following an experience.

Merger (econ.)—a combining of existing corporations wherein one corporation buys up all the stock of the other corporations, dissolving them, and assuming ownership of their assets.

Metaphor (psych.)—a concept that indirectly symbolizes another idea.

Middleman (econ.)—a trader who buys commodities from the producer and sells them to the retailer, or sometimes, directly to the consumer.

Migration (anthro.)—the deliberate movement of people from one place to another, definite destination.

Military industrial complex (econ.)—an alleged collaboration between the Department of Defense and some segments of the business community whereby business uses its political influence to assure the appropriation of large sums of money for the military, and the military in turn spends these funds with the businesses in question.

Modeling trials (psych.)—a study according to a certain set of specifications, or model.

Monopoly (econ.)—exclusive or near-exclusive control, possession of, or access to a commodity or service permitting the regulation of its supply, distribution and price by one enterprise.

Monosyllabic behavior (anthro.)—talking with a vocabulary of one syllable words.

Motive (psych.)—the mental representation of a desired event.

Mutation (anthro.)—a sudden variation in a certain important characteristic or characteristics by the offspring from its parents.

Myth (anthro.)—an authorless, unverifiable and usually picturesque traditional story about the origin and meaning of things and events which are important to people.

National income (econ.)—the total income of all the citizens of a state in the form of profits, salaries, wages, rents, dividends, interest, etc., during a specified time.

Norm (soc.)—a rule for conduct.

Nuclear family (anthro.)—the husband, wife, and their offspring.

Occipital neurons (psych.)—nerve cells in the visual area of the brain which are located in the back part of the skull.

Oligopoly (econ.)—the control of a market by a few competing producers or suppliers each of whom can influence the price of a given commodity to some extent.

Ontogenetically (psych.)—pertaining to the life cycle of a single organism.

Opportunity cost (econ.)—the goods, services, or activities which must be foregone in order to provide some other good or service.

Orienting reflex (psych.)—a postural and autonomic reaction that occurs when a person becomes suddenly aware of a new event.

Paradigm (psych.) (anthro.)—a pattern, example or model.

Participant observation (soc.)—a method of research by which a researcher becomes a participating member of the group or community which he intends to study; as an accepted insider, he studies the activities of those around him.

Personal adjustment (soc.)—the condition of being in harmonious relationship or satisfied with one's social roles and statuses.

Glossary 519

Personality (psych.) (anthro.)—the functional integration of all the learned behavior of an individual arising out of his roles in various groups which makes him a unique person; it is a construct that includes the person's goals, attitudes, opinions, habits, moral ideas, and his conceptions and evaluations of himself.

Personality factors (psych.)—basic dimensions of personality.

Pharmacologically aroused (psych.)—altered states of arousal produced by drugs.

Phobic (psych.)—pertaining to a persistent, irrational, and uncontrollable fear which has a neurotic origin.

Phonemes (anthro.)—a set of phonetically similar but slightly different sounds in a language that are heard as the same sound by native speakers and are represented in phonemic transcription by the same symbol.

Physical Anthropology (anthro.)—the study of the biological origins of and the variability among, the hominids.

Planned Economy (econ.)—an economy in which a central agency decides how the economy's resources will be used.

Pluralism (pluralistic society) (pol. sci.)—(1) the existence within a nation or society of groups distinctive in ethnic origin, cultural patterns, religion, or the like (2) a policy of favoring the preservation of such groups within a given nation or society.

Political socialization (pol. sci.)—the process whereby the different political beliefs and practices of society are passed on from generation to generation.

Politically traumatized (pol. sci.)—the state of being immobilized politically and of the opinion that little change will occur politically.

Polyandry (anthro.)—a form of polygamy in which a woman may legally have two or more husbands at the same time.

Polygamy (anthro.)—a form of marriage in which one partner has more than one spouse.

Polygyny (anthro.)—a form of polygamy in which a man may legally have two or more wives at the same time.

Population (anthro.)—an aggregate of individuals defined with reference to spatial location, political status, ancestry, or other specific conditions, like time.

Poverty (econ.)—the absence of some culturally determined minimal quantity of material resources.

Power elite (econ.)—an imprecisely defined group of individuals who, through their wealth, their formal or informal political strength, or their positions of leadership or influence in key institutions of society, are felt to be able to exert considerable influence over the organization and operation of that society.

Practices (anthro.)—what people do in contrast to what they believe.

Price structure (econ.)—the relationship between the monetary values attached to goods, services, and resources within an economy.

Primary group (soc.)—a group whose members generally have face to face, physical contact with each other.

Private property (rights) (econ.)—the exclusive right of a person or group to control and use wealth as they choose. It implies legally recognized ownership as well as possession.

Proactive interference (psych.)—the process

by which an event in the future interferes with recall of an event in the past.

Production possibility boundary (or curve) (econ.)—a graphic representation which attempts to illustrate, via geometric symbolism, the alternative output mixes which an economy can achieve with its given resources and technology.

Production (theory) (econ.) (soc.)—the sum total of the processes involved in the creative phase of the self-maintenance of society. The extraction of raw materials from the land, and the conversion of them by the application of labor, capital, and organization into forms useful to man, either as production goods or consumption goods, with the latter as the final objective. An explanation of the process which allocates the society's resources among the various goods whose production is possible, and which determines how these resources will be combined to achieve this production.

Projective (psych.)—describing the tendency to assign to others one's own attitudes, wishes, fears and characteristics.

Property (econ.)—ownership of a thing or things; the right to possess, use, and dispose of something.

Psychodrama (soc.)—the technique of analyzing and dealing with personal problems by having the patient act out his difficulties before an analyst.

Psycholinguistics (psych.)—the study of the psychological factors involved in the perception of and response to linguistic phenomena.

Psychopathology (psych.)—the study of the causes and development of mental disorders.

Race (anthro.)—any group of people having the same features, ancestry, family, lineage, etc.

Racialism (pol. sci.)—a doctrine of teaching, without scientific support, that claims to find racial differences in character, intelligence, etc. that asserts the superiority of one race over another.

Random sample (soc.)—a sample derived in a systematic manner so that each case in the sample is selected purely by chance.

Receptor surface (psych.)—sense organs which receive stimuli.

Recognition (psych.)—identification of some person or thing as having been known or seen before.

Recognition techniques (psych.)—the technique of applying recognition of things or events to determine memory capability.

Reinforcement ratio (psych.)—the ratio of the number of reinforcements to the total number of responses made.

Religiocentric (soc.)—relationships or organizations in which a dominant role is played by religion, and where persons usually distinguish each other on the basis of religion.

Repossession (econ.)—the act of taking back from a buyer a thing for which he has failed to make payments.

Representation (pol. sci.)—the fact of representing or being represented in a political process or decision-making situation.

Revolution (soc.) (pol. sci.)—a sweeping, sudden and comprehensive change in the basic practices and ideas of an institution or society.

Ritual (anthro.)—an act, allowing of no deviation, which symbolizes a complex popular attitude, and which is performed only on certain extraordinary occasions.

Role (soc.)—the function or expected behavior of an individual in a group, usually defined by the group or culture.

Role conflict (soc.)—role relationships between individuals where the norms for the role occupants are not congruent, and do not mesh.

Role model (soc.)—a person who serves as an example for others.

Role playing (soc.)—the act of doing what is expected of one because one holds a certain position in a given group or society.

Satiated (psych.)—having had enough or more than enough.

Scarcity (econ.)—the fact that something does not exist in sufficient quantity to permit its free and unrestricted use by all who wish to use it.

Schema, Schemata (pl.) (psych.)—an abstract representation of experience.

Secondary group (soc.)—A group whose members generally have only formalized or institutionalized interaction with each other.

Segregation (soc.)—the practice of restricting or setting apart racial and cultural groups in a population either by conscious social purpose or by unconscious use of personal and cultural influences.

Self-determination (pol. sci.)—the right of a people to decide upon its own political status or form of government without outside influence.

Semantics (anthro.)—the study of meaning.

Semi-participant observation approach (soc.)—a researcher who looks at social phenomena from the outside, as opposed to the inside.

Sex (anthro.)—physical characteristics that distinguish male and female.

Significant (psych.)—meaningful.

Social adjustment (soc.)—(1) those types of relationship between personalities, groups, culture elements, and culture complexes which are harmonious and mutually satisfactory to the personalities and groups involved. (2) those processes which tend to produce such relationships.

Social behavior (soc.) (anthro.)—human activity which occurs in response to the conduct of others, or which is meant to stimulate meaningful responses in others.

Social change (soc.)—any variation, modification or change in the ideas, norms, values, social roles, and social habits of a people or in the composition or organization of their society.

Social class (soc.)—Groups of individuals ordered vertically and valued differently because of their characteristics or behavior.

Social control (soc.)—the sum total of the means by which society makes its individuals and groups conform to the avowed social norms. Control may be institutionalized or informal, and its two main forms are coercive control and persuasive control.

Social disorganization (soc.)—a situation in which behaviors and conditions that exist are rooted in the goals and aspirations of a few individuals rather than linked to the social norms of the community.

Social distance (soc.)—reserve or constraint between individuals or groups of people because of cultural, racial, religious, economic or other differences.

Social group (soc.) (anthro.)—a number of persons between whom exists a psychic interaction and who are set apart by that interaction in their own minds and in those of others as a recognized entity.

Social institution (soc.)—the sum total of the patterns, relations, processes, and material instruments built up around any major social interest.

Social organization (soc.)—(1) a social group, or society; (2) the organization of society into an interrelated hierarchy of groups and status levels; (3) the process whereby all the groups and persons in a society cooperate in their willingness to give allegiance to their value system; (4) the condition in which there is a high degree of order and integration (singleness of purpose) in the social practices, values, and ideologies in a society, with a minimum of ambiguity and conflict among them; (5) the customary, and regular relationships among people; the regular ways that people usually behave toward each other.

Social processes (soc.)—social changes or interactions in which by abstraction a common pattern can be observed or named.

Social psychology (soc.)—the study of the individual in relation to his group behavior and social relationships.

Social relations (Social relationships) (soc.)—the interactions of persons that take place with some purpose and which are guided by a set of norms.

Social Sciences—the general disciplines which deal with the behavior of people, their interactions and the environment they share.

Social stratification (soc.)—(1) the arrangement of societal elements into groups along different (usually vertical) dimensions, (2) the establishment of status in terms of varying superiority and inferiority.

Social structure (soc.)—(1) the orderly organization of the social roles and statuses in a society; (2) any degree of regularity in the way that people act toward each other in a given group.

Socialism (econ.)—any of the social philosophies or idea-systems which are based on the principle of collective ownership of all productive property and natural resources.

Socialization (soc.) (anthro.)—the process of developing a personality; it refers to the way that people learn the habits, attitudes, social roles, self-conceptions, group norms and universes of discourse that enable them to interact with other people in their society.

Society (soc.) (anthro.)—the largest social grouping having permanence through generations of people who adhere to a common culture, tradition, and value system, who have a status system and a division of social functions, who have modes of control over their social conduct, and who are conscious of being a unique grouping distinct from all others.

Socio–linguistics (anthro.)—the study of the relations between language and society.

Sociometric choice (soc.)—positive and negative ratings of persons with respect to given behaviors or characteristics.

Sovereign power (pol. sci.)—political power wielded by an ultimate decision-making person or group beyond which there is no appeal.

Specialization (econ.)—the division of labor, by biological, geographic, institutional, industrial, vocational, or other bases, so that a complex task may be separated into its component parts, allowing greater proficiency in each of the component tasks.

Spot price (econ.)—the price of a commodity at an exact moment.

Sovereignty (State) (pol. sci.)—the notion that the states hold the ultimate decision-making power over the federal government.

Status (Social Status) (soc.)—the relative position or standing of a group or individual in the social scale, along with the privileges, rights, and duties associated with that position.

Stratigraphy (anthro.)—in archaeology, the inference of chronology from the various layers of ruins.

Sub-cultural (soc.)—pertaining to the culture that is peculiar to a particular group of people who form a part of a larger society, and who also share in much of the culture of the larger society.

Subsidy (econ.)—a payment made by an outsider (usually the government) to a production unit which is unable to cover its full production costs.

Symbiotic (anthro.)—pertaining to mutual subsistence relationships between species.

Sympathetic activity (psych.)—activity of the sympathetic branch of the autonomic nervous system.

Sympathetic nervous system (psych.)—a part of the nervous system that reacts to fear and stress.

Symptom (psych.)—a complicated product that involves feelings of distress and anxiety as well as the notion that one is not adjusted to society.

Synesthesia (psych.)—a process in which one type of stimulus produces a secondary, subjective sensation.

Taboo (anthro.)—a social rule prohibiting certain acts under the threat of supernatural reprisal.

Totalitarianism (pol. sci.)—the body of ideas and practices which seeks to implement the concentration of absolute and unimpeachable political powers in a central government, enabling it to control all the important phases of public life.

Tribe (anthro.)—a type of large social unit, usually made up of several clans, villages, bands or other sub-groups, which are politically bound together by a chief or common council, and normally have a definite territory and a common language and culture.

Trust (econ.)—an association of corporations for the purpose of avoiding competition.

Valence (psych.)—the attractiveness or desirability of a thing, a person, or a group of people.

Value (soc.)—any object, situation, ideal, principle or norm that a person or group of people consider desirable and worthy; (econ.) the capacity of an economic good to be exchangeable for other goods.

Value pattern (soc.)—a related set of values that guide behavior in a particular area of social life.

Value system (soc.)—the interrelated pattern of values that exists in societies.

Verbal deprivation (anthro.)—being deprived of normal amounts of verbal stimulation.

Verdicality (psych.)—that which corresponds to reality, or facts.

Veto (pol. sci.)—an executive disapproval of a legislative bill or a joint resolution.

Vicarious extinction (psych.)—the process by which the strength of a response weakens through observation of an organism which is being extinguished.

Vicarious reinforcement (psych.)—the process by which a person observing a model being reinforced behaves later as if he were the person being reinforced.

Visual-verbal synesthesia (psych.)—a process in which visual-verbal stimuli produce secondary, subjective sensations.

Witchcraft (anthro.)—the practice or art of influencing the well-being of another person or his soul by using supernatural techniques.